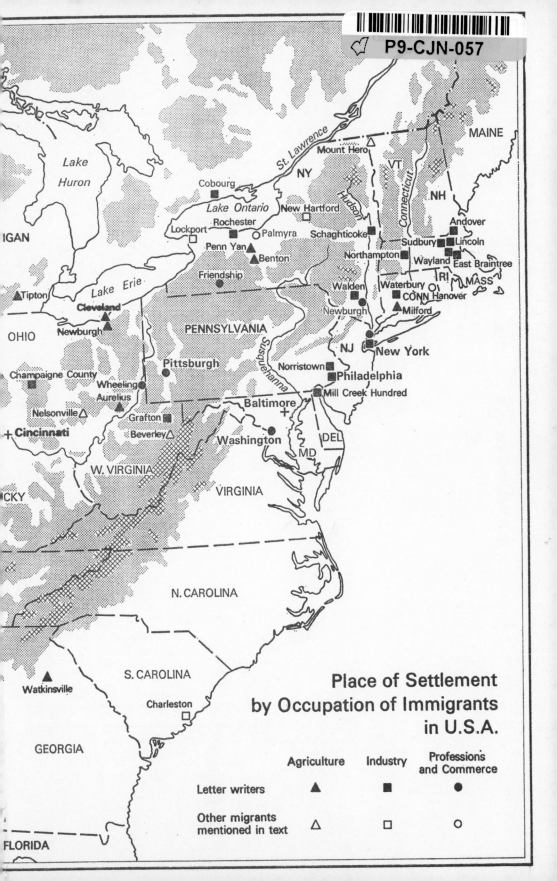

Place of Settlement
by Occupation of Immigrants
in U.S.A.

Invisible Immigrants

Invisible Immigrants

*The Adaptation of English and Scottish
Immigrants in Nineteenth-Century
America*

Charlotte Erickson

UNIVERSITY OF MIAMI PRESS
Coral Gables, Florida

Contents

PART III   THE UPROOTED: IMMIGRANTS IN PROFESSIONAL, COMMERCIAL AND CLERICAL OCCUPATIONS

Letters from Immigrants in Professional, Commercial and Clerical Occupations

Illustrations

Page references for these illustrations refer to the facing page.

ACKNOWLEDGEMENTS

Illustrations 8, 9, 10, 11, 12, 13, 14, 16 and 17 are reproduced by courtesy
of the Radio Times Hulton Picture Library. Illustrations 1 and 2 were provided by the Peoria Public Library. Numbers 3, 4 and 5 have been reproduced
from prints lent by Miss Jessie Thompson. Number 6 is reproduced by
courtesy of the United States Naval Institute of Annapolis, Maryland.
Number 7 is printed by permission of the National Maritime Museum at
Greenwich, and number 15 by courtesy of the American Antiquarian Society.

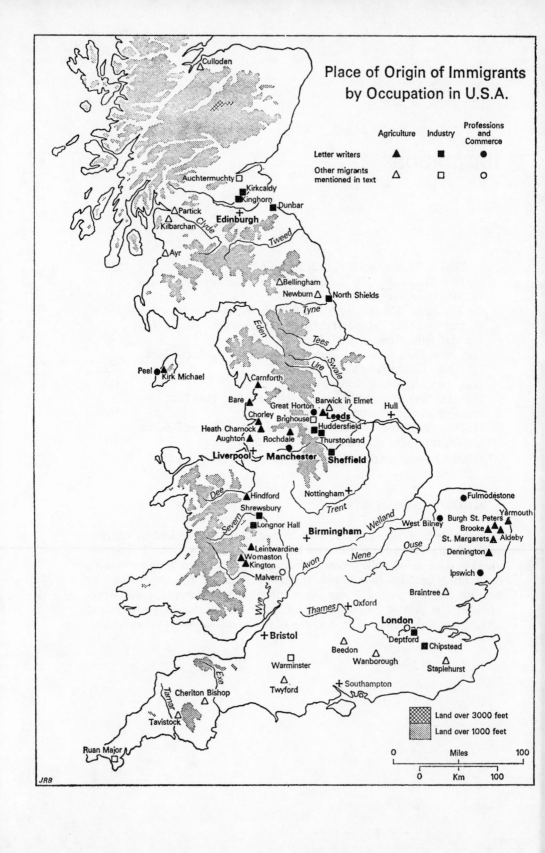

Place of Origin of Immigrants by Occupation in U.S.A.

	Agriculture	Industry	Professions and Commerce
Letter writers	▲	■	●
Other migrants mentioned in text	△	□	○

Culloden

Auchtermuchty

Kirkcaldy
Kinghorn
Dunbar
Partick
Edinburgh
Kilbarchan
Ayr

Bellingham
Newburn
North Shields

Peel
Kirk Michael

Carnforth
Bare
Great Horton
Barwick in Elmet
Hull
Chorley
Brighouse
Leeds
Heath Charnock
Huddersfield
Aughton
Rochdale
Thurstonland
Liverpool
Manchester
Sheffield

Hindford
Shrewsbury
Nottingham
Longnor Hall
Birmingham
West Bilney
Fulmodestone
Yarmouth
Burgh St. Peters
Brooke
Aldeby
Leintwardine
St. Margarets
Womaston
Kington
Dennington
Malvern
Ipswich

Braintree
Bristol
Oxford
London
Deptford
Beedon
Chipstead
Warminster
Wanborough
Staplehurst
Twyford
Southampton
Cheriton Bishop
Tavistock
Ruan Major

Clyde
Tweed
Tyne
Eden
Tees
Ure
Swale
Trent
Welland
Nene
Ouse
Avon
Dee
Severn
Wye
Thames
Exe
Tamar

Land over 3000 feet
Land over 1000 feet

0 — Miles — 100
0 — Km — 100

JRB

Introduction

Manuscripts of emigrant letters constitute a unique historical source material. The act of emigration led many ordinary working people to record their actions and attitudes. From such letters we can gain some knowledge of the inner social history of the nineteenth century, of the motives and ways of looking at their world of people who did not lead armies or governments or business firms, but who participated in the greatest movement of people the world has ever known, journeying overseas as individuals and families with little or no outside assistance in taking this great step.

Few of these letters may be said to have literary merit, though some contain good examples of the native wit of the writer's region of birth and most unfold stories that are fascinating in themselves. The letters also have importance as historical documents. The character of English and Scottish overseas emigration during the nineteenth century is not yet fully understood, partly because of the paucity of good statistical records of the movement.[1] The statistics collected at the ports did not report the part of the country from which intending migrants came. Changes during the century in the mode of collection of these port records leave some doubt as to when the emigration was heaviest. Earlier writers concluded that the emigration movement,'had passed its peak in England before 1850'. Many writers were influenced by the obvious causes of emigration – over-population, rural poverty and technological unemployment – which could be cited for the period from the close of the Napoleonic Wars to the Repeal of the Corn Laws.[2] The emigration of these years was probably grossly under-recorded. Yet statistics of emigration suggest that both relative and absolute peaks in the overseas movement from England and Scotland occurred during the 1850s and the 1880s. If the emigration actually increased after England and Scotland reached industrial maturity, and, indeed, supremacy, then it was at least in some respects different from the movement of people from Germany and Sweden which declined as industrialization provided alternative opportunities at home.[3]

1*

Reliance on government documents, pamphlet literature, and the immigrant and trade union press in the United States as source materials for the history of British emigration may have given us a distorted picture. In particular, we know more about cases of government-assisted emigration, and the projects and colonies of speculators, trade unionists, socialists, and the British Mormons than we do about the individuals and families who emigrated on their own initiative without special schemes of assistance.[4]

Obviously emigrant letters cannot entirely redress the balance or complete the picture. In the absence of good migration statistics they constitute one method which may be used to find out more about the emigration from England and Scotland in the nineteenth century. The particular types of bias which they introduce must be considered and analysed.

Another aspect of the historical interest of emigrant letters is the knowledge they provide of the process of migration and the impact of the experience upon the migrant himself. Because of the predominance of American historians in the writing of migration history, as Frank Thistlethwaite has pointed out, the emphasis has most often been placed upon the impact of immigrants on the economy and society of the receiving country.[5] This one-sidedness is not altogether attributable to the blind spots of historians. The dearth of historical documentation has kept the emigrant and his experience out of the centre of the historical accounts. Some of the attempts which have been made to concentrate upon the experience of the migrant himself have come close at times simply to imagining the migrant's reactions.[6] The classic work by Thomas and Znaniecki is still the richest source of knowledge about the experience of ordinary migrants from Europe to America.[7]

Even when migrants moved into another society which used the same language and had many similar institutions, migration required considerable risk-taking, a high level of adaptability to changing circumstances, and often a break with family and community. The migrant had many adjustments to make if he did no more than change his residence within an emerging national culture, as when Britons moved within the British Isles or the native-born within America.[8] In 1901 the Devonshire Association asked for information about emigrants from Devon in the Colonies and the United States. One of the letters they received in answer read:

seeing in the Evening Paper that you would like to know about the old Families of Devonshire my Father and Mother Mr and Mrs Bayes lived on Lord Taylers estate East Ourgal Near Newton Abbot I left home 40 years ago as I wanted work i got work at Hartlepool and was there five years under the

North Eastern railway and i left there to come to York under the same company in witch i have worked for 40 years i remain etc. P.S. Sir if you her on any one off the name of Bayes Kindly let them See thiss Letter as it may be Some of my Bruthers or some of there children as i Should like to hear from them.[9]

Mr Bayes regarded himself just as much an emigrant as the man who went overseas.

As between England and the United States variations in attitudes arising out of cultural differences were sometimes masked by language similarities. Indeed the immigrant who came to an utterly different culture might have had a built-in shield against painful encounters with members of the receiving society and an aid to accommodation in his obvious need for leaders of his own nationality who could help him by mediating for him as an immigrant The Englishman in America, like the Irishman in England, was more exposed because his difficulties were not so apparent.[10]

Manuscript immigrant letters sometimes provide us with the clues needed to study this process of migration, from the old country to the new. They often enable us to ascertain the social and economic position of the writer and his family in the neighbourhood from which he emigrated. In some instances the letters give information about the motives behind the decision to emigrate. One can trace the network by which the migrant found a job or established himself on the land in the United States. In some cases one can assess the migrant's social and economic adjustment in the light of his background, his own statements and the characteristics of the place in which he settled.

Private emigrant letters contribute a different sort of historical knowledge than do most of the collections of emigrant letters published heretofore. Broadly speaking, the collections of emigrant letters published in recent years shed light on two subjects. They provide information on local conditions at a single point in time in the regions overseas to which the emigrants went. Indirectly we sometimes obtain clues as to what the emigrants were looking for in migration, according to whether they emphasized the material, political, or social inducements or deterrents to migration. In the second place, these collections tell us something about the type of information which was available to the prospective emigrant, information on which he may have based his decision about emigration.[11]

Many of these collections, to which the scholars of Scandinavian migration have contributed the greatest variety and quantity, are subject to certain limitations as sources of knowledge of the process of migration. The letters included in them were often written expressly for

publication. The writer sought a wide audience because he wanted either
to encourage or to discourage emigration. For example, immigrants who
had bought land hoped to realize an appreciation in land values or an
increase in the local market for their produce by stimulating further
settlement in their area. Alternatively, trade union members tried to
prevent an increase in immigration in their trade or locality by describing the hardships of an immigrant. In a great many instances these
possible sources of bias cannot be offset by identifying the writer, his
background before emigration, or his precise situation after immigration. Thus a lot of the testimony of migrants in letters to the press cannot be appraised because the witness is unknown. When it is possible to
identify the witnesses, as in the case of John Hales' *Settlers* and some of
the leading figures in the volumes edited by Conway and Blegen, this is
because the writers were part of an educated, socially prominent elite
who had access to newspaper columns and publishers in the countries of
their birth.[12] The story of these elites, in every immigrant group, is indispensable to an understanding of the adjustment of immigrant
groups.[13] Their leadership in promoting or discouraging immigration,
in assisting or attempting to impede the gradual identification of immigrants with the values and attitudes of the countries to which they came,
is obviously central to immigration history. But the experiences of
more obscure migrants are also important and interesting.

Collections of emigrant letters culled from published sources also
reflect public controversies about migration at the time when the letters
were written. In order to try to discourage further emigration, William
Savage, the printer for the Royal Institution, published in 1819 letters
written by English emigrants in Kentucky during the 1790s. William
Cobbett, on the other hand, selected letters which showed migration as
a success when he wanted to prove, at the end of the twenties, that there
was no alternative for the excessively tithed and taxed English farmer
except emigration.[14] The policies of newspapers influenced their choice
of letters for publication. One could not find a letter which advocated
emigration in the columns of *Rylands Iron Trade Circular* during the
1860s, while newspapers for trade unionists, such as the London
Beehive, published letters encouraging emigration.

Private letters were no more unbiased than published ones. No witness
is entirely unbiased. While one emigrant might write for the press a
letter calculated to assist his own economic interests, another might
justify his emigration to an unsympathetic family with similarly selected
and garnished facts. The one advantage we usually have in using private
letters, is that of being able to identify witnesses, even when they were
obscure people. Thus we can compare their statements with inde-

pendently obtained facts about their background and situation. Just as migrants wrote to newspapers to advance their own interests as well as to report, so they wrote to their families and friends for various reasons, some interested and some disinterested. Three main purposes lay behind the writing of the private letters of English and Scottish immigrants in the United States.

In the first place letters were written to arrange the migration of other members of the family who wanted to come to America. In contrast to published letters these private letters rarely encouraged migration. The phrase 'I will not encourage anyone to come' was a *leit-motif* of the private letter, even when migrants declared themselves to be satisfied with their own decisions. A variant of the planning and advising letter was the one written by an emigrant who had not decided whether to remain permanently in America or not. Often he was a scout for his family who waited upon his decision either to help them join him or to return home.

A second motive for letter-writing was to obtain financial help from home. This feature of the British immigrant letters stands in sharp contrast to the usual stereotype of the immigrant from Ireland, Poland or Italy, saving assiduously to send remittances or free passages to his family. If these letters be any guide, the English and Scottish immigrant was not prepared to make his way unaided if there was a possibility of importing capital. In many instances we owe the existence of letters to this search for capital. A need for capital, or the prospect that it might be obtained, could reinvigorate a correspondence after a lapse of many years.

Finally some letters were written merely to report and to keep in touch with family at home. Lloyd Reynolds pointed out many years ago that the emigrant letter was characteristically written by the unassimilated immigrant.[15] He wrote home so long as he felt himself to be an outsider. There is much evidence of this motive in the letters published here. The immigrant pleaded with his family to send him news from home. More subtly, the letter provided him with a means of remaining himself and justifying himself when he felt most disorientated. The simple loneliness of the immigrant is the explanation for some of the long series of letters which we have from single men. Other series of letters were produced by the desire of older immigrants to re-establish contact with their homes, sometimes after a silence of many years. Contrary to the generalizations which have so frequently been made about the ease of their adjustment in America, these letters suggest that English and Scots immigrants in the United States often, at least for a long time, accommodated to their new environment rather than assimilated. Although they were not in open conflict with Americans nor suffering harsh discrimination, they had to rely on other immigrants for help and friendship.[16]

These three themes in the manuscript letters raise the question of how typical of English and Scots emigrants as a whole these particular individuals were. This is an experiment in micro-history, and one is very conscious of the dangers. Certainly the word typical has been used very loosely in connection with immigrant letters. One could avoid this thorny problem simply by noting that these were historical cases, whether typical or not. While recognizing that it is impossible to assess their representativeness with any precision, I cannot leave the question entirely at that. Certain features of the letters should be emphasized. Obviously not all emigrants wrote letters. Any sample of immigrant letters places undue emphasis upon people who failed as immigrants,[17] and upon those who did not break their ties with the homeland. Letters will under-represent orphans, for example, and whole families who emigrated at the same time, as well as others who had no desire to retain ties with their former homes. It need hardly be said that illiterate emigrants, or those who could read but not write, will not be represented. This is one reason for believing that the poorest emigrants, those who may have emigrated for the most straightforward economic reasons, will not be found among letter-writers.

The second hazard is the chance of survival of letters once they were written. This may not be an entirely random factor either, since letters were probably kept when a family did not move too frequently, or when someone happened to be interested in family or local history, or when the letters had some bearing upon the settlement of an estate. Many letters probably still survive in private hands, and it is to be hoped that more of them will gradually find their way into libraries. A number of American libraries contain collections of immigrant letters which had been brought by later migrants because of the information they contained. Since my opportunities for searching for letters in America were limited, I am sure others survived which I have not used.

Finally there is what one might call the bias of selection. I have tried to dig deeper into the social structure of the migrant population than has been customary in publishing collections of emigrant letters. This has meant omitting long collections written by more literate and better-off immigrants. Thus I have selected relatively short collections of letters which contain enough detail to make possible a treatment of the migrant's background and adjustment, but which do not require so much cutting that my own judgement of what is significant could become the over-riding feature of the selection. While a number of very rich and interesting series of immigrant letters have been published in historical journals, I have selected unpublished materials in order to add to the stock of such materials available to historians and others. If the letters selected do not tell us much about the least privileged people who emigrated from Britain to the United States, they do reveal something about the attitudes and hopes of people somewhat lower in the social scale than appear in most published collections of emigrant letters and memoirs.

The letters of farmers, handicraftsmen and small traders are included, but ordinary labourers from both town and country are clearly under-represented. So much attention has been given to the skilled worker who emigrated from Britain,[18] that it is often forgotten that common labourers formed the single largest group of migrants, larger among the English overseas migrants than among the Scots. While labourers were probably not very important in the unassisted emigration before about 1840, when costs of emigration were still highly unpredictable, they formed the largest occupational group in the last half of the century. During years of American boom, such as the early 1880s, their share rose to as high as two-fifths of the immigrants who stated occupations on arriving in the United States.[19] Few of the letters of this huge segment of British emigration, especially of people who found jobs in American industry, have been found.

More letters have survived from emigrants who left Britain during the first half of the nineteenth century, before emigration to America reached its peak, than have been found from the latter half of the century. This bias reflects in part the same 'class' bias noted above, since the emigration of the last half of the century contained proportionately a much larger share of ordinary labourers.

The letters have been divided into three groups according to the occupation the immigrants entered on arriving in the United States. The first group contains letters of people who went into agriculture; the second, letters from immigrants in industrial occupations as manual workers; and the third, letters from individuals who entered commercial, clerical or professional work in America. This scheme of organization has been adopted because the migrants differed in their motives for emigration, in the network of distribution in which they moved, and in their behaviour in America according to the occupation which they intended to follow after emigration. This organization does not coincide with the occupations of the emigrants before they left Britain, since many of them changed occupation on emigrating.

In focusing upon the adaptation of immigrants in America, the study differs from that of W.I.Thomas and Florian Znaniecki, who were able to work with letters from people in Poland to immigrants in the United

States collected at the time the migration was in full flood. Nevertheless, I have tried to ask some of the same questions about attitudes to family, to land, to work, towards government and religion about which Thomas wrote in so masterly a fashion. Thomas developed a model of the traditional peasant society in Poland, and examined the ways in which it was being transformed by economic change in the years before World War I. He believed that the traditional peasant society in Poland survived only where people had been settled 'at least for four or five generations in the same locality and admitting no important changes of class, religion, nationality or profession'.[20] A peasant society in this sense was simply not to be found in England in the early nineteenth century. Indeed, it is difficult to speak of a 'survival' of peasant attitudes and values because nothing like the stable Polish system, based on the kind of family solidarity which Thomas and Znaniecki described, existed in the English countryside, even in the seventeenth century.[21] The curious fact then is that many English and Scottish emigrants who chose to enter agriculture in America expressed an adherence to some of the values which Thomas and Znaniecki associated with their traditional peasant model. They regarded land as worth acquiring for its own sake at the expense of commercial advantages. They looked upon work as an activity necessary for gaining a living, not as a means to a higher standard-of-living or to satisfactions gained from a skilled job well done.[22] Thomas and Znaniecki remarked that 'there is hardly another distinction so profoundly rooted in Polish consciousness as that between independent work on the person's own property and hired work'.[23] Such a distinction, and such a definition of independence, was also made by British immigrants who went into agriculture, and notably by emigrants from urban areas. While these English emigrants did not come from a disintegrating peasant community, some of them tried to become peasants in America. Even some who went into industrial occupations showed vestiges of these attitudes, a confidence that land would provide a living shielded from economic fluctuations and that independence was a more laudable goal than economic advance. However, those who remained in industry differed in several respects from farmers, and more of them acted upon purely economic calculations. Much as I should have liked to organize these materials on a spectrum from the peasant attitudes to the mood of economic advance, this was not practical. In too many cases, we do not have letters just at the time of emigration which might make such an experiment possible. Yet to a remarkable extent the organization by choice of occupation does coincide with differing motives for emigration.

In editing the letters some passages have been cut, but I have indicated the nature of the material omitted. In the rather unpleasant task of cutting, I have omitted references to letters, to health, and messages from other immigrants and to other persons, once the network of friends and acquaintances of the immigrant has been established in the early letters. I have also cut most accounts of ocean voyages, most lists of American prices and some rather shallow descriptions. This material is not without interest, but is not central to the themes of this book. To increase readability I have introduced paragraphs, some minimal punctuation and removed excessive capital letters. In order not to sacrifice all guides to the level of education of the various immigrants, I have retained all original spellings, even when these are confusing.

It will be evident to the reader that I have exploited the published census materials of the United States and the United Kingdom to help specify the background of the letter-writers and the nature of the regions to which they went. Since this information is easily available, and there should be little doubt as to where to find it, I have not provided notes for facts taken from published census records.

Nor have I given precise references to the many manuscript census returns which I have consulted on both sides of the Atlantic. Reference is made only to the census years in which I found material relevant to these case histories. Should any reader want further details, I will be happy to supply them, and they will be obtainable in the uncut version of this book deposited in the British Library of Economic and Political Science.

I am very conscious of the fact that, with more time and travel and work, I might have found out even more about some of these families, and I would almost certainly have discovered more emigrant letters, especially in American libraries. Instead of intensifying the work on the genealogical side, I have worked on census manuscripts, county histories and port records in order to reach judgements about the entire population from which these few case histories are drawn. The results of these efforts are being published elsewhere.

I have many debts to acknowledge. In 1949, when I was in England as a Fellow of the American Association of University Women and the Social Science Research Council, and later a Fulbright Fellow, Edith Fox, who was then Curator of the Collection of Regional History at Cornell University, put a small grant at my disposal to search for and copy letters in private hands. I am also grateful to Bernard Crick for initiating a new search for such materials, which now forms the basis of the collection of emigrant letters in the British Library of Economic and Political Science, when the United States Information Service made a grant to the British Association for American Studies for the *Guide to Manuscript Materials relating to America in the Libraries of Great Britain.* Copies of most of the letters reproduced here are either at Cornell or at the London School of Economics, though the original manuscripts may still be in private hands or in other archives. Above all, I am grateful to those people who saved and treasured such letters and have permitted them to be used. They are acknowledged by name in the appropriate place in the book. The book could not possibly have been completed but for a grant from the John Simon Guggenheim Foundation for the academic year 1966–7 which enabled me to complete some of the necessary research in the United States and to prepare a draft of the book free of the distractions and time-consuming interruptions of full-time teaching. Those individuals who have pointed out particular collections of letters to me are acknowledged in the text. I am grateful for the help and encouragement, at various times, of Professor David Glass, Professor Oscar Handlin, Professor Paul W. Gates, my colleague Dudley Baines, and Susan Ritter. For the maps, I am indebted to Mrs E. Wilson of the Drawing Office at the London School of Economics for advice and to Mrs Janet Baker for preparing them. Mrs Prudence Collins, Mrs G. Cornwall, Mrs Joan Lynas and Mrs Jill McClare have helped with the difficult business of typing drafts and reproducing errors accurately. My sons, Thomas and David Watt, have helped as well in checking these spelling errors in the letters to be sure that they are rendered accurately, and David has searched for many an obscure place-name in atlases for me. My colleagues at the LSE have been very patient as I indulged my interest in these nineteenth-century migrants. Without the help of my husband, G. Louis Watt, rendered in innumerable ways, the book would never have been finished. I myself am responsible for whatever errors may still remain.

London, September, 1971   Charlotte Erickson

PART I

THE SAFETY VALVE: ENGLISH AND SCOTTISH
IMMIGRANTS IN AMERICAN AGRICULTURE

1

How Typical are the Letter-Writers?

More than half of the collections of emigrant letters which have been found were written by people who intended to go into farming in the United States. They were some of the most faithful letter-writers, who wrote frequently and over many years. This fact suggests that the letters present a one-sided view of the immigrant population, since so much attention has been given, in recent years, to British industrial workers who helped to develop American industry.

The apparent bias of the letters towards farmers can be explained on several grounds. The loneliness of immigrants on isolated farmsteads may have prompted them to write letters, as did also the uneven pace of work on a farm, particularly a subsistence farm only marginally in touch with commercial markets. Another reason is suggested by the content of the letters: the relative stability and unity of family structure among emigrants who chose to enter agriculture. Family members remaining in Britain looked to the immigrants for advice as to their own future emigration, and the immigrants themselves could sometimes expect financial help from relatives in Britain. Both sorts of transactions kept a correspondence going.

Other evidence suggests that the preponderance of letters from farmers was not simply a function of their circumstances. Before the depression of the late 1850s, most English and Scots emigrants probably went to the United States with the intention of becoming farmers. Three out of four of the English-born inhabitants of the United States in 1850 were living in the band of States which ran from New York and Pennsylvania westwards to the Mississippi River. Nearly half of them were living in the mid-Atlantic States of New York, New Jersey and Pennsylvania.[1] Many of the English-born residents enumerated in New York and Pennsylvania in 1850 were probably on their way further west, as was John Fisher when he stopped in Palmyra, New York, before proceeding to Michigan, and as were the members of the Morris family during their stay in the Philadelphia region before settling in Ohio. The letters are full of examples of settlers in the Old Northwest who had tarried for a few months or years in the east before moving west of the mountains. That this was common practice is suggested by the appearance of New York and Pennsylvania as places of birth of children of British immigrants settled in Wisconsin, Ohio and Illinois. The frequent mention of years spent in the east in biographies of English and Scots farmers in county histories in these states is further evidence. A few ship captains, conscientious enough to complete all the details in their passenger lists, tell us that of 105 English and Scottish farmers they carried to the port of New York before 1854, sixty-six gave one of the eastern States as an immediate destination.[2] New York, in particular, represented to many British immigrants the gateway not to fortune, but to a farm. As late as 1870 the English were still very well represented in the agriculture of New York State.

Beyond New York lay the rich agricultural regions which were achieving commercial development through increased population, transport innovations and market opportunities in other regions. Twenty-eight per cent of the English-born and twenty-seven per cent of the Scots were living in Ohio, Indiana, Wisconsin, Michigan or Illinois in 1850. No other state except Utah ever had so large a share of English immigrants in its population as did Wisconsin in 1850, and no other state has produced so many immigrant letters from that period.

The English and Scots immigrants continued to direct their steps, either by primary or secondary migrations, towards the Old Northwest during the fifties. As the remaining attractive public lands in this region were incorporated into farms, as the reasonably well-drained prairie lands were finally rushed into production, the share of the English and Scots inhabitants increased in these states. No other state, not even New York, experienced so large a net increase in its English-born population as did Illinois. Not yet a manufacturing state of any consequence, Illinois reached the position of leading wheat-producer of the nation during this decade. The continued attraction of agriculture for British immigrants is also suggested by the striking gains in English and Scottish inhabitants recorded in Iowa, Minnesota, Kansas and Nebraska. The West North Central States as a region increased their share of the English-born people from 3·3 per cent in 1850 to 6·5 per cent in 1860, and of Scots from 2·6 per cent to 6·2 per cent.

In 1850 more than half the labour force in these States worked in agriculture and three-quarters of the population lived on farms or in towns of fewer than 2500 inhabitants. The success achieved by English and Scots immigrants in settling there is a strong indirect indication of the attraction which agriculture had for them. It should be noted, however, that the English were particularly strongly represented in the lead-mining counties of Wisconsin and Illinois and in the iron and copper-mining counties of Michigan to which Cornishmen and Yorkshiremen came in large numbers.[3] Yet the census of 1870 indicates that the English were very well represented in the agriculture of those two states, and both emigrant letters and county histories make it clear that many immigrants regarded mining as a means of obtaining a farm.

After the mid-century, one may speak of a 'new immigration' among the English. In 1850 only one in ten was living in New England, the region most likely to attract immigrants intending to enter industrial occupations. This new immigration was beginning in the fifties when the English slightly increased their representation among the foreign-born in New England. The most striking redirection of the English towards the industrializing parts of America came during the sixties, however. From that decade onwards the New England states increased their share of English-born residents in every decade, those of heavy as well as those of light immigration. Pennsylvania, which had been in sixth place in its increase of English-born inhabitants in the fifties, came forward to first place and was again in first place in the eighties. The far western mountain region, where mining was more important than agriculture, also began to increase its share of the English-born population during the sixties and seventies. As new arrivals after the Civil War tended to settle in industrial states, the share of the English-born living in the East North Central states bordering the Great Lakes fell. Wisconsin actually experienced a net emigration of English inhabitants during the sixties. A subsidiary stream of English immigrants continued to seek out the agricultural frontier after the Civil War. The share of the English immigrants living in the Plains states west of the Mississippi River rose from three per cent in 1850 to a peak of eleven per cent in 1890. But the English never attained the relative concentration among the foreign-born of the Plains that they had in the Old Northwest before 1860.

The location of the immigrants in agriculture whose letters have survived seems to be quite typical of English and Scots settlers. Most of the letters from emigrants who arrived in the United States before the mid-century were written from Ohio, Illinois, Wisconsin and Michigan. Two collections have been found of families who arrived in Iowa during the fifties. The Bonds, who went to Kansas in the seventies, while part of a greatly diminished flow of English immigrants into agriculture, were typical in their choice of Kansas as a place to try to realize their ambition at that time. Kansas ranked fourth among the states and territories of the country during the seventies in its absolute net increase of English-born residents.

Only four collections of letters have been found written by settlers in the South, where, until the eighties, British immigrants were under-represented even among the foreign-born. The few examples we have of migrants who remained in eastern agriculture were men from poor families, people who had very limited resources when they came to the United States.

The letter-writers also reflect the pattern of emigration from Britain: 1819, 1826, 1830–1, 1839–43, 1849–50 and 1869 were all years of tem-porary peaks in the flow of people overseas from England and Scotland. Considering the reduced movement of English and Scots immigrants to the more purely agricultural regions of the United States after 1860, one can also say that the more meagre survivals of letters from farmers who emigrated late in the century also accords with the general pattern of migration.

It is more difficult to assess the representative quality of the letter-writers with respect to their social and economic background in Britain. Almost certainly more immigrants from England and Scotland attemp-ted to enter agriculture in America than came directly from farms. The main tendency of the nineteenth-century outpouring of people from Europe was to transfer people from rural neighbourhoods and occupa-tions to more urbanized and industrial regions. However, an un-measurable segment of the British immigrants between 1815 and the 1840s moved from secondary and tertiary occupations and from cities to primary production. The agrarian myth which directed many indus-trial workers, manufacturers, professional people, clerks and retail traders to the American frontier in the twenties, thirties and forties, had lost some of its power by the 1850s. No county in England or in the Scottish lowlands, however remote from the gathering industrial revo-lution, was so little urbanized, or had its labour force so heavily com-mitted to agriculture, as the states of the Old Northwest before 1850. Immigrants who made their way west of the Appalachians were deli-berately seeking out a less developed economy and less complex society than that which they left.

The letters from migrants in agriculture have been divided into three groups according to the migrants' background in Britain. The first four collections were written by people who came from farming families. For this group it was possible to select a few collections from a larger number which have survived, and I have drawn upon these other collections in my discussion.[4] Most of the letter-writers from farming families emi-grated before 1840 from counties outside the industrializing regions of England, from Hereford, Essex, Kent, Norfolk, Dorset, the North Riding of Yorkshire, Westmorland, Inverness and the Isle of Man.

None of them had been very large-scale farmers by British standards. The farms they left were between one and two hundred acres in size. In nearly all cases, these were rented farms, cultivated with the aid of employed labour. Thus although these farmers left the more backward counties of England and Scotland, they came from a developed, commercial agriculture. They were not peasant farmers whose families had cultivated the same land from one generation to the next, for whom the departure for America would have constituted a first uprooting from particular land with which the family had long-standing ties. We have only one case of a traditional community which overseas migration disrupted for the first time, that of the Corletts who left the Isle of Man in 1826.

The second group of letters presented was written by people who had been town-dwellers before they came to America to farm. The industrial workers in this group came from the more developed and diversified parts of the British economy, areas where industry was serving national and overseas markets or where steam-powered machinery had been introduced. Samuel Mearbeck, a metal plater from Sheffield, emigrated in 1817 before the social structure of that city had been much modified by industrial change.[5] Power loom weaving was in its infancy in Lancashire when the Morris family emigrated and in Yorkshire when Abel Stephenson decided to try to escape from its impact. Peter McKellar, whose letters are too voluminous to be reproduced here, had already lost his job as a hand printer of cotton goods near Glasgow many years before he decided to try farming in America in preference to the lumberyard work he had been doing in the interim.[6] Published a generation ago, the letters of Edwin Bottomley tell us about a man who had been a pattern designer in the Huddersfield woollen mills which his father managed.[7] Other craftsmen from Lancashire who turned to farming in America included Henry Woods, a blacksmith, and John Morris, a carpenter. The career of William Freeman, a cabinet maker who had worked in Buckingham Palace before he toiled with his sons on a Wisconsin farm, can be traced in the letters of his daughter, Catherine Steel, a woman of good education, whose letters are also too numerous to include in this selection.[8]

Wilbur Shepperson dedicated his history of emigration from early Victorian Britain to his great-grandfather, a London solicitor, who emigrated to a farm in Missouri in the 1840s. As his case illustrates, the prospect of farming in the American West attracted people from many levels of English society other than farmers and manual workers. While the former industrial workers lost their interest in American agriculture after 1850, some individuals from professional and commercial families continued to be drawn to the West until the terrible winter and poor harvests on the plains in 1886–7.

Our knowledge of some of these people is far more extensive than it is of ordinary farmers, labourers and industrial workers who tried to become farmers in America. This is partly because they participated in trying to establish English colonies in America. Richard Flower, Morris Birkbeck's original partner in inaugurating the English colony in Edwards County, Illinois, had been a brewer in Hartford. In addition to the farm labourers and mechanics drawn to this settlement, a number of settlers from a higher social rank arrived. A merchant tailor from Hatton Garden, a London doctor, a merchant from Plymouth, a gentleman from London, a copyist or scribe from London, and various others came to Albion in 1818 and 1819.[9] The journal of William Hall, owner of a large water mill at Ewell, Surrey, amateur botanist and ornithologist, who emigrated to Wanborough, Illinois, in 1821 has been published.[10] A few letters from Deborah Pritchard, whose home was mentioned by Hall as the meeting place for the Miscellany Society in Wanborough, also survive.[11]

Professional people and independent businessmen also participated in establishing the English colony, not far from Birkbeck's, on the Wabash River in Vanderburgh County, Indiana. It was founded by Saunders Hornbrook, Jr, in 1817 because Birkbeck's prices for land were deemed too high. Hornbrook Sr, who arrived in the summer of 1818, had been a woollen manufacturer and ironfounder in Devon. Other early settlers included the son of a Baptist minister, John Ingle, in whose cabin William Faux stayed for five weeks.[12]

In 1819 Robert Hutchinson Rose, the wealthy son of pre-revolutionary Scots immigrants, succeeded in attracting a few English families with capital to a bleak, remote, beautiful part of Pennsylvania, near the upper reaches of the Susquehanna River. Among the settlers in this abortive colony were C.B.Johnson, a Shropshire doctor, who let his name be used on a promotion pamphlet, and Thomas Deakin, said to have been a wealthy fur dealer before he emigrated.[13]

Still another attempt at founding an English colony during the disturbed years just after the Napoleonic Wars was made by George Courtauld who managed silk factories in Essex and London. After visiting the States to purchase land in 1818, he took his children and their spouses to a wilderness of forest and vines in south-eastern Ohio in 1820.[14] After George Courtauld's death in 1824 and the retreat of his children to England, James Knight carried on the attempt to attract immigrants to Nelsonville, near Courtauld's rapidly disintegrating settlement at Englishtown in Athens County. Before he emigrated in

1821, Knight had been a maltster and shopkeeper in Wisborough Green, Sussex.[15]

Another professional man turned farmer whose letters have survived in great profusion was Thomas Steel.[16] Thomas Steel's father, James, the son of an unsuccessful Scottish farmer, had started life as a weaver in Glasgow, where he attended lectures by Dr Birkbeck at Anderson's Institution in the evenings. As a sergeant in the army in 1803 he met several excise men and managed to secure an order of instruction and gain entry into the service. After serving in various parts of Scotland he moved to London as surveying general examiner in 1823. Thomas Steel was born in Inverkeithing, Fife, in 1809 and trained as a doctor in London and Glasgow. Immediately after qualifying in 1833 he emigrated to Canada and the United States but returned to England within a few months, his money gone, and worked for several years as a ship's doctor on vessels trading with India and China. In June 1843, Thomas Steel again set out for the United States, this time in a party of London tradesmen, clerks and others who had pooled their resources in a co-operative society to establish a socialist community in Wisconsin.

Every one of these people from commercial and professional families, caught up in community-building projects, came like our farmers, from outside the industrializing North of England.[17] In contrast, the letters selected for inclusion in this volume came from families of more modest means from the growing towns of Lancashire, Yorkshire and London. They were less profuse in their letter-writing, and their story is more briefly told. On his first voyage to the States in 1834 Thomas Steel assured his father that he was by no means the least prepared of the English migrants for the undertaking:

I wish I could transport you here for one half-hour to see some of my fellow emigrants all full of hope and Spirit. yet from the regular John Bullism of their nature as unfitted for such an enterprize one would think as their greatest enemy could wish – composed chiefly of clerks, Haberdasher apprentices – chemists & druggists and one bookseller from Dover. Yet such is the class who are pouring out to America in thousands. . . .[18]

The fate of one such family, that of George Poulton, an army pensioner from Hounslow, Middlesex, has had to be omitted,[19] but Rebecca Butterworth's letter, which is included, may be said to represent the tragic situation of some of these urban middle-class people from Britain who came to rural America totally unprepared and unfitted for the experience. The American census manuscripts make it possible to trace the career of Joseph Hirst from Leeds in the town of Equality in

Gallatin County, Illinois, in the country of 'rank, unwholesome vegetation', and 'wan and wretched inhabitants' which Dickens described in *Martin Chuzzlewit*. By the decade in which Hirst died, the 1840s, the population of Equality was declining sharply.[20] The letters of Ann Whittaker, the wife of a provision dealer from Leeds, are reproduced, since they say a bit more than does the single letter from Hirst about her attitude to a fairly indifferent farming career in Illinois.

Many English and Scots immigrants sought to become farmers in America with no prior experience of agriculture. Their letters reinforce the hints in travellers' accounts that there was a backward element, economically speaking, in the migration from Britain. For quite a large number of British emigrants who hoped to become farmers in the United States, land in the American west was a safety valve against urban and industrial discontent.

The third group of letters from immigrant farmers was written by men who had been rural handicraftsmen, agricultural labourers or farm servants before they emigrated and who, like the farmers, knew something of the way of life they were choosing. The letters of Robert Smith, a shoemaker from Norfolk, who joined his brother-in-law in Lenawee County, Michigan in the 1830s are reproduced here. Smith and his family were far closer to destitution before their emigration than were the industrial workers from Lancashire, Yorkshire and London who contemplated careers as farmers.[21]

Very few letters from former agricultural labourers have turned up. A number of letters from farm labourers who emigrated to the United States and Canada were published between 1818 and 1834 in pamphlets designed to stimulate emigration;[22] but only four manuscripts have been found which have not been included in this collection.[23] These labourers emigrated at a later period than the farmers. The Griffiths emigrated in 1840, Edward Gilley in 1843, the Bishops about 1857, and the Bonds in 1869. The geographical origins of these labourers also contrast with those of the farmers. While the emigrants from farming families came from the less developed parts of England and Scotland, these few rural labourers came from neighbourhoods where non-agricultural jobs were probably expanding quite rapidly, though not perhaps at the very moment when they left Northumberland, Shropshire and Berkshire in the forties and Lancashire in the sixties. In these counties lived some of the more favoured of England's agricultural employees. They came from areas where pastoral husbandry was emphasized, where the labour force on any particular farm was relatively small, the work more varied and the wages higher than in the grainlands of the southeast.

These generalizations do not fit the Bishop family, who left Suffolk in the late fifties, a decade in which the population of that county actually declined. These letters had the lowest standard of spelling and grammar of any which have been found and are among the most interesting. Their very existence suggests that improved transport and information, as well as Britain's prosperity, were by this time making it possible for very poor labourers with ambition and intelligence, but with little schooling, to venture overseas without paternalistic assistance.

2

Motives for Emigration

In assessing motives for emigration from emigrant letters one must be careful not to infer reasons which were *ex post* justifications, made from the point of view of the migrant in America. Since it is necessary to rely on letters written about the time of migration, not all of these collections illuminate this subject directly. Indeed, immigrants were not likely to comment in detail about the reasons for their emigration when they wrote to members of their own family, who presumably were well-acquainted with the facts. Yet some clues can be garnered from statements made by migrants and from a consideration of their background.

The most purely economic motives for migration can be traced among some of the farmers and sons of farmers who left parishes where population was either falling or stagnant. Local opportunities appeared limited to these men, especially when there were several sons in the family. Yet, so far as we can judge, they did not leave because of actual economic hardship. They were all able to take capital with them to the United States. In most cases one brother remained on the farm in England. Others made their adjustment to the diminution of local opportunities by moving within Britain and entering other occupations.

A large number of English farmers, from Morris Birkbeck to the men of more modest capital whose letters are included in this volume, hoped to get a better return on their capital, invested in American land or employed in agriculture, than they did in England. They felt that too much of the return on their capital and labour was paid out in rent, in taxes and in tithes. The theme had not changed much from the eighteenth century when English farmers appeared on American shores because they objected to making improvements on other men's land, to tithes and taxes as well as to the limitations on the freedom of their farming operations sometimes incorporated in their leases.[24] So James Flint found English farmers in New York state in 1818 who told him that they had declined to renew their expired leases because they feared having the paternal stock and savings of many years divided between landowner and tax collector.[25] John Burlend had taken a farm in Yorkshire in 1817 on a fourteen-year lease at a rent fixed too high, in his opinion, in relation to the price of corn. He managed to make his payments until the lease expired, but, as his wife later reported, they 'had to see the diminution of their little property' to do so.[26] A farmer from Dorset in the 1830s stated simply that he and his wife had left because they were 'not doing themselves much good'.[27]

These people expressed a discontent arising out of economic ambition. The prospect of owning land seemed to suggest that the return would be greater, since it would accrue more fully to themselves. Few of these farmers recognized in advance that, where transport and markets were lacking and labour dear or unavailable, the cash return might be less than in England. This motive of economic advance is most pronounced in John Birket and Thomas Wozencraft, both of whom were quite as ready as Americans to take their return through capital gains in land values rather than from farming operations. One former Scots farmer wrote from a prairie farm forty miles from Chicago in 1845:

Had you come here with money you have it would have been more than doubled by this time Money lent on mortgages draws interest from 12½ to 50 per cent. Illinois is filling fast with inhabitants ... We were 2 years too long in coming out. Land has encreased in value more than 700 per cent within the last 3 years ...[28]

Some of these farmers who came from slowly growing parts of Britain exhibited highly developed commercial and speculative attitudes.

Speculative impulses may have moved some of the middle-class community builders as well, although they were inclined to stress non-material benefits when they discussed their motives. No one elaborated the spiritual blessings of agricultural life more than George Courtauld, who nevertheless confessed to his son, Samuel:

... I purchased land, having reasonable evidence of its being, in common acceptance, a good bargain, and (as I thought) sufficient evidence that *part* of it would be *immediately* resold for immediate payment at a very handsome advance. I certainly had fair ground for this conclusion, but it has prov'd fallacious.[29]

Yet the theme of economic advance was most pronounced in the letters of immigrants who came from farming in England to farming in America.

Economic ambition also stimulated agricultural labourers and farm servants to find their way to the United States. A rather straightforward economic motivation is expressed in the following statement by the son of an agricultural labourer about the reasons his parents emigrated from Devon to New Jersey in 1866:

In 1866 my father and mother began to think very seriously about going to America. Their children were growing up and becoming old enough to realize that if they wanted to be some bodies in this world they must work, and while we were all very willing to work, we at the same time felt that the labourer is worthy of his hire . . .[30]

The motivation was not quite so simple in the case of the labourers whose letters we have found. These people came from districts in which population was growing and alternative means of employment opening up about the time they emigrated.[31] They did not look about them very much before they left. Considerations other than a simple estimate of relative economic return influenced their decision to emigrate. Mormon recruiting activities formed part of the background to the emigration of the Griffiths from Shropshire in 1840. In the case of the Gilleys and the Bonds, whose fathers had been farmers on a very small scale, the emigrants may have aimed at avoiding sinking to the status of day-labourers.

Economic factors contributed to the emigration of urban and industrial workers as well. Unless they were prepared to change occupations, the cotton handloom weavers who left Lancashire in the 1820s and the woollen weavers who left Yorkshire at the end of the thirties had good reason to take a gloomy outlook on their future.[32] But their emigration to farms in the United States was not dictated primarily by hopes of economic advance. These people made little attempt to find other work at home. Much more bleak were the local prospects for a man like Hannibal Lugg, born on a poor farm in Cornwall, apprenticed for six years without pay as a carpenter, only to find that he could not find work in his trade in the neighbourhood in which he lived.[33] The craftsmen from Lancashire and Yorkshire and the Scottish lowlands had not only more resources but also more complex non-economic reasons for seeking to become farmers in America than did emigrants from less developed regions. Sometimes their own relatives, who sympathized with their desire to emigrate, could not understand what induced them to become farmers. Peter McKellar, a former cotton printer who cleared his own farm in Iowa, was warned by his brother: '. . . it is true that there is plenty of land to be had cheap but in that case you give up all social society and believe that is too high a price to pay. . . .' His sister, the wife of a blacksmith in Charleston, SC, advised him on his son's future: '. . . it would be much beter for Archd to lern a trade than follow what he is at now as at best farming is a slaving business'. After Peter's death she was even more perplexed: '. . . what induced your father to purchase ground lying between two Prairies in the North East Corner of the state of Iowa. what inticed him to that remote spot was it the world's deceipt. . . .'[34]

The letters provide some insights to the motives which propelled industrial workers like Peter McKellar to toil on isolated farmsteads. At the outset they did not take a speculative attitude towards land values nor pay much attention to the prices of farm products, but aimed rather at acquiring land in order to gain a subsistence from it. We find such attitudes among some of the farmers, nearly all the industrial workers and urban people from developed counties in Britain, as well as among immigrants from commercial and professional families. To these people land ownership was not an avenue to economic advance or status improvement but a means of getting the necessities of life. This was true not only for poor urban dwellers like the Whittakers, but even for emigrants who came from comfortable circumstances in England. Shortly after he had established his family on unimproved land in Wisconsin in the forties, Edwin Bottomley wrote home:

> . . . I do hope to place myself in circumstances one day or another so that I can see my children smileing around me in contentment and be able to assist their parents in theire Declining Years . . . which is worth all that I can do and no more than I Desire and with no other object in View Did I emigrate to this country . . .[35]

Some of the immigrants from farming families professed not to be looking for economic advancement in the United States. Morris Birkbeck claimed that he hoped eventually to live as he had in Surrey, as a well-to-do farmer, 'but emphatically not as a fine gentleman'. And Robert Bowles assured himself, 'If I had ever so fine a house I should meet with no more respect and I am sure that respect which is caused by a fine house and handsome establishment I have no wish to cultivate.' Instead he would ultimately cover his cabin in his 'rural shady bower' with vines, roses and morning glories.[36]

How can one explain the emigration of people who recognized that it would involve hardships, that it would mean, at least for some time, a reduction in their standard of living, and that in the long run it might do no more than bring them back to the economic position they had at the time of emigration?

One explanation lies in the fears these emigrants felt about the future. They were hardy pessimists, certain that things were getting worse and that in the long run they would get much worse. 'My flight allowed me to escape destruction,' wrote Robert Bowles. Bottomley referred to his 'dark forebodings' about the future. Believing that their country was in the throes of a long-run decline, they regarded emigration as a defensive measure, a means of not slipping backwards as the nation did. Both Robert Bowles and Thomas Steel were readers of Cobbett, who believed that England had been at her zenith at the time of Edward III, and that her decline had been more precipitous since the Glorious Revolution of 1688 'until she has become the land of domestic misery and of foreign impotence and contempt; and until she, amidst all her boasted improvements and refinements, tremblingly awaits her fall'.[37]

Some feared that while revolution was inevitable in Britain its outcome would bring no improvement. William Hall listed among the reasons for his decision to follow Birkbeck to Edwards County, Illinois, in 1821:

> That as there could be no prospect of amelioration in England without the total subversion of all the existing relations of society & Government the convulsion caused by such a change would almost to a certainty involve persons in my situation in total destruction & all the Horrors of Civil War ... for altho some individuals might rise to Glory & Eminence in the contest should it prove successful yet the prosecution of it must be destructive to everything like domestic virtue & Religion in the rising Generation ...[38]

Although this theme was strongest during the years just after the Napoleonic wars and in the 1830s, a Scottish-born doctor advised his father, a civil servant in London, as late as 1847 to buy land in Wisconsin as a hedge against the probability of revolution in England.[39] No reader of emigrant letters can wonder at Karl Marx's prediction of an impending revolution in England.

These fears about the future had a social as well as an economic aspect. Some emigrants doubted that they could maintain the social status of their family at home. George Courtauld did not like his daughters to seek employment as governesses, and they chafed at being made to feel like employees. Edwin Bottomley feared the future because he could envisage no other occupation for his children than as factory workers. A clergyman assured his son who had emigrated to the wilds of Indiana before 1820: 'Had you stopped here you would have lived somehow, but you could not have continued in the society you have been used to. Here the smaller stations of property appear gradually wearing into pauperism and the prospect before us is unpromising indeed.'[40] A fear of loss of status in one's own society helped produce a willingness to undergo material privation in another.

High on the scale of priorities of the industrial workers from Lancashire and Yorkshire was a hope of escaping from trade fluctuations. This attitude led Samuel Mearbeck to turn down profitable offers of work in his trade after he arrived in New York in 1817. It led the Morris family to exchange jobs in Pennsylvania textile mills in which they were saving money for farms in Ohio where cash was very hard to come by. Edwin Bottomley urged his father to come to Wisconsin 'wher you can meditate on the mercies of God without anyone to interfere and Disturb your meditation' rather than hazard the fluctuations in income from his investments in cottage property in Huddersfield.[41] In addition to his escape from landlords, parsons and tax gatherers, Robert Bowles, congratulated himself on being able to 'go to bed at night equally free from care or trouble – No brooding over the trials of Business' in Ohio.[42] Interested only in escaping from commercial life such businessmen and craftsmen did not contemplate becoming commercial farmers in America. Although they did not join communities, they were seeking an agrarian utopia.

No other goal was mentioned so frequently as that of independence. Almost without exception these immigrants believed that farming was the most independent life. To them independence meant gaining a livelihood without having to work for, or take orders from, anyone, be he employer or landlord. Independence meant being self-employed. 'You may depend on a better way of living here than any tenant-at-will on the Coloden estate,' wrote one immigrant, 'especially more independent'.[43] To both manual and clerical workers the term 'independence' meant freedom from an authority or master.[44] The prospect of 'independence from all supercilious and brow-beating superiors' was a stronger inducement to farm ownership for some of the less commercially-minded immigrants than were the prospect of capital gains from land or profits from agriculture. Immigrants to American agriculture sought to escape from unwanted social relations arising out of economic dependence.

Other meanings of the word supplemented this central one. To some, private land ownership constituted independence.[45] To the middle classes it might mean freedom from having to work at all. To James Steel, one's 'glorious privilege' of independence was jeopardized if one were in debt.[46] To the readers of Cobbett, raising one's own food constituted independence which was even more complete if one made all one's consumer goods as well.

Is it not an invaluable acquirement to be happy possessing nothing? But to meet the case more fairly, is it not delightful to acquire the art & ingenuity abundantly to supply all our wants with a seeming paucity of materials? Enjoyment *so* obtained has a sweeter relish, is less encumbered, more independent, & has a firmer base.[47]

Emigrants who placed a high value on securing independence did not use the term in the same way as did middle-class publicists who urged the poor to show their independence by staying off the rates.[48] Some letter-writers who went to America to achieve independence had no

hesitation about seeking aid from the Overseers of the Poor to do so,
just as immigrants from a higher social class took continuous subsidies
from their families while they tried to attain that goal.

Ann and Betsey [wrote two immigrants to their wives in Britain] you must
exert yourselves with all your might, you must throw yourself on the Parish
or they will not do anything for you. . . . Do not let the Parish know that you
can work at the Needle, as they would Say you could earn your own living.
You must push with all your strength . . .[49]

The value of independence sometimes conflicted with rational
economic behaviour in the sense that individuals were willing to forgo
better economic opportunities to gain it. George Courtauld tried to
persuade his son, Samuel, to leave the profitable business of silk
manufacture in Essex for an Ohio farm:

Let us hope [he wrote to another son] . . . that he may be able with prop^y to
make the change, from A Business & circumstance that must be v^y distressing
& follow us where a more simple state of society & which offers to persons in
moderate circumst^s a greater portion of comparative independence than is
easily obtained & retained by such persons here. . . .[50]

In search of independence skilled industrial workers turned to primary
production and rejected more productive ways of using their labour
and talents.[51]

To many a British immigrant the desire for independence was
connected with a longing for leisure. It seems incredible that people
with a high preference for leisure should have contemplated clearing
farms in America, but this was another of their less realistic aims.
Immigrants hoped that they would find the leisure on American farms
they believed their forefathers had enjoyed in Britain. Published letters
from immigrants in American agriculture often noted that in the United
States one had to work only three or four days in the week to support a
family. Farm labourers in the United States and Canada sometimes
commented that, although one had to work from sunrise to sunset, one
could take it easier during the day than one could in England.[52] The
statement that 'the Americans . . . live well and work little' not only
appealed to the high preference for leisure among prospective emigrants
to whom it was directed; it also reflected the low incentive to hard work
on a western farm whose markets were so limited that there could be
little return for extra effort.[53] The letters of John Fisher, Mrs Whittaker
and Andrew Morris contain expressions of this longing for leisure
which was gradually eroded as they began responding to commercial
opportunities in America.

Resistance to the dispersal of the family through the migration and marriages of children was another motive which led people into American agriculture. Although immigrant farmers occasionally mentioned the opportunities for the 'rising generation' which America offered, more of them hoped that a farm would form the basis of a family economy which would make it unnecessary for their children to disperse in search of a livelihood. This motive can be seen in the Morris series. George Courtauld carried on in the face of severe difficulties in clearing his Ohio land with an image of improving social evenings to be spent with his sons and daughters gathered around him.[54] Mrs Sarah Mytton Maury, the wife of a cotton trader, gave this as the reason for her desire to emigrate to an American farm:

I see English parents daily parting from their sons, without a hope of seeing them on this side of the grave. Surely it is wiser and happier and more in accordance with the laws of God for all to seek together a land where they may retain the blessings of kindred, and of domestic and undivided intercourse.[55]

All of these attitudes – distaste for commercial life, desire for independence, love of leisure, resistance to family dispersal and faith in subsistence farming – were to be found among craftsmen, domestic workers such as handloom weavers, and also among some farmers, professional people and even manufacturers and merchants in Cobbett's generation. These attitudes conflicted directly with the optimal requirements for an industrializing society. Some of the speeches of early English socialists equally emphasized the longing of workers to be free of the uncertainties of bad trade and their desire for land on which they could 'raise the necessaries of life'.[56] An interest in socialism was expressed by some of the immigrants on American farms but not by those in industry. A farm in the west was a means of escape for some of these frustrated people who did not want to come to terms with changes in their own society. One cannot say how much of English and Scottish emigration to American agriculture served this function of safety-valve to discontents felt because of social change, but the letters suggest that it was an important part of the movement. Emigration did not always select the most ambitious people, or those most responsive to economic incentives. Many of the British who went to American farms in this period of social unrest in Britain were social conservatives who clung to a partly idealized view of the past which was their agrarian myth. Simple faith in agriculture can also be found in the letters of other immigrants who did not succeed in establishing themselves on farms in America.[57] It can rarely be found in letters from emigrants who left Britain after about

1850, however. At least these later migrants did not justify their actions in phrases which seemed to be derived from Cobbett. These attitudes, especially the desire for independence and the longing for subsistence farms, did not altogether die out, but people less frequently expected to fulfil their dreams on American farms. One reason for this must have been the discouraging reports sent back by industrial workers who had tried to do so.[58]

English and Scots immigrants did not place equal value on all parts of the vast spectrum of benefits America has been said to have signified for Europeans in the nineteenth century. Except among a few of the better-known publicists such as Morris Birkbeck, no evidence of religious motivation has been found. Although many immigrants were nonconformists, they did not complain of the political and educational disabilities which they still suffered in England. Whether Anglicans or not, many immigrants in agriculture showed pietist leanings. To them religion was not primarily a social institution but an intensely personal concern. John Fisher seems almost to have hoped that farming in America would shield him from some of the temptations of life. Nor were these immigrants so badly informed as to expect to find an efficient school system in a young agricultural community.[59] They were more interested in the moral training of their children than in their secular education. Those who put a priority on education, like Isaac Goodchild, remained in the East.

In her study of Norwegian immigrant letters, Professor Semmingsen concluded that political democracy was one of the features of American life which attracted migrants. She expected to find a relative indifference to politics, a desire to be free of government and authority altogether, among immigrants from more backward societies like Ireland and Italy.[60] One can find little evidence of a yearning to live under a democratic government among these English and Scots immigrants. They wanted to escape from the authority of government and especially from taxes. When they spoke of liberty in the United States they usually referred to its low taxes and want of tithes. They showed little interest in participating in government. Edwin Bottomley begrudged the time and energy he had to devote to public duties in a small township in Wisconsin.[61] Thomas Steel hesitated to take out citizenship papers because of the declaration 'abjuring in the strongest terms my native country'.[62] Robert Bowles consciously withdrew from opportunities for political leadership:

You speak of my obtaining civic honours, but I assure you I have no wish of that kind to gratify – were I to thrust myself forward for preferment I am sure that it would, if obtained, cause me more trouble than pleasure and I have no ambition for that – besides if I had I know that my temper is too irritable to bear that freedom of attack which the Americans will make upon opponents of their friends.[63]

They did not cite a want of democracy as a reason for leaving Britain. While holding pessimistic views about the future in England they had no clearly formulated views about reform. Nor were they strongly nationalistic; a man who felt the strong loyalties of Cobbett did not emigrate.[64] One is inclined to associate their social conservatism with an unwillingness to participate in movements of social protest. Emigration, rather than protest, was the means with which they met unwanted changes.[65]

British immigrants who went into agriculture in America did not emigrate in order to try to save or contribute to the improvement of a family farm in Britain. Only one of them mentioned the possibility of helping to pay the rent on an English farm. Taking a farm in the United States was not a means of being able to send cash back across the Atlantic. Undertaking no responsibility for family or enterprises left behind, the emigrants to American agriculture made a clear break. One of their strongest assets was the fact that most of them had decided to remain in the United States permanently before they emigrated. Though they hoped to visit England, even this intention was frustrated as the cares and expenses of farming piled up.

3

Networks of Distribution

It is customary in discussions of the distribution of immigrants to refer to projects and colonies, to emigrant guidebooks, and to various kinds of emigrant recruiting agencies, from state governments to railway and steamship companies and land associations. All of these left published evidence of their efforts to influence the distribution of migrants. The emigrant letters indicate that these activities were much more noisy and conspicuous than effective in prodding prospective immigrants to particular decisions.

The only reference in the letters to a railway land company's work is in a long letter written in 1871. The writer, John Dixon, who used the land company offices of the Burlington Railway in Liverpool to purchase his tickets seemed not to have had the slightest feeling that by using the services provided by the railway company he need look at any of its land. He went to Iowa, it is true, but to the family of the friend with whom he travelled.[66] So far we have found no one who became interested in the USA through the propaganda of recruitment agencies.

Many of the would-be founders of colonies were no more disinterested in advising emigrants than the various recruitment agencies which have been denounced over the years, by government officials, reformers and historians, for doing so much harm to migrants. Their influence upon prospective emigrants was perhaps slightly greater than that of commercial recruitment agencies. One occasionally encounters a reference to Birkbeck as the source of an interest in emigrating to the USA. His colony at Wanborough and that of the Flowers at Albion became an established part of the British travellers' grand tour of the United States during the 1820s, though few of the reports they published were friendly.[67] As time went on private accounts supplemented the public condemnations of Morris Birkbeck as an emigrant adviser. In 1833 an English Quaker from Birmingham visited a cousin who had been one of the early settlers at Wanborough. He reported to his brother that over the fifteen-year period since Wanborough was founded only twenty-one families (118 persons) had come from England to settle there, along with

about thirteen American families. He concluded that 'they have committed a great error in going so far to follow the fortunes of Morris
Birkbeck who was *very ignorant as a practical farmer*'.[68] So little influence did the publications of Birkbeck and the Flowers have upon the
distribution of British immigrants in the USA in the long run that in
1870 not quite six hundred English, Welsh and Scots-born inhabitants
were enumerated by the census in the whole of Edwards County,
Illinois – about eight per cent of its population.

Like Birkbeck, all such prospective colonizers wrote guidebooks.
George Courtauld produced his when he returned to England in 1819 to
recruit settlers for his colony in Englishtown, Ohio. His successor, the
man who managed the Courtauld lands after the family had retreated
to England, also published an invitation to immigrants in the form of a
'letter' in an emigrant guidebook.[69] But James Knight was not content
with this means of reaching prospective settlers. In order to direct
English migrants to the hilly, wooded lands of Athens County, Ohio, he
also wrote for English newspapers the kind of emigrant letter which
prospective emigrants learned to distrust. 'The Emigration to the
United States this Year has exceeded treble usual Years', he wrote to
George Courtauld in 1831, 'But we can have none to join us here'.
Knight began to turn his efforts towards diverting some of that stream
to Nelsonville, Ohio, where he owned land and kept a country store.
'During the past two years,' he explained to Courtauld in 1833, 'I have
perhaps wrote fifty [letters] on the subject of Emigration to various
enquirers – several I learn have been published – some you may perhaps seen – I want to make this if I can an English settlement.'[70] Probably as a consequence of these efforts, in the spring of 1832 forty
English emigrants from Wisborough Green suddenly arrived un-
announced at Nelsonville. All of them were young people, some with
families, whom Knight had known when they were children. At about
two hours' notice Knight had to set to work to feed them all, house
them temporarily in cabins and warehouses which he owned, in order to
try to keep them long enough to influence their land purchase.[71] Even
this modest success was based in large part upon the personal contact
of the immigrants' families with Knight before he emigrated, not so
much upon his advertising efforts. Neither Englishtown nor Nelsonville
flourished. As early as 1830 James Knight had to report to Sophia
Courtauld that at Englishtown 'now most of the cabins are gone or
going to ruin. And the faces of relations and friends and the lively
prattle of children are heard no more'.[72] He died in 1837, before his own
efforts at Nelsonville had borne much fruit. In 1870 only 258 English
and Welsh-born people were living in the whole of Athens County, Ohio.

2*

The British formed a smaller share of the population of that county than they did of the state of Ohio as a whole.

The greater concentration of English immigrants in Vanderburgh County, Indiana, where another agricultural colony had been founded by people attracted to America by Birkbeck's writings, resulted from urban growth rather than successful publicity by the colony's founders. Within twenty years not a single inhabitant was left at the agricultural colony in Saundersville, Indiana, but many of the immigrants had moved to the growing town of Evansville nearby. There one of these erstwhile farmers, John Ingle, started an ambitious project for influencing the distribution of English immigrants. The immigration bureau which Ingle inaugurated at Evansville, some time before 1850, provided several services which migrants from England usually had to arrange for themselves. It forwarded money through an English banker to enable immigrants to assist friends and relatives to come to America and also to help old or needy relatives in England. The bureau also aided immigrants in collecting legacies in England.[73] This innovation did not bring a flood of English immigrants into the area, although more English and Welsh-born people were living in Vanderburgh County in 1870 than in either Edwards County, Illinois, or Athens County, Ohio. With 729 immigrants, this Indiana county had a higher concentration of English people than did the state of Indiana in 1870; but urban growth had come to the rescue of the colonizers. Little can be attributed to the colonizing efforts themselves.

Prospective colony builders were able to attract either people from their own immediate families or neighbourhoods or else rather literate and romantic middle-class migrants who did not make good frontiersmen. The immigrant letters suggest that little attention was paid to such projects by the ordinary emigrant, unless he had some sort of personal contact with a sponsor or settler or had no other means of emigrating. A Scotsman in Wisconsin in 1850 noted in a letter to his brother that he had seen a prospectus of a plan to induce people to come to Wisconsin, 'But I could not give my approbation to it. The Emigration Society may do if a person could not do any better', but he advised his brother to try to come on his own. Only then could he buy land at the cheap government price. Moreover, he pointed out, colonies were quite unsuitable in Wisconsin where neighbours did not settle close, as they did in Scotland, but scattered to find range for their livestock.[74] Though the many colonies projected and advertised in England have considerable interest, they have received more attention from historians than their importance in the distribution of British emigrants merits.[75]

Emigrant guidebooks were one mode of advertising colonies. The infrequent mention of any guidebooks in the letters suggests that emigrants did not often use them as a source of disinterested information. They were wise to be suspicious of the early guidebooks, many of which were simply plugs for a particular tract of land or fronts for projected colonies closely associated with someone's land speculations. Moreover, every literate traveller, however limited his experience, seemed to think writing an emigrant guidebook a good way of trying to pay expenses. A young merchant by the name of James Stott, on arriving in New York City in 1820, wrote to his wife that he intended to write down his advice about sea-stores, quarantine, tips, the condition of immigrant vessels, 'things which would render "Knight's Emigrants" guide more than double its present value'.[76]

By the early 1840s a few guidebooks began to appear in Britain which could make a claim to being disinterested and which at the same time were often better informed. The publishing houses of William Strange, William and Robert Chambers, Thomas Tegg and John Cassell, which brought out books for the large working-class market, each produced an emigrant guidebook.[77] Prepared as possible bestsellers at a low price, these guidebooks drew on quite a few different sources for their information. Chambers' first effort was in *Information for the People* in 1842, long before either of the brothers had visited America. In separate pamphlets they provided information on the USA, Canada, Australia and other fields of emigration. When these more accurate guidebooks did discuss the United States they tended to favour the rapidly growing states of the Old Northwest. Here was a source of influence on the distribution of British migrants, since the only guidebook to be actually mentioned in these private letters was, in fact, Chambers' *Information for the People*. Catherine and William Freeman, the children of a radical London carpenter, Dr Thomas Steel, son of an exciseman, and Ann Whittaker, wife of an urban provision dealer, consulted the Chambers' pamphlets.[78]

Thus neither colonizers, emigrant guidebooks nor published emigrant letters had a great deal of direct influence upon the decisions of those emigrants whose private letters have been preserved. For most of them the principal source of information about the United States and the chief instrument of their distribution was the private emigrant letter. Again we come up against common misconceptions. The following remark is so typical of the view usually taken of private emigrant letters as to appear simply self-evident: 'for two centuries, letters from former neighbours and acquaintances who had emigrated had been eagerly received and often circulated among the inhabitants of entire communities'.[79] This picture of the widely circulated letter has been painted

in words for villages in every European country which produced overseas migrants. At least in England and Scotland by the nineteenth century it was probably an inaccurate one. These immigrants who entered
American agriculture did not forbid their relatives from showing letters
to anyone outside the family quite so often as did some of the immigrants presented in Parts II and III; but they definitely wrote private
letters, not intended for oral 'publication' in the village. 'Do not permit
the perusal of any of my letters outside of our own family,' wrote a
young doctor farming in Pennsylvania in the 1820s.[80] In the 1880s a
farmer's son from Yorkshire in Iowa, writing to a cousin, asked that
the letter be read to his grandparents; he did not assume that it would
be read to them.[81] British immigrants took the view that if, like James
Knight, they gave an invitation to immigrants to come to them, they
would be obliged to be their hosts when they arrived. The immigrants in
agriculture were willing to do this for relatives. Indeed, they often
looked actively for young relatives who might provide some labour as
well; but they did not so often offer hospitality to others, and when they
did the invitation was specific.[82] This may be the reason that the most
content and complacent reports on America were usually followed by
such a remark as 'I will not persuade'· or 'I will not invite' anyone to
come. The British emigrant letter was not meant for general consumption. Partly because of this an emigrant could say that he would trust
nothing except private sources of information.[83] The English and Scots
people knew how to discount puffs in published letters. Only the private
letter was important in the process of distributing immigrants to
American agriculture. Here was where the planning was undertaken,
the advice given as to what to bring, when to leave, what to provide on
shipboard, how to avoid runners, how to get to one's precise destination, how much to save for freight of luggage inland. Such letters have
not been reproduced, but they are numerous and typical.

   The immigrant letter was used for these purposes because, for the
immigrants who intended to take up farming, the family provided the
main network of distribution. Most of the farmers in this volume went
to join relatives who had emigrated earlier. Some British soldiers who
deserted in New London, Connecticut, during the War of 1812, when
asked where they were going as they set off on the road out of town,
are said to have replied gaily, 'To our uncles!' Uncles were the family
member whom immigrants most frequently sought on arrival in the
United States. The uncles kept the migration option open in a family
from one generation to the next. Emigrants were expected to accept and
to assist nieces and nephews who might want to emigrate.[84] The enlarged family thus continued to have at least this function in English

and Scots life. In Britain, young boys were often sent from parental farms to town by apprenticing them to an uncle. Other family connections were also used in the network of migration, though less frequently. Young men emigrated with or to in-laws, either their own wife's family or the family of a brother's wife or sister's husband.[85] In the few instances found in which immigrants did not go to relatives when they arrived in America they went out unmarried. Sometimes two or more brothers set out together, as did the Gilley brothers. Father-son combinations, as in the case of the McKellars, were also to be found in the passenger lists and county biographies.

Among these people attracted by agriculture as a way of life, not only was the preservation of the family often a motive for emigration; the family also fulfilled important functions enabling this great voluntary migration of the nineteenth century to take place. Because the family as a social and economic institution was generally strong (in Britain as in other European countries), the weakness of the various agencies for aiding and protecting migrants *en route* did not matter quite so much; and inadequate local welfare services in receiving countries were not continuously over-stretched by the great immigration into rural areas. After all, a city was better equipped to handle infinitely more immigrants than was a purely rural area, especially one which could generate almost no cash, as was characteristic of so many of the communities to which these British immigrants came. Families accepted the responsibilities over long distances towards relatives – not simply siblings, children and parents, but also brothers' and sisters' children, relatives of their spouses and their siblings' spouses.

It would be interesting to be able to gain more insight into decision-making in these families. John Birket condescended to his father's views, twenty years after emigration, accepting verbally his aged father's authority whilst ignoring it in practice. Nevertheless, Birket did believe that he should ask his father's permission on matters of importance after he was married and had a family of his own. In the Morris family, once the old parents had been brought to the United States, the seat of family authority also changed. Andrew Morris wrote to his oldest brother, who had not joined the rest of the family in America, 'We consent to your remaining'. In the case of two Scottish families, for which we have letters travelling in both directions across the Atlantic, more consulting and less unquestioning adherence to a tradition of patriarchal authority appeared. Peter McKellar asked the permission of his son to remarry, since the decision would affect him. 'We want a housekeeper, and I know Persis Butler wants to become my lawful wife; she could make all our cloths, socks and suits; she has likewise got considerable money which would help to give us a good start. . . . If you have any objections to the above. I will think no more of it; I would not do anything to make you uncomfortable. . . .'[86] James Steel, whose permission his son in Wisconsin sought before marrying, seemed to regard that marriage as displacing himself as his son's mentor; at that point his wife and her father became his son's advisers, even though James Steel continued to subsidize the Wisconsin farm.[87]

Unable to contemplate making any remittance to family members left in England, immigrants on farms continued to express some sense of responsibility by actually aiding relatives who did emigrate, by offering advice and injunctions about caring for dependent relatives in Britain, by sorrowing over evidences of family disunity and attempting to avoid disagreements, especially about money.[88] In contrast with immigrants in Part III who entered commercial or professional employment in the United States, family disagreements did not constitute a major reason for the emigration of these prospective farmers. The only one of these agriculturists who clearly was totally at odds with the rest of his family was Thomas Wozencraft, who became a slave owner in Georgia. Wozencraft was unusual also in settling in an area containing few other British immigrants. In this also he resembled some of the emigrants of Part III for whom family disruption was part of the background to emigration.

The family loyalties of these people were not based upon a farm or other landed property in England or Scotland from which relatives might expect some economic security. The situation was very different from that described among Polish peasants in the early twentieth century by Thomas and Znaniecki. Nor was it comparable to a landed family in Britain itself. Yet in spite of the want of a central economic function for the family, its vitality was strong enough in these cases to carry the main responsibility for the movement of people from England and Scotland to agricultural areas in America. Because there was no landed property to be nourished in the homeland, remittances did not flow from these immigrants to their families at home. One might reasonably doubt that immigrant farmers of any nationality were able to save for passage money or other types of remittance. Though offers to support relatives in the United States while they looked for land or jobs were common, prepaid passages were rarely mentioned in the farmers' letters.[89] The remnant of the family in England was to care for dependants there; if that remnant became too small the old folks were brought to America, where many elderly Britons ended their days with one of their children on an American farm. Only people who could emigrate without feeling that their families in Britain might need, and have a right to claim, their financial help, and who were not committed to trying to maintain some family property in Britain, could feel free to try to realize their desire for a farm of their own in America. The very fact that there were so few landowning yeomen in England made it easier for English and Scots rural people to try to becoming landowning farmers in America.

Only in the more exceptional circumstances, when prospective emigrants had no relatives to travel to or with, did other networks come into use: the socialist colony in the case of Thomas Steel; the Mormon Church in that of the Griffiths family; a Liverpool chapel with the Whittakers. So also a known member of the immigrant's community might provide the link with a particular destination as when James Knight's writings brought Sussex people to Athens County, Ohio, or when the Corletts and other families from Kirk Michael on the Isle of Man followed a local schoolmaster to Newburgh, Ohio. Peter McKellar and his son, Archibald, probably made their way by water to an impossibly remote corner of Vermont, Grande Isle in Lake Champlain, through information provided by Scotsmen already settled in the village of Mount Hero. Nevertheless, the enlarged family was the principal instrument for distributing these English and Scots people to farming regions in the United States.

4

Economic Adjustment in Agriculture

Sources of Capital

A successful economic adaptation was the indispensable basis for an immigrant's adjustment in America. Although each of these families was in some respects unique in its situation, the letters do suggest some patterns. The English and Scottish immigrants all had far-reaching adjustments to make in coming to farms in the United States. Even those who had been in agriculture in Britain found the methods in use in America different from those with which they were familiar. Moreover most of them were engaged in clearing new farms, a task for which none was prepared by experience.

Many of these people either brought capital for land purchase with them from Britain or left their savings in Britain until such time as they had selected land. In preparation for departure farmers sold what property they had in the form of farm implements, livestock, household goods and sometimes even government bonds, collected anything they could for improvements on their farms, and put the proceeds towards land purchase in the United States. Others came with an inheritance, a 'portion' given them in young adulthood, or savings. Immigrants in America generally advised relatives to bring as much cash as they possibly could rather than carry household goods and farm implements across the ocean.[90] Others converted savings into merchandise which they attempted to sell on arrival in America to put the proceeds into land.[91]

While the immigrants with substantial capital were doubtless a minority of all immigrants, they were conspicuous in the undeveloped areas. Herman Blennerhassett built a $40,000 home on an island in the Ohio River near Marietta in 1797; Robert Hutchinson Rose constructed a Regency-style house on the banks of a lovely lake in northern Pennsylvania before 1810; Morris Birkbeck was said to have had the finest house west of the Appalachians in 1820; James King built a log house with a magnificent view in frontier country at Sand Lake, Lenawee County, Michigan. When such men spent their fortunes in these isolated areas a considerable local multiplier was generated at least temporarily.[92] From a farm village thirty miles west of Milwaukee, a village without a store, a post office or a decent road, Thomas Steel commented in 1846, '. . . the only money in the country seems to be brought out by Englishmen. . . .'[93]

Immigrants who were unable to bring enough cash with them to buy land immediately often went to work in the eastern states.[94] Lancashire and Yorkshire weavers and cloth finishers were willing to work in American factories in order to save towards land purchase. In this respect, they were not unlike the Polish immigrants who worked in American industry at the end of the century to provide themselves with money to buy land in Poland. Possibilities of land ownership could provide the incentive to a handicraftsman to enter factory employment which he wanted, in the long run, to avoid. It is a comment both on their thrift and on American wages that the Morris brothers managed in two or three years of work in eastern factories to save enough money to think of buying land. Three hundred dollars saved in three years of employment in a textile mill in the 1830s represented the same kind of frugality for which Polish immigrants were later criticized. Married men were aided by their wives' earnings, and unmarried men could more easily save out of their own earnings. Nevertheless, these would seem to have been prodigious savings. On the other hand, such a sum was an exceedingly small capital on which to begin farming. None of these people who worked to accumulate their farm-making capital after they arrived in the United States waited until they had acquired the thousand dollars historians have cited so often as the minimum amount necessary to enter farming on the wooded frontier.[95]

Not all were successful in securing enough savings through industrial work in the east to enable them to buy land. Peter McKellar had once been a calico printer, but for ten years before he emigrated he had worked at shipbuilding and in a lumber yard. His son, Archibald, could not be said to have had a trade at all. Landing first in Grand Isle County, Vermont, where they worked for farmers, saving very slowly, the McKellars decided to go back to more developed territory for some cash:

> . . . Last fall we came down to boston and stayed about three months bussiness was pretty much at a stand and we could get very little to do I was in several [cotton] printing shops but they were doing very little. Archie wrought some time in a saw mill but could get no regular employment. . . .[96]

When they set out for Iowa the following spring, Peter had enough money to pay one-fourth of the money down on 135 acres of unimproved land. Archibald went up the Mississippi to Taylors Falls,

Minnesota, and took what work he could find, looking after horses and sawing wood, in lumber camps and blacksmiths' shops, in order to make some money for the farm while Peter worked away at clearing and planting for two years without a team of oxen.[97] Year after year Peter's pleas for money and for his son's physical help at harvest time became more and more strident: 'I cannot be here alone and have so much to do and money I must have come from where it will. . . .'[98] His son did not at any time question the view that all earnings obtained in cash or banknotes beyond his keep should be assigned to the farm's expenses.

Opportunities to save were therefore by no means wanting in the Old Northwest in this period, although cash payment was not so certain, especially on isolated farms, construction sites or lumber camps. The uncertainty of cash payment was one reason given by the Courtaulds' erstwhile share-cropping tenant, John Rochester, for not stirring himself to take employment on the Ohio Canals.[99] Perhaps similar considerations kept the English and Scots immigrants from railway construction work. The only letter-writers to use canal construction as a means of saving for land purchase were the Corletts from the Isle of Man. Very few references are to be found in county histories to construction work as a means by which English and Scots immigrants secured farms. Nor were jobs on canal, river or lake boats mentioned. One Scotsman in Iowa in the early fifties remarked ruefully that the sons of his Irish neighbours were earning higher wages than his own son, and in cash, on the river steamboats.[100] British migrants without trades who came west hoping to save for farms were more inclined to engage in teaming or lumbering. Most frequently those with neither trades nor capital secured employment as agricultural labourers.[101]

A man with a trade could, in the same way as a medical doctor like Thomas Steel, exchange his services for the labour and materials needed for farm-making, even when he could not secure much cash return for his skills. Several such cases are to be found in letters and memoirs.[102] County histories provide examples of wheelwrights, blacksmiths, harnessmakers, bricklayers, carpenters, plasterers, shoemakers, weavers, shipbuilders, gunsmiths and bakers who were able to save for land purchase and farm-making through employing their skills in western towns and villages. The most frequently mentioned ladder to farm ownership among English and Scots immigrants in Wisconsin, Illinois, Michigan and Ohio was mining and stone-quarrying. Some, like Robert Pollock, made a trip to California.[103] A few worked in Pennsylvania coal mines or in the Michigan iron or copper mines; work in the lead mines of Wisconsin and Illinois was more commonly a means by which land-hungry Britons satisfied their longing for subsistence farms.

This is the same kind of phenomenon as the remittances of Irish industrial and construction workers which went towards shoring up marginal farms in Ireland. Polish peasant farms were subsidized by the industrial earnings of young adults in Germany and the United States. The motive may have been different. To the Englishman the farm was a means to independence, and the impulse was entrepreneurial rather than attached to family solidarity. In America the savings of one's youth or even of a lifetime would be plunged hopefully into an unimproved farm, as in England they might be put into a small retail shop or public house, acceptable means of obtaining independence in England. While this investment had a different meaning to the English and Scots industrial worker or professional man than it did for the Irish or Polish peasant, the economic effect was the same. Savings generated in the secondary sector were transferred into primary production. The effect was to limit the accumulation of the most productive capital. This is the economic aspect of what has been called the safety valve.

Immigrants without capital were also able to become farm owners by working in agriculture after they came to the United States. English immigrants were more likely than the Scots to go to work immediately after arrival as farm labourers or sharecroppers. In regions where cash was scarce, sharecropping agreements, under which the immigrant rented a farm in return for part of the crop, the landlord providing all or most of the capital, were common. Only in the more developed commercial farming areas could employment be found as agricultural labourers, and many English immigrants worked as farm labourers in the east before going west to get land of their own. References to labourers and sharecroppers who later bought land for themselves appeared in letters, in county histories and in the census.[104]

Only experienced farmers, recognizing at the outset how little land represented of farm-making costs, withheld enough of their capital for the purchase of other necessities, especially livestock. Many of these immigrants were woefully short of animal labour and animal products at first. Both the inexperienced and the experienced continued to call upon their relatives in Britain for loans or outright subsidies as the voracious appetite of a young farm for capital became apparent. Even the best farm manager among the letter writers, John Fisher, borrowed from his mother so as not to have to sell his cattle, in order to build a house and stable. For many years James Steel sent off five pounds in his fortnightly letter to his son in Wisconsin, in addition to larger sums earmarked for special purposes transmitted by bank draft. Legacies were as carefully sought as any other remittances. Richard Birkbeck wished he had 'some good old maiden aunts and bachelor uncles – I would not want much. Two or three hundred pounds would make me independent forever.'[105] Considerable amounts of capital flowed into American agriculture from England and Scotland in this way.

One doubts that the family in Britain ever received a return on such loans to family members, made frequently without security. You will but 'change the mode of investing your money' Thomas Steel assured his father in London.[106] The idea that an extra injection of capital at the outset would lead more quickly to independence (because markets were not considered in the calculation) was the argument used at first by Thomas Steel. 'With a little assistance from you for a short time I feel sure of being independent in a few years. . . .' But gradually, when fifty pounds did not bring the hoped-for result of independence, Steel shifted his ground: 'If you would let me have a small sum every quarter say £10 til we get fairly afluent – we will soon be in the most flourishing circumstances. . . .' Within a month of this, Steel made clear his desperate dependence on his father's regular remittances when one failed to arrive: 'I do not know what to make of it probably it may arrive in a few days but I almost despair – it has driven everything else out of my head. . . .' Yet the next year he calmly assured his father that a capital sum for land to be purchased in his sister's name 'will secure Lilly an independence should she come to reside in this country'.[107] The Courtaulds, Edwin Bottomley and Thomas Steel eventually used the argument that they were preparing a future home for their relatives and that normal investment criteria should therefore be suspended.[108] Less rationalized were the religious arguments with which John Birket, Thomas Wozencraft and others – less well educated and less urbanized – interspersed their requests for money.[109] Both Birket and Bottomley succeeded in raising for church schools and chapels small amounts of money which they borrowed without apology for their own purposes.[110]

Such loans, subsidies, legacies and annuities came from families who had money in the funds, rental income, or relatively high entrepreneurial industrial incomes. Immigrants and their families accepted without question that industrial profits be used to subsidize farming: 'I was so delighted to think that as Sam's business improv'd & he could spare a little money to enable your father to make his house comfortable . . .', [111] wrote Mrs Courtauld. The English immigrant did not regard himself as cut off from family windfalls by emigration. Immigrants from families of industrial or agricultural wage earners, on the other hand, did not try to make such levies upon their families.

Loans and subsidies were often used to provide more comfortable housing sooner than would otherwise have been possible, to start out with a frame house rather than a log cabin or sod dugout. But subsidies were also used for land purchase, for simple living expenses, and to hire labour to make improvements or help in farm operations. Sometimes grants were made to service loans already contracted in the United States at a higher rate of interest.[112]

A source of additional capital or credit in England was not always an unambiguous asset to the immigrant farmer. It did not encourage him to make his farm enterprise self-sufficient at the earliest possible date. It seems unlikely that Edwin Bottomley or George Courtauld or Thomas Steel would have struggled so long on their farms without family assistance from Britain. None of the immigrants whose letters appear here was able to draw so regularly upon his family for assistance. Most migrants found that they could borrow locally even in remote areas, though they had to pay high rates of interest. Robert Bowles found his credit as good at the country store in Ohio as it had ever been in England and did not complain of the terms.[113] One reason that they could borrow without great difficulty was that others in the immigrant community had money to lend. Borrowing and lending among immigrants themselves was common. When friends and relatives borrowed from each other in America the terms were probably lenient.[114] Often those with easiest access to credit complained most bitterly of their need for cash. One is inclined to think that the English agricultural labourer, who came to America with neither savings nor credit, had two advantages over his better financed compatriot in his adaptation to farming in America. In the first place he tended to rely on his own resources because he could not borrow on particularly favourable terms. Secondly, the fact that he had no money for land purchase on his arrival may have helped him purchase more wisely when he did, with a better knowledge of the circumstances of American agriculture.[115]

Farming Methods

Marcus Hansen's view that immigrants served as 'fillers-in', purchasing improved farms from native-born Americans who moved elsewhere, has rarely been questioned.[116] Emigrant letters supplement other recent evidence that Frederick Jackson Turner's schematic model of successive waves of specialized settlers, from pioneer to capitalist farmer, is wrong. The letter-writers were not mainly fillers-in. They were pre-empting land in advance of sale, buying unimproved land from the federal government and taking over claims on which little effort had been expended.[117] Most of the families to whom we have referred spent years clearing and bringing land into cultivation for the first time.[118] Few of the manuscript letters come from people who bought improved farms which were going commercial concerns.[119] Possibly emigrant letters exaggerate the pioneering element among British immigrants because of the social isolation on the frontier and the need for capital. But a sampling of county histories confirms an impression that the British were helping in the tasks of clearing, breaking and fencing new land. Samuel Mearbeck bluntly described his early efforts at clearing: 'About the middle of May I went to my land which was all woods, took an axe with two or three other necessary tools with me, made myself a camp, covered it with bark in the same way the hunters do, and then fell to work at chopping down trees. . . .'[120]

The search for cheap land brought these migrants to the edge of the frontier. To British immigrants a farm of 80 to 160 acres was not a very large farm. With limited means, they had to get to a region where government land or undeveloped speculator-held lands were still available, to satisfy their aims with respect to land purchase. Some who settled first on the east coast later moved farther west because they found the price of land too high.[121] Former industrial workers shared this initial proclivity for unbroken land for the same reason, because they wanted a larger farm at a low price for the land. Even in Vermont, Peter McKellar reported 'land here stands about twenty-five Dollars an acre we must have it at a lower price. . . .'[122]

Since the main consideration drawing these people to the farming frontier was their search for cheap land, many did not select their land with great wisdom, either with respect to its suitability for subsistence agriculture or its future prospects for commercial farming. Few chose land quite so blindly as Samuel Mearbeck, who bought land in the wild rness in a Washington land office, but even George Courtauld, who contemplated an extensive purchase and who actually did see the land before he bought it, was influenced primarily by the low price asked for it. Rejecting more fertile soils because they would require drainage, the settlers at Saundersville, Indiana, bought high and rolling ground which they expected to be more healthy but which was also more easily eroded. Several immigrants tried to select what they thought would be healthy terrain. The inexperienced also tried to find land which had a road nearby. Industrial workers did not hesitate to buy hilly, broken lands.[123] The best choices were made by farmers who arrived with capital, but this may have been partly fortuitous. The Birkets, the Corletts and John Fisher settled in frontier country near sites which later became important towns. The handloom weavers from Lancashire, as well as

Mearbeck, the Courtaulds and the Birkbecks settled in what came to be arrested frontiers. Immigrant labourers and industrial workers who, like Robert Smith, were unable to buy land immediately after their arrival in America, or in the west, and who worked for other farmers until they had the savings to become landowners, had a better chance of buying land wisely than did industrial workers who bought land immediately.[124]

If the search for cheap land brought them to the frontier, the difficulties of clearing farms from woodland soon led a large number of these immigrants to try to add a little prairie land to their original purchase or to try to buy prairie lands in the first instance. The attraction of the prairies was a persistent theme in the English immigrant letters from the time of Birkbeck and Flower onwards, before the American suspicions of these lands had been overcome. Thus in the 1830s English and Scottish immigrants were persistently taking up oak openings, as letters in these collections illustrate. Thomas Steel's reaction to his first sight of Wisconsin prairie in 1843 was in keeping with the Birkbeck tradition:

... leaving Prairie ville we traveled about two miles farther when we reached the most beautiful tract of country that I have yet seen – everywhere as far as the eye could see the most beautiful park like appearance presented itself – with a rich sward – the trees arranged in clumps as if laid out by the hand of man for a park – the country was not level but what they term here rolling . . . .[125]

The English and Scots immigrants used the prairie land for their arable farming, not simply as pasture for livestock. Before they had time to assimilate the American mistrust of the prairies, the British immigrants not only responded to their natural beauty but also seized upon smaller ones to save the work of clearing. Those who tried to wrest a farm from thickly wooded land became terribly discouraged.[126] Thus the prairies of the middle west were an asset in the adaptation of British immigrants to western farming.

Whatever ideas about good agricultural techniques they brought with them from Britain, their chief problem in America was adaptation to local conditions.[127] Too great a commitment to a certain cropping pattern or a rigid view that English farming methods were best in some absolute sense, not to be modified by labour or capital shortage, a severe climate or a want of market opportunities, were handicaps. Like other immigrants just after their arrival, confident that English methods would succeed whatever the economic circumstances, Hugh Nudham poured scorn on the techniques he observed in use in the States.[128] Yet once immigrants had spent some time in America these condescending and scornful attitudes began to soften. The view began to be expressed that a rigid adherence to English farming methods would not pay in the United States. 'The mistake of many English who settle as farmers', wrote Joseph Pickering, an English farmer who spent six years in the United States and Upper Canada during the 1820s, 'is that they are so fond of their own opinions as to attempt the introduction of English husbandry, and entail a heavy expense upon themselves for their folly.'[129]

At first those who knew something about farming in Britain showed a determination to introduce improvements on American methods. Thomas Steel planned that 'my horse and cow when I get one will supply me with manure'.[130] Immigrants from regions where livestock farming was emphasized tended to save some of their capital to get animals immediately. Thus Edward Gilley, who had worked as a farm servant in Northumberland, noted: 'I was obliged to keep a good part of my money back to buy farming implements and stock and provisions to last until I growed enough for my maintenance. . . .'[131] Immediately after their arrival, before markets meant much to them, British immigrants in Illinois in the thirties and Wisconsin in the forties, men who had prior knowledge of dairy farming, thought that 'probably dairy farming would be the most profitable'.[132] Others had projects for drainage and ditching. Birkbeck, who had a lot of money, could indulge his passion for ditching. Thomas Steel, on the other hand, who bought marsh land with the express purpose of draining it for pasture and who disapproved of the poor work done by American ditching machines as compared with hand labour, had to postpone his plans for want of capital.[133] The British immigrants also planned experiments with hedges soon after their arrival, when they observed the insecure modes of fencing in common use. Thomas Steel proposed to try the black locust which Cobbett recommended, and John Birket experimented with hawthorn.[134]

The American environment destroyed many of these early resolves. It is not perhaps surprising to find William Hall, who had been a mill owner in England, seizing upon the information that 'The French had long been settled in that neighbourhood & the Common Field has been regularly Cropped without manure for a Century without any perceptible diminution in its fertility. . . .'[135] But even experienced farmers like the Burlends, after seventeen years in Illinois, explained to English readers that in America 'cattle are inured' to being turned loose to forage for themselves even in winter; that the 'soil of woodland is always more valuable than that of the prairies'; that they did not use manure or raise turnips because 'tillage would rather injure than otherwise'.[136] 'Everyone from England to this country has much to learn – I have gone through that ordeal,' commented James Knight about farming methods.[137]

The adaptation of experienced farmers to local practices and circumstances is evident in many letters. John Fisher noted, after four years on his Michigan land, that he could not farm it in the English fashion.[138] There was no impetus to specialization in Wisconsin, according to John Thomson from Fife. 'A farmer here must reap a little of all kinds'.[139] While a well-informed traveller like William Oliver could be convinced that 'a good Scotch plough, with the share much broader than in common use, would break prairie much better than any of those I saw at work in Illinois', a Scots immigrant on the prairies wrote home: 'Tell Dr Taylor to bring no plough with him if he comes to the prairies; scotch ploughs will do in a barren farm. . . .'[140] As late as the 1880s Fred Pickford's uncle in Iowa lost eighteen hogs on a cold winter day from their smothering each other to keep warm. 'Most people are now building places for them in winter,' he commented, but these recently arrived, penurious immigrants from a Yorkshire farm, had, of necessity, to go against both their own better knowledge and the practice of better-off neighbours.[141]

While former farmers abandoned such practices as manuring the soil and stall-feeding of livestock only when forced to by shortages of capital and labour, the inexperienced farmers, who were trying to gain their independence on American farms, could do no more than try to learn from their neighbours. As for Thomas Steel, his father tried to act as tutor from his home in Holloway, London, from the knowledge he gained as a youth on a Scottish farm and his extensive reading of agricultural literature. James Steel, who was reading von Liebig's *Soil Chemistry* in 1845, thought he knew something about farming. Not only were his letters full of advice, but he also sent articles from the agricultural press from which he thought his son might profit.[142] Thomas had to reply that all of this was very interesting, 'though we are not in a situation yet to avail ourselves much of improved methods of farming'.[143] Until he secured the help of his father-in-law, a carpenter, and two brothers-in-law, equally novices, Thomas Steel was not able to get his twenty acres into cultivation. Even then his difficulties, arising partly out of their want of experience, were manifold. Having bought a cast iron plough for seven dollars they set to work in 1846; 'the third furrough the nose of the plough got under a root the oxen pulled and the beam snapped like a carrot – having been made of poor and brittle oak nicely painted over. . . .' After his father-in-law had fixed a new beam of tough ash, 'Alfred and William then had a trial – when alas in passing the root of a tree some how or other one of the cast iron plates was [shattered] in pieces – so here we are in a fix – probably I may be able to get a new casting at Milwaukee – the truth is I should have had a wrought Iron plough – . . . .'[144] Harvest-times proved equally harassing. Unable to afford the American-type cradle, they used two scythes and a billhook to cut their grain.

as I am no hand at stack building never having seen it done I must endeavour to get it thrashed as soon as possible for fear of accidents – I intended to have it thrashed by hand – which we are now doing to a small extent to take to the mill but find we get on so slow – and having no barn are exposed to all sorts of weathers that I believe it will be my wisest plan to get it thrashed by a machine or a skillful hand – particularly as there are so many other necessary things to be done . . . .[145]

They made mistakes as well in the handling of their livestock. With his father's money Thomas Steel had been able to put up a shed for his oxen within two years of his arrival, but stall-feeding meant little when fodder ran short before the end of winter. In 1845 he had to turn his horses out to shift for themselves. Two years later, in spite of purchases of hay, he found his oxen too undernourished to be able to undertake the spring ploughing.[146]

After three years of poor wheat crops in the late forties, when their yield per acre went down to six bushels, Mrs Steel reported, 'Father is preparing to plant Indian corn on a part of the ground where wheat should be. . . .' This former cabinet-maker did not change his cropping patterns readily with the appearance of rust and fly on the wheat, combined with low prices.[147]

The disappointments of Peter McKellar, another relative novice at agriculture, were of this same order. In describing his harvest of 1855 he wrote to his son:

I had not time to do every thing right and there was no help to be had for money and a great part of my work had to lay behind til it was too late hamilton got his corn off the ground before me then he went and bought 26 sheep and put in his own land and they came over on my corn and destroyed about 30 bushels of it. . . .[148]

The shorter collections included in this volume do not provide quite such circumstantial details of early disappointments encountered by inexperienced farmers in the west. Yet among the cases considered, those with experience succeeded more readily on American farms, so long as they were willing to change their methods when appropriate. Robert Pollock, Robert Smith and the Morris brothers indulged in constant cropping, failed to treat the soil, were grateful not to have to plough the land for a year or two to get a scratch crop, and did not seem to be aware of the clear signs of declining fertility in their lands.[149] The Morris family followed their American neighbours in turning to tobacco as a substitute for wheat.[150] The men with farming experience in Britain – the Birkets, the Griffiths, the Corletts and John Fisher – did better than industrial workers partly because they had more capital, partly because they made better choices of land, and partly because they combined their experience with a readiness to adopt American methods when appropriate.

Standards of Living

Another aspect of the immigrant's economic adaptation, which depended on his background in Britain and his attitudes at the time of migration, was his relative satisfaction with the standard of living he was able to achieve in America. People whose motives for emigration had been largely non-economic were willing to accept a reduction in their standard of life, because they hoped to gain independence, family unity and leisure. Such values sustained Samuel Mearbeck, the Morrises, the Whittakers and John Fisher. A substantial English farmer who had a strong ideal of a peaceful, independent retreat was Robert Bowles, who settled in the hinterland of Cincinnati in the early 1820s.

Tis true [he wrote] that for some time we had many inconveniences, and many sacrifices. We had trials to undergo as necessary attendants on strangers and wanderers in a new country, in search of a home, without friends to apply for instruction or advice, and with the consideration that one false step might prove inevitable ruin. . . .

When that period was finished he was content 'surrounded with abundance of everything but money and that we have little occasions for. . . .'[151] Men with economic ambition, like Joseph Hirst, John Birket and Thomas Wozencraft, were less likely to undergo privations willingly.

Sometimes the farming idyll was inadequate to withstand the onslaught of objective conditions in a relatively undeveloped territory.[152] A greater advantage for successful adaptation to the conditions of the frontier was the memory of a relatively low standard of living before emigration. This may be one reason why English immigrants who arrived in Edwards County, Illinois, during the early years of its settlement, when England was in the grip of a post-war depression, seemed more content than those who came five or ten years later.[153] Both Mrs Whittaker and Mrs Butterworth had agrarian dreams, but Mrs Whittaker, whose husband had been a petty provisions dealer in Leeds, showed more fortitude during her early years in America than Mrs Butterworth, whose father was an estate agent in Rochdale.

Immigrants from both rural and urban places had to accept a lowering of living standards in some respects during their first years in the United States. In only one respect did few immigrants complain about the standard of living on a western farm in the twenties, thirties and forties. This was the standard of diet. When immigrants referred to America as a land of abundance, they meant food. Five years after he had arrived in Wisconsin, Edwin Bottomley wrote with satisfaction, 'I shall have bread for my Children and Pork sufficient for them also.'[154] Nevertheless, one Yorkshire farmer's wife thought the general standard of diet among the natives around her in Pike County, Illinois, in 1831, rather low. The Illinois settlers, she wrote, lived very differently from the English peasantry. They had only three meals a day and rarely ate fresh meat, which they could never obtain, as in England, by going to a butcher. Yet once they had put in their ten or fifteen years of hard, unabating work, she was completely satisfied with the diet they achieved on their farm, all 'within ourselves'.[155]

To immigrants who had experienced or seen food shortages in England the ease of gaining food in the west compensated for other privations. Delayed in Wales after a shipwreck on his way to America in 1816, Samuel Mearbeck, the metal-plater from Sheffield, wrote to his mother, 'Wales is a most miserable country. Many of the inhabitants live on barley bread and are very ignorant and dishonest.'[156] Somehow American poverty did not strike him as so deplorable because it was accompanied by independence:

The country people live on very coarse food and there are a number of familys near my land that live on bear bacon, venison, wild turkeys or anything they can get, and spend their time hunting instead of minding their land. The woomen make all ther own clothing; the men tan their own leather, make their own shoes and nearly all their own farming utencils. They are the most independent people I have ever seen.[157]

None of the British farmers, whose letters we have, complained of an absolute shortage of food. Nor do they appear to have been bitter about the need for substitutes for some purchased groceries. They had to use corn meal instead of wheaten flour to make bread. Roasted Indian corn had to serve as a substitute for coffee. Necessities in England became luxuries in the west.[158] Thomas Steel described efforts to imitate local methods of breadmaking in Wisconsin without yeast.[159] Similarly, English immigrants on the plains, later in the century, wrote, 'I believe the real reason we appreciate treacle so much here, is that here we have no butter or jam, and very little sugar, and it acts for all three. . . .'[160] None of these British immigrants wrote with the bitterness of John and Sarah Kenyon, immigrants from New England in Iowa in the late fifties, that they would 'dread for our neighbours to come to see us', with 'no butter no sweetening', 'no tea or coffee no spices no grease. . . .'[161]

The standard of dress which immigrants could achieve depended less upon their own farm produce and much more upon their opportunities to obtain a cash income and the progress of American manufactures. English immigrants in the east during the first half of the nineteenth century thought that both fine clothes and cheap clothes could be purchased for about the same prices as in England.[162] One young girl expressed her delight that in New York she could wear silk and crepe 'without a parish grumbling about it'.[163] Such acquisitions were not to be made by subsistence farmers in the west. Mrs Burlend recorded that after they had been in Illinois for a year their clothes were tattered; they had less warm clothing than when they arrived. Thomas Steel found that the long grass in Wisconsin cut up his trousers sadly.[164] On farms which tried to rely upon homespun cloth and homemade clothing, immigrants who regarded anything homemade as morally superior were predisposed to accept a lower standard of clothing than they might have had in England.[165] And others adjusted to it. A visitor to the English prairie in Illinois in the early 1830s observed:

you would smile at the extreme simplicity of dress in these parts; we look rather singular by being dressed in broad cloth. Stockings seem quite out of fashion as a common article of dress and shoes also when they are quite free from Company in summer weather, even the women think it a luxury to go barefoot. . . .[166]

Immigrants learned to call some items of common consumption in England 'artificial wants'. Most immigrant farmers continued, throughout the period before the Civil War, to advise their friends and family to bring clothing with them in excess quantities when they emigrated, and to ask for gifts of stockings and worsteds.[167] They noted the appearance of cheap domestic cottons in the country stores of the west. As early as 1828, an immigrant farmer in southern Ohio reported that he thought American-made cotton goods 'nearly as cheap as they are in England, and of a much better quality [than imports]. . . . Your manufacturers have ruined themselves in this country by sending too many showey goods filled up with Starch and well pressed to look firm. . . .'[168]

Most British immigrants seem also to have had to accept a lower standard of housing in their early years in the West than that to which they had been accustomed. Few were prepared for the reality of a log cabin or dugout. The house on the small farm in Cornwall where Hannibal Lugg was born had only two rooms, a dirt floor and a thatched roof. Its walls were made of cob, a mixture of clay and straw, and it did not have glass windows. The first home he had in Wisconsin was made of mud.[169] Few English immigrants could say, soon after their arrival in America, as did one Norwegian, 'I and my Norwegian neighbours now have just as good cabins as we did in Norway'.[170] Mrs Burlend was shocked to find the man whose private letters to his brother had induced them to come to Pike County living in a 'house . . . more like the cell of a hermit who aims at super excellence by enduring privations than the cottage of an industrious peasant'. 'It is by no means to be understood', she warned, 'that an American log house equals in comfort and convenience a snug English cottage.'[171] To live in a house without proper floors, without plaster, fireplace, windows or furniture was hardship for most English and Scottish immigrants, some of whom felt themselves to be, as Faux said, 'barbarizing in a log hut'. Those who with family assistance were able to make a start on a frame house or to buy land containing one, also suffered relatively since they were likely to have known an even better standard in England.[172] Improving the standard of housing was an important step in the economic adjustment of these immigrants, if the search for cheap land had led them to a primitive region. It provided an economic incentive where immigrants had not previously felt a strong one. Fifteen years after they arrived in America, Mrs Burlend confessed that, although they now had a new house and better furniture than in their early days in America, if these were the principal means by which possessions were measured, 'there are after all few cottagers in England who would not be on an equality with us except that their house would be rented.'[173]

Beyond the necessities of food, clothing and housing, British and Scots immigrants who were farm-making in the Old Northwest in the period before the Civil War noted a wide variety of articles which had been both cheap and easily purchased in Britain but which were too dear, too poor in quality, or simply unavailable in their new situation. Some of the lists which they sent home, itemizing their requirements, remind one that the standard of consumer goods in this region was probably little better than that on southeastern plantations after the Civil War. Immigrants from London and the manufacturing districts of England sent the longest lists, advising other intending immigrants to bring iron tools of all sorts, including lathes, hammers, saws and chisels; fire irons and candlesticks; basins, pots, china and cutlery; featherbeds, needles, tapes and laces.[174] Thomas and Catherine Steel, who came from London to a village thirty miles from Milwaukee in the early

migrant's own capacities combined with the opportunities offered by
the trade cycle. Migration to another region or out of agriculture altogether were considered when farm prices were particularly low. Investing in land in the hope of capital gains or entering supplementary occupations were more likely to be adopted in times of rising prices.

The evidence of the emigrants' letters suggests that English and
Scottish immigrants were not so inclined as their American neighbours
to sell out and move farther west if success was limited or land showed
signs of declining fertility. Many of them exhibited considerable mobility
before they actually bought land. Once they had finally invested in
farmland, these letter-writers showed a high degree of persistence.
Some former urban and industrial people exchanged their first claims
after a short time for land in the same neighbourhood. 'I have sold all
our land to McCaffery for our claim and improvements 200 dollers and
all the money we had paid in back besides. I think we can get a farm with
better land and we can start on a clear footing . . .'[192] wrote Peter
McKellar. Thomas Whittaker also bought and sold farms in Monroe
County, Illinois, as opportunity offered.

A hesitation to move to another region and begin farm-making again
is evident in many letters. Andrew Morris was tempted to follow his
neighbours as they set out for Illinois from southern Ohio in the early
forties, but he did not go. Robert Bowles would have liked to look at
Indiana prairie land, but was persuaded by his wife not to try to begin
again. After he had sold his first claim in Clayton County, Iowa, Peter
McKellar considered trying Minnesota land, but bought another claim
in Clayton County instead. Other immigrants in Fond du Lac, Wisconsin,
invited by friends to come back to New York, replied, 'as a rolling stone
gathers no moss we think we can do better hear at least we intend giving
it a fair trial. . . .'[193] In so far as we can trace the attitudes and actions of
these migrants, they did not follow the American pattern of continued
migration. Migration was resumed by the second generation. The children of the immigrants, some of whom were British-born, were one
source of the British migrants who kept appearing in each new farming
region. Several of our families – the Morrises, the Corletts, and the
Birkets – saw their children established on farms near their own. One of
John Birket's sons went to Kansas, however. The Bishop family in
Yates County, New York, had three children established nearby, but
others moved to Kansas and Michigan.[194] The first generation immigrant was unlikely to want to repeat the prodigious task of farm-making
Since he often came with an idea that a farm of his own would end all
economic uncertainties, he was inclined to pour all his efforts into that
first farm.

If he could not gain a livelihood from his farming operations he was more likely to try to diversify his activities on the spot than to try again on another farm. Henry Woods, a Lancastrian blacksmith in southern Ohio and Hannibal Lugg, a Cornish carpenter in Wisconsin, both found their industrial skills so much in demand that they never actually farmed the land they bought.[195] Others who had some pre-industrial craft, or even just a mechanical aptitude, turned to other occupations in combination with farming.[196] In the American West this type of adaptation did not require a knowledge of industrial skills on the level of an English artisan. Aptitude and flexibility were more useful than a thorough training. The crafts most useful were village crafts, not the new skills of the industrial revolution. Edwin Bottomley was trying to construct a jenny and a loom from parts sent by his father from Huddersfield, just as Walter Birket considered building a machine for processing flax.[197]

More economically ambitious immigrants tried to diversify their economic activity by entering other businesses in addition to farming. John Birket is perhaps the best example of such a man. But on a more modest scale, a Berkshire immigrant in Rhode Island, with much smaller means than Birket, added to his earnings by buying poultry and taking them to market. This man had also bought a threshing machine to thresh for others.[198] Some found storekeeping an occupation which could be mixed with farming. James Knight complacently visualised himself as the benefactor of the improvident natives.

I had considerable Corn coming into me last year from many families to whom I had supplied some two months or less before they could gather their Crops, by letting them have 3 Bushel to receive four after gathered – the greater part of this was to the very same persons that had been selling of corn to me 3 or 4 months before – this is the way you know the Americans live – and how happy they must think themselves to have an English person to provide for them.[199]

Unsuccessful farmers who did not take on other occupations sometimes adapted without further migration by land speculation or money lending on a small scale, as did John Birket. James Knight did not long keep his monopoly position as store-keeper at Nelsonville, Ohio. When competition spread from Athens, he turned his attention more and more to property.

Most of the immigrants whose letters appear in this volume did not invest in land as a source of capital gain, however, but as a means towards a livelihood through production. For this reason, instead of moving on and beginning farm-making in another region, they were more likely to leave agriculture altogether, if they could not achieve, through farming or diversification, a level of success on the land commensurate with their expectations. Those who had a trade, such as William Morris, did not have much difficulty in recovering from their mistakes, for they were able to earn a living in nearby western towns. The behaviour of the English mechanics and artisans who tried to establish a colony at Melton, Iowa, in 1850, was not unlike that of many skilled workmen whose agrarian dreams dissolved in America. Locating at different points in the west, one after another they returned to their separate callings.[200] Some were even prepared to return to factory employment after experiencing disillusionment with farming.[201]

For people who had left Britain in order to try to find Eden, a period on the land was sometimes a detour in the movement into industrial occupations. Experience of farming in America whittled away their resistance to change, and they were able to accept changes they had hoped to avoid. The letters of families who went through this cycle, such as the Morrises, probably helped to modify attitudes in England and Scotland as well, by diminishing the resistance to change among members of their own families.

Men without a trade were less easy to absorb into the economy of the Old Northwest. Clearly, opportunities were available for men who enjoyed taking risks and had some business ability. But often the immigrant did not see them. One Cambridge-educated merchant's son wrote from Upper Canada, a region not very different in many respects from parts of the Great Lakes states in 1844,

The complaints are universal of the difficulty of making a living by farming, and I feel no doubt . . . that in the present state of affairs it is not to be done. . . . Ways of making money there doubtless are, but almost any I can think of involve the necessity of moving to a more civilized neighbourhood.[202]

With some the desire for independence diminished as the glamour of farming faded. John Rochester became willing to take employment as a clerk in a store in Logan, Ohio.[203] After a well-educated friend of his family arrived on his Wisconsin farm, Thomas Steel had to admit: 'Edward seems never to have been accustomed to the use of his hands in any shape & his ignorance of all connected with agriculture and horticulture is complete. . . .' This young man went back east to try to find employment as a clerk.[204]

An immigrant with a good education, but without manual skills or aptitude, was also likely to give up and return to Britain. Such a course required that he have resources of his own or from his family to draw upon, if he were unable to realize the cost of his investment in land and improvements. An immigrant who had poured all his savings into land was unlikely to be able to return home. His higher standard of life in Britain also dictated that the better-off migrant should be the one who gave up in despair, as did the Butterworths.[205]

If these few case histories be any guide, immigrants who had been in agriculture in England were the most successful in adapting to the conditions of farming in America. William and Walter Birket, John Fisher, William Corlett, John Birchall, John Burlend and Brazilla Smith all succeeding in gaining a livelihood from agriculture, which they considered adequate, in the region in which they first bought land. In contrast with the less successful Morris Birkbeck, none of these farmers' sons brought a very large capital to the United States; nor did they grow up on very large farms, by English standards. They were unable to continue to gain subsidies from their families in England. Most of them had the additional advantage of having settled near a place which was to become, before very long, a considerable town. They were willing to work very hard themselves, and did not expect to find labourers to undertake the major part of their farm-making tasks. The letters also provide instances of men who had been farm-labourers or farm servants in Britain and who remained on their farms in the United States throughout their careers. This was the case with Isaac Goodchild from Berkshire who settled in Rhode Island; of the Bishop family who came from Suffolk to Yates County, New York in the 1850s; and of Edward Gilley in Wisconsin, the Griffiths in Illinois, and the Bonds in Kansas. Those whose early life had been spent on a farm had the greatest chance of making an accommodation on a farm in America, however different the specific tasks and circumstances, and in spite of an initial diminution in living standards. This experience was more important than capital in achieving an economic adjustment, which was, in the immigrants' own terms, satisfactory.

Farming in the United States also served as a safety valve for urban and industrial workers from England, dissatisfied with what they knew of city life and industrial work. County histories give evidence that large numbers of such individuals did manage to claim, buy, clear and farm unimproved land in the United States; and instances have been found of industrial craftsmen who managed to remain on their farms—Samuel Mearbeck, Andrew and Thomas Morris, Henry Woods and Robert Smith. Other emigrant letters indicate that subsidies from Britain or a comfortable way of life before emigration were factors which worked against the successful operation of the safety valve. It was clearly possible, before 1860, for a mechanic to arrive in the United States almost penniless and still succeed in acquiring a farm of his own. Yet among these people were many who found that independent farming was not so easy and secure a life as they had imagined. Some of them were absorbed into secondary and tertiary occupations in the regions in which they had bought farms. The better-off returned to England or Scotland.

5

Social Adjustment

If they succeeded in making an economic adjustment on the land, few
apparent obstacles blocked the social adaptation of these English and
Scottish farmers. In rural society, they were unlikely to feel many
pressures from the native-born population to conform with American
customs and attitudes. They did not meet discrimination in employment in the regions, so short of labour, to which they brought useful
knowledge and skills. They were accepted in the frontier churches, and
could take an active part in political life, once they became citizens, if
they so desired. Indeed, it is difficult to imagine circumstances more
propitious to the rapid assimilation of an immigrant group than these
British immigrants met in rural America.

In spite of these obvious advantages, many of them experienced
difficulties in adapting to American society. Those who emigrated as
adults rarely forgot that they were immigrants. The most successful
adaptation was achieved by immigrants who remained within an immigrant community, relatively insulated from the society round about
them. While the British were not notably successful in establishing large
rural colonies, a community of thirty or forty immigrants, many of
whom might in fact be relatives, was enough to stave off the worst loneliness and to provide adequate social satisfactions. Apart from the exceptional men who derived pleasure from leadership and responsibility, immigrants who had the most opportunities for contact with
Americans were the least content with their situations.

If social conflict was not a problem for British immigrants in agriculture, loneliness was sometimes quite intense and the feeling of strange-
ness profound. Few of the letter-writers questioned the correctness of
their decisions to emigrate; but many commented on the differences
between Britain and America and their feelings of being strangers in a
strange land. As one Scotsman wrote, 'I must confess this is a plentiful
country, altho it is different in the most of things from the old country'.
To immigrants, differences were more apparent than similarities. 'The
English tongue is practically all that is English in America', wrote one.[206]

They hesitated to advise others to emigrate because 'there is few who like it at first' and 'there are so many homesick complaining English folk in this country'.[207]

The most serious problems in adaptation were experienced by women. Women often resisted taking the first step of emigration. As Rebecca Burlend said, but for her dutiful obedience to her husband, she would never have crossed the Atlantic. The opposition of his wife was an important factor in Jonathan Morris's decision not to follow his brothers and sisters to America. Cobbett recognized this female resistance and devoted a section in his emigrant guide of 1829 to advice on how to persuade, tactfully but effectively, one's wife to emigrate.[208] Once having arrived in America, women were loath to continue to move.[209] Edwin Bottomley distinguished between the physical problems of adjustment on a farm in America and the additional dimension of hardship which women felt by virtue of their want of social accommodation as immigrants.

... we are contending with the Difficulties attendant on an emigrants life which generaly appear more Difficult than they realy are owing to them being in a forien land and amongs strangers and I must hear state that the woeman in general are the most Disatisfied with theire situation . . . .[210]

As in the case of Mrs Butterworth, it seems clear that fears of childbirth, without female relatives or midwife services, heightened the terrors of women immigrants. Mrs George Courtauld recalled her own experiences in the United States in the late eighteenth century, when she was a young woman:

I had many difficulties that you have not. I began to breed soon after I got there; I had never been used to work of any kind but ordering others, but by far the severest burthen I had no friend with feeling like my own, no brother or Sister to whom I could speak of my heart sickness, my pains & my fears.[211]

After several letters in which he failed to mention his wife at all, Robert Bowles finally reported optimistically 'Mrs B too I think begins to feel more comfortable, she only wants weaning and she will feel as I do. . . .'[212] Even weaning did not reconcile some women to remaining in America. After a residence of sixteen years, during which time they had never altogether given up the idea of returning to England if conditions there seemed to improve, Charles Streater finally had to inform his sister in Hampshire: 'I regret to tell you that Mrs Streater does not like the situation I have chosen for my future residence & she is set against a residence altogether in the Country, so much so that I am apprehensive no circumstances will tend to reconcile to remain. . . .'[213] Middle-class women, unaccustomed to manual labour and conscious of status, did

3*

not make good migrants. But women of all classes were more likely to express their unhappiness as migrants.[214]

Impediments to assimilation of the first generation immigrants did not arise mainly from hostility on the part of Americans. From the letters, one can judge the attitudes of the native-born only as the immigrants perceived them. Few newcomers thought they encountered either hostility or indifference on the part of Americans. John Fisher found them friendly and openhearted. Mrs Griffiths described them as 'good neighbours', particularly helpful in times of severe difficulty. 'In America no one will ever want for anything if they are willing to work', wrote immigrants newly arrived in Wisconsin, 'and if they are not able to work the Yankees have better hearts than the English, and would never see any body want, but would readily help them in any part of America'.[215] Thomas Steel was pleased to find that the socialism of himself and his companions encountered no opposition among the neighbours.[216]

These were first reactions, coloured by the expectations of the immigrants. Usually these lyrical expressions of gratefulness diminished with the passage of time. During the first few months of his residence in Wisconsin, Thomas Steel was pleased to find that there were no more rogues among Americans than one found anywhere else, and that while the 'Yankies have their own peculiarities, . . . upon the whole they are not a bad sort of people – '.[217] Necessary contacts with a neighbour who, they thought, poisoned their dogs and misled them about the location of a road, led the Steels to become more critical of American character in general: '. . . a better acquaintance has not raised the Americans much in my opinion – there is I am sorry to say a total want of principal amongst them particularly in political matters. . . .'[218] When the political agitation over the Oregon question was at its peak, they thought they would have to retreat to Canada, in the case of war, and spoke of their situation as 'disagreeable if not dangerous', even if Thomas were to declare his intention of becoming a citizen. 'I have been much vexed several times to see the spirit [the Americans] exhibit towards their transatlantic brethren even females for everybody is a politician . . .' wrote Catherine Steel.[219] Although this proved merely a temporary peak of anti-British sentiment, the Steels found the Americans less interested in social contacts with them after they had been in Wisconsin for seven years than they had at the outset: 'we have made friendly advances enough to [our Yankee neighbours] and have given it up in despair of being met in the right spirit.'[220]

After some years in America, other immigrants also thought the Americans hostile to them. Writing seventeen years after their emigration about their reception when they arrived in Illinois with limited money to spend, Mrs Burlend warned that the Americans were 'exceedingly hospitable to gentlemen who may be making a tour, likewise amongst themselves as neighbours; but when they know a person really must trouble them, they appear to be aware they are conferring a favour, and expect an equivalent.'[221] Another family, who might have given the impression that they did not have money to spare when they arrived, were the Bonds, agricultural labourers from Lancashire, who lived in Connecticut for a few years in the early seventies. They too thought the Americans a distant people, 'who dont thinck much of John Bulls'. Years later, during the Populist period in Kansas, the Bonds encountered what they interpreted as outright hostility from the community, when their barn was burned one night. In the main, however, few complained of their treatment by Americans. This absence of conflict probably reflected a low level of contact with Americans rather than the assimilation of the immigrants.

Of greater importance in their adjustment were the expectations and prior experience of the immigrants. Accepting emigration as an irrevocable step, as did many who entered agriculture, was an advantage in enduring whatever circumstances they found. Preconceptions about independence were also useful. The men who so much admired economic independence sometimes prided themselves as well on their independence of the need for much human society, as did both Thomas Steel and Robert Bowles, though obviously not even they actually lived for long in isolation.

Immigrants such as the Whittakers and the Morrises, who were accustomed to hard work, had an advantage, not only in a physical sense, but also because they felt no loss of status through attending to household and farm work without servants. Those who expected to rely mainly on their own labour and exertions were not so likely to be perplexed and offended by the indifference of American neighbours to their day-to-day difficulties. Mrs Courtauld, senior, had insight into the obstacles arising out of too great expectations of assistance from the host community when she chided her daughters:

I hope ere this your unsubdued feelings of Pride and prejudice have given way to a better and juster way of thinking and gratitude for the kindness you own you have received without abusing people for not showing you more than they thought proper, or more than you certainly had any clame on them for And as for your father's being impos'd on, I understand his severest losses have been by his English friends.[222]

One of the greatest obstacles to assimilation was the difficulty some British immigrants experienced in accepting the attitudes of social equality which Americans expressed so aggressively. Here too some British immigrants were adequately prepared for the experience. Political radicalism probably contributed less to a willingness to accept social equality than did membership in one of the weaker Protestant sects, outside the respectable strongholds of the Church of England and the Wesleyan Methodists. The best example of the influence of religion in dissolving ideas about deference is John Fisher. Because he felt himself to be still an unredeemed sinner, Fisher showed a deep respect towards his brother-in-law, Robert Smith, in spite of the latter's rather indifferent economic success. Within his own household, Fisher accepted his labourers as his social equals.

Those who did not welcome the social democracy in America were part of a minority from the more comfortable classes in England, people who had been accustomed to having servants and who were not influenced by religious denominations which put a great emphasis upon humility. These people came to America convinced of their own superiority to Americans, expecting to find them ignorant and crude. Consequently, they wished to avoid contact with them. Some of the famous English settlements were founded in part to make it possible for the better class of Englishman to live without having to mix with Americans. In these letters, Mrs Butterworth illustrates these attitudes. Rebecca Burlend, a farmer's wife and a Wesleyan Methodist, confessed that she and her husband were suspicious of their neighbours and 'scarcely knew whether to wish for increased acquaintance or seclusion'.[223] The Courtauld ladies felt that they had nothing in common with the people around them. 'I want *Society*, not company', complained one of the daughters.[224] Such immigrants did not want to meet Americans on terms of social equality; they positively resisted assimilation.

Finally, the attitude of the immigrant towards the United States and Britain affected his adjustment. Readers of Cobbett, from farmers like Robert Bowles and John Fisher to a handloom weaver such as Andrew Morris, accepted the notion before they emigrated that America was a land of liberty and low taxes, and that they were fleeing from 'tyranny', 'despotism' and 'bondage'. Wives like Ann Whittaker and Jane Morris, who shared their husbands' views in this respect, were able to make a positive contribution to the family's social adjustment. Travellers warned immigrants that they would regret leaving Britain in time, even if they felt themselves to be rejecting some of her institutions when they left. 'Whether or not we may feel our patriotism very strong while in our native land, we are sure to have it greatly increased in a foreign country and to burn with indignation at hearing our own decried or

abused in the least degree.'[225] This was, undoubtedly, a common experience. Nevertheless, travellers probably exaggerated this tendency
among British migrants of the generation after the Napoleonic wars;
they certainly exaggerated it for migrants who were fortified for migration by having absorbed the slogans of the Radical attack on Old
Corruption. Emigrants who left because of serious dissatisfactions at
home, whether these were economic or social, were not tormented by
homesickness nor inclined to feel more pride in Britain as the years
went by.[226] Migrants of the last part of the century, such as John Bishop
and Catherine Bond, who had not grown up under the tutelage of the
radical literature, were more willing to express their feelings of loss. Yet
even when homesickness was felt, in the difficult early years of farm-
making or, as was frequently the case, in old age, it was expressed in
terms of a sense of loss of family and friends, familiar places and
particular pleasures, rather than in terms of national patriotism.[227]

These immigrants in agriculture had to come to terms with the
migration experience without assistance from formal ethnic institutions.
Charitable societies for aiding distressed English and Scottish immigrants already existed in the port cities in the early part of the century,
but the rural areas, to which these people made their way, had not the
resources to establish St George's or St Andrew's Societies. The large
concentration of immigrants from the Isle of Man in the Cleveland area
after 1826 made it possible for them to organize distinctively Manx
mutual aid societies in 1851.[228] By the time such organizations were
created by English and Scots immigrants in Wisconsin towns, nearly
thirty years after immigrants began arriving in the territory in large
numbers, the English-born population of the state had already begun
to decline.[229] Thus English and Scottish immigrants in rural areas had
no obvious ethnic leaders to interpret American society for them, no
existing institutions they could join, and no strong consciousness of
an English-American or Scottish-American identity. They had to find
resources within themselves to withstand their transplantation.

When they did band together to emigrate in groups wider than the
family for mutual assistance, the experiment almost invariably broke
up in a welter of suspicion and recrimination.[230] 'What is everybody's
business is nobody's business', commented Thomas Steel on the socialists with whom he emigrated. The family was the only institution which
could bear the demands made upon it by new arrivals from Britain.
This fact makes the Mormon success among British immigrants the
more remarkable.

When a large family succeeded in establishing itself in an area, the
immigrants relied very largely on their own kin for social contacts. 'At

first it would seem a little lonely for Albert', wrote one young immigrant in Iowa in the eighties, 'but after he got to know cousins he would be quite satisfied at least I am.'[231] The Birket, Morris and Corlett letters suggest that the kind of network described in this passage, from a Quaker visitor to America, in 1856, was rather typical of the social contacts of English immigrants. The writer was visiting Jane Plummer, the clerk of the Ohio Weekly Meeting. He found, 'besides my Aunt and her dear Husband, there is an older Sister and a brother of my Mother with their families, and several of their Married children living near each other in the Country, a few miles from Mount Pleasant.'[232]

Beyond the immediate family, English immigrants sought to associate, not with Americans or other foreign-born people, but with other English immigrants.

i thought i should never see any of you again and i should never have friend nor acquaintance any more in this i was happily mistaken for on monday we had an english lady come to see us who came from hornsey near hull 2 year since. they have one son and two daughters we were all so glad that we got acquainted the first week as if we had been neighbours for 10 years and they have been our companions ever since . . .[233]

These were the sorts of contacts appreciated by newly arrived immigrants. It was satisfying to be able to write home, 'There are so many English people here that it seems much like home'.[234] Most of them longed for an English colony to develop spontaneously around them. Among the immigrants, social barriers, which might have been present in Britain, came down:

. . . you know that most who come out here from England are neither the rich nor the better classes – neither are they always the most moral – they come out here and we can only judge them from their mode of conducting themselves amongst us – what they have been or what they may be on returning to England we can know nothing. . . .[235]

Their own families and a small circle of friends from the homeland constituted the most valued companions of first generation immigrants. The families of Robert Pollock and six other Scotsmen were virtually the only non-Norwegian people in the township of Cambridge, Wisconsin, by 1880. The Whittakers, in the hinterland of St Louis, were surrounded by Germans as early as 1860. Even when they had Yankee neighbours, their social contacts with them were minimal, if other immigrants were present. Describing a round of parties he had been attending after they had been in America seven years, Thomas Steel remarked that they were 'amongst our own country people for with the Yankees we have no intercourse of the kind. . . .'[236]

Immigrants who did not succeed in joining such an informal community were less content. Peter McKellar was appreciated on both sides of the Atlantic as a good man to make a social gathering cheerful and amiable. Settling first in a Vermont township, where there were only three other Scottish families, he worked for a Canadian family and was thoroughly accepted by them. He received warm and friendly letters from them when he moved on to Clayton County, Iowa, to a neighbourhood where native-born migrants from the same Vermont township were going. Acceptance by this Yankee community did not save Peter McKellar from miserable loneliness on his farm. Immigrants such as Thomas Wozencraft in Georgia, who settled in regions where so few compatriots were present that they could not create a 'little England' or 'little Scotland' for their social life, had more social contacts with the native-born, and in this respect, seemed to have been more socially assimilated than most first generation immigrants. More of these isolated individuals will be considered in Part III.[237]

If they settled in what became a small group of their countrymen, the English and Scots immigrants nevertheless encountered Americans in commercial transactions, and sometimes as employees or lodgers. But they did not often participate in social gatherings in which they met Americans. House-raisings and husking bees were rarely mentioned, except with reference to the immigrant group. Robert Bowles did, rather unwillingly, organize two husking parties, with about eighteen people present at each, for the sake of his younger brother, but he clearly disapproved of the fact that the huskers wanted neat whisky every half hour.[238] Similarly, the Steels went along rather reluctantly to a fourth of July celebration in their ninth year in Wisconsin:

. . . we are engaged to go to a tea and ball got up by the Jenkinsville people for tomorrow being the anniversary of the declaration of independence, the greatest day in the year with the Yankees – we do not anticipate any great gratification but thought it policy to go as we have to live among them and there has been a good deal of talk on different matters between us instances prejudices &c &c. . . .[239]

The other informal organizations and social events mentioned in the letters were centred on these small immigrant communities. The Huddersfield immigrant, Edwin Bottomley, noted that although they 'had no so many Publick houses where we can meet and chat over public affairs, we enjoy ourselves By meeting at one anothers houses and a more chereful party than we are you cannot find anywhere we amuse ourselves by reading and Singing . . .'[240]

During the winter in Wisconsin, the Steels and the Freemans attended a round of parties given by themselves and immigrant friends. To some of these a few Americans were invited, and on one occasion, Irish immigrants were included because an extra fiddler was required. Mrs Steel felt, however, that the Yankees disapproved of these parties because guests stayed all night to avoid the dangerous roads and because married folk participated, in contrast to the Yankee custom whereby parties were for the unmarried young people.[241] Other social events – such as the Miscellany Society meetings in Wanborough, the Saturday afternoon gatherings in Saundersville, Indiana, to discuss agriculture, and the Burns anniversary dinners, which Thomas Steel attended in Waterville and Milwaukee in the early fifties, relied upon the presence of well-educated urban immigrants in the community.[242] Few of our farm immigrants had the cultural interests to support such societies. Although they were all ardent newspaper readers, not many mentioned wider literary interests.[243] Unless an individual found other immigrants settled near him with cultural interests similar to his own, he found no basis for social contact based upon them. This is why the migrant who played the flute or the fiddle was so valued.

Given their preference for continued association with their own country people, marriages were not common between immigrants who arrived in America as adults and Americans. The evidence we have on immigrant marriages in the nineteenth century seems conclusive that the British married Americans more frequently than did other immigrant groups.[244] Yet the letters remind us that this step was not taken lightly. Adult immigrants tried very hard to find English or Scottish wives. Each non-British marriage was justified on special grounds. John Fisher, who did not like Yankee girls, accepted his widowed brother-in-law's marriage to an American on the grounds that his numerous family dictated marriage at any cost. Peter McKellar, who in desperate loneliness and intense need of help announced to his son, 'I will take home a wife early in the spring and I will buy a cow', married a woman who had been deserted by her husband. In the few cases of intermarriage, there is little record of any subsequent contact with the wife's family. The wives of George Gilley and John Birket were orphans.

Their British-born children did more frequently marry Americans or non-British immigrants, though where an English or Scots settlement of any size persisted, as at Wanborough, Illinois, and in the Manx Settlement in Newburgh, Ohio, intermarriage could be avoided even in the second generation. When Henry Newman visited Wanborough in the 1830s, he could describe the marriages that had taken place among his relatives in the knowledge that both partners, or their families, would be known by the family in England.[245]

First generation immigrants were sometimes defensive about their children's easy absorption into American society through marriage:

... We could not see why you should laugh so much about Clara. She is in her 19th Year and is a Woman Grown. She is now Mrs Hulse, Respectable Young Farmer, as got a Large Farm and plenty of good cattle, and in fact the Yankee is a first rate chap. . . .[246]

The principal social contacts of these immigrants with Americans came through churches. Religion was something which most Scots and English farmers had in common with the native-born. Like the Americans, they came from a variety of Protestant denominations including Presbyterians, Episcopalians, Wesleyan Methodist, Primitive Methodist and Baptist. Without exception, the immigrants in agriculture, whose letters we have, professed religious beliefs. Finding an opportunity to attend religious services was as important to most of them as finding English friends. If they were too close to the frontier, or cut off from the town for part of the year by poor roads, they noted the loss.[247] The first visit from a ministering English Friend was a signal event to the Quakers at Wanborough.[248] Both John Fisher, in Michigan, and the Meatyards, in Illinois, in the 1830s welcomed camp meetings. 'I felt camp meetings the greatest means of grace to my soul I would advise all that felt themselves sinners to [attend] them at every opportunity and Prayer meetings as well . . .[249] Contrary to the impression created by travellers, not all British immigrants were shocked by the excesses of frontier religion in America. Many of these letter-writers, even Presbyterians and Episcopalians, were very piously inclined. But whether evangelical or not, they shared a highly individualized type of religious faith, which enabled them to remain on the fringes of civilization during the period before regular church services were available. In this their attitudes contrasted with those of James Grayston's wife, an Irish Catholic, who would not remain in Kansas without a Catholic church nearby.[250] The reactions of the more piously inclined to the absence of religious provision was to try to start churches of their own, by securing the services of itinerant ministers and raising money in England. In such cases, the church was likely to coincide with the same immigrant community on which other social contacts were based.[251] When they found churches already established, they suffered no discrimination, and several of the migrants held offices in the churches which they joined.[252]

Although most of these people longed for religious observances and tried to secure church services if they were not available, a minority, among whom former urban dwellers and Unitarians were conspicuous, had so individualized a religious faith that they preferred not going to church to participating in services of which they disapproved. Shocked by the 'sorrowful exhibition' at camp meetings, 'weary of the yoke' of the Presbyterian church before they emigrated and suspicious of piously inclined people, Thomas and Catherine Steel went to church only when they visited Milwaukee, where there was a Unitarian chapel.[253] Similarly Unitarian immigrants in Iowa from the West Riding explained their want of church attendance:

there is no church of our belief in Nora Springs though there are 4 churches there. So we do not go often but we attend Sunday School in the school house almost every Sunday. We do not think religion consists at all in going to church or sunday school but in living right and doing ones best to be happy and make others so . . . I would rather stay at home and rest or read some good book than go and hear what, to me, is a poor sermon. . . .[254]

Immigrants who had no evangelical leanings were more inclined to be critical of American practices, and to remain aloof from them, than were the Primitive Methodists and the Baptists, who more often found the church a point of contact with American society.[255] Beyond this, there can be little doubt that their religious beliefs helped these immigrants to sustain reverses and to live separated from friends and relatives, in the confidence that they would meet in an afterlife.

Since most of these immigrant farmers were much more deeply concerned with religion than with politics, political activity afforded fewer contacts with the rest of society than did church-going and camp meetings. Wherever the English and Scots settled, however, some of them held township offices and a few served in state legislatures. If they were willing to undertake that kind of work, they did not have to organize ethnic parties in rural America to get themselves elected. Thomas Steel was not elected a magistrate as a Scotsman; nor was Edward Gilley elected to township offices as an Englishman. The politically active immigrants were among the most completely assimilated of the immigrants. Yet it is interesting that James Knight, who found it 'really a pleasure to enjoy the confidence of the people – even in the backwoods', began concerning himself with canal improvements, railway petitions and local politics, after the community at Englishtown, where 'all that I knew and respected in America used to live', had dispersed.[256] It is possible that political activity constituted a means of succeeding, and thus of adapting, for those who were not able to find an English or Scottish colony around them. A lifetime of community-building and political activity in the village of Endicott, Kansas, did not save the bachelor, Edward Hawks, from spending his last years alone, in dire poverty, taking laudanum to suppress his rheumatism.[257] This can be no more than a suggestion; political activity was rare among our unassimilated letter-writers.

The fact that some of them fled from government, which to them meant merely taxation, in emigrating, may partly account for their low level of interest in American politics. Few of them grasped eagerly the opportunity to become citizens which was open to them. While most of them did eventually become American citizens, they did not rush into it. The oath abjuring monarchy made some hesitate. As landowners and taxpayers, they eventually decided that it was in their interest to become citizens and to have a vote.[258]

Immigrants found themselves unable to join in the excited and intense discussions of politics which were characteristic of the pre-Civil War generation of Americans. James Knight, who favoured Adams's re-election in 1828, nevertheless noted that 'for myself I am utterly disgusted with the Subject'.[259] Those who mentioned politics at all continued to comment quite dispassionately on American politics, without identifying with political parties, for many years after they had emigrated.[260]

On one issue nearly all these immigrants of the pre-Civil War generation, those in agriculture as well as those in other occupations, had an opinion. On the subject of slavery they had formed ideas before they emigrated. Their remarks about slavery in their letters often appear to have been elicited by questions addressed to them by their correspondents in Britain. English and Scots immigrants living in the north condemned slavery, and assured friends and relatives that their neighbours shared their views. Indeed, their own favourable response to anti-slavery agitation may have coloured their interpretation of the opinions of their neighbours. James Knight went so far as to predict that the slave insurrections of 1832 would open the eyes of the inhabitants of Virginia and North Carolina 'to the propriety of emancipation'.[261] An immigrant in the south, on the other hand, isolated from both family and any community of his compatriots, felt a strong compulsion to adopt the views of his neighbours. Both Thomas Wozencraft and Nathan Haley, who expressed pro-slavery views, were in this position. Archibald MacLeish, a Scots blacksmith in Charleston, was also a slaveowner.[262] As a young man travelling alone and looking for work in Kentucky, even Thomas Steel, who later avowed socialism, noted that he was being attended by a slave and that slaves were well-treated in Louisville.[263]

The outbreak of the Civil War stirred these immigrants profoundly. While some of the northern immigrants accepted the view that the aim of the war was to preserve the union, and others saw it as a struggle to prevent the extension of slavery, they fervently hoped for a northern victory. The struggle led some of them, for the first time, to speak of themselves as Americans. Anti-slavery agitation and the Civil War made some British immigrants loyal Republicans, and thus speeded their social assimilation by leading them to identify with a political party.[264] The few agricultural immigrants who arrived after the Civil War, and whose letters we have, evinced no interest in American politics: the Bonds in Kansas during the eighties and nineties did not once mention Populism in their letters.

Ironically, the Civil War also brought English and Scots immigrants in the south to a fuller identification with their adopted society. One merchant in New Orleans wrote home on 19 April 1861:

All foreigners resident here are joining and even the English have come forward en masse – it is a remarkable thing that no foreigners who have been here more than a month or two but sides heart and hand with the South – Although Englishmen never become American citizens, they now that there is real work possibly, if not in prospect, come forward to defend New Orleans.[265]

While not living in ghettos, immigrants on farms did protect themselves in their early years in America, by insulating their social lives from the society around them. Those whose religious demands were not too sophisticated probably approached real assimilation through participation in church life. Immigrants living in America during the early sixties experienced a strong pull towards identification with the United States. Yet most of the letters reflect accommodation rather than assimilation. Not fully members of the society around them, they were not in conflict with it. Nor is there much evidence of serious disruption of families or individual breakdowns as a result of migration in this group of letters from people in agriculture. The immigrant most likely to find himself in conflict with American values and customs, the individual from a family of some means in Britain, could usually make his way back home.

One aspect of this successful social accommodation is the relative absence of evidence of conflict between the generations in these letters. The Birkets, the Corletts, the Smiths, the Griffiths, the Gilleys, the Bonds, the Bishops, the Morrises, the Stephensons and the Burlends all had at least some of their children established on farms near where they had settled. They had no worries about economic dependency in their old age. In several cases, the aged parents came to live with one or another of their children. Even the Bonds' son, who, disillusioned with farming, left Kansas for Colorado for a time, eventually returned home. As we have seen, these people arrived in America with strong views about family unity and loyalty; and they were able to maintain this point of view and to pass it on to most of their children in a rural environment. The parents met little competition from the host society in shaping their children's attitudes. Many of their children married into the small local immigrant community. A Scotsman in Wingville, Wisconsin, was delighted with his daughter's marriage to an Englishman: 'so now you see I feel that I think more to see some of my friends now'.[266]

Among the farmers who clung to an immigrant community, the only instances of some conflict between the generations are to be found among immigrants whose children were subject to urban influences in America. Hugh Nudham had been in business in Cincinnati for a time when he first came to the United States. His son, described by his father as 'too ambitious', had run off to an unknown destination before Nudham finally bought his farm. Not so serious a disagreement arose between W.T.Corlett and his father. Brought up near Cleveland, the son put more value upon education than did his father, and criticized his father's investments in urban property, which precluded him from helping to finance Corlett's training as a doctor. John Birket also had a disagreement with one of his sons as to the latter's career. Birket firmly intended that one of his sons should be a clergyman, but when Arthur Birket agreed to attend the Episcopalian College at Peoria if he might then decide on his own occupation, his father relented and allowed his son to go to England to train as an engineer. The only other case of an estrangement between father and children is the apprehensive statement by Robert Smith, at his daughter Harriet's marriage, that she moved in higher social circles than he. Smith's other children settled on nearby farms, and even this daughter returned to the family circle. The prolonged and bitter quarrels which Thomas Wozencraft, the immigrant in Georgia who did not belong to an immigrant community, had with his children, stand in sharp contrast to the easier transition of the other migrants.

The letters from farmers share another common characteristic which indicates an absence of serious social maladjustment. None of them mentions drunkenness. While a few immigrants alluded to temperance agitation, they did not go on themselves to moralize about the evils of drink or to make fervent temperance resolutions. Drunkenness did not appear as a problem for them. This was not because they all abstained.[267] These people in agriculture had sufficiently organized and stable lives, and achieved enough satisfaction in their situations, that they did not drink excessively, although liquor was cheap and easily available and they did not abstain from the cup that cheers.

Accommodation to their social environment was possible for migrants in agriculture largely because they felt so few pressures from the Americans. Many of them hardly noticed American society and felt no particular need to conform to it. These people were remarkably individualistic and self-reliant; they placed a high premium on independence, and were able to support a relatively isolated existence by drawing comfort and companionship from family life and a circle of immigrant friends, and from their religious faith. Although emigrant letters themselves, which were an instrument of accommodation, inevitably emphasize the difficulties, there are many statements in them which denote a satisfactory adjustment. Yet in spite of their knowledge of the English language and their Protestantism, social adjustment was not easy. Successful adaptation for the first generation immigrant depended more upon living in an immigrant group than it did on opportunities for participating in American life. Referring to another sort of community to which he was committed, William Owen saw the difficulties of the adult migrant, after he came out to New Harmony:

Did I not expect that those who were brought up in a community, shall continue to live in that manner, will enjoy more happiness than I anticipated for myself, and more than they can experience when brought up and living under the old mode of society, I should not be disposed to promote the formation of a society, as I at present am inclined to doubt whether the happiness of the present generation will be increased. . . .[268]

Letters from Immigrants in Agriculture

Birket Series 1833–56

The migrations of the Birket family started from the tiny village of Bare, near Fleetwood, Lancashire.[1] John Birket and his wife, Anne, were born in Bare, and the family maintained links with family and friends there for more than a generation. Among these was Thomas Wharton, towards whom the migrants showed a deference developed in their childhood. The migrants turned to Wharton, a man of independent means, as a patron for loans and gifts many years after they had arrived in Illinois. From Bare, John and Anne Birket moved to a rented farm in Westmorland, probably near Kendal, where two of their children were born in 1794 and 1801. Their children were brought up on farms in this relatively under-developed part of England. After his sons had emigrated John Birket moved to another farm, farther south, at Carnforth, Lancashire, near the coast of Morecambe Bay.

By the time John Birket leased this one hundred-acre farm at Carnforth, all his sons had left home, except one of the younger ones, Thomas, who was born in 1801. Thomas Birket, to whom many of these letters were addressed, never married and continued to manage this farm after his father's death. When the census enumerator came round in 1851, he was still working this farm, employing four labourers and supporting his aged mother and an unmarried sister. The population of Carnforth township did not grow between 1821 and 1851. The district was committed very largely to agriculture, and no perceptible change occurred in its occupational structure during this period.

Only one other of John Birket's sons remained in England. Charles Birket left the farm and the stagnant village of Carnforth for a more rapidly developing part of the county, one very near the family's starting point at Bare. In 1833, he was living at Walton Hall, two miles east of Preston, where he was employed by Henry Bold Hoghton. From there he moved to Plungington, just outside Preston, where in 1851 he described himself as a surveyor and civil engineer. Charles Birket was investing in town-sites in the fast-growing town of Peoria, Illinois, during the 1850s. By 1855, he had become land and estate agent for the Earl of Derby. Charles Birket prospered following his migration to the industrial part of Lancashire. His career was, in certain respects, similar to those eventually followed by his brother John and his two nephews in Peoria, Illinois.

Although the letters say nothing about the reasons why the other sons emigrated to America, the timing of their emigration, during the depression just after the Napoleonic wars, suggests that they emigrated for economic reasons. No doubt the outlook was discouraging for a family of five sons in a relatively stagnant part of Britain. Since letters begin fifteen years after their emigration, it is impossible to know their mood on emigration. Yet one cannot fail to notice that the letters do not contain the socio-political overtones found in the letters of English emigrants who entered American agriculture from southern Lancashire and the West Riding of Yorkshire. The Birkets did not seem to have been out of sympathy with the society they left. They remained Anglicans, continued to express deferential attitudes towards the Whartons, and mentioned American politics only in so far as they directly touched their economic interests. The first to emigrate was William, in 1816, at the age of twenty-two. His elder brother, Walter, followed the next year when he was twenty-five. The younger brother, John, the most ambitious of the three, who had been trained as a carpenter before he emigrated, went out in 1819 at the age of twenty-one. None of them was married, and they all went directly to Ferrysburg, Vermont, where two of their father's brothers, Thomas and Walter, were settled on farms.

Dissatisfied with farming prospects in Vermont, the Birkets sent a family scout to investigate western lands. Instead of stopping in New York state, as did so many emigrants from Vermont during these years, William Birket, the first to leave, journeyed in 1821 to Fort Clark, which later became Peoria, on the Illinois River. Four years later, his younger brother, John, set out for the west, stopped briefly in Plainsville, Ohio, and then continued his journey by wagon, peddling tea, coffee and calicoes as he went. John Birket arrived at Fort Clark in 1826, when there were still only six white families settled there. Land had not yet been put up for sale by the federal government, nor had the Indians been cleared from the area. Here John Birket bought a claim for 154 acres of land, and he remained in Peoria trying to develop this land. He probably acquired some capital through his marriage, in 1831, to the daughter of Colonel John Thomas, who had been killed in Indian Wars. But Peoria's growth during the thirties was very modest. Steamships reached this point on the Illinois River in 1831. The next year the village still had only about fifteen to twenty log cabins. Between 1833 and 1837 some growth took place, but the town stagnated again in the late thirties and had fewer than fifteen hundred inhabitants in 1840. John Birket arrived in Peoria one boom too early for successful speculation in town lands. Not confining himself to agriculture, he started the first orchard in Peoria in 1831, worked at his trade of carpenter, lent money to other settlers, encouraged men to dig for coal on his land, let his farm on shares, and was even said to have made crude ploughs for settlers who had not brought them from Pittsburgh.

Meanwhile, his brother who had visited Greene and Madison Counties, decided to settle in Tazewell County east of Peoria and invited his eldest brother, Walter, and his two uncles to come out from Vermont. They all claimed land in Washington township. Settled first by southerners, Tazewell County already had a population density of seven persons per square mile, but only four other families had settled in Washington township when the Birkets arrived, pre-empted land and began the labour of farm-making.

When growth slackened in Peoria in the late thirties, John Birket bought 400 acres of land in Washington township near his brothers. From there he resumed his correspondence with his family in England in 1841, after a silence of six years. John Birket was finding it difficult to hold his land through this long depression. Vexed by increased property taxes, unable to sell his land at what he regarded as a good price, nor to collect on debts owed him because of the stay and bankruptcy laws passed by the state legislature, he looked to family and friends in England to help him find a way out of his dilemma. His scheme was to try to raise money to develop his lands for the purpose of providing his own children, and those of his brothers, with a school. The letters indicate the direction in which he hoped for economic development, not from farming, but from flour-milling, wool-carding and fulling mills. Using timber from his own land, he even started a sawmill to try to help pay the teacher's salary. While his economic drive was clearly bound up in this project, he was also profoundly religious and at the same time suspicious of the other denominations which were growing in the area. He wanted an Episcopal church and Episcopal school for his family. During these ten difficult years which he spent in Tazewell county, from 1839 to 1849, by which time he had been in the United States for thirty years, John Birket, his brothers, and their families formed practically a self-contained community as they struggled to provide their own church and school.

The growth of Peoria finally gave John Birket scope to realize his economic ambitions. From a population of 1,600 in 1844, it reached

5,095 in 1850 and 14,045 in 1860. In 1849 John Birket moved back to Peoria and began a career of building and real-estate development. During the fifties, he laid out what came to be known as the Birket addition in Peoria. By 1870, when at the age of seventy-two he described himself as a 'retired farmer' to the census-taker, he was living with his son, John, who also described himself as a farmer. According to his own valuation, his Peoria real estate had risen from $5,000 in value in 1850 to $53,250 in 1870, four years before his death.

Two of John Birket's children continued his work of real estate development. His eldest son, John Charles Birket, who wrote one of these letters, married a Lancashire girl and never travelled outside the state of Illinois. The youngest son trained for a time as an engineer in Lancashire and then returned to Peoria to take up several municipal and county appointments, though his main interest was also Peoria real estate.

The growth of Peoria also helped William and Walter Birket by providing the farmers of Tazewell county with a market. The Birket brothers had concentrated on livestock and dairy farming from the outset. Their background in a pastoral farming region in England prepared them for agriculture in an area where there was no outside market for wheat. Until the Illinois–Michigan canal was completed in 1848, this area had to find its markets to the south *via* the Illinois River. More than most farmers in their township, they continued their commitment to livestock and dairy farming. They valued their livestock, per improved acre in 1860, at just about the average for the township; but only two others, among 28 British immigrant farmers, owned so much livestock as the Birkets. William and Walter were still living in Washington, in retirement on farms operated by their sons, in 1880. Having been the first English farmers to arrive in the township, they were, by 1880, the only English-born farmers remaining there. At this time, there were no fewer than eight farms in Washington township operated by Birkets. Four sons of William and Walter, a son of John Birket who had moved out to his father's land in 1862, and four grandsons of Uncle Thomas Birket, who had died in 1838, were all established on farms in the township.

The originals of the Birket letters are in the Lancashire County Record Office, Preston, and are reproduced by permission of the County Archivist. Photostats are in the British Library of Economic and Political Science.

Letter from Walter Birket to Charles Birket, Walton Hall, near Preston, Lancashire

Tazwell County, Illinois, 6 May 1833

DEAR BROTHER AND SISTER,

I hope this letter will find you and your little famely in good health, allso all of ower friends in England, as thank God we all engoy here at present, excepting Williams wife is a little unwell, but no more than might be expected. They, rather he, were married I think in November last to a pretty little girl 20 years younger then himselfe. Johns wife has had the misfortune to have the second miscarriage in Januarry last, but is now got well again. They have boath married respectable women.* I have long neglected writing to England but have regularely heard from there and I frequently wrote to William and John and expected they would informe you of me. I will informe you of my journey in 1831. The 28 or 29th of August I started to go into Cannada and travelled 300 miles on horseback, and on the 7th of September I started with Uncle Thomas and his famely to the State of Illinois, and our journey by water was about 2,700 miles. I will mention some of the principal places on my way so that if your cureosety should lead you to trace it on the map you may the better find it out. In the first place we took a steem boat on Lake Champlain near Vergennes; from thence to Whitehall where we took a canal boat to Schenectedy to Utica to Rochester to Buffalo on the grand western canal through the state of New York. At Buffalo took a steem boat through Lake Erie to Cleaveland in the State of Ohio. From thence took a canall boat on the Ohio Canal to Zanesville on the Muskingum River. From thence took a scaw boat down the Muskingum to Marietta on the Ohio River. From thence took a steem boat to Cincinnati to Louisville where we travelled 2 miles by land past the falls of the Ohio River. From thence took a steem boat to the mouth of the Ohio. Then took the Mississippi to St. Lowis in the Missouri. From thence by a steem boat to Pioria on the Illinois River. I have chosen 400 akers of land as a clame which I intend to enter or buy when it comes into market. 160 akers of its is prierare [prairie] goining to William; the other is timber land. I have commenced making a farm this last winter and spring. Goining to Williams my field is 61 rods North and South and 61 rods East and West. The way that fenses are made in this countrey is to cut timber about 10 feet long and split it into pieces so that each piece will rase the fence about 4 inches and then lay them one uppon another in a zi-zag form thus [sketch]

I have found this countrey as good as I had ever heard it reccomended and I expect it is as good as you ever heard it reccomended. Uncle

* Both William and John Birket married American-born women.

Thomas has settled near to William and myself and has got some buildings up and is makeing a farm. . . . [about a letter directed to another immigrant who knows their family in England] I have boarded with Uncle Thomas last winter and now I bord with William. I have engoyed the blessing of good health since I have been in this countrey, more so then I did in Vermont. At this present time I am with John in Pieoria but am going back today. I am verry fulley engaged as you may expect makeing a farm and takeing the land in its state of nature without fences or buildings. . . . [Greetings to relatives and friends] From your wellwishing Brother,

WALTER BIRKETT.

. . . Tell Mother her glasses has come here in Richards chest. [on envelope] Enquire what sort of land prierie is, of what it is constituted &c. Raising hawthorn for fences.

Letters from John Birket to John Birket, Carnforth, Lancashire

Peoria, Ill., 7 Dec. 1834

DEAR AND HONOURABLE PARENTS, . . . [Letter received. Sickness in family]

Walter was over here last Sunday but only stayed long enough to get his dinner, etc. He is verry busy building a house and afraid he will not be able to get it compleete before winter. Walter says William and himself have each secured one hundred and sixty acres of land by premtion. Therefore they are safe of a home and both doing well. Therefore I shall not state any more perticulars so I expect they will one or both write soon. George Stewardson wishes to be rememberd to you. He has had the misfortune of loosing his wife and he is now living with me again. G.S. has secured to himself eighty acres of land or upwards by peremtion. Richard Benbow is well and doing tolerably well. He stayed at my house one night last week and was talking of trying to get premtion wright but has not done it yet. He appears to be verry careful and verry industrious, but rather swearing, boasting carracter, considering his education etc. I think it is poorley bestowed upon him. I am glad to hear that you have removed to Carnforth and I hope you have got a better farm than the one you left and should you at any time fall short in raising your rent you might perhaps get it off Richard Benbow's father or uncle as he says he expects them to remit him some more money soon and this letter shall be your securety for my paying it to the said Mr Benbow, that is to the amount of one hundred pounds sterling. Should you receive any money in this way write me immediately and I will account with Mr Benbow for the same . . .

[Thanks for gift for his son] I think perhaps I may rent my farm next year and go and live with or near Walter and William next summer, as my health has not been verry good for 2 years back. However I have no reason to complain. I am comfortable and able to work a little, and I have 5 hands to work for me at the present time digging coal of nearley or quite as good quality as that in Whiteheaven, England. Last winter I sold 1,000 bushel. This winter I have sould 2,450 bushels, Winchester measure. I cart it $1\frac{1}{2}$ miles and receive 8 cents per bushel. I pay $1\frac{1}{2}$ cents for digging and a good hand can make $1.50 per day or 6s. 9d. sterling. By this calculation you can see that the vilage of Peoria is rappidly increasing in population. About 4 weeks ago we had an Episcopalian Church established by the name of St Jude's Church. One Dyer is our clerjeyman. Therefore this may answer the question asked by my mother in a former epistle 3 or 4 years ago, have you any churches or places of worship. I answer we have a place of worship but no church as yet. Only we meet in the upper room of a tavern. Would it not be charity indeed if some of your rich men in England would send us 5 or 6 hundred pounds sterling which to build us a complete church in this countrey? You have no idea of settling a new country. Suppose 100 familys were placed on a piece of land in the sea and had 10 cows, 15 horses, 4 or 5 sheep, no money, as only the poorer class would go, and it takes all they have to get them there, no houses, no fences, no tools, 1 mecanick, the rest farmers, the land to pay for and everything to do. Which would be the most necasary at first? We remain your obedient and loveing children,

JOHN AND MARJORY BIRKET

A blacksmith is a very good trade in this country and might procure tools easier than to bring them. I am fattening 36 swine, but I have had bad luck with them this summer. Nearley one half died and 1 horse also.

I have secured 2 more pieces of land by premtion, say perhaps 120 acres, which I expect to pay for next year.

Please give our best respects to all enquireing friends and relations. I should be glad if you could send me some ditching spades such as you used in Westmoreland if you have an opportunity. I would give any price for them and send the money in a letter if I thought you could get it exchanged. I want you to write and let me know whether it would be of any use to put a bit in my letter or not.

Peoria, Ill., 7 May 1835

DEAR AND HONOURABLE PARENTS,

I received your letter of Feby 15th and am glad to hear that you are all well as thank *God* this short epistle leaves all of us. . . . [progress of his children] Walter has not got his house finished. He keeps Bachelor Hall in a room with Uncle Thomas. They are all well. I did not go down to see Mr Bamber people. They live about a mile from the rest. They are all well and their son is with them. Mrs Bamber does not like this country. She says she will write to Ann and tell her never to come. Therefore you may know what is comeing from such a rattler. I have rented my farm and I let the man have my stock, also husbandry utensils of every kind he needs, and find him seed, and feed for the team this spring and summer, and he gives me half the products of the farm, i.e. I take oats and hay in the stack, corn in the barn, hogs and cattle are divided in the spring. Butter, cheese, etc. he sells and gives me half the profit. George and myself what little we do is in opening and draining the stone coal and prepairing for winter.

Dear Brother, I am sorry to say that all my hopes are blasted of securing to you before your midsummer rent day the money anticipated in your letter, and this is the reason, that R. Benbow wanted to buy a piece of land off me and have me take my pay in England as stipulated in my last, a plan I thought would answer verry well on both sides, although it appears not. However should you be in want go to Mr and Mrs Wharton with this letter and tell them the circumstances and I think they will let you have 50 or £100, and I will be accountable for the same to them or their order as soon as the spring of 1836 and I will pay them 6 per cent from the time they let you have it till the time they receive it from me. Give my best respects to Mr and Mrs Wharton, and tell them that when I was a little boy they were not affraid to entrust me with money when I used to bring home silver and brass that I had received for apples, etc. Also when Mr Wharton's pocket got too heavy he used to send home the cumbersome load by me. Tell Mr and Mrs Wharton that I am as true to my [word?] now as I was then and should we not any of us live [to?] it repaid I will keep a writeing in my house from the time I hear that you have received the money, authoriseing my heirs, executors, administerators or assigns to pay the said money to Mr and Mrs Wharton, their heirs, executors etc.

I have the money by me at the present time but I have two reasons for not sending it at the present time. First is that I should have to go to Philadelphia (which is 1100 miles) to pay it into the bank or otherwise get a draft on that bank from a branch in St. Louis (which is 200 miles distance) and write to Philadelphia and then it would be optional with them whether they would send it or not. We cannot place so much confidence in our banks as what you can in England. Therefore it is impossible for me to get it to you by midsummer. A second and great reason is, that at this time money is worth 50 per cent per anum, and should I send you that amount William would have to borrow at 50 per cent to pay for his land. I believe that I tould you in my last that we had each of us secured by premtion a little land – Walter 160 acres, William 160 acres, George a fractional piece perhaps 80 or 90 acres, myself 2 fractions probably 120 acres: and now the land sales for this state is advertised to be on the 15th day of June and we are oblieged to have the money before that day or lose our land. God be thanked for his goodness I have the money to pay for mine with, and enough to pay for 160 acres for William and perhaps a little to lend George S., and Walter I believe is ready and perhaps a little to spare. Therefore we are all doing well, should we meet with no disapointments in colecting. George Stewardson says that should you fail in getting money from Mr Wharton that you might probably get it off his mother Mathews and it would be a great saving of traveling expences. To go to Philadelphia the cheapest way I could it would cost me £10 at least and there would be no certainty of your getting it by midsummer any other way. I expect to start to the land office shortley which is a distance of 150 miles. . . . [asks for letters] from yours etc.

JOHN AND MARJORY BIRKET

Letter from John Birket to Charles Birket, Plungington, near Preston, Lancashire

Mount Pleasant, Illinois, 25 Dec. 1841

DEAR BROTHER,

This morning I prepared and started to go to Tremont 18 miles, to commemorate the birth of our Dear *Saviour*, and I found the whole face of the earth in one glare of ice and my horse having no shooes on his hind feet I considered it not practicable and returned to write this letter, (May it please *God* to send His blessing along with it), in which I will endeavour to give you some idea of the state of things in this country.

I recd your kind letter of Septr. 23rd. In it I find that you have had the Whigs to rule, and they proved incompotent. On the contrary, we have had the democrats to rule, and are now trying for a Whig government. Those things are an alegory, and leads me to think that the government is not altogether in the fault, but that *God* is angry with His people ..nd takes this method of chastiseing them. For instance, in this country *God* has seen fit of His great goodness to send us plentifull times and money plenty for years back, and we have laid it out for treasure in this world and forgot the *Hand* who gave it. Therefore the moth doth eat etc., or in other words Silver is mine and gold is mine saith the *Lord*. But where am I wandering? The democrats ruled this State till they run it in debt, I know not how much, at the same time crying, down with the banks and give us specie curency. At this cricis the banks stopped specie payments which threw all things in stagnation, our paper not good, the silver and gold gone, and a large amount of intrest to pay, which raised our taxes about 8½ per cent on land, and every other kind of property in proportion, this throwing down the price of land so that many poor people who had not got through with paying for their land will be sold up for less than they had payed towards it, and loose all: and others who thought themselves more fortunate feel the efects verry sencible.*

I for one had been carefull enough to keep out of debt and had money by me to pay for 320 acres of land (which I call Mount Pleasant with a beautifull situation for 2 or 3 mills or factorys which will be of great value shortly) also having money out for colection to have built a mill. My farm at Peoria rented for 10 years at 400 dollars per annum when (lo and behold) a law was passed to stay everyone from colecting debts contracted before the 1st of May 1841 which, with my tenants leaving their farm and others failing and others puting their property out of their hands, has put a stop to my building a mill and is likely to make me have to borrow money or sell land at a verry low rate, the latter of which I should prefere unless some of our connections was likely to come out and want it, and for this reason, money in this country bears a verry high intrest, and the land pays a high tax at present. My farm at Peoria will not rent now to pay its taxes of about 40 dollars per annum and would 5 years ago have sold for 100 dollars per acre and now would not probably fetch 5 per acre, although in the course of 2 or 3 years when the state debt is paid, it will in all probability be of its former value.

I do assure you that there perhaps never will be so good a time again as the present for people to buy land in this country. I should be glad if some millwrights would come out and build me a mill and take his pay in land, as I have sold of most of my stock, my health being such as not to permit farming any longer, and that makes my income small till I can build one. I suppose about £150 would build one.

Respecting the building of a church I do not know what to say. The Bishop of this diocese was in England about 5 years ago and received £18,000 for the building of a colege, most of which he laid out for land

---

* Illinois had not only a large debt on the Illinois–Michigan Canal, but also an additional internal improvement debt of $5,600,000 in 1840. To begin to pay the interest on this debt, after the default of 1839, an act was passed on 21 February 1841, which increased the property tax by ten cents on every one hundred dollars' worth of property and established a minimum valuation of three dollars per acre on all land subject to tax in the state. This tax was reduced in 1842.

to support it.* Three years ago he went through the southern states to colect money for building it, and this summer he has been through the northern states to colect more, and we feel afraid that he will think it will interfere with his geting money and therefore do nothing for us. If so, I see no way for us to get a church unless some young clergyman in England would colect money and come out here as a missionary and build one. We have paid an Englishman for one year. He comes 12 miles every other Sunday and preaches 2 sermons. As yet we meet at my house and it is commonly crowded to overflowing now in the winter, and in the summer I have a butifull grove of trees by my house that we can get under, and before the year expires I hope and pray that *God* for us will provide a better way. Mr Douglas, who preaches for us, is a missionary and talks of going to the state of New York where he lived two or three years to colect money for the building of a Church in Tremont. It would surprise you to see and hear what our eastern brethren are doing for the church in these westeren wilds. If the English people would come here to build mills, fulling mills, carding machienes, factories, etc., and at the same time to assist in building up the true Church of Christ, it would be more honourable than to go to help Joseph Smith to build his temple, and I conjecture that some of those hundreds of people who came from England have found it so. I send you a paper with this which will give you some idea of their leader and I will send you one every week if you will accept them. The Mormons are a set of almost lawless fanatics and have been driven from pillar to post ever since they started. They have been dispersed 2 or 3 times and it is expected that they will be removed by government before long. . . . [Greetings from William and Walter] I remain yours etc.

I thought for us all to sell here and buy again near Bishop Chase, but Walter thinks it so much trouble to begin again that he will die where he now lives.

My coal mine has run out except it can be found deeper which would require more capital than I am posesed of. [not signed]

Letter from John Birket to John Birket, Carnforth, near Lancaster

Mount Pleasant, Illinois, 28 Nov. 1842

MY DEAR FATHER,
   Having adressed our nearest friends and relations both in England and Vermont, for information as to the best mode of erecting and

---

* Bishop Chase established Jubilee College in Peoria County as an Episcopal College in 1839. John Birket gave an acre of land to this college. The buildings still stand in a park outside Peoria.

building up of a Church and still receiveing no decisive answer, I feel humbled to the dust that I have wandered so far from my duty as not to ask your advice at first, but waited till I had formed a scheem of my own, and the only appology I have to make is that I always expected you, my Dear Parent, saw all my letters: and if you saw anything in them deviateing from the rule of Christianity you would correct me of your own accord. Now, having in remembrance your advice at the time I left Vermont (on my speaking of building on a sandy foundation your advice was: you hoped that I would seek and build upon a *Rock* next time). I never have built since, only a mere hovel to shelter us from the storm, not fit for a stable in England. Neither do I have any desire to build a house for myself till Ive another object under way, that is, a building founded on that *Rock*! and my Bible tells me that every man ought to take heed how he buildeth thereupon for other foundation can no man lay than that is laid which is *Christ*. Therefore like the penitent Prodigal I return for advice and will endeavour to lay all my plan before you: you know my ignorance and want of education, (but not my heart) and I hope you wil answer me soon as convienient and correct any and every eror that you see in me, or the plan formed. Here follows a copy of the plan formed by my own hand which no person has seen but my wife and brother Walter.

This Indenture made the first day of May in the year of our Lord 1842 Between John Birket of the Township of Washington and County of Tazwell, state of Illinois, partie of the first part, and all the people now and forever, living in the aforesaid Town of Washington and being members of the Protestant Episcopal Church of the United States being parties of the second part.

Witneseth that the said partie of the first part for and in consideration of the foundation of an Episcopal school in which is to be taught, (or caused to be taught), by the aforesaid Episcopal society the Holy Bible, the Prayerbook and Church catechism, and governed by Trustees elected by said Society for that purpose, and should said society be so unfortunate as to elect at any time Trustees that shall deviate from the true Episcopal Doctrine the Bishop of the diocese shall have power at any time to overrule said Trustees and bring said School to a healthfull state of Episcopacy again, by electing or appointing others, or as the Bishop may deem propper on the part of the said Episcopal Society, To which may be aded, at any time, by any well disposed person, any money, real or personal property, which may be deemed necessary for said school, or for the erecting of a Church, He the said John Birket hath given, granted, aliened, remised, released, enfeofed, and confirmed, and by these presents do clearley and absolutely give, alien, remise, release, enfeof, and confirm, unto the said parties of the second part, forever, all the right, title, and interest, (dower, right, title, or claim of dower,) claim or demand whatsoever, in law or equity, of the said partie of the first part, of, in, and to, all that certain Tract, Piece, or Parcel, of land, situate lying and being in the State of Illinois and known and described as the west half of the North West quarter of section No. twenty-seven, in Township No. twenty six, North of No. three, west of the third principal meredian, containing one hundred acres, To have and to hold all and singular the said Tract, Piece, or Parcel of land, with the rights members and apurtenences thereunto belonging or in any way apertaining unto the said parties of the second Part. and . . . own propper use benefit and behoof forever. And the said John Birket for himself and his heirs, the above described and hereby granted, and released premises, and every part, and parcel thereof, with the apurteneces unto the Parties of the seccond part, against the said partie of the first part, and against all persons whomsoever lawfully claiming, or to claim, the same, by, from, or under him, the said partie of the first part, his heirs or assigns or any or either of them shall and will warrant and by these presents forever defend: In witness thereof the said partie, of the first part, have hereunto set his hand and seal this day and year above written. John Birket.

Brother Charles wished to have me see the Bishop before I wrote again. I have done so, but he thinks that we could not call on the good people of England again so soon for so trivial a flock (or I might say for so few scattered sheep). Therefore we must labour or faint. When I wrote last things wore rather a gloomy aspect but according to the above plan or something like it, I think I see a brighter prospect, so much so, that buying the land that I thought to be the worst thing I could have done, is likely to prove the best thing I could have done, (for *God* is able to Make all things work together for good to those who love and fear Him). I think in this way we might be the humble means of building up a Church in this wilderness, (that is by God's assistance) and should it prosper to need more land we can add more at any time, but I think 100 acres is enough to begin with or I would give more. (The Bishop finds his three thousand acres for his school a burthen at this time when money is so scarce and taxes so high). I do not see why people should not feel anxious to assist a thing like this for it would be of itself, and in the hands of the people, and the people would be under the controle of the Bishop, so long as they deviated from the true Episcopal faith, and no longer, the Bishop then losseing his power. Although it is a small thing it might grow great for *God* regardeth the day of small things as much as the laws of nations. This we see in the widow's two mites, and although

I who am but a poor worm, and that of the baser sort, would have to be trustee, treasurer, etc. at present, yet when other people joined and we get a church organised they would be in like power, till the number of trustees was compleete. Then they can be incerporated into a body and enact such laws and regulations as was necessary, the small pittance of £100 carefully laid out with what labour would be given in the place might set it on foot, so that it would grow slowly of its self. Principal things wanting would be a house for the teacher and a school house, which would answer for a church some time. We are only 5 communicants at present, my two brothers, one American, my wife and myself, Some little fencing and a well diging etc., then for the stocking of it, we have abundance. It would get plenty of them *gratis*. I would give 50 sheep which I think would be the most profitable of anything to stock it with now, seeing we have got a tarif to protect our manufacturers, and we have so good a situation for machinery. If manufactorers of wolen cloth would come here to settle in place of going to Nauvoo to help Joe Smith, I think they would do better. If I could sell my place at Peoria I would not ask any person to help us, but all that I could do with it at present would be to give the rent of it to support it etc.

Now, my Dear Father, I have begun at the top and studied to the bottom, and find no other foundation to a Church than our Saviour's first charge to Peter, *Feed My Lambs*. The second is *feed my Sheep*, which appears plain to me that our first duty is to feed the lambs of *Christ*. I submit it to you as my guardian, for perusal, for correction, and for reproof: should you deem it on the right foundation and plan and any one sees fit to asist me, I pledge myself and property to do the best in my judgment in laying it out, *i.e.* what they give for the purpose they give it etc. I most earnestly beg for all your prayers to *God* to assist us to plant a church in Mt. Pleasant. I remain, Dear Father, your affectionate, and for the time to come, dutiful Namesake, Amen.

JOHN BIRKET

[A letter from John Birket to his brother, Charles, 14 December 1842, giving further details of this project and of their difficulties, has been omitted]

Letters from John Birket to Thomas Birket, Carnforth, Lancashire

Mount Pleasant, Illinois, 2 Feb. 1843

DEAR BROTHER,

I had almost despaired of hearing from any of you since I have spoken of trying to build up a Church to the living *God*, but ... I feel as though it was a matter of serious consideration and I wish the advice of you all. I received a paper from Charles and hasten to return thanks for so small a token of friendship, at the same time give you some further view on the subject in consideration, and whilst I do so may it please the great Jehovah who rules the heavens to guide my heart and direct my pen. I asure you that what little has been said has caused considerable exitement here even amongst the fiew that call themselves Episcopaloons, each wishing to have it his own way: but the most part think it best to strike out catechism. I say let us all be Episcopal (or none Episcopal). If the church has doctrines or catechisms, that is not fit to be taught to childeren, let them be rooled out of her . . . [God's will] Others here say that the Bishop will not take charge over it, to which I . . . answer, that makes no difference to us only it leaves so much more for the trustees to do in keeping it pure; and Pastor says that if it is once begun the Bishop will take charge of it. I understand that our good Bishop has doubts as to our geting a church here, being so few in number and having so many enemies. Therefore we need not expect to get one short of begining with a school, which I consider the true foundation of a church: and can we be so fortunate as to build the lower story, the next generation may build the upper one . . . [Trust in God]. If you had seen what I have of men living amongst heathen or savages or, as I might say, without church or school, then I would attempt to describe what men will relaps to; but as it is, it would beggar all description. Therefore I shall not attempt it, but proceed to show what has been done. We have agreed on a name for our church and begun a reccord as follows. Only I omit the form in this letter.

1841 Rise and Progress of Trinity Church, Mt. Pleasant.

Sept. 28, Rev. Wm Douglas, Missionary, had Divine service first time and baptised Marjory Birket, adult, Ann A. D. Birket, John B., Margaret B., Marjory B., Walter Thomas B., John Charles B., and Wm Armstead B.

Nov. 15, John Birket furnished Rev. Mr Douglas a horse worth $75 for one year service, on which Walter Birket paid $5 in pork, Wm. Birket paid $15 in work. Cyrus Parker gave in adition some corn, had some cloths made etc. I have not acertained to what amount.

1842 May 5, John Birket deeded 100 acres of land for a school.

May 8, first Confirmation, Marjory Birket, and received the same at Tremont.

July 10, Holy Communion administered first time at Mt. Pleasant, and for want of house room, had Divine service under some shady tree.

August 7, first funeral Wm. A. Birket, not baptised

Sept. 28, Rev. Wm. Douglas no salary after this time, only some small presents such as provisions, clothing, etc.

January [22nd?], Arthur Thomas Birket baptised. Born 10 Jan 1843.

A true copy of reccord, by which you see that after a laps of 7 years, and my dear Wife, 42 years old, the Lord saw propper to add another member to my family, for which we feel very grateful. You will also see how we have to do things in this country. We are makeing a verry weak begining, but I most earnestly solicit all your prayers (if no more) that *God* may prosper us in the undertakeing. And I do not want you to be discouraged from so small a begining, for we can add as we are able, and this is what we want a little aded to enable us to add more. I wish you to look upon it as I do upon my Babe, that if it please God to bless him (with a little of my asistance) he will make a man, after all our discouragement. . . . [Describes circumstances of his son's birth]

The government of the United States has given 640 acres of land to each township all through this country which, if cultivated, is sufficient to teach all the childeren, but some of the townships have been so foolish as to sell the land and put the money at intrest.* This town for one had done so; however each school draws its share of that money every year according to the number of scholars. Therefore a school of this kind, by being made free or nearly so, would be apt in time to get the largest number of scholars, thereby drawing the greatest share of the school fund, which is now for the most part paid to the support of the Universalist schools, and by keeping a record as above it would always be to show to the world and other might follow the same steps, and by this means throw some of the school lands, or school money, into the hands of the church where I think it ought to be, to train up the childeren in the way they should go etc. Now Christ declares himself to be the way, and that *all* will be with His church to the end of the world. Therefore that church must be the way, and if that church is not Episcopal I cant find it. But in this case we see the Kingdom of Heaven suffer violance. . . . It is contrary to the laws of the United States to sell the school lands. I have never seen a true churchman yet in favour of selling the land; but other denominations, being the strongest party, convert it to their own use. I wish you, my dear Brother, to circulate these letters amongst our old friends and nieghbours, wherever convienient, to see if any of them will render asistance; and should any person wish to plant their name in America to the end of time they can do so by makeing the largest donor etc. whose name the school will bear, my name excepting. Lord Kenyon and Lady Gambier, has planted

* A law passed in Illinois for taxation for common school in 1825 was repealed in 1827 because of the populace's objection to taxation. Birket here refers to a state law, passed in response to pressure from 'squatters' on school lands, ordering townships to sell the lands reserved for schools. The proceeds from these sales were lent by the townships to the state which eventually had to tax to meet interest payments.

theirs in the state of Ohio* I have tryed to get the building place spoken of before and failed. I think it might be got for $100, prhaps less. This is all we can do at present, and I leave it with the good people of England to say if we shall swim or sink . . . [More requests for aid] So no more at present but we all join in love to you all. And the Lord grant that we may not have asked amiss.

J. BIRKET

[Letters from the school teacher and a clergyman, 13 April 1843, to Charles Birket, near Preston, asking for aid for John Birket's projects, are omitted.]

Mount Pleasant, Illinois, 19 May 1843

MY DEAR BROTHER, . . . [More requests for assistance for the church and school]

The next thing I come to is sending me a hind. What I meant by that was I had just received a Preston paper from Brother Charles in which I saw that the best of men were hireing at Kendal market for £2.10s the winter half year, and I thought I could give a young man and woman a better chance than that either to live with me in my house or to live on my farm as George Stewardson did, although wages is low in this country, from 8 to 10 dollers per month or 50 cents, equal to 2s 3d per day, I am sorry that ould comrades in Westmorland has not courage to come here and work for land. G.Stewardson has got 240 acres of good land and well stocked with cattle, horses, etc. and verry little in debt. He owes me 56 dollars which he ways he expects to pay shortly. He was married last fall to a widow with 4 childeren and is now likeley to have an heir of his own . . . [News of other families from their district]

I hope that your tythes may do well for you and I think it will. For there is no prospect of this country reduceing your markets, for the wheat crop is principaly cut off as far as I can hear from, owing to the hard long winter, the hardest and longest I have seen in the United States. Wheat and corn both is smartly on the rise all through this country, and I think on the whole everything looks a little better, *i.e.* people are geting out of debt. The stay law that was passed last winter and to be in force 3 years gives those that are in debt a good chance, that is, they are able to keep people from collecting their money for 3 years and that without cost to themselves. Others have taken the benefit

---

* Kenyon College at Gambier, Ohio, was founded by Bishop Philander Chase, with the aid of twenty thousand dollars raised in England in 1823. It was incorporated by the Ohio Legislature in 1824 as a Theological seminary. Lady Gambier was the widow of Lord Gambier and Lord Kenyon was the Second Baron of Gredington, County Flint. Both were members of the evangelical party within the Church of England and active in many charitable societies.

4*

of the bankrupt law. I shall loose perhaps $100 by the bankrupt law and I do not know what by the stay law. One man that I have had a note against for 5 years of 265 dollars sent me word that if I would take 150 dollars for lumber (*i.e.* sawed timber) he would pay it, but the lumber would be 25 miles from me and no sale for it at any price in money. Therefore I may as well loose the whole or wait the three years. Those 2 laws passed by our wise legislature make hard times here where people have been borrowing money to pay for land etc.

Dorithy seems anxious to have Walter sell out here and go to Jubilee Chapel or in the neighbourhood and I think should that take place we had better all do so and should that be our destination I will do all in my power to provide a place for you since you are doing that which we cannot do, that is provideing for our Dear Parents. Had we a settled church and school to go to I should be happy to welcome you to our soil but I do asure you we do not any of us wish to see you go through the privations that we have done, although our prospect brightens, to either get a foundation laid here or to get to some other place, either of which I shall be satisfied with. Brother William is building a barn this summer, a thing that has long been wanting considering the number of stock that he keeps. Brother Walters farm keeps him slaveing and working verry hard and he talks of building a flax or hemp machiene this summer. I hope it may do well for him. . . . [Greetings from brothers and news of cousins] No more at present but I remain etc.

                                                              JOHN BIRKET
My Dear Wife wishes to be remembered to you all but begs to be excused from writeing for the want of education.

                                                Mount Pleasant, Illinois, 4 Feb. 1845
DEAR BROTHER,
I have undertaken 2 or 3 times to write you but as yet have always failed to get through, things in this neighbourhood wear so gloomy an aspect, that is respecting school and Church. At Easter 1843 here was a letter wrote in my house and, as I understood, requesting you and Dear Brother Thomas to try to raise for half the expence of building a saw mill, myself to be at the other half of the expence; and one half the proceeds of this mill was for the purpose of supporting a school, improveing the land I had offered to the township etc. To accompany this letter I wrote another requesting you, my Dear Brother, that if anything had been raised on previous letters sent by me, that it should be turned over to the company and *not* sent to me, since that time I looked to that company to do as they thought propper. I was then requested to try to

get the mill built by selling some of the land. I did so. Then last June they chose to begin a free school and $\frac{1}{2}$ the proceeds of the mill was to pay the teacher and half the expences of atending the mill, and I was to be at the other half of the expences. Accordingly a man was hired to tend the mill but it pleased *God* to take him away. Then the widow wanted her pay. Then it was proposed for me to take the sheep and the mill and to pay the widow. I did so. Next comes a proposition from all quarters to stop the school, but the teacher must have damages; and it could not be acertained what those damages would be till the end of the year. Therefore the damages might be as much as the school bill. I thought best to have one years schooling. Then the Church meeting was brought back to my house (for it had been removed $1\frac{1}{2}$ miles distant for nearly 2 years) and I am trying to raise the school bill by attending the mill. Should it please God to give me health and strength to raise the amount, it may be the means of raiseing the droopeing spirits and we may go on again. Otherwise we shall undoubtedly have to stop the first of June. You may suppose the work I have to roll logs of 3 to 4 feet in diameter and 12 to 18 feet long, into the mill, and when sawed to carry out of the mill in plank, joints, beams, etc. and all this to do by hand, and no one to help (I may say) for I have only received 25 days work in asistance from the begining and that was mainly in repairing a breach in the dam caused by some evil person pulling a plank of the head gate and by this means leting the water through at a high time which tore away the head gate and the whole creek came through the mill, for about 24 hours like to take everything away; but it pleased *God* for it to stand fast with less damages than could be expected.

How shall I get you to look upon these things as I do? Perhaps by refering you to the 132nd and 133rd psalms of David which was read here the first time that the church service was read on this hill, and 8 baptisms (remember I live in the woods) and from the time that the meeting was taken away till it came back there has been no change taken place till it returned. Then the first week was a weding Elizabeth Norris that came with Mr Bamber, (has done verry well) Now read the 6th and 7 chapters of the 2nd book of Samuel. Not my will but thine be done *O. Lord*.

I have now a letter before me . . . in answer to your kind letter of June 12th 1844 praying for the money you had been so kind in raising to be sent if convienient through some banking house in New York, and it has waited for signers ever since and I find but two names to it, Mr Wm. Douglas, missionary, and John Birket, and it is still waiting. I have now endeavoured to explain matters as well as I can, not daring to say one word what shall be done, Amen.

.... [About his parents, births and deaths]. Therefore we now stand thus, Walter Birkets family consists of 3. Wm. A.Birkets 7, John Birkets 5, Wm. Birkets 4, in all 30 souls. We have 23 scholars in school and have had off and on upwards of 30, some of which have had no schooling but what they have got here and others verry little; however I do not wish you to think that I am complaining, for my children are doing verry well. Charles, who is 11 years old yesterday, can beat me in ciphering and write about as well as I can; and Wm. who is 9 years old, begins to know his tables and write a little. I think [he] will shortly beat Charles.

You will undoubtedly have heard that Joseph Smith, the Mormon prophet, was shot by the mob when brought to trial for·some of his actions. Guns and pistoles were fired from every quarter that it was impossible to tell who killed him. Something like 24 or 25 balls had hit him if I recolect the story right. This session of Congress have taken the charter from them for their city at Nauvoo, also granted a charter to Peoria that you see it is now the City of Peoria and likeley to become the Seat of Government for the State of Illinois. When we have had the taxes raised to pay the indebtedness of the State, which they are trying to do this sesion [and should?] it take place it will sell a great deal of [land?] at a verry low rate.* Last month I had an offer of $1000 for one lot of land bordering on the lake and adjoining the City of Peoria. I felt quite encouraged, for half the sum would have carried me through the pressure handsomely with the rest; but news came that the tax was going to be raised 16 or 20 per cent and the bargain failed. Thus we see many a slip between the cup and the lip, and all for the best. On the whole I think things wear a brighter prospect in this country than they have ever since the bankrupt law and stay law have been done away with. You would hardly realise if I should tell you that for years past men who we had obliged by crediting them or lending them money could send us a letter saying that he had taken the benefit of the bankrupt law and was discharged from his debts. Thus by makeing us pay the postage of a letter thousands of dollars was paid. But no more of this painful subject. I would be glad to hear of your prosperity in Old England and how all our relations at Bare is getting along, and conclude with my love to them all. Believe me to be your ever loveing Brother,

JOHN BIRKET

---

* A new tax law was passed on 1 March 1845 providing for a levy of one mill on each dollar of property valuation to be transferred from the county to the state. In 1844 the Barings agreed to take the full amount of a new bond issue on behalf of European creditors to complete the Illinois Michigan Canal, provided the state restored this 'interest' tax.

Our schoolmaster has $200 for 1 year services. He is an excelant teacher but considerable in debt and now sued at law. Therefore he must have his pay whenever it becomes due. We have a very dry warm winter so far which makes water scarce at the mill. I can only saw a day now and then.

Fragments of a letter from John Birket

Peoria, Illinois, 8 March 1853

DEAR BROTHER,

It becomes my painful duty to inform you that four more of our dear friends has gone, whence they will not return. . . . [Records deaths]
Yours ever truly, J.

People in this country are anxiously engaged in making railroads. We are likeley to get one from here to Philadelphia east and another Pacific to the west. The one going east is surveyed closed by the mill I built in Tazwell County, say, within 200 yards or less.

Letter from John C.Birket to his Uncle, Charles Birket, near Preston, England, with a Postscript from John Birket

Peoria, Illinois, 31 July 1856

MY DEAR UNCLE,

I beg your pardon for not having written sooner but I had nothing to write, but I have now resolved that I will try and if I do not do justice to the subject you will please pardon me.

Last fall you asked me to send you the prices of lots in our City. Since then money has been bound prisoner and times have been very dull. There is no business doing in real estate, for it is hard to get money enough to pay honest debts without speculating in land. I have however within twenty months past heard of as for sales as follows.

On the corner of Main Street 25 ft. by 72 ft. on Washington Street sold for $4500, and there is now a building in construction in it that the basement is said will cost $1000. J.Brothers Sons Addition lots are offered for $330 a piece and adjoining they have been sold for $630, per lot.

In Frye's addition on the Bluff which is situated on the S.W. qur. of the N.E. qur, of sec. four (4) lots sold from $80 to 310 dollars a piece. And on the third tier of blocks from the N.E. in Birkets addition lots sold for $221 in cash and 275 dollars on four years time.

I will draw a plot of a part of section 3 showing the division and lots and the size of the same so as to give you a true idea of the [upper ?] part of the town. For to tell you the truth those maps you have is not quite correct it being drawn to serve his and whose name it bears. We have not sold any lots yet but I wish to sell a few (which are a gift from dear Father) which I offer as follows, at low prices, being situated on the Rail Road and the River as they are. My prices are $331 as follows, fifty dollars down and the balance in one, two, & three years with 10 per cent provided they build immediately; if not it will [be ?] thus 400 dollars, 100 dollars down and the balance as above. To factories of any kind (except of liquor) I would offer the following inducements: I will sell them a lot for their work thus: I will give them a bond for a deed and wait one year before I will ask for a payment provided they will begin opperation on their buildings as soon as possible after they have obtained a lot and push it with vigour till completed.

I think a good cotton manufacturer would do well if he would try an experiment, for we have in the spring a good chance to ship cotton from the South by water, and soon, that is in a few weeks. We can bring them at any time by rail road and in the course of a couple of years we can bring them by rail road direct, their being one laid out direct to St. Louis . . . [Father's visit to Uncle William in Washington] All join with me in kind love to all. Yours ever truly,

                                                        J. BIRKET

P.S. The cause of Dorothy's illness is from a fall that she got on the ice (in 1855) and, not being let blood, the blood has settled inwardly and has been growing ever since, which takes the nourishment that ought to support the body and has reduced her to a mere skeleton. They have had the advice of five doctors but they are not agreed on the place where it is settled; however, they are agreed that she will not recover without it being taken away which cant be done till cooler weather, and I am afraid that should she be permitted to live till that time she will not be able to bear the operation. This puts a dark cloud over our oldest brother. Not my will, but thine be done. Charles is waiting to take the letter to the Office or I would write more. Still I remain, Your affectionate Brother till Death,

                                                        JOHN BIRKET

Corlett Series 1831–47

Unlike the Birkets, the Corlett family had farmed the same land in Kirk Michael parish, near Peel, on the Isle of Man, for at least five generations. The unenclosed farm, called Orrisdale, consisted of about forty acres in scattered strips. In 1827, at the age of forty-four, William Corlett, who wrote the three letters which follow, sold his land, which as the eldest son he had inherited, and used the proceeds to take his family to America. William Corlett's grandson described him as not a particularly ambitious or aggressive man. 'During his lifetime [he] had been in the habit of taking things as they came without fret or worry – nor was he given to an over amount of exertion.'[1] Like the Birkets, he appears to have emigrated entirely for economic reasons. The difficulties of providing for a family of four sons and two daughters on the Island, with its limited land resources, made the idea of emigration attractive. In the early 1820s small farmers, especially in the northern parishes of the Isle of Man, where the Corletts lived, faced adverse conditions. With no industrial growth in the Island, the parish in which the Corletts lived declined in population during that decade. William Corlett was also very much aware of the discontent caused on the Island by new taxes during the Napoleonic wars, since his father had been one of the envoys sent to London to protest. A new tithe of 1817 actually produced rioting in the Island.

Other members of the Corlett family also considered emigration. One of the main purposes of William Corlett's letters was to advise them about America as a field of emigration. By the 1840s, conditions had much improved on the Isle of Man, partly through the growth of tourism and partly through continued emigration. William Corlett's brother, Thomas, a weaver, to whom these letters were addressed, remained in Kirk Michael parish, and eventually married a much older woman, who inherited some property from her father. A sister married a local farmer. But William Corlett's other brother and sister left the Island. His brother John went to London, where he worked as a tailor; and his sister Mary married a carpenter and moved to Liverpool. Some of his nephews emigrated to Manchester. No other members of this family went to the United States.

In company with a party of fifty emigrants from the parish of Kirk Michael, the Corletts went directly to the Western Reserve district south of Lake Erie in Ohio. At least three Manxmen, including the brother of the Vicar of Jurby, had visited the Western Reserve before this and sent back accounts of the area, which interested Manx farmers who contemplated emigration. The immediate link for these emigrants from Kirk Michael was a local school teacher, who had settled in Newburgh township, about six miles from Cleveland, in 1826. Cleveland was then a village of only six hundred people and its site was considered unhealthy; consequently the Corletts went to join their fellow townsman, William Kelley, at Newburgh.

The farm of fifty acres which William Corlett acquired, first by leasing and later by purchasing it from the state of Connecticut, had already been cleared of trees. He had enough capital to save himself the labour of clearing, but he was only the second person in Newburgh to buy land from Connecticut's Western Reserve.

The Corletts arrived at a favourable moment, and their material success was underwritten by the rapid growth of the area in which they settled. Now linked by water with the east, Cuyahoga County more than doubled in population during the thirties, rising from 10,373 in 1830 to 26,505 in 1840. The city of Cleveland, already four times as large as Peoria by 1840, increased in population from 6,071 in that year to 17,034 by 1850. The inflow of new settlers and the rapid growth of so large a town near their farms helped the Corletts and other Manx farmers become commercial farmers by enabling them to obtain cash for the produce of their farms. William Corlett's letters do not tell us much about his farming operations. It is to be noted, however, that while he complained about the fly on his wheat crops in the late forties, the more progressive farmers of the Western Reserve were taking advantage of the growing urban market by expanding their dairying operations.[2] William Corlett showed no interest in speculative gains to be made from land and remained on his original small farm until he sold out in about 1865, at the age of eighty-two, to spend his last years with his children in Cleveland. Expecting little more than a living from his farm, and having come to a favourable location, he seems to have achieved his economic aims quite easily. In 1860, he valued his land at only $2700 and his personal estate at $400.

William Corlett did not attempt to provide his own children with land. His eldest son, William, who was seventeen when the family emigrated, worked on canal construction and at clearing land to save money to buy land. He bought a farm in 1843 which he sold to buy another when he married the following year. This farm of 110 acres was in Orange township, twelve miles east of Cleveland, also in the Western Reserve. Most of it was 'primeval forest', which he cleared himself. On his second marriage to a Devonshire immigrant in 1850, William Corlett moved from a log cabin to a frame house. By this time he was forty years old and had been in America for twenty-four years. In 1860, he valued his farm at $3300. William Corlett does seem to have been attracted, late in life, by land speculation. He retired from farming in 1872, at a much younger age than his father, and bought speculatively an allotment just outside Cleveland. Unable, because of this purchase, to pay for his son's education as a doctor, William Corlett had to wait until the suburban boom of the eighties, with the coming of electric trams, before his little speculation realized a capital gain. He, too, spent the last years before his death, in 1901, in the home of one of his children.

William Corlett's second son, Thomas, who went into the Episcopalian clergy, training at Oberlin and the Theological Seminary at Gambier, Ohio, later became rector of St Paul's Church in Cleveland. The other sons became carpenters, an occupation much in demand in a rapidly growing city. John worked for his brother-in-law, John Gill, a Manx immigrant who became a successful building contractor in Cleveland. After a journey to California in 1852, Charles also settled just outside the city to work at his trade.

While the Corletts who had been born in the Isle of Man remained in farming and the building trades, the next generation moved into the professions and other tertiary occupations. William Corlett Jr's son, William, eventually became a doctor, though his father wanted him to remain in farming. The children of his sister, Mary Corlett Gill, were working in Cleveland in 1874, one as a doctor practising medicine, another as a book-keeper and a third in an insurance office.

Thus the Corlett family showed the same strong cohesiveness as the Birkets. They remained in touch with the family in the Isle of Man, but never attempted to gain financial help from them. William Corlett, like John Birket, a devout Episcopalian, was active in securing both church services and a school for the Manx children in Newburgh. A preacher from the Isle of Man, Patrick Cannell, who emigrated in 1827, held church services for some time on the Corlett farm in the log schoolhouse. Little interested in American politics, Corlett did not become a citizen until 1836. His social contacts seem to have been entirely with friends and acquaintances from the Isle of Man. William Corlett made a satisfactory social and economic adjustment because he had very little need to change his way of life greatly; nor did he feel any pressures to assimilate with the host community. In 1852, his son, Thomas, reported to William Corlett's brother in the Isle of Man: 'The old stock are about as they ever were. The young people are in no way different from the people of this country.' William Corlett did not want to lose touch with the Isle of Man. Again, in the words of Thomas referring to his parents: 'They feel very anxious to hear from you. I think as old age creeps upon them, they think more and more of their friends on the other side of the ocean.'

In Cleveland, where his children settled, the largest centre of Manx immigration in the United States, the immigrants created social and mutual aid societies, which kept the Manx community distinct and somewhat separate for a much longer time than was the case with the small group of English settlers in Tazewell County, Illinois. The Manx immigrants were able to keep alive their language and to remain as clannish as they desired. This clannishness, for which they were renowned, was an advantage in accommodation. Other immigrants from England and Scotland, who settled in as primitive a spot in the first instance, were unable to secure enough followers to establish so strong an immigrant community. The Manx emigrated in a community network, rather than simply in family groups as did our other emigrants to agriculture.

The originals of the Corlett letters, including the letters of Rev. Thomas Corlett, are in the Manx Museum in the Isle of Man, and are published with the permission of the Librarian-Archivist. These extracts have been made from photostats in the British Library of Economic and Political Science.

Letters from William Corlett to his brother, Thomas Corlett, of Orrisdale, Kirk Michael, Isle of Man

Newburgh, Cuyahoga Co., Ohio, 12 May 1831

DEAR BROTHER,

I received your letter the 29 of April 1831. I did not get that letter you sent last year. This is the first letter I ever received from you. I hope these few lines will find you in a state of good health as I am at present. Thanks be to God that my wife and family are in a state of good health ... [portion missing] my house, and we are to keep school in.* Old neighbour Patrick Cannell is in good health, and family, and desires to

---

* A log schoolhouse was built on land donated by William Corlett from his farm in Newburgh. The log building was replaced in 1842 by a frame building. Reunions continued to be held in connection with this school until 1923.

be remembered to Father and to all enquiring friends. Mr Quayle* desires to be remembered to you, and Phinlo Corlett. Also Mrs Quayle desires to be remembered to you. All my neighbours does very well and encreasing every day. We are about ninety persons in the neighbourhood, all from the little Isle of Man, and we all attend to hear the Gospel preached every Sabbath Day. It is like we shall not meet in this vail of tears, but if we meet at the right hand of God, all is right. . . . [portion missing]

I am to give you a little information about my situation. I do prefer this country for my own part; and if I should be in the old country now I would soon come out. I would be very glad if some of my relations would be here; but I dont encourage any person to come. Let every person make their own mind up about that.

I have thirty-two acres of improvement, eight acres under wheat and 12 acres ready to sow in. . . . [portion missing] on the Lake Erie sails about one hundred schooners and 11 steemboats. Also there is a steem mill which grinds seven hundred bushels in twenty-four hours, and there is one hundred and fifty thousand bushels waiting for the mill to grind is not half the wheat that is in town of Cleveland. They import and transport ten times more than the whole Isle of Man. There is three churches in, and building a new church and it is to be made of stones; and Wm. Cain from Peel is to be the general mason. . . . [portion missing]

Dear Brother, give some account of this to Mrs Cain, grandmother, and give her all the information you can understand out of this letter. . . . [Long list of persons to be greeted]

When I write again I shall give you a little more satisfaction about the country, and I will give you a little more information about my situation and neighbours. . . . [More greetings] So no more at present. You must excuse me for my bad writing.

WM. CORLETT

Newburgh, 9 Nov. 1842

DEAR BROTHER THOMAS,

I hope these few lines will find you & family enjoying good health as they leave me at present. I am glad to hear from you and all my old friends. The death of my father reminds me of the shortness of time; also that of my aunt Finlow Corletts wife. Thanks be to the Lord for all his goodness to me and family in preserving our lives to the present time. I am sorry to hear of the sickness of John Cain, yet let us trust in

* John Quayle, born 1770, emigrated from the Isle of Man with the Corletts. He was listed as a farmer in the population census for Newburgh township in 1840 and 1850.

the Lord for all his ways are right. My health has been good since my last letter; my wife & children are all well; I have removed in my new house.* My neighbours [are?] all well. John Quayle is well. He is building a new house. Mr Philip Shimmon B., my old friend in Orrisdale, has removed near us. John Cannell, son of my neighbour John Cannell,† was drowned last July while swimming. In regard to John and Ellen coming out next spring I will say as I have said before that I think they will do well. I know of no one of the Manks who are not doing well. I believe they have plenty of work and pretty good pay. There is no regular wages established yet. I believe the wages for shomakers, joiners & other tradesmen is from one dollar to one & a half per day. Money is getting better and the prospect is that in a few years the money will be good. All the disturbances between this government & Great Britain is settled and now universal harmony and peace reigns through the States. Crops has been very good here this year. . . . [Prices]

This country is a fine country for farming and mercantile business, not however so rich as some of our good friends wrote to us the first years when we heard that bread grew on the trees & ginger root was the worst weed here. I am not sorry I came out here, but I am very glad that I have come. Permit me to say amore as I have said before, that the country is a good country & no one need be poor here if he or she is well & endustrious. I might say many things about the soil and forests & the way of clearing off the forests, but perhaps it would not be best as you know enough about the country to judge for yourselves. I have endeavoured to tell you the simple truth about this country, and I think if you will come out you will find it about the same as I have written to you. And I wish this plain so that you may not be disappointed when you come here. You can rely on what you find in this letter. I tell you these things about the country from fifteen years experiance. The country is growing more & more healthy, the state of society more & more moral. There are great revivals all over the country & thousands are turning to the Lord. The Lord is working powerfully in all this land. Temperance sweeps all before it. Millions have joined the tee-total temperance society. All things go to show better times for which we bless God. I should be glad to have John & Ellen come out next season. All that I have said they can rely on. I would say to them come. I wish they would bring the late history of the Isle of Man. I will pay them for it when they come. Remember me & family to all my old friends. Write to me before spring. I remain your affectionate Brother,

WM. CORLETT

* Thus, after fifteen years he moved from a log cabin to a frame house.
† John Cannell, 49, farmer, was listed at Newburgh in the 1850 census.

Newburgh, 28 Oct. 1847

DEAR BROTHER THOMAS CORLETT,

About one year and a half since I wrote to Wm Cain but have received no answer as yet. I thought perhaps the letter was miscarried, and yet I did not know but you might think that we had mooved from the fact that the letter was mailed at Oberlin. We are living in the same place yet and probably shall not moove. The reason why the letter was mailed at Oberlin was Thomas was going there and took the letter with him . . . [Gives correct address, health]

We are all well, at present. My son Wm. is still living on his farm near me. Mary is living in Cleveland. She has three boys & one girl. My son Wm. has four little girls all well. Son John is living at Cleveland. He works with Mr Gill, Mary's husband. Thomas is at home now. He has just finished his studies and in a few weeks will be either preaching or teaching. Charles is working in Cleveland, at his trade. Jane lives in Cleveland, with Mary. Eliza has been teaching for two years past near home. My children are all doing well. For which I feel to bless God.

The Manks around us are doing well. Last week my son Thomas called on a number of Manks families in Painsville about 30 miles east from where we live. They were all well and doing well. This year has been a very sick year. All over around here some have been sick but not so many as in large cities. The crops for two years past have been fair. All but potatoes and wheat this year have been good. The wheat is very much injured by the fly; the potatoes rot badly. . . . [Prices] The war with Mexico has caused some changes here. It is so far from us that about here it has not been felt much. It still go on and may continue some time yet. Daniel Cannell called here after he came to America. From what he said I fear that you may be in doubt about coming here. To remove any such fears if you have them I would say you need have no fears about doing well here. With industry and economy no one need be destitute long of a good home. All can get it. There is plenty to do and good pay. Daniel Cannell and his cousin John Christian are doing well. They work in Cleveland. Tell my b in l Wm Caines children* they need have no fears about coming here. I have no doubt but that they would do well. I should be happy to see them, if they come let them come to Cleveland, they will be then within five miles of my house. . . . [Greetings] My respects to all. Write soon! Your brother,

WM. CORLETT. . . . [About another friend]

---

* William Caine, born 1781, landed proprietor farming thirteen acres, was the brother of William Corlett's wife.

Fisher Series 1830–38

John Fisher was born on a farm in St Margarets, Suffolk, during the first decade of the nineteenth century.[1] His family had already migrated within England before John Fisher emigrated to America in 1830. At that time, his mother and brothers were farming rented land at Brooke, a village in the northeastern part of Norfolk, in the broads west of Yarmouth, seven miles southeast of Norwich. During the 1820s, the population of this small village had increased rapidly by about a hundred souls to reach just over seven hundred inhabitants. This growth was not maintained in the thirties, when migration carried off the population increase. Brooke was an entirely rural parish, its whole occupational structure geared to agriculture. In 1851, more than three in five of the men in the surrounding census district were employed in agriculture.

Although opportunities for employment, other than in farming, may have seemed limited in his immediate district, John Fisher cannot be said to have emigrated because of economic necessity. In contrast with the Birkets and the Corletts, he came from an area of large farms and progressive agriculture. In 1851, agricultural labourers outnumbered farmers by a ratio of six to one in the area around Brooke. At that time, his elder brother was farming 201 acres of land and employing ten labourers and three waggoners.[2] Francis Fisher, who did not marry, and his mother also employed three indoor domestic servants. John Fisher was able to take enough capital to the United States to buy land shortly after his arrival there and to hire labour to begin his farm-making operations. This capital possibly came from his father's will. His father had died, before he emigrated, leaving a widow, Lydia, and four sons. The eldest of these sons, William, died in 1854. George, who seems to have been regarded as a ne'er-do-well, probably also emigrated. John Fisher was a younger son who emigrated, in part, to satisfy his desire to have a farm of his own, a goal which he did not think he could achieve at home. This is not to say that such a goal was unattainable in Norfolk in his generation. One of his friends, Palmer Leader, progressed from sheep dealer to farmer and cattle dealer, and eventually became a landowner in his own right during the years that John Fisher was farm-making in Michigan.[3]

Since his letters began right after his arrival in America, it is possible in this case to gain some idea of the frame of mind in which John Fisher left his homeland. He visualized the United States as a land of liberty, which to him meant that it was free of 'parsons and poor', as did his Uncle Brazill Smith, who emigrated with him. Evidence of a pessimistic view of England's future is also to be found in John Fisher's letters. After he arrived in America, he continued to take an interest in political news from England and in the progress of reform, but his letters do not betray any involvement in American politics.

Like the Birkets, John Fisher's destination in the United States was determined by relatives who had emigrated earlier. When he arrived in Palmyra, New York, he found that some of them had already made a second move to Lenawee County, Michigan, and he followed them. Although the lands of the federal government had been on sale in Lenawee County since 1823, it was still true frontier in 1830, with fewer than two inhabitants per square mile. During the boom of the thirties, population flooded into the county to raise the total from 1,491 in 1830 to 17,889 in 1840. This rapid increase in population was one reason why John Fisher found a ready sale for his crops, as soon as he was able to grow a surplus. Tipton, the village from which his last letters were posted, was about forty miles from Monroe on Lake Erie. Fisher's choice of location made it possible for him to become a commercial farmer within a couple of years of his arrival in America. The fact that wheat was to be an important market crop in the agriculture of this county for a generation enabled him to manage his farm with certain modifications of Norfolk methods. More conscious of the possibility of declining fertility with constant cropping in wheat than some of his neighbours appear to have been, Fisher kept his soil manured. His attitude towards livestock contrasted with that of the immigrants from Westmorland. Fisher regarded his livestock as a source of power and of fertility for his soil, and thought livestock farming required too much capital.

An outstanding feature of John Fisher's short career in America was the speed with which he was able to clear unbroken land. His record in this respect was far better than that of any other immigrant whose progress we have been able to trace. Discouraged by the task of clearing the eighty acres of timbered land which he bought in the first instance, he added eighty acres of prairie, which he proceeded to break and use for his crops. In eight years he cleared nearly a hundred acres, and in the single year of 1838 added twenty acres to his improved acreage. This achievement was made possible, not only by his taking up prairie lands, but also by his more ample capital, which enabled him to hire labourers and buy ten bullocks.[4]

During these years of abundant opportunity for commercial wheat farming in Michigan, John Fisher's economic aims were gradually changed. When he first arrived, he seemed to look forward to the time when he could let his farm and live a retired life with his books. Year after year he planned to return to England for a visit. As his enterprise prospered, he found himself too busy for such a visit. Investing all of his earnings in farm improvement, he worried that he was concentrating too much of his attention on material gain. By 1838, the life of leisure was no longer in sight, or even contemplated.

Although John Fisher encouraged other members of his family in Norfolk to join him, the only ones who came to Michigan were his brother-in-law, Robert Smith, a shoemaker, and his family.[5] Most of Fisher's other associates seem to have been English immigrants. The labourers who worked for him were English-born, as was the woman he married. Fisher's increasing interest in religion may have been influenced by the American part of his environment, though this is difficult to say. He probably had nonconformist leanings before he emigrated. There were nonconformists in his Norfolk village, where a Baptist chapel was built in 1839. Clearly with his Methodist wife and brother-in-law, the latter a class-leader and active in the local revival of 1838, one does not have to look for American influences to explain John Fisher's responsiveness to this revival. The Fisher letters do suggest how close the attitudes of some emigrants from rural England were to those of immigrants to the Old Northwest from rural New England and the Burnt Over district of New York.

John Fisher was listed in the 1840 census at Franklin, Michigan, still on the land he bought when he arrived ten years earlier. At that time he was employing three agricultural labourers. He probably died soon after that, as his letters ceased and he was not listed in the census of 1850.

The Fisher letters are in the East Suffolk County Record Office in Ipswich and are published with the permission of the Archivist.[6] Photostats of some of them are in the British Library of Economic and Political Science.

Letters from John Fisher to his mother, Mrs Lydia Fisher, Brooke, Norfolk, and brothers and sister

Palmyra, NY, 20 June 1830

.... [Beginning of letter missing] Quebec is a flourishing town, the prevailing religion Catholic, language French. The town appears full of emigrants, 7,000 having arrived this spring & my uncle went away in the steam packet for Montreal. I would have gone with him but could not get my luggage out of the ship. Thursday, 10th, went to the Catholic Church which is the most splendid edifice I ever beheld, like Solomons Temple, inlaid with gold. The service was performed by 126 men all dressed like [andrews ?]. Their superstition and ignorance is beyond description. The priest caried an immage of gold representing the Saviour on the Cross, 126 men with lighted candels, some before and some behind. When nearly all knelt down I did not, when a godly old woman pulled my coat and endeavoured to make me understand what she meant, but I would not.

Friday, 11th took my leave of Quebec, had bad accomodation on the steam packet and cold nights. Sunday, 13th, arrived at Montreal. The river from Quebec to Montreal is interceted with islands. The scenery was beautiful and pictersque. The Church at Montreal is more splendid than at Quebec, religion and language the same. Went on board the packet [for Lappare ?]* [got of o clock arrived at Lappare] . . . and had 18 miles land carriage. At 12 at night succeded in hiring a cart to carry my luggage to St. Johns, the road very bad. Arived at 4 in the morning, went on board the steamer packet on Lake Champlain, had very bad accomodation on a fine packet. Tuesday 15th, saw the Catskill Mountains, arrived at Whitchalk,† the Custom House Officer to examine the goods. He opened only my little box. I had nothing to pay, went on board the horse packet for Albany, had better accomodation. Thursday, 17th, arrived at the junction, went on board the horse packet for Palmyra, had good accomodation, the country hilly and wilden, the canal convey & over the River Mowhawk. Come to a place were the canal cut through the solid rock which is done by gunpowder, holes being bored down and filled and then set on fire, which blows of large masses of rock. Friday, came to Utica which is a beautiful town, the streets strait and wide.

In toward Palmira, the land more level and fertile. I was excedingly tired of travelling long before I arrived. Monday 22nd, the land fertile, my [heart ?] boyant with expectation at the thought of meeting my uncle in a fertile land, but judge my feelings when I arrived at Palmyra and I found my uncle gone to Michigan teritory, 500 miles further up the country west and could not get his address. Tuesday, 23 June, was

---

* Probably refers to La Prairie, Quebec, one hundred miles south of the city of Quebec, on the Salmon River, just north of the Quebec–New Hampshire boundary.

† Probably Whitehall in upper New York state east of Lake George on the Champlain canal. If so, the mountains were not the Catskills but the Adirondacks.

very much disappointed and felt myself a stranger in a foreign land but met with many friends. 24th, went to Marion where my uncle lived and found many kind friends who invited me to stop all night, had a letter from my uncle and found that he had bought 80 acres of land in Michigan, got his address with an intention to folow him. But my uncle arrive with his family and met with every kind reception at Mr Pooleys brothers.* Later my mind was much aggitated to determine wether I should go to Michigan or stop here, but after a while, blieving the bounds of my habitation where fixt, I felt more comfortable. My Uncle Brazill Smith intends [to] settle here at Marion, has hired a house and a little land and is going to work. He was excedingly disappointed when he found Pooley was gone to Michigan teritory. He likes the country much better than England and met with very kind treatment from Pooley's numerous friends. [not signed]

Bachelor's Hall, Tecumseh,† Mich., 12 July 1831

MY DEAR MOTHER,

. . . [Letter received] When I wrote to you before I was in an unsettled state. I left Palmyra for Michigan on the first of July and arrived at Mr Pooley's on the 16 July after travelling through a very fertile country. I like the land about Mr Pooley and bought 80 acres for 23£ in a wild state. It is mixt soil, partly timbered and part openings and look like a gentlemans park. I admire the providence of God in providing such a country for the rescue of the distressed of all nations. I bought 2 yoke of cattle and one cow and 2 calves. I found hay in great abundance on the marshes in a wild state. I plough with cattle, horses being very dear in this country. I intend sowing 3 acres of oats, planting 2 acres of maize, sowing 1 acre of spring wheat and planting 1/2 an acre of potatoes. Though this may appear a slow way of farming, it is a certain one. As we have nothing to pay to the parsons or poor, for the industrious poor man is not known in this country, for here labour has its own, and the rigours of taxation are unknown.

But my cup was mingled with bitters for I was taken sick with the billious fever after which I had the fever and ague the whole of which lasted nearly 3 months. Though these are not distressing complaints they kept me from work until the winter. I have great reason to bless God that he has still preserved me in the land of the living.

* This uncle, Brazill Smith, remained in Palmyra, Wayne County, New York, and was listed in the population census of 1850 as a farmer with $4,500 -worth of real property. Two of his sons were established on farms near him by 1860. The two brothers were Edward and Nathan Pooley. Edward Pooley's wife was the sister of Brazill Smith.

† Tecumseh was organized as a township in Lenawee County, Mich., in 1827.

I am situated in a country where I see but little of the noise and bustle of business and hence but little of what is going on in other parts of the world, but here I enjoy peace at home, having nobody to disturb me. I live alone, do my own milking, churning, cooking, and sometimes washing and mending; but I do not much like it. I think I want a wife but see no chance of getting one in this country as I do not like the Yanke girls. I esteem my books a great treasure, for though I live alone I can converse with a Milton, a Young, and many more excelent writers which adorn my libery. This settlement began last spring. Now there is near 20 familys within 3 miles all aggreing to help one another along, borrowing and lending all they have. I should very much like to see some of my friends in this country. I think my Uncle George had a great deal better come to America as he would be conferring a lasting benifit on his family.

I had a letter from Mr Brazill Smith who is living in York State near Palmyra. He and family are doing well. He talks louder than ever about the enormous taxation of England and the devouring Clergy who for their bellies sake creep and intrude and [clime] into the fold. [Mr Pooley ?] is returned to York state on account of his wifes sickness. I am very glad I come to this country and should any ask if I should not like to make England my final settlement I would tell them no, not if I could sway the sceptre. I have a good share of the comforts of this life, and may say that

> My land my cattle and my cow
> Add to my comforts here below
> And should not this a comfort be
> My lands from tythes and near from taxes free
> My lands my own no tything Parson share
> Nor mean exciseman is admitted here
> The prospect of this country I love
> Its liberty and laws approve
> Its Government simple every subject share
> A vote for members who the truths declare
> Free and unbiassed every subject feel
> His liberty and laws his intrest still.

But this kind of cant won't do. As my dumplings are [done ?] enough, I must go to dinner.

I must give you a little account of my travelling since I wrote to you before at Palmyra. I have travelled about 500 miles and about 1154 miles from Quebec not costing more than £3 besides board. I had only 18 miles land carrage from Quebec to Michigan. Tell my friends I am much obliged to them for writing to me. They wanted to know if the gospel was preached where I lived. It is preached by Mr Smith, late from England. He is of Mr Wesley persuation and though not a man of very bright talents he is a sincere Christian. . . . [About another migrant]

I should be glad if you could borrow 50£ for me and give security for it. I would pay the intrest and if my health is spared I have no doubt but I could pay the whole in 2 years. I have bought my land and cattle and furniture and things fit to go on with, but I want to build a house and stable this summer and have no money to do it with. I shall build this summer and put of my pay until I hear from you again. If you can get the money for me it will be a great advantage to me. If not, I must sell my cattle to pay it. This will materialy hinder me in farming. If you can get the money, pay it in some bank in New York. Inclose the receipt in the letter you send to me.

I should very much like to come to England again to see my friends and if I dont get married, and I see no like[lihood] of that, I think I shall come to England again in the course of a year or 2. I should like to see some of my friends to tea with me at Bachelor Hall and I should very much like to meet my friends at the Book club. Every full moon reminds me of it. I think if my Brother Mr Smith like to come to America he would do better than he can in England but I would advise none to come but such as can work.* Here was 2 poor Englishmen come into this settlement last spring with little or no money. Now they have got 80 acres of land each, to be paid for in 2 years. There is a great many Indians in this teritory who live entirely by hunting and fishing. They are poor, distressed creatures and refuse every attempt to civilize them. As the country get settled they flee back to those immence regions of the West. Give my respects to all my friend. Teell them to write to me and not be affraid of making me double postage as my last letters cost me no more than 13 pence and can cost no more if it is sent from East to West in the United States. . . . . [Directions. Prices. Greetings]

I remain your affectionate Son,

JOHN FISHER

Bachelor's Hall, Franklin, Mich., 11 June 1832†

DEAR MOTHER,

I have just recieved your letter with the greatest pleasure and am glad to find you are all well. I have enjoyed good health since I wrote to you before and have built my house but have not quite finished it. I have

* This is Robert Smith who was married to John Fisher's sister, Harriet. When he emigrated with his young family in April 1834, Robert Smith lived with John Fisher in the latter's log cabin.

† Franklin, Michigan, was incorporated as a township in 1833.

drawn the timber [for] my barn and expect to build it in about a month. My crops look well and I think I shall have abundance.

I thank you Dear Mother for all I enjoy of this earths goods and Oh may God grant that I may be enabled to enjoy the blessing of an intrest in the blood of his son who died on the cross to redem sinners of whom I feel myself to be the chief. I know that I have lifted up the arm of rebelion against my great Creator. I have fought against him to whom I am indebted for every breath I draw. Dear Mother do thou pray for me that I may be enabled to lay down my arms of rebelion and ceace to fight against God my Maker that I may be enabled to enlist under his banner and fight the good fight of faith laying hold of the helmet of salvation looking unto Christ the author and finisher of my faith. . . .[His brother George's conversion]

You were very rongly informed as to the American character respecting the Sabath. We have meetings every Sunday and once in the week, all of which are well attended. The laws of this Teritory strongly prohibit working on the Sunday and are well enforced. But if there were no laws or concience in the way, believe me the Yankees do not like work well enough to work on the Sunday. I am sorry to hear that the colera is making such ravages in my native place & likewise in France. I have the priveledge [of] reeding 3 of the best nusepapers in America. We have recieved accounts from London down to the 26 of April and Paris to 25, all of which state that the colera is still spreading and who knows where it will stop. It has not yet visited our highly favoured land but it is much feared it will. Adieu, my dear Mother. I fear I shall not see you again in this world. If not, may God grant that we meet in the realms above where sorrow and sighing shal be done away, where the inhabitants shal no more say we are sick. Desire an intrest in your prayers. I remain your affectionate Son,

JOHN FISHER

DEAR BROTHERS,

I must give you my opinion of this country and draw some comparison between them. I have left England and its gloomy climes for one of brilliant sunshine and inspiring purity. I have left the country cowring with doubt and danger, where the rich man trembels and the poor man frowns, where all repine at the present and dread the future. I have left this country and am in a country where all is life and animation, where I here on every side the sound of exultation, where every one speaks of the past with triumph, the present with delight, the future with growing and confident anticipation. Is not this a community in which one may rejoice to live? Is not this a land in which one may be proud to be recieved as a citicen? Is not this a land in which one may be happy to fix his destany and ambition? I answer for one, it is. Am I asked how long I mean to remain here? I answer, as long as I live; yet, my dear brother, I have a respect for my native land and much more so for my friends and eagerly recieve all accounts from that country and feel an intrest in its wellfare, and why? It is my own, my native land. I see the reform bill has had a second reading in the House of Lords by a majority of nine. I am affraid it will not pass.

I must give you some account of what I have been doing here. I arrived here in July 1830. I bought one farm [of] 80 acres and went to work on it, but finding it had too much timber on it and I could not chop very well I bought 80 acres more clear openings, something similar to a pasture. I still own both of them and have but a small morgage on one, about the amount of 22£. The first I bought is worth nearly double the money I gave for it. The last, which I farm myself, is worth 5 times what it cost. I am very buisy. I should be glad [to get ?] here people to work for me at the same rate you [pay] but that is the difficulty as almost all are farmers. [You may] say were are the poor people? I answer . . . [illegible passage] *the industrious poor man is unknown.* How would [the] labourers of Old England rejoice if they could be . . . [illegible words] I have seen some who [were sent] over by the parish some 8 or 10 years since now [in] circumstances far preferable to those who sent them. [I advise] all to transport themselves before they are [risk the necessity] of being sent by the parish. I would advise [none to come] to America but those who can work for a living [or] have plenty of money. I think if any of you my brothers think of farming you would do well in America, but I feel very delicate in giving advice of this sort as you might blame me should you come and not like the country. . . . [Greetings] I remain your affectionate Brother,

JOHN FISHER. . . . [More greetings]

MR AND MRS SMITH, DEAR BROTHER AND SISTER,

I cannot thank you for your letter for I have not recieved one, but I wish you well. I think you would do well in America as you have a growing and increasing family. We pay very high for all kinds of labour. Leather is cheap and shoes are dear. But perhaps, dear sister, you are afraid to cross the mighty deep. If that is all the scruples I hope they wont detain you. You will say you cant leave your friends. I confess that was the most I had to contend with, but althow I left my friends I hope I have not lost their friendship, & I have found friends in this country so that I have friends in both countrys. The Americans are a warm hearted people, friendly in distress and affliction, free and openhearted. They know nothing of the over-bearing tyranical power of the rich and are equely destitute of the spirit to crush the poor and keep them down. . . . I remain your affectionate brother,

JOHN FISHER

Bachelors Hall, Franklin, 18 July 1833

DEAR MOTHER,

I recieved your letter and am glad to find you are all well. I have enjoyed good health since I wrote to you before and am getting along very well with my farm. I wish you could come and drink a cup of tea with me and see how [neat ?] bachelors hall looks and fetch along some of my old acquaintances with you. I should very much like to see my old friends again and if you will not come and see me I think I must come and see you in the course of a year . . . if life is spared. I should like to be present at a [meeting ?] of [the] book club. The thought of the pleasure I enjoyed often [is] present with me. I have recieved a letter from Mr Brook Roberts. With he informed me you were all well and that the Lord had pleased to convince [word illegible] & David of the error of their ways. I wish I could say that I enjoyed the same peace of mind which he says they do.

Dear Mother I wish you and my brothers wear in this country for I hear that [word illegible] is hard home in England. Besides I know that you could own more land here than you can hire there and the richest land I ever saw and our crops here sell nearly as high as there. Than there is no rent, poor rates, or taxes and money is worth more than doubel here. I have borrowed money and paid thirty per cent and then made it answer my purpose. I have worked but little since I came to this country and you know I had but littel money and I have got one hundred forty acres of land, good comfortabel house and barn, stabel, forty acres of land fenced and nearly thirty under a good state of improvement, and am in a sure and easy way of living. All I appear to want is a wife to make me comfortable which I can get as soon as I please, but I dont like to give up the notion of seeing England once more and if I ever do see it, it must be before I get married. . . . [News of friends and relatives in New York state. Greetings] I almost forget my friends names as I have not seen any person from the same [county?] since I left [N?] I should like to hear how William Fisher is getting along and Penced Gearman and all my friends. I will answer Williams letter in the course of a week or two.

I am very busy and must conclude. We have nearly done harvest. July 24: our harvest is a little earlyer than yours. We have had very hot weather for the week past. The thermometer 100 degrees all day; yet I feel no difficulty in working in such weather as there is generally plenty of air stirring. The climate of this part of the country agrees well with English people who generally have good health. I should like to come to England this autumn but I cannot arrange my business so as to leave this country this year, but I would come if I thought I could persuade you to sell and come to this country. For I think it would be the best thing you could do to come while you have money to come with. I hear that farmers are breaking and I am afraid that would be the case with a great many before many years. I must conclude. There have been a great reformation in religion in this country during the past year, and many have flocked to Christ, the captain of their Salvation. I remain your affectionate son,

JOHN FISHER

Franklin, Mich., 23 July 1833

TO ROBERT SMITH. DEAR BROTHER AND SISTER. . . . [Letter received. Advice about emigration. Prices]

Here is plenty of feathers, but they sell very high. You had better bring your beds along with you. Here is plenty of timber to make chairs and tabels and all kinds of furniture. Tabuls and chairs very cheap.

Dear brother and sister, I am glad you are coming where you can have the benefits of your labour and if you cannot furnish money enough only to pay your passage to my residence, do not be discouraged. You and I can get a living to-gether as I have got my farm in a cultivated state so that I raise my own living and live as independent as your richest farmers though not in such great style. I never heard you had any increase in your family untill I received your letter. They will be a blessing to you in this country. Here is good schools and very cheap. Every child is liburally educated. I do not know that I have seen a Yanke but had some education. Bring your clothes along with you as they are a little more durabel if not a littel cheaper. Do not bring any breeches as trowsers are universally worn. Your friends in religion (as there are many Methodists in this settelment) are anxious to see you and I believe you will have a joyful welcome to this fertile country. How pleasing tis to see people of every country rejoicing in the same God & Saviour uniting with heart and hand in spreading the Saviour's name. . . . [Write]. I remain your Affectionate Brother,

JOHN FISHER. . . . [Letter from brother William]

Franklin, Mich., 7 Oct. 1835

MY DEAR MOTHER AND BROTHER, . . . [Letter received with news of death of brother William]

I have made much improvement on my farm in the past year so that I cannot leave my buisiness without a great loss. I have 75 acres of improvement, 35 acres of wheat, 5 acres of rye, the rest for spring crops. My crops the past year were good and are selling well. Wheat is selling for 18s. per comb*; oats, 9s. 6d. per comb and other things in the same proportion. The above is given in English money. *Reccolect* no *Tythes* nor *Taxes*. I cannot say that I make much money, for I lay it all out in improveing my farm which will eventually repay me. My farm is worth more than *four* times as much as the money I brought with me from England. I cannot farm it in the English fashon, for instead of 10 horses I have 10 bullocks to work it with; but I think the time is not far distant when I shall exchange my bullocks for horses. Horses are not so usefull in improveing a new farm as bullocks, but better after it is improved to work it with.

Mr Smith lives with me. He has married a Yankee wife. He has worked for me for half a year passed. He has bought 40 acres of land and made some improvement; will build him a house on it this fall. John Hurry works for me & and has done all summer. He too has bought a *farm* but I think I can persuade him to stop a year longer with me. I have hired an Englishman for a year from [Dereham] Norfolk. I pay John Hurry 138 dollars a year (30£ English) and board him and pay for his washing and mending. He has had more wages before he came to me, but he likes living with the English best. I find much trouble in hiring men for any leangth of time as they soon get to be farmers themselves.

It is very likely that the next letter you recieve from me will inform you I am married as I find it difficult to hire a woman to do my work in the house. I have long paid my addresses to a young lady in this vicinity (from Yorkshire in England) of a very respectabel family. She has been very sick lately but it is with great pleasure that I see the glow of health begin to reanimate her countenance.

[About Brazill Smith]. . . . Mr White is comeing to Michigan in the spring to settle and I think that it wont be long before Mr B.Smith comes too as he has not bought land in York State. Land is very dear there. This country is improveing faster than it has done in any past year as the people are getting more able to improve their farms and build better houses and barns, &c. I am going to dig a well this fall. I have had to fetch water from a creek nearly forty rods for the past year. I have had many difficultys to struggle with for five years past but I begin to surmount them now & recieve the reward of my labours. My prospect is cheering as far as the good things of this life go. My

---

* Comb, a variation of coomb, a dry measure of capacity equal to four bushels or half a quarter.

5

improved land would let for 300 dollars per year, quite sufficient to support me without work, but I think of improveing forty acres more next year. Land rent here for nearly £1 per acre. Its true that crops do not sell so high here as in your country but farmers make more money. The fact is here is no *tythes, taxes*, no *poor rates* to take away the profits. And yet I have been very much blamed for inviting people from England to this country althou I have never extended my invitation to any but those that had to live by their labour, but I now say that capatalists would double their profits by emigrating to this country, for money is worth more than double the intrest here that it is there, often 14 per cent.

Mr Smiths children are all well. 5 of them are living with me and one (Elizabeth) is staying a short distance from here with a respectable family. People have been very kind in taking the children untill Mr Smith got married. His wife is a religious woman and behave very kind to the children. He is more comfortable than he could have been unmarried with his family. They are playing about the room while I am writing, all in good health. I wish you could see how much they are grown. They are promising children. Mr Smith is digging a sellar and will shortly build a house for himself on his own land ... [Messages from John Hurry and Robert Smith]

I have sometimes indulged myself in writing some pieces of poetry which are circulated far in this timbered world; but my buisness is pressing, my time nearly all employed in work so that I have little time for poetry. I take a weekly newspaper printed at New York so that I have all the political news from your country sooner than you could send it by letter. Accounts from Ireland are distressing. Many perish by starvation. From your country accounts are rather flattering but I now it too well to believe that the lower class of people fare as they do here ... [Message for a friend. Directions. Greetings] I remain your affectionate Son and Brother,

JOHN FISHER

Franklin, Mich., 30 Nov. 1836

DEAR MOTHER AND BROTHERS,

I have recd your letter some time since, but have waited till Mr Smith recd his money from New York. He recd it a week since. I and wife are well and getting a comfortable living. Providence is supplying all our wants. Mr Smith is well and so are all his family. He has another daughter, a fine fat baby. He named it *Marthy Jane*. He is working at shoemaking and has a hired man working on his farm. He makes nearly one pound ten a week and board besides. He is getting along well. He has bought a yoke of cattle &c. Land is rising very fast in value and Mr Smith has 40 acres of his own. John Hurry is living with me yet. He felt very bad about his mother and sister being transported.* It is not known in this part and he feels anxious to keep it a secret. I wish you not to mention it in any letter to Mr Smith. It might probably get out if you did. John has bought eighty acres of land and has nearly money to buy eighty more ... [Friends from Norfolk stopping on way west] I suppose you have entirely given up all thought of coming to America. I think while you can do well there and get a good living it is hardly worth while to travell so many thousand miles as this is, but should any of my brothers think of settling for life I think they had better come to America. For my part I should never advise my mother to come to this country (though I should very much like to see her) for there is considerable differance in the manners and customs of the country and old people cannot so easily bear the fatague of a long sea voyage and land travvel as young ones, nor as easily change their homes so as to be more comfortable. For it always takes a year or two to get things round them comfortable after they have settled in this wild country.

I now begin to reap the benefit of my work though I have ever since I have been here had a good living. Still all the money I could get I have laid out in improveing my farm. I have just had the thrashing machiene to thrash out 100 combs of wheat and 20 combs of oats and have about 25 combs wheat and 50 combs of oats more. Wheat is worth £1 2s. per comb, oats, 9s. I grew 3 acres of barley to fat my hogs with, the first I have sown in this country. The crop was good. They allways fat hogs on Indian corn in this country. I have got a pair of as fine gray horse as the most of your country gentlemen drive in their carriages. We feed them all the oats they like to eat. All our waggons are fixed the same as your coaches with a pole instead of shafts so that we drive horses abreast with reins. Our waggons are lighter than your carriers waggons are; yet we carry heavy loads on them. Our farmers crop their land every year till they cannot get but small crops. Then they say that the land is poor, but in this new country they have not had a chance to reduce the land yet. New land will bear cropping ten years without any manure. But I have not neglected to manure mine. My crops have been good. As yet I do not see that they fail any. I have two hired men and work hard myself, but times go a little better with me than they did a year or two ago. I could live without work now. Since I have been married I have lived more comfortable than ever I did before in my life. I should have been married before but for the desire I had to see my friends in England once more, which desire I still have but I think I shall never see them

* This probably means that they were sent out as paupers.

unless they take it into their heads to come to his country for I am so situated that I could not come to England.

We have preaching twice every Sunday 2 miles from my house by Presbeterians, Methodists and Baptist alternatly. They all unite in this country. The divesian wall is not so high as it is in Eng. There I hope it is pulled so low that they can reach over and give one another the right hand of fellowship, but here one preacher resign his pulpit for one of a different denomination and the same congregation will sit and hear Methodist, Presbeterian and Baptist. Once in a while one stiff in his own faith will leave with the precher of his own [denomination ?] but not often. My wife belong to the Methodist church but we stay and hear all the different preachers, and I do feel more at home since we have had preaching regular. Mr Smith attends at the same meeting I do sometimes and sometimes at one nearer his house, Baptist. . . .

Your affectionate Son and Daughter,

JOHN AND E. FISHER

Franklin, Mich., 5 Sept. 1837

DEAR MOTHER AND BROTHERS, . . . [Letter received. Birth of son]

I have been very busy this summer building a large barn 34 feet wide 46 feet long. I built it on a side hill so that I have stables under nearly two-thirds of it. From the foundation to the eaves, it is 25 feet high. It cost me a great deal of money. It is built something like the old Saint Margarets Barn on the farm where I was born. My crops were good this year but we have had a very wet harvest. I have not quite finished yet. I have five acres of oats out yet. My greatest difficulty is to find men to work for me. They are nearly all farmers themselves. I pay 3s. your money a day for plowing and harrowing and such work, and board. John Hurry has left me a few days since. He is gone to the Territory of Wisconsin, 360 miles from here, to buy more land. He told me to send his best respects to you. When you write again tell me how Hurrys father and family are. Hurry has been a faithfull servant to me. I am afraid I shall not find another like him yet.

I shall sow wheat next week. I have cleared, fenced and plowed 20 acres more this year. I have nearly 100 acres plow land improved now. It has cost me so much improveing my farm that I am short of money the most of the time, Mr White built my barn. He and family are well. Mr Brazill Smith was out to see me this summer. He is comeing to live in Michigan in about a year. . . . [News of mutual friends in Palmyra] I think I shall build a new house another summer if crops sell well. Times are not quite so good as they have been owing to the derangement of the currency. Our government is trying to put down banks and substitute gold and silver currency. I think they cannot accomplish it. If they do there must be a fall in every kind of marketable commodity. I see by my newspapers that your good King William is dead and you have got a *Queen*. I must say that it seems strange that among so many great and able statemen as you have, a girl of eighteen should be called to rule the destinees of a hundred and fifty millions of free men, but so it is . . . [Asks for letters] Pray for me that the acquireing of the things of this life may not engage the whole of my attention but that I may seek first the kingdom of God and [illegible words] I am afraid that business is gradually [turning my] thoughts from God and religion. But may God [grant] I may be aroused from my state of lethargy [before] it is late . . . [More religious hopes] My wife joins with me in love to you all. Your affectionate son and Daughter,

JOHN & E. FISHER

I built my barn so that we drive in on the uper side. The waggons run over one of the stables. It is a very convenient building. I hope to have all good buildings in time but they cost so much I have to build one at a time.

Mr Smith & family are well and send their respects to you all. He has got 15 acres of land more improved which he will sow of wheat next week. The children are all well. Yours truly,

JOHN FISHER

Tipton, Mich., March 1838

DEAR MOTHER AND BROTHERS . . . [Letter and clothes received]

Mr Smith and family are all well. The children are grown very much and look healthy. They have all been to school this winter and have learned very fast. Little John did not know his letters when he commenced but now is in the words of two syllables. Harriet is through the geography, the rest in proportion. I know you would like to see them. They look clean and nice. John is about as large as William was when they left England. I have a fine little son about a year and a month old. He walked alone when he was eleven months old. He begin to talk a little. I should like you to see him. He very much resembles our family. Mr White and family are all well and send their respects to you. John Hurry is just returned from Wisconsin. He has bought 160 acres more land. I think Hurry will do well in this country.* Charles Pulfor and Benj. Edge have travelled to the west with the intention of buying land. They get high wages and like the country well.

* In fact, John Hurry settled in Franklin. He was listed in the 1860 census as a farmer with $3000 worth of real property, married to an English-born woman.

Our country is in a prosperous condition but there is war in Canady now. The people are rebelling against their government. They want to establish a republic government similar to the United States but I do not think they will suceed. They do not unite. Religion divides them. The Catholicks and Protestants will not fight together. The United States troops a restationed along on the lines to maintain nutrality. There is great talk about war between England and the United States but I think there is no foundation for it. I think either nation will deliberate well before they declare war. It would be a great loss to the comerce of both nations, but I do not think there will be any war. At least I hope not. I have had good crops this year. Corn is selling well. I have nearly a hundred acres of plow land improved, so that I think I can get as good a living on my small estate as I could in England on the same quaintity. I am going to build a new house in the spring. I have been getting timber and boards ready for it this winter. I shall build it 32 feet wide and 34 feet long and shall have five rooms below. I think it will be quite convenient. I should like after I have finished my house to have you make me a visit. Tis true tis a long way but I should like very much to see you. I think tis a great chance if I ever come to England again. Mr Smith is getting along something better than he has been other years. He has 15 acres of wheat sown. He has rather hard work to pay his way at present but I think he will do well after another harvest. I have sown 36 acres of wheat this year. It looks well. I think I shall have a good crop. This is truly a land of plenty. Here is no want of the common nesesarys of life, but this is not a country abounding with luxurys like England. At present we have but few orchards large enough to bear much fruit. I think that this is a better climate for fruit than England, but we have plenty of beef and pork and good wheat and good gardens.

We have regular preaching once on a Sunday within a mile and prayer meetings on Thursday evenings amongst the Methodists. We generally attend with the Methodists. They are very zealous in the cause of religion. Mr Smith is considerable of a speaker at their evening meetings. I rather expect Brazill Smith will come to Michigan to settle in the spring. They were all well when I heard from them last, Scottens also. ... I live very comfortable much [more so] than I did before I was married. My wifes sister [travelled ?] nearly 800 miles last fall to make us a visit with the intention of returning in the spring. She is a very clever girl. In this country people frequently [travel ?] from 500 to 1000 miles to make their [relations ?] a visit, stay two or three months, and return again, and think less of it than you would of going to London. Tis suprising to think of the extent of this country. People are constantly travelling west to settle. I supposed I had got to the far west when I came here but now they talk of cities rising up 1000 milles west of me and I suppose there is settlements more than 2000 miles west in the United States. I believe this country was destined by Providence as a refuge for the poor of all nations. . . . [Pray for me and write] I remain your affectionate son and brother,

JOHN FISHER. . . .

P.S. You write that you hope we shall free the slaves in the United States. You could not wish it more sincerely than I do and a majority of the population of the nortern states are in favour of abolution of slavery, but the southern states are powerfull in the councils of the nation. Adieu.

JOHN FISHER

Tipton, Lenawee County, Mich., 29 May 1838

MY DEAR BROTHER,

I received your letter some time about a year ago and I must confess that I am ashamed it has laid so long unanswred, but I think I can tell you somthing that will pay you for all this waiting. The Lord in his infinite goodness has seen fit to pluck me as a brand from the everlasting burning & thanks be to His holy name, I am enabled to rejoice in the righteousness of Jesus Christ. I was first induced to think seriously of my future state some time in April. Brother Robert Smith and [a young?] Methodist preacher commenced holding prayer meetings close by my house once a week.* I attended these meetings with my wife & as I came home from one meeting I said I would go to no more of them, but when the time came for the next I had a desire to go. I attended them all often & saw that they appeared to be greatly conserned for the salvation of souls. I then began to consider and examine my own heart and found that I had sinned against God all my life long & that I deserved to be sent to hell. This brought me deep and lasting conviction. About this time at an evening prayer meeting they said that if there were any present that they had sinned against God & desired the prayers of the congregation they might make it known by rising. I with six more rose and espressed our desire for an interest in their supplacations. This was a bold & decisive step with me. I found my convictions deepning to an alarming extent so that I could not rest. I then began to seek God in

---

* According to Charles Johnson (*The Frontier Camp Meeting*, Dallas, 1955), Michigan camp meetings of the 1830s reflected a mature stage of revival practice and were relatively sober in character. While John Fisher seems to have been converted at Methodist prayer meetings rather than at a camp meeting, it is probably worth noting that practices associated with these evangelical gatherings in Michigan in this period were probably not such as to shock immigrants from rural England.

reality, but I had many temptations to grapple with from the enemy and from my own heart. I found great consolation from the promises of God & reasloved [resolved] that with the assi[s]tance of God I would seek till I died and if I did not find before that religion which would stand the test of a dying hour & a judgment day. I soon began to have a hope that God for Christs sake would pardon my sins & in less than a week I was enabled to rejoice in a sin pardoning God. My load of guilt was gone & I was enabled to rejoice in my God and Saviour. My Dear Brother, praise the Lord for He has taken my feet out of the money clay & placed them on the rock Christ Jesus. He has put a new song in my mouth, even praise to the Lord & this is not all. He has been visiting my neighbours & friends & we have witnessed that the arm of the Lord is not shortened that He cannot save. Neither is His ears heavy that He cannot hear. Dark as the prospect has been the day dawns & we see the morning of better days. For three weeks after the revival commenced the people did very little besides attend prayer meetings, going from house to house. Some made deep convictions enquiring the way to Zion; others telling what the Lord had done for their souls. We have had prayer meetings not far from us almost every day in the week. In the evening we seldom close them till near midnight. Then sometimes with such rejoicing as I never saw or felt before. When we go visiting we generaly close our visits by holding a social prayer meeting, for nearly all our neighbours in this revival are made, I trust, subjects of saving grace. We have two excelent preachers living amongst us. They preach every Sabbath and tis surprising to see the congregations that get together to hear them in this wild country. Our meeting house will not hold all who attend but we talk of holding the meeting in my barn this summer. We still continue to hear the voice of some enquiring the way to Zion. The work is spreading from heart to heart from house to house & I pray God it may spread from town to town & from city to city till all shall know the Lord from the least to the greatest. We have seen the drunkerd, the deist & the old hardened sinners turn to the Lord & find forgiveness.

As it regards my worldly affairs I am geting along as well as ever. The Lord is bountifully suppling all my wants. I am just commencing building a new house 32 feet by 34 with 5 low rooms which I think will be a very convenient house. I hird Robert Smith to improve for me this summer 20 acres more land. Brother Smith is getting along well, better that he has before, since he has been here. He really enjoys religion. I, my wife and my wifes sister have joined the Methodists & Brother Smith is our class leader. . . . [Greetings], I remain your Affectionate Brother,

JOHN FISHER

Wozencraft Series 1843–9

As in the case of the Birket series, we owe the existence of the Wozencraft letters to a search for capital in England by immigrants in the United States during the depression of the early forties. The difference is that John Birket had left farming and was embarrassed because he was unable to collect on debts owing to him by farmers in the neighbourhood, while Thomas Wozencraft, as a farmer, owed large sums and was losing his land bit by bit. Both men had bought more land than they could carry comfortably during the deflation of the early forties.

Thomas Wozencraft also came from an agricultural village outside the main region of England's early industrialization.[1] Like the Birkets and the Fishers he had migrated in Britain before he went to America. Born in South Wales, he was living in the village of Leintwardine, a few miles north of Kington, Herefordshire, in 1790 when his son, John, was born. Thirty-five years later, when he emigrated, he was farming land that he owned, 172 acres at Womaston, three miles northwest of Kington.[2] Railways did not penetrate as far as Kington until the 1850s. As late as 1851, sixty-eight per cent of the labour force in the surrounding census district was still in agricultural occupations. Farmers here used less labour than did the Fishers in Norfolk, partly because of the emphasis on livestock husbandry. In the district as a whole labourers outnumbered farmers by less than two to one. Thomas Wozencraft's son was, therefore, rather a large farmer for the district, since he was employing five labourers in 1851. Population in this district had remained stagnant for a generation before this. The village of Womaston itself returned 181 inhabitants in 1821 and 186 in 1831. This was the decade when Thomas Wozencraft emigrated. Kington continued to lose population during the following two decades, the census authorities ascribing the decrease vaguely to 'emigration'.

When Wozencraft left for America in 1825, he let his farm to his son, John, who was then about thirty-five years old. Wozencraft himself was nearly sixty years old when he emigrated. In this respect he was already an exceptional emigrant, though there were quite a number of elderly

5*

people who emigrated from Britain with their children to American farms. The fact that Wozencraft left alone, without his family, is even more remarkable and may have been preceded by some sort of rupture of family relations. At least the letters make quite clear that Thomas Wozencraft did not bear any great love for his children in Herefordshire.

Though he referred to his wandering in the United States, Wozencraft had arrived in Watkinsville in Clarke County, Georgia, before 1830.[3] By this time he had also remarried, bought land and six slaves. Clarke County, created in 1801 and situated in east north central Georgia, already had 7,628 inhabitants in 1810. In an older cotton producing region, it was no longer growing rapidly by the twenties, when Thomas Wozencraft settled there. Its population rose slowly from 8,767 in 1820 to 10,176 in 1830, and during the thirties it became a region of net emigration, for its population rose by fewer than four hundred people. According to the 1840 census, all the employed population of Clarke County was engaged in agriculture. Thus, like other immigrants to be discussed later, Thomas Wozencraft chose an area which did not continue to grow nor to diversify its economy as the westward movement swept past it. The largest town in Clarke County, Athens, had a mere 1,658 inhabitants by 1850.

While his choice of a region whose growth was to slacken and his role as a 'filler-in' in the wake of the westward movement of Americans were probably not unusual among British immigrants, his selection of the south was highly exceptional. In 1850, there were fewer than seven hundred individuals of English birth living in the whole state of Georgia. Clarke County's total foreign-born population was only sixty-six in that year. Watkinsville itself, which was the town nearest to Wozencraft, returned only two other English immigrants in 1850, a Methodist Episcopal minister and a merchant. His isolation from relatives and other immigrants is reflected in the letters. Unlike our other cases, he makes no mention of acquaintances from home in his letters. He had married a Georgia woman and was raising a large family (of six children, apparently in 1840), though none of them was mentioned in his letters to England. Furthermore, in sharp contrast to immigrants in the north, he positively discouraged relatives and acquaintances from emigrating. When one of his daughters did come out, he refused to permit her to live with him.

Partly because of this self-imposed isolation, Wozencraft seems in some respects to have become more completely assimilated by the American community in which he settled than did most of these immigrants in the first generation. Watkinsville was deep in the piedmont cotton belt. It had more Negro than white inhabitants in 1850. In writing to his son he referred to his Negroes as 'servants'. His justification of slavery is most interesting, especially in the light of the general condemnation of the institution by English immigrants living in the North. The fact of his owning slaves undoubtedly contributed towards his adopting the views of his neighbours, as did his isolation from an immigrant community.

Wozencraft's motives for emigration probably combined economic and personal factors, but did not have social and political overtones. Like John Birket, whose motives were also largely dominated by the hope of economic advance, Wozencraft evinced a speculative attitude towards land. Having bought additional land in 1839, he had grossly overextended himself, and was losing part of it during the period when these letters were written. Also like John Birket, Wozencraft mingled his requests for money from his relatives with religious exhortations. In all four of these long series, Birket, Fisher, Corlett and Wozencraft, one can detect a theme, during years of depression and money tightness, of God's punishing an overly materialistic people and evidence of heightened religious fervour during hard times.[4]

At the time of the 1850 census, Wozencraft was still on the same plantation, though his land holdings were reduced from the five to six hundred acres he reported in his letter of 1843 to three hundred acres. He now owned only four slaves, as compared with six twenty years earlier. Only six other slaveowners in the Farmington district where he lived had so few as five slaves. By this time his son, John, born in Georgia in 1831, was helping on the plantation. Wozencraft's farm operations also differed in other respects from those of his neighbours. His ratio of labour to land was closer to that of his son in Herefordshire than to that of his neighbours in Georgia, and he was also placing more emphasis on livestock in his operations than most of his neighbours. With eight cows and forty swine he was carrying more livestock in relation to the size of his farm than was usual in Clarke County in 1850. The value of his livestock per improved acre was nearly twice as great as that for Clarke County farms as a whole. Although still growing cotton, he was also raising corn and oats for his animals, and food for his family and slaves – wheat, peas, beans, potatoes, and sweet potatoes. In an area known for its failure to diversify its agriculture, Wozencraft was running a mixed farming enterprise. Unfortunately, one cannot say how much his reverses of the forties and how much his early experience in Herefordshire contributed to this fact. Although he had only improved 150 of his 300 acres, the value of his improved acreage exceeded the average for the county.

The Wozencraft letters are published by permission of Mrs Helen

Rogers. Photostats are in the British Library of Economic and Political Science.

Letters from Thomas Wozencraft to his son John, Kington, Herefordshire

Georgia, 10 Oct. 1843

MY DEAR JOHN,

I hope this will find you in health, as it leave me at present. My not having recd a line from your side of the Atlantic for I think upwards of two years precludes my knowing anything of your affairs & circumstances there. The news here, with the exception of some of us having *as yet* a sufficiency of food & raiment of some kind, is all *worse than the worst I ever knew*!!! I do not feel disposed to enter into particulars. Time, paper & patience would all fail. I suppose you have occupied the Perthy Farm five years previous to the 25 March last. I hope you have paid for your three sisters £15 a piece annually. If not, please pay it as soon as convenient. *Up to Lady Day last, no longer.* You say in yours of 29 Novr. 1840 (which is now before me) that you will pay for Perthy according to Mr. Sayce's valuation, £50, which I think is rather low. As times are with you it is certainly worth £60. You will recollect that when I told you or your Uncle to pay them the £45 a year, I desired that the ballance might be reserved till I advised what disposition to make of it, ... I am now under *the disagreable necessity* of requiring you to pay immediately into the hands of my brother or Mr Vaughan the sum of £75, being the ballance due me for the last 5 years, together with £30 for half a years rent up to Michaelmas last, totall £105. The interest on the £15 will overballance the difference between us. I want no evasion, equivocation, or quibbling mystification about the business. Do not tell me you have not the money in your pocket: every body knows that in your country you may obtain it if you choose, at less than one eighth the interest here. *I enjoin you particularly* to write me soon as this comes to hand. My wants are pressing beyond measure. I had bought a plantation and other property adjoining me in 1839 payable by instalments, which I could easily have liquidated, but that in 1840 our crops for a few square miles were destroyed by a storm of hail or rather ice, so that instead of receiving 800 or 1000 for cotton I had not one pound of cotton to sell!!! So true it is, that Man *Pro*poses, but God *Dis*poses of all. I had to borrow money at from 16 to betwen 30 & 40 per cent!!! The Sheriff sold a part of my property some months ago for cash, at less than 1/7th the value. Having sold 2 lots I stopt the sale and gave security. But the low price of cotton ever since, being about 2d p. lb.

instead of from 10d to 15d some years ago, now disabled me from doing justice to my [illegible] men by paying them their just dues. That last news from Europe to the 5th of last month has caused the prospect to brighten a little. It is now selling at about 4d. Should it advance to 6d I think I should be able in a little time, with genial seasons and the blessing of a kind Providence, to pay what I owe, and save what property is not called mine.

I possess and have paid for between 500 & 600 acres of good land without any incumbrance. The situation is healthy, and the spring water as good (I believe) as any on the surface of this globe. Springs & streams of water in every field, and I have as yet a few good servants whose labour I have purchased & paid for to work it. They fare as well as I do. I can well remember the time when the majority of the farmers in [Hansthead ?] did not eat as much meat in a week as my servants eat every day, except Sunday. I can't tell how they fare then, for they are always from home (except one or two) either at meetings or visiting their friends &c. They feel none of the pressure of these times, of course. They are in some sense the happiest of mortals here, beyond all comparison. Never since the Creation according to any history extant, has any state, kingdom, or empire, suffered such a change as this. Suppose that in the British Empire every kind of property should be reduced 75 p cent. How would the interest of the national debt be paid? Every body knows it would be impossible. I shall write to your Uncle Rees in 10 days. I wish you to see him afterwards to consult about remitting the money to Liverpool. Perhaps some of your acquaintance in Kington can assist or direct you. I shall direct him about remitting it to Savannah or Charleston. I shall be glad to hear of the wellfare of all our relations, connections, & acquaintances, or as many as you can find room for. Hoping to hear from you soon I remain, my Dear John,

Your affectionate FATHER

P.S. Perhaps I may see you in Wales in the course of one, two, or three years at most, when I have no doubt I shall find every thing correct. T.W.

[Letter dated 8 January 1845, to his brother-in-law, David Lewis, Carmarthen, asking for a loan at eight per cent on security of his Georgia land and also for help for his daughter, Livia, who is separated from her husband, has been omitted]

Cedar Hill, Georgia, 10 May 1845

MY DEAR JOHN,

I desire you will write me *soon as possible* after the receipt of this. Let me know may I draw upon you for a year's rent, payable on the 1st October. Also what amount you can afford to pay? I should think 50 guineas would be about fair. That would make it even money to me, 250 dollars. I wish you to be *explicit* and *punctual*. I don't much relish having to pay £13 11. 6. for *Protest* &c. I should be glad to hear *as much of the news as convenient*.

Let me know how your nephew John, Betsey's son, is likely to succeed in his business? I was astonished to hear of his making choice of that. I have travelled considerably in this country during the last 20 years, and of course formed many acquaintances, but have not as yet seen a chemist or druggist in the country. The physicians here I suppose purchase their drugs of the wholesale merchants, and compound themselves. Much as I should like to see him, so far from encouraging him to come here, I would dissuade him from thinking of any such thing. I should be at a loss to conceive what he could do for a living here.

At the present time I believe this to be the most distressed country of any on the surface of the globe. The planters get next to nothing for their produce, cotton 2d p lb. Mechanics cannot get employment, doctors & lawyers in a state of starvation.

A few years ago I possessed some few thousands worth of property the value of which is so much depreciated that if all I own were to be sold tomorrow, I am doubtful whether the amount would meet the demands against me. We have heard of people dying their own executors. That undoubtedly will be my case. *Perhaps* by the indulgence of my creditors, I may be allowed food & rayment, during the few days I may have to remain here. I wrote to David several months ago and desired an answer, but he has not thought proper to comply with my request. Perhaps he thinks he is sure of all he can get from me. I hope you will not follow his example, but write me by the first opportunity. My distress of mind is truly indescribable. Yours affectionately,

T. WOZENCRAFT

12th Whitsun. Monday, we are favoured with a little rain this morng but our crop is so withered that much of it can't revive, even if the rain continues sometime. Let me know whether London or Liverpool will suit you best to pay the money, I have frequently deposited in the Kington or other banks in the country, and taken a check on their connexions in London and vice versa. I wish you to enquire if the same may be done at present, or what other way with *the least trouble and expense*. T.W.
11th May
We are likely to be involved in war with the British, Brazilians, &

Mexicans all at once! We have had little or no rain in nearly 3 months. The land is as hard as the high road. Our crops withering and dying daily, so that we have war & famine staring us full in the face ! ! ! All this and much more we richly deserve. Being the most highly favoured of any nation we are (at least 7/10th of us) the most greedy worshippers of Mammon, the most selfish, and most ungrateful to the Dispenser of all Good, that ever lived on the surface of this globe!!! T.W.

1 July 1845

MY DEAR JOHN, . . . [Again asks for £50 rent]

If you knew my circumstances you would not be surprized at my anxiety or hurry. I have many payments due at Christmas, and if I cannot get that little from you, I know not what I shall do. I am now at the mercy of two gentlemen. Everything I possess may be sold at 30 days notice! I had expected to be able to pay a part of what I owed with the present crop. But you know the uncertainty of all human calculations. *Nothing certain, but death & taxes!* From early in March to the present day we have had little or no rain to penetrate the earth an inch deep! ! ! In some parts of the country a few hundred miles from here sufficient rains have fallen to injure the crops! ! ! Wheat is commonly ripe here in May, the straw was too short to tie, the oats too short to cut, having had *no rain since it was sowed.* Maize (Indian corn), commonly from 8 to 10 feet high, from 4 feet down to 9 inches; cotton, from 8 to 9 inches high. I have a sufficient quantity of land planted with maize to have from 15 to 1800 bushels, but instead of having 8 or 900 bushels to sell, I shall have some hundreds to buy, as that is our principal dependance (from the earth) for food and support for man and beast. You will perceive by this what are our prospects here, bad times, and no doubts worse coming. I mentioned in my last that I should like to hear what business your Nephew Betsey's son is engaged in, and thought that perhaps he might wish to come here. Some years ago I might have fixed him in some profitable business. But in the present state of things here, I advise him by no means to think of coming to America. There are thousands of emigrants here from Europe that rue the day they first thought of crossing the Atlantic, and such is their distress that they would most gladly return if it were possible that they could procure the means. I do not know how soon I may have to leave here, nor to which point of the compass I may direct my course from here. The World is all before me, where to choose, and Providence my Guide. I desire an answer *soon as possible.* I need not tell you that I have *no particular wish* to be again disappointed and to have to pay such an amount for Protest &c. Let me know the *earliest date* to suit your convenience on which I may make the bill payable, with the amount. I remain Yours affectionately,

T. WOZENCRAFT

25 June 1847

MY DEAR JOHN,

Yours of 26th Apl came to hand about the 1st Inst. Also advice from our agent that the amt. of my last draft was recd., by which I am much obliged; for, tho small, the amount it was a great accommodation to me in my present circumstance. I had in my haste forgotten to put my signature to the first receipt. I afterwards recalled the circumstance and sent you another duly executed. You mention something about Livia's poverty. I had been led to believe that she lived with her husband. I wish you to inform me on the receipt of this where she is, and how employed. She caused me no inconsiderable expence in coming here. Nothing else would do, come she must. Having got a good situation with an opulent, kind family where I thought she had a prospect of doing well, she engaged a neighbour to carry her things to Augusta, without ever consulting me on the subject till after she had concluded the business. I am pained to think of her being in straitened circumstances, but at this time it is out of my power to afford her relief. The advance in the price of cotton has revived my hopes that in two years, with good seasons, I may be clear of debt. I have only 40 acs of cotton planted. The weather during the spring sea[so]n has been very unpropitious; much of the seed rotted in the ground. Hail storms, worms, flying insects, & grasshoppers destroyed much more. About one half of mine looks very fine, the remainder very indifferent. Many have plowed up their land & planted over again with corn. From present appearances the crop will be very deficient.

In order that you may have the full control of the Perthy Farm, & manage it in your own way, I will again make you the proposition that for 200 guineas I will give you an immediate & indisputable title to that farm. I think it would be a good and safe investment for you, and a very great accommodation for me, so great, that if cotton should again be reduced to the price it has been of late years and the seasons unfavourable, it would perhaps save me from total ruin, as far as the transitory things of this life are concerned. I am now in entire dependence on the indulgence of one mortal individual, who could in the short space of 30 days bring all I possess here to the Sheriff's hammer, and as of course it would be a cash sale, perhaps the whole would amount to very little if any more than sufficient to meet the demand. I beg you will think of it. And I trust that my God and the God of our Father's, who has the

Hearts of all Men in his Hands, will through the Influence of his Spirit upon your mind, incline you to comply. From all present appearances, it will be a very *profitable* investment for you. My grandfather lived to be near 20 years older than I am at this time, and I am confident that I enjoy as good health, and am possessed of as much strength & activity as he did at my age. Ever since I have declined the use of ardent spirits, my health has improved . . . [Greetings] . . . I remain, Dear John, your affectionate Father

T. WOZENCRAFT

Received of John Wozencraft the sum of Twenty Six pounds 5/ Sterling in full for half a year's rent of Perthy farm, due the 25th of March last. June 25th 1847 THOMAS WOZENCRAFT

[Letter of 21 September 1849 omitted.]

20 Dec. 1849

MY DEAR JOHN, . . . [Letter received]

I shall be glad to learn who are your sapient advisors that put it the notion into your head to retain the rent of Perthy for the interest of mortgage on Beilybychan? You took an assignment of the mortgage, and have of course all the title deeds in your possession. The law and custom in your country when the mortgagee fails to get his interest or wishes to receive his money is to foreclose, pay himself, take his due and return the ballance (if any) as directed. I have no more to do with it than the Man in the Moon, if there be such a man.

I am truly astonished at D's improvidence. The rent of the farm 15 years would be much more than double what he paid for Building &c.

If I live here that long, I shall forward a draft for the Lady-days rent, which if not paid will impel me to resort to such means and measures as in such cases are made & provided. *The rent I must have.* Had you complied with the proposal I made you some time ago, I should have been out of debt, and you would have the farm without any incumbrance. I am truly sorry and much grieved for D. G. L; but they made their own contracts, without any persuasion, advice or consent from me.* It is totally out of my power to assist them. Interest of money ruins thousands of honest men in this country. I have paid from 16 to $33\frac{1}{3}$ p. cent p. annum. I thought that about 500 would have covered all I owe, but from accts. I received last evening it will require upwards of 800. I

---

* This no doubt refers to David Lewis from whom Wozencraft had asked for a loan in 1845. Lewis appears to have lost a farm through foreclosure. The census of 1851 lists Sarah Lewis, haymaker's widow, living with a daughter who was a laundress, at the same address, Bank, Llandelofawr, to which Wozencraft's letter of 1845 was addressed.

have perhaps worth about 600 of cotton by me unsold. I remain Yrs affectionately

T. WOZENCRAFT. . . .

Let me know where Mr Thomas Lawrence resides, son of Mrs Chas. L. now or late of [Stanelweth ?] Hall. T.W.

Morris Series 1829–46

The next few migrants to be discussed were industrial workers or urban dwellers before they emigrated. Since they were seeking out cheap undeveloped land in the USA during the same years as the farmers we have looked at, they will be considered before the agricultural labourers who emigrated at a later date. While the farmers and labourers were closer to each other in terms of their occupational preparation for agriculture, the industrial workers resembled the farmers in two respects at least. First of all, they usually had acquired savings before they came to the region where they expected to settle on the land and were inclined to buy land rather quickly rather than to rent land or work as labourers. Secondly, they had some business experience before their emigration. They were not pure wage-earners, but often bought their own raw materials and tools and sold their products themselves.

The Morris letters enable us to trace the careers of three Lancashire handloom weavers, Andrew, Thomas and William Morris, who emigrated between 1829 and 1832, as well as those of their two brothers-in-law, Henry Woods, a blacksmith, and John Birchall, a farmer. Their faith in farming was undoubtedly nurtured during the 1820s, difficult years for Lancashire weavers whether they were immediately threatened by competition from power looms or not. By the time of their emigration they exhibited peasant attitudes towards land in that they refused to be deterred from reaching their goal by attractive opportunities for industrial employment in Pennsylvania. Once they had earned what they regarded as enough money to begin farming, they went to the land, though they had had experience of incentive schemes, overtime, and wage increases.

The Morrises came from a rapidly changing part of Lancashire. When the eldest son, Jonathan, was born in 1804, the family lived at Heath Charnock, a village of some five hundred inhabitants, two and a half miles southeast of Chorley. The little village began to feel the impact of the rapid growth of its neighbour some time after the end of the Napoleonic Wars. While Heath Charnock added only twenty people to its population between 1821 and 1831, the nearby parish of Chorley very nearly doubled its population. The local census enumerators attributed this rapid growth to the establishment of cotton factories in the town and the opening up of coal mines. Lying between Bolton and Preston, Chorley was situated in the weaving district of southwest Lancashire. As cotton factories were established, there was for a time increased employment for handloom weavers as well as factory operatives.

In the early 1820s, the Morrises joined the flow of migrants from neighbouring parishes into Chorley where John Morris, the father, followed his trade of carpenter and joiner on Water Street,[1] and continued to train up his eldest son, Jonathan, in the trade. His other sons, as well as his daughters, sought employment in Chorley's expanding cotton industry. By 1831 Chorley had one thousand two hundred men, three-fifths of its adult males, employed in cotton manufacture. As power looms spread during the following decade, jobs for men in the cotton industry contracted to just over nine hundred and fifty, while employment of women and children expanded. Employment for men continued to expand in other directions during the thirties, however, and by 1841 the Bolton and Preston Railway was being built.

The Morris brothers had good reason to begin to think of some alternative employment to weaving. E.P.Thompson has argued that opportunities were non-existent for men brought up to weaving. Unable to get into the artisan trades for want of proper training, they had 'neither the "great bodily strength" nor skill in any factory craft' to enable them to obtain factory employment, and they had not the strength to compete with the Irish in heavy unskilled labouring occupations.[2] All three of the Morris brothers proved able to stand up to the physical strain of factory work in Pennsylvania, and two of them, to the heavy labour of farm-making. There is no evidence that they cared to examine other possible occupations, so strong was their urge to acquire farms.

The eldest son of John Morris was the only one of his children to remain in Lancashire. This son, Jonathan, probably left home about the time his brother Andrew emigrated. In that same year, 1829, John Morris removed from Chorley to a tiny industrial village three miles southwest of Chorley, whose population was actually declining during the twenties.[3] In the same year Jonathan was living at Tyldesley, near Leigh, a town between Manchester and St Helen's, almost directly south of Chorley. On the way to Leigh from Chorley lay the village of Hindley, where Jonathan's wife was born. At Tyldesley Jonathan carried on his own (and his father's) trade of joiner, making not only coffins, but also lathes and shuttles for the expanding cotton industry. His traditional craft was being transformed into that of 'mechanic', as the term was used in Lancashire.

For many years, as the rest of his family, including father and mother, gradually left for the United States, Jonathan considered following them. To his indecision we owe the continuation of this series of letters up to 1846. That Jonathan did not fall in with this family decision seems to have resulted from the opposition of his wife and her family, for he continued to move about in Lancashire and to discuss emigration in letters to his brothers. During the thirties the town of Tyldesley where he was living lost three hundred people out of a population of five thousand. Jonathan Morris and his family left Tyldesley for Hindley, his wife's native town, amid talk of emigrating, and there Morris got a job as a 'mechanic' for the Hindley Twist Company at Pennington Mills. His brother's letters from Ohio in the early forties offered no inducement to emigrate. By the time they became more optimistic, in 1844, Jonathan had found a better position at Barlow's Factory in West Leigh, a cotton and silk manufacturing town near his wife's village. Jonathan Morris obtained eventually the same goal of independence, which the rest of the family sought in America, by turning shopkeeper at West Leigh, dealing in bread, flour, groceries and beer.

No immediate economic crisis seems to have prefaced the emigration of the rest of the Morris family. The Morris brothers appear to have been fancy weavers, as no doubt most men who stayed in the trade as long as they might have been. They made no reference to having suffered hardship themselves before they emigrated, though they did find food more abundant while they worked in mills in the Philadelphia region. In so far as they had economic motives it was their poor assessment of the future for themselves and their children which prompted their emigration. Scraps of evidence also point to social factors in the decision. Urging his aged father to join him in Ohio, Thomas reminded him, 'you used to say you could like to occupy land of your own'. There is more than a hint in these letters of a feeling that by remaining in England they would find their social standing reduced. John Morris had received a painful snub in public at his sister's funeral from relatives whom he described as having gigs and fancy clothes. The sensitivity of at least some members of the Morris family to social distinctions may be suggested in their mentioning that Thomas had been 'made an Esquire' and in Andrew's emphasis upon the distinctions made in England between the working class and the rich. This is the only collection of manuscripts in which the early English socialists are mentioned, by William Morris in 1841. At the time of migration, the brothers used the radical rhetoric about America as a land of liberty free of 'kings, priests and tyrants'; but their real goal was to acquire land, to see their children also established on farms, and to get sufficiently prosperous that they need only work for part of the year. They maximized income in the short term in order to obtain and remain on land in the long term. Only William gave up the quest for a farm before this series of letters stops, and he was handicapped in reaching the goal by asthma.

Andrew Morris was the first to emigrate, probably at the age of thirty-two, in 1829. His brother, Thomas, who was thirty-one in 1830, followed in that year with his family. Their sister Ann and her husband, John Birchall, a farmer, arrived in Philadelphia in May 1832, by which time John was thirty-five years old. The parents came out with their youngest son, William, later the same year, as did also another daughter Alice, with her husband, Henry Woods, twenty-seven, a blacksmith. All except Thomas, who had enough savings to buy land immediately, went first to the Philadelphia region to find jobs. The Morrises clearly could not command easily the ready cash to emigrate. Andrew paid £9·50 (£9 10s) on a packet ship, but had to borrow money to get away. The Birchalls paid £5·75 (£5 15s) in a regular packet in 1832. John Morris had to delay his departure because he could not raise the fare.

There are few instances in these letters of a large family so closely knit as the Morrises. So similar was their outlook, that they made the same decisions sometimes (e.g. in 1837), without even consulting with each other. Mutual help was taken for granted, and for that reason, they had to bring out their old parents when they all decided to leave England. Before they emigrated the father constituted a clearing house for family information. Later William became the chief co-ordinator of information for the family for a while, though Andrew, the eldest son in America, resumed the task in the forties. After emigrating, they depended on other relatives both for aid in finding jobs near Philadelphia and for land scouting in West Virginia and Ohio. Both Thomas and Andrew went to uncles when they first arrived in the States. Though they seem to have depended entirely on family contacts for securing jobs and land, an unsigned letter in the Morris collection from 1830 points out that there were a great many Oddfellows in Philadelphia, twenty-five lodges within three miles of the city, which would relieve a 'dishelped' brother. Years later, Andrew wrote to Jonathan that the Oddfellows would help him find work in eastern cities. Thomas Morris became a charter member of the Lodge of Free Masons chartered in Aurelius, Ohio, in December 1850. Here was, at least, a source of institutional help of which they were aware.

The Morrises and their relatives showed considerable flexibility with respect to occupation as they moved around in the region about

Philadelphia for the next few years, attempting to save for land purchase. As soon as they arrived, Jane Morris went to work on power looms, but the men accepted work offered as handloom weavers. Andrew remarked that although there was no fancy work done, 'it is very good to learn' to do plain goods. The farmer, John Birchall, also worked as a weaver in order to buy a farm. In trying to give new heart to a discouraged emigrant, Andrew weighed up the latter's chances as a blacksmith, a weaver or a farmer. Sometime later when their employer moved to Brandywine Creek to introduce power looms, the Morrises went with him, showing no hesitation about moving from hand weaving to power weaving. It was only when they found that their wages were to be lower than those in other similar establishments that Andrew and William, the weavers, left and found work easily enough elsewhere. Thus, they also showed during these years a willingness to move in response to wage differentials. Yet in 1836, when wages were rising, they still declared their intention of taking up land.

Their brother Thomas, who set out as soon as he arrived in America in 1830 to buy land, was also alert to economic prospects. In selecting land in Washington County, Ohio, Thomas paid attention to the availability of road and river transport, market towns, to the lay of the land and to the presence of cattle drovers to market livestock – as well as to the water supply and healthiness of the spot. Washington County was no longer true frontier, since there were about eighteen persons per square mile in 1830, but federal land was still available when Thomas arrived. The land he bought was located in Aurelius township, inland from the river and about fifteen miles from the small market town of Marietta, which had about three thousand inhabitants by 1850. Population was increasing in Washington County during the thirties and forties, after having remained practically stationary during the twenties. By 1850, the population was nearly three times what it had been when Thomas Morris arrived. Aurelius, in the extreme northern tip of Washington County, had been constituted as a township in 1819. While the Morrises admitted that there were 'high ridges and deep gutters' in the township, they perhaps understated the case. A local history describes the topography thus:

> The hills [in Aurelius township] are rather high knobs with rounded tops, and separated by narrow ravines with almost precipitous sides. The West fork of Duck creek, the principal stream of the township affords comparatively little bottom land, the valley being, perhaps, not more than a half a mile broad in its widest part. . . .

The soil was partly infertile sandstone; the best soil was to be found on the ridges. The people of Aurelius had to build their roads 'not always where they are needed, but only where they can be built'. It was very beautiful. However, the Morrises had not chosen an ideal spot to realize their conservative goals.

To this township came the others, Andrew Morris and his family, William Morris, John Birchall and Henry Woods and their families, and old Mrs Morris in 1837, the famous year of the safety valve. Here were a number of industrial workers who went, not back to the land, but to the land for the first time in their careers, during an industrial depression. They did not leave the east because of industrial unemployment; rather they observed that the onset of the recession was a good moment to take their savings in order to carry out a decision, long since made, to become landowners.

In spite of their modest economic aims, these families did not find that the thinly settled, broken country of Washington County could provide them with what they regarded as a livelihood. Henry Woods and Thomas Morris took up industrial by-employments, and William Morris gave up the project of becoming a farmer before he began clearing the land he bought. At first they seem to have expected to concentrate on livestock farming, a decision consistent both with their background in Lancashire and the market opportunities they found in Marietta and among the cattle drovers. But the Morrises expanded their livestock at a painfully slow rate. Their land-clearing also proceeded slowly. Resisting the temptation to adjust to their difficulties by emigrating farther west, Andrew and Thomas Morris and John Birchall turned to tobacco as a commercial crop.

The tobacco craze in these hilly counties of southeastern Ohio had begun as early as 1822. In 1825, it was said to be the most profitable cash crop in Washington County. After it was abandoned in other parts of Ohio, tobacco remained important in eastern Ohio during the thirties and forties. The output of Washington County rose from 11,390 pounds in 1839 to 540,392 pounds in 1849, by which time it produced ten per cent of the state's output.[4] Since tobacco was a crop that required little capital outlay, the Morrises turned to it hopefully in the mid-forties, clearing new land to expand their production.

It was the poorer areas of the Ohio Valley that turned to tobacco in the 1840s.[5] Many farmers found that their large crops of 1844–6 did not sell for enough to pay the freight to Baltimore. By 1850, it was generally recognized that tobacco-growing in eastern Ohio was 'an enterprise of dubious merit'.[6] The Morrises, the Birchalls and the Woods were all still there in Aurelius Township at the time of the 1850 census. Except for the blacksmith, Henry Woods, they were all still heavily committed to tobacco. Thomas had produced 2,300 pounds of tobacco in 1849, Andrew, 600 pounds and John Birchall, 1,800. None of them raised much grain of any kind, beyond what was needed for their animals and themselves. Producing both butter and cheese they were all still engaged in dairying in a small way, as Thomas had been as early as 1835. The experienced farmer among them, John Birchall, who had farmed in Lancashire, produced over twice as much butter and cheese per improved acre as the average for the township, though he had only five cows. Thomas, with four cows, was very close to the township average and Andrew well below it. By 1880, it was recognized that farmland in Aurelius was not good for much more than sheep and orchards. All three of these men had some sheep. Thomas, who had more than the others, reported thirty-one sheep to the census enumerators in 1849. But after twenty years' of work, Thomas Morris could place a value of only $2,000 on his real estate, that is about twelve dollars an acre. Andrew's farmland, after thirteen years, was worth $1,500. And John Birchall, who had made the outlay for an improved farm in 1837, valued his eighty acres at $600 in 1850, about seven dollars per acre. He had paid $400 for it, and had only found it worth his while to clear an additional twenty acres in thirteen years. These immigrants were not worse off than their neighbours. Of the sixteen English-born farmers in the township in 1850, only one other could value his farm at as much as $2,000. The average cash value of farms in Washington County in 1850 was about eleven dollars an acre.

Thus the Morris family succeeded in getting on the land, but with indifferent economic success because of a poor location and a hesitation to move on. By 1850, these men were over fifty years old. They were having trouble finding farms for their sons in the area. By 1860, not a trace of any of them, or their children, is to be found in the census returns for Aurelius township.[7] Only four English-born farmers were left in Aurelius by 1870.

Little can be said about the social adaptation of these people. So long as they remained in the Philadelphia area, they had frequent contacts with immigrants from their own neighbourhood, as well as other members of their family. Once in Washington County, unlike our farmer immigrants, they did not discuss church attendance in their letters, though we do know that Thomas was an Episcopalian lay reader. By the close of the series, their children had begun to marry. One daughter had married a German immigrant, and Andrew's son, John, married a Maryland-born woman.[8] Since tobacco is such a labour-intensive crop, one suspects that they had little time for society, apart from the close network of related families who had settled so near to each other.

The Morrises tended to reverse the spelling of 'their' and 'there', to drop their 'h's' occasionally in their writing, and to omit the final 'y' from 'they'. Some of their more curious spellings have been translated for the reader in the text. The originals of the Morris letters are in the Lancashire Record Office, Preston, and are published by permission of the County Archivist. Photostats are in the British Library of Economic and Political Science.

Letter from John Morris to his son, Jonathan Morris, Tyldesley Banks, near Bolton, Lancashire

Coppull, Lancashire, 30 Nov. 1829

DEAR SON,

We have the satisfaction to let you know that we have recived a letter from your brother Andrew. And we have also the sorrow to tel you that brother John & sister Ann has had their house broken and nearly all their clothing stolen besides his watch and many other things to the amount of 25£ in value or upwards. We are all much as usual.

Copy of Andrew's letter to John Birchall

Bristol, 19 Oct. 1829

DEAR BROTHER AND SISTER,

I take the oppertunity of writing these few lines to you hoping they will find you all well as they leave us at preasent than God for it. When we got to Lieverpool *Zetis* was bound for Quebeck but had not commenced loading. The man that I ingaged with did his indeaver to send us to New York but we would not. We got the money that I deposited and then had to looke out for another ship. We got a pasage in the ship *Telegraph* for nine pounds ten shillings. We sailed on the 7th of June and after a long but very good passage we landed at Philadelphia on the 30th of July. We was only 13 passingers so we was not throng*.... [Seasickness] We had plenty of provson and fresh water. We had not much difficulty in finding your uncle Henry. He treated us very well. I hired with him on the 7th August for 9 dolars per month and found† tel Christmas. Jane is weaving on the power looms and can earn about 10

*According to the ship's list of the *Telegraph* which arrived in Philadelphia from Liverpool on 30 July 1829, Andrew Morris, weaver, was twenty-seven years old, his wife Jane, twenty-four, and their son John, a year and a half. There were sixteen passengers on the ship.

† Board and lodging.

dollars per month. She and the child is boarding at your uncle John's and pays 2 dollars per week. Your uncle John and his family is all in good health and doing very well. They send their kind love to you all. They all say they are very glad that they are in the Land of Liberty. Your uncle Henry is doing very well. He is still farming on shears [shares]. His two eldest daughters is mairried. He has one at home and four sons. He also sends his kind love to you all.

You will wish to know somthing about the weaving but we have not had an opertunity of trying it but by what I can see and hear I could earn a dollar per day at least. There is not any fine work wove in this country yet. There is verious kinds of coarse such as check, gingam, wooling cloath, flannell and many other kinds but it is all very good to learn. If you had your family here you might do very well. . . . [Prices.] Give my respects to Samuel Marsden and tell him I have inquird about a farm. There is none at liberty about here at present. Tell brother Jonathan that carpenters has 1 dollar and a half per day. We are very desirous to know when brother Thomas is coming. If my father and his family was here they might do very well. You desired that Jane would tell you her mind about this countey so I leave her to conclude.

From Jane Morris [but same hand]
I find this countrey very much like Andrew often told us. There is plenty of work, plenty of victules, and clothing is nearly as cheap as England. Tell my father and sister Betty and brother William that I am in better health and better spirits and more content than ever I was before but I am sorry when I think that all our relations is in such an oppresst land. . . . [Greetings]

ANDREW AND JANE MORRIS. . . .

Letter from Andrew and Jane Morris to Samuel Marsden, Chorley, Lancashire*

Germantown, Penn., 19 Nov. 1830

DEAR FRIEND,
I recived your welcome letter dated August 4th and am very glad to hear that you are all in good health and that you intend to come to this

* Samuel Marsden lived in Eaves Lane in Chorley in 1841. His family had moved from agricultural to industrial occupations in the generation when Samuel considered emigration. Also living in Eaves Lane were John Marsden, aged fifty-five, farmer, and two men by the name of James Marsden who were agricultural labourers. John Marsden's daughter of fifteen had started work as a power loom weaver and a son of fourteen was an agricultural labourer. All the other Marsden families had become cotton manufacturers, most of the men as weavers and the children as warpers.

country but am surprised that you intend to come in January it being as I think a very improper time to cross the Atlantic for you can expect nothing but very cold and s[t]ormey weather at that time of the year. I should advoise you to come in the spring. . . . [Letter from Thomas] You say you want me to send you the 6 pounds but if you are determined to come so soon it would save the expence and risk if you would come to me for it, but if you do not intend to come write as soon as you get this and let me know and I will send it as soon as I recive yours. You say you want me to let you know how we are all geting on and how trade is going on with us. We are all in good health and spirits and perfectley satisfied with this country. Our Jane says she would not live in England again if any body would give her an estate. Trade is going on very well. A good weaver can earn 1 dollar per day on any sort that is made in Philadelphia. So I conclude with saying that if you come you will see for your self . . . [Greetings] If you come would you please to settle with John Birchall and Brother Jonathan and I will pay you all as soon as you come and you will oblige yours

ANDREW AND JANE MORRIS

Letter from Thomas and Jane Morris to his father, John Morris, near Chorley, and family

Brook County, Virginia, 12 Nov. 1830

DEAR FATHER AND MOTHER, BROTHERS AND SISTERS, FRIENDS,

I sit down with pleasure to write to you because it resembles talking to you, at the same time, hoping these few lines will find you in good health as they leave us at preasent, thank God for it. You desire me to give you some account of our journey so I begin. May 15th we got to Liverpoole and found the [packet ?] overstocked with passingers. So we was transferred to the ship *Jefferson* for Baltemore. Captin Robert Leslie. May 19th in the evining we sailed into the River and lay at ancor all night. 10 in the morning we had the rool called over wich amounted to 107 Passingers. At 10 o Clock weighed ancor with a fair breese. At 6 o Clock was in site of wails [sight of Wales], at 8 oclock Skerres light house in sight. . . . Sea sickness ceased [seized] nearly all the passingers in the forenoon. 22nd a good wind but a heavy sea at night the ship began to rool rather heavy wich made some of the boxes tumble about in the steerige which alarmed the whomen and children. A greate many prayed and wished themselves at Liverpool or at home again. One man fell down in the steerige and wanted the Captin to hold the ship still wile he got up again and placed his boxes. . . . [Weather each day reported]

26th a fine morning with a good wind, in the evening a head wind with a heavy sea. It washed over the shithouse we had on deck. 27th a head wind, 28th the same, 29th a pleasant day with a head wind, 30th a fine day but calm. 1 ship in site in the afternoon. We saw a good quantity of grampares or black fishes. At 6 oclock at night we had a preaching with singing and prayer by a wesleain precher. . . .

3rd a fine morning with a good wind. Before breakfast was ended a sad disaster broke out. Our whomen began to find a live stock of gray horses [lice] which had strayed from a few Irish men, so we made them bring out their beds and beding wich we found very throng. 1 of their blankets we put overbord and a bed the steward hung by a rope outside the ship to air but Jack a sailor boy cut the rope and said let the bugar go and be d—d to it. In the afternoon we had a head wind. The day was a day of great slaughter among the Irish horse for we made the Irishmen examin all their body clothing; at night we saw a quantity of gramposes.

5th a misty morning and very calm, we saw a wale. 6th a fine day with a good wind. A ship named Robert Curr passed us from Belfast for Quebeck. We spoke her. She had 404 passingers on bord. At night we had a pareaching with singing and prayr. . . . [Description of journey]

14th, a fine day but very cold, a head wind, 2 ships in sight. We sounded and found the bottom at 40 fathom on the banks of Newfoundland. A man caught a dogfish about 6 pounds. We had a mass seafowls about us. We shot some for divirtion. 15th a fine morning but cold, a head wind, 2 ships in sight and a many fisherbotes. We bayed too and sent out our boat to a French fisher and they gave us a good quantity of codfish. A good wind in the afternoon. At midnight a rough squall till the 16th in the morning. Then a strong wind with a heavy sea.

17th, a head wind with a heavy sea, sometimes water on deck. A man struck his wife. So we called our comitty to try him and sentence him and his sentance was that there should be 6 whomen chosen and give him 6 slaps each with a handsaw on his backside. So the began and laid him on a barrel. But Mary Fairbrother being the 4th and being inraged, gave him 7 slaps wich made his friends fly in. So it was agreed to let him go. . . . [Description of journey]

28th, a misty morning with a head wind. Tea leaves, rope, yarn &c. became substituts for tobacco with many. 29th a fine day, but calm. 30th a fine morning with a head wind in the afternoon, prity good sailing. July 1st, a fine day with a head wind. 2nd, a head wind. One of the passingers broke an old black pipe and mixed it with tea leaves for smoking tobacco. . . . [More about journey. Chesapeake Bay]

7th, a fine morning with a small head wind. On the sides of the bay apeared a pleasant countrey, small hills and deals with great quantities of grean [grain ?], with clumps of trees, houses, stacks &c. In the bay there was sevral ilands covered with trees, and ships, brigs and small crafts. At 2 oclock in the afternoon a fair breese. 8th, at 3 oclock in the morning let down the ancor to wate for daybreak lest we should get fast on the sands. At 5 oclock weighed ancor with a head wind and heavy rane for about 3 hours. We cot [caught] a little fast on the sand but soon got off; at 12 oclock a fair wind which soon give us bouityfull prospect of Baltimore; at 2 oclock we got to the curantee [quarantine] ground and got the doctor on board. We had no sickness so we went right to the warffege. 9th, we stayed in Baltimore. At 11 oclock the custom house oficer began is overall [of] our boxes. We left them in the ship all night. 10th, we ingaged a wagon and loaded our logage.

July 11th, we began our [word illegible] to the road. We saw on the road sides immence woods with large spaces cleared abounding with weat, oats, rye, flax, Indan corn, fruit, &c. It was very warm travling. The people told us it was hotter than ever they had known it in there lives. When we stoped in the towns the people would shake hands with us and bid us welcom to a free country. On the road sides there was grate quantities of aples, ripe cherres and peaches. We got as many as we wanted and [left] thousands of bushels behind.

We got to Thos. Sharplesses on Saterday the 24th July. The received their relitives and friends with joy and tears of gratitude, and treated us all well. On Tusday the 27th of July I rented a house of Robert Marchall Esqr. and went to work for him. He gave me 8 dolars per month and found and gave us as much milk and as many aples as we could use. I worked for him till about the middle of October when his work was pretty well done on his farm. So then I went to work for the neigbours a few days. I am living on Bufellow [Creek?] 1 mile from Wedsbury in Brook County, Virginea, near the place where Henry Marsden lives.*

On the 30th of Oct. brother Henry Fairbrother and me went out to look for land. We went about 80 miles into Ohio. We found an English setlment in Washington County, Ohio, where the people treated us very well and shewed us the Congress land. We went to Zanesville and bought at the Land Ofice each of us a quarter setin [section] of Land. Fairbrothers amounted to 164 acres and ours to 162 acres, better land than ever I saw in England. Our land is half a mile square. Fairbrothers is 1 mile long and a quarter of a mile wide. We paid 1 dolar 25 cents per acer. I agreed with a man to build us a house 24 feet long and 18 feet wide for which I am to pay 20 dollars. I intend to move to my farm with

---

* Brooke County is in the tiny neck of what is now West Virginia which extends northward between Ohio and Pennsylvania, along the Ohio River. It is a small county of only eighty-six square miles.

my family in 5 or 6 weeks. Fairbrothers intends to move in the begining of April and with the blessing of God we hope to do well.

Near Wellsburg* the land sells very high from 8 to 20 dolars per acre and it is very hilly and broken. If the people can sell their farms at a high price the move back and buy Congress land and by doing so get a deal of mony; the land we have bought is generaly prity level and well timbered and exilant springs on it. There is within a mile a saw mill, a grist mill, a blacksmiths shop and a store and distilerey. There is a county road goes through Fairbrothers land from Woodsfield to Marietta and another county road goes within 10 or 15 yards of my land from Barnsville and striks the Marietta road a little below Fairbrothers land. Our best market will be Marietta, a river town on the Ohio side about 100 miles below Wellsburg.† If we can rise cattle, horses, sheep and hogs, there is drovers comes through the country often and will give good prices for them.

We like this country better than we expected we should, and we got through the toil of coming better than we expected we could do. We had a good passage, a kind Captin, good natured sailors and agreeable passingers. On the 1st of Octr we had a fine daughter born, and calls her Ann. All that came along with us are in good health and doing well and wether have writen or are going to do so you will get to hear of them all. Give my respects to Lawrence Bragg and tell him he might do well in this country. So might any industrous man. Give my respects to Wm Calderbank and tell him I take a weekly peaper for 2 dolars per year without a red patch on its corner‡. . . . [Greetings]

THOS. AND JANE MORRIS

Letter from Andrew and Jane Morris, to their brother-in-law, John Birchall, Chorley, Lancs.

Germantown, Penn., 19 Nov. 1831

DEAR BROTHER,

We received the letter from my Father on the 27th of April and we are very glad to here that you were all in good health and doing pretty well, but we are surprised that brother Jonathan has not been to see you since June 1829. He says you have heard bad accounts of this country and I am not much surprised, for there is some people that will not be satisfied

---

* Wellsburg is in Brooke County, West Virginia, then of course, Virginia.

† Marietta had one thousand two hundred inhabitants in 1830. It was within fifteen miles of the land which Thomas Morris purchased.

‡ i.e. no stamp duty.

anywhere. There was two men that was passengers in the same ship with us that seemed to be in great spirits about America and after talked what great things they would do when they got to America, but when we landed the first thing they got drunk instead of looking for work. They stayed in Philadelphia about two weeks and got drunk almost every day and then began to curse the country and all that was in it. They went back. They had not money to pay their passage, so they sold themselves to the captain untill their father come to Liverpool and pay their passage. So I leave you to gess what tales they would tell when they got home, and as for John Shaw, he came to Philadelphia about two weeks before he cut his throat and sent for me to meet him at the Sign of the Plough. So I went and was with him near half a day. He said things was not as good as he expected to find them, for weaving in New York did not earn more than about 18s English money per week. He said he had upwards of 300 dollars and asked me which was the best way to lay it out. I told him the best way was to go into the country and buy some land but he said he was too old to go a farming and blacksmithing was to hard work for him and his sight was not good enough to weave, so he gave up to the [illegible words] when he had not the least occasion to. I suppose fearing lest his money would be done before him, he cut his throat, but he soon got better and is now living in Philadelphia and weaving check. As for what Henry Marsden said about bugs and mis-kitoos [mosquitos], it is only a joke. We are not troubled at all here with misskities and people may keep the bugs down if they will and we have no flees at all; but you see how easy it is to make people believe anything bad about this country and how hard it is to make them believe anything good about it. They may believe what they will but if any man intends to find a better country he must leave the earth for there is not a better country on it.

My Father wants to know whether this country would do for brother William and him or no, to which I answer Yes, it will do for every person that is willing to work for a living as there is plenty of work and good wages. I am very desirous for William to come as he is young and if Father and Mother & him was here and living together they would do very well, and if they do come we will do what we can for them; but if Father concludes not to come it would be well if William could come with your Uncle Henry. We have received no letter from brother Thomas since May. I sent him a copy of my Fathers letter and am expecting one from him every day. He got to his land at Christmas. He gives us good encouragement to go to him. He said if we would go to him I might either join him at farming so he would give me a part of his land for 10 or 12 years or untill I could get a farm of my own. He has

BIRKET LETTERS

Peoria, Illinois, in 1846,
reproduced from an oil painting.
John Birket settled in this town
on the Illinois River in 1826
(pp. 85–9, 101–2).

John Birket (pp. 81–102).

John Birket

GRAYSTON-BOND LETTERS

above right: Peter Grayston, agricultural labourer of Aughton, Lancashire, father of emigrants Catherine Grayston Bond, Ann Grayston Moran and James Grayston (pp. 209–10).

above left: Robert Bond, son of Catherine and James Bond, photographed about the time he left the Kansas farm for Colorado. See Catherine Bond's letter of 1888 (pp. 222, 212).

Labourers' cottages in Long Lane, Aughton, Lancashire, like that in which Peter Grayston's family lived before their emigration (pp. 209–10).

bought a sow and 8 pigs, 2 months old, for 4 dollars. I have no doubt but we could do very well in the western country but we are doing well here and I think we had better stay as we are a while, as weaving is very brisk in Philadelphia and likely to be so. If I can [tend ?] a 100 looms I could have work for them all. . . . [Another son born]

From Jane Morris

DEAR BROTHER,
   please to tell my Father that I should be very glad if I could go over to see him sometime, but I never want to see him in that country. I would much rather he would come and see me. I am often uneasy when I think about him having so large a family to maintain in that country while there is a free & plentiful country so near. If he was here he could get 5 dollars per week at the paint works or bleach works or he could earn as much with weaving; and provision is a great deal cheaper than it is there. If sister Betty was here she could do very well, for girls is badly wanted and servants get from a dollar to a dollar and a half per week; and this would be the very place for brother William; but if they will not come tell them not to be uneasy about me for I am well of, for I have good health, a good house and a good husband and am perfectly satisfied with the country. . . . [Greetings]

                                        ANDREW AND JANE MORRIS

Letter from Thomas Morris, Aurelius Township, to his father, John Morris, Heath Charnock, near Chorley, Lancashire

          Aurelius Township, Washington County, Ohio, 7 Feb. 1832
DEAR FATHER AND MOTHER,
   I received your welcom letter of July 3rd on the 15th of Octr and am very glad to hear that you and all our brothers and sisters are in good health. And thank God we are the same. We are very glad to hear that brother John and sister Ann are doing pretty well and have such a good stock, but I doubt they are grate slaves to do so. I am very sorry that you are yet in an opressed countrey. It is pitty that such a pritty, senseable, goodlooking boy as Thomas, my nephew, is should be kept to the loom every day, and I may say every night too almost, wile boys in this country of 15 or 16 years old are going to school. We are also glad to hear that brother Jonathan is doing well, but you say it is with hard work. You say he talks of coming to America if he lives; but how long must he live before he comes. A resolution is wanting, and if he make a

6

resolution praps [perhaps] some of his wives ralations will cry and knock it all on the head again. I hope there will be no ofence at my aprupt way of writing. We are glad to hear that our brother Henry and sister Alice are going pretty well, but we think the would do better in this country. We are also very glad to hear that brother William is doing pritty well and has got a new shirt of clothes and a [watch ?] You say he could like to see me in the Land of Liberty, but talking abought it will never bring him or you to this country or we should all have been in America long ago. . . . [Births in family]

We have had 2 letters from brother Andrew and he seems to be doing very well. He did talk of coming to us in one letter but in the latter he had changed his mind. He wants to get money with weaving and then come out here and buy land which I think he will manage in a year or two. In his last letter he sent me a coppy of your letter to him of the date of March 18th in which you informed him that Samuel Marsden is not coming to this country, of which I am very sorry to hear. You seem to take notice of what Henry Marsden said about never going to bed on account of the bugs and muskities. I have never seen nor felt a bed bug since I have been in America, niether a muskitte. Their are a few knats on a fine summers evning, but I have never felt them near as bad as I have in England, but you know Henry has a soft skin so that if a fly or a flea or a knat tuch him he will swell up like he was mustle stung . . . [Where parents should live] . . . You said in your letter to my brother Andrew that you did not know wether it would do for you and William to come to this countrey or not. You are afrade to leave your sick club, but if you will take my advice you will not hesatate 1 day. If you can by any meanes get as much as will buy your sea stores and pay your passage over I would advise you and my mother and William to come, the sooner the better. You never had has good a chance in your life. If you could sail for Philadelphia you would have your own son within 5 miles to receive you, and if you had not the meanes to come on you might stay awile with him and he says a weaver may get a dolar per day on any sort that is maid and I know he would be very glad to receive you and if you could buy any meanes come forward to us I should be particulerly glad. Yes, if you will come to us I can promis you shall never want common nessersaries of life wile I have health to rase them off my own land. You used to say you could like to occupy land of your own. If you will come to me you may have as much as you can make use off wile you live. If you will come to me you may ether live with us or I will build you a house to yourselves, just which you like best, and you may have free access to our vituals and you may have as much timber to work at or to burn, or you may have [plenty ?] of coal to burn as we have plenty very good to get, as you pleas. Bring nothing with you but your cloths, beds, and beding and your Burkett and Bible and a few choice books. Your cooking utencels you will want on bord. You may think you are too old but there was older looking men and women than you [on ship] with us and did very well. So now I will invite you tenderly, once more to imbrace the opertunaty and make a start. Remember their is the same God at sea as on land, yes, the God that says ask and you shall receive &c. . . . [Deaths]

You talk of better times in England and a reform bill, but I see in my news paper that the Lords rejected the bill and disturbances and mobs began and are still incrasing. As for me and my wife, we are very well satisfied that we are got to this happy country and would be still glader if all our ralations and friends were hear also. We live in our own house on our own land. We have cleared a little land. We raised about 100 bushels of corn and about 40 bushels of potatoes and about 8 bushels of cucumbers and about 10 bushels of pumkins besides beans, peas, turnips &c. last year and I erned 21 bushels of wheat with mowing & reaping, &c. at 10 bushels per day. We have 2 cows, 2 bull calves, which I intend to have for a yoak of oxen if the have luck, 2 sheep and 14 hogs and 3 we have killed for our winter and spring meat and 13 head of poltrey and a dog and cat. . . . [Greetings]

THOS. AND JANE MORRIS

Letter from Andrew Morris to his brother, Jonathan Morris, Tyldesley Banks, near Bolton, Lancashire

Philadelphia, 24 Sept. 1832

DEAR BROTHER, . . . [Letters received]

You say I promised to write to you indevidualy which I do not remember, but having my mind tossed whith the jurney and our disapointment at Liverpool I might easely forget it and I thought one letter would sofice for all. We are sory to hear of the long continuance of your law job but we hope it will soon be decided to your advantage. Brother and sister John and Ann Birchall had a very good passage and landed on the 14th of May. I understood from Henry Birchalls letter that they intended to come and cusion Samuel Goodwin landed on the 11th of April and came to our house. He tould us that they had given up the farm before he left England for the porpuse of comeing so I took two houses joining together at Philadelphia, one for them and the other for us, the rente of which is 50 dollars per year each. The houses are new and well finished, 4 stores high, joining to no other. We have a small yard to ourselves. I also got a promis of work for them before they landed, though weaving is not near so brisk as it was when Henry Birchall sailed for England. John and Betty is weaving what they call Wilmington stripe. It is wove with 5 tradles [treddles]* ¾ wide, 60 picks on the inch, 4½ cents per yard. The weft is dark blue and in the scain [skein]. I am weaving 3 shuttle plaid. It is 4/9 wide, 70 picks on the inch, 7 cents per yard. Ann is begining the same kind as mine.

We have had the cholera here which cased considrable of a stagnation in bisness. It never was known to be in America before last June when it made its apearance at Queebeck and visited almout all the towns in its way to this place where it was very alarming for about one month. It took from 30 to 70 off the stage of human action in 24 hours. Mr Smethart of Chorley, comonly called old salt, lived neabour to us and [kept] cows. He was at our house on Saterday morning with milch and on Sunday he died of cholera. It was far worse in New York then here, this being a hopen clean and healthey city, but I thankfully state that it has nearly left us and that the numerous tradesmen, merchants and store keepers &c that had left the city on account thereof have returned and resumed their wounted occupations, and trade seems to be on the mend considrably.

You seem desirous to know some perticulars about your trade. There is but few sled shuttles used. Wheel shutles is from 1 dollar to 1¼; a new laythe for 1 shuttle, 1½ dollars; 1 for 2 shuttles is 4½ dollars; 1 for 3 shuttles is 5½ dollars. A coffin for a grown person is about 8 dollars and I belive yours to be a very good bisness as there is a great deal of bilding carried on here. I understand brother Henry Wood wants some information about his trade. Please tell him I cannot give him many perticlars as I have had no dealings nor am acquaint with any blacksmith except John Shaw of Chorley. He does not give it a good word, but what he says is nothing to go by for he has not a good word for any thing; but him and his son James is both working at one blacksmiths shop and he had 7 dollars per week standing wages. Is son James is working piece work and earns from 8 to 11 dollars per week, so I leave [you] to judge. But Shaw says they are not working at the proper blacksmithing bisness but are fiting up stove doors &c.

I do not know what to say about Father and Mother comeing. I am afraid a sea voyage for two old people like them would be rather teadious except they had some body to take care of them in case of sea sickness or rough wether. It could be better if you could make it conveniant to come together. You might be of advantage one to another perticularly

* Several treddles were needed for figured weaving. Five were needed to make a striped dimity.

to our old pearants. One thing I would say if they can by any means get comfortably over we will do what we can for them. We join with you in the congratulation of brother and sister Thomas and Jane Morris in laying the foundation of rural happiness not only for themselves but to the inconceivable advantage of their children so we think it would be well if you had a garden of your own as your stock of May flowers seems to increase. . . . [Gifts of tobacco. Greetings]

ANDREW MORRIS

Letter from William Morris to Jonathan Morris, Tyldesley Banks, Lancashire

Philadelphia, 14 Dec. 1832

DEAR BROTHER AND SISTER, . . . [Account of voyage with his mother and father]

About six oclock at night we steped on to the Land of liberty. We stayed at New York one day. We got our luggage entered at a steam packet warehouse for Philadelphia, the freight of which was 75 cents per cwt. The nex day we went to Philadelphia by a steam boat to Brunswick, by the stage to Trenton, and by a steam boat to Philadelphia, for which we had to pay three dollers each. My Mother stayed at Philadelphia all night, but my father, John Smith and I went to Germantown, but on enquire we found that brother Andrew had moved to Philadelphia, but his friends, though strangers to us, treated us very well and gave us super, bed and breakfast. The next morning we were joyfully, but surpriseingly, received by brothers and sisters, as brother Andrew has not received the letter you wrote of our comeing to this country. Cotton buisness has been very slack all sumer but it is now brisk again. We are liveing with brother Andrew. John Smith and me is weaving what the call Willmington stripe. A good weaver will earn five or six dollars per week. We like this countrey very well, and I am very glad to think that we are in a free countrey, free from the oppressive tyrants of King, Priests and Lords. . . . [Letters and greetings]

WILLIAM MORRIS

Letter from John Morris, Philadelphia to Henry Woods, Oak Tree, Coppull, near Chorley, Lancashire

Philadelphia, 26 Dec. [1832]

DEAR SON AND DAUGHTER, . . . [Landing at New York on 4 November]

We are liveing at Philadelphia with son Andrew and we all like the countrey very well. The working mans industry is much better rewarded here than it is with you. Weavers will earn 5 or 6 dollers per week with ease but the weft is to wind from the [h]ank. You wished me to inform you of the rate of wages in your trade but I can give you no perticulars but I believe the earn very liberal wages. You might do very well in this neighbourhood if you could come and set up a small shop of your own, but I should be more glad to see you in the state of Ohio with a house and shop on your own farm as it is the intentions of us all to go and settle there at some future period, if life and health permits.

Philadelphia is the finest citty I ever saw. The streets are set out streight for 7 or 8 miles in length. You would be surprised to see the countrey farmers come to town rideing eather on horseback or in their light wagons which the call dearburns. You would be surprised to see the market houses set out with such immense variety of meat and vegetables. . . . [Prices] We do not set down to such a table here as we did in poor old England. Here the table is spred with plenty of boiled and rosted meat, cheese, bread, butter, rice pudens [puddings], pies and various other eatables to teadious to mention and that of the best quality. Our tea, bread and poark is much better than any you can get in England. If you come be cautious how you ingage your passage. It is the surest way to ingage to come in a packet ship as they generly sail at the apointed time. The ship we came in was first advertised to sail on the 24 of August before which time sevral passengers was ingaged and had paid there passage money. These poor emigrants was forced to stay at Liverpool till the 26th of September during which time several ships sailed for New York with passengers. . . . [Greetings]

JOHN MORRIS

Letters from William Morris to his brother, Jonathan Morris, Tyldesley Banks

Rockdale, Penn., 8 March 1834

DEAR BROTHER AND SISTER,

You well know I am slow at speaking so now you find I am slow at writeing. I received your welcom letter in May which now I undertake to answer. The last time I wrote we was living at Philadelphia, but hand-loom weaving being irregular on account of the wonderfull increase of power looms, we concluded to try the power looms. The man we was worcking for at Philadelphia, was starting a power loom mill on Brandywine Creek, about 40 miles down the river from Philadelphia in the State of Delaware. He wished us to go there and so worck for him still. So brother Andrew and John moved their familys down to Brandywine, but the commenced to pay lower wages than was paid elseware. We tryed to get an advance but could not. This was a great loss and disapointment to us all for the man had made us very fair promises. So we went to Rockdale which is about 18 miles from Philadelphia by land and about 14 miles from Brandywine and about 7 miles back from the River Delaware. Their is 4 powerloom mills in this neighbourhood, 2 more starting, 2 of them containing about 150 looms each. The others are but small; the all go by water. We got worck at an old established mill caled Philipses Mill, but John Burchel declined moveing for this winter. So brother Andrew is living at Rockdale.* Me, John Smith, and two other men is boarding with him, all working in the mill. Their is both double and single looms in this mill and a good weaver on 2 single looms will earn from 4 to 5 dollers per week, and on 2 double looms the will earn from 5 to 6 dollers per week. Jane has to attend to the children and boarders & they had another fine son born in September which the call Thomas. John Birchall is living at Brandywine, him and family all working on the powerlooms. Father and Mother is liveing with them. Mother is keeping house for them. You wish to know if they have ever wished themselves at Johnsons farm again. They say they would rather go farther west than to return to the old sod again. The wish you to know that they did not all pigg together on board the ship, though they where all cloos neighbours.

B and s Henery and Alice Wood are living at Philadelphia. He got worck the first day he enquired for it and has had constant worck ever since. He has 1 doller per day and the privelege of worcking piece worck at nights which enables him to earn from 7 to 9 dollers per week if he has a mind to work over time, and I believe the are both well satisfyed with the countrey.

We received a letter from brother Thomas in August. . . . He states that their is plenty of wood worck in that part of the countrey and the wages is from one to two dollers per day. He states that he has 6 acers of corn, 3½ of wheat, ½ an acer flax, 1 of potatoes, 1½ of grass, 1 of buckwheat and a few oates, besides peas, beans, onions, pumkins, squashes, parsnips, cucmbers, cabage, &c., 1 mare, 7 head of horned cattle, 3 sheep, 10 hogs, 2 cats, 1 dog and about 40 hens and chickens. The had another fine son born in March which the call Jonathan which he thinkes a greater blessing than all the crop he has raised besides. . . .
[Greetings] Yours affectionately,

WM. MORRIS

* Rockdale was in Delaware County, Pennsylvania, just west of Philadelphia.

.... [More greetings] Tell my friend John Oaks that I would like to go over and see him if I could come here again tomorrow for I could not be satisfyed to live on the tyrants sod again. Pleas to give my respects to Miss Horsefield and tell her that I have indeed seen a great number of fine accomplished young wemen in this countrey which makes me sometimes almost to forget all that ever Ive seen in England, but then I come to my reccolections again and then I sing, Old Lang Syne.... [Greetings and directions]

Rockdale, Penn., 27 Feb. 1835

DEAR BROTHER,

Though the distance is great between us, yet we feel for you in your troubles with the true feelings of sympathy, but alas what can be done when the death warrant comes. We must only advise you to look forward with an eye of phylosophy and still hope for the future, but alas you have now to lament the loss of your dear father. He died the 8th of Janaway at one oclock in the morning. He was liveing at Brandywine with Bro & S Burchells. His health was much the same as in England, only more feeble and infirm with old age. He was only sick about $2\frac{1}{2}$ days. It was the third time he had been suddenly struck with the same kind of sickness but had quickly got better the two former times. We can give no name to his sickness but a kind of faintish numness. He seemed to suffer little pain. He did not talk much nor enquire for any of us. He was deacently buried in a graveyard in that neighbourhood where he had wished to be buried if he died at Brandywine.... [Letters acknowledged]

The mill at Rockdale was stoped five weeks to put in a new waterweel. So I went and got three looms at a mill in Manyunck, a village laying 7 miles northwest of Philadelphia.* I liked the place pretty well so I stayed there till the present date. B & S Andrew and Jane are still living at Rockdale and doing very well. He is working in the mill on a pair of double looms and wile the mill was stoped for a waterweel he got worck with a neighbouring farmer at 50 cents per day and found. B & S John and Ann are still living at Brandywine and doing very well, him and famaly all working in the mill. Mother is keeping house for them.... [Sickness] B & S Henery and Alice are still living at Philadelphia and doing very well. He is still worcking at the same shop and has now got is wages advanced to 7 dollers per week and he says the longer he is in the countrey the better he likes it. We received a letter from B & S Thomas and Jane in June. The was doing very well. He

* Manyunk, a township in Philadelphia County which had over six thousand inhabitants in 1850.

stated that they was still trying to enlarge there farm, had 1½ acres of wheat, 1½ of meadow, ½ an acre of flax, ¾ of oats. The had planted about 3 acres of corn and was going to plant 6 acers more, and ½ an acre of gardening. The intended to plant their new piece with potatoes, cucumbers, pumkins &c. They had 7 head of horned cattle, 1 mare, 3 sheep, 14 hogs, 1 cat & 1 dog beside poltrey. Their was a great stagnation in the American trade last sumer on account of the United States Bank being put down, but it has been brisk again all winter and is now very brisk.

You asked me a few questions. Rockdale is a small vilage, a countrey place laying in a vally by Chester Creek containing 1 power loom mill, 1 store, one grist mill and upwards of 30 houses. The vilage of Pennsgrove is joining up to it over the bridg in the township of Pennsgrove containing 2 power loom mills, 1 store, 1 masheen shop, 1 blacksmith's shop, 1 Post Offis and about 30 or 40 houses. Their are also a number of mills and houses and little firther up the creek &c. The length of days in factoris is from sunrise to sunset in sumer and in winter from sunrise till 8 oclock at night with ½ an hour for breakfast and an hour for dinner. Here is no fetching up lost time, and our rools are not so strict as with you. Our machinery is good; we are paid in good bank notes and silver; rents are not very high. Brother Andrew pays 25 dollers per year a house with a small seller and 3 bedrooms. Fire costs him about 16 dollers per year, board wage is 2 dollers per week for men and 1¼ dollers for girls or wemen. And this climat agrees with me as well as England, but I am still weakly as usuel. We should like to see you in this country but it would be a troublesome jurny with your family. . . . [Greetings] Yours affectionately,

WILLIAM MORRIS. . . . [Further messages and greetings]

Rockdale, Penn., 30 May 1836

DEAR BROTHER, . . . [Letter received]

Mother is in a tolerable good state of health considering her age but very conceited and hard to pleas. She is now living at Philadelphia with Henry and Alice Woods. Brother and sister Andrew and Jane are still living at Rockdale. . . . Brother and sister John and Anne and famaly are all in good health and doing very well. The are now living on Chestercreek, about a mile above Rockdale. Himself, Thomas and Alice are worcking on the power looms at Mr Croshers Mill. Brother and sister Henry and Alice Wood and their daughter Mary are all in good health and doing very well. He is working with a steam boiler maker in Philadelphia. His wages is 8½ dollers per week and the hours of labour is only 10 hours per day.

6*

We received a letter from Brother and Sister Thomas and Jane in March. . . . They have made him an Esquire. He is also Master of the Sundy Scool and lea [lay] reader of the Episcople Church in that neighbourhood. Trade is very brisk and has been ever sinc I wrote last and wages is very considerable advanced in every branch of buiseness and hands are badly wanted all over the country. Their is also an advance in the prices of victules and clothes of all descriptions. . . . . [Winter. Fire in New York City] You say you would like to come to this country and if you was here now you might do very well, for turners and filers and machine makers wages is about 2 dollers per day and plenty of worck to be got . . . You say you often wonder if we have all given up the notion of farming which I answer no, we still intend at some future peariod to go to the western country and buy land if life and health will permit . . . Pleas to let me know what length of days you now make in factoryes since the short time bill was passed for a law. Mother, Brothers and Sisters all join with me in sending our love to you all, from your affectionate brother,

WM. MORRIS . . . . [Greetings]

Since I finished writing this Sister Ann returned from Brother Henrys at Philadelphia where she had been on a visit and brought word that Henrys wages is raised to 9½ dollers per week.

Providence, 4 June 1837

DEAR BROTHER, . . . [Comments on letters received]

I am living in the township of Providence about 2 miles from Rockdale and working at John Bancrofts woolen mills, a flannel manufactory. My work is twisting in and drawing in all they have and to make out my time at a wide powr loom which will weave 4 pieces of flannel in the width. I am on piece work and can earn about 6½ dollers per week. B and S Andrew and Jane left Rockdale about the middle of last October. It seems that his employer was a wealthy man and thought he could make more by some other kind of speculation. So he stoped the greater part of his machinery. B Andrew was thrown out of employment. He could have got plenty of work in the neighbourhood but they thought it best to go to the western country. So they had a publick sale and then packed up for their jurney. They got a wagon to take them to Philadelphia and stayed there a few days. They took their passage on the railroad and canal line from Philadelphia to Pittsburgh for which they paid 7 dollers each and children half price. I went to Philadelphia to see them start. Mother went along with them and is liveing with B Thomas.

We have received two letters from Andrew since he went giveing us some account of is jurney and success. They left Philadelphia on Sundy morning; got to Columbia that night, a distance of 82 miles by the rail-road; got their things on board the boat before dark and slept on board that night. They started next morning about 10 oclock and got to Holydaysburgh [Hollidaysburgh] on Thursday morning before day where they took the steam cars again and started about 8 oclock the same morning and at night they slept at a tavern on the top of the Alleyganey Mountans. They got to Johnstown on Friday about 3 oclock and in half an hour was under way on board another boat. They got to Pittsburgh on Sundy night about 8 oclock and slept on board. On Monday morning they got a passage in a steam boat to Marietta for 2 dollers each and the 3 children counted on[e] passinger. They payed 50 cents for hauling their things to the steam boat which was about a mile. The saw Samuel Goodwin. He was working at the Glass worcks but they had very little time for talking as the steam boat started at 10 oclock. They got to Marietta on Tusday morning at daylight. They got a wagon to take them out to B Thomases for which they paid 6 dollers. It was 12 oclock when they left Marietta and they got to Thomass at 8 oclock that night. So you see they was 10 days on their jurney.

They got one of Thomases neighbours to go with him two days to look for land who knew all the land in that neighbourhod and the numbers of it. He [paid ?] him a doller per day. The land is laid off in 80 acer lots and 40 acer lots for the acomadation of people who is not able to buy more and to prevent speculation. No man can get more than two 40 acre lots nor that without oath that it is for his own culta-vation, but any man can buy as many 80 acer lots as he can paye for. He took the numbers of some of the best lots that was not taken up, and then Thomas went with him to the land office at Zeansville, a dis-tance of 50 miles. He bought one 80 and one 40 acer lots laying together for which he paid 150 dollers. He hired two men to assist him in build-ing a log house. It is 1¼ miles from Thomases and he is one of his nearest neighbours and their is a publick road between the two places. He says that neighbourhood lookes rough at first for the land runs in high riges and some of them rather steep but it is good land and very healthy and they like the place very well. He bought two sows with pig for 11½ dollers and he intended to buy a cow in the spring as soon as food began to spring, and he intended to plant 5 acers with corn and potatoes.

B and S John and Ann wished Andrew to buy them a place and had sent some money for that purpose. So we received a letter about the last of Apriel stateing that he has bought them an improved farm, 80 acers of land, from 15 to 20 acers cleared, 8 acers fenced, a log house with 2 rooms and a poarch, 2 out buildings and a good spring cloose to the door, and something done towards a barn which must be finished in the bargain. The barn is to be 2 twenty feet square buildings 12 feet appart with a thrashing floor between and a roof over the whole. The price is 400 dollers, 100 paid down, another 100 on or before the 1st of October and the other 200 on or before the 1st of October 1839. It joins to Thomases land. He rented it for this season for one third of the grain. So they could eather go now or stay till they had got more money. If they went now the could have possession of the house and be prepareing for another season. If they stayed he thought he could still rent the farm for them. But times got bad here and they concluded to go and are now on their jurney. Ann has been sickly for some time. She is now better and is far advanced in pregnancy.

B Henry was over here two weeks ago. Imself, Alice and Mary all well. He was in full work at 9½ dollers per week and doing well. I was in Philadelphia yesterday to see them but to my surprise they [had gone ?] along with B John to Ohio. We have had very brisk time since I wrote to you before, plenty of work and good wages; but provisions has been very high. Flour has been from 8 to 13 dollers per barrell &c. I pay 2½ dollers per week for my board, but times has been very dull for six or seven weeks past. Some cotton mills have stoped, some runing half time and some full time and their is a great many manufactorers and mechanicks out of employment. This pressure of the times is oweing to the bad regulations of the currency for since the United States Bank has been put down from being a national bank, it gave rise to many petty banks. These encouraged a high run of speculation and everything demanded high price but the foreign merchants demanded payment in hard money which [strained ?] the banks and then the merchants and speculaters began to fail which [led to a] great stagnation. . . .

WILLIAM MORRIS

You say you have tould us your sercumstances and why not? We tell you ours. I have only saved about 300 dollers. I have not had the best of luck but I have had a better living and more time than ever I had in England. B Andrew had about 300 dollers when he left Rockdale and I dont know what the others had. You say you often wonder if you had come if we could have entered into any kind of trade jointly or separatly that would have done us any good. To which I answer we have had no intention of entering into any kind of trade in this country. It is attended with many changes and fluctuations. We think it most sutable for such folks as us to get a piece of land and live upon it for this houlds out a permenent and encourageing prospect. We should be glad to see you in this countrey but their is no encouragement in your buiseness at present, but if you was in Ohio you might buy a good place with your money.

Aurelius Township, Ohio, 30 Dec. 1838

DEAR BROTHER,

I wrote to you in the spring of 1837 and have received no answer. . . . When I wrote to you I think I stated that I was working at a woollin factory in Provedence township about 2 miles from Rockdale. . . . [Reviews contents of earlier letter] I continued at Mr Bankrofts woolen factory through the sumer of 1837 and went to great expence in trying to get a compleat cure for my old complaint the asmatic. Their is a new system of medicine found out in this country which is far superior to the old one. It was first found out by Samuel Thompson, a farmer in New England, and practised with great success.* He at length got a patent right for his new discoveries though bitterly opposed and persecuted by the old scool of doctors. He published books of derections with all his receipts [recipes] and discoveries and sells them with a patent right for a famely at 20 dollers each. I put myself under one of his practising agents in Philadelphia for a few weeks, but finding it very expencive and a cure uncertain I bought a book of derections with a famely right for my own use and information. I then bought a stock of medicins and started for Ohio in September. I got to brother Andrews in about 9 days. I boarded with them about 7 months and treated myself with the new system of medicin, but I found my complaint too deeply seated to get a cure but I got some better. It cost me a great deal but I am highly pleased with the new system of medicine and would not be without the knowledg of it for any sum of mony. If I had known what I know now when I had the pleuracy at Tyldesly I could have cured it in 2 days without bleeding, blistering, or purging or takeing poisonous medicines.

Last spring I went up to Jefferson county to get work at the factories for their is no factory about Duck Creek in Washington County. I got work at a woolen factory where I wove sattennet, flannel, and casemeer. Their is 8 woolen fa[ctories] in Stubanville and a number of small ones in many parts of the state.† I went over to see our folkes again this fall

* See Samuel Thompson, *Narrative of Life and Medical Discoveries*, Boston, 1822. His botanic system offered a single treatment, vegetable drugs, for every illness. Such systems flourished during this period, when public confidence in doctors was at a very low ebb; the old remedies of bleeding and purging with calomel were under attack, and doctors had no other universal cures to offer.

† Steubenville, near the wool-producing region of eastern Ohio, early became one of the most important centres for the manufacture of woollen cloth in the Ohio Valley. By 1845 there were five woollen mills in the city.

and stayed about 2 weeks. I bought a 40 acre lot of land at 1½ doller per acre with a county road and a stream of water runing through it. It is about a mile from their places going towards Maryatta. B & S Andrew and Jane and famely was all well. They had a fine child born September 2nd which they call Maryann. They have 1 horse, 1 cow, 2 calves, and a few hogs and have got about 11 acres under cultavation by clearing off the small timber and deadening the large which is here called cleared land.

B & S John and Ann and famely was all well. They have a fine daughter which they call Elisabeth. They are liveing on their place and makeing some improvements. They have one horse, 2 cows, 1 calf, and a few hogs. B & S Henry and Alice and their daughter, Mary, was all well. He has bought a 40 acre lot of Congress land joining to Andrews place. He has put up a log house and blacksmith shop on it. He has got 2 acres cleared. He has more work in the shop than he can do. They have a horse, a cow and a calf. B & S Thomas and Jane and famely was all well. He was puting up a small grist mill to go by horse powr. Mother was as well as can be expected at her age but is generally complaining. The land here is hilly and broken. It runs in high ridges and deep gutters but it is rich and productive and there is generly enough of good laying land on a place for ploughing and the steep is very good for grass or woodland and their is good water, cole and limestone. I have given up the notion of agriculture for my imployment and think I can live easer by working at the manufacturing buisness. I am now working at a woolen factory in Belmont County, 6 miles from Wheeling and 5 from Santclairsville,* near the National Turnpike, and see numbers of famelys with wagons passing every day going to the far west. Land is fast advancing in value in these parts of the country in conciquence of it being taken up so fast. Improved farms in some of the old settled and more improved places sells at from 15 to 30 dollers per acre and it is fast advancing. In Washington county where our folks is the Congress land is nearly all taken up and the price of land is advancing 20 or 25 per cent per year without improvements. . . . [Letters]

We have had dull times in the manufacturing districts ever since I wrote last but the are graduly reviveing and the banks has resumed specie payments; but I understand you have had a very great stagnation of trade in England which is very bad for the people of England as it is their whole depenance but a stagnation in the manufacturing business in

---

* St Clairsville, Belmont County, had a population of 1,025 in 1850. Wheeling had only 1,218 people. Belmont County was more thickly populated in 1840 than Washington County where the Morrises had bought land. However, Washington County's population was growing more rapidly during the 1830s and 1840s.

this country is but comparetively a small loss as the greatest number of people are not depending on it. Farming is very good now for such as have got large cleared farms as grain and provisions is rather high. I would like if I had capitle enough to comence manufacturing in a small way on my place. If I had a carding machine fixed to go by horse power and a spining machine and loom; but I can not yet. I think you stated in your last that it would be a great consolation to be settled in the same neighbourhood with our folks so that you could often see and converse with mother, brothers and sisters; but I think you would not like farming. But if you was here peraps you and I could join at manufactureing a few corse woolen goods or you might do very well by working at your trad in some of the towns. We should all be very glad to see you in this country and think it would be advantageous for you and especially for your childran. But there is so many homesick complaining English folks in this country that we do not wish to advise. . . . [Write] from your affectionate Brother,

WILLIAM MORRIS. . . . [How to address letters]

Barnsville, Ohio, 14 July 1841
DEAR BROTHER, . . . [Letter received. Death of mother]
    I am liveing at Barnsville, Belmont County, Ohio, and weaveing in a woolen factory and doing reasonably well at present.* My health is much usuel.
    Barnsville is about 35 miles from Aurelious township where our brothers and sisters live. I was over there to see them about a month ago and found them all well. B & S Andrew and Jane are improveing their farm and increasing their famely. They have 3 sons and 2 daughtere, John, William, Thomas, Maryann and Elisabeth. They have about 24 acres of land cleared. They have 4 milck cows, 1 horse and a number of calves and young cattle and hogs. They had a cow died in the spring, soposed to be poisoned by eating a poisonous vegetable called Buckeye. He is rather enclined to sell out and go to the State of Illinois to get perary [prairie] land. B & S Thomas and Jane and famely are in good health. Their youngest childs name is Thomas. They have a horse mill which runs by a cupple of horses on a tramp wheel. They have $\frac{1}{8}$ of the grain for toll and the customers finds their own team. They have 2 horses, 2 or 3 milck cows. They have some young cattle, sheep, hogs, chickens, &c., but I dont know how many. B & S John and Ann and famely are in good health and still improveing their farm. They have 1 horse, 3 or 4 milck cows and a number of calves, young cattle, hogs,

---

* Barnsville was a township in the western part of Belmont County.

chickins, &c., but I dont know how many. B and S Henry and Alice and daughter are in good health. They are still improving their place but he works the greatest part of his time in the blacksmith shop at his trade. They have 1 horse, 3 cows and a few young cattle and hogs.

Times has been rather dull in America for this last 4 years and some macanics have been out of work at their own trades; but their is one advantage in this countrey and that is in such times their are a number of mecanics moves back to the land where their is plenty for them to do and this gives more room for the others. Their are some conflicting intrests in this countrey. The south is oposed to a duty on imported goods without which the ballance of trade will go against this countrey thus dreaning out the specie and destroying the corency. Their is two great politicle partyes called the Whig and the Demacrat parties and people of the same intrests are very much devided in opinions and party spirit runs very high before the elections. Their are also a party in favour of the abolishion of slavery and a party oposed to the abolishion of slavery. Theese contending parties makes the prospects of American manufacturers somewat uncertain and changeable but considering all the disadvantages as well as advantages I think their is still a better prospect in America than in England. But I think you have done right in not changing certientyes for uncertantyes for I belive it is best to be satisfyed as long as you are doing well, but if not doing well to be redy to come. If you come to this countrey I think you would not like to go to the back countrey and go to clearing land and farming but you might do well in or near some of the eastern cittyes working at your trade. Or if you could start a macheene shop of your own in some of the western towns but for furnework [furniture ?]. I believe the neighbour-hood of Philadelphia or New York is the best. . . . [Has not received his letters]

The factory where I work runs by steam. They have 4 carding machiens and cards wool for the farmers at 6 cents per pound. They carded about 800 dollers worth of custom work last year. Their custom work at fulling and finishing amounted to nearly the same. Besides this they manufacture some goods for sale such as cloths, flanels, sattenats and jeans. It is a good buiseness to them that can get a small establish-ment of their own. I would like to try it if I had a good partner. I have been informed that you have gained some steps of reform in England and also that there is a new society there called Sochilestes [Socialists] which have increased very fast and got very numerous. Pleas to let us know if their is many of them about you. . . . [Greetings] Your affectionate Brother,

WILLIAM MORRIS. . . . [Prices]

I heard from John Smith about a year ago and he had left the factory and had rented a small farm on Chester Creek about ½ mile from the factory where he had been working. Himself and famely was well and doing well. . . . [Address]

Letters from Andrew and Jane Morris to Jonathan Morris, Penningtons Mill, Hindley, near Wigan, Lancashire

Aurelius, Ohio, 13 Aug. 1842

DEAR BROTHER,

After reflecting, studeing and consulting about what could be the cause that we heard nothing for so long from the only branch of our family remaining in England, we received your truly welcom letter on the 18 day of April, dated Feby 26th. We are sorry to hear that times is so bad in England and that their are so many people out of imploy, but it is nothing but what we expected, knowing as we do the smallness of the island and emance population and that all the property belongs to the rich and they having the makeing of the laws can consequently do as they pleas with the working class. There is no prospect ether for the presant or riseing generation. Things is very different here although times is wors than ever they was known to be through bank failurs and scarcity of money; yet there is an excelent prospect for both the presant and riseing generation and perticulary the latter as there are hundreds of miles of first-rate land in excelant climits for 1¼ dollers per acre.

If you should come we do not know wether it would be better for you to come to us or stop in some of the manufacturing districts. If times was as they used to be the latter would be the best, but as money and trade is in a bad state we do not know. You ask if we have good roads. Our roads are good considering the newness of the country. You ask are we far from a town or vilidge. We are 20 miles from Marietta, a very nice town on the bank of Ohio River at the mouth of the Muskingam River. It is pleasantly situated and has 2 market days in a week. We can go with a wagon in half a day. The market hours are from daylight until 9 oclock Wedensday and Saterday. We frequently go in the night with butter &c. in the wagons, sell out in the morning and come home the same day. Their are three little vilidges nearer. You ask if the country is pleasant. What is pleasant to me is unpleasant to another. It is broken or rowling and a great deal of the land is prity steep. So we answer it is pleasant for a broken country. You ask if there any farms on sale part cultivated, to wich we answer Yes, plenty. You ask can we sell our produce and get money for it, to wich we answer Yes, there has not been a time since we came here that we could not get money for produce though at presant it is very low. You ask can we injoy society, to wich we answer Yes. Our neighbourhud is quite throng enough. You ask is there any railways near, as to wich we answer No. You ask is it considered a healthey spot, to wich we answer Yes. You ask are we much trubled with reptiles or wild beasts or bugs or fleas or midges, to wich we answer No, there are no wild beasts except some wild turkeys and a few dear; bugs are not as bad as in England. Fleas we have none and midges are not near as bad here as there. We have some snakes but not many. You ask do we consider we have made a good choice. We should think so if we did not hear of so many other parts that is so much supearier, but if times gets better we shall very likely some of us go and look and if we like sell our property here and go. You ask do we live in rude log houses. We answer Yes. When people buys Congress land in the woods they build what they call temperary log cabins untill they get a farm cleared and fenced and cultivated so as to grow produce enough for there own use and some for market an where they find themselves able they can build a house to there own likeing. There is hewn log, brick and frame houses in our nabourhood which are all very comfortable. You ask how we spend our time. We have plenty of work and are likely to have untill we get enough of land cleared and our farms in good order and then we think we could do very well by working one half or two thirds of the year.

B William was over to see us about the 1st of June but only stayed one night. He is living about 30 or 40 miles from us. He is intending to buy some carding machines and start a small establishment of his own. His health is about as usuel. B Johns family is all in good health. They have 2 horses, 4 milch cows, 3 two-year olds, 5 one year olds, 2 calves, 6 sheep, 27 hogs. Brother Thomas' family is all in good health. He has 2 horses and a coult, 2 milch cows, 2 two-year olds, 2 one-year olds, 3 calfs, 11 sheep, 20 hogs. He has a horse mill that gos by tramp weel which grinds for almost all the nabourhood in dry wether if they find their own team. He takes $\frac{1}{8}$ for toll and if he finds horses he takes $\frac{1}{4}$. B Henry has one mare and colt, 2 milch cows, 2 one-year olds, 2 calvs, and 3 hogs. He has plenty of work in the blacksmith shop. We have one horse and one year old colt, 4 milch cows, 3 two years olds, 4 one year olds, 2 calvs, and 27 hogs. If you come here you can come from Philadelphia to Pittsburge by canal and railroad and from Pittsburge to Marietta by steamboat. . . . [Greetings] From yours affectionately,

ANDREW AND JANE MORRIS

Aurelius, Ohio, 5 Feb. 1844

DEAR BROTHER,

I received your welcom letter on the 30th of March last dated January 19th and am very glad to hear that you are all in good health and doing well. You intimate that we may think you rather changeable. We think the changes of yourself and family does not extend very far or you would sometime find yourself from under the dominion of Queen Victoria. However, we think you acted wisely by imbracing the chance that offered perticularly at that time when scarcety of money and very hard times prevailed almost all over the civelised world, but times was not near so bad here when at the worst as in England for provisions was very cheap and very plenty, but report says times is very good now in the East. The factorys are all runing full time and some of them night and day with two distinct sets of hands to fullfill there orders; but we know nothing about the wages.

Wether it would be better for you to come to this country or not we cannot tell. It would depend on your mind. You can do well there and I dought not but you could do well in this country also ether here or about Philadelphia, but as you have never been much accustumed to farming work it is hardly reasonable that you would like it; Philadelphia is very handsum city and the surounding country also is very pleasant and there is vast numbers of Oddfellows there who would help you to a good situation if it were posable. We should be very glad to have you and your family among us, but if it is more to your advantage and satisfaction to live elswere we consent and we do not think it wisdom for any one to move so long as they can do well, injoy satisfaction of mind and good health; but for my part I could not live contented in England were there is so much distinction between the working class and the rich, so many people in a state of starvation or beging from door to door, and besids there is very little prospect for the preasant generation, and for the riseing generation there is absolutely none allthough there seems to be great exsitement on the subgect of reform and the Irish repeal, but I do not think they will make good times for the working class long at once.* For to secure a perminant market for British manufactures with their immence amount of hands, meshinery and capital it would be ne[ce]ssary to have corespondance with some other world besids this small planet of ours.

Brother William was over to see us last sumer and we received a letter from him a few weeks ago. His health is about as usual. He is living in Stubanvill. He has rented a loom, is buying wool; geting it carded, spun,

* The agitation for outright repeal of the union between Great Britain and Ireland, led by Daniel O'Connell, was at its height in the early forties.

and colord at the big factorys; and weaving jeens for himself. He writes that he intends to go down the river to Cincinnati with a box of jeens in the spring and call and see us coming back. He left B Thomas to sell his land if he could. Accordingly he has sold it for 110 dollars, it being none improved. He is going to write to him soon and let him know. B Thomas was sick last summer of the intermitant fever but has got well. John Birchalls daughter, Alice, was maried a year ago last Christmas to a Duchman or a young man from Germany whos parents lives near Birchalls.* They own a great deal of land and he seems to be a very fine yung man.

Brother Thomas, John, and myself are going into the tobaco bisness and in fact almost all the rest of the nabourhood. B Thomas has raised two crops; B John and me each one. From presant appearances there can be more made by growing tobaco than any other crop, provisions being still very low. Good ground, well managed, will produce from 800 to 1,200 pounds to the acre and this year it has sold from 4 to 5 dollars per hundred to the merchants who packs it into hogsheads and sends it to Baltimore, but I intend in future to pack my own if I cannot get 5 dollars per hundred here.

Their has been a great excitement in this nabourhood for two or three years on the subgect of emigrateing farther west to the level rich perraire [prairie] countrys. A great many sold out and went but almost all of them came back well satisfied with this part, many of them having run through what they had with traveling, fixing and unfixing &c., which caused land here to be sharply looked after and all the Congress land being took up. Of corse improved places must rise in value before long.

A few perticulars on the culture of tobaco: the seed should be sown as erly in March as the ground will permit and tranceplanted something like cabage from the 1st of June to the 1st or 10th of July, seting the plants about 2 feet apart each way, and if the season be good the first planting will be ripe by the last of August. The stalks grows from 5 to 7 feet high and the leavs from 1 to $2\frac{1}{2}$ feet long and from 1 to $1\frac{1}{2}$ feet broad with about 20 leavs on a stalk. When ripe we strip of the leavs and string them on sticks and hang them up in tight houses built for the purpous with a flue across the bottom of the house with the mouth outside to make a fire in. We have to keep a fire under it till the sap is dried out of the stem of the leaf which takes about a week. Then, take it out and bulk it down in some other building, fill the house again, &c till the crop is finished. It takes about 2 houses to 5 acres. Brother Henry

* Alice Birchall was nineteen when she married. By 1850, she had five children and her husband valued his farm at only three hundred dollars.

Woods has as much work in the shop as he can do and could have a great deal more if he could [do] it. . . . From your affectionate Brother

ANDREW MORRIS

Aurelius, Ohio, 21 Feb. 1846

DEAR BROTHER, . . . [Letter received]

I packed my tobacco last year and sent it to Baltimore. I had 5 hdds [hogsheads]. One sold for 9 dollars per hundred, one for 6, one for 5½, one for 3¼, and one for 3. I put about 750 lbs in a hdd on an avrige. When the expence of fright, commission &c was taken out it avriged me 4 dollars and 58 cents per hundred in cash. I have last years crop on hand which I intend to pack and send off this spring. Brothers Thomas and Birchall have each a crop of tobacco on hand. They have not packed any yet but are talking of doing so this year, for the merchants round here that buys are crying it down very much.

There familys are all in good health. Thomas Birchall is maried to his cusin Margret Morris. Andrew Morris is also maried to a girl by the name of Martha Ann Miller. Brother Henry Woods had his shop burned down last spring but he has built a new one. He has as much work as he can do and well payed. He keeps 2 and sometimes 3 cows, 2 or 3 young ones, one horse and some hogs. He grows hay, corn, potatoes, and sometimes wheat. His family are also in good health and so is mine.

Brother William came over to see us last fall. He had hired a peddling wagon, came through the country peddleing jeens of his own manufactureing. He is living at Steubenville. . . . [His health]

Andrew Morris has rented a part of his fathers land and is living near him. Thomas Birchall has rented a farm joining to his fathers. Alice Birchall is living joining to her fathers on land belonging to her father-inlaw. She has two children, Thomas one and Andrew one.

I have just returned from a visit to Thomas Sharples, a distance of 80 miles. I went on horseback, started last Wednesday morning a week ago, got there on Friday forenoon. They did not know me nor me them except him it being over 27 years since I saw any of the rest of his family. They was very glad to see me. I found them very well fixed and well satisfied. He owns about 500 acres of land in that nabourhood. The farm that they live on is 200 acres with 100 under cultivation. They are 9 or 10 miles from Cochocton, a cash market for all they have to sell.* There brotherinlaw Danial Johnson and Elen has got a very

---

* Coshocton, Tuscarawas Township, Coshocton County, Ohio, had 1,226 inhabitants in 1850. This region had an outlet to the north for its grain via the Ohio Canal after its completion in 1833.

pritty farm of 100 acres joining them. Sharples and me went to see them on Saturday. They came back to Sharplesses at night and stayed until bedtime, talking over old times about Gray Eights, Johnsons place, Crosshall, Limbrick, Chorley &c. &c. On Sunday we all took a ride over to his oldest daughter Marys who livs about 2 miles from them. She knew me after looking at me a long time. She is maried and has 4 or 5 children and a very good farm. His oldest daughter by his second wife is maried and has 4 or 5 children and a good farm. She was about 2 years old when I saw her before. I saw James Holand. He is single yet, boarding with Daniel Johnsons brother. He works at stone quarying and erns as much in the sumer as keeps him through the winter too. He does not pertend to work any in the winter. I started back on Monday after dinner and got home on Wednesday night. I payed Sharples 100 dollars for the money that he let me have when I first left England. When Sharples moved to were he is now 12 or 14 years ago he could get plenty of land for 3 dollars per acer and now it cannot be got for less than 20 in that nabourhood. He told me that he bought a farm some years ago for 300 dollars and sold it again for 900 dollars without doing anything on it, makeing 600 dollars by his bargin. There is no chance for the riseing generation to get land there now without paying a high price for it. In this part also all the Congress land is bought up. Consequently it is riseing in value and is likely to do so more after a time. . . . [Prices. Potato rot]

We have not done much work this winter, the ground haveing generaly been covered with snow and the boys has been going to school; but we shall have plenty to do when the wether comes fine, for we want to clear some new ground for tobaco beside haveing to pack our last years crop and haul it away to Marietta, a new tobacco house to build and ten acres of logs to rowl that we cut down last fall, besids puting in the spring crop of oats, corn, potatoes, &c. But I think I may as well quit for the presant for I am out at a side. Our Brothers and sisters and there familys all joins with us in sending our kind love and respects to you all from your affectionate Brother and Sister,

ANDREW AND JANE MORRIS. . . .

Butterworth Letter 1846

Rebecca Butterworth was the daughter of William Whittle Barton, a land surveyor, of 62 Toad Lane in Rochdale, Lancashire.[1] In 1846, when she wrote this letter to ask her father to help her and her husband return to England, she had been in Arkansas for three years or more. This little settlement of Outland Grove, not even listed in the census, and which Mrs Butterworth called 'The Backwoods of America', contrasted in every respect with the growing and thriving town from which she came. Here is an example of an urban family who tried to settle on a frontier farm. In spite of the help of her husband's family, settled nearby, the Butterworths were ready to give up. Mrs Butterworth was physically and temperamentally unprepared for the dangers and hardships of farming in such a region. An illustration of the want of preparation of this family for a farming existence was their complete reliance on doctors in sickness. No one in the family had even an elementary knowledge of midwifery. The reliance on calomel (mercury), as prescribed by an old-fashioned doctor of her day, contrasted with the botanic remedies used by working-class immigrants, who had not been accustomed to consulting doctors.[2]

The original of this letter is owned by Mrs Isobel Preston of Bishop Norton, Lincoln. A photostat is in the British Library of Economic and Political Science.

Letter from Rebecca Butterworth to her father, W.W.Barton, Rochdale, Lancs.

Back Woods of America, [Outland Grove, Arkansas], 5 July 1846
MY VERY DEAR AND TENDER FATHER,

I have been long in answering your and my dear sisters letters. The reason is I was taken sick a month since today. I commenced with bilious intermittant fever which nobody thought I would get over. Thomas was with me nearly all the time. He did not expect me getting over it. I was almost covered with mustard plasters, had a large blister on my back and I cannot tell you what kind of medcine. On the Thursday Thos said their was no help but [salination ?]. If not he said before 24 hours it would reach the low typhoid [grian ?] and then if preamature labour came on it would be certain death. Well, I had nearly 60 grains of calomel steamed bricks put to me. I had a burning head, my extreamities getting quite cold. My feet they could not get warm at times. Well, the result was the mercury had a happy effect. I had one of my cheeks cut half way through. Indeed it would have scared you to look in my mouth. On Sunday the 14th of June labour came on. I had a many came to see me expecting it almost the last time. I was insensible at times. We did not know I had labour and John and Sarah would have been alone with me on Sunday night but Thos and his wife got very uneasy about me at 9 oclock and concluded to come and sit up that night, knowing John and Sarah were weared down which I know I attach to a kind Providence. I suppose I had a dread few hours still not knowing I was in labour beside having ben so prostrated a whole week with fever. However I suppose about 3 oclock on Monday morning my dear baby was born. Not 5 minutes before they say I forced myself out of bed and from sister and run round the bed to a pallet on the floor. Well our little Wm Barton was born and crying like a child at full time. Thos did not like to help me as he had not studied midwifery much. I had to remain in that situation for two hours before the doctor could be got, the little dear boy crying all the time and alarmed at what would be the result. Doctor Howard come when he took the little darling and gave it to sister. In about ten minutes after he took his flight to heaven above to join my other 3 little angels. I know it is the Lords will. We are quite resigned. Both Docter Howard and Thos said I may be very thankfull I am spared myself, for if I had lived to come to my time the child was so large I could not of borne it. You would have been astonished to see. He is laid beside Polly and Rebecca. She would often tell tacky they were going to have another little broder Billy. So they have and seen him too. I felt when I heard him crying so if I could have him in my arms and put him to his breast I would be glad, but the Lords will be done and not ours.

I am now again able to sit up about a half a day at once. I have had another sever attack this past week which threw me down again owing to a dreadfull thunder storm and wind which scared me and threw the blood to my head. I have ridden on horseback to Thos once since. John had to lead the horses head and with being worse again I could not sit on a horse. Mary Ann is out, came in a buggy, so Thos brought last Fridy and took me to his house. I am so nervous that riding when able helps me. Yesterday he brought me in his carry all to Fathers. I am their now Inded if it aint for him through the providence of God I expect I would have been in my grave now. You would hardly know me now. I am so pulled down but am out of danger now but has to be very careful. My dear Father and Sisters. . . . Be very thankful to God for shewing us so many mercies. The family have really all been very kind to me in this sickness. Father & mother shed tears when he helped me in his house. I can forgive all the past. He wished me to tell you to be kind enough to see James and tell him the have not had an answer to his letter and are very uneasy for fear it has miscarried. Mary Ann is well and going to have a baby middle of September. I have not heard of poor Ebijah which makes me feel bad for fear he is dead.

John is not satisfied here. What little corn we had the cattle as jumped the fence and eaten it so that it will not make even cattle feed. We are [dammed ?] up in corner. We have not bread to last above a week and no meat, very little coffee, about $\frac{1}{2}$ lb of sugar. John can milk one cow which makes us a little butter but the other wont let him. He as had to be with me a month. We try to put our trust in the Lord knowing he is able to open the way. We want to sell the horse but cannot meet with a customer. If we could we think we could get along untill spring. We are going to do our best to part with the place. If we sell soon and the Lord spares us, we will be out in fall; if not, I will write again soon and if you can help us along without hurting yourself we should be glad to get home.

We want to [go] through Philadelphia. Mr Moore got there in 2 weeks & 2 days. It will cost very little more by taking deck passage. Will you try to get to know what Captn West charges steerage passage from Phildia to England? He knows you and would perhaps favour us. Now, Father, John is in good earnest, you may depend. Please do your best and if we are spared let me meet you all again. I feel a pang, that is leaving the homes of our 3 little ones but I cannot see their faces. Docter Howard charged 5 dollars but expect to pay him with a big 2 horse plough. Thos as given me a deal of medcine beside attention twice a day. Indeed the whole family was afraid of having done. His charege is nothing but a little sewing of bridles which is nothing.

Tell my dear sisters not to feel slighted I have not written. I fully intended to do it, am not yet able. You see how my hand trembles. I have had to rest in doing this. Excuse a long letter as I am so weak. Please write immediately when you get this and advise with us for the best way. Coming that way we can see more of America and get home in 3 weeks less sea. When Mr Moore comes back we can get to know pretty near price to Philidelphia. When I get your letter I will write and say what it is. My love to all and every one as if mentioned. Tell my sisters to think of us. John would have written this letter and . . . [illegible word] Sisters to but I though[t] if I could do it any how I would, and now my dear father may our God bless us all and give us more grace to receive chastisement and trust more in him. What is this world without a hope of a better? May he at last take us all to meet with him and all our dear children and Mother. Wont that be a blessed time? Bless you all with a kiss for you sisters and not forgeting little John. Ask him what I shall bring him. I wish I had one of the children with me. Mr Massel, the post master, sent you 3 newspapers, which was very kind in him. Now I must conclude as I have had hard work to write so much from your poor weak daughter,

                                        REBECCA BUTTERWORTH

Whittaker Series 1849–56

The Whittakers were another urban family who took up farming in the United States. Ann Whittaker was, almost certainly, born in Leeds. Her brother, James Smith, to whom these letters were written, had been born there in 1814, and was enumerated by the census-taker in 1841 as a warehouseman on St John's Place in Leeds.[1] It is not clear when or where Ann and Thomas Whittaker were married; but in 1839, when their last child was born, they were living on Standish Street in the port district of Liverpool. Thomas Whittaker reported himself as a provision dealer when he registered the birth of their daughter, Mary Jane. He was not able to sign his name on the birth certificate. Standish Street was lined with shops and workshops, and the presence of a considerable number of Irish agricultural labourers suggests that it was a neighbourhood of migrants. For the Whittakers it was a stopping-off place, where they lived, perhaps even so long as a few years, before continuing their migration to the United States. They had probably left for America before the 1841 census was taken.

Both Leeds and Liverpool were growing cities when the Whittakers emigrated. However, they probably left during the cyclical downswing of 1838–42, when hardship in these developing cities was more severe than at any other time in the nineteenth century. Someone like Thomas Whittaker, who was without industrial skills and also illiterate, and who had a large and growing family, was likely to be among those who felt the impact of unemployment and high food prices. But this is only conjecture. The Whittakers seem to have had 'a little to begin with', that is, some savings when they arrived in the United States.

Because her husband could not write, Ann Whittaker wrote the letters. While they are perhaps more banal and more concerned with domestic trivialities for that, they reveal an exceptionally happy and content English woman in subsistence agriculture. Although she had the interest in newspapers and world affairs of an urban woman, she did not fit the persistent report of travellers that English women were 'the most discontented people in the New World'.[2] Her attitude contrasted markedly with the resigned sense of duty evident in Mrs Bottomley's letters from a Wisconsin farm about the same time, or with the terror of Mrs Butterworth.[3] Perhaps because she had not lived so comfortably in England, Mrs Whittaker took a more positive attitude towards her new life. Though she did not have to adapt to the want of servants, it should be noted that she had four daughters. Mrs Whittaker's letters are among the most disinterested which we have; they were written neither to ask for aid nor to encourage immigration. The main purpose was that of reporting on their progress and keeping in touch with family in Britain.

The Whittakers settled on broken, hilly land, as had the Morrises. Their choice may have been influenced by the writings of William and Robert Chambers, in the early editions of their *Information for the People*. The Chambers recommended the highlands of Pennsylvania, the territory of Michigan and the counties in the Ohio and Mississippi River valleys in Ohio, Indiana, Illinois and Missouri.[4] Monroe County, south of St Louis, in the southwestern part of Illinois, where the Whittakers went, was attracting more foreign-born immigrants in proportion to its population than the state as a whole. In 1850, more than a third of its inhabitants had been born outside the United States, as compared with thirteen per cent of the population of the state of Illinois.

Partly because of this large foreign immigration, Monroe County was growing fast during the forties and fifties. In 1840, it had 4,481 inhabitants – about twelve persons per square mile. While it was not frontier in the technical sense, uncleared federal land could still be obtained in the county when the Whittakers arrived. The county population reached 7,697 in 1850, and 12,832 in 1860. The letters thus cover a period during which new arrivals provided a market for farmers in the neighbourhood, in spite of a want of urban or outside markets. The largest town in the county in 1850, New Design, had only 1,442 inhabitants. Waterloo, near the Whittakers, was a village of 791 people in 1850 and 1,435 in 1860. St Louis, thirty miles away, could be reached from Waterloo by wagon or horseback, but it was too far away, by these forms of transport, to serve as a commercial market for the farmers near the Whittakers. Thus, relatively isolated from outside markets as this county was, only about a third of the land in farms had been improved by 1850.

The optimism and satisfaction of Ann Whittaker in her letters of 1849 and 1851 must be seen against this background. Though a relatively old river settlement, Monroe County's farms 'in the hills', away from the river bottoms, were not highly commercialized when the Whittakers arrived. Circumstances changed quite rapidly between 1851 and 1856, however. Increasing material success and opportunities for commercial farming contributed to Mrs Whittaker's continuing complacency in her letter of 1856. By this time, they had rail connections with Chicago and were able to buy many articles, like cheap cotton prints, which they had advised immigrants a few years earlier to bring with them from England. Under this stimulus, they increased their wheat acreage from ten acres in 1849 to sixty acres in 1856. They sold their first farm in 1849 for $400, and the next year Thomas Whittaker reckoned the value of the real estate on their new farm at $480. By 1856, Mrs Whittaker thought that their 240-acre farm was worth between $5,000 and $6,000.

Mrs Whittaker's social adjustment did not arise out of intimate contact with the American community. She visited only the members of her own family and friends from England, so far as one is able to judge from these letters, though the Baptist Church probably formed a link with the local community. During the fifties, however, German immigrants were pouring into their neighbourhood. The early contacts with other immigrants from Liverpool were supplanted, as the hoped-for English settlement failed to materialize, by a close-knit, rapidly growing family in the next generation. By 1856, two of their daughters had married and settled near them.

This, then, would seem to be an instance of very satisfactory economic and social adaptation in the United States. Their economic success was satisfactory in the light of their limited aspirations. Mrs Whittaker was proud of their success, a pride partly reflected in the preaching tone evident in her religious injunctions to her family, even her mother, in England. While they never sent any cash to England, they offered to absorb into their household any number of children whom the family might wish to send to them. This offer also tended to give them prestige.

No letters survive after 1856. The question arises as to whether this family ever again achieved their peak of economic success of 1856. Did Mrs Whittaker stop writing when times became more difficult? After the panic of 1857, land values were brought down. In 1860, we find the Whittakers still living near Waterloo (soon to be re-christened New Hanover by the German immigrants), but now Thomas Whittaker reported his farm as worth only $2,000. Showing always too much appetite for land at the expense of intensive investment, Thomas Whittaker had added another forty acres to his farm since 1856. His position as a commercial farmer was not strong in 1860, and would have required a considerable new adaptation for continued success. Yet by this time he was fifty-five years old. Only 70 of his 280 acres were improved, and he was still emphasizing wheat in his cropping. His livestock had not increased since 1856. Valuing his livestock at $600, Thomas Whittaker was keeping fewer pigs than he had had earlier, and still had only six cows and ten other cattle. His farm implements were worth only $100.

Their son-in-law, Samuel Isles, had a farm of forty acres, valued at $500.

We do not know what happened to the family after this. Neither Thomas Whittaker nor Samuel Isles appeared as farmers in the Waterloo area in 1870. The decade of the sixties saw no continued influx of settlers to Monroe county, which added only 150 to its population between 1860 and 1870. Town growth and economic diversification were arrested. By 1870, only ninety-seven English immigrants were left in the whole county. Today there are no paved roads within about fifteen miles of the place where their farms were situated in 1860.

To read Mrs Whittaker's letters one must remember that she is very liberal in her use of the letter 'h' and added it to words like 'as' and 'is' very frequently. The Whittaker letters are owned by Mrs M.L. Harris of Harrogate, Yorkshire, who has kindly given permission for them to be published. Photostats are in the British Library of Economic and Political Science.

Letters from Ann Whittaker to her brother, James Smith, in Leeds

State of Illinois, Jany 1849

MY DEAR BROTHER,

I doubt not but by this time you will have wondered why I have not answered your dated Decr 16th 1847. Well I must say neglect tho I must say it has not been out of sight out of mind for I feel has tho I could not wait long enough for this to be answered. Do not I entreat you serve me has bad has I have served you. But write by return of post and send me all particulars. We are all in good health at present and have great comfort in send you word that we have had a great revival of religion in our neighbourhood. It commenced in September last. There has been a great many of the wickedest characters brought to a knowledge of the truth. We have a church about three quarters of a mile from our house and 4 of our family has become members of, myself, Thos, and Elizabeth, and Samle Isles the orphan which I named in my last. His sister has got married twelve months since 28th of last Decr. She was married from our house. I can truly say I feel more satisfied the I ever did since we came into the country. Thos was ordained for 1 of the deacons of our little church last Sunday. We belong to the Baptists. I find for my own part that there his nothing like living to God for then we have the promise of this life and also of that which his to come. Godliness with contentment his great gain. My dear Brother, if you have not begun to serve the Lord it his high time to be up and doing. The judgment of God are abroad in the land.

We have had sad accounts of the ravages the cholera has made in New Orleans. They average 1 hundred and fifty in a day dying of that awfull disease. It has also made its appearance in St Louis at this present time and I fear if it continues untill spring we shall see or hear tell of awfull calamities. We have had a great many very sudden deaths in our neighbourhood and there has a great many familes suffered thro the late war which is all settled some time since. It seem to me has tho there was all loud calls for us be ye also ready for in such an hour has ye think not the Son of man cometh. Methinks it will be an awfull change for the ungodly. Oh my dear Brother, let us live as for Eternity. You are favoured with great privileges such has we have not been favoured with since we left England untill the present. May we improve our time and work out our own salvation with fear and trembling because the Lord has said he will come has a thief in the night, and blessed his that reverant whom his Lord when he cometh shall find watching. I should like once more to have a few lines from Sister Jane. Give my kindest love to my dear Mother and tell her I do not forget to pray for her and I do hope and trust that she his ready with her lamp trimmed ready to enter in to the supper of the Lamb. Oh how I would like to see you all but I expect it will never be unless some of you come to America. But if we live heaven we shall meet in heaven. There his not a doubt of that thank God for it.

The Gentleman I mentioned in my last letter returned safe back to America and he said he could not make you out. I expect you will have a visit from an old gentleman the name of Ross. He his a close neighbour of ours. I intended writing when he came but he started before I was aware. You can send anything with him with the greatest safety if he should call. I directed him to York Street. You wished to know the price of land. It his 1 dollar and 25 cents per acre in its rough state. We have sold our first farm to a relation of Thos. It his a counsin. She his married and they have 2 children. We got 4 hundred dollars for it. We have 120 acres on the farm we now live on and a beautifull orchard. We have 3 small houses or rooms and we are about to [put?] up a large house this spring if we live, and we have plenty of stock such has cows, calves, oxen, horses, and hogs. We killed our hogs for our years provisions which was 13. No rent to pay, no fireing to buy. We are out of debt and a shilling to spare, so if we are not has happy as we need to be I know not. If a person can have a little to begin with and have their health they may get along in this country. Our children are very much altered since you saw them. . . . Children. Greetings] Affectionate Sister

                                      ANN WHITTAKER

16 March

. . . . Yesterday I made about one hundred weight of soap and today I am going to make more. We make our soap in the spring to last all year. The young woman I named in the beginning of my letter came over to our house to spend a week or two and died with us on the 6th of Feby of a dropsy and confinement. She had been married 14 months so you see in the midst of life we are in death. But death his nothing if we are prepared. I have been sitting up with sick woman last night who I do not believe has long for this vain world. But she his happy and submissive and rejoicing in hope of her immortall bliss. Yesterday we heard that a great revival of religion has broken out in Saint Louis. Three hundred has joined one church in six months. When you write send me word [how] the professing part of mankind his getting along with you. I believe I must conclude has the men his about to start for Waterloo this morning. Give my love to all and accept the same yourself from your affectionate sister

ANN WHITTAKER. . . .

State of Illinois, 23 Jan. [1851 ?]
MY DEAR SISTER AND BROTHER, . . . [Health]

We have removed since I wrote last to a beautiful situation about a quarter of a mile from where we was before. Our house stands at the top of a hill and we have bought eighty acres of land. We have got 10 acres of wheat which will be ready in August and we are getting ready for our garden and potatoes and Indian corn. We have 2 cows, 4 calves, 2 horses, 24 pigs, 2 dogs and I cannot tell you the number of chickens. Before you get this letter we shall have more young pigs. So you see our stock keeps increasing continually. We killed a fine fat pig for Christmas. We had some mince pies. I wished many a time we could send you some . . . [Names of cows] I still like the country. We have a larger house than we had before and Thos is getting ready to build another to join it. The climate is much the same has England, very little different. . . . [Weather. Earthquake] We had Mr Thos Isles of St Louis at our house. He boards and lodges with us when he comes into the country. He has bought a great deal of land about us and his building houses and intends to let it off for farms. If any of you should come to America I should like you to come to St Louis and enquire for Mr Thos Isles, Seventh Street, and he would soon put you into the way to find us. [Chaffins ?] Landing has washd away since I wrote last and it would be the cheapest and best way to come to St Louis and then by land to our house. It is a waggon road all the way.

EMIGRANT SHIPS

The *James Monroe*, 424 tons, was the first packet vessel to sail from New York to Liverpool for the Black Ball Line. Edward Phillips sailed from Liverpool on her on 23 August 1819 during her second year of service and arrived in New York on 7 September 1819 (p. 267).

The *Persian Monarch*, 3,900 tons, iron steamship with sail auxiliary, owned by the shortlived Monarch Line which entered the emigrant trade from London to New York in 1881. The vessel was new and furnished with outstanding steerage accommodation for the time when Ernest Lister made the journey on her in 1881 (p. 383)

Interior of the Cathedral in Quebec which so shocked John Fisher according to his letter of 20 June 1830. Photographed by William England in 1859 (p. 113).

View of Washington, looking down the Mall from the Capitol about the time Thomas Petingale came to the city. Photographed by William England in 1859 (pp. 456–7).

Brother James wants to know the price of land. We cannot buy less than forty acres and that cash 10 pounds. There are hundreds of acres bought since we came. There his likely to be an English settlement here very shortly. I have been once to St Louis on horseback. Thos was over since the members of Liverpool Church came. He has seen Greenhouse and the rest of them. They are in St Louis yet. They cannot get any farther up the river for the ice. The best time for coming his the time we we came has the water his high up the Missisipi and the ice all gone. There his other misfortunes at the fall on account of the water being so low. Send word all particulars and write back as soon as you get this. Let me know the names of your chicken.* Elizh was in great study about it for some time has I did not tell her the meaning of it. She says after she would not like to come back [to England] and indeed she may well for we live better and our minds his not care and we have not so much work. . . . [Greetings] I do wish all the poor familys was in America, but it is no use coming without something to begin with and then they can grow every thing they want almost. Mr Masters family his wearing dresses and other clothing that was on the chaps back when we came. If any of you should come, be sure and bring plenty of shoes and each a pair of clogs. I should like a pair of good warm winter boots myself. They make their shoes and very dear; and part with nothing but furnyture. I should bring [Dolly ?] and [tub] if I was coming again and plenty of muggs. We want some blue cups and saucers if you should come. Pack all your muggs and books. We have more time for reading. And seeds of every kind. There are seeds here which you have not and you have seeds which we have not. We want some slips of gooseberry trees and currents. There are none here and some strawberry roots. We have plenty of squirrels running about and deer and rabbits and hares. We eat squirrels. They are beautiful meat and wild ducks and geese. We have no coal but I like the wood fires very well. We have a fine yoke of oxen, a sled to haul wood upon. We plough with oxen in this country. Thos can drive them first rate. We call one Rock and the other Tom. If any of you should come bring farmers tools with you, has you will find you will want them. . . . Our field of wheat is green. So you see if all goes well we shall have plenty of flour. It is selling at 3 dollars a barrell, that his 12/ of your money. Get James to read *Chambers Information to the people* and get Sister Betsy to drop a line as I did before has I should like her to send me the Leeds *News* and you the Lpool. We can have the newspapers free if you would favour us with one. You can rent a farm, that his do a certain quantity of work upon it from 1 years went on you can buy your land and the neighbours helps each other to build the houses. They can

---

* Slang for children.

7

put one up in one day if the logs are cut down ready for them and then you return the compliment if any of them have a house or stable to rear. . . . [Greetings] Beef is selling a 2 cents per pound that is 1 penny of your money. I make all my own candles. We grow our own coffee, at least what we drink for coffee, and it is very good. It is roasted corn [rest of letter is missing]

State of Illinois, Monroe County, 24th June 1851
MY DEAR BROTHER AND SISTERS, . . . [Deaths in family in England]
You stated in your letter the cholera had been ragging all over England. It was the case here. Oh the distress! I cannot begin to pen it. We had 1 case in our family which was Ann but she got well. We had no doctor. We undertook to attend her ourselves and were fortunate with Gods help to restore her to her health again. The cholera his takeing rapid strides in this country again. We heer from St Louis and other parts that it is very bad. Our neighbourhood has not suffered with it yet. You will hear no doubt by the papers about the flood again. The river his now rising and has been for more than 2 weeks and his driveing the inhabitants of the American bottoms out of their homes. They made their gardens, planted their potatoes and corn, and now all his under water, thousands of acres. Some of the richest farmers lives in the bottoms and it is expected they will be broke entirely up by the loss. They have had to move out their familys in skiffs. It his a most distressing time for hundreds of familys. I believe the cause his on account of so much snow falling in the north and his now melting and overflows the rivers. I am happy to say that it does not interrupt our farm has we live on the hills.

We have a good prospect of a plentiful harvest which will soon be on. We have about 30 acres in wheat and not much less in corn. We have a fine show of potatoes. Last year potatoes failed most everywhere but we had a good crop. We raised about 2 hundred bushells. We had a good crop of turnips and an excellent garden. We had beets in our garden that weighed from 8 to 11 pounds. I weighted them through curiosity. We have a good garden this year. Also last year we had a great deal of fruit. It was supposed we had 4 hundred bushels of peaches in our orchard and cherrys and apples. The trees were propped. They could not bear their weight of fruit [again] & many of the trees was broken down. This year we have not so much fruit. We had some very late hard frosts which killed the fruit in the bud.

I received your newspaper and would be glad to have them often and I will try and send you one. They dont cost anything for postage. We are all well at present and I trust and hope you are the same. Elizabeth was married to Samuel Iles on the 19th of last June and his now nurseing a fine son which we call Thomas.* He his 11 weeks old. They are still liveing with us. . . . [About her children] Send a paper about the worlds fair which will be very interesting to us, and my brother I want you not to sleep once after you received this letter untill it is answered and send all particulars respecting our family. We have received 2 letters from William and he wants us to send him money to come which we cannot do. I should like to have Janes children if I could get them here. I would take care of them has long I lived. He named in his letter about Betseys money being in Wms hands when he died which I hope you have settled in a proper way. Mother was the most proper person to enjoy it. But you are aware, my dear Brother, that I do not like difficultys and about dead peoples property. But I hope this has all settled. . . . [Greetings] We have 2 hundred and 40 acres of land and our stock increases every year which blessing we have a right to praise and thank God, for we have seen many of our fellow beings suffer in many ways whilest we enjoy plenty of every thing and above all other blessings good health. I must conclude with mine. All the familys love to you all from your ever affectionate sister

ANN WHITTAKER

Write back immediately.

State of Illinois, Monroe County, May 1856
MY DEAR BROTHER AND SISTERS, . . . [Excuses for not writing]
I suppose you think it is not worthwhile to send any more newspapers. I have not had any for some time and I love to read them. We should send you papers if we had a chance. But they are printed in St Louis which is 32 miles from us. The Waterloo paper is small and not worth sending. . . . [Her daughter Elizabeth and her family] I have not seen Jennings and Ann for some months. They are liveing nearly 40 miles away from us but they are well. We had a letter from them a few weeks since. They have a girl. She was 1 year old on 30th of Novr 1855. We have had a very hard winter. Snow fell the week before Christmas and we never saw the ground clear of snow untill April. We had good crops of every thing last year but this year before was very dry. Potatoes and Indian corn failed. A great many of our peaches trees had died through the severity of the winter. We have plenty of plum and apple bloom but

* In 1850 Samuel Isles, the orphan referred to in Mrs Whittaker's first letter, was living in Thomas Whittaker's household. A 'farmer without a farm', he had been born in England, and was then twenty-two years old.

no peach. Last year we had abundance of peaches for market and to feed to the hogs. Our weat crops looks well. Everything looks green and pleasant. Elizabeth and Mary Jane his busy with their young turkeys and chickens and Thomas his as busy and has anxius has he was the first day we come. He his fenceing and clearing new ground every year. He looks fresh and well and Grandpappy to death nearly. . . . [Grandchildren] Thos says if Mary and Ellen will come he will keep them has long has they live. We have raised 4 girls larger by the head and shoulders than myself. I am has heavy again has I was wen I left Liverpool.

Farms are worth 3 times as much as they was when when we came out. The country his very much improved. We have saw mills and flour mills very convenient to us. Our farm his worth 5 or 6 thousand dollars. The land his all enterd around us. We cannot buy 40 acres of Congress land for a great many miles from us. We have 60 acres of wheat growing which looks very well. By the time you get this letter we shall have harvest close upon us. One of our cows has just had a calf. We shall milk 8 cows this summer. . . . [Prices]

Wearing apparel his cheap. Prints his from 8 to 10 and 12½ cents per yard. I often wish I could take a peep at you all and you peep at us. We have plenty room to tirn round in. When I go to St Louis I think I should take very badly to the city. They look so smothered up. When the weather his hot, we sleep with all the doors and windows open. We dont lock or bolt our doors in the winter. So you see we are not in fear. We have four good dogs. We still keep on labouring for the bread that perishet. May we labour also for that bread of life. We shall soon have done with all things here below. Oh may we give our hearts to God who his the giver of all good. What shall it profit a man if he should gain the whole world or what shall a man give in exchange for his soul. . . . [A hymn]
26th May. . . . [Greetings]
We have had Jennings and Ann to see us last week. They are well and their little also his well. I must conclude my pen his bad. Write an answer has soon as you get this and believe me your affectionate Sister

ANN WHITTAKER

Smith Series 1851–60

In the next few collections, the experience of a few more emigrants from rural parts of England will be considered. These people had not had farms of their own before they left Britain. Like some of the urban emigrants whose careers have been examined, most of these emigrants were unable either to continue to raise funds in England or to buy land as soon as they arrived in America. Among these rural emigrants were many industrial craftsmen, such as Robert Smith, as well as agricultural labourers and farm servants.

Smith was the brother-in-law of John Fisher, whose career was discussed earlier. Although his wife, formerly Harriet Fisher, died in October 1834, a few months after the family arrived in Lenawee County, Michigan, Fisher continued to regard him as a brother. As the Fisher letters indicate, John Fisher helped Smith to get a start before Smith settled on a farm next to him.[1] By the time this series of letters begins, in 1851, Robert Smith's children were coming of age and claiming inheritances from the Fisher family. These particular letters were saved because they acknowledged receipts of money from the Fisher estate.

Robert Smith was the youngest of nine children of William and Sarah Smith. His father had worked as a coachman as a young man, but became a farmer and gardener, renting land for himself, before his death in 1842. Robert Smith was born in 1800 in Burgh St Peters, Norfolk, a village lying between Norwich and the coastal town of Yarmouth in East Anglia. At the age of sixteen he was apprenticed for three years to a shoemaker in Yarmouth, and thereafter moved around practising his trade. In 1825 he married Harriet Fisher. Through the birthplaces of their six children, one can trace the continued migrations of this family before their departure for America. Two children were born while they lived in a village in Suffolk in 1826 and 1827. Then the family moved to Aldeby, Norfolk, a few miles west of Lowestoft, where they lived from 1828 until their emigration in 1834.

Acquiring capital after his emigration by working for John Fisher and practising his trade of shoemaker, Robert Smith started buying land.

He began with 40 acres of unimproved land in 1835, and as the Fisher letters indicate, had a hard struggle in the early years. After Fisher's death, he bought more land, for he at one time owned 270 acres. By 1850, this was down to 240 acres, and in 1860 he owned 160 acres, of which 80 acres were improved. It may be that he bought more land than he could improve or farm himself in order to help his sons.

One suspects that Robert Smith reinvested too much of his earnings in land. His life as a farmer was not easy. In 1850, his farm, valued at $2,400, was worth only two-thirds as much per acre as the average for the county. He had only twenty-five dollars' worth of farm implements, and was dependent upon wheat, wool and butter for his cash income. In spite of declining yields, he continued to grow wheat, and to mention this aspect of his farm operations particularly in his letters to Norfolk. By 1860, when he was fifty-nine, he valued his farm of 160 acres at $4,000. He was now beginning to shift his farm operations more in the direction of dairy farming, for he had six cows as compared with two in 1850, and produced 500 pounds of butter. Reporting no Indian corn in 1849, he produced 300 bushels in 1860. As compared to some of our urban immigrants, his opportunities for adaptation were better, because the population of Lenawee County continued to grow from 26,372 in 1850 to 45,595 in 1870. Under the circumstances, his economic success was modest.

In some ways, he seems to have been more assimilated into an American community than most of the other immigrants we have considered, though it must be remembered that we gain glimpses into his life after he had already been in the United States for seventeen years. Widowed with six children in 1834, he married a New York-born woman, whose parents were born in Massachusetts and Connecticut respectively. His wife's mother was living in his household in 1860. Smith was also a pillar of the Methodist Episcopal Church in Franklin, where he served as a class-leader for forty-three years.[2] Having settled in an area where farming prospects did not contract, as they did in the Ohio River counties, he was able to see his family established round about him, as did the Birketts in Tazewell County, Illinois. His three sons became farmers in Franklin, and four of his daughters married farmers in the same township. All of his children married young people who were born in the States. In 1870, he was still on his farm, with his eldest son, Robert, and his family living in the same household. The letters make clear that he maintained his contacts also with other immigrants from East Anglia, including those who had remained near Palmyra, New York. Again, we have the combination of strong religious faith, family unity maintained throughout the life of the first generation immigrant, and modest economic ambitions providing the basis for a successful adaptation. Robert Smith never moved from the farm on which he settled in 1835.

The Smith letters are in the Fisher Collection (2815/1–4) in the Ipswich and East Suffolk Record Office, and are published with the permission of the County Archivist.

Letters from Robert and E.Smith, Franklin, Michigan, to Francis Fisher, Brooke, near Norwich, Norfolk

12 July 1851

DEAR SIR,

I take this opportunity of answering your letter received on 12 inst (this being an uncommon rainy day). Glad to find you & mother were well though struling with hard times in consequence of your Corn Laws & the revolution going on in England the wich I hope will ultimately result in general good. . . . [Health] We have got in about 12 acres of hay (mens wages very high) clover and other tame hay, intending next Monday to commence harvest & have but 18 acres of wheat as my health was very poor last summer. I hope it will be good quality though thin on the ground. The price of wheat is low this year by reason of abundant crops in many places on clay & stiff lands. Prices about 3/6 your money. Oats and corn or maize as you call it is in good demand, butter & eggs very cheap. Here is the contrast: everything low, mens wages extremely high, excepting horses 20 pounds, sheep 5 lb & hogs 6, tolerable good price this summer.

Dear friends, I believe you would like to hear about the children. Harriet at last was married on 25 of June at our house, had a splendend show of trimmings on all the sweet cakes as I never saw before, most 3 days in preparing.* In atendance all the Conklin family besides others, in all between 20 and 30 guests. I believe they are going into a Seminary about 70 or 80 miles a little north of west from home. They move amongst the higher circles. I hope they will realize their expectation. Robt and Wm have their farms.† Their wheat is very good. Robt work at his trade generally. Hiram Learned, Elizabeths husband, bought him a farm in the same place for 700 dollars, calculating to move on in Oct.

* His eldest daughter, Harriet, born in Suffolk in 1826, married Alonson Conkling, probably the brother of Charles Conkling, a New York-born farmer enumerated in Franklin in 1860.

† Robert, the eldest son, born in 1827, was apprenticed to the trade of carpenter. He was not listed in the 1850 census of agriculture. William, born in 1828, had 65 acres in 1850, of which fifteen acres were improved, and valued his farm at $1,500.

next.* Angelina & John are living at home at present. They are pretty well at this time. My 3 younger girls are with us.† Mrs Smith health is but moderate, has the rhuemetism some. Notwithstanding this I think you would enjoy a visit with us around our humble home to see how green & healthy the fruit trees look. We had about 100 bushels aples last fall besides peaches, curants, &c. We have a pretty stream of water a few rods from the house. Now, Sir, it is not difficult for a person to live when once out of debt, but so many necessary improvements to keep one back.

Dear Sir

I do hereby acknowledge the receipt of fifty pounds by Draft inclosed in letter dated April 12 1851 from Mr Francis Fisher Executor of Francis Fisher deceaced, late of Brooke Norfolk Eng.

Hiram Larned
Elizabeth F. Larnerd

Received of Mr Fisher 4 pound 10s interest money

Robert Smith

DEAR F AND MOTHER,

Notwithstanding the distance & space between us I want to communicate my sympathys to you in your turmoils and disappointments in life, hoping God will still be your guide & solace in trouble. What a priveledge it is to pray to God in the name of Jesus who is full of sympathy for all that love Him in truth. Whe are now having a thunder storm, heavy rain with some hail, producing a great flood in some places. I hope you will excuse mistakes. Angeline will be 21 year, a year from next October. If you have money to let I will give 7 per cent. Interest here is as high as 10 the wich law alows. I hope you will write as soon as convenient. We join with love to you.

R AND E SMITH

Letters from Robert Smith, Franklin, to his Brother [in law?]

Franklin, 14 April 1860

DEAR BROTHER,

I received your letter 31st inst wich brought the mourful tydings of

---

* Hiram Learned (or Leanard), born in Vermont, had already married Elizabeth Smith, Robert Smith's fourth child, before 1850. His father, James, born in New Hampshire, was a farmer in Franklin Township. On Elizabeth's death, Hiram married the next younger daughter, Angeline.

† These were the daughters of his second marriage. Two of them were to marry farmers in Franklin, and the eldest one settled in Montcalm, Mich.

dear mothers death. I had indulged myself with a hope of hearing from her once more, but God has otherwise determined to take her home to rest. I hope & pray that we may be wise to follow her as she followed Christ. I know, Francis, you must feel the loss of one you have spent your life with so comfortably, so quietly. Though you have had your trials in common with others, you have one consoling thought mother died in peace. I assure you I never can feel sufficiently thankful for the instruction & advice she imparted to me at different times by word & more especially by letter. Now I feign would sympathise with you & dear Daniel, for we must submit to the unalterable decree it is appointed unto man once to die. Nevertheless it is painful to part with beloved friends. Still I hope we only part to meet again. . . . Our children are usually well settled on their farms within a mile of us. Robt has but 16 acres. He works at his trade, carpenter.* Harriet, as you will perceive, lives in the village. My health is a good deal [impaird ?] by incesant labour & years. I am in my 60 year. With respect to the money left for the five children at the death of Mother, I am instructed by Daniel to inclose & send you their orders to forward the amount stated, say £50 each to Robt Smith senior, Franklin, Tipton p. o. Lenawe County, Mich. We have though it would be better to send it in one draft if practicable as it will be as safe as any other form or deposit. In regard to the firm in which you deposit the money your judgment will best dictate. The last we recieved I believe come in this way and was safe all right. When so done they will send you their receipt for the same as they have done before. I must close so farewell dear friend. Yours most affectionately,

ROBERT SMITH

Franklin, 22 Oct. 1860

DEAR BROTHER,

I have to inform you I had no difficulty in the way of getting the childrens money. The bill of exchange with your letter came to hand allright. It was thought best to send it to New York to ascertain correctly what it was worth. I indorsed it, sent it the day after receiving it, waited a week for the returns, found it to be 1 cent & ½ on the dollar premium wich was so much more than we had been getting heretofore. Robt was down to town just at the time it came in by mail from New York. So he took it in goods, funds & specie from our exchange office

---

* By this time, Robert Fisher Smith, the eldest son, had married a Canadian-born woman. His sixteen acres of improved land were valued at $600 in the 1860 census. William had married a Michigan-born woman, and valued his real estate at $1,000 by 1860 (eighty acres). The youngest son, John, had also married a Michigan-born woman and appeared as a farmer in the 1860 schedules. By 1870 John valued his real property at $5,600, considerably more than the value placed on the farm operated by the elder son for his father.

7*

an divided it with his brothers & sisters agreeable with their instructions. I should have written before but been so very busy thrashing and carrying of our grain wich fetch us about 4s/6d your money per bushel. Crops tolorbly good this year. In addition to this we put in about 40 acres this season of wheat. The weavel, a insect, I hope may not be so destructive as they have been. We are trying to get more into the English system of farming though it dont always have the same effect in this climate it does with you. It has been a very busy time with us I assure you. I hope you will excuse my delay and write again as soon as it is convenient. I shall want to hear how you & Daniel get along and would just tell you that Mr & Mrs White, Mrs Wheathead had been down to York state to see their father N.B.Barzila Smith. When they returned to my surprise I found Uncle Smith had not heard of mothers death. He is getting an old man but abundantly able to live without work. Has been a very prosperous man. His children rent the farm of him so he live easy. Robt Fisher is living not far from them.* I believe they were all well when Mr White returned after harvest. Mr White too is one of these rich men. The fact is money is more plentiful now that it has been. Percentage will not be so high & thing not any more now, Brother. Remember me to Daniel & family. Tell him to write as soon as he can for I shall take care of his letters for I love to read them. My children are all pretty well at this time. My health is better than it was in the fore part of the summer so that I have been able to work. I shall inclose my receipt for the amount of money received and divided amongst the children and if that will not suffice they must send this acknowledgement for the same if it is required. I remain yours most affectionately,

ROBERT SMITH

August 1860

Received of Mr Francis Fisher two hundred forty seven pounds ten shillings and equally divided amongst the proper heirs,

ROBERT SMITH

* There was a clan of Fishers and Smiths also settled in Palmyra, Wayne County, New York. The census of 1860 listed Barsilla Smith, seventy-five, farmer, with $3,200 worth of real property; his son, Barsilla Smith, forty-one, was in the next household, a farmer with $7,000 worth of real property. Robert-Fisher, referred to here, was probably a recent immigrant from Norfolk to this community in 1850 when he appeared in the census as a labourer, aged forty-five, with $500 worth of real property. Palmyra would seem to have continued to be a stopping-off point for some English immigrants bent on getting into agriculture, since there were in 1860 a lot of English-born day labourers and farm labourers returned in that township.

Griffiths Series 1840–65

With the next series of letters we begin the consideration of a few more immigrants who moved from agriculture in Britain to agriculture in America. None of these people had operated farms of their own in England, but they did have first-hand experience of agriculture as labourers or farm servants. The Griffiths family came from farther down the economic ladder of rural society than did the farmers whose cases we considered first. Their economic adjustment as independent farmers in America was better than that of any of the urban immigrants we have looked at, and rivalled that of the farmers. They are also the first family whose last letter reflects a strong identification with the United States as 'our country'. Written at intervals over a period of twenty-five years, these three letters were sent mainly in reply to requests for advice about emigration.* The long gaps in the correspondence may in themselves, be evidence of a satisfactory adjustment, for the immigrants did not rely upon letters from England.

John and Margaret Griffiths and their brother-in-law, Charles Williams, the writer of the first letter, emigrated in the autumn of 1840 from Hindford, Whittington Parish, Shropshire. John Griffiths was twenty-eight, and his wife twenty-three, when they emigrated; they did not yet have any children. Margaret Griffiths's father, Edward Roberts, was an agricultural labourer, as were her brothers. They had all been born in Shropshire.[1]

The economy of the Oswestry district, in which Whittington Parish was located, had already become somewhat more diversified with respect to occupations than were the rural districts from which came the farmers who wrote some of our earlier series. In 1851, fewer than half the men over twenty years of age in this district were employed in agriculture. The emphasis on livestock husbandry in the district dictated a lower ratio of labourers to farmers than was found in southeastern England. Labourers outnumbered farmers by a ratio of three to one. Most of the occupations listed in the Oswestry district, apart from agricultural ones, were traditional rural crafts: sawyers, blacksmiths,

* The first letter dated 24 December 1840 has been omitted.

wheelwrights, carpenters, shoemakers and tailors. The principal sign of change in 1851 was the presence of 251 coal miners and 56 railway workers.

The decades of the 1820s and the 1840s both witnessed considerable emigration from the parish of Whittington, the population remaining almost stationary. During the thirties, in contrast, although emigration had continued, the population of the parish increased from 1,788 persons to 1,919. It seems likely that the Griffiths left for America in the wake of a period of growth and expanding employment in their immediate district.

Thus there were two points of contrast in the background of the migration of the Griffiths, as compared with our families of farmers. In the first place, the Griffiths were still living in the county of their birth when they emigrated to the United States. There is no evidence of prior migrations of any distance within England. Furthermore, growth and diversification of the economy had become somewhat more marked in the districts from which these poorer emigrants left than was the case in the agricultural areas, districts with stationary or declining populations, which produced the emigration from farmers' families in these series.[2] This growth in itself may have helped provide migrants with savings for emigration; but it also marked them as people who wanted to try to continue the old way of life.

The Griffiths may have been in contact with the Mormon Mission in Britain, in its very early days, for they emigrated directly to Nauvou in Hancock County, Illinois, on the banks of the Mississippi River, four years before tragedy again overtook a Mormon settlement.[3] While most of the Mormon missionary activities were concentrated in the industrial cities of Britain, this village in Shropshire may have presented an attractive field because of its high incidence of nonconformity.[4] With a total population of fewer than two thousand persons in 1858, Whittington Parish contained three independent and two Primitive Methodist chapels. The Griffiths did not remain with the Mormons. When the rest of their friends and neighbours trekked west to Salt Lake after the lynching of Joseph Smith, they stayed behind.

Hancock County had been settled during the 1830s. By the time these Shropshire immigrants arrived it had a population of nearly ten thousand people, about twelve persons per square mile. Its growth during the forties was not rapid, by the standards of a newly developed river county, because of the withdrawal of the Mormons. The largest town in the county, Nauvou, had been depleted to just over a thousand people in 1850. During the fifties, the population of Hancock County increased more rapidly, from 14,652 in 1850 to 29,061 in 1860. The second letter in this series was written by Margaret Griffiths in 1850, as this boom, in which the county population doubled, was getting under way. The growth was principally an expansion of agriculture. Town-growth in Hancock County was very limited during the 1850s when the river town of Nauvou itself grew more slowly in population than the county as a whole. The final letter in the series, written in 1865, reflects the prosperity which Civil War prices brought to these English immigrants, who were able to build a new house, get free of debt, and save something in addition.

The Griffiths letters emanate a spirit of contentment and satisfaction with economic circumstances in the United States. The explanation for this contrast with many earlier series is in part cyclical; that is, the years 1850 and 1865 were good ones for Illinois farmers. The tone of the letters suggests that the Griffiths waited for a good year before writing home. They wanted to be able to give an encouraging report to relatives who might be thinking of joining them. Even more striking is the fact that they offered to assist other members of their families with the expenses of migration, something they were able to do at the time these two letters were written, but something which few other English immigrants in American agriculture in these series considered. The letters suggest that emigrants from the poorer sections of English agriculture expected, as did the Irish immigrants, to try to help other members of their families with assisted passages. In contrast to our farmers, the Griffiths did not expect to be subsidised or to raise money at low rates of interest on the other side of the Atlantic.

The Griffiths settled in Hancock County because of a religious connection, but it proved to be a rich agricultural region. In contrast to urban immigrants of limited means, like the Whittakers, John Griffiths used his meagre initial resources wisely. He invested more of his profits in improvements, machinery and livestock, and less in land. He remained on the 80-acre farm, which he bought in 1847, for the rest of his life. By 1860, he had increased his acreage to 180 acres, but 160 of these were improved. In spite of the recession of the late fifties, he valued his farm at $5,400 in 1860. Perhaps his English background had something to do with his early emphasis on livestock. He valued his livestock at $700 in 1855 and at $1,100 in 1860. He had invested $200 in farm implements – far more than had the urban immigrants whose careers we have been considering. Although his corn/wheat ratio was lower than the average for the township of Appanoose, he emphasized corn in his cropping pattern, for in 1859 he had produced 205 bushels of wheat and 1,500 of corn, along with oats and barley. His responsiveness to market opportunities is also suggested by his shift from pigs to sheep during the sixties and towards more wheat as the Civil War changed relative prices.

By 1870, John Griffiths valued his farm at $8,000. The Griffiths were not among the thousands who left Illinois farming during the seventies. Though the population of Appanoose declined during that decade, John Griffiths' eldest surviving son, John, born in Illinois in 1847, continued as a farmer in the same township. He had bought a farm of 160 acres, worth $5,000 by 1870, but had as yet little livestock or farm implements. By 1880, he had invested in cattle and pigs. His arable enterprise was almost entirely subordinate to livestock raising and dairying. He was continuing the same emphasis his father had made from the outset.

By the close of the Civil War, John Griffiths felt himself to be an American. But the letter of 1850 reveals considerable loneliness on the part of his wife, as they lost contact with the large group of friends and relatives with whom they emigrated. There were still six English-born farmers in Appanoose township in 1870, however, and the county contained 359 natives of England and Wales at that date. When his wife died in the 1870s, John Griffiths married a Kentucky-born woman. The Griffiths provide a case in which appropriate farming experience, not too high a standard of living before emigration, and a fortunate choice of location made possible a successful career as a farmer in America and a social adaptation which might be called assimilation.

The originals of the Griffiths letters are in the possession of Miss Ray Dorien, the novelist, who has kindly consented to their publication. Photostats are in the British Library of Economic and Political Science.

Letter from John and Margaret Griffiths to Edward Roberts, Hindford, near Whittington, Oswestry, Shropshire

Nauvoo near the Big Mound, Hancock County, Illinois, 4 March 1850
DEAR FATHER AND MOTHER,

After a long silence I now sit down to write a few lines to you hoping these will find you and all our dear relations well as it leaves us at present, thank the Lord for his mercies to us. I hope you will forgive for not writing before but I had not courage to rite after Joseph and Ann and all our English neighbours went west and left us behind; and the reason that John did not write because every letter that came from England was directed to Joseph.* But he did not prevent me from writing. I would have gone west but John would not go and neither

* John Griffiths's brother.

mobs or any one else never molested us. We are still on the same settlement that we came on first. We live a mile from where Joseph used to live on the side of the road seven miles from Nauvoo. We have a farm of our own that we have been living on three years in a pleasant healthy place. We have 80 acre of land in cultavtion and pleny of land to turn our catle in the summer.

I feel satisfied to live and die here but we should feel better satisfied if you were here. We have four children . . . [Names] . . . We have been blessed with good health for we have not had a docter in our family but once we sent for one to little John when he was but seven months old. His father was sick at the same time. The docter said he had the billious fever but he says himself he would have got well sooner without the docter. I was not very well last summer. I went three times to see a docter for the first time in this country. I never enjoyed my health so well in England as I have in this country. For this cause I have no desire to return to England as well as for many other reasons. For this is a good country for a man has a chance to become independent if he has his health. We should like to hear from my father and mother and all my friends and relations. If any of them would like to come to this country we would help them. We would let them have land and house room and provisions untill the could raise ther own. Dear father and mother, we should like to see you all once more but I ham afraid we shall not but I hope we shall meet in heaven where parting is no more. I have spent many lonsome hours while I have been thincking about you all in England; but thank the Lord, though we be absent from all our dear friends, we live happy and comfortable. We have good neighbours. We are learning Harret and Joseph to read. The cares of our little family take our attention and passes away our time. If we had no family we would come to see you. There is nothing in the world would give me so much joy as to see John meet his mother. . . . [Asks for news and letters]

We have acquainence in Nauvoo that came over the ocan with us. They lived in Liverpool and belonged to the Mormons. Ther names are Charles and Harriet Chandler. Mrs Chandler is a midwife. We lived together in St Lous six weks before we came to Nauvoo. We hold them as relations. She is one of the best women I ever saw. Her husband drinks and she maintans the family. She is respected and loved wherever she goes. She is talked of where she is not known. I heard her name in the Church before I knew her. All on this setlement is acquainted with her. She has three girls. She has been talking of coming to live by us but I do not know whether she ever will. She has a great deal of buisness in the city. We feel [lost ?] at times and think if we where to be taken from our little children what would the do. Our little ones tells us the would have Mrs Chandler for a mother. I often look at them and shed many a tear and pray that we may be spared to see them grown. But why should I pine. The same hands that feeds the young ravens would surly feed them.

I hope you will write back us soon as you can and let us know of the welfare of all our dear relations. John is still the same as ever. He believes in the doctrine of Mr Manning.* He is a good kind husband, a tender father and thank the Lord we have plenty to make us comfortable . . . your Affectionate son and daughter,

JOHN AND MARGARET GRIFFITHS

Letter from John Griffiths to his brothers and sister

Appanoose, Hancock County, Illinois, 23 April 1865
DEAR BROTHERS AND SISTER,

I once more take my pen in hand to inform you that I am still in the land of the living and enjoying good health at present myself, thank God for it. And before giving you any details of my family, I must inform you of the reason why I did not answer Mosses† last letter, which I received in 1860. In the first place we, the American people, were contending for our Constitutional liberty against a Slaveholding Arristocracy which as turned out to be one of the bloodiest wars that history as recorded, and I did not want any of my relations to come here untill I saw which would gain the victory, Slavery or Freedom. I thought at the commencement it would not last above one year at the furthest; but it has turned out to be a bloody strugle and there has been great lamentations in the land. But I think it is about over. But there has been great sacrifices made to preserve the life of the nation. But thank God it is safe and the victory is won and Liberty is triumphant and slavery is dead. But in dying it made some awfull strugles, and has killed some of the noblest champions of liberty that ever lived, and amongst them our Beloved Pressident Abraham Lincoln, a man that was loved more than any other man in the nation. But though his body has fallen his Spirit lives in the hearts of the people. He did not fall in the field of battle but by the cowardly hand of the bloody assasin. We was rejoysing over our victory when the sad news reached us of the sad calamity and cast a glom over the whole nation. There never was such a mourning on the continent of

* Probably the Anglo-Catholic beliefs of Henry Edward Manning, 1808–92, before he became a Roman Catholic.
† Moses Roberts, born 1825, brother of Margaret Griffiths.

America as last Wensday. There was funaral sermons preached in almost all the churches in the free stats and large processions. So now we have a free cuntry to offer to apressed of all nations, the home of the free and the land of the Brave. So no more at pressent about the Strugle. May the Lord santify it to us all that we may esteem liberty more than ever.

Dear Brothers and Sister, now I will give you a short history of myself and family and of our welfare. I think when I wrote to you last, my family consisted of my wife and six children and we have had two since, but the yongest died before we named him. He was four months old when he died and I think Harriet was sick when I wrote you last. She died on Good Friday in 1861 and Almira died 4 weeks after so we have now but 5 children all well except Joseph. He has not been well since last harvest. He is in the room as I write. He is able to walk about but I do not know wether he will recover or not. He would be glad to hear from you. John is in the army. We had a letter from him last night. He says he is stout and hearty. He got 450 four hundred and fifty dollars bounty and twenty five dollars per month. He enlisted for one year. He was seventeen when he enlisted on the last of March. William is 10 next June. He is large enough to plow with a quiet team, but I have to plow myself for labor is verry high an hands scarse . . . [Other children] Now I have told you of my family. We are still living on the same farm and we have got a new house, a verry good frame house, something of the shape of Mr Groughall's. The front is two storis 18 feet by 34 feet and a kitchen 18 feet by 27 feet and a good cellar under the larg porch. So we are in tollerable good circumstances as to this world's goods. Indeed any industrius man can make a good living in this cuntry. You asked me in your last if I would advise you to come to this cuntry, but I could not then as I did not know how things would settle. And now I leave to yourself to choose for yourself.

You wanted to know how much it would cost for a man to come. The second cabin pasage to New York is thirty-five dollar or about seven pounds five shillings, the steerage about five pounds four shillings; and if any of you would like to come now I could help any of you as I have a little money after paying all my debts. It has been a good time for making money in the north since the war began. Everything has sold so high. I sold four hundred bushels of barley at two dollars or eight shillings four pence per bushel. But I expect everything will fall soon, but we shall be very glad if we can have peace in our cuntry again . . . [Deaths of his brother, Joseph, and brother-in-law, Charles Williams] . . . I am ashamed that I have not wrote to [relatives] in all this time, but I have been engaged heart an soul against this wicked rebellion and thanks be to the Lord for his providential care over us and that he has slain the monster slavery, I hope never to rise its blightining influences over the land again. . . . I remain your affectionate Brother

JOHN. . . .

Bishop Series 1872–4

The next collection consists of a few letters written by immigrants who had not kept in close touch with their family and community in England. The illness of their father, and his unhappiness, led them to try, with considerable zeal, to re-establish contact after they had been in America about fifteen years.

We cannot establish exactly when the Bishop family emigrated from Dennington, Suffolk, a village about seventeen miles north of Ipswich. The evidence suggests that they emigrated about 1857 when John Bishop, the father of the other migrants, was fifty-four years old. John Bishop was probably the son of John Bishop, weaver, who was listed in the census at Dennington in 1841.[1] Before he accompanied his family to America, John Bishop worked as a farm labourer. One of his sisters married a butcher, and another married an agricultural labourer in Dennington.[2] During the fifties, when this family emigrated, the population of the parish fell from 1,047 to 895 souls. Both this fact and the tone of Caleb Bishop's letter suggest that economic motives were very strong in the migration of the Bishop family.

With John Bishop went his daughter Emily, who married John Tongate, also from Dennington, son of a farmer of fifty-two acres, who employed only one labourer. In 1851, John Tongate's older brother, Charles, was living away from Dennington, working as a grocer and draper. But by 1861, he had returned to Dennington to take over his father's small farm. John Tongate, whose wife wrote the third letter, became a butcher in Penn Yan, Yates County, New York, a few miles from the township where his father-in-law settled.

John Bishop's son, Caleb, who wrote the first letter and may also have been married before they emigrated, became a harness-maker in Penn Yan, and was still there at the time of the 1880 census, then a man of fifty. The youngest son, Thomas, who was only fourteen in 1860, lived with his parents on their farm in Benton, Yates County, until just before the first of these letters was written. By 1880, he was established as a farmer in Benton, the only one in the Yates County part of the family to marry an American-born woman, the New York-born daughter of German parents.[3]

The Bishops emigrated to an old established region, by American standards, in the mid-nineteenth century. The population of Benton, where John Bishop settled was declining during the 1850s, when this family arrived. So ironically, this family emigrated from a parish in England whose population was falling to an American township which was also losing population. This family acted as 'fillers-in' in the wake of the westward expansion of American agriculture. It does not seem that John Bishop was able to buy a farm as soon as he arrived, however. He was listed in the 1860 census at Benton as a farmer, but claimed no real estate and a personal estate of only $400. His success, which made it possible for him to return $4,000 worth of real estate and a personal estate of $1,000 by 1870, was achieved by very hard work according to the immigrants.

Benton township had a sizeable English-born population, estimated at 127 in the New York State census of 1855. In 1850, 5·5 per cent of the labour force in the township were people who had been born in England; this had increased to 7·7 per cent in 1860.

Though Yates County was relatively isolated from the most vigorous growth in New York state and had remained largely agricultural, the Bishops were well-satisfied with their economic success. One of the chief points of interest in this collection is the sheer boasting about economic success, especially by Caleb. Yet in spite of their prosperity and settlement in a township with a significant sprinkling of English immigrants, John Bishop became very lonely, self-pitying and depressed in his illness. However, family solidarity was maintained among these immigrants, and the children in Penn Yan looked after their ageing and sick parents. Both John Bishop and his son Caleb had become American citizens by 1870.

The Bishop letters have been reproduced by the kind permission of their owner, Mr Dennis Baldry of Epsom, Surrey. Photostat copies of the letters are in the British Library of Economic and Political Science.

Letter from Caleb Bishop to his cousin, daughter of Thomas Bennett, Dennington, near Framlingham, Suffolk

Penn Yan, 23 Dec. 1872

MY DEAR CUSSON,

Yours receved a few dayes since with joy and pleasure to hear from you for I was so glad to hear from some of my realitaves in England. I have wrote to sevearel of my cusons in England and never had no answer from them, but little did I think of getting a letter from one that I never had writen to. The reasen I never had writting to you because you was very small when I left England. I think it a great kindents of you in wrigten to me. How did you know my adress?

    Send word.

You wanted to know how we are getting a long. We are getting on first rate. It was a fortchen to my farthe and mother when they left England and sailed for America. My farthe have got a nice farm of 60 akers and good house and barns on it and is spleaned [splendid] land and it is all paid for. He can take one hundread and twenty five dollers per aker, it wold be twenty five pounds of English money per aker. My farthe is well of[f] now. He have had to work very hard indeed, but he have made money fast. Now I must tell you a little about my self. I have got a good bissens and I keep 3 men to work all the time and I am doing first rate. I have made money fast since I have been in bissins for my self. I have got a good house of my own and all paid for and a good shop and money out to interest. This is the cuntrey for yong peapple to make money. Your farther and mother can do well if they were hear. If it did not benefit them it wold thare children.

Dear Cuson, I am sory to tell you my farther and mother have been very ill this last three months. We did not think they wold live one day after a nother. Fathe had the asme so bad and mothe had the feaver, but Thank God they are got better now, so they can seat up part of the day. It have been very hard for us for we have had to seat up with them all night for this last three months.

I no you think America is a wild cuntrey, but it is not. It is a spleanded cuntrey. I like it very much indeed. I was a little home sick at first, but I soon got over it and I feal as hapy as a lord in England. I have the best the world aford. I see my farthe and mother to day. I told them I receved a letter from you. They ware surprised and told me to tell you to give thare love to your farther and mother and all inquire frinds. I wold like for you to come and make us a visset. It shall not coast you enything when you get hear. You must excuse this for I am in a hurry to go to a large partey. So no moore at present from your loving cusson

                    C. W. BISHOP. . . . [Asks for news]

Letter from John Bishop to his family in Suffolk

                                             25 Febr 1873

DEAR SISTER AND BROTHER,

    I now take the oppertunety writ a few lines to you hooping thes few lines will find you all well as it leaves me quite sick, not able to work. I

have to doctor all the time with the astemea and coff. I have sutch a
time to get my breath. I have not been out doors but little as three
months, so whee have a great boy to work. Whee have one of Mr
Pendles boy from Worthington to live with us now. My wife send her
love to you all and she hope when theses lines reach your hands they will
find you all well as it leaves her better than she has been, for she had to
be taken bead for wheeks just like a child. So whe have had a hevey
afeliction this winter. Whee both was taken down ill in one night and
whee neither of us cud not help ouirselves for wheeks. But Thank God
my wife is better now, but I cannot get out to do nothing.

I have been farming all the time ever since we left England. Whee
bought a small farm 5 years agoo of about 40 acres of land, a veary nise
place for fruit of all kinds. Whee have about three ackers of my orched.
But, Dear Sisters, ouir children are all maired and left now and my
helth is so bad and I cannot tell where I can work aney more. Therefore
whee are a gooing to sell this spring. Whee raise all kind of things as you
can in England, but Dear Sisters, whee have veary long winters hear.
Whee have had snow and frost ever since the begining of November.
Ouir winter last pretey well up to the first of April. Now I will tell you
how mutch cattle whe have. Whee have milked 4 cows this last time
and whe have a heffer cuming in and whe have two horses and a yong
calf. I have butchered 2 hogs [weighed ?] over 6 hundreds pounds and
whe are a going to butcher 3 smaller ones in a few days. Poork have a
been selling about 20 shillings of English money for a hundred pounds.
Butter is now 13 pence of English money, eggs 15 pence. My crops have
been veary good this year.

But, Dear Sisters, whee prefard Engelent to live. Mericke is good
hardworking people to live in beacause there is plenty of hard work to
do in a short time. Dear Sisters, whee live 5 miles from Peny Yan. Ouir
2 gairls and Calep lives thear. Emerley Husben butcher all the time. He
get all the meet he whant to use and so mutch a wheeak. They have got
a good house paid for. They heave 3 children. They yongest is 11 years
old. Alies husben keeps a livery stable and they have a nise house to live
in. Thomas live 2 miles from us. He is working a farm. Arthur lives at
Misigan about 5 hundred miles from us. Walter is living Kanses about
2 thousends from us. They was all over to ouirs 4 years last Crismes.
The time semes so long since whee see them.

Ouir Calep is a doing great bisenes. He plye [employs] always 2 men
and som times 3 men to work. Calep have a veary largh house of his
own and whe can live in a part of that if whe like. . . . [Asks for letter
and news of family] Dear Sister, I have put everey year of not writing
up to thir present time, but Dear Sister whe may not have theses excuses

no longer, for behould now is the time to work while whe have the oppertuenety. For whe have all a hasenetng to ouir maker and Dear Siste I hope whe shall be [pre]paired for that chang. Dear Sister, the longest of my time is but short. Dear Sister, that has been my falt of not writing before now. Therefor I pray that all of you will forgive my falts. Dear Sister, if whe are speard a few years whe have a nuff to live on. Dear Sister, I cannot think of aney more at present, so no more from your Brother and Sister

BISHOP. . . . [Asks for news]

Letter from Emily Tongate to her aunt and uncle in Suffolk

Penn Yan, 23 Sept. 1874

MY DEAR AUNT AND UNKELL,

I thought I would try and write a few lines to you both to let you now we air a live at present. We hope these few lines will find you and your family well as it leves us all as well at the present time. We would like to see you or here from you. John would like to now ware unkell is butching yet or what is he doing now and how much family have you now. . . . [Her family] John and I have talked quite a good deal about you all and wondered you did not try and come to America with your family. You could have done well out here. This is a good country for working people if they will try they can get a long well by their work. John is butchering. He kill three beefs and sheep and lambs and calves every week, besides fowls. So you can tell they do a good busseness in their market every week. Penn Yan is quite a town for busseness. We live these five minnits walk of the depot so we can see every train that come in and it is very plesent. Indeed we have quite a plesent home. . . . [Weather and harvest] We have plenty of fruit here, all kinds of it and it is quite cheep to. People use quite a good deal of fruite here. Potaters and wheat is quite cheap here now. I would like you to see all our stuffed birds and animals whitch John did. We have got a room full of them now.

We surpose Denington look quite different now what it did when we left England. We would like to come and see you all once more if we live, but we cannot tell ware we shall, but we hope and trust by the blessing of God we may, but if we do not we hope to meet in heaven. I hope you will excuse this bad writeing. I will try and do better the next time. You must not blame mother because you have not had eny letters from father. It is not her falt. She have wanted him to write to you all times – and again but he did not and now he is got so very sick and he is not able to do it for he can not dress himself nor undress himself. Mother and father is stoping with us now and have been this last five weeks. . . . [Father failing] Dear Unkell, we wish you would be so kind as to send word ware Mother Tongate is a live or not, for we do not get eny letters from her now, nor from Charles. He never write to us so we wish you would find out all you can and send it to us for we feal very ansious to now about them and how they get along and how things look around the farm, but we do want to now about mother – perticler. . . . How we would like to see you all. . . . [Again asks about her husband's mother. News of her brothers and sisters] John and my children join with me and send our kindest love to you both and family and hope to here from you soon. We hope to remain your well wishing neaices

EMILY TONGATE. . . . [Prices]

Letter from John Bishop to his sisters, Caroline and Betsy

Penn Yan, 23 Sept. 1874

MY DEAR SISTER CAROLINE AND BETSY,

I now write these few lines to you both hopeing they will find you both well as it leves me very sick indeed, but it leves my wife better then she have been, but I myself shall never be eny better. I got my daughter Emily to write these few lines for me to you to let you now that I am alive, but I do not think I shall be here on earth long, but I hope and trust to meet you both in heaven. I am not able to dress nor undress my self now, nor I do not expect I shall eny more, but I only want to be perpared to meet my savour and I feel quite willing to die when I am called, but if eny thing should happen to me some of the family will write and let you both now. We air liveing in Penn Yan now with my daughters. All our children air well, the best of our knowledge, and I hope your familyes air well.

Since I have sold my farm we feel quite strange to be out of busseness but we was not able to tend to it and that is the reason we sold it. We have three children live in Penn Yan, so it is very plesent to us to see them so near us. Our youngest son live in Benton on a farm and one in Michigan and one in Kansess and the one in Kansess is comeing home this fall as soon as he can get ready to come. I hope you will write to me just as soon as you get this letter so if I live I can here from you once more, and when you write to me direct your letter to my daughter. My wife join with me and send our love to you both and to your familys and hope to here from you soon, so I will close. I hope to remain your loveing

BROTHER JOHN BISHOP

Grayston-Bond Series 1870–99

This outstanding series of letters was written by two members of the Grayston family of Aughton, Lancashire. Aughton was a village ten miles northeast of Liverpool, a station on the Lancashire and Yorkshire Railway. In many respects Aughton was still an agricultural village in the mid-century. Most of its inhabitants were farmers, labourers or the usual village craftsmen and retailers. Yet in contrast with the districts from which so many of our farmers emigrated, Aughton was growing and changing in response to the vigorous economic growth in the region around it. The population of the village showed an increase in every decade in the nineteenth century. During the sixties and seventies, when these emigrants left, its population increased from 1,870 in 1861 to 3,145 in 1881. The proportion of men over twenty who were still in agriculture had fallen to less than half as early as 1851 and continued to decline. Other employment opportunities were appearing in the Ormskirk census district, of which Aughton was part. The 1861 census recorded significant increases in cotton manufacturers and coal miners. Employment on the railways rose from fourteen in 1851 to nearly a hundred in 1861. The increase in market gardeners during that decade also indicated a response in local agriculture to urban growth nearby.[1] Thus it was no absolute want of economic opportunity nearby which formed the background to the migration of members of the Grayston family. They seem to provide another example (like the Griffiths) of growth, rather than decline of incomes locally, as making possible the emigration of people from lower income groups.

The grandfather of these emigrants had been a small farmer at Aughton. His eldest son, Robert Grayston, a man of sufficient standing to be listed in local directories, took over the parental farm, and in 1851 was farming sixty-five acres, employing three men and a boy.[2] A younger son, Peter Grayston, was working as an agricultural labourer at the time of the 1851 and the 1861 census-takings. Peter Grayston is said to have worked as a railway labourer while the railway was being built in the neighbourhood. He was the father of these emigrants.

Peter Grayston already had seven children by 1851. One of them, Isaac, though only thirteen at the time of that census, was working as a farm labourer, living in the household of a farmer of fifty-two acres. By 1861 he had married and described himself as an 'agricultural carter'. The occupations of Robert and Peter, other sons who did not emigrate, cannot be definitely established. Robert had left home by 1861, and his younger brother, Peter, was then only ten years old. According to a descendant of this family, these Grayston sons who remained in Lancashire gained a competence by changing from labouring to gardening on wealthy estates. Their father was employed as a gardener by the early seventies. A younger sister, Sarah, who was a girl of thirteen when the first group of emigrants left, had her own business by the nineties, when she twice visited the American branches of the family.

The first of Peter Grayston's children to emigrate was his daughter, Catherine, who, like her sister Ann, was put into service while still a young girl. While Catherine was in service, she met James Bond, son of a Liverpool pawnbroker who later became a farmer in the nearby village of Sefton.[3] In 1869 James Bond was a farm labourer at Sefton. Given the assumptions that James Bond wanted to remain in agriculture and that he was unable to find a tenancy in the district, the motives for emigration of this young couple were economic. As Catherine Bond wrote, they wanted more than a living, though they intended to save any extra income they obtained for land purchase, not to gain a high standard of living immediately. The Bonds sold their furniture to help raise passage money and Catherine's father lent her the money to travel cabin class, since she had an infant, Robert, when they emigrated in 1869. Their jobs in Milford, Connecticut, were probably arranged for them beforehand, in much the same way as they, in turn, advised relatives at home of particular situations they were asked to help fill.

There were about three thousand English-born people in New Haven County when the Bonds arrived in 1869. The English were more concentrated in this county than they were in the state of Connecticut as a whole. In spite of this, Catherine Bond complained of loneliness, though they were well pleased with their situations as servants of a Philadelphia businessman on his farm in Connecticut. While they were thus wage-earners, they even sent small sums of money home to Peter Grayston and his youngest daughter, Sarah.

In the mid-seventies, the Bonds moved to Kansas, during that state's great population surge. By 1880, Kansas had eight thousand more English-born inhabitants than it had in 1870. The rate of increase of its foreign-born population was only a little less rapid than that of its population as a whole. Russell County, where the Bonds bought land, is situated in the central part of the state, the part where the Populist movement had its great strength. The letters of Mrs Bond record their struggles in this marginal farming country during the eighties and nineties.

A change in Mrs Bond's attitudes can be traced through these letters, written from the unpredictable circumstances of Kansas farming. As late as 1884 she still maintained that it was better to be independent than working for hire. By 1888, however, she was no longer sure of this. Valuing their farm, stock and implements at less than the savings they had brought with them from Connecticut fifteen years earlier, Mrs Bond thought they would have had more 'pleasure of life' if they had remained in England, even if only for daily wages. If Mrs Bond wrote any letters during the peak period of Populist strength, they have not survived. By 1897 she was resigned to life in Kansas as her home 'as long as I am on this earth'. Having come to a very risky farming region, the Bonds held out, unlike many of their neighbours, and remained on this farm for the rest of their lives.

The Bonds do not seem to have had much social life. They did come to the township in Russell County which contained most English people, however. With five per cent of its labour force English-born in 1880, Center township contained about two-thirds of the 150 English immigrants who had settled in Russell County. The mention of a Christmas party for the children at their school house was the only reference Mrs Bond made to a social occasion. More assimilated into her environment of the 'light' Kansas air than she was to American society, she relied greatly upon her children for companionship.

Catherine's older sister, Ann, fell in love with an Irish railway labourer, Pat Moran, whom she met while she was in service in Lancashire. The family in Lancashire disapproved of this liaison. Pat Moran went out first to Grafton, West Virginia, where he had relatives. This town in Taylor County in the north central part of the state was the largest town in the county, with a population of 1,987 in 1870. Pat Moran worked at first on the railways, but by 1880 he had established a blacksmith shop and thus secured his independence.

When Ann became pregnant, the family let her go to Grafton to marry Pat, and her brother James accompanied her. In 1861, James Grayston had still been living in his father's household, working as an agricultural labourer. When he arrived in West Virginia, he worked as a railway labourer with his brother-in-law, but during the depression of the seventies he was unable to secure steady work. He married Pat Moran's sister in time. He had come to a community which contained a lot of Irish immigrants, but very few English. Like the Morris family,

James Grayston moved west during a period of industrial unemployment in the east. He arrived in Russell County, Kansas, in September 1878. When the census was taken in 1880, he and his family were living near the Bonds, James working as a brickmaker, but with hopes of becoming a farmer. Since his Irish wife objected to the want of a Catholic Church (and, it would seem, did not get on too well with Catherine Bond) James was forced to retreat eastward as far as Bates County, Missouri. There as a teamster in the brickyards, employing his own team, James Grayston achieved a kind of independence.

This was a family in which the urge to emigrate was not the result of absolute hardship or of absence of economic opportunity in the immediate neighbourhood from which the emigrants came. Migration was a way of contracting out of adaptation in the neighbourhood. A social attitude which condemned working for others and a prejudice against Irish Catholics combined to push these three families to America. Catherine and James Bond and James and Catherine Grayston never seem to have become part of a community in America. In their loneliness, they kept up contacts with the family in England. Grayston's last letter, in which he emphasized the importance of brothers and sisters staying together, is particularly interesting from this standpoint.

The Grayston and Bond letters have recently been given by their owner, Miss Jessie Thompson, to the Lancashire Record Office, and are reproduced with her kind permission. Copies have been in the Collection of Regional History at Cornell (861) since 1949. Though few of the letters are dated, the dates when they were written may be estimated roughly from Catherine Bond's regular references to the age of her son, Robert, who was born at Sefton, Lancashire, in July 1869.

Letters from Catherine Bond to relatives in Lancashire

Milford, Conn., 5 July 1870

MY DEAR BROTHER,

You will thinck me unkind not to write before now but I shal beg forgiveness and hope you will not be so long in answering mine. You will be surprised to hear that we have got James Berry here.* He is living with us and likes very well. It is a splended country and we all have our health so far. . . . [Her baby, Robert] Yesterday was a great day here. It was the day they keep in memory of the proclamation of independence. There was fireworkes and guns like we have on the four November. You

---

* James Berry, twenty, farmer, born in England, was enumerated in 1870 in the household of James Bond.

wished to know if our master was a Yankey or an English man. He is a Yankey, but I think his parents was English. He is a real nice man. If there was plenty like him in England there would not be so many poor people. He is keeping the farmer on this year, for Mr Fowler was to have sent him a man in January so he did not thinck it rite to turn him away when he had gone so far in his year. But it will be a great expence to him for their is nothing growing on the farm and thar is 160 acres of land and fourteen cows and two oxen and three horses and about eighty sheep and he will have to buy food for them all winter. You wish to know how far we are of New York and I should thinck we are something like being at the Isle of Man from Liverpool. The steam boat comes every other day from N York. I have had a letter from sister Ann. She says we shall be about five hundred miles from where she is.* But that is not thought far in this country. How is brother Robert getting on? You did not say anything about him in your letter. Tell him this is the country for them if he gets spliced. The Yankes tell us if there would more English they could send some Irish back. Tell my Father we are a great deal better of than being at Sefton for we have all our wages clear and no expence. . . . [Write] Your affectionate sister,

C. BOND

[Letter of 5 July 1870 to sister, Sarah Grayston, omitted]

Milford, Conn., 11 Oct. [1870?]

MY DEAR BROTHER, . . . [Letters received]

. . . . have been kept very busy the last three month. The master [family] has gone back to day and Bobby and me has to go to their house in Philadelpha for a week in a fortnight from now. He took the young ladies and me and Bobby for a drive this morning. Their is not such scenery in England as their is here. But they dont come up to England in farming. If they did their would not be a country like this. . . . [Fishing] You whished to know if we had any [churches?] here. We have three just over the river, but no Roman Catholic. They will not have any their. . . . I will write as soon as we come back and will send something for father . . . [Greetings] Your loving sister,

KATE BOND

Milford, Conn., 1 Dec. 1870

DEAR ELEN, . . . [Letter and son, Bobby]

It is not winter here yet, but the Master tells me that it is very severe when it comes. He has given me two pairs of drawers and two wollen

* This is a reference to Ann Moran, living in Taylor County, West Virginia

stockens for this winter and the Mrs has given me a black scarf shalle for a Christmas present. I had a real nice time of it when I was at the Masters. He took me to the cemetry where his first wife was burried. We was too soon for the train so he took me for a drive in the city. Then he went with me to West Chester 30 miles out of Philadelphia to see a dairy. I staid their 2 days and then went back to his house. They churn with horse power and the Master has one to churn and cut hay and wood. I went to Church last Sunday for the first time since I was at Aughton. Jim took me acros in the boat and Boby in his carriage, for J.Berry was in his sulks. He is often in them. I thinck he will not stop long here. The master is paying him 25 dollars a month. That is a pound a week and board. Is the new Church finished yet? It will be Christmas when you get this. I suppose you will be having a gay time of it their. I dont know what sort we shall have here for we have not got acquantied with any one yet. The Yankes are very distant peopel. They dont thinck much of John Buls, but we have lots of mutton and the master said we was to kill a young pig for Christmas. So we dont care much about them. . . . [Write] Affectionately,

KATE BOND

DEAR BROTHER,

I must not forget to tell you that Jim has begun plowing after his team of long tails. The master is quite pleased. He says he is the best ploughman he has ever seen and he thinck three times more of him. Now I sent sister Sarah a five dollar bill. I hope she will get it for I can send it better that way than English money. I would have to get it registred and have to go to Bridgeport. I am sending a two dollar bill in this for father. It will buy them something for Christmas day. We have plenty and want for nothing. . . .

YOUR LOVING SISTER

Milford, Conn., 30 Dec. 1871

DEAR ELLEN, . . . [Having children vaccinated, though it is not compulsory as in England. Asks for news]

I dare say you will have heard that Berry has gone back home. We heard he had got safe their. You will see us coming some day, but not yet for we shall never come back to work for our living. But Jim tels me when we have been here five years I may go back and see you all. But I am quite settled hear. Our Master has taken some pigeons to the show and Jim is to have the prise they get. . . . [Greetings] Your ever affectionate freind,

KATE BOND

Milford, Conn., 11 July 1872
DEAR BROTHER, . . . [Aunt Ann's death. The children]

It is haytime and we have a first rate crop, more than the stock will [use] this year, and they have always had to buy before and their is plenty of fruit to. But it is so very hot now the men can hardly stand out to work in the midle of the day. . . . [Asks about brother Jim] Is father with Martin yet? I often thinck of him when I see our old gardener here. He has such nice times and gets his 50 dollers a month, and father is working from morning than 9 and 10 at night for a good deal less than that and he is a older man than father and not as good a gardener. But this is his last year here. The Master is building a new house here for himself. He will be living here next year. He is giving up buisness. It is a large house build of brick, but he is going to have painted. But I thinck it will spoil the looks of it for it is build of patent brick. . . . [Asks about brothers Isaac and Peter] from your loving sister,

KATE BOND

Milford, Conn., 3 Sept. 1872
DEAR BROTHER, . . . [Photographs]

Our Master is on here now and a freind of his has been asking him if he knew of a man and his wife that could take the management of a farm. Their is a very large dairy and his wife will have to take the charge of it. But it is a good place. He asked for Richard that was here, but you know he is single and no sings [thinks] of being married; and I thought if you was thincking of being married it would be a good opening for you. It will be no less than a hundred a year, I know, and that is better than a farm in England, for their is no loss and if you are carefull you may have a farm of your own in a few years. The farm is about half way betwen our Ann and us and we could go their in a day and that is not thought far in this country. I would not miss the chance if I was you. I know it has been a good thing for us coming here for if we had stayed in England we should only have got a living and scarcly that and here we can get everything we want and save plenty of money. Jim told me to write to you. It will be spring when the other man leaves. He has been their a good while and has got tired. I suppose he has enough to start for himself. I dare say Father will not like you to leave him, but if you come if I was in your place I would bring Sarah and him on with you. I dont know wether one woman can do all herself, but you will only have your own family in the house. Please to write to us soon so we can give the master an answer. But I hope you will come for you may never get such a chance again.

I thinck Jim will be on this winter. He cant be spared now for their is so much work going on here and in the winter there will not be any men working here so it will be the best time to go. . . . [About brother and sister] If Isaac had not had such a large family it would have been a good chance for them, but I dont know whether they will like children or not. Any how if you dont make up youre mind to come it would be a charty to help Isaac, for he will always be a poor man where he is. Write soon if you dont wish to come. We will ask for Isaac and send you full paticualrs next time. With kind love Elen and yourself, I remain your loving sister,

C. BOND

Milford, Conn., 22 Dec. 1872

DEAR ELEN, . . . [Bad roads prevent them from going to Church]

I have not been off the place since the 28 off last month. That was Thanckgivings day. It is a great day here, as much as Christmas day in England. We went to a freind of ours. They are an English family. They are sevearl here. I dare say you will thinck that Jim does not mean coming, but he has to wait than the workmen have finished in the house. He is quite disapointed for he thought of having his Christmas in Old England. I dont know when he will start, but I thinck it will be in two or three weeks at the latest.

I had a long letter from Peter Taylor last week. He gives a very bad acount of the weather and the crops. I am afraid it will be a hard winter for the poor folks. I wonder if the gentleman has written to Isaac yet. I gave Mr Hubbell his address. I did not ask him before spring. It will be a good place for him if he can get it, and Jane is very foolish for if she stands in his light. I know it has been a good thing for us coming here. I dont regret it, for we have all we want and are very comfortable. The only [regret is that] we are so far from our freinds, but we must not thinck to always be with them. We can write to each other and wherever our lot on earth is cast the[re] is the same God and I trust a meeting in Heaven to look forward to where we shall never part. I thinck that is it that makes me so contented here though I have my children for company. . . . [About children] from your Afectionate Freind,

KATE BOND

Milford, Conn., 24 May [1873?]

DEAR BROTHER. . . . [No letters]

You will be surprised to hear that we have left Mr Hubbell. Jim has been shad fishing since he left, but will be through with it in two weeks more. Then he is going out to Kansas where I hope he will buy a farm;

for the next time we move I hope will be to stay for good. We have got another little one, a boy. We have called him John after Jims father. . . . [Asks about relatives] I should very much like to see you all again. But it is hard to say weather I shall or not for we shall be two thousand miles further out if Jim buys land out at Kansas, but if we do well there I can see no reason why I cant visit you. He can get 160 acres of land at 5 dollars an acre and there are plenty going now. If we could get brother Jim along with us I thinck it would be a good thing for us both, for Jim is doing nothing where he is and if we can get along together he will have a chance to start for himself in a few years and it will be company for us both. . . . [Asks about brothers] Your loving sister,

KATE BOND

Milford, Conn., 28 Nov. [1874?]

DEAR BROTHER. . . . [Letters received. Children]

Last Saturday the children and me went over to the grave yard to look at Johnnies grave. I cant forget the little fellow though I know he is far better off and happier than I could make him, but he went from us so quick. You say there is a great many dying around you. It is the same here and very sudden too. Last week a man was out peddeling one day and died the next. He worked here two years. How many children has brother Peter? Sarah told me he burried one lately. . . . [Would like to see them] We are very glad to hear that Isaac is doing so well. . . . [Children and requests for news of relatives] Jim seems in good heart and if times would only brisk up I thinck he will do well, but every thing is so slack everywhere. Last week was Thanckgiveing here. It is kept all over the country and is as much thought of as Christmas. We had a turkey for dinner. We always have one for Thanckgiveing. I have all the fowl to pluck so I have got me a nice feather bed. . . . [Greetings] from your loveing sis,

KATE BOND

Three letters from James Grayston to his sister in Lancashire

Grafton, W. Va., 29 July 1877

DEAR SISTER, . . . [Letter received]

I am glad you like your new place so well. I am sure it must be very plesant were there is so much music every day. I have not heard a good band of music since I left old England. I am same as you in regard to Aughton. I think there is know place like it – at least I have not seen it yet. . . . [About relatives] What kind of time have you got in England

8

now? It is very dull here. Will, Pat and me as been out of work for five weeks, but is going to start a shop of us own, for the railroad is nothing to depend on now days. All the railroads are on strike and there is nothing at all a doing. Everything is stoped, not in this place only, but all over the country. There is nothing runing but the passenger trains. They reduced the pay of the men on the first of the month so the majority of them struck work and [they] would not let them work that would work. You ought to have seen the commotion last Sunday. One of the bosses & an engineer succeded in geting out a freight train, what you call a goods train in England, & the strikers went after them & brought it back, the train; but they did not get the men as they left the train standing over the track and hid in the wood. The best thing they could have done, for the strikers took a rope with them to hang them if they caught them which they would have done, for they run into the train with the engine that they follow them with and heard three of the strikers. I was on the platform when they ran on and was talking to one of them and he swore they would have hung them if they had caught them. I am sending you a paper with all the news of the strike in it. I must now conclude with kind love from Kate & myself and a kiss from the children. We remain your aff brother & siss,

J. AND C. GRAYSTON

Grafton, W. Va., 27 June 1878

MY DEAR SISTER, . . .

I dare say you will think it strange that I have not wrote to you before now, but I have been waiting to send you better news; but I have not as I have not had any constant work since last June. I have been working on the saw mill for a few weeks, but we have run out of logs so that I am doing nothing but working at home. I have taken a three years lease of a few acres of land & put up a house on it. I get it for clearing it, so that I have no rent to pay nor fire to buy as we have plenty of wood to burn. Work is still very dull here & in fact all over the cuntry. . . . [Aunt Margaret's death] Were are you living now? Are you all together yet? You answer let me know when you write again. I had a letter from Sister Kate a short time ago. They all very well, but she say they onley just making a living now, but that is more than a great many is doing. Sister Ann husband is doing very well in his shop. He has all the work he can do. . . . [Asks about brothers and father] I remain your loving Brother,

J. GRAYSTON. . . .

Bunker Hill, Russell County, Kansas, 26 Jan. 1879

DEAR SISTER, . . . [Letter received]

Suppose you know that I have got out to Kansas. We come here in September. It is a fine country, no trees to bother you, nothing but the wild prarie but is splendid for growing wheat. We are living with Sister Kate at present. There is plenty of work out here, but I am going to farm with James this year. Next year I expect to have a place of my own. We like it out here very well. It is a very healthy. . . . [Have another son] Kate & Jim is quite aristocrats, at least they would think themselves so if they were in England and had a hundred & sixty acers of land and a house of their own & twenty acers of wheat, two horses, and a cow and kill all our own game, plenty of hares, rabbits, prairie chickens, geese & wild duck. . . . [More about deaths in England] I see by the papers that there is hard times in England. Hope they wont last long. I think the worse of the times is over here. . . . [Relatives] We are about twelve hundred miles farther west, a long way is not? But as I told you before it is a fine country and land is chiep. You can buy it for fifteen to twenty shillings a acer. . . . [Greetings] from your loving brother & sister,

J. AND C. GRAYSTON

Letters from Catherine Bond to relatives in Lancashire

Bunker Hill, Kansas, 26 June [1881?]

DEAR BROTHER, . . .

We have had two very bad years out here, but we have pulled through them and this year is better so far. We are very busy harvesting wheat. Ours is very good, but some is very light. I thinck there is a great deal in putting it in. Jim has got a self binder. He has cut his own and has ninety acres to cut on the next claim as his machine has paid for itself. If we have as good crops every year we shall do well. Jim is going to build a barn this fall if all keeps well. He has the stone ready as he has only the timber and labour to pay for, and I thinck the wheat ought to do it. How is the crops in England? In some states here there is nothing with the dry weather and in some they are flooded out. . . . Hundreds are destitute and the farms ruined. We are needing rain here now for the corn is suffering. It is so hot that it dries so qu[i]ck. But it looks like a storm. We have very heavy thunder storms here, but you can get used to them. I like a Western life. They have kept me busy the last three weeks, for the men have gone out at five in the morning and left me with cows pigs and all to see to. We had one sow had six little ones and she killed every one. But we have two more to come in. Yet we may have too many if the corn crop fails more than we can seed. But if the corn does well it pays better to feed pigs than sell corn. Meat is a good price now. We killed severl last winter and we have most of the meat yet to sell. You have to smoke your meat here for sale, but for our own use we have it like Old England. I wonder if I shall ever see Old England again. . . . [Children and relatives] I have not heard from either Jim or Ann since Jim left here. He was in Kansas City last I heard. His house that he build when he left us is there yet and I dont thinck he has got paid for it yet. He sold it to the miners. He will do well if ever he gets the money unless there is a great change. Jims wife did not like the prarie. There was no Catholic Chapel and there is very few Irish round here, but there is plenty of English.* But she has got where ther is plenty of Irish and Chapels too. I often wonder what mother would have thought if she had been liveing and could have seen his wife as I saw her. None of you see her after marriage. Than is the time to know what they are. She has Jim as good a Catholic as herself. All his children are christened at chapel. . . . [Children] Our children have no notion of singing, but I blame the schools for that. There is no singing like there is England. . . . your loveing sister,

KATE BOND

Bunker Hill, Kansas, 4 July [1884?]
DEAR SISTER AND BROTHER, . . . [Children]

I would very much like to see Old England again, but I am afraid I never shall. Bob also talks of going when he grows up, but he may change his mind. Jim and Bob are away harvesting. They will not be home for a week yet. We have very heavy wheat crops this year. We have had very heavy rains all spring. Every thing looks well. They head most of the grain here; 20 acres a day is about what they cut. Jim has a wire binder of his own, but he thought Bob was not strong enough, to shock and pitch the bundels and men are so scarce you cant get hands enough, so they go with a header and our own 3 horses. We had them one day and we shall have them 3 days next week. We have two kinds, one earlier than the other. I wish you could see them. Maggie and me have enough to do home. We have six cows to milk, 8 pigs and about 2 hundred chickens; but they are no trouble for there is wheat enough round on the ground to feed them.

We have 22 head of cattle, but we only milk six of them and sell the cream. Butter is 2 cent a pound. Thats a penny your money. Cream is 10 cents a inch, so it pays better and not near the work. I wish you was

---

* There were only five Irish working people returned in Center Township in 1880 as compared with twenty-three English, most of whom were farmers and farm labourers.

out here and fixed on a farm. We have had very poor crops the last two years, but still it was better than working for another. . . . [Relatives and their children] Give our love to father. I wanted to send him something for Christmas, but I was sick in bed. We had a little boy born the 23 of December. He lived to be eight weeks old. As soon as harvest is over and things straight I will not forget him. We have not wanted for any thing, but it has been all trade, no money stiring. . . . [Please write] Your loveing sister,

KATE BOND

Bunker Hill, Kansas, 9 Jan. [188 ?]

DEAR BROTHER, . . . [Apologies for not writing]

I wish we was nearer so that we could see each other some times. I feel lonely many a time so far from you all. We left to better ourselves, but some times I thinck we should have done as well if we had stayed. We have our own home and our children are all with us; but there is a lot of care. Last year the crops was a failure and there is the expences to meet just the same.

There is no sale for any thing. We have over forty head of cattle and six horses. They are a lot of work. Jim thought of selling some last fall, but he could not get what it cost to raise them. The market was glutted. The drought has been so bad in the Eastern states that there was neither water or feed, so they crowded their stock into market. But I thinck by spring there will be a change. . . . [Health and weather] I had a letter from brother Jim a few weeks since. He was well and seems to be doing well. He was working in the Brickyard and two of his boys with him. He has two horses. I have not heard from sister Ann for a long time now. Tell your little folks that their was a Christmas tree at the school house for the children. An Christmas Eve all of ours young ones went there. Lots of presents hung on the tree. I dont know weather you have them trees or not for the young folks. . . . [Sympathy and best wishes] From your Affectionate sister,

CATHERINE BOND

Bunker Hill, Kansas, 1888

DEAR BROTHER, . . . [Apologies]

There is one thing, Robert, that I have thanked God for many a time since you wrote me of father's death and that is that I had a father that tried to teach us to do what is right to all, our enemies as well as our freinds. If it had not been so things might have been worse for us today. Jim or me did not thinck we had any enemies until they set fire to our wheat stocks last fall and burnt a good part of it. There are not very good neighbours when they do that. It was a big loss. It made me feel bad to see all that wheat burn and hundreds wanting bread. But we have not wanted for food. There is good prospects for wheat and rye so far and we have had good rains this spring. You asked what sort of a country this was. It is all right for any one that has money, but for any one that has to work his way it is no place as things are now. If we was to sell all we have should not have what we brought from Connecticut after working all these years. I often tell Jim we should have more pleasure of our life if we lived in Old England even if he only had his days labour for he got payed for it but we work many a month and dont get any pay. Last year we had not a ear of corn out of all planted. We had to buy all our grain for our horses. More than half the people have left Russell County.* They mortgaged their farms to live and could not pay the intrest or mortgage and have gone out with nothing to try and get work to live. All the towns in the Eastern states are full of men wanting work. Our Bob left home last Nov. He has been running an engine in a lumber camp in Colorado. I don't thinck he will come home to stay any more. He has got discontented and says there is nothing made farming. . . . I remain your loveing sister,

KATE BOND

Bunker Hill, Kansas, 5 July [1890?]

DEAR BROTHER,

I will now take the pleasure of writing to you. Jim and Bob are away harvesting. Jim and a neighbour own a header between them, so they work together. It takes eight horses and seven men to run one so you see when two work together it goes better. They have cut ours. They was four days. They is poor crops of wheat this year. It will hardly pay for cutting and thrashing. We have had very little rain this year. I suppose you have heard of Maggies death.† I miss her so much now that they are away. They dont come home at night and it is so lonely without her. But I supose we should have parted if she had lived and perhaps it is better as it is, for I know where she is now and wants for nothing. She give herself up at the begining and I thinck that made it worse, for the medcine took no efect on her. But she was ready and willing to go and missed a troblesome world. How is your boy getting on. I often thinck of you. It seems to all come back today. Yesterday was Bobs birthday.

---

* Actually the population of Russell County simply remained stationary during the eighties, which meant some outward movement. Center Township, where the Bonds had settled, did lose about a third of its population, however. It declined from 1,619 people in 1880 to 1,170 in 1890. So Mrs Bond was more accurate about the situation in their immediate neighbourhood.

† Her daughter, Maggie, born in Connecticut in 1871.

He is twenty one. How the times goes. He is well and strong now, but he had a hard pull. Jim is not so strong as he used to be. He had a spell of sickness and pulled him down and last winter. He had to take care of the stock and Bob was sick and not fit for work much this spring. But he seems more content at home now. . . . [Greetings] [Letter not signed]

Bunker Hill, Kansas, 3 Feb. 1891

DEAR BROTHER AND SISTER, . . . [Apologies]

Bob and me went on a visit to Virginia. Ann and her family are well. I dont see much change in either [her] or Pat only they are older like myself. We had a very nice time while we were there only it rained nearly all the time and here we dont have rain once a month or once in three months. We have had snow on the ground for two weeks, but it is gone and the frost is severe yesterday and last night was a fissler. It frose the water in the kettle on the stove. Today it is pleasant. That is the wor[s]t of Kansas. It is so changeable. We stoped at Kansas City to see brother Jim. Jim looks little and old. He has worked hard at brick-making and last winter he had the chills all winter and the boys too. They had been working on the bottoms where it is always damp and mudy. He was hauling coal when we came back, but it is heavy work. He has a good team of his own. He had his back hurt and he is as humpt back as Cousin Jim Grayston. But he is in good spirits and thincks he will rent some land and grow garden truck. His two boys are both able to help him. . . . [Sister Sarah's impending visit] From your affectionate Sister,

KATE BOND

Bunker Hill, Kansas, 21 August [1891?]

DEAR BROTHER AND SISTER,

We received your welcome letter. We was glad to hear from you, but sorry to hear of your loss. For I know it is a loss that none but a mother can feel. But, Ellen, when the first pain is over you will thanck God in your heart that it has pleased Him to take him out of this world of sin and sorrow. He has been a great sufferer as you say and he must have had the best of care or he could not have lived as long as he did. I dont know how you have kept up so long. But it seems as though there is extray strength given us for our trials. The other children will miss him, I know, but you must try not to fret too much for their sakes. Peter is in Heaven and at rest and it is those that are here that need our care now. If it had not been for my younger ones I thinck they would have laid me beside her before now. So thinck of yours now and it will help you in your trouble. . . . [Impending visit of Sister Sarah] I would have sent you the money now, but Jim sold his corn to our neighbours that had none and they would pay him when they thrashed and we have to keep a little money to work on. We may get it in a little while, but I did not want to wait so long before I wrote to you. We have plenty of every thing. We have good crops. It has been a good year for wheat, but there is a good deal spoiled in stacking. The weather was so wet. . . . [Asks for news] Your loveing sister,

KATE BOND

Bunker Hill, Kansas, [Spring, 1892?]
DEAR BROTHER AND SISTER, . . . [Sister Sarah's five month visit]

I could never go to England to live now after being here in Kansas. The air is so light here. I supose you will be planting potatos by this time. We shall plant some this week. Wheat looks green now, but two weeks since you could not see it. But it grows so fast here. . . . [Sickness in England] We have our troubles and there is a time for us all if we are only ready when the time comes. We are a great way apart from each other. Still I always feel the same affection for all of you though I know we shall never meet here on earth, yet I feel shure we shall in heaven. It was that thought that kept me up when I lost Maggie. Its only for a little while and theres work for me here or I should not be left here. . . . [Greetings] Your loveing sister,

KATE BOND

Bunker Hill, Kansas, 14 Oct. 1897
DEAR BROTHER,

You will be sorry to hear of my husbands death. He died on the 2 of Oct. He had been suffering for a long time with Brights Desease and Diabetes. He has wasted to nothing but skin and bones. I had seen for a long time he would never get well and he knew it himself. He plenty of time to prepare for the change that he knew was coming. The last words he said was its all right. He has been a good father and a kind husband and has left a good home for us. Bob has come home, so the boys will work the farm and keep every thing together. The children are all grown, but Jim he is only eleven. He is going to school, and Sarah too. She is sixteen, but they go to school longer hear. . . . [Asks for news] Your loveing sister,

CATHERINE BOND

Bunker Hill, Kansas, 7 June [1898 ?]
MY DEAR SISTER, . . . [Consoles her in loss of her husband]

I would like to see you, but I shall never leave Kansas. This is my home as long as I am on this earth so we must look forward to the meeting in a better world. This life is not for long for either of us at the longest. I have not heard from Sister Sarah for a long time or Ann either.

I had a letter from brother Jim last week. Bob wrote for his boy to come and help them harvest, but Peter is married so Tom is coming. We are asking for him this week. The wheat crop is heavy and hands are scarce. There is great many gone to Cuba. . . . [Her eyes failing] from your loveing sister,

KATE BOND

Bunker Hill, Kansas, [1899 ?]

MY DEAR NIECE, . . . [Letters]

We have had a very severe winter here, and a long one [compared] to what we most always have. Some people have lost a good deal of stock but ours are looking well. We have forty head of cows and calves and eight horses. But there is nothing to do but take care of the stock in winter here. You say you are teaching school. Our Sadie is going to school. She is trying to get through with the examination. She is 17 years old, but there is only six month school here. We never have any school in the winter. But our children have better learning than we had. You are doing better than hireing out as we did for nine and ten pounds a year. . . . [Wants letters and news] . . . this is my home now as long as I live. If it is Gods will to spare me untill Jim grows up. He is 13 years old. But I thinck they have it tougher in this country than in England if they are left to do for themselves. Jim is going to school now, but when it is out he will work with the boys on the farm. . . . [Greetings] from your loveing Aunt,

CATHERINE BOND

Letter from James Grayston to his niece in Lancashire

Rich. Hill, Bates Co., Mo., 4 June 1899

MY DEAR NEICE,

I received your letter some time ago anounceing the loss of your dear Mother and was very sorry to hear it for it is a sad loss to be left without those you love best in this world, but we must all go sometime when it pleaes the Lord to call us away. I hope you and your sister and brother are getting along well together. You must try and stay together if you can for it will be better then being seperated. I hope your brother has got a good possition where he is working. If he has you will get along allright, but it not be like having your father & mother with you. How

8*

is your Aunt Jane and Uncle Peter getting along? I never hear from them at all. I suppose they are still living in Aughton yet. Remember me kindly to them and tell them I would like to hear from them. I got a letter from your Aunt Sarah today. She is staying with your Ant Kate Bond in Kansas, that is about three hundred miles west of where we live. I suppose you would think that a long way in England, but this is a great country and it does not seem so far. I will now close for this time, hopeing you all well as this leaves all here at present. . . . [Greetings] I remain your aff Uncle

JAMES GRAYSTON

P S Many thanks for the funeral card you sent me. J G

PART II

TRAMPING ARTISANS: IMMIGRANTS IN
INDUSTRY

1

How Typical are the Letter-Writers?

The first census to compile statistics of immigrant occupations, that of 1870, reported forty-seven per cent of the English and Welsh immigrants and forty-six per cent of the Scots as engaged in manufacturing, mechanical and mining jobs. Since industrial workers do not make up anything like half of the writers of letters which have been found, they are under-represented in the surviving documents. Yet what we do know about the distribution of British immigrants in the States before those first occupational statistics were published for 1870 suggests that a smaller share of those in the country in 1840 had entered industrial occupations. The fact that more letters survive from people who emigrated during the first half of the nineteenth century, when more migrants were going into farming, helps explain the paucity of letters from industrial workers.[1]

The British immigrants formed a much larger share of the labour force in certain basic industries – mining, textile manufacture of all kinds, iron and steel manufacture and engineering – than they did of the labour force as a whole in 1870. They also made up an inordinately large share of the labour force in a few smaller industries which were also well developed in Britain. Among brass-founders, potters, copper workers, tool and cutlery makers, the British were conspicuous.[2] Unfortunately the surviving emigrant letters tell us little about the transfer of skills and techniques associated with the industrial revolution from Britain to America. The letter-writers were not part of an elite cadre of advanced industrial workers. We have no manuscripts from English or Scottish workmen in American iron and steel plants; only one small collection has been found from a coal miner; and most of the textile operatives whose letters we have made the adaptation to power-driven machinery after they went to the United States.[3] Even the group of Sheffield cutlers to whom we are introduced found a more highly mechanized industry in Connecticut than the one they left. The letter-writers may be characterized more aptly as bringing pre-industrial skills to America. We have letters from a carpenter, a sign painter, handloom weavers, a tailor, knife cutlers, a stone quarrier, a lead miner and a coal miner, a brush-maker, a flax hackler, a piano maker and a cabinet-maker. None of these occupations was a nineteenth-century creation, an occupation closely associated with industrial changes taking place in England. Thus the letter-writers were not spreading new industrial skills in the American labour force, although in so largely agricultural an economy as that of the United States, their specialized pre-industrial skills were useful and valuable. Several of these migrants entered factories for the first time after they arrived in America. Through the letters we learn something about the adaptation of a few industrial workers with traditional handicraft skills to growth and change on both sides of the Atlantic.

Other immigrant letter-writers who entered industrial jobs in the States had no previous industrial training before they emigrated.[4] They form part of the evidence that many British immigrants who came to work in America's basic industries did not have the full craft qualifications which would have given them an entrée to the best jobs in British industry, or came as boys and learned their trades in the United States. Take, for example, the case of Henry Edward Price who had spent most of his youth in the workhouse in Warminster, Wiltshire. One day a carpenter, in need of an apprentice, had come to the workhouse and selected Price for a trial period of a year. But, as Price recounted in his autobiography, the man did more gardening, coal selling and shop-keeping than carpentering, and he sent Price back to the workhouse when the parish stopped paying eighteen pence a week for him. In 1842, an unskilled worker of eighteen years of age with a keen desire to become a cabinet-maker, Price arrived at his grandmother's house in New York City. In New York he managed to pick up some knowledge of the trade from a German cabinet-maker and worked in several other shops, each of which specialized in the making of one article of furniture. After eight years in America, his training was hardly equivalent to a proper apprenticeship, as he found when he returned to London and tried to find work as a cabinet-maker. After six weeks he found a job but

noticing that i poughed the Drawer Sides for the bottoms as we used to in America [the boss] told me I had split them. Left job after 3 days & found another with a cabinet maker making cases for pianos. I was to clean up the ends, then to mould doors. Having got them in as I thought all right, He examined them. Its not exactly the thing says he I told him I thought they were all right What is the mater with them with that he brings a piece of silvered glass and places it behind the metres of course the silver could be seen through the joint . . . he told me I should not do for London shops. You had better go back to New York. . . .[5]

Because so much attention has been paid to the transfer of industrial technology from Britain to America by way of immigrants, these letter-writers with traditional skills, or no skills, might seem to be quite untypical of the English emigrants to the United States. Yet if one looks at occupations given in port records, rather than at occupations returned by English or Scottish-born inhabitants to census enumerators, the two most important groups of skilled immigrants were building trades workers and miners, who together made up more than a third of the skilled emigrants from Britain during the last half of the nineteenth century. The building trades workers, though not the miners, are fairly well represented among letter-writers. The letters introduce us to somewhat neglected aspects of the emigration of industrial workers, and these obscure migrants may be more typical than are the more famous British immigrants who helped teach Americans new industrial techniques.[6]

The letter-writers were certainly typical in the dates they emigrated. Almost without exception they left Britain during years of high emigration: 1819, 1829-35, 1839-42, 1848-53, 1857, and 1882. Most of them emigrated during the first mass exodus of the late forties and early fifties. As the century wore on, not only did more British immigrants go into industrial occupations in America, but also a larger share of those arriving gave their occupations as common labourers. The fact that less skilled people, from both industry and the countryside, the kind of people who would have had neither the resources nor the information to emigrate unaided during the first half of the century, constituted a larger share of emigrants after 1850 partly explains the dearth of letters from emigrants in the last half of the century. As the volume of emigration grew, the emigrating individual from any particular town or family became less extraordinary. His action was not so much in the nature of an adventure into the unknown. Similarly, as information about shipping and about the American labour market became more widely available in the press, the information provided in letters became increasingly superfluous and was no longer to be treasured by family members who were themselves undecided about emigration.

Most of the literate immigrants who wrote these letters came from in or near growing industrial centres rather than from agricultural villages in the less developed parts of Britain. Henry Edward Price who emigrated from Wiltshire, George Martin, a carpenter from Sevenoaks, Kent, and George Fewins, another carpenter who left a village in Devonshire about 1850 are the only representatives from regions of rural exodus whose experiences can be chronicled from these materials. The largest group of letter-writers came from the textile and metal-working cities of the West Riding of Yorkshire, the county which had shown the highest rate of emigration at the time of the 1841 census.

These Yorkshire cases were concentrated in the mid-century period, from 1839 to 1853, precisely when the mix of industries was changing in this region, and new methods of working were spreading rapidly through the traditional woollen manufacture. The other towns represented among the emigrants whose letters we have were also relatively late starters, as compared with Lancashire, in industrial change: Brighouse, Yorkshire; Kirkcaldy in Fife; Shrewsbury, Shropshire; North Shields, Northumberland and London itself. No letters from emigrants from decaying industrial towns have been found, and only two collections of letters from workers in Lancashire industry. Like the few agricultural labourers whose letters we have, most of these industrial workers left regions of growth and change, where alternative opportunities were by no means absent in their own neighbourhoods. Unfortunately, there is no comprehensive way of assessing the representativeness of such regions as origins of industrial emigrants to the United States.

2

Motives for Emigration

Economic considerations dominated the migration of most of these industrial workers. In this respect, these people were more similar to farmers and agricultural labourers who became farmers in America than they were to the urban and industrial workers who changed their occupations to try farming after they emigrated. But before discussing the nature of their economic impulses, something needs to be said about the distinctively non-economic considerations which influenced some of them.

Those emigrants who did write in such a way as to reveal non-economic motives left England during the same years as did the urban people who went into agriculture, during the twenties, thirties and forties; and they shared some of their attitudes. They wanted to make a complete break with their old way of life and to gain independence from employers. Some shared the belief that farming was the only sure route to independence.

Indeed, the political views of some of these industrial workers who emigrated before 1850 were both more explicit and more extreme than any encountered in the agriculture series. They shared the belief with many agriculturists that the government of England was tyrannical and that America was the land of liberty. While he was working in Oswego, New York, in 1847, Henry Edward Price, the would-be cabinet-maker, wrote verses about the 'land of freeborn men who spurn oppressions thrall'.[7] These industrial workers, however, tended to be more vitriolic in their denunciations of tyrants at home. Whereas a number of farmers feared revolution and sought to escape it, Abel Stephenson, a hand-loom weaver from Thurstoneland, near Huddersfield, who left a scene of Chartist agitation in 1838, assured his relatives from afar that acceptable changes could never be achieved by petition, only 'by dint of metal and steel'.[8] Just as thorough in his denunciation of both government and power-driven machinery was William Winterbottom, a carpenter who emigrated from nearby Saddleworth in 1840. Writing many years later to a cousin to defend and explain Luddism, he spewed forth – not altogether coherently – the bitterness he had felt:

In 1831 Earl Gray killed the old Borrow Mongers Cobden & Bright & steam looms that was then the best taxed people on earth tax from the cradle to the grave Even if you lived in a pig stye you must pay for light so old Edmund Sung in is songs, and as for Bright & Cobden did thay ever do one thing to better the sons of toil no never it all the Love of gain & Self reduced man to the level of a machiene when they had built there Big Factories. . . .[9]

Just as certain of the need for revolution in England, as late as 1848, was George Martin, a carpenter from Sevenoaks, Kent, though he objected more to the 'longnos'd gentry' than to the abominable machines.

More of these industrial immigrants of this period were interested in voting. '. . . [w]e was planted and reared on what we know to be a verry small Island furnished with Lords Barons Kings and we thare dependants & Subjects we had no say in the mater only work and Obay just animals.'[10] Some industrial workers explicitly referred to the fact that workingmen could qualify for a vote in the United States as a point in its favour.[11] Some had actually been in touch with political agitation at home before they emigrated. James Roberts, knife cutler, had been involved with Chartist agitation and knew some of the Chartist councillors in St George's Ward, Sheffield.

The industrial workers as a whole took more interest in political questions and more frequently discussed issues which did not directly touch their own interests. In this respect they differed from most of the farmers. Yet the emigrants of the twenties and thirties were distinctly more strident and dogmatic in their views than those of the fifties. While nothing suggests that any of them left England specifically for political reasons, their extremism in politics was linked with a want of faith in gradual change, which made them good candidates for cutting out completely from their own society. Though more extreme in their political views than the farmers, they shared the same hopelessness about the future in England.

Elements of an agrarian myth can also be found in the letters from industrial workers who emigrated during this period. Perhaps no one was more confident about the joys of subsistence farming than Jonas Booth, the son of a Bradford stuff manufacturer, an emigrant of 1829:

> The trade is very brisk in bed-ticking and calico but the farmer is the most independent. They grow all they want; they spin their own yarn and weave their own cloth and make their own soap and candles and makes their own sugar and molasses from a tree they call sugar maple.[12]

Some of these people even tried to gain independence through farming. Edward Phillips, who emigrated from Shropshire in 1817, remained as a woollen worker in Delaware only long enough to bring out his family and save for a farm. Abel Stephenson, who believed that no one should come to America except to farm, went so far as to buy land in Jefferson County, Iowa; but this village radical appears to have gotten cold feet once he arrived on his land in 1840. He left it to a brother, who had a family, to discover the joys of a farming life. Vestiges of the same beliefs can be seen in the letters of the tailor from Northumberland who encouraged his brother to bring his savings to put into western land, though Hails admitted the possibility that his brother might want to do this simply as a speculation. This was not the pure agrarian myth. The waning strength of the myth can also be seen in the letters of Titus Crawshaw, a wool finisher from Huddersfield, who went to Wisconsin in 1854, attracted by the farming idyll, but with little determination to realize it.

A brief encounter with the realities of farm work was enough to undermine Titus Crawshaw's vestigial agrarian dream. Discouraging reports like his, and those of some urban people who had a longer exposure to farming, perhaps helped destroy the myth of farming as a utopian final solution to problems of social and economic change. To these industrial workers farming was not the only avenue to independence, however. A shift in emphasis can be seen in the letters of Colin Houston, a textile worker from the Glasgow area, who flirted with emigration for many years. In 1851 he wrote to a cousin who had already emigrated: 'Dear Cousin it wold give me grate pleasaure to be with you and I hope the time will soon be when we will be together on a little farm of our own then we will be like the lords of old. . . .'[13] Thirteen years later, after one visit to Canada, Houston still half-wanted to emigrate. Independence was still a goal, but now there was no reference to a 'farm of our own'.

. . . the reson that I left Canada the truth was that I was a littel homesick and that is a very bad truble to be bothered with when from home but I am thinking by this time that I would have been better to have tried and made a home on your side of the world it is still in my mind that I would like to try something to be independent but there is littel chance here for that. . . .[14]

The letters included here tell part of the story of the unsuccessful efforts of Titus Crawshaw and Edward Phillips, both woollen workers, to go into business for themselves. Our Sheffield cutlers left jobs in which they were getting on swimmingly, to set up a co-operative factory. Some emigrants who remained in the employ of others – like George Martin who worked for a carpenter in Rochester, New York – felt it necessary to defend themselves for their failure to gain independence.[15] The persistence of the hope that emigration would make it possible to work on one's own is suggested by the misguided attempts of Ernest Lister, a London sign painter, to take contracts for himself in New York City in the early 1880s.

As the mid-century approached, when economic pressures to emigrate should have been somewhat reduced in England and Scotland, the motives for emigration suggested by migrants in their letters tended to become more purely economic. The change can be seen partly in a shift in attitudes towards the possibility of returning to Britain. Emigrants in agriculture, though often cherishing hopes of paying a visit home, usually migrated with the intention of remaining in America. So also the industrial workers of the early period, whose emigration had social and political overtones, expressed a determination to remain in the United States. This may have been partly because they had had difficult and dangerous Atlantic crossings in sailing vessels. Stephenson, who so hated power-driven machinery in the woollen industry, looked forward to the appearance of steam in Atlantic shipping. But their intention to remain in America was also consistent with their rejection of the tyranny of English life, as they saw it, and their hopes of becoming independent farmers. The new, more economically oriented immigrants did not go to the United States with the fixed intention of staying there. Even among those who did remain, the possibility of returning to Britain constituted an active alternative choice for a long time. They emigrated to see whether or not they did better than they had in Britain. After the mid-forties, industrial emigrants often appear to have left on a kind of speculation, whether times were good or bad. In fact, Colin Houston planned to come out if times remained brisk in 1851 because this would enable him to pay his passage.[16]

This is not to deny factors of economic push. The prospect of technological unemployment haunted Abel Stephenson. When John Ronaldson left Scotland in 1853, his trade of flax hackler was entering a short depression, and his occupation a real secular decline. Although new methods and machinery were not yet affecting skills in the traditional Sheffield metal trades in the late forties, the pocket-knife making branch, in which the Roberts family were employed, was seriously depressed when they emigrated. These people did not look about them for other work, but, like many of the agriculturists, emigrated to escape change, to try to remain in familiar occupations.

Complaints of poverty and distress before emigration were relatively rare, even among those who showed the greatest symptoms of economic motivation. Jane Martin, the wife of a piano maker, referred to the 'struggle we had to live in London' before they emigrated in 1851, but these people were not favourably impressed by the standard of living of the native Americans in Rochester, New York, and soon scurried back to London.[17] Joseph Hartley, a stone quarrier who left Brighouse, Yorkshire in 1857, had regarded his life as materially unsatisfactory before emigration and expressed classical economic drives when he wrote from Lockport, New York: 'i shall go where they are giving the most wages for i am bound to make money before i come back to england agen i am not going to come back as i left it.'[18] So far as we can tell, these people were economically ambitious and chafed at the want of prospects they envisaged in England or Scotland more than they suffered real want. This hope of economic advance seems to have been the single most important reason for emigration of industrial workers, at least from the forties onwards. Abel Stephenson referred to the 'gloomy prospect for a poor man before i left'; John Ronaldson thought his 'prospects are far from good in Scotland'; George Martin thought 'there is more chance for a man to do something for himself here than there is in England'.[19] 'I came away a little in debt,' wrote another, 'but if I had stayed it would have been worse.'[20] Just as strong potential motives for emigration were expressed by some individuals who did not go. Jane Peebles wrote to her father from Scotland that 'the Mill is not paying us very well this year and think Partick Mill will be don up altogether soon'.[21] She and her husband, an engineer, considered emigration, but did not go. So also Henry Edward Price, after he had returned from his eight-year sojourn in New York State and finally found a job in London, recorded that he kept working hard, paying debts, never losing an hour's work and at the end of fifty-two weeks was not forward at all. This inability to advance turned his thoughts to emigration again, and he said he would have gone if he could have raised the money. Once he lost heart in the struggle. When his wife had had smallpox, a baby had died, and the nurse had used their credit to run them into debt, he ran off to Portsmouth hoping to escape to America, but thought better of it.[22]

Thus the economic motivation of these people can be more accurately expressed as a hope of economic improvement, rather than a flight from impoverishment. Most of these people used all, or practically all, of their savings, to get themselves to American shores. Jonas Booth claimed to have arrived in New York City in 1829 with no cash. George Martin left Kent with thirty-seven pounds but had only five pounds remaining when he arrived at his destination. Richard Hails referred to having two pounds when he landed in Boston. John Ronaldson wrote that he arrived with seventeen shillings and six pence. A brushmaker from Mile End had only twenty-five shillings left when he landed in the port of New York in 1857.[23] Titus Crawshaw had to borrow to emigrate, and lived at the expense of a friend when he first arrived. Having invested their savings in the venture, only economic improvement could justify the speculation.

The outlines of their economic ambitions are seen more clearly when we notice that these industrial workers did not speak about getting a living or a livelihood as did the farmers. In fact, one immigrant weaver from Yorkshire, who was living in Fairfield, Iowa, in the sixties, expressed rather succinctly his dissatisfaction with an activity which brought in no more than a living when he noted that his brother, 'Samuel is not doing very well at farming. He is not more than making a living.'[24] Most of these men were not satisfied with their jobs unless they could save money. If they could get no more than a living from industrial work in the United States, the immigrant life was not worth the effort.

The specific aim of saving differed from one individual to another. Family responsibilities were one reason. Those who left wives and children behind in Britain saved in order to bring them over, or to return to Britain with a supply of cash. It seems quite clear, from the Crawshaw letters, that single men who went out to America were expected to continue to send money to their parents as they would have done had they remained at home. Joseph Hartley, like Titus Crawshaw, was nineteen and unmarried when he emigrated. His letters, for the first few years, were punctuated with this kind of apology: 'I shud like to send you sum Money but I donot see any chans this summer but I wil do my best to send you sum. . . .'[25] Similarly, Richard Hails, though he was married, sent money to try to help his brother keep their parents out of the workhouse. These responsibilities were felt more keenly by the economically motivated immigrants; our most bitter and alienated emigrant, Abel Stephenson, did not send the single remittance he once promised his father. This expectation on the part of parents, that their unmarried sons should provide them with remittances, may be one reason for the paucity of letters from industrial workers. Both Hartley and Crawshaw indicated that they neglected to write home when they could not send money. Workers who felt this as a duty which they could not, or did not want to, fulfil might simply cut themselves off on emigrating to satisfy their own economic ambitions without such awkward requests.

The other pronounced use of industrial savings was to get a house and garden. Linked with the hope of establishing security for old age, this aim might be fulfilled either in America or by returning to Britain with industrial earnings from America.[26] This dream was in a way parallel to the agriculturalists' confidence in land as providing a livelihood. It was connected with hopes of a future time of leisure, which was also to be independent. This seemed to be George Martin's idea when he urged his brother to keep his good job at Lord Stanhope's, to save as much as he could, and then to come to the States and invest it in such a way as to live with very little work.[27] It was also evident in Richard Hails's advice to his brother.

Although these people tried to be exemplary savers, none seemed to be aware of the Smilesean exhortations to workingmen to save in good times to tide them over the bad. In their overriding purpose of saving from industrial earnings and their view that life away from home was not worthwhile unless they could do so, these English and Scots immigrants exhibited traits which Thomas and Znaniecki ascribed to Polish peasants. There is little expression in these letters of the higher motives which Thomas attributed to former peasants infected with hopes of economic advance. Only rarely does one get a glimpse of anything like work for its own sake, or pride in a job well done, or alternatively, a desire to display one's economic success through fine dress, or treating, or lavish furnishings in the home.[28]

One can contrast the close-fisted attitudes of most of these letter-writers with the remark of Richard Hails, 'I intend to keep within my means but I like to enjoy myself as far as is right & needful,' and John Ronaldson's exhortation to his wife not to live mean and ruin her health. 'Spend the money. You must all take more pleasure. Take a jaunt some opportunity.'[29] In both of these instances, chronic ill health had interfered with work, however, and these options in favour of more present leisure and pleasure were taken in the interests of restoring health. On the whole, although their actions were based upon economic calculations of relative wages and cost of living, their goals were directed towards the non-material ends of independence and leisure, not so much towards the acquisition of a higher standard of life in terms of material goods. In the case of a few of these migrants, one can trace a modification of these aims after they had lived in America for some time.

This minute sample of industrial emigrants provides at least a hint that they were more responsive to economic incentives than the urban emigrants who chose to enter farming, and that they did not think a situation right unless they were able to get more than a living from it. Though they aimed to save rather than spend money, they did not outline any elaborate uses for the savings. Instead, some of them tended to project their social ambitions upon their children. In this, too, they showed attitudes which contrasted with the agriculturists. They shared with them a general belief that in America a man could look after a large family better than he could in England. But the industrial workers tended to place more emphasis on the value of education, and to be

more alert to the advantages of free education and short apprentice-
ships. They took pride in their own literacy and wanted their children
to obtain a good education. Some even wrote of the ease with which a
college education could be obtained in the United States.[30] Through
education their children would be able to make their own way in the
world. Thus, those of the industrial workers who had occasion to discuss
this question in their letters did not anticipate keeping their children by
them all their lives, as did so many farmers. They regarded schooling
and a chance to learn a trade, rather than a bit of land, as the best thing
they could arrange for their children.

While some of their remarks may have been merely rhetorical and one
cannot be altogether certain they were not influenced by their short
residence in America, some of these industrial workers let their imagina-
tions expand when they began to think of what their children might do
and what they might be preparing for them through their emigration.
Hails, Martin and Phillips all made statements about the chance of
one's children becoming the first in the land in America. It is perhaps
not altogether fanciful to see in their attitudes towards their children a
more individualized love for them. They were at the same time less
possessive of them, not planning to rely upon them in old age, and more
interested in them as individuals. They did not fear the upward social
and economic mobility of their children, but rather favoured it. In this
they contrast with such farmers as Robert Smith and Hugh Nudham
and a farmer's wife like Catherine Bond. It is also suggestive that some
of these craftsmen made remarks indicating that children were not to be
regarded simply as acts of God and taken as they came. Richard Hails
and Titus Crawshaw seemed to consider the idea of family limitation,
Hails when he expressed the hope that his wife would not have to have
children so rapidly as did his sister-in-law, and Crawshaw when he disapproved of his brother Alfred's having so large a family when he did
not have steady work.

3

Networks of Migration

Individuals who sought industrial employment in America were more likely to go out as single men than were emigrants who tried to establish themselves on the land. Most letter-writers were young men who had not yet married when they emigrated: Edward Phillips, the younger, Abel Stephenson, Richard Hails, Titus Crawshaw, Henry Edward Price, David Laing, Joseph Hartley and Ernest Lister. James Roberts was a widower. Those who were married tended to leave their wives and families behind them, as did Jonas Booth, John Wilson, John Ronaldson, George Fewins, Frank Johnson and Fred Cheyney. George Martin had been advised strongly not to take his wife when he left for America in 1834. Sometimes emigration was a means of escaping from an unhappy domestic situation. Jonas Booth wrote of his wife's family, 'that infernal crew . . . which has been the cause of all my trouble . . . wished me a thousand miles off, but I got four thousand miles from them'.[31] Relatives of another young man warned the family in America not to assist him in emigrating: 'I believe [he] is inclined to go out to you he is Married to a deacent wooman and so far as is understood is not very kind to her She has a nice boy to him and it is rumoured that he would like to get away from hir and it. . . .'[32] One emigrant, waiting in Plymouth harbour in 1839 for his ship to sail to Australia, reported that the emigrants were virtually imprisoned while the ship was in harbour 'lest any married should think proper of leaving his wife to continue her journey by herself, . . .'[33] There were also obvious practical reasons why a man seeking industrial work should travel alone. He could be more mobile in his search for work, and the return to Britain would be cheaper should he decide not to remain overseas. Furthermore, since so many of these industrial workers emigrated very young, before they had the resources to contemplate marriage or emigration with a family, success in America was to be the means of enabling them to marry or to reunite with their families.

If they had the resources, industrial workers who travelled with their families behaved more like intending agriculturists and made for the west where provisions were cheaper.[34] Indeed, it is highly probable that English and Scots immigration to the United States was much more of a family movement in the first half of the nineteenth century, when agriculture was the goal of a large share of the migrants. In the latter half of the century, as industrial work attracted an increasing number of migrants, British emigration looked more like the 'new' Italian and Polish immigration, as more and more single men travelled alone – both ways – on the Atlantic. Ships carrying English and Scottish immigrants in the eighties often carried quite a balanced complement of men, women and children, so that the published totals made it look like a family migration. These shiploads were made up of many split families, young men on their own, along with the wives and children of other emigrants, presumably already established in America. Those who travelled without families in the early period were more often industrial workers.[35]

Once a man gained a toehold in an industrial community in America, various other members of his family might follow. Obviously he tried to send for his wife and young children first, as did Edward Phillips, who hoped later to bring out his married sons. A young emigrant from Ashton-under-Lyne in Lancashire travelled to East Liberty, Pennsylvania, near Pittsburgh, in 1848, with his mother and three sisters. Two brothers were already there, prepared to receive them.[36] The group with whom Joseph Hartley emigrated included two cousins and the mother of another relative who was to meet them.[37]

This emigration of other relatives was frequently assisted by remittances from America. While emigrants in agriculture only rarely assisted relatives by paying their fares or part of their removal expenses, industrial wage earners did do so, since they had far more opportunity to find ready cash. The hackler who lent John Ronaldson his passage money was probably a brother-in-law. Jonathan Oakes promised to send for his brother Joseph, and Joseph Hartley also offered to pay his brother's passage out.[38] Another immigrant promised, 'If James [his brother] as not enough to pay his passage money make it up amongst you and I will send it you again by john Butcher.'[39] Would-be emigrants asked relatives in America for aid, though they did not always get it. In 1846 Henry Edward Price had this request from his mother: 'Henry is very wishful to come to America and if you can do anything towards his coming he will be very glad he will come in the spring and what you pay he will endeavour to pay you again if god willeth. . . .'[40]

The letters give the impression that English and Scots immigrants were not so generous in providing free tickets to relatives as Polish and Irish immigrants. We have no instance of brothers and sisters who migrated systematically, one after another, each in turn aiding those left behind. Offers of aid to relatives were often simply, as with the farmers, the promise of a house to come to temporarily and assistance in finding a job on arrival.[41] The higher *per capita* incomes in Britain, as compared with other parts of Europe, meant that it was easier to obtain passage assistance from relatives in Britain. One middle-aged Scottish woman, who was a textile mill worker herself, offered to pay the passage back to Britain of a favourite nephew if he were not happy in America.[42] Edward Phillips and John Wilson both asked their families in Britain to provide some of the cash necessary for the emigration of their own wives and children. George Fewins asked the Guardians of the Poor to send out the rest of his family. When Henry Edward Price decided he would like to join his grandmother and other relatives in New York City she wrote to the Guardians in her village in Wiltshire begging them to send him out, and he was given passage, outfit and a sovereign.[43]

One of the outstanding differences between these letters and those from immigrants on farms was the extension of the network of advice and assistance beyond the family. Sometimes migrants merely carried letters of introduction or recommendation to prospective employers. John Ronaldson had with him a piece of paper on which were the addresses of prospective employers in and around New York City. John Wilson's father, a worsted manufacturer in Halifax, had business contacts in Lowell, Massachusetts, who helped his son find work.[44]

Most of these people found jobs with the help of workmates and friends from their own communities. George Martin went to Cobourg, Upper Canada, in 1834 at the invitation of a friend. Richard Hails was assisting friends in the Boston area in the early 1840s. When John Ronaldson arrived in Skaghticoke, New York, in the early fifties, there were twenty of his acquaintances in the town. Titus Crawshaw was met in Philadelphia by a former workmate who paid his bills until Crawshaw found a job. Disappointed that the expected relatives did not meet them in Medina, New York, Joseph Hartley and his companions found plenty of 'John Bulls' who had previously emigrated from the quarrying town of Brighouse, Yorkshire, to the quarries of Medina.[45] So also, our Sheffield people had friends in both New York and the Connecticut towns to which they made their way. George Martin was helping both relatives and acquaintances to establish themselves in Rochester, New York, in the late forties. Contacts with workmates were fully as important as family connections among these industrial workers who sought jobs in America after about 1840.

Some of them emphasized the difficulties to be encountered by a skilled British workman who tried to find suitable work quickly without such contacts.[46] These individuals may have wanted in this way to swell their own importance by offering to aid immigrants. Yet the letters of Richard Hails describe his very real problems as a skilled worker who arrived during a year of trade depression without contacts in his trade.

These non-family arrangements frequently turned sour. George Martin is in many ways the prototype. He was seriously disappointed with the inadequate assistance rendered him by the friend whose invitation to come to Cobourg he had accepted. Fifteen years later Martin in turn thought that the friends he helped into employment in Rochester expected too much. Complaints of ill-usage, of loans not repaid, of migrants exploiting each other, of embittered personal relationships are to be found in most of these series where friendship was relied upon as the network of migration. The instances are too common to believe that this was simply a matter of personal difficulties. Indeed, this persistent theme of petty complaints about the misdeeds of workmates may be another reason why few letters from industrial migrants have come to light. Families may have felt that these were really entirely personal idiosyncrasies which reflected badly upon the migrant. It seems clear that the economic ambition of these industrial workers made it more likely that they should get into such arguments over money and services than did farmers. But the explanation must go beyond this. Under these circumstances, customary relationships, which were not designed to meet the strains which migration placed upon them, broke down. Individual immigrants did not know what they were expected to do for friends; nor did recent immigrants know how much they ought to receive. So long as these actions remained within the family, there was usually sufficient trust and confidence on both sides of the transaction that expectations were fulfilled. Outside the family, individual immigrants could not serve as trade society branches, aiding travelling members. Consequently the granting of aid was not commensurate with expectations.

Even the family as an agency of migration had greater burdens to bear with industrial migrants, and the signs of strain are evident in some of these series.[47] Thomas Martin and his wife condemned their cousin George for his treatment of them. John Ronaldson had some difficulty in persuading his wife to accept his travels meekly. It probably was more difficult to aid either relatives or friends in industrial towns than it was in a farming area, mainly because lodging and food had to be paid for in cash. Moreover, an immigrant in an industrial area was likely to find himself confronted with generation after generation of migrants who knew friends of friends or of his family, if he remained in a town for a long time, as did George Martin. Immigration did not dry up in many of these places, as it did in the farming areas to which most of our agricultural migrants went. Thus, new migrants seemed to constitute a never-ending threat to savings. As the mid-century mass immigration hit him personally in Rochester, George Martin suggested that further people from home get in touch with a good immigrant agent whom he recommended.

One by-product of the extension of personal relationships outside the family was an insistence upon the privacy of the immigrant letter. Few British immigrants seem to have written letters, in any case, which were intended to be read out in the public house or in chapel, or passed around from house to house. Industrial immigrants positively enjoined their families not to show letters to anyone other than the addressee, to keep certain sections private, or to let only specified individuals see them. One reason for this reserve was the desire to prevent accounts of bitterness which had arisen between former workmates from passing beyond the private knowledge of a particular member of the family. Another reason was the self-consciousness of these migrants about their writing and spelling. 'Please to let Wm. A. Booth, my son look at this letter' wrote Jonas Booth to his brother, 'but do not show it to every person because it is badly written and worse spelled'.[48] These men did not want their weaknesses exposed.

In addition to the network of the trade, occasional references were made to other institutions which aided British immigrants. It was in the no-man's-land between these institutional aids and family migration where there were no customary norms, that the breakdowns in social relationships occurred. English migrants in the Philadelphia region referred to assistance to be obtained by Masons or Oddfellows as early as the 1830s. David Laing used his lodge connections in establishing himself in a town in Indiana. One group of immigrants from Sussex in 1828 obtained jobs in a cotton factory in Hudson, New York, through a chapel they attended in New York City shortly after their arrival.[49] By the 1880s, when the last great wave of English and Scottish immigrants arrived in the United States, these institutional forms of assistance were available in all of the port cities as well as most large inland towns. The immigrant could look to them for assistance in finding work and lodgings if he had neither friends nor family to meet him. In the present state of our knowledge we have no way of knowing how frequently the labour exchanges set up by steamship companies were patronized by British immigrants. If they did use them, this was another respect in which they too were 'new immigrants', in the sense in which the term was used in the debates over immigration in the United States. One suspects that the British immigration of the eighties was not only more largely composed of unskilled young men who came without families than that of previous generations, but that also more use was made of labour exchanges by the migrants of that decade. It may, however, simply be coincidence that Ernest Lister, our sole representative from that bumper immigration, found work through the agent of the steamship company with whom he travelled, and that the Sons of St George invited him to purchase the right to their insurance benefits within a few months of his arrival in New York City. Another Englishman, who entered the United States from Alaska in 1898, has written that when he arrived, jobs were obtained by paying a dollar at employment offices, suggesting that this was the usual method for even British immigrants to obtain work.[50]

4

Economic Adjustment

During the first two or three years they spent in America, most of these young industrial immigrants were artisans on tramp. Although none of these letter-writers moved within a trade union tramping system or had received an emigration benefit, they did come to America partly to see more of the world and partly to find a better job. One young man from Glasgow who was in Boston in 1841, the period when the trade union tramping system was at its peak in Britain, actually used these words, 'I am on tramp at present'. The next year he cautioned his brother, 'You must not come out yet I will be through with my travels in a short time I will then come home and if you should think of travelling a little I should be proud to accompany you.'[51] Throughout this period in their careers, when they regarded themselves as looking around for a job which would enable them to save money quickly, they showed a remarkable willingness to change location in search of work. They were likely to continue to travel within the States after their arrival. Most of them expected to return to Britain upon the conclusion of their travels. The states of New York and Pennsylvania, through which most British immigrants passed, were starting points for eastward moves into New England as well as westward migrations.[52] Some British miners kept up a high mobility for several years after they came to America. For example, one young immigrant from Tavistock in Devon, who arrived in New Jersey in 1860 to join his father and brothers, continued to travel with them to Columbia County, Pennsylvania, in 1864. From there this young miner went, in 1869, to Weston City, Nevada, for three years, then back to New Jersey until 1876, then to Bloomsburg for a year and to McIntyre, Lycoming County, Pennsylvania, until 1884. In 1892, at the age of forty-eight, he finally settled down, buying property in Clearfield, Pennsylvania.[53] Such a high degree of mobility was perhaps rare, but the willingness to move about was a characteristic attitude of these migrants, though few considered travelling as more than a temporary phase in their lives.

Judging from their behaviour, one would conclude that these skilled workers preferred to change location rather than job, since few of them made moves which involved a change of trade. One Durham miner in Tennessee contrasted the English miner with the American in this respect. The Englishman knew nothing but mining and was less likely to work at other jobs when work was scarce in the mines.[54] While this may have been true of Durham miners, the Cornish miners in Wisconsin were quite prepared to mix farming with lead mining. This was the reason that Jonathan Dawson from Northumberland could report in 1849 that although he had made nothing in lead mining for two years, he and his family were still living comfortably.[55] Several of these industrial workers recognized the potential advantages of versatility of occupation. Hails said that he regarded it as a 'principle' and a 'duty' to try some other occupation if he did not succeed at tailoring, and Abel Stephenson considering 'turning [his] hand to some other business'.[56] Titus Crawshaw exclaimed at one point, 'I must go at anything', but he hesitated to take harvest work for fear of the sun and seemed to reject railway labour out of hand.[57] Joseph Hartley was determined never again to practise his trade after he reached America. A year after he had arrived in New York, he wrote, 'When I do work it will never be in a quarry', and he did take farm work for a few years.[58] Furthermore, changing occupation did not seem very difficult once they had arrived in America and observed the want of specialization of workmen there.

The intertwined goals of a search for a job in which saving was possible and the achievement of some kind of independence kept these men mobile, both in job and location, for a time. Several of them tried farming, and others an independent business venture; but none showed the single-minded devotion to that goal of some of our farmers. Their attempts at independence were incidents of the tramp. In spite of their stated willingness to change occupation, moreover, most of them, in fact, moved geographically within the same trade, while the farmers stayed put geographically and varied their sources of income.

In coming to America, they were usually unable to find work in their own trades exactly like that which they had done in the old country. In a wide variety of trades, methods were found to be different. Perhaps it is in the very nature of the immigrant letter that through it one does not encounter direct, successful transfers of skill from Britain to America or an easy economic adjustment, successful both from the standpoint of the immigrant and the needs of American industry. The only one of our immigrants who obtained easily just the kind of job he sought was a Lancashire engine fitter. Richard Hails was unable to find work as a custom tailor in the Boston neighbourhood when he arrived in the early forties, and subsequently took work as a cutter in a large workshop.

Crawshaw, who regarded himself as a wool finisher, had difficulty getting into finishing rooms in American factories. On arriving in New York City, Alfred Green found that 'brushmaking is no account here. They don't hardly use any. They use whisk brooms for sweeping so that our trade is not much account here'.[59] Even building trades workers found modes of working and materials different. Ernest Lister reported that to get work as a painter in New York City, he virtually had to learn the trade anew.[60] Though he had worked in a sawmill in Scotland, Archibald McKellar had to take work in Minnesota below the going rate because he 'had no experience in the woods'.[61] On the other hand, John Wilson, who had been a book-keeper in Yorkshire, was given a job as an overlooker in a carpet factory, for which he was not prepared by experience.[62] Few complained of discrimination against them because of their inexperience, though most appeared to have worked at first for rather low wages.[63]

Edward Phillips and Henry Edward Price, who emigrated in order to be able to learn crafts, found that mobility was essential to picking up knowledge in America. Price went so far as to sign up for an apprenticeship as a cabinet-maker on Long Island at the ridiculously low wage of a dollar a week with board for the first year, rising to a hundred dollars a year in the third. Like others, he found the arrangements for training fully as casual as in the abortive apprenticeship he had served in Wiltshire. Although his employer called himself a cabinet-maker, he made only bureaux. After fifteen months, Price left to find other work in order to widen his range a bit.[64] Another young immigrant from Lancashire believed that he had apprenticed himself to a mechanic in Allegheny City, Pennsylvania, but when he turned up was told to come back in a month to see if the boss had work for him.[65]

Several factors combined to make the first few years in America a period of intermittent and unsteady work for most of these men: their own assumption that they should continue to move for a while, the discovery that work methods differed, and the failure to find a long-term industrial training which they understood as an apprenticeship. Obviously, the immigrants were not themselves responsible for many of their difficulties in finding steady work. Emigrating in 1858, Joseph Hartley arrived in western New York to find work scarce and wages lower than he had anticipated. Similarly, James McKellar reported from his tramp during an earlier depression, 'Trade is very dull here at present Taylors and Shoemakers are doing nothing and [cotton] printing is no better than at home in Scotland and worse than in England. . . .'[66] Yet even in good times, some of these men complained of irregularity of work. This was partly a consequence of their mobility. They were the

9

first let off when they had been the last hired. Crawshaw had the misfortune to have an employer go bankrupt, owing him money; but he did not say why his employer's successor refused to take on any of the old hands. After much travelling, Henry Edward Price returned to his old employer on Staten Island, only to have him die shortly thereafter. Their early inability to keep steady work was to a great extent the result of the instability of the economy and of small employers. It is, nevertheless, rather remarkable that those who came with skills had this experience. In addition to the tramp psychology which kept them on the move looking for something better to turn up, certain other characteristics of these immigrants made for irregular employment. George Martin, Richard Hails, Titus Crawshaw, John Ronaldson and Abel Stephenson had to give up jobs at some time because of sickness. This was a particular hazard for the immigrant on his own. Henry Price left a decent job in Oswego, New York, when he became ill, in order to get back to New York City where he had relatives. The very instability of their lives while they were on tramp enhanced the chances of sickness, as did also their residence in cities when the cholera epidemics struck. At times in Crawshaw's account, one cannot sort out whether he was unemployed because of sickness or because the employer had 'turned them off'.

Although they were very conscious of wage rates and reported them frequently, in only two instances did a man specifically state that he left a particular job because he wanted more money. Price left his exploiting master on Long Island for this reason, and Titus Crawshaw threw in a job in 1857 when wages were reduced by fifteen per cent. The immigrants also considered hours of work in assessing a job. George Martin complained of the twelve and a half hour day in Cobourg, Upper Canada, and John Ronaldson thought that factory hands were not paid 'in proportion to the work performed' in Skaghticoke, New York.[67] These men did not chafe at long hours nearly so much as some of the correspondents with English newspapers, however.[68] Jonathan Oakes, in New York in 1841, and Crawshaw, in Philadelphia in 1854, noted that they were working a ten-hour day.[69] One might have expected more irritation at long hours. In fact, the main grievances for most of these men at first were not low wages or long hours but irregular employment and the difficulty of securing wages in cash. The prevalence of wage payments in truck and irregular payment of cash wages made it difficult for workers to assess the meaning of wage rates.

Some of them commented that employers were not so tyrannical as in England. Employers were either kind or tyrants in the vocabulary of most of these immigrants. Change of job was more frequently related to the assessment of the employer's intention than to strictly cash

criteria. Stephenson left one job because he thought his English employer a tyrant. Martin left Scottish employers whom he considered
mean. Joseph Hartley, on the other hand, was induced to remain a
second year with an employer from whom he had received no cash
wages because the employer was good to him.[70] The Roberts and
Bradley families left the Waterville Manufacturing Company's employ,
in spite of the unaccustomed amenities, good wages and regular work,
because they concluded that the bosses were becoming more tyrannical.
For all their goals of saving, in practice these men responded to kind
treatment and to respect, even at the expense of optimum economic
gain.

Sometimes they changed jobs for more trivial reasons. They took off
with a friend who had found a job in another town.[71] Ronaldson left
Skaghticoke partly because it was 'nothing but a colony of Irish'.
Crawshaw gave up a job in Delaware because it was a slave state.
Joseph Hartley did not expect to work during the first winter he was in
America and spent it with friends in a rented house with nothing to do
but 'to eat and drink and smoke throo winter'.[72] When Titus Crawshaw
left for Wisconsin in 1854 to see what the west was like, he was in full
employment and making better wages than he was to obtain for the rest
of the decade. Thus their mobility was frequently not used purposefully,
and it did not get them much ahead.

Throughout this tramping period these young men had to live most
of the time in boarding houses, though occasionally they rented houses
with friends for short periods, and sometimes had jobs which included
board. Several of them resented what they paid out in board and felt
that they could live more cheaply if they had someone to keep house
for them.[73] This discovery was often a prelude to settling down.

In several of these collections we get a glimpse of the migrant only
during this rather unstable period while he was living in lodgings and
changing employment rather frequently. Only two series (Hartley and
Martin) continue until the rather premature death of the migrant, well
after he had settled down. Attempts to import capital did not give rise
to sudden spurts of letter-writing as in the farming series. The only such
case was Edward Phillips, who tried to rescue his faltering business
venture in Illinois during the depression of the early forties.[74] There are
fewer cases than in the agricultural series of a lapsed correspondence
resumed in old age, though the Laing series, begun in the seventies
when David Laing had been in America for nearly twenty years, is
representative of several short collections which we have from the
depressions of the seventies and the nineties. The period in the industrial
migrant's life when he continued to write letters was (we may assume) a

phase in his career marked by both ambition and restlessness. These migrants did not send back letters urging people to emigrate. Crawshaw, after six years in America, thought he would have been better off had he stayed in Huddersfield, and Ronaldson advised, 'them that is anything right to stop where they are'.

More mature migrants, who had fought their way through and remained in America, commented on the characteristics necessary for success. George Martin warned people not to wait until they were three thousand miles from home to see 'how much better you could have done there if you had only tried'. In his view, after sixteen years in America, the individual who arrived with nothing and had to begin immediately a struggle for survival was more likely to adapt than the one who arrived with savings. As old William Winterbottom said, 'in a strange Land you have your trials and it takes tim to sucseed the word is press on'.[75]

A vast number of English industrial workers did not press on, but returned home having seen enough. Some of those who returned were men, like Lister and Ronaldson, who had been able to save something during their travels. Ronaldson referred to those who stayed in the United States because they would lose face if they returned with nothing. Both Hartley and Crawshaw were waiting to get some savings before returning, and the moment passed. Others simply went home because of poor health or fears for their health, as did Thomas Martin and Henry Price. We know that many British industrial workers returned home during depressions, and also that the annual migration became a feature of the lives of a number of building trades craftsmen, including stone masons, especially during the 1880s.[76] Many British industrial workers completed their tramp by returning home, but we know little about the subsequent careers of such men.[77]

For those who remained in America, it was a matter of settling down. Joseph Hartley had decided in a couple of years that he wanted to remain in America and that he would only visit England if he had enough money saved to return to the States. His adjustment was achieved in three ways which were characteristic of the men whose careers we know.

First of all, Hartley returned to his old trade of stone-quarrying. This happened during the Civil War, when, presumably, wages of twelve shillings a day simply could no longer be forgone to remain with his kind farmer-employer at $130 a year. The men who remained in American industry returned to their old trades, if they had flirted with farming or private ventures. Once this had been accepted, and they stuck to an employer, they had more regular work. This was the case with both Hartley and Martin. Hartley became foreman of the quarry by the end of the sixties. Martin stayed with Jonathan King, afraid to exchange a 'certainty for uncertainty'. Crawshaw also kept returning to woollen textiles, though he accepted what was in his view a down-grading of occupation each time he came back. At first he tried for finishing rooms; a few years later he had to confess to his handloom-weaver father that he was now only a weaver on power looms. After the Civil War and his disastrous attempt to set up on his own account in Canada, he was reduced to spinning. In spite of their initial attitude which favoured change of occupation, these particular men stayed in their trades. The only acceptable alternative to them was the independence of a farm or their own business, and experience eroded these hopes.

The second aspect of Hartley's settling down was to acquire property in the United States. In his case, this came about almost by chance when his employer offered to give him an acre of land in lieu of unpaid wages and Hartley had a house built on the land. Property, a house and garden, became the focus of the economic organization of the household from this point on. The advantage of living in the United States was that there he could get not only a living but also a house of his own. When his income as a foreman of the quarry came in regularly for a few years, beguiled by the idea of a secure livelihood, Hartley invested in a thirty-acre farm as well. Then came his death and the depression of the seventies, with eight hundred dollars still owing on the farm.[78] A foundry worker in Mount Washington, Pennsylvania, was also trapped by his property during the depression of the seventies:

... I calculated when we purchased this lot and erected a good house upon it, that by this time it would fetch five thousand dollars, but, alas, we should be glad to get one half of that amount for it now, after spending all my savings in prosperous times, I am now receiving no benefit but all is melting away like Snow ... if I only had the money I laid out in this building I could speculate in something else, or I would come back to the old country.[79]

The fulfilment of a dream of home ownership was clearly one thing that held migrants in the United States.

With a steady job and property came marriage. This meant not only a prospect of cheaper living by housekeeping, but also supplementary earnings. Without exception these industrial workers expected their wives to work. They took it for granted that their wives would contribute to the family budget, though it must be remembered that we have no evidence in the letters about the attitudes of men in heavy industry. Edward Phillips and John Wilson sent for their wives only after they had found jobs for them. John Ronaldson was looking for work for his wife as well as a satisfactory berth for himself. Those who married after they came to America, Richard Hails, Titus Crawshaw and Joseph Hartley, also mentioned the contribution their wives made, and were expected to make, to the family income. Not only in these textile families, but also among the Sheffield cutlers, it was accepted that women should work in factories. There is not a single expression of regret at this situation; nor is any hope recorded that one day it will not be necessary for their wives to work. At times women could get jobs more easily than male immigrants. John Williamson's sisters obtained work more quickly than he did:

we have not begun of any work yet our girls might have had the first work but we was living at Eastliberty they have had a deal of sewing to do we come a living to Alleghany on the 2nd of June there is one Mill which they would rather go to they are new looms but they are not ready for them yet Boss said that if he could not find them work next Monday he will pay them their wages there is about 6 Mills in Alleghany so they might have had work any day but this one Mill is reckoned the best.[80]

If a woman did stay at home to keep house, she earned something with her needle.

5

Social Adjustment

Certain of the attitudes expressed by industrial workers gave them advantages, as compared with some of the British farmers, in adapting to American society. None of them professed to feel superior to Americans; nor did they hesitate to associate with them. Whereas American agriculture attracted some families who expected deference from their workpeople and who were careful about the society in which they mixed, these industrial workers, when they commented on this subject at all, welcomed the atmosphere of social equality they expected to find in America. Jonas Booth, son of a Bradford worsted manufacturer, reported from Oneida County, New York in 1829:

Men servants ... eat with their Master all at one time if they be iver so rich, which they call him their Boss and they are called Mr and the women servants is called waiting maids if their Mrs Bids them do anything its be so good as to do such a thing There is no such a thing as scoulding them. ... The girls that works in the Mill is dresst as fine as any of the others and is thought of with much respect with the rich they are different from England for they are all workers. ... [81]

In this respect their attitudes were the reverse of those of the more fastidious English farmers. Industrial workers were sensitive about how they were treated themselves, objected to tyranny in employers, and were proud of receiving such marks of respect from them as being provided with heat in winter while they worked and with soap to wash with at the end of the day. [82] A few of them did show a fear of having to mix with the Irish, but their contacts with them were limited primarily to sharing transport facilities. [83]

A bit more unexpected is the want of any conviction of the superiority of British techniques and methods of working. Migrants who had been farmers in Britain were much more likely to arrive in America with the attitude that they had better ways of farming than the Americans. These industrial workers did not emigrate with firm intentions as to their future occupations. This attitude predisposed these free-lancers to adapt to new methods of working. They reported on different techniques of working, sometimes with outright approval, rarely with a conviction of British superiority.[84] Of the particular migrants whose cases are presented here, those most resistant to changing methods were the Sheffield cutlers, who settled in a community in Connecticut in which there were perhaps as many as a thousand other immigrants from Sheffield. Such communities of English workmen may have resisted change and clung to traditional work methods, thus giving the English workman in America his reputation for being conservative and rigid. That these attitudes were not characteristic of all British industrial workers in America is amply documented in these letters. Men like Abel Stephenson, who condemned power-driven machinery as such, criticized the trend in manufacturing industry on both sides of the Atlantic.[85] The adaptation of even such men, in time, is suggested by the following remarks of a Yorkshireman, who left a Luddite sympathizer but wrote, after nearly a half-century in America: 'whould you if you could go back to old times its out of the question I saw a labouring man with a plaining maschine cut more good Mouldings in one day than I could in 12 days better & truer than man knows how.'[86] Most of these men seemed to have been willing from the outset to learn new ways of doing things.

Nor did they show much prickly British nationalism, which might have hindered their adjustment. The early radical emigrants like Martin, Stephenson and Winterbottom were critical of both Britain and America, as when George Martin denounced America's war with Mexico as evidence of the 'Anglo-Saxon spirit of aggrandizing territory'.[87] The later, more purely economically motivated industrial workers complained bitterly of homesickness; but as with farmers from poorer families, they expressed a longing for the locality of their birth and childhood, for lost friends, family and certain celebrations like Christmas which were not given the same attention in America, not a strong sense of national identity.

These industrial workers exhibited a richer variety of interests than did most of the farmers. Their newspaper reading was both more discriminating and more extensive, though the exchange of newspapers was a prominent feature of both groups. They relied on newspapers not only simply for news from home, but also to satisfy objective interests in the outside world. They made more reference to books, and some evinced an interest in natural history. Those who had such cultural interests had an advantage, as compared with many farmers, for this was one means of assuaging the loneliness they felt at times.

Fewer of these industrial workers relied so much as the farmers on religious faith as a means of accepting difficulties. The immigrants of the first half of the century all expressed some religious faith, but none of them had the kind of evangelical tone in their letters so noticeable among the farmers, nor the tendency to mix religion with every aspect of life. Without exception, these particular industrial workers were either nonconformists or non-church-goers. Less evidence of religious faith, and thus in the possibility of churches and chapels as institutions of accommodation, appears in the letters of the migrants of the second half of the century. Crawshaw, Ronaldson, Green, Laing and Lister made no reference to religion at all. One textile worker in Iowa expressed a position on the margin between belief and disbelief:

If it is true that there is a future happy state of existence after we leave this world, and if it is true also that friends and relations who are so happy as to get there will know each other, and I have no reason to doubt it, it will certainly be a great pleasure to me to meet all of them there. You probably know that father always thought there was.[88]

Not all of these industrial workers had the confident faith in an after-life which helped most of the farmers through their difficult early years in America and brought them in touch with Americans in churches.

Their geographical mobility was another obvious disadvantage in social adjustment which contributed to their continued feeling of being strangers in a strange land. Their ambivalence about whether or not to remain in America, and the growing dominance of purely material motives which, coming from a relatively advanced and comfortable society, they could not easily satisfy, also worked against their easy assimilation. As Alfred Green, the brushmaker from Mile End, wrote home shortly after he arrived in America: 'Give my love to Emma, Bill, Amelia, Mary Ann and Clara. Tell them I dont think they would like America much. There is not the comfort there is at home.'[89]

The attitudes of Americans towards them can only be seen indirectly through the letters;[90] but, just as in the agricultural series, few references to Americans and to American institutions appear in the letters. Another similarity is that the references to contact with Americans were made early on in the migrant's stay in the United States, as when Jane Martin referred to her friendly Yankee neighbour shortly after her arrival in the United States.[91] David Whyte, a Scots weaver, wrote home within four months of his arrival in the United States about some of his encounters with the Yankees. 'It is useless to try to turn round or beat a Scottsman once he takes up his position,' wrote Whyte. When the Yankees tried to tell him that the States were superior, he reminded them that their ancestors were likely to have been convicts sent out from Britain. 'All the difference betwixt them and I was that they or their Fathers had come sooner from the Home Country than I had.'[92] After a few encounters like this, no doubt, some immigrants, less sure of themselves than David Whyte, became more wary of mixing with Americans. Although it is possible that migrants simply did not mention encounters with Americans in their letters, as being of less interest to their correspondents in England, none of them wrote that he had an American friend or that he exchanged visits with Americans at any time during the correspondence.

The industrial migrants had two points of secondary contact with Americans, however. Some of them worked for American employers, and for George Martin and John Wilson, these were satisfactory relationships akin to patronage, for which the immigrants were grateful. While most of them lived in boarding houses kept by British immigrants, those who lived in American homes, like Laing and Lister, were very well satisfied with the treatment they received, and met a positive friendliness to which they responded.

All of these immigrants settled in towns where churches could serve as agencies of assimilation. David Whyte and his wife, Margaret, joined the Congregational Church in Watertown, Wisconsin, within weeks of their arrival: '. . . in the Evening service there was sung There is a land of pure delight I says to Magt you see we are not so fare from home. . . .'[93] So, in New York City, Henry Price found both friends and acquaintances in the 16th Street chapel, which he attended from the early days of his sojourn in America. He alone, of all these industrial immigrants, professed to have been influenced by American revivalism. Writing of the 1840s he noted, 'it was the custom in New York in the winter to get up Revival meetings and was led to believe that I was a great sinner.' So he was baptised through immersion in the East River. Later in life, as a carpenter in London, Price discarded the literal belief in the Bible, which he had acquired in the village in Wiltshire where he was born, from attending street corner meetings in Bristol with his mother, and from these revival meetings in New York; but he thought religion was 'my best and only friend in my youth and when far away in a strange land'.[94]

Religion was not so frequently a central part of the lives of these industrial workers, however. As we have seen, some of the tramping artisans did not mention going to church. George Martin, a strong Unitarian who refused to have his child baptised in spite of criticism, found no Unitarian Church when he came to Rochester in 1838; but whereas this led Unitarian farmers to avoid going to church, Martin visited other churches in Rochester to 'hear their different opinions'.

Approval of the mutual toleration of the many denominations in America was an attitude expressed by several of these people.[95] The letters suggest that churches were not so universally agencies of assimilation as they were among the farmers.

Urban immigrants had other opportunities, however. Two of these young men joined political demonstrations long before they could become citizens. Joseph Hartley had such a good time visiting a torchlight parade of the Wide Awakes in Buffalo in 1860 that he joined a Wide Awake Club in Lockport. As a young man he was having a grand time participating in a parade every few nights.[96] So also, Ernest Lister got involved in the Republican election activities in New York City in 1882, through the Americans with whom he boarded. For these young men, the social and carnival side of election antics was attractive. The immigrants of longer standing did not concern themselves much with American politics, however. The radicals Stephenson, Martin and Roberts, like the farmers who arrived in America with strong political views, did not plunge into American political agitation or citizenship. Most of their political comments were made as uncommitted outsiders. George Martin was quite strikingly misinformed about North American banking. Abel Stephenson's hostility to paper money and Richard Hails's distrust of banks were notions they brought with them from England. Few immigrants commented at all on American politics, except to note that election years were likely to be dull ones for trade.[97] Though both David Whyte and Titus Crawshaw expressed objections to working and living where there were Negroes, the Civil War called forth feelings of identification with the northern cause among workers resident in the north.[98]

In spite of the greater opportunities which these settlers in towns had for contacts with Americans, their letters indicate that, at least during the period of their lives when they continued a correspondence with the old country, they relied upon other immigrants for friendship. Less frequently settled in a large family group, they sought friendship, in the first instance, with people from their own county or neighbourhood at home. Joseph Hartley wrote home in 1860, two years after he had come to western New York state, that he was now not so homesick because Charles Hartley, his cousin, was living in Lockport and working for the same boss. When Charles returned to England about six years later, the Hartleys began a persistent attempt to get other relatives to come out. 'Joseph is very lonesome without some of you', wrote his wife, and Joseph himself asked for pity because 'I have no frende of mine in this country to help me'. This difficult period of about four years, straddling Joseph's eighth to twelfth year in America, finally ended in 1870, when

Charles returned, as well as another family from home. Their appearance meant daily visits for a while and trips to Rochester to visit Charley. The difference which these friends made to their lives and outlook is a striking feature of the Hartley letters.[99]

When the migrants did not succeed in settling near either family or friends from home, they did form new friendships, but every such case cited in the letters was a friendship with another immigrant. Abel Stephenson from Huddersfield found a shoemaker from a village near Leeds when his travels brought him to Northampton, Massachusetts. George Martin, from Sevenoaks in Kent, referred to his friendship with a Londoner, whose father was a retired clerk in the India office. Titus Crawshaw met a Scotsman, John Wilson, in his boarding house, and the friendship was made even more secure when Wilson married a girl from Farnley Bank, near Crawshaw's home in Yorkshire.[100] One of the reasons why Crawshaw retreated from Wisconsin was that friends and neighbours were scarce. He thought 'everybody appeared as if they were most as dead as trees' and was glad to get back east where he could 'converse with someone I was acquainted with'.[101]

Their marriages were consistent with this pattern of friendships made with other immigrants. Few of the unmarried industrial immigrants felt such a pressing need to marry as did the unmarried farmers, who had to marry both for companionship and for the labour of a wife. When Henry Price was keeping company with the mistress of his boarding house in Oswego, a widow whose husband was said to have been killed in the Canadian Rebellion, his mother wrote to warn him that thirty was quite young enough to marry.[102] At the age of thirty-five, Titus Crawshaw married a woman from Northern Ireland. Richard Hails married a Welsh girl, and Hartley, an immigrant from Cambridgeshire. The two of our immigrants who married native-born women arrived in the United States very young. Edward Phillips was fourteen when he joined his uncle in Delaware. By the time he was twenty-five, he had married a fifteen-year-old Virginia-born girl. The only one of these letter-writers who became completely cut off from even a small informal immigrant community, Phillips wrote to his father after eighteen years in the United States: 'I have been like a lost sheep, a long time stranger in a strange land'.[103] David Laing was also in his teens when he emigrated from Scotland, a labourer. Before he was twenty, he had married a Pennsylvania-born woman, and this is the only instance of a broken marriage, (in spite of the lengthy separations some of these families endured while men were seeking work) in either the agricultural or the industrial series.

Only in communities where large numbers of English or Scots industrial workers were settled was it possible for immigrant communities with institutions and recreations to develop.[104] The Sheffield cutlers in Waterbury played cricket together on Shrove Tuesday, and the Yorkshire quarrymen in Medina, New York, had their traditional rush-bearing while the Americans celebrated the fourth of July.[105] What is more noteworthy in these emigrant letters is the paucity of references to formal ethnic institutional life even among migrants settled in large towns. In all the letters there is but one single reference to a branch of the Sons of St George, and only one immigrant mentioned reading a newspaper produced for the English-American reader.

In spite of the fact that these immigrants did not participate in any formal ethnic community life, these letters do not provide evidence of tragic personal disorientation. None re-emigrated with the bitterness of the Butterworths. Contrary to the reputation which British workmen gained in areas where they settled in large numbers, these particular migrants did not assuage their loneliness in excessive drinking, if we are to believe their letters. Very few references to drunkenness are to be found in the letters. One coal miner in Pennsylvania confessed to his niece: 'well Annie you have had your sports we have none here but the 4th of July and i had a visit to penn station about 70 miles and had a week spree the only one since I came back to America. . . .'[106] According to John Ronaldson, when he and his hackler friends had time off, they went to Boston and visited the theatre and museums. Henry Price amused himself while working on Long Island by buying pigeons and bathing in the sea.[107] Among our farmer immigrants, drinking was rarely mentioned as a serious problem. The industrial workers, on the other hand, regarded excessive drinking as a serious potential obstacle to success. Richard Hails hoped his father had stopped drinking and would, thus, be able to stay out of the poor house; Ronaldson boasted that he had only touched liquor twice since coming to America; Crawshaw claimed that he was a teetotaller and Alfred Green described himself as 'almost' one.[108] Drink was obviously more of a menace to the savings goals of these workers than it was to farmers, who made their own liquor. In fact, they hesitated to spend money at all when they first came to America, except for the minimum necessities of life. Their tendency, once they had set up households in America, was to invest in livestock, houses and garden plots, rather than in pleasure expeditions or clothes or fine furniture. So long as they had a specific savings goal, they kept their consumption to a minimum, except apparently in the matter of food.[109] The similarity in their economic aims to those of the farmers is suggested in this passage from a letter of

Daniel Stephenson, a weaver in Fairfield, Iowa, twenty-four years after he had come to America:

We have four fine children, three boys and one girl. the oldest is big enough to wind bobins and spool in the Shop. we have got a new house with five rooms in a garden with plum, Cherries, Apples, and pair trees in, and a cow with strict economy, hard work and pretty good management and the blessing of God we have got along very well.[110]

Unfortunately, the letters of industrial workers do not in many cases enable us to follow through the migrant's adaptation, especially after he had settled down. We are unable to trace what happened to their children. Those who finally settled in large communities of English or Scottish workmen, in cities like Fall River or New Bedford, and who were more successful in developing their own institutions and distinctive modes of recreation, do not appear to have been letter-writers. These letters introduce a few men and women who, for shorter or longer periods of their lives, were thrown more completely on their own resources. They too reached an accommodation to life in America, largely through small, informal groups of immigrant friends. Their pronounced individualism and self-reliance helped them sustain years of loneliness, convinced that they were materially better off than they would have been in England. Most of them were pretty well shielded from the kind of experience which Titus Crawshaw had in the army during the Civil War, after which he felt that the Americans did look upon all immigrants as inferior to the native-born.

Letters from Immigrants in Industry

Phillips Series 1820–45

Edward Phillips was a handloom weaver of cotton cloths. He was born near Shrewsbury, Shropshire, but his wife and children were living in Manchester when the first of these letters was written arranging for them to join him in America.[1] At least forty-five when he emigrated alone in 1817, Phillips had found work at the Roseville Cotton Works in Newcastle County, Delaware, before 1820. This firm was employing about thirty men and a hundred women, boys and girls at that time, operating two thousand spindles and twenty-five handlooms, producing cotton yarns and also finer fabrics like muslins, plaids and stripes. Phillips's English employer helped him to send for his wife and younger children, consisting of three boys and two girls. Though the Phillips family were enumerated in the census of 1820 in Mill Creek Hundred, where the Roseville Factory was located, they moved to Wilmington soon afterwards, and it seems most unlikely that he remained with his employer long enough to repay the passage loans. From the outset, Phillips was thinking of buying land. He apparently realized his dream a few years later in Chester County, Pennsylvania; but we have no further information about him.

The last four letters in the collection were written by his nephew, also Edward Phillips, who had been sent to him in 1821, a lad of fourteen, by his brother Phillip. This brother worked at Longnor Hall in St Chad's parish, about four miles from Shrewsbury, for Robert Burton, who had been sheriff of Shrewsbury. Owned entirely by Robert Burton, Longnor was a tiny township which returned only four houses and thirteen inhabitants in 1841. The nearby town of Shrewsbury, whose manufactures were produced for local markets, had grown a bit in the early part of the century, but from 1821 to 1851 its population was stationary. Shropshire was, of course, within the band of counties in which farm servants were relatively well paid, and Phillips's father was able not only to pay his son's passage but also to lend his brother money towards the journey of his family to America.

Phillips is an example of a skilled British workman who learned his trade in America. The handloom weaving of cottons was not a much better occupation in America than it was in Lancashire, especially as firms working in the finer branches felt the impact of British competition during the 1820s. Setting out for the west about 1826, Phillips picked up a knowledge of the various branches of the manufacture of woollens in factories in the Ohio Valley. He became a chronic migrant, never settling for long in one place, and seemingly seeking out the least commercialized places, well away from either of the major water routes to the west, in order to set up a small woollen factory of his own. Having married, in 1833, a Virginia-born woman of about fifteen, he lived for a few years in Champaigne County, Ohio, a few miles west of Columbus. This location must have been on the National Road, and by 1842, he had continued westward from that place to Greenville, Illinois. In 1845, he was living at Vandalia, a few miles east of Greenville, in Fayette County. By Illinois standards, this was a backward county. Vandalia itself had only about four hundred inhabitants in 1850. The population of the county increased very moderately from 6,328 to 8,075 people between 1840 and 1850. The value of farm land and buildings per acre was well below the average for the state in 1850, and there was a high rate of illiteracy in the county.[2] Again trying to start in business as a country wool carder and spinner during the difficult years of the early forties, Phillips begged for help from his Shropshire relatives. The letters end with this immigrant unwell, discouraged, and as he wrote 'very needy'. In 1850, he was still in Vandalia, a man of forty-two, but now described himself to the census enumerator as a cabinet-maker. The prairie lands around Vandalia were put into production more rapidly during the fifties, when the population of the county doubled and the town became a station on the Illinois Central Railway. But neither Edward Phillips nor any of his family could be found in Vandalia in 1860.

The Phillips letters are in the papers of the late William Phillips, presented by the executors of his estate to the Public Library in Castle Gate, Shrewsbury. They are published by kind permission of M.F. Messenger, F.L.A., Borough Librarian. Most of the letters are copies which appeared in a letter book when the Phillips papers were given to the Library, and it is not known who made the copies. Thus, it is possible that changes in spelling were made. One original letter of Edward Phillips survives in the collection, the letter dated Buck Creek, 7 May 1845.

Letters of Edward Phillips to his brother, P.Phillips, Longnor, Shrewsbury

Stanton, 5 January 1820

DEAR BROTHER,

I embrace this opportunity of writing to you hoping this will find you, my brother Thomas, an John in good health, and their families. I got to Liverpool on the 23rd of August after parting with you. I sailed from there on the 7th of September in the ship 'James Monroe', in company with James Haslum, who returned home in August following. We landed in New York on the 17th of October, left there for Philadelphia, got there on the 20th, went to work the day after with a farmer, where I remained six weeks. Then I got employment in my own business in Philadelphia. I came to this place on the 12th day of last August; this is a small village in the State of Delaware, six miles from Wilmington, and 34 from Philadelphia. Trade here is rather dull, yet my employer has kindly agreed to send for my family, by giving a note for £31.10s British, which is the cheapest passage I could get. It would be no object if I once got them here, as provisions are cheap, and he will find me a house and employment for them all. On the other hand I could never think of sending for them if it was not for this opportunity, as board &c. is so heavy that a single man can save very little except those that have regular monthly wages. As for me I sent what I could to my family, from time to time, as I knew the distressed state of working people in England. I expect my family to come in either the 'William Penn' or 'Kingsinton', I cannot tell which of them, as they both belong to one company. The merchant tells me that he expects they will be here in four months from this time. My wife sent me word that they would be assisted with a trifle to pay their expenses to Liverpool, yet sea stores I am afraid they will be ill provided to prepare for themselves, as they must be badly off for clothing. Dear brother, if you would send them a trifle you would ever oblige me and them; and it should be gratefully acknowledged, and returned as soon as possible after. I would get them here with what you have done for me before. My two sons that are married are likely to be left behind at present; but with the help of God I hope it will be in my power to send for them soon. It will be sufficient to break my heart if they are prevented coming for want of means, as I have gone to such extremes to get their passage agreed for, and perhaps would never have another chance. Please to have the goodness to write to them as soon as you receive this, for I think the time will be very short.

I met with three men in Philadelphia from Shrewsbury. They were all joiners, and they all knew you. I have forgotten their names except one, his name is Edward James. They left home about the same time I did.

. . . I like this country very well for many reasons, particularly the attention paid to Religion, and the freedom a man may use in adoring his Maker in his own way. I have known them in the city of Philadelphia to put chains across the street at time of service to prevent coaches or carts from disturbing the congregation. I conclude by giving my best love to you my brother and all friends, wishing you all every happiness, both spiritual and temporal. Such is the ardent wish of your ever affectionate Brother,

EDWARD PHILLIPS

Roseville Factory, 22 July 1820

DEAR BROTHER,

I take this opportunity of writing to you, and I hope these few lines will find you in good health, as it leaves me and mine. They landed at Philadelphia the 15th of June, all in good health, after a passage of 49 days. I got to hear of the vessel going up the river, and was in Philadelphia the day after they landed, which is a distance of forty miles, and was happy to see them all in good health – happier than I can express in words to see them all well after an absence of nearly three years. We got here in three days after they landed, and were kindly received by our employers. Edward, Jean, and myself are weaving, George and Ann at present are winding. I am much indebted to you for your kindness in assisting my family to come to me. I am sorry to hear of my brother John's troubles, but I hope they will be all for the best. I am informed that they think of coming to this country, but let him know that the weather here is very hot, the thermometer often stands at ninety-five degrees, but as he has been used to working in the fields he may perhaps stand the climate well enough. Markets being very low the farmer is not able to give the labourer so much wages as formerly. Wages at present are from eight to ten dollars a calender month, and found in board and bed. If he thinks proper to come I will do everything that is in my power for him. As for your son, if you should send him I will use him as one of my own. As I intend sending for my two sons next spring you can have an opportunity of sending him along with them. And if my brother John thinks of coming, let them all come together.

The Government in this country I think is excellent. In the first place the people have the chusing of all the Governors from the constable to the President. The Magistrates are chiefly the working class of people, and are chosen annually. As there is no established religion there are no tithes, and every profession pay their own clergy. We are comfortably situated here, markets are low, . . . [Prices]

I have written to my sons [the last word torn] to know from them whether they are willing to come and leave their families for the present till an opportunity serves to send for them. When I agree for their passage I will send you word, and if they chuse to come all together it may perhaps answer well. Give my best respects to my brothers John and Thomas and his wife. I hope you will answer this as soon as possible. No more at present, from your affectionate brother and sister,

EDWARD AND M. PHILLIPS....

Rosevill near Newark, 6 January 1821

DEAR BROTHER, . . .

I have this day wrote to my sons, and have agreed for them and their families their passage, as I hope to see them do well here, where industry is encouraged and seems to improve.

I have to pay 150 dollars for both families; if you still are intending your son coming you may get his passage for about £3 along with ours. If my brother John is still in the humour for coming he may come for about £6 finding his own stores. If you do send your son I shall use him the same as my own. At present weaving in this country is the best business. I feel very grateful towards you for assisting my family to come over, as it has altogether completed my happiness. At present things seem to favour us beyond expectation. I feel completely at home. My employer is an Englishman and is very kind, and offered to assist me in geting my sons over, and I hope very soon to see them. He has advanced 30 dollars to be paid in England, likewise their passage, which is 150 dollars. There is an acquaintance of mine, James White, from Manchester, has bought 40 acres of good land at 25 pr acre, improvements, log house, barn &c., in which is high cultivation. The tax on this land does not amount altogether to more than £2 per year. You may buy land here out and out for what you have generally to pay in rent & taxes in your country for one year. I request you will write to my son John to make a bag and put his shuttles and bobbins in, and put them in his bed till he gets out to sea. If he has a side engine he may take it and conceal it under his berth. Tell him to keep on good terms with the Customs House Officer. But if you are in anyway afraid to risk it, do not attempt to do it. . . . [Prices. Weather] My family seems to be comfortable. Plenty of oak wood to burn, and no tax gatherers with their books, every week at the door. We have a good deal of money to pay for furniture, and other things, but we have every day more encouragement. . . . [Thanks and greetings]

Your affectionate brother,

EDWARD PHILLIPS

Letters from Edward Phillips, the younger, to his father, Phillip Phillips, Longnor, Shrewsbury

Urbana, Champaigne Co., Ohio, 10 February 1838

After an absence of seventeen years I send you a few lines, which leave me and family in good health, and I hope they will find you enjoying the same. I will not attempt to give you a history of what has happened since I last saw you as it is uncertain whether you get this or not. If you do get it please favour me with an answer. I will be more explicit when I write to you again. I have not heard anything of Edward for several years and do not know where he is. If you have his address please sent it to me. Remember me to all my friends, and send word how they all are. I say no more at present but subscribe myself your ever gratfull and affectionate son,

EDWARD PHILLIPS

Kings Brech, 4 October 1838

DEAR SIR,

I received your letter in due time and am very sorry to hear that you are in so bad a state of health. As for myself and family we are in good health at present. My family consists of 5 persons, we have three children, one boy James William, a hearty little fellow going on 5 years old, two girls, Sarah Ann two years old, and Amondy Maria six months old. As to my history it is as follows:—I landed in Philadelphia after a passage of seven weeks, and arrived at my Uncles in a few days after. He was then living near Newark, but shortly after moved away to Wilmington, where I learned to weave, and I staid with him five years. About that time he hired me out to a farmer, business being bad in the w[e]aving line. I never saw my uncle but once since, but I heard that he has since moved into Chester County, Pensylvania, and bought a small farm. That is the last I heard of him. I lived with my employer on the farm about 6 months, and then with a light heart, and pockets as light, started to seek my fortune in the West. I went to Pittsburgh, about 300 miles off. I walked there in 10 days, and was tired enough. I lived there about six months, and then started down the Ohio River, one of the finest rivers in the world. I landed in Cincinati in about 10 days, 500 miles from Pittsburgh. I worked journeyman-work at a great many factories for several hundred miles round, and learned a little in every one until I got to be a good workman at weaving, spinning, carding, and dyeing. In 1833 I married and began to do a little business for myself. In 1835 I rented a farm for 7 years containing one hundred acres of land, with a small factory on it for carding wool for the country people. I pay

100 dollars rent yearly. I made a spinning machine, and looms, and buy wool and make it into cloth of different kinds. I hire a hand to tend the carding machines and get my weaving done. I spin and prepare the yarn for the weaver. This is my imployment for the present. The farm I get farmed on share, giving two thirds of the grain, and one half of the grass for the farming.

This is a good country to live in; every man that will work can get a good living, everything is plentiful and low. . . . [Prices] All the necessaries of life, and a great many luxuries are raised in the country. A great many vegetables grow here that do not grow in England. Sweet potatoes as sweet as sugar, melons of different kinds, plenty of apples, pears, peaches, cherries & plums grow wild in great abundance, and are very good. Fruit is never sold in the country in the same season. People that have orchards alow anybody to get as much as they please, but in the fall they sell apples at [figure omitted] per bushel on the trees. In fact, I think with you that my lot is happy to be in America. But there is a great difference in the parts, and where my uncle lives in Pensylvania things are double as high there as here.

You complain of the Government of England. This Government is in a bad state at present. The President and Cabinet have for a few years been making experiments on the currency of the country, which has been very oppressive on the merchants and traders in general, but the people have the power to remove it, and are begining to set themselves to work, so we shall have a new government in a little while. I suppose you are acquainted with the nature of this government, so I shall not attempt to say anything on that head. Suffice it to say that I think you would do well to come here. My reasons for thinking so are first you can get your choice of millions of acres of good land at one dollar and a quarter per acre, five shillings and two pence halfpenny; climate of any temperature you please, by going north or south. The laws are excellent, within the reach of every man, and every man of 21 years of age has a vote in choosing the law givers. There is none to high that the law cannot reach him, nor none so low that it will not protect. The path to science, to wealth, and to honour is open to all. Industry will always command competence, and virtue respect. Your sons have the privilege of becoming the greatest men in the nation. In fact this is a free country, and I wish you to think of the advantage it would be to you and your children to come here. If what I have said meets your approval and you wish it I will give you all the information you require in my next. Please send to let me know how my uncle John is, for I very much respect him, and let E. Williams have my address, for I should like to hear from all my old friends. I have been like a lost sheep, a long time stranger in a strange land. But I must conclude. I hope I shall see you here before long, but if we should never meet here I hope we shall meet in a better world. I am very sorry to hear that your lady is in so bad a state of health, and hope she will soon get better. Accept my best wishes for the welfare of your whole family, and believe me I shall ever remain your most affectionate son,

EDWARD PHILLIPS

Grenville, 10 Dec. 1842

DEAR FATHER,

I received your letter of 9 July and am very glad to hear from you, but sorry to hear you are such a cripple. These few lines leave us all in good health except myself, & I am very much troubled with sore legs, and have been for several years. My eyes have been well ever since they broke out. We have an increase of family since my last – a boy, we call him Charles Edward, he is now 7 weeks old. I have not received uncle William's letter, but he may possibly have written, as I have moved 350 miles since I wrote the letter to which that was to be an answer. I should like to hear if he wrote to Urbana or not, or if he sent the £10 or not, so that I could send for it. All letters remain in the Post Office over three months are sent to the General Post Office, and if it has gone there it will be some trouble to get it. You say that I got £10 when I came away. I hope my uncle will surely pay the interest on the money he has had the use of so long. Money is always worth the interest. The £20 at 5 per cent for 14 years before I came away would be £14, making £34. Take 10 from 34 it will leave 24, which at 5 per cent for 22 years would be £26.8s, making in all £50.8s, which I claim as my right. The interest I put very low, for money is worth 25 per cent here, and cannot be got for that without the best of freehold security. Now is the very time I need money, more than I ever did, as I am building a woollen factory. I am at a stand for want of money. If you can get Mr Williams to send it on in the spring it would do me a very great favour. He can get his banker to procure a draft on New York, and send it on as soon as possible in the spring, as it would enable me to get my building done in the summer. If my uncle has not the money ready, and you can let me have a little till he has it ready you will very much oblige me.

You wish to know something of my Uncle Edward. I am sorry to say that I can give you very little information about him at present, as we live about one thousand miles apart. I think he lives in New Garding Township, Chester County, Pennsylvania, but I will endeavour to find out where he lives, and let you know. He may be a thousand miles from there by this time, as the tide of emigration is westward, and people are continually changing their residence. You say that John & James talk of coming to America. For their information I will give you a brief description of this part of the country where I live. In the first place you will notice that there is a great difference between the Eastern and Western parts. Times are very bad all over the United States owing to the scarcity of money, which causes all business to be very dull. Bricklaying in good times is a very good trade, and men can make from 2 to 3 dollars a day, and when wages are good, but work here is scarce. There are no servants in this country, so it is necessary to have some trade, or to be a farmer. Farming is very bad at present and provisions low. It is 60 miles from where I live to St Lewis, the nearest market town. I will give you a list of the prices of provisions at St Lewis. . . . The place where I live is 10 miles from Greenville, the country is principally prairie or vast plains, void of timber, but covered with grass which affords fine pasture for cattle and horses. Here almost every man keeps a horse, as the distance to mills and towns is so great that they cannot doe without one. There are a great many Deer and turkeys in the country. Any man may shoot if he pleases, and plenty of smaller game, such as rabits, squirrals, partriges, prairie chickens, a fowl something less than the common dunghill fowl, and equally as good. I shall be glad to see the young men [in this] country. There is no doubt that they will do well here. Prudense and industry are all that are necessary to insure success. . . . [Greetings]

Your most affectionate son,

EDWARD PHILLIPS

Buck Creek, Illinois, 7 May 1845

DEAR FATHER, . . .

The times are very bad in this country at this time, and I stand very much in need of a little pecunary asistance. I have not been able to comence my buisness for the want of funds. I have been verry lame for almost a year, and have not been able to work, which makes me verry needy. I am afraid, dear Father, that I am getting to trublesome to you, but I hope you will look over that, and answer this letter as soon as you get it. And if you will try to have that monny sent over to me I shall consider it as a verry great favour.

Give my love to all my friends, and accept my best wishes for your own wellfare, and that of your family. So no more at present, from your most obedient son,

EDWARD PHILLIPS

Martin Series 1834–52

George Martin came from Chipstead, a hamlet in the parish of Chevening on the Darwent River near Sevenoaks, Kent, a mere twenty-two miles from London.[1] Chevening and nearby Brastead, where other members of the Martin family lived, were predominantly agricultural villages when George Martin emigrated in 1834. Well over half of the working people in these parishes were employed in agriculture, most of them as agricultural labourers, since this was a district of relatively large farms. George Martin's father, who had been born in the county of Kent about 1785, was a carpenter, and all three of his sons were brought up in the trade.[2]

Unlike most of our industrial migrants, George Martin took his wife with him, against the advice of his family, when he emigrated at the age of twenty-three. There is little reason to suppose that his emigration was induced by severe economic pressure. The population of the parish of Chevening actually increased from about 901 people to 1,003 between 1831 and 1841. His two younger brothers both remained in Chipstead. Alfred, who was only fifteen when his elder brother emigrated, was still living in his father's household as a journeyman carpenter in 1841. By 1851, he had married a local woman and set up on his own account as a carpenter. He worked for some time for Earl Stanhope of Chevening House, the largest landowner in the district. A younger brother, Peter, also working as a journeyman carpenter in his father's business in 1841, had similarly set up his own household and business of carpenter and joiner in Chipstead village by 1851. With George Martin's letters as a guide, these men were unlikely seriously to consider emigration to the United States.

In so far as there were economic factors in George Martin's decision to emigrate, his belief that a man had more opportunity to 'do something for himself' there classed him as an economically ambitious rather than a poverty-stricken migrant. His political views may also have encouraged him to leave the land of his birth, for he clearly regarded England as a country of 'oppression'. Like Edward Phillips, he set some value upon having a vote, and he became a believer in republican government, though one cannot be certain that this was so at the time of his emigration. In religion he was not an outsider in his village, since a Unitarian Chapel was built at Chevening some time before 1846. One can imagine that George Martin was rather an angry young man given to verbal outbursts against established institutions at home. Not surprisingly a disagreement with his parents, the nature of which the letters do not make clear, also formed part of the background to his emigration.

Although the Martins landed in the port of New York, they made their way immediately to the village of Cobourg on the northern shores of Lake Ontario in Upper Canada, where George Martin had a friend, a carpenter, who had held out inducements to him. Hoping to be able to get a house with enough land to keep his own livestock, Martin went on west to Hamilton on the western side of the Lake by 1837. The following year he retreated to a slightly more developed part of North America, to Rochester, New York, just south of the Lake. There he found work in November, 1838, without the help of other migrants, simply by approaching a builder who was working on a brick building. This man, Jonathan King, gave George Martin relatively steady employment from that time until Martin's death.[3] Martin had come to a fast-growing city where, except during the winter months, his craft was greatly in demand. The population of Rochester more than doubled during the thirties, and increased by eighty per cent to a total of over thirty-six thousand inhabitants between 1840 and 1850, under the impulse of the opportunities afforded by the Erie Canal.

There are several points of interest in the letters which George Martin wrote from Cobourg, Hamilton and Rochester. Among them was his inability to get on with other immigrants. Objecting bitterly to the treatment he received from his friend in Cobourg, he, in turn, found himself beset by immigrants from Chevening and London in the late forties and early fifties. The letters show both his annoyance at their inability to find work and housing unaided and their disgust with his failure to help them more than he did. These disagreements, as well as George's feeling that he had been unjustly treated in his father's will, arose, at least in part, out of a want of custom to regulate new sorts of social and familial relations which accompanied emigration to American cities. Recent immigrants believed that their contacts in America should provide them with free housing and good jobs. The family in England took the view that emigrants had cut themselves off from more than a token payment by way of inheritance. As an emigrant of long-standing, George Martin accepted neither of these views.

George Martin did not succeed in achieving the goal of independence. As the years went on, he became increasingly defensive about his failure to go into business for himself. He clearly lost face both with his brothers in Kent and with other immigrants to Rochester because he remained in Jonathan King's employ. His savings and his spare-time effort all went into the house he was building for himself in Rochester. When he died in 1852, this house was still unfinished, and the Martin family in England had to contribute over $500 to get it completed for his widow. After George Martin's death, Jonathan King wrote to the family in Kent: 'never can I tell you the hard struggle he has had to sustain his family and try to secure a home for them and he was in a fare way to accomplish it if his life had bin spard'.[4]

It might also be said that the Martin family were assimilated immigrants by the time George Martin died in 1852. It is true that he had visited England in 1845, and continued to have most of his social contacts with other immigrants and to rely upon them in times of difficulty. Yet at the time of his death, only his American employer undertook any responsibility for the widow and her children. Martin also evinced more interest in American political life than most of our immigrants. In Rochester there was no segregation of the large immigrant population by ethnic enclaves. On the street in Ward 8 where the Martins lived, the other residents were born in Canada, Ireland, New York, Switzerland and France. No doubt his persistent clashes with recently arrived immigrants during the last three or four years of his life also enhanced his feelings of identification with America. He showed definite anti-immigrant leanings during the great immigration of the mid-century. Like several of our immigrants in Part III, who also left England partly for personal reasons, George Martin did not achieve his adaptation through the immigrant community.

As the Phillips family had a branch in Manchester, so the Martin family had also established a bridgehead in a large English city. One part of the family was living in Woolwich by the 1840s, and George Martin's uncle, Thomas Martin, was engaged in business as a piano maker in Fitzroy Square in London. We have a few letters from Thomas Martin's son, who emigrated with his wife, Jane, to Rochester in 1851. These migrants planned to prepare the way for their father and his daughters to join them in America. This plan was not fulfilled, however. Although they complained of the hardship of their lives in London, Jane Martin was thoroughly disgusted with the poorer class of migrant they found on the ship bound for New York; Thomas Martin objected to the standard of food among the native-born in Rochester; and when cholera struck the city in 1852, they scurried back to London.

The originals of the Martin letters are in the Sevenoaks Public Library in Sevenoaks, Kent, and are reproduced with the permission of the Chief Librarian. I am also grateful to Dr Felix Hull for assistance when the Martin Letters were still lodged in the Kent County Archives.

Letters from George Martin to his parents, Mr and Mrs William Martin, Chipstead, near Sevenoaks, Kent

Cobourg, 30 Sept. 1834

HONOURED PARENTS,

I write to inform you of our safe arrival at Cobourg after a tedious voyage of 8 weeks, and of our circumstances since our arrival here, not knowing whether you wish to hear or know any thing about us, and I have stopt thus long before I write from illness, and from wishing to know how things would succeed before I wrote to you, that I might write the truth, and if there is any bitterness of feeling on your side still existing pray let it be forgot in the dangers and troubles I have encountered since the morning we parted but let all this be forgot.

And now for our voyage, we left London as you may know on Tuesday the 8th of April, in the packet ship George Clinton, for New York with 170 passengers on board. . . . [Account of voyage, storms and seasickness]

Monday Morning May 19 4 o clock made land a part of Long Island, sailed along the side of the island for some time, and then bore out to sea again having made the wrong side of the Island. Tuesday 20 Great quantities of fishing boats and fishing for Mackerel. We bought some mackerel alive. They were beautiful eating and came very seasonable for I was very near laid up from eating salt provisions so long. The scurvy made me very ill so that I had nothing to eat much for I had left off eating the salt provisions, and we had no pickles nor any such things, which are very necessary in a sea voyage. In the afternoon we entered the mouth of the North River, the scenery on the banks of the River the most beautiful that ever was seen, no pen can convey any idea of it, the sight seemed to repay us for all the troubles in coming over.

Arrived at New York 9 o clock in the evening and anchored off Whitehall Stairs. Wednesday afternoon landed at New York after rough passage of 6 weeks, took lodgings at a tavern, went to bed about 9 o clock. Scarce laid down in the bed before I was attacked by the bugs which were of 2 sorts the flat London bug and a long round bug 3/8 of an Inch long. My eyes and nostrils and all my body was swelled to a great size. I was obliged to walk the rooms all night. The Tavern was kept by English people who were very uncivil people.

Thursday obliged to attend the ship to have our luggage searched. The Custom house officer's were very gentlemanly men, so very obliging they just opened the lid of my clothes chest, and said they would not trouble me to open any more. I had no duty to pay at New York whatever. New York is a very large and fine city and full of fine broad streets lined with rows of trees on each side which look very green and gives the streets a very pleasant appearance. There are some very fine buildings of white marble, and a great many churches, which instead of a clock in their steeples they have a painted face to mimic a clock. Broadway is the finest street in New York 3 miles long and very broad and Straight, and rows of fine shops of all sorts on each side but built very irregular, some 2 stories, some 3 some 4 and 6 which is a very great defect in the city. Some old wooden buildings dropping down joining to a fine brick building was very frequent in the city, but the new streets are more regularly built, and they were very busy pulling down and building up fresh streets. There was plenty of trade and employment for carpenters at 12 to 14 York shillings p day, 7½ English money. There are no docks for the shipping only what they calls Ships which are long platforms of wood running out in the river, at a certain distance apart between which the vessels are moored in rows, We landed at one called peck Ship. There are no fine warehouses along side, only a parcel of whitewashed wooden buildings of all heights and sizes.

Friday moved the luggage on board an Albany tow boat, Saturday went to deliver the letters, took a place in an omnibus, paid 20 cents to find out Mrs Marten a distance of 3 miles, found the street in a very pleasant retired part of the city. The Street lined with weeping willows and horse chestnuts in bloom; they appeared to be not very well off in circumstances. Mr Marten was very poorly and he seemed fast sinking to his last home. I left Mr Colgate's letter to their son with them for I could not find him out. I went to find Mr [Mepham's?] brother but he was moved from the place where he did live to No 21 Scammel Street which was several miles off so that I had not time to find him out. So I put fresh directions on the letters and put them in the post office. Mr Bennet was likewise moved so I left Mr Anscomb's letter at the place for them to forward to him and if I came over 20 times to New York, I would never bring any more letters for anyone without it was to put them in the post for it is a common practice for people to leave their houses and move to another in the month of May which was the case with them.

Saturday afternoon left New York in the steamboat commerce for Albany. New York is situated on the south east end of Manhattan Island, which is about 2 miles across, and several in length. North of

Hudson River runs on one side and East River on the other, at the end of which they join. A very great number of all kinds and sizes of vessels laying at the wharfs on both sides the town, and a great deal of business going on very much like London only not so fine nor yet so smoky. There are plenty of omnibus's and hackney coaches (not old things like those in London but fine new ones) with beautiful fine horses driving in all directions.

Saturday night sailing up the Hudson saw some of the most vivid and brilliant lightening I ever saw, Sunday evening arrived at Albany a distance of 145 miles. Monday morning left Albany in the Steam coach for Schenictady distance of 16 miles on the railroad. In one hour took passage in a canal boat for Rochester, a distance of 270 miles, $4\frac{1}{2}$ days, stopt at Rochester 3 days for the steamboat, went with one meal a day to make money last. Monday left Rochester for Genesee, a distance of 3 miles, had my bed and blanket stole from the ware house, could get no remuneration from loss, went on board the steamboat Constitution and arrived at Cobourg Tuesday morning 7 o'clock June 3rd 1834, exactly 8 weeks from the time we left London. We had a very rough night across the lake, nearly all the passengers sick, landed and found George Winn in a new house on a quarter of an acre of land which he had purchased for 50 pounds, 4 years to pay it in.

He made us welcome as he could and seemed pleased to see us, got me work in 3 days at the new Scotch Church, but did not make any agreement for wages, so they cheated me at the end of the job out of 2 Dollars or 5/– each, which I mean to make them pay if I can. We worked from $\frac{1}{2}$ past 7 in the morning till 8 at night, and I could not get a dollar a day for all those hours of hard work. The masters were a set of whiskey drinking, negro driving Scotchmen, did not care how the work was done so has they got through it. I worked for them $8\frac{1}{2}$ days and then the job was finished, went to work for some more Scotchmen at 4/6 p day for $9\frac{3}{4}$ Days. The weather was so hot and the work so hard, for instance look at matching $1\frac{1}{2}$ in flooring together with $\frac{1}{2}$ in match planed, and I was very weak so that I was attacked with the Cholera of the country which is vomiting and purging attended with the cramp, which attacked me so violently that had not the Doctor been fetched instantly, and every means tried to stop the cramps before it reached my stomach which it was fast travelling you would never have heard from me; but by the blessing of God, I recovered, but it left me so weak that I could not work for a week. All together I have been laid up a fortnight and I have enjoyed very ill health since I have been here. You wished me to come by myself but I am sure you will recal that wish if you wish me any happiness, for when I was ill they could get no one to come and help my wife. Directly I was seized with the cramp Mrs Winn run away frightened to death, and I had no one to rub my legs and put hot water bottles to my feet but my wife. If I had been by myself I should have been taken to the hospital where I should have been sure to have died, for all that go there sick with the cholera never came out again alive. Neither could they get any one to sett up with me to help my wife during the nights but Mr Phelp's servant maid, a kind hearted girl of 18, so afraid are the people of the Cholera, and it is no joke here, I can tell you. Mine was the first case in the town, but since that a great many have died with it. Just an instance or two out of the many, A man, his wife and child been at Cobourg about 8 weeks from England seemed both well in the morning. The man went to work, and dropped down as he was going to breakfast and died soon afterward. The wife was taken ill soon after he left her and died soon after and neither knew the other was dead, the child died 3 Days after. Another, and I have done, to which I was witness. After I left the Scotchmen a month I went to work for a Cornishman at 5/– a day. One morning we had 2 Coffins to make by 11 o'clock, and he had left part of his house to a tinman just arrived from England. About $\frac{1}{2}$ past six this man was waked in the morning and directly he began to move he began to vomit and he was along time before he would have a doctor who, when he did come could do him no good, for the cramp had got to fast hold of him, and by 4 o'clock in afternoon he was a dead man and we made his coffin, and he was buried by $\frac{1}{2}$ past eight at night. The night before he was alive and well and talking to me.

Aug. 31 Sunday morning. Mrs Martin was delivered of a son, both doing very well. The child was said to be the prettiest little fellow ever born by every one that saw him. He was small but perfect in every limb and the Doctor said he was a complete model. We had a good many come to see me. He lived to be 12 Days old when the Cholera carried him off. I named him Peter after his Uncle. I got into a fine row with the old nurse who was a Methodist because I would not have the child christened. She called me over at a fine rate; there are a great many Methodists in Cobourg.

Cobourg is a neat little town built on the shore of the Lake Ontario of which we have a fine view as far as the eye can reach, nothing but water, very much like the sea, only the water is fresh. There are 8 steamboats plying on the Lake that touch at Cobourg and take in wood for fuel, 2 or 3 of a day, besides schooners &c from the States. The Lake is about 70 miles across at Cobourg. Cobourg is a neat town about the size of Brasted.* It contains 2 Churches 1 English & 1 Scotch, a Methodist

* Brasted, Kent, near Chevening, had 964 inhabitants in 1831.

Chapel, several other donominations meeting in private houses, such as Bible Christians, Universalists, Millenarians &c but no Unitarian meeting, so that I cannot go to any place of worship only now and then to one and the other to hear their different opinions. The houses are principally frame houses boarded outside with $\frac{1}{2}$ in[ch] board about 6 in[ch] wide, called Clap boarding which is the same as weather boarding only the boards are all of one thickness. The frames is mounted on 4 or 6 Cedar stumps, which is allowed to last longer than Oak (it is what you call Arbor vitae and grows to very large timber trees and as a very strong smell;) the floors are laid of $1\frac{1}{2}$ flooring matched together, the roo boarded with 1 in[ch] board and then shingled with fine shingles; and the inside lathed and plastered. The lathing is done by the Carpenters principally. They take wide pine board 3/8 in[ch] thick and split it all over with an axe into narrow strips about 1 1/8 in[ch] wide then take and nail it up, opening the splits with a wedge as joining on. The price for nailing on is 2d p yard. There are several stone land brick building, the roofs covered with tin which keeps as bright as when first put on and as a very glittering effect. Ther is also a very fine large brick building with tower and domes covered with tin called the Upper Canada Academy. It remains unfinished for want of money which is very scarce here owing to the Banks being robbed of several 1000 pounds last year.

The country round about Cobourg is very low and flat so that you cannot see a 2 miles around you. The soil is a light sandy clay, with a great many swamps where nothing but the Cedars grow. The timber is beach, ash, butternut, basswood, iron wood, maple of 5 different sorts, hickory, cherry, birch &c and Yellow Pine which is the most used, the houses being all built of it outside and in; there are 3 kinds of Oak grown, Black White and Red. Land is rather dear round Cobourg £50 for a quarter of an acre, or what they call a town lot for building on. Pine boards 1 in[ch] thick are 4 Shillings a 100 feet, and some less; the houses have all of them sash windows, the price of which are 4 per square finding timber, a pane of glass 8 by 10 in[ch] 4 p pane.... [Describes currency and prices]

All ironmongery is dear, tools of an inferior quality and very high priced. A pair of flooring planes cost 16/– shillings and they dont use the common auger here at all. They use nothing but the twisted ones, which sell at 1/0 p 1/5th which are preferable in framing of pine, the sashplates here work the moulding and rabbit both at one time so that theres no need of a sash filister.*

You must not place much dependence on what George Winn writes home for I have found things quite different from what he wrote home,

---

* A sash filister is a plane used in preparing bars of windows for sashes.

10

though when we first arrived there to find him, he behaved very kind and made us up a bed in the top part of his house as well as he could, though it was in an unfinished state, and the bed was straw. He got me work as I have said before, and when that job was finished we went and took a job of flooring together 15/9 p square. We went and begun and he worked $\frac{3}{4}$ of a day and then he took and left it and went off to a man 160 miles further up the country that had sent to him to come to work for him long before I got here, and left me to finish the job as well as I could, being strange work and his job. When I had done that and worked 4 days longer for the same man, I was out of work. We had settled between us to build a little room joining to his house about 12 feet square and he was to build the chimney and do part of the lumber and help build it, and I was to have possession of it for 2 years rent free; and he went off up the country and left me to build it myself, and I was out of work for 6 weeks so I built it to save rent which is very high. I was ill with the Cholera 2 weeks out of the 6. It appears by his own account that when he wrote that last letter inviting me over and to have part of his house, he was in lodgings and did not no what to do for a house himself and said he never wrote home any such thing, and again after he had been up at Dundas 2 months he came back to see his wife, and on the Sunday night he called me into his house to sign an agreement as he said, and I was to have it for 2 years. After I had built the room and made it comfortable and cost me £5 then wanted to cheat me in that manner, and I would not agree to any such thing. So he said I should have it for 18 months, and I agreed to it hoping to get away from him as soon as I can, for I do not mean to stop at Cobourg longer than that if I do so long. He has not done so well even as you might expect. He has got a $\frac{1}{4}$ of an acres of land for 55 pounds and a house for so much more it is true, and he is to pay for it in 4 Years with interest, £10 down on poassession and he has only paid £3, and he owes a great many more debts but be sure you dont say anything about what I have wrote about him, for if he should hear of it by any means it would make things very unpleasant indeed. I only tell you the truth so say nothing to nobody besides yourselves.

I have been at work for the last 6 weeks for a Cornishman, a kindhearted old man at the rate of 3/– [dollars?] p week. I have taken a job of flooring to do for him and after that I do not know how it will be. Winter is coming and we have not got a blanket to keep us warm; nor have I any warm clothes for the winter and I do not know that I shall be able to get them, for woollen things are very dear. Worsted is 4 shillings a pound; when I left Chipstead I had £37 in my pocket and when I landed at Cobourg I had £5 left which is all gone, and when my debts are paid I shall have about £2 left at present, and winter and a cold one too is very near at hand for this morning Sept 27th we had a very white frost as white as snow and it was very cold. Cordwood is 7/6 p cord and there is nothing else to burn for there is no coal and the Blacksmith's use charcoal; it cost us for living about 7 shillings p week and the common price of board and lodging for a single man is 10/– dollars 3 p week and pay for washing besides; we live very close to get along as well as we can, sometimes bread and potatoes for dinner and sometimes meat pudding, 1 lb of meat lasting us 2 days and we had a leg of mutton of 7 lb, cost 2s & 8d which lasted us 6 days. We have not got a chair to sit on, only some 4 legged stools that I made. We lay on a bed of shavings, a feather bed being no easy thing to get without you buy a flock of geese; but we have no rent to pay thats one blessing, and my room is paid for except the plastering which I am going to work on, but for all these difficulties I thank God for All that we do possess, and I hope by his blessing, if I have my health, to get through all these difficulties. If I can but get through the winter without starving, for work is very scarce here at present and they say there's nothing much during winter so I do not know how it may be yet, over head and ears in debt, if I go with one meal a day or less. But I hope things will turn out different to what I expect.

Mr James, that is my master, and I have 2 jobs in view to go partners in, and if we get them we shall manage very fair to rub along. They are 2 houses to finish, one of the bare frame and the other which is 7 miles off, is only the inside work, to be taken out in wheat, pork &c in part and some cash, but they are not settled yet. Money is very scarce at present which makes trade dull. We get half cash and the other half store, which is rather disadvantageous. Storekeeping is a very good thing, for they all get on well at it, and there are a great many in Cobourg. Tell Mr Mesham that the Custom house officers are not very strickt at New York, if you give them no suspicion by number of packages. There is a great deal of smuggling carried on between the Canadas and the United States and that store keeping is very good anywhere in the Canadas. Children's shoes of all sorts and sizes would sell well. Ladies do I cannot say much about, but I believe they would sell very well, but the women have 9 out of 10 of them such large feet through going without shoes or stockings, which is so very common that scarce any children wear them, and even the Store Keepers daughters, fine lasses, go without indoors, and I have seen washerwomen washing clothes out of doors by a public road with their clothes hitched up to their middles, which I am told is a very common practise with the French Canadians.

We have had a very hot summer indeed the hottest ever felt in Canada the newspapers say, the presperation running off you in streams as you sit at meals, but I did not feel the heat so much as I did in the States. When you write to me send us plenty of news and also the French Polishing recipe, and pray take care of my books that I left behind, for there are no such books to be got here, and if anyone is coming out in the spring that you can trust, be so kind as to send them to me by them and likewise the Penny and Saturday Magazine and Guide to know-ledge for 1834* bound, for there are no bookbinders here, and also a diamond for we do all glazing in the houses, and a good many more things I want but its no use saying anything about them, for I do not expect you will have the chance of sending any of them, but if you do I shall be thankful for anything. I mean to go up the country further when my time is out for it is much better about 300 miles farther up, and if I can manage to get a little piece of land and a small house, so that I can keep a cow and pig, poultry and geese, there is our living directly, which I hope to accomplish some day if I have my health, for though I am in difficulties at present I hope to rise above these all yet, and I say, as I always have, that there is more chance for a man to do something for himself here than there is in England. Labouring mens wages are 3/9 p day. If a man comes here he must work and hard too. We remain your dutiful Son & Daughter

GEORGE FREDERIC AND ELIZABETH MARTIN

Hamilton, District of Gore, UC, 7 June 1837
DEAR FATHER, . . . [Weather]

I have sent you inclosed a view in a street of Montreal, and the same may be seen in the streets of any town or village in Canada during winter. I have also sent you a picture of a Radical grindstone which might be used with effect on such long-nos'd gentry as Wellingtons and also on Whigs as well as Tories, for 'they are all rogues aleek', as King Jamie says, just want grinding and shaving up pretty close to make any thing of them fit for use; you must be in a miserable state all through the country by that new Poor Law Bill; and I do not hesitate to say, that if such a thing was put in force here, that they would be fetched off their perch, every man jack of them and sent to roost in not quite such a comfortable place. 'I guess' as the[y] . . . say. You say that it is the general opinion at home that we must take up liberty and fight for it,

---

* The *Penny Magazine* had first appeared on 31 March 1832. Both it and the *Saturday Magazine* were edited by Charles Knight for the Society for the Promotion of Christian Knowledge. Although aimed at a working-class market, their concentration upon useful knowledge and exclusion of fiction limited the circulation to shopkeepers and skilled workers, like George Martin.

which we would soon do were they to begin to oppress us, but as we have so little to complain of at present. It is only the true Canadians in the Lower Provinces that [illegible words] I think it would be very foolish to kick up a row for nothing at all. We are not taxed so much as our neighbours in the States, more than one half less, and I do not see but what our government is nearly as good as theirs. To be sure there is a great deal of room for reform in ours, and so there is in theirs.

You seem to think that the States is much better than here, and I will agree with you there in one point, that is, that there is more spirit of enterprize carried on there than here, but this is a new country from what the other is, and is only just now growing in to commercial consequence; but they are arising from their lethargy and have begun to see the advantages of public improvements; and there are more improvements to be made this year than ever has been before. The House of Assembly granted this year £200,000 towards our Great Western Railroad to go from Hamilton to Port Sarnia at the outlet of Lake Huron a distance of 146 miles, and they are now busy surveying the route and when it is completed it will make this town rise above any other town in Upper Canada, and bring . . . tract of country into cultivation, which is of no use now, and as the . . . and best route from the Eastern States to Michigan and Illinois is through . . . part of Upper Canada, we shall draw all the Yankees to come through our country instead of going so many more miles by Lake Erie, and the Americans are going to commence a railroad as a continuation of ours on the opposite side of the water . . . through the State of Michigan to the River Illinois, which is navigable for . . . down into the Mississippi river just above its junction with the Missouri which will open to us a direct communication with New Orleans and the Southern States, a distance of 2,000 miles or more, which we could go in about . . . days, so that some of these days perhaps you may hear from me at New Orleans or thereabouts.*

I have been pretty well ever since last Autumn, and I might say I never was better most of the time, I am getting along pretty well; and I have not lost much time for the want of work for the last 6 months. I managed better for work this last winter than any winter I have been here before, all indoors work pretty much; I could not save any thing though for provisions have been so high this winter as never was since the war – bread 1 shilling per lb, beef 7½d, butter 1/6, and every thing in proportion, potatoes 4/– per bushel. They are getting a little lower now, I hope if I have my health well to get along better this summer than ever

---

* The Great Western Railway grew out of a charter granted in 1834 to the London and Gore Railway Company. Little progress in building the railway was made until 1847, a new charter having been obtained in 1845.

I have, because I have got the most of my building done, or I can make shift with doing very little more at present, so that I hope to be able to pay by next September £[50?] towards my Lot, which if I can manage will save one 3 Dollars of interest for the next year, and I shall only owe $150 Dollars, which I have 3 more years to pay that in, but I should like to pay it before if I can, for to get my deed for it in my own hands, and when I have done that I think I shall be happy, when I can call it all my own, for I am just now getting it pretty comfortable. I have let one of my rooms off for the last 3 months for 7/6 per month which helps a little; and I have bought a good cooking stove, which is so much more comfortable than a fire place. It does not burn so much wood, and it keeps every thing so clean, and there is a nice oven in it besides, large enough to take 2 large loaves of bread. We bake all our own bread. It [the house] cost 32 dollars, furniture &c complete. I paid for it in work, and I got a feather bed this winter too; I was offered 600 dollars for my house & lot a little while ago, but I did not want to sell. Besides I would not sell it for less that $800 which is £200 pounds and if I keep it for 2 or 3 years longer it will be worth $1000 dollars or more, if I can but get it my own, and then I have a vote to send a member to Parliament.

You say in your letter that a great many are coming over to the States. Now if this letter should get home soon enough for to give them my advice, I would candidly advise them to stop till next year, and see how things turn up then. For depend upon it, so sure as the come there, they will wish they had stopt at home, for never was there such times in the States before since they have become United States, and if it was not that the Parliament of England had lent them £2,000,000 there is no knowing where would have been the end of it. As it is they do not know how it will be yet. Americans threaten to kill their President Van Buren whenever they can light of him. You see the Americans owed to the British merchants $30,000,000 Dollars; and Van Buren to hinder them making their payments good, took all the money belonging to the States and lodged it in a bank of his own raising, so that the merchants began to fail in all directions. There were . . . failed in New York alone, and nobody knows how many at other places, and since that Van Buren's Bank has broke and lost the States money and they threaten vengeance on him, and he must look out or he'll get it. We are just now beginning to feel some of the effects of it here. They keep coming back from States, because there is nothing doing and hundreds out of employ, but I am in hopes it will not check us much here.

Good Bye and I wish you all manner of happiness.

P.S. When I write for any plans again draw them in the letter, and not send them enclosed as you did the last. They charged me for a triple letter. If you have a newspaper particularly to send, send it folded with the ends out and put no writing inside. They will cost about 2d, I believe, so you can send me one and I will send you word whether you are to send any more or no.

[Signature illegible]

Letters from George Martin to his brother, Alfred Martin, Chipstead, Kent

Rochester, NY, May 1844

DEAR BROTHER, . . . [Apologies]

It is now ten years since I left home and after struggling through sickness, and slaving through health, I have for the first time in ten years had a steady winter's work, which as proved a great blessing, for I have had a very expensive winter from so much sickness and one thing and the other; and I should have been very hard run if I had not been favoured by fortune for once in my life. And if I had not so much building to do, which runs away with the money so, I would come over and see you all, for I can get from here very cheap now. I reckon with £25 or $100 Dollars in my pocket I should have money enough to pay my passage both ways and some left to spend when I was over there; or come as a Royal Visitor and have my expenses paid by the Government, as the pauper King of Prussia and others do. Why not? But I suppose I may as well neither think nor say any more about it, for I do not expect I should be a very wellcome visitor and it would cost to much money to be repaid with sour faces. Father never writes, and it takes you boys from 1 to 2 years to answer a letter and in your last you never so much as mentioned mother's name. . . .

6 August 1844

You must have heard by this time that we had got another little boy for he is now nearly 10 months old, a real fine fat boy and as hearty as a little pig and I have named him William after his grandfather, and we have only him and the little girl now, and she is not so hearty as she used to be, and I begin to fear that I shall not raise any offspring to perpetuate the name of Martin. Betsy is very sickly and none of the doctors seem to do her any good, and I am very much afraid that consumption as marked her for his own. I have suffered considerable myself in bodily health for this 4 months past but I am considerable better now, and hope to be in as good health as it is possible for me to be very soon. But something hangs on my mind and say that a very few years hence and not one of us will be among the living, but what grieves me the most in this case is that after a wearisome and toilsome life in getting so many nice books and other things together and have nobody to leave them to but strangers. You cannot imagine what the feeling is to think that you will die, the last of your race, in a foreign land far from your kindred and home, and no friendly hand to close your eyes, that would give more than a passing sigh and then forget you. I wish very much that some of you were over here, but I must not press you to come; and these may only be gloomy forebodings, that may vanish like a mist before the morning sun never to return; but which ever way it may be, let us learn to say, 'Thy will O Lord be done.'

A particular friend of mine by name Charles A. Wheeler, a native of London, is now returning to London to reside there and I take this opportunity of sending this letter and some trifle to father & mother, my means would not enable me to send much. Nor could I trouble the person much. Mr Wheeler thinks that he shall pay you a visit in the country when he gets settled, and if he does I hope you will give him a welcome reception for my sake. He is a very fine man and I think a great deal of him. (His friends are well to do in the world. His father is a retired clerk in the East India House on a pension of £600 a year) and he has had a good education; and if any of you should want to see him before he comes down, he will call on Uncle Thomas and leave his directions there so that you can find him, if you want to have any talk with him about me. . . . [Exchange of papers and business conditions]

So no more at present from your affectionate brother and sister,

GEORGE F. AND ELIZABETH MARTIN. . . .

Rochester, NY, 16 April 1848

DEAR BROTHER,

It has been the mildest winter I have seen in North America. It was pretty good for mechanics. I was quite busy althrough winter, but it was a miserable winter for the city merchants. In fact, it was ruination to several of them. Through the quantities of mud, the roads were impassable at times and the country farmers &c could not get to the city to trade and spend their money with us and we buy their produce, for when we had a spell of good weather and no sleighing, the weather changed so quick that any one living at a distance was afraid to venture, for fear of being catched in a scrape. It made all kinds of provisions very high with us all winter and they still keep up. In this country we want plenty of snow and good sleighing as all that makes merry times, and any one thinks nothing of going 50 or 60 miles in a day to market. Any person then that as good wood for sale which is almost useless to them in some situations, think nothing of runing in 40 miles with a load and turning it into cash, and so with any other marketable commodity, and if nothing else for pleasure trips.

Spring has opened very fine and this month of April as been very fine so far, and business is very brisk, so much so that every one is completely crowded at present. Every body appears to have something wants doing and they all want it done at the same time, so that we do not know which way to turn. I am working for the same old 'boss' as usual.

You talk about your new kind of asphalted roofing. We have got a new kind to talk about, which at the end of twenty years is said to be better than the day it was put on. It was discovered some few years ago in natural kind of basin in the earth of a great extent, at Sharon in the State of Ohio. It is dug in the first place in a soft state and is then ground and allowed to dry and is then ground again which reduces it to a slate coloured powder, which is then fit to mix with linseed oil and makes a black paint which is both fire proof and water proof. When painted on canvass or straw board it is said to make a good and cheap roof covering, and we are using it to some extent in this city this year. It is called Blake's Fire and Water proof paint. It consists of about one half of silicia, one fourth alumina with proportions of magnesia, black oxide, sulphate of iron, lime and carbon. When first dug it is of the consistency of tallow, but it hardens in a few days like slate, and then as hard as any rock. If they do not grind it in its soft state, they can do nothing with it afterwards.

Our (in)famous war with Mexico is now supposed to be at an end, as a treaty of peace has been signed and sent off to Mexico for the Mexicans to ratify, and the 'poor devils' can't help themselves, if they are [robbed?] of one third of their country; and I feel very glad indeed to think that we have escaped with taking so small a piece, for I was afraid that the Anglo-Saxon spirit of agrandizing territory, inherited from her mother, would not satisfy the daughter without taking the whole of Mexico. I have sent you a paper along with this containing the speech Dan Webster made in Congress on the peace question which will show you what is thought of this iniquitous transaction by a large portion of the intelligent community of this country.

But I say what a flare up in France. Learnt Old Phillip how to dance, 'sarve him rite'. I hope they will have the pluck to establish a Republican Government on a firm basis; but I am afraid of them for they are up today and down tomorrow. It is about time that folks got rid of their hereditary race of fools, that gnaws at their very vitals and devours them by inches. Only see at that infernal Lord John Russell wanting to increase that infamous income tax, to put more money in the rich mans purse out of the poor mans pocket. It is about time you had a

10*

revolution in England, and pay no such expensive salaries to have a little woman reign over you and laugh at you to think how well you keep her and her husband and all her young rats that will be eternally gnawing holes in your pockets, if you don't choke them off like other vermin. Give justice to Ireland, and that is, make her free and hang every Irishman that you find in Great Britain after 6 days notice for they are ... all the world over. So no more at present from your affectionate brother,

GEORGE F. MARTIN ...

P.S. John Whitehouse talks of coming out this season if he can raise money enough. If he should come I wish you would send me a sort of that pure flavoured rhubarb. If you can a dry root would come the best.

Rochester, NY, 7 Jan. 1849

DEAR BROTHER,

I here present you with a likeness of our new President, [President Taylor] and I hope and trust he will be every thing that his friends predict him to be, and if so, we shall have a first rate old fellow that will be a blessing to his country. . . . [Winter makes business dull] I have scarce earned any thing this last 4 or 5 weeks. Howsomever I have plenty to do to my own house, but self is a bad pay master; but its the way to turn lost time to profit. I raised up my different [pieces?] of building this summer under one roof, and now I shall have a good house, and plenty of room, and some to spare, when I get finished, which I shall rent to a suitable tenant, which will be some help if I can once get it in that situation. But it cramps me up rather tight, but the old boss is helping me some, so that I can do as much as I can whilst business is dull, so that I may be ready to go ahead as soon as work commences and that will not be long first I hope.

I am glad grandfather's business as got settled at last. Better for father to lose what he did then to go on any longer in the way he was going. Uncle Tom wrote me full particulars last July, and I had another letter from him dated Dec.r 1, which gives a deplorable picture of things in England and his prospects there. And I think the best thing he can do is to sell out and come to this country in the spring, for he can have work at the pianoforte manufactory in this city, for they want to get a hand from London, and the girls could do well at straw work. John Whitehouse* is very much pleased with the country as far as he is acquainted with it, and he and Tom are steady to work making flour

* Musician, aged fifty in 1850, who had emigrated from Chipstead after Martin's previous letter.

barrels, and Tom has just told me that he made 22 barrels last week and his father 25 do. at 10 cents a piece which is a low price, and as coopering is very dull indeed this winter, it is very fortunate they can earn that, which has insured them till the first of April, and a higher price p barrel should they rise. At the present price they average a sovereign p week, which at the rate provisions are here is worth as much as two sovereigns would be in England, and the 2 girls were very lucky in getting a job of sewing, making up ladies cloaks for a store (along with a dozen more girls), and they earned 45 dollars in 7 or 8 weeks, and on the 1st of March to go again to help make up summer goods such as visiters &c. John blesses himself to think he was enabled to get over here, and contrast this winter, with his last in England. It was lucky for him he found such friends, for he must have had something considerable left when he got here, but I never could find out how much (that would have been too confiding). He told me he had a little left. I tell you what he would have found some difference if he had had to work his own way among strangers. They are living about a mile from us now. (Didn't John catch a tartar when he married Ann Bligh??)

I am obliged to you for the rhubarb plants, but I doubt very much if either of them grows. One root had sprouted a little, but the large root appeared entirely eat up with the dry rot. I planted them in the richest soil in the garden, and time will solve the riddle. The wooden toys rotted asunder and the tin toys rusted, and the pewter toys smashed. Quite a chapter of casualties.

I received a letter last week from one of Betsy's uncles in London, Henry Maddams, No 10 Wood Street, Tabernacle Walk, Finsbury, asking for information about this country and he says if my views meet his, he shall not be long before he his over here. He has had a milk walk for a good many years in London, and I expect has got some property. You can learn at Riverhead when he intends coming, and you can then send any thing by him if you wish too. . . . [Sickness]

Emma helps her mother considerable but she is troubled with such rotten gums, that she bleeds at the mouth almost every night, and I do not know what to do for them. Father used to have a recipe for such a case. I wish if you could find it, you would send it when you write again. . . .

What has become of young Ned Young? You never mention his name. I didn't know but you might be off to California digging gold, where you can sift it out the soil by shovelfuls and is making every body almost crazy here. You will see by the papers that the cholera as reached these shores, and as been raging very severely at New Orleans, and as now reached Cincinatti and I expect when warm weather comes will kill thousands of us off, and who will escape God only knows; but it is no use being frightened. We must take our chance. You must excuse all blunders and I have made a good many, for it is written in haste and if I have forgotten anything you must forgive the omission. So no more at present from your affectionate brother,

GEO. F. MARTIN. . . .

Rochester, NY, 14 May 1849

DEAR BROTHER, . . .

You labour under a mistake in saying that the mail only leaves once a month in the winter, for it left England every other Saturday from November to May and left here every other Wednesday and is now leaving England every Saturday and this country every Wednesday till next November. I am glad to hear that you had such a mild winter, for we had a very sever one, only we had such good sleighing. . . . [Prices]

Business opened very brisk this season and is likely to continue so although money is scarce and hard to get at, but every steamship from England brings from 20,000 to 25,000£ apiece, so that money will not be so scarce long, and the tide of emigration this year beats all the preceding years, by thousands, but one bad thing in it is that so many come entirely destitute, that it swells our pauper community to a great extent, increasing crimes and raising taxes. Only a week or two back 88 persons from one ship sent over from Ireland by Lord Besborough* landed entirely destitute so that on landing at Albany 14 of them had to be sent to the poor house right off, and the rest would not be long before they [were in] the same condition. 6 or 7 years ago there was scarce a beggarman in the country; now they are quite common, mostly Irish and Dutch.

You can tell Charles Lentchforrd that if he has an inclination for this country and is good for anything as a carpenter, that he cannot fail of doing better in this country, than he can in England; but he must make up is mind not to be scared at trifles when he first gets here but puts his shoulder to the wheel with a strong determination to conquer, and he will then be sure to go ahead, and that is all the information necessary for him or any other mechanic, and it is too hard work for me to write letters to be answering all *creation*. You can tell Ned Young that it is not very easy for strangers to get a clerks place in this country. There are so many standing ready that are not strangers, but still there are many ways to get a living here if he is not afraid to work. Give my respects to him. You think 10 shillings a week for Tom to earn a week

* Lord Lieutenant of Ireland in 1852, warm friend of O'Connell, who had the reputation of administering his Irish estates well.

in our land of promise, a most miserable low price. Tell me where an apprentice boy in England would get as much and then again that 10/– in the way of living was as good to them as 20 shilling would have been down to Riverhead. . . . [Greetings] I have not seen John for more than 6 weeks. They have moved 3 miles from us but not out of the city. Tom comes round every Sunday. He and his father play the violin at the Free Will Baptist meeting house, a small congregation; with the idea of getting something as usual, but what they get I shall never know nor I don't care. I have helped them to a first start and they have got to go their own way now. The better they do, so much more shall I be pleased.

I am sorry to see by the papers that trade is still in a bad way in England, but I hope father as got enough to keep them busy. Its lucky for you getting so good a place at Lord Stanhopes,* and I should advise you to keep it as long as you can and be as saving of your money as possible; and then if you live long enough to get through there, you can come over here and you can invest your money in such a way so as to live with very little work. . . . [Greetings]

. . . [Cholera expected] My old boss as got married again and it makes him feel quite young again. We have had a most lamentable riot in New York on a most foolish subject which as ended fatally to 25 persons, and I have sent you a paper with full particulars by this mail. I likewise enclose you an advertisement for transporting emigrants in this country and if you hear of any one coming to this country be sure and give them the directions to John Allen, for he will save them many a dollar, and tell them to listen to one but him or they may get suckt in. I know John Allen well he . . . more from your affectionate brother,

GEORGE F. MARTIN

Rochester, NY, 25 May 1850

DEAR BROTHER,

Let me congratulate you on deserting Old Bachelorism and putting on the silken fetters of Hymen; and which I sincerely hope may always continue such, and never become changed into thorns. I am not any ways surprised at the news of the birth of your son; for I knew last June that you were married, and that the prospects of a crop of the rising generation was promising. Now I knew all this without your writing, so I was not any ways astonished at the confirmation of the news.

We were very glad to hear that Harriett had such a good getting up, and that the dear little fellow was thriving so well. But if you begin to

---

* Cf. Aubrey Newman, *The Stanhopes of Chevening*, New York, 1969.

despair at the birth of the first child, what you shall do with your family if it increases, I do not know what you will say when you have a dozen of them. If your prospects are so gloomy as you forebode, it is about time you tried another country where you can get your children educated for nothing, and so enable them to work their way in the world; but if you ever make up your mind to emigrate you must do it before your family gets to large and when you do start, you must make up your mind . . . a new country, and you find that the folks of that country will not conform to your ways; but if you wish to succeed you must learn their ways and conform to them as soon as possible. I really have no patience with such chicken-hearted people. Henry Clarke is one of that kind. He came here braging what he would do. He knew every thing about the country, and nobody could tell him any thing . . . [illegible]

. . . about it got scared and went home without trying any thing. Mr and Mrs Franks arrived here safe on the 11th of April after a tedious passage. I met them in the street going to look for them. I am sorry to say that John Franks as been sick ever since he has been here and he is no better at present. He as not been able to do any work since he came here, so that the importance of getting him out here early as been all lost. They send their respects to you and Harriett. Charles Lentchford arrived here 2 weeks after Franks. He is strong and hearty and all his family are well, and he likes . . . well. I got him lodgings right off when he came and got him work for a spell at the same shop as myself – and he is working there now. He sends his respects to you. George Thorbridge and 3 others hired out to farmers in this neighbourhood and are doing well. You would be astonished to see the quantities of emigrants going. . . . So no more at present from your affectionate brother,

GEO. F. MARTIN

Letter from George Martin to his brother Peter

Rochester, NY, 9 Feb. 1851

DEAR BROTHER,

I received your hurriedly written note last November and being very much harassed in my domestic circle I did not answer it before this, and indeed I had not thought much of doing so: for, thinks I, Peter never expected me to answer that scrap of paper, and I have been expecting ever since to hear more fully from you or Alfred, but it appears I was doomed to be disappointed.

. . . . [Arrival of some immigrants and return of others] Truly this last year past and gone as been one of great trouble, anxiety and expence. I commenced the year with trouble and I ended it the same, and what with doctors bills, lost times, and continual outgoes, it as cornered me up pretty close; but with good health and the blessing of the Almighty and many endeavours I shall soon overcome them.

I suppose you will have heard long before this that we have had an increase in our family. On the 28th of August Betsy was safely delivered of another daughter and was doing very well for 3 or 4 days when child-bed fever ensued and we had a tough job to save her. For five weeks Mary and me had to watch every night with the exception of 3 nights when we had neighbours assistance, and a kind neighbour took the baby for 2 or 3 days and that was a great help; for 3 weeks I had but a few hours sleep and poor Mary wasn't any better off. It was a great blessing that she was in the country. She was not living with us then but 10 miles off at a farmers of the name of Hodges from Sevenoaks Weald, where they are now stopping. She came in the first week of August and stopt till the end of the first week in November, when Betsy could just crawl round. When John fetched Mary away he would not let her stop any longer and as she would not take any pay I could not ask her to, and she as never been anigh since although an omnibus runs within 2 miles of where she lives and cost only 6d English for the ride. I hired a woman to do the washing every week all the time and still do: but Betsy as never regained her health yet, although she gets about better than she did and I am in hopes when warm weather comes she will get as well as usual, but she never would have got along so well if she had not tried an excellent preparation of sarsaparilla and [Woahou?] syrup (manufactured here and sold two quarts for a dollar) which purifies the blood, and sthrengthens the whole internal system, and makes healthy nurse so that the baby as thrived wonderfully and is as fat as a little pig, but as cross grained as 'Dick's hatband', a real chamber organ as you say. I wish you had it.

I have not seen John Franks since the third week in October when he was at my house one Sunday and his health was no better and Mary and he then concluded they would go back to England in February: but when two weeks after he fetched Mary away, he felt so much better, that he concluded they should not go home, and he has called twice since, the last time about 4 weeks ago and he said then he was never in better health in his life. I did not happen to be at home, ne'er a time when he called so thats the reason I did not see him. Neither have I seen John Whitehouse for the same length of time, but he as not been anigh the house. It was a hard matter to offend them, but I managed it at last. His she devil of a wife came to my house during Betsy's sickness, when she could not bear the least noise, kicking up a row about her daughter Betsy. So I told John afterwards that if Ann could not behave herself better I never wanted her to enter my doors again, and as they had found out sometime before that they had suckt all they could suck out of me, the whole lot took offence and never came near, and all the harm I wish them is that they never will any more.

Tom called in yesterday to see his Aunt and said his father had had a severe fall on the side walk which had shook him considerable. But a truce to such confab, just to give expression to my thoughts, which is that if I cannot have more pleasure than I have had in folks coming to me here, then I wish I may never see another face here I have known in England. Why don't folks ask themselves the question? Am I fit to emigrate? Am I fit to go to a new country to leave my old ways behind me, and begin life anew with everything strange about me, new manners, new customs, and I wedded strongly to my old customs! And if answered in the affirmative why not go manfully to work with a strong determination to go through thick and thin 'never say die', and not wait to see after you have got 3000 miles from your dear old home, how much better you could have done there if you had only tried. . . . [Weather]

I am still working at my old place. I sometimes think I am doing wrong in not leaving and starting for myself, but I hate to leave a certainty for an uncertainty and as long as the old man uses me as well as he does. I have work if there is none for anybody else, and a promise of it as long as he carries on business, and when he gives up for me to take it, and he will help me if I stand in need. But promises are like pie crust made to be broken; and I must go on the old way as long as it suits.

If you should have a chance, just send me 2 or 3 first strings for violins, for you must know that I have begun to fiddle a little again for the amusement of the children as they are all good singers, as singing is part of our common school education, one hour every week. An excellent teacher attends so that Emma is quite a good singer and Willy is pretty good, and Julia too, and then comes the little shaver, Georgiana, not quite 3 years old, sings as well as any of them. You would laugh to hear her sing to the fiddle and sound the keynote she never fails nor do. How pleased poor father would be to hear their sweet little voices singing in unison with the fiddle, some of their sweet songs. I bought one of the tune books on purpose. They have all been tolerably well in health this winter with the exception of bad colds now and then. They all send their love to grandpa and grandma, and the rest of you. We have named this last shaver Ellen. . . .

Young Tom and Jane talk of coming to this country in the spring. I have written to them. I have held out no inducement to them, but there is plenty of room and plenty of chances to make a good living if they will only try in earnest. Mrs Bennet says she as enquired round the city and she as no hesitation in saying that if Uncle Tom and his daughters where here that the girls could earn a first rate living for themselves and him too; but as I tell them, glad as I should be to have them here, I will not hold out any inducements for them to come but leave it to their own free choice. They know what I think of the country, and if they are a mind to try it on the strength of that and put their shoulders to the wheel they are sure to succeed; and they will not be so ignorant when they get here that they cannot see what benefit the country can be to them, and sit down and pine & cry and get home sick and try nothing. It is the best thing in the world for emigrants to learn them wisdom and keep them from getting home sick not to have a sovereign in their pockets when they get to their journeys end. It brings them to their senses right off and tells them pretty plainly what they came for. I have spun you a long yarn about not very interesting topics, but if it fails in giving you satisfaction you must forgive me, for it is so seldom we have a confab that it takes a long yarn to clear our throats ready for operation and then my papers full.... [Greetings] From your affectionate brother,

GEORGE FREDERIC MARTIN

Letter from George Martin to Alfred Martin

Rochester, NY, 18 Jan. 1852

DEAR BROTHER ALFRED,

Under the circumstances of the case as you state it I accept of your apology for not writing before, and your after conduct will decide what kind of a bond of amity will exist between you and me. Till then I call you Brother and thank you for the copy of Peter's will, not fathers. I was not so much surprised at poor fathers death, because all the accounts I heard of his health and feebleness of body led me to anticipate such an event; but I certainly was astonished at the delay, in writing to me of the sad event, but I am not any ways astonished now, that I am acquainted with the facts of the case. Everything goes to show Peter's villainy. I don't wonder now at not receiving any letter from him last year, the scoundrel. He had not the face to write to me after making that will. It was well for him and myself too, that I was not present at the reading that said will for I might have left such a mark on him that he would not have forgot in hurry, and I might have been sorry for in a calmer moment. Now read my principle testimony for the view I have taken of the case. In his last letter but one to me dated Feby 10th 1850 sent by Mrs Franks, he thus writes of father.

'Father I am sorry to say cannot now attend to anything, his nerves are so weak, and his mind appears so confused, that it is with difficulty you can make him understand any trifling thing'. Now that was father's state of mind 9 months before that will was dated, and Tom saw father in October and he was in no better state and Tom says he should not consider him capable of making a will, and our firm belief here is that Peter wrote that will to please himself as near as he could in relation to you on the spot, and deprived me of my birthright, (who he thought was to far off to trouble him), and got father to sign his name to it without his understanding what was in it. Do you think he would have left mother so completely in Peter's power that he can compel her to give up the business to him, just when it suits his convenience to do so, and she can't help herself. No, he would not no more than he would have deprived me of my inheritance. If I was not so far off I would certainly come home and stand a suit at law and set that will on one side. I do not wish to wrong any of you, of a red cent; but I what I demand of you all is my rights, and till you can show me good and sufficient reasons for the provisions of that will in relation to me, I shall continue to demand them. I should have been just as well satisfied if he had cut me off with a shilling, for that would have settled the matter at once and I should have been as likely to receive one as the other, for I don't expect to ever see any of it. Now, as I acquit you all of having any hand in Peter's villainy, what I have got to say to you and Mary and Emma and Frances is, that you are not bound by his rascality, and you can tell what amount of property father has left and what will be the amount to be received by each of you and what would have been my share by an equal division, and then you can tell what additional amount each of you will receive by my share. Now mind what I say. I shall hold each and every one of you accountable for that amount to me and whoever appropriate that said amount to their own use is guilty of robbery, as much as if they went into anybody house and stole that amount of property. Now if you are my brothers, you will see justice done your injured brother, and you will see Mary and Emma and Frances and talk with them and find out what they will do and let me know when you write again, what is your determination, and if your answer should be in the negative, (or you should not all agree to do so then let each one answer for their own iniquity), and you cannot show me any good and sufficient reason for so doing, I shall not consider any of you brother or sisters of mine, the same as I no longer consider Peter any brother of mine, and don't come anigh me for heavens sake! For we should only quarrel. Now I say nothing about the division of the books, and much as I should have liked to have had some of them but let them go. But I see Peter as got the lion's share there too, and it's a lucky thing for you that you was not over here or we should have been paid off with £50 stock apiece which would have been a much greater loss for you than being deprived of your share in the business.

You wish me to advise you about your coming here. Now glad as I should be to have you here as this must depend entirely upon the course you take in respect to what I have said. Now as I cannot act the hypocrite I would rather not say any thing on that subject till I hear from you again. Or shall I have confidence that you will be my brother, I think I will and trust to Providence for the result. Now I am perfectly aware of the evils you state of a constant place of work, and Uncle Tom's case is in order, and sorry I am for him; but still my case is different from his, for I am steadily laying by something for a rainy day, and if my life and health should, with the blessing of God, be spared to me for some years, and my family expences are only in bounds, I shall have eventually something to make me comfortable in my old age, and when you have got 7 mouths and bodies to fill and clothe and all the &c and only one pair of hands to do it all, you will appreciate some of the benefits likewise, and you will be very cautious how you leave a certainty for an uncertainty and risk the losing of all your savings. Now I have two considerations in view. In the first place as I say I can do no better as a journeyman; secondly, I am headman, and the boss as promised me the business. It was only last week that we were talking it over again, and he said, if it was not for one or two things, he would give the business up to me right away, but he should not carry it on much longer, and that he would not sell out to anybody, and that he would find me money to go on with if I needed it, and help me all he could. So you see that my being in business for myself is not an impossibility; and if you should come and we could agree perhaps, as you say, we might do something together. But I have said that I would not write for any body to come here again, for whether they sink or swim my thanks are very small. Nevertheless, if you should make up your mind to come this spring I could promise you work with me for a certainty to begin on, and a home to come too, where you would be made welcome, and if you have the wish to come to this country, the sooner you come the better. You need not fear that there are not plenty of ways to invest a small capital profitably. Betsy thanks you for your washing recipe, but guesses she will not try it because she uses a soap, a patent article, which does up the business as well as yours I guess, with $\frac{1}{2}$ an hour soaking and costs us $3\frac{1}{2}$d English a week for our washing which enables her to get through with it or she would not be able to do it. We are all pretty well in health, and hope to remain so. . . . [Winter and news of immigrants] So no more at present from your affectionate brother,

GEO. F. MARTIN . . .

[Two letters from Tom and Jane Martin, 27 July 1851 and 16 May 1852 from Rochester, NY, have been omitted]

Stephenson Series 1838–40

Abel Stephenson was described by his nephew as an honest but singular man. Stephenson was, if anything, even more irascible and violently inclined in his views than George Martin. Critical of the new Poor Law, a man with almost an *idée fixe* about the evils of paper money, a firm opponent of power-driven machinery in his own trade, a believer in farming as the only independent life, Stephenson may have seemed singular to his young nephew, but in fact he adhered to a bundle of ideas quite common among emigrants, especially from Lancashire and the West Riding of Yorkshire, during the thirties and forties.

Since his two brothers, James and David, had been born in 1799 and 1805 in the clothmaking village of Thurstonland, an upland weaving fold in the West Riding of Yorkshire, south of Huddersfield, it seems very likely that Stephenson, like Martin, left the town of his birth when he went overseas in 1837.[1] Most of the families of Thurstonland were employed in the manufacture of woollen cloth. According to the 1831 census, 170 of the adult men in the town were engaged in manufacturing or in making machinery, while only 43 were employed in agriculture and 38 in retail trades or handicrafts. Stephenson referred to himself as a clothier, but in his part of Yorkshire that meant little more than that he sold the cloths he wove himself. The population of Thurstonland was increasing during the decade when he emigrated, from 1,098 people in 1831 to 1,826 in 1841. At the time that he left, power looms had already appeared in this village; and he emigrated recognizing that his craft was becoming obsolete in Yorkshire.

The other members of his family, to whom these letters were written, stayed in handloom weaving throughout the decade of the forties. His brother, James, was listed as a clothier in the census in 1841 and 1851. James's sons, Amos and Abel, who were sixteen and thirteen years old in 1851, were being trained up as handloom weavers of woollen cloth, in spite of the spread of power looms. Another brother, David, was still described as a weaver in 1851. Thus, the members of the Stephenson family who remained in Yorkshire did not readily adapt to changes there, and suffered the full impact of power looms in the woollen industry during the forties and fifties. They were among the few families represented in these letters who actively sought remittances and inheritances from emigrants in America. David in particular, a woollen weaver of fifty-four years of age, tried very hard to get a share of the full improved value of the farm that Abel Stephenson left in Iowa, though the American courts decided against him.

Arriving in the United States just at the onset of the depression of the late thirties, Abel Stephenson spent his first two years moving from one place to another. Finding power looms well established in Northampton, Massachusetts, in 1840, he was reduced to spinning for a livelihood. These experiences may well have fortified his dream of becoming a farmer. He may, in fact, have bought his land in Jefferson County, Iowa, as early as 1840, while he was still working in textile factories in the east. Jefferson County was organized in 1839 from the western part of Henry County and the Indian purchase of 1837.[2] Abel Stephenson's 160 acres were uncleared government land. He seems to have sought first the help of another English immigrant by the name of Robert Stephenson, who arrived in 1841 in the township of Lockridge, where Abel Stephenson's land lay. So far as one can tell, Robert Stephenson, who became a prominent citizen of Lockridge, was not a relative of Abel Stephenson.[3] In 1845, Abel Stephenson persuaded his brother Richard, another handloom weaver who had emigrated to New York State in 1840, to come west with his family. Richard Stephenson settled on 80 of Abel Stephenson's 160 acres; and from that moment, Abel Stephenson disappeared from his family's ken. He announced that he was going off to Canada and that he would be back in about two years, but he never returned.

Jefferson County expanded very rapidly in population during the forties to reach 9,904 by 1850. There Richard Stephenson raised his three sons: Samuel, who remained on the farm; Abel, who was killed in the Civil War; and Daniel, who moved to the county seat of Fairfield and established himself as a weaver of blankets and coverlets. Thirteen years after his brother had given him eighty acres to farm, Richard Stephenson and his son, Samuel, had succeeded in clearing only fifty acres and in breaking, ploughing and fencing forty acres.[4] Neither Abel Stephenson nor his brother Richard seems to have found farming a really acceptable alternative to their obsolete craft. Richard continued to weave in Jefferson County, Iowa, until the end of his days.

Copies of the Stephenson letters were made from manuscripts owned by Alderman Clifford Stephenson of Huddersfield, and the letters are published by his kind permission. Photostats of the letters are in the Library of the London School of Economics and Political Science.

Letter of Abel Stephenson to his nephew, Abel Stephenson, Thurstonland, near Huddersfield, Yorks., and other relatives

Pittsburgh, Penn., 18 April 1838

DEAR FRIENDS AND RELATIVES,

I now take my pen to write a few lines to let you know that I am in a moderate state of health, and on perusing those few lines you will be enjoying the same blessing. I am still working for Joseph Haigh. . . . [Letters] The letter says that he has given my father five pounds has we proposed, but I am most ancious to receive a letter from you to know how my father and Joseph is coming on. By the accounts that comes, times is no better but worse then when I left you. I gave an account of my voyage in my last letter, so if you did not get it, so it will be left for time to reveal it, what was in it. I am going to send this letter by a man who is going into the neighbourhood of Thurlston from Pittsburgh.

I can give no good accounts of the times in this country in the manufacturing business. The rotten corrupt banking, it is a curs to this country. Since the suspension of specie payments, there has scarcely been any silver to be seen. There is some banks taken their notes and pays silver. It does not mean what form of government there is as long as this rotten corrupt paper system exists, it gives great liberty for all this band of idlers, usurers and speculators. They are a cankerworm, preying on the very vitals of the working class, as well as the aristocracy of England. I shall give no encouragement to come to this country except they turn into the land. A man could buy a large farm for a 1000 dollars wich will keep him and his family in a state of comfortable independence. Machinery is increasing fast in this country, so that in a little time it will be as bad as it is in England. I shall not advise to come to this country to work in the manufacturing business, for times in the New England states is nearly as bad as they are in the old country; but it is better in the western country. Yet power looms is increasing rappidly.

It is very winterly at the time I am writing this letter. It snows pretty hard. I have stood the climate very well so far on the weather is very changeable. I have done better in America than I did in England, but I shall not settle in this part; for I am going to leave and go down the River and I think of going to New Orleans in autumn. It is situated at the mouth of the Mississippi River, 2000 miles from Pittsburgh. I shall turn my hand to some other business. . . . [Arrangements for receiving letters]

I shall never come back to Thurstonland to be a clothier again. I may come back sometime to see you, but not to stop. So I wish you all good luck and I hope you are all doing better then I expect. They call the man William Shaw who is going to bring this letter. He will put it into the post office nearest to Thurstonland from his way from Manchester to Thurlston. I suppose Brooks as only got 27 power looms yet. By the news that comes, there is not better a prospect of a change then ever for the better. The new poor law bill still goin on. Yet but I hope there is none of you got to . . . a union workhouse. So if I cannot to suite me well I shall go to New Orleans and try some other business. So I shall conclude with my best respect to you all, dear friends and relatives,

ABEL STEPHENSON . . .

Glens Run, Ohio, 26 Nov. 1838

DEAR RELATIVES,

I received your kind letter with much pleasure on the 12th of November. I gladly embrace this oppertunity to let you know that I am in my usual state of health, and I am glad to hear of my father and Joseph and the rest of the family been in their usual state of health as when I left you, except Elizabeth Lockwood. I hope she is gone to that place where there is no trouble nor sorrow nor anxiety exists. If I never see you again, father, forgive me, if I have done anything wrong to you and pray to God to forgive me. We are all frail mortals by nature and subject to passions. I hope we shall all be prepared to meet at Gods right hand, were tyrants and oppressors will not be admitted to drive a poor man away to a foreign land as they do in this world. I suppose times is still getting worse. I saw there was a gloomy prospect for a poor man before I left. I was determined I would try my luck in America and I do not regret it, thank God. I could not bear the thought of been brought to a state of destitution and starvation amidst plenty. I would do anything that is necessary to be done in exterminating that vermin which is the cause of all the distress and misery that exists, so universally throughout the earth.

I left Haighs on the 7th of August. I should have left sooner but on account of expecting a letter from you. They got your letter on the 1st of September. I left my chest with them till the river rose. I should have gone sooner but the river was so low that steam boats could not run till into this month. I am near Wheeling. It is about 20 miles below Pittsburgh on the bank of the river Ohio. It is three miles from Wheeling. John Hobson from Hagg, near Holmforth, Joseph Earnshaw from [Leeds?] rents the factory that I am weaving and spining here. Old Haigh, he his a little tyrant. He charged me 5 dollars the pound. The difference in the value of money is 6s. 6d. to the dollar, the standard value. He said he had as good a right to the profit of exchange as the money changers. He says the labouring class is too independent in this country. He says as much as any man against tyranny and oppression and he his as bad as any man according to the power he has, so no more of old Haigh.

I suppose by the newspaper called the *Old Countryman,** a New York paper, gives an account of large and numerous meetings being called for the purpose of petitioning for universal suffrage, and the speakers, it seems, is for agitating the question only and no other till they get that. It is very good, but they will not get it by petitioning. The aristocracy will not give up their plunder, they have robbed the people of but by dint of metal, lead and steel. The sooner it is done and the better for the labouring class. Democracy is gaining ground a little in this country. I think the banking system will be reformed. The people seems to see into the evil of it. There as not been much loaning paper out to speculators since the resumption of specie payments, so that money is rather scarce. The limits of a sheet of paper will not allow me to say more on the subject. I begin to like the country better than ever. The climate as not taken any effect on me. If my father had come when he was young he might have had a large farm now if he ad had health and good luck and he would have been independent now, and he would have been reaping the fruits of his labour. If he his in the want of some money, send me word in your next letter and I will see if I can send him some. I should not wish him to come to endanger his life on a voyage to America, for it probably would; so I advise him to prepare for a better country then America where I hope we shall meet never to part again. If he be spared a few years longer I shall come to see him. I cannot come yet. My circumstances will not allow it at present. When there is lines of steam ships established between England and America the passage will not be much, then I will come. . . . [Remainder of the letter missing]

Northampton Factory Village, Mass., 18 April 1840

DEAR RELATIVES,

I take this oppertunity to write to you to let you know where I am. I am sorry that I could not write sooner on account of very bad times and sickness at the time I got your letter. I was sick of the fever and ague. I was taken sick in July and continued till the middle of October and then I left the place on account of it being unhealthy. I liked the place very

---

* This is a reference to a shortlived newspaper for English immigrants, which apparently existed earlier than the date of 1842-8 given in the *Union List of Newspapers*. This is the only reference to a newspaper for British immigrants in any of these letters.

well if it ad been healthy. I should not have left there, as fine and good behaved a man as any man need work for. I got your letter on the 8th of October and I left on the 26th of the same month and that is the reason I did not write sooner. The times is and as been so bad this last 6 months in the manufacturing business that I cannot give you any encouragement to come at presant. It as been as bad last winter as ever it as been since they got their independance, without any prospect for the better owing to the rotten and corrupt paper system and unsettled state of the currency. Brother James, I am sorry that I cannot fulfill my promise at presant relating to the money I promised thee. I was sick nearly three months and after I left the last place I worked at I was out of work till January. I am spinning at the place I am at now. They weav all by power here. Wages is very low here. I shall not stop here any longer then till times begins to revive again. I shall go back west again. I have ad another attack of the fever and ague this spring. I have got better again. Sickness and been out of work it is nearly taken all my earnings. Times in the manufacturing buisness is very dull and likely to continue till there be a radical reform in the currency.

I am glad thou did not let John Bottomley look at the letter. I should not like any one to see my letters but yourselves. I have not got any one on to my land. I shall go on to it myself as soon as I can. I send my best respects to William Stephenson. Tell him to let me know how he is coming on. America is a fine country for a farmer. It is a sure and independent living. Dear Brothers, I am sorry that I cannot give you any encouragement to come and depend on the manufacturing buisness. Fancy goods is imported from England cheaper then they can make them here. Out in the western country there is nothing of the kind wore except a little in the towns. Manufacturing will always be a poor buisness in America till they have to compete with England and a better currency in the country. When they buy Congress land they pay all down at once.

There is a man from Lower Wortley. His name is William Swift. He is a shoemaker. He is going to send for his family. We enjoy ourselves together very well. Lower Wortley is near Leeds. I hope this letter will find you all enjoying good health. My health is not so good as it was when I sent my last letter. I can do my work I am not got right well again yet. So I conclude for the presant, Yours affectionately,

ABEL STEPHENSON . . . .

Hails Series 1848–9

This series of letters begins when the writer, Richard Hails, had been in America for six years. The final letter reviews his emigration in 1842 and his early history in the United States. In this case, it is difficult, if not impossible, to distinguish between attitudes held at the time of his emigration and the modifications or changes in them after the migrant arrived in America. While his economic adaptation had not been outstandingly successful, he regarded it as satisfactory. In other respects he showed no evidence of uneasiness, and his homesickness was not excessive. Hails did not directly mention American friends, though he spoke of friendly neighbours, and none of his friends at the time these letters were written were people known to his family in England. He had married a woman, who was probably Welsh-born, after he came to America.[1] Thus, in so far as these letters provide clues, Richard Hails appears to have made a very good social adaptation within a few years.

Hails emigrated from the town of North Shields in Tynemouth Parish, Northumberland. His father and his brother, George, appear to have been pottery workers at the North Shields pottery. Very few pottery workers of any kind were listed in the 1841 census at North Shields, though by 1851, sixty-six earthenware manufacturers were enumerated there.[2] With one in four of its adult males employed in coal mining in 1851, more men were also working in iron manufacture and shipbuilding in Tynemouth than were engaged in agriculture. By the mid-century, North Shields was fast becoming an area of heavy industry, but this growth had been quite recent. According to the census records, its population had actually declined during the 1820s. While it increased from 6,744 in 1831 to 7,509 in 1841, it had not yet recovered the level of population reported in 1821. The growth of population accelerated during the forties, after Richard Hails had emigrated. Like the other industrial workers whom we have discussed, Hails did not leave a stagnant rural parish but an industrial area whose long-run growth prospects were good and where new opportunities were being created with economic diversification.

The letters provide no direct information as to the reasons for his emigration. Hails had himself served an apprenticeship as a tailor. The number of men and boys in the tailoring trade in Tynemouth Parish had expanded with extraordinary rapidity during the thirties, if the census figures are to be believed. During that decade, while the population grew by eleven per cent, the number of adult tailors and breeches makers increased from 58 to 166. If such an expansion in tailoring did, in fact, take place, it may help to explain Hails's emigration, for even if this growth began in response to rising incomes in the area, the very rapid growth suggests that the occupation was becoming overcrowded by the end of the decade. The trade showed very little further expansion during the forties, when population increased by sixteen per cent. It need hardly be added that the year of Hails's emigration was one of considerable hardship and unemployment in industrial areas like North Shields.

The inference that his emigration was largely economically motivated seems to be supported in the letters. Richard Hails made no references to politics in Britain or America; if he fled from England, as did Stephenson and Martin, as from a land of tyranny and oppression, these thoughts were gone by the time he wrote these letters. In discussing the question of his brother's possible emigration, Hails concentrated on economic criteria, emphasizing above all the opportunities afforded children in America and the ease of providing them with trades. Although he encouraged his brother to buy land in the west, he did not accept uncritically the view that a farmer's life was easy and independent, but weighed the possibility of investing in land as a speculation and warned his brother not to plunge into farming without seeking some prior experience of work on the land. It is interesting that by 1849, Hails did not even want to be bothered with the garden in the large house which he was renting. He does not seem to have been propelled towards the particular goals which guided the radically oriented industrial workers, who went into agriculture or who centred their lives around the acquisition of a house, an allotment and a few animals. His behaviour seems to have been more economically rational.

Nevertheless, Hails shared some characteristics with the other industrial immigrants we have been considering. His letters traced frequent changes of location during his first years in America. These three letters of 1848 and 1849 were each written from a different small village in Middlesex County, west of Boston. Wayland and Sudbury each had over a thousand inhabitants in 1850. The town of Lincoln, where the last letter originated, had only 719 people. This was an almost entirely agricultural village, with no industry other than that of craftsmen such as blacksmiths, carpenters, and tailors. While it must be admitted that his indifferent health governed his decisions to a great extent, it is interesting that Hails was managing to avoid the industrial revolution, even in Massachusetts. He could not be found at Lincoln in the census of 1850, and we have no information about his later career.

Hails also expressed a willingness to try another occupation if need be, though he had not done so by the time these letters ended. One cannot tell whether or not this approval of change of occupation was an attitude acquired before emigration. Whatever its origins, his comments upon the ease with which one might pick up another trade and his observations on the want of specialization in American trades are significant. After only six years in America, Hails was not a man who was rigid about work methods nor secretive about the mysteries of his craft.

The same pattern we have observed of a break with friends who had promised to help him in the United States and with others whom he had aided is repeated in the Hails letters. It should also be noticed that he felt some responsibility for the welfare of the family left in England, especially for his parents, though he almost certainly did not regularly send remittances home and revealed some curious breaks in logic when he discussed these questions..

The original Hails letters are in the Collection of Regional History at Cornell University (865), and they have been used by permission of the Archivist.

Letters from Richard Hails to George Hails, North Shields Pottery,
Northumberland

Wayland, [Mass.,] 24 July 1848

DEAR BROTHER GEORGE,

I now sit down to answer your kind letter that I receved from you last week, but sorry to hear of my uncles loss in the death of my Aunt Jane and of his sickness. I hope that the Lord will sustain & comfort him in his sickness & affliction; if he has much to depress his spirits he has more to sustain him, even the promises of God. I hope he will have the comforts of all the Christian graces as he has sustained the Christian charracter.

And sorry I am to hear of my father's lameness. I hope he will not be laid of work. True he is getting old so that according to the corse of nature he will not be able to work long, but I hope he will not let them go to the work house. Let us do as well as our good uncles have done befor us, do all the good we can. Thare is four of us. Can we not do somthing for them? Can they not sell some small articles & so let us strive together? I hope he has laid aside the foolish habit of drinking. I would be glad to keep ether Father or Mother, but I could not keep them both as I am but a poor man with very uncertain health. Besides it would be rong to part man & wife. Then the expence of comeing here. In a word I will do all I can for my poor parents. If anything hapens to them I hope you will write an answer to this and let me know what can be done.

Now to inform you how we get along. My health has some improved since I last wrote to you but am still unable to sew on account of a pain in my side and down the part of the right shoulder wich makes it quite a loss for me. I have a garden and raise my own vegetables and potatoes wich enables me to get along pretty well. I have had plenty of work but can not do much; but still I think after plastering & blistering & doctering I may get better.

My Dear Wife has recovered from her sickness pretty much and I hope she may be a well woman. So you see that I have had to struggle against advers circumstances in a strainge land. Perhaps you may not be much disapointed in your kind wishes as befor long you may be the uncle of a live Yankee. I expect my wife will be confined befor long, but I hope she will not have to have them as fast as your wife. . . . [About mutual acquaintances] My dear Brother, will you do a kind office for your brother in enquireing something in reference to some of my old companions in your next? It will interest me much as I often think of them. My Sister Bell perhaps can furnish you with some account of them. You can not realy think how I feel sometimes as I look back on the past. It is a requst I have often made anciously looked for an answer but could never gain any intelegence of them. Do not feel angry with me for trubling you, for I would do much more for you if I could. You might get some very thin papper and send me 2 instead of one at the same price and bare in mind that whatever news I receve from England does interest me much more than any I can send you as it is from the house of my childhood. I do not altogether dispair of paying you a visit before many years or as soon as I can spend some time, that is over a summer. I shall have to send this to Boston so I can not send our portrats, but I will try to find some way of sending them as soon as I can. Now, Dear Brother, we send our love to you & wife, Father and Mother and tell them to trust a kind Provedence, to Brothers and sisters. Tell them to be good & kind to each other and if they will be happy, to love God. Remember me to my uncles & aunt. I hope if we do not meet again we will meet in Heaven. I want to tell you how much I love all butt I want to see you then. Until then I remain yours affectionatly Brother,

RICHARD HAILS

P.S. You see I am not used to write many letters so excuse all faults . . . .

Sudbury, [Mass.,] 21 May 1849

DEAR BROTHER GEORGE,

I receved your kind letter yesterday and was glad to hear of your good health and that of your famely, and glad that you receved our portrats through the hands of Mr Clark, as it may be somewhat pleasing to my dr mother and father & friends. As to the liknesses, it is said that the single one is most correct because they can take a single one better than with two, but the way of taking them generaly makes the features larger than the origanl one, but that is to take them single. As to the truble of my side, I have had it for 30 months so that I have not been able to do so much as I could otherwise; but I find that it is leving me so that I think I shall be well again soon. As to me coming there now, I think it not best for the present; but it is in my mind and hart to visit my native land, and as soon as I think it best I will come. You speak of my father sickness and about him not being as cheerful as formerly. I am sorry. I hope that he will not be down cast or dishartened, for it will be best for him to look at the best side of things. Do, my Brother, ask him to forgive me if I have done any thing that may have displeased him, and I hope to hear in the next letter that he is recovering from his sickness to health and cherfulness. I would like to see you all an especly my dear Mother! Oh! How I would hug her, but never mind. She can visit me now every day if it be but in dumb silence. You may say my mother is in as good health as when I left home. If you recolect then she was not in good health and for some time back she had been very sick from disseness? Is she not better than she was then? Tell mother not to fret of seing me, for I think I can see her often in my imagings. As to my wife being a good partener, God know she is all that I could wish and I think I am happy in my lot. Now, my dear Brother, I will send you £5 pounds with this letter and would send more but times is hard now. I think we shall have better times and when you receve this you will send word back directly so that if it does not come safe I can make it right.

In respect to your question of this place, I do not think it may be quite as healthy as England but if a man is careful he can keep helthy. I have been here 7 years I think and I have not had sickness but the liver complaint and I think it was brought on by hard work and [imprudence ?] and so of most of the sickness I see round me. The people here are not as careful in respect to diet as they shold be. You know the proverb, to much of a good thing – good for nothing. In respect to my plans, if you were to come here there is a good many things that I would or could take hold of for a living. But I do not know that you would like them. It is a principle with me if I cannot do one thing I will do another. When I come to this cuntry first it was in bad times and I got into wrong hands and could hardly pay my way; but I think you would not be situated so. I would be kind to you as far as I can and do not think that thare would be any fear that your childreren would cry for bread in this cuntry. For, my Brother, thare is land to be had for about 5 or 6 shillings an acre and, if you had but a small captal, here is a good chance for so long as land increeses in value (*whare I am speaking* is west). As to education, your childern can be educated free of all expences to be fited for coladge, and if they wanted a coladge education thare is a way for them to have that by there own industry and a chance for them to be the first of the land. I could not, my Brother, write all pertickulars wich and what way. You could get along as that you would judge for yourselfe and measure your own capabilities. Any how I can give you a house untill you look round and gain a situation, but you will not blame me if you do not like. I would like my sister Hannah to come here as I think she can have 5 times as much wages as she can have at home and may be that she would be better situated. . . . [Greetings] I remain your affectionate Brother,

RICHARD H.

My Wifes love to you all.

If you should to come here, let be in the spring of the year so that you should be sure to have something to do, and as to your sons they are the best property a man can have in Amaraca. Yours, R.H.

In my next I will tell you what can be made in some kinds of buisness that you could do, but do not expect to live without work for they work hard in this part of the cuntry.

Lincoln, [Mass.,] 31 July 1849

DEAR BROTHER GEORGE, . . . [Letter received]

First, I am much pleased that my father is doing so well, but very sorry that mother is so unwell. I hope that she will be better soon, that by next letter I may hear of her recovery. Let them know that I often think of them and would like to see them happy and comfortable. As to the time I left you I went to Liverpool and arrived at dead of night, when up steps an Irishman and would have had me go with him to stay over night. I did, and slept in a room by no means very inviting. I stayd I think one day and night and he would fain covet over me but I got him to take a little of his price. But the first thing I saw was 2 men without sherts and I felt for my wacth and mony, for I managed always to sleep with them consealed on my person. However I was not molested. From thare I went in pursut of my vesel (and mind I name these little partickulars in order that you will be exceedingly caucious into what hands

The Battery in
New York City
from Trinity
Church, 1859
(p. 278).

Quay side on
the Battery in
New York City.
Photograph by
William
England, 1859
(p. 278).

THE EMIGRANT ROUTE WEST FROM PHILADELPHIA

The Columbia Railway Bridge across the Schuylkill River, viaduct 984 feet in length, two miles from the commencement of the Philadelphia and Columbia Railway, opened in 1834, which was the first link in Pennsylvania's early canal and railway route to the west (pp. 162–3).

you may fall, and befor you engauge any thing done for you always enquire the price. This I wish you to remember for you will not travel long befor you will find out as the best way) and thare was not any to start for Boston as they engaged. So I was obliged to bord myself 2 weeks and sleep in the ship witch made my expences come down more hevy than it would otherwise would be. Then they did not find me enough bed clothes and the provisions wich they allowed me was not enough, for they promised to find me al my provisions. I had to be [buy] more and what more I did buy was just done when we arrived, and if we had not made such a short trip I would have sufered. Besides if I had kept my money in hand and bought my own provisions I could have done better and not been so long detained in Liverpool. Besides instead of shiping me for Boston they sent me to New York wich cost me more than they allowed me for my fare. So you see how we pay for our igornance.

But at last we set sail and that night I will not forget. 1 man fell over bord as we started, but I think we hauled him in; but all night such a rumpis at the tops of our berths. Thare was all kinds of tin ware [hung ?] and legs of ham and many other artickles and boxs, barells, sacks and a medley of every thing left not fast as the ship reeled all night. Those things came all out of place and such a racket I never heard. Some of the men began to imatate cocks crowing, others bellowing like that anamal we call in England a Hudy and all kinds of sounds that they could make, for we could not see any thing nor put any thing to rights untill next morning, and you may be sure there was many things among the missing. Well we got righted as well as we could and we found for a few days it was plesant as we went allong the Irish-Channel. The wild look of the Welsh costs, so diferent from what I had been used to see; as the land receeded from our vew they left many [bitter?] feelings to many. Very little could we find to break the dull monotney of the time. Sometimes we could see a sail. Such a circumstances was a great releaf. The sea sickness was very bad and the passangers were all Irish and they were so filthy that it was enough to make any sick. I was sick 2 weeks so that I could not get any thing to lie on my stomack, but the next 2 weeks I fleshed up very much. I worked at my trade 2 weeks on my passage when I had a chance. My dear Brother, you have an idea of the mity ochen at Shields. But Oh! from land with no vew of hewman habetation except the small comunity of wich is confind to such a small surface roling and tumbling in such a wide expance of water whilst the sun is withdrawn from our vew wich makes it have some efect on our sences and the dashing of the spray over our heads, it must strike the landsman with a solemnety wich nothing els can impart. But thare is somethings wich is very interesting. Thare the rising of the sun on the watters wich is the most butiful sight that mortal ever saw. Thare [wanders?] in the fish tribe somtimes. They are like a pack of hounds dashing through and over the watters. Then thare is so many crouded in a small space wich gives a good opertunity of seeing human nature as it is in a short time and many other things wich I cannot for want of time [relate?] heare.

But sufice it say that you may know that I have alwas been receved with much kindness whareever I have been except by 2 or 3 indeviduals after I left Liverpool up to this time and they wer my own cuntrymen. 1 was Thomas Furguson, the man I had a letter of interduction by J. Taylor with whom [I] lived. I will not recount the behaviour he showed me. The other was a Mr Melville from Newcastle, a friend of J. Tailor, as I thought he was poor and I even gave him my situation and let him have about 8 or 9 pounds in trust and tried and obtained the charety of my friends here to send him west as he was or pretended to be sick 2 years since. I supose I never will gett it. Did he write to me for more, the first I had not got it or he would have it. The next I suspected his honesty and wrote to him accordingly. Since then it is about 2 years since. The next was John Tailor. I spent much time getting him 2 situations and [he] did not use me as he should, but he was harmless in comparison to the first 2. I name him not so much on account of anything he has [done?] as to let you know that from any other sourse I never had the least provacation nor disrespect from any one. I do not want you to let any one know out of our family any thing I have said in respect of the last person, for he is one of a vain, silly, fopish turn of mind. I do not think he intends to hurt anyone, so do keep this to yourself. In fact I would not be so partickular if you had not requsted somthing of my history.

Next I will give you an accout of what has transpired since I came to this cuntry. When I gott to Boston trade was very low of all kinds so that I could not gett work much that winter for 3 or 4 months, and when I got work I could not get good custom work in this cuntry. You must understand with my buisness a man must work in the best way he can until he gets aquanted or be introduced. So for the first year I got work I never worked so hard nor receved less, for after paying my debts I do not think I had more than £2.0.0 left after working 8 or 9 months. After that you must understand that [I] found out better how to do to get work and I then worked for 2 years for about £1.0.0 or £1.12.0 pr week. Then I left thare and went to school, stayed 2 months and some-how or-other they got me out by giveing work wich kept increasing so that I left school, stayed 4 months, made about £2.0.0 pr week.* I left that

---

* The term 'going to school' is defined in the *Slang Dictionary*, 1874, p. 279, as 'a knot of men or boys, generally a body of idlers or street gamblers'.

place and got married, did not go in to work for 2 months as I had worked hard to that I neaded a rest. So I went to Manchester, New Hampshire, a large place, and let my selfe for 18s.0 pr week steady and thare was the place I lost my health from working so hard. I did cutting for 12 & 14 hands and did the pressing for the same number, 2 mens work. Any man here will say the same. I had a bad disentry and continuing to work so hard while so much reduced down I brought on the liver deseas, and I could hardly lift my arm to work and I had a pain in my side and down my shoulder so that I could hardly lie in bed, could not but on my back for 1 year or more. I was obliged to quit thare and did not work that winter for 3 months. I think my wife was sick both at Manchester and here in all as much as 4 months if can remember, so that I was much afraid she would not live. For the doctor thought she would not. For he thought [it] was consumtion of the blood.

After that I thought I would not work so hard and I went to keep house and had a nice garden to work in when I got tired in the shop so that the exercise in the open air greatly assisted me in recovering. The house I had was a very plesant one with 6 rooms and ½ an acre of land, rent £8.10.0. I stayed thare until this spring. Two years I did not work very hard, saved after all my expences was paid I think £40.0.0. I left that place to work still esier for a stated wag of £65.0.0 per year. He gives me 1 month for recreation and all I have to work is not more than 6 or 7 hours pr day, sometimes not that. The rest of my time I use for walking and reading &c. The house I now live has 5 rooms and verey plesant sorounded with an orchard, the most plesant house in the vilage and good large rooms. 2 of them are £7, no garden as I did not want to hire it. Have the privledge of eting all the fruit I want. I somtimes make more money, for my wife erns considerable by her needle, 5 or 6 shillings pr week on an average. Then I have caps manufactured and sell them wich I make may be a good part of a liveing. Now, my Brother, I have been induced to let myselfe for so low wages in order to get my healh again, for stil my side trubles me but I may not give way to much dispondency. If I am not better next spring I will ether go to school or take a voyage to see you. I am very happy, have as good a home as I want and as good friends. I am now going a jurny with my wife and child up in the cuntry, will be gone 1 month. I intend to keep within my means but I like to enjoy myselfe as far as is right and needfull. I have ben partickular in leting you know all I could as I was afraid you were more concerned about me than you need be. I hope to get well again but I am somtimes afraid I never will gett wholy rid of the side ake and if not I can not nor will not follow my trade but shall think it my duty to try something else. . . . [Greetings]

Let me hear from you in your next letter. Tell my Mother that I feell very much for her sickness. I thought that she was entirely better when I heard 10 month after I arrived here. I would be glad to be near her but she out to console herself that I am better of here and shurly it is her gratest wish to see her childeren do well. I know it is. Tell Father to be cheerful and happy. I am much plesed to hear that he is getting stout and young again. Let them know that they have one of the best little grandchildren that ever was O! Now I must not say so befor so many to contrdict me. Never mind. I supose you woud give a little to se the strainger. He is very fat and [strong] and hansom, very active and can now stand alone. My wife is not so well. She is very thin owing to the child being so hevey. We have to feed it ever since it was a fortnite old as my wife's brest was broken on both sides. She had a very sick turn of it. I have a little babys caradge wich I draw her out often and we have good times togeher.

The land wich we have here at 5 or 6 shilings pr acre is not here but at the west whare it is not so well populated. It is the best land for farming in the cuntry or perhaps in any other cuntry. It is fast filling up by emegrants and every year it is rising in value. So, dear Brother, the mony put out on the land thare would be a profitable investment. You can have land for $1\frac{1}{4}$ dollar pr acre of Government land and pay it when you can, and if you cannot pay for it thay cannot sell it with out allowing you for all the improvments made on it. Is not that a good chance for a poor man? But you would not get so much money perhaps as in the north, but you would have all the comforts of home and your land would be increasing in value and is not that better and safer than putting it in a bank? I supose that Jane's husband could discribe the land and so forth better than I could.* About here you can buy a farm for from £150 to £400 to £1,000 with building on them, but the land is rockey and not so esy to coltivate as west and a man can live esier than he can here. Thare is a stock of cattle to get thare. You can raise horses & cows as cheep as you could hogs whare you are and you can raise hogs for nothing. You can shoot as much game as you want. As to the health of the places, they vary. Those on high land is suposed to be the healhiest. Those on low land are not healthy. Peple often buy farms here and pay for them when thay can. But it not be best for you buy unless to speculate untill you could tell whether you would [like] farming and

* His sister Jane had emigrated with her husband, Jonathan Dawson, to the United States in 1840. Living for a time in Illinois, Pennsylvania, and Iowa, the Dawsons had settled in Shullsburg, Wisconsin, farming and lead mining, by 1848. Jonathan Dawson appears to have been dead by the time of the 1850 census, and we find his widow, Jane, who could not read or write, still living in Shullsburg with her four children. In 1860, she had only three hundred dollars' worth of real and sixty dollars' worth of personal estate.

that you could find out by hiring one for 1 year. Besides it would be new buisness could not expect to make so much as you do now untill things agoing.

Your boys here when they get a little larger could be of grate assistance to you, and if you put them to a trade they can suport themselves from their wages. Look at the difference. When I went to trade I had but 2 shillings pr week and one more for every aded year for 7 years. If I had to be trade here I might had 6 shillings the first year and kept and an increese of wages as I advance in time and 3 years is all that a man or boy need for a trade. Dose not that make a vast diference? Of your advantages cast up the diference and make all the allowance you can and see what is best. Then the diference when a boy has to lern a trade so quick he will lern faster. You have 4 boys and may have more. When they are lerning trads in England they will come hevey on your hand if you cannot cloth them as they ought to be. It somtimes crushes a young mans spirets. But I will not perswaid you to come. You have good wages whare you are but on account of your children if it were me I think I would come if I could but get along at first. I know men that came over here. At first they had hard times to pay thier way, but thare are now very well of and that is a common story.

Thare is a grate many small poterys whare they make brown ware heare such as jars and bottles and I think that you could change your hand in a short time so that you could do well to start for yourselfe. Thare is a village in New Hampshire whare they are all potters.* I have been told it is a good trade. I think from the prise of ware it might be. My father might give you a few lessons or you could keep your eyes open. I do not know personly about your trade but from hear say I could lern you in a fortnite to cutt caps, umberellas, carpets bags. I think somthing could be made at it. The women sew most every thing here. You could do that certianly when you could do nothen els. You could work on a farm or take the first kind of a job that comes along untill you see your way clear. I would not advise you to leve your famly because you would be homesick. That I am certian if you love them as I love mine. Things may, dear Brother, be that we may com together and be happy yet as a famly. I think it would be best for you to try and work in a potery some whare or take a job on your own account as soon as you should see your way clear; then buy a pece of land and pasture a cow and keep a hog and a good garden. It would go a long way to keep your Famely. Now sir, thare is every chance for your boys having a first rate education and a priveldge of holding any of the most honorable situations under Government. Books and papers ar plenty and cheep.

* The 1860 census listed only nineteen potters in New Hampshire.

Now I think I have given you a very long letter but you ask how much capatal you would require. I do not know if you have a little, all the better, butt if you have none you will be better of than I was when I came here. I had £2.0.0 to grace my pocket. I have had much sickness, no friends. I will engadge that if you come I will find as much provisions as you and your famely will need, if you get sick of your bargan and return on your return; and more than that if you should come soon my house is open to you and yours. Why I say soon I do not know I will do my selfe next year. If you should come next spring I would go west if you would to buy land and buy land. I would like you to know as much as you can about my Uncle John's effects for certainly it [is?] naturly that I should like to know. Write me a long letter. Let me know what your wife thinks of crossing the watters. I think she would hardly stand such hard usage. Give my love to all. Do not any thing in a hurry. Your affectionate brother and sister,

R. AND A. HAILS. . . .

I do not wish every one to read my letters and I supose that it is best for you to keep things to yourselfe in respect to your intentions and in respect to what I told you of my il usage. I did not tell to make truble among friends but only to answer your inquires, so I hope nothing will be said to their friends but forget and forgive. I no doubt have done many things wrong. . . .

Roberts Series 1849–52

James Roberts was a widower of fifty-nine when he emigrated from Sheffield in 1849 with his son James, a young man of twenty-six, his daughter-in-law Mathilda, another young woman by the name of Mary Wilson and her illegitimate son. Both father and son were in the trade of pocket-knife manufacturing. In Sheffield, with its advanced division of labour, cutlers such as the Robertses were engaged in assembling and adjusting the various parts of a knife. In the main, their work consisted of fitting blade to handle.[1] James Roberts may even have been one of the many small masters for which Sheffield was famous. At any rate, he had a wide acquaintance among the small masters and skilled artisans who qualified as voters under the Reform Act of 1832. The immediate background to the emigration of this family was a year of great difficulty for spring-knife makers during which the Chartist minority on the Sheffield Town Council pressed unsuccessfully for an inquiry to be made into the conditions of workers in this particular trade.[2] John Loxley, Roberts's son-in-law, to whom these letters were written, was a knife forger and son of a builder and joiner.[3] He never emigrated.

The Robertses found their way easily into a network of Sheffield cutlers already established in the United States. A prominent group of Chartist cutlers had gone to America in 1839 to escape arrest.[4] The town in Connecticut where they arrived in the summer of 1849, after a brief sojourn in New York state, was well known to Sheffield cutlers. Waterbury contained, in 1850, a variety of English-born workmen, including button-makers and machinists; but the largest single group were the cutlers. Sixty-one English-born cutlers were enumerated in Waterbury in 1850, as compared with forty-seven who had been born in Connecticut. The census schedules confirm the impression one gains from James Roberts's letters, that the Sheffield cutlers were living in a compact community in contiguous dwellings.

The Waterville Manufacturing Company, which employed these people, was a joint stock company, like other manufacturing concerns in the industrial town of Waterbury. Making only pocket cutlery, the

firm differed from a typical Sheffield undertaking in that it manufactured the product from beginning to end. With no similar factory for
miles around and stocks unobtainable in an emergency, everything
possible was made on the premises; and the firm employed grinders and
forgers as well as setters-in and cutlers. Portions of pocket-knife manufacture, which in Sheffield constituted trades in themselves, were at
Waterbury 'produced in the ordinary routine of business'.[5] About a
hundred people were employed by the Waterville Manufacturing
Company in 1854.

James Roberts found that he could make more money here than he
had in Sheffield, and appreciated certain amenities provided by the firm.
There is no evidence in the early letters of any resistance to different
methods of work. In fact, Roberts positively welcomed the greater use
of power to aid them in their work. No deterioration in their economic
position had been experienced when a considerable group of these
Sheffield workmen suddenly became discontented with their situations
early in 1852. A new requirement that they must find their own tools
(which they would certainly have done in Sheffield) and the threatened
introduction of more native-born workers convinced these immigrants
that they were being subjected to, or would shortly encounter, 'tyranny'
on the part of their 'masters'. The letters indicate that these Sheffield
men were doing part of their work in their homes. The requirement
about tools may have constituted an effort by the firm to get them into
the factory and to enforce greater discipline. The immediate challenge
to which the immigrants responded was a threat to their status, rather
than to their pockets.

A group of these cutlers, among them James Roberts senior, determined to gain their independence by setting up a co-operative knife
factory. This answer to their dilemma had been imported directly from
Sheffield, where, in 1848, three branches of the spring knife trade had
tried co-operative production.[6] When George Wallis, the English engineer, visited Waterville, two years later, only a few Sheffield workmen
were left at the factory. Many more drifted away, in addition to those
involved in this particular co-operative venture. Although the population
of Waterbury doubled during the fifties to reach more than 10,004, the
Waterville Manufacturing Company was a victim of the depression of
the late fifties. It is impossible to say what part the loss of their skilled
workmen may have played in this event. In 1860, twenty-nine houses
owned by the failed firm were standing vacant.

James Roberts and the rest of this group of co-operators moved, in
1852, to Matteawan, Dutchess County, New York, where they organized the New York Knife Company. In 1856, they shifted their

location to Walden, a village in Orange County incorporated the previous year. There they bought an old building, formerly a cotton factory,
which had stood vacant for some years, on the falls in the Walkill River.
Twenty-two English-born cutlers, knife grinders and blade-forgers were
living in Walden by 1860, of whom at least seven had come thither from
Connecticut. Both the firm's president, Thomas J.Bradley, in whose
household James Roberts was living, and its secretary, Joseph Rowland,
were among these immigrants from Connecticut.

The firm enjoyed a modest prosperity. By 1870, Thomas Bradley was
worth $13,200 in real and personal property, ten times as much as in
1860. After the Civil War, the firm imported labour (as well as parts)
directly from Sheffield, through the good offices of James Roberts, the
younger, who made an extended visit to the city. By 1870, reinforced by
fresh immigration, forty-five English-born cutlers and workers in the
knife factory were reported to the census taker. In spite of the establishment of a rival American firm in 1870, the Walden Knife Company, the
New York Knife Company continued in existence, employing 250
workers making 'table and knife cutlery of every variety' in the 1880s.
When Thomas J.Bradley himself had suffered a stroke by 1880, Thomas
Walker Bradley became president. The firm carried on until 1927.[7]
Transformed rather early from a co-operative to an ordinary joint stock
company, the firm was successfully conducted on a larger scale and
with less specialization than its leaders had known before they emigrated. Thomas J.Bradley became a pillar of the community in the little
village of Walden. These letters provide a good example of the strength
in adaptation afforded by a small but clannish community of
immigrants.

The Roberts letters are the property of Mr F.L.Preston who has
permitted copies to be made for the Collection of Regional History at
Cornell University, the British Library of Economic and Political
Science, and for the Connecticut State Library in Hartford, Connecticut.
The originals are lodged in the Sheffield Central Reference Library. The
Roberts letters are reproduced by the kind permission of Mr Preston. It
should be noted that James Roberts quite consistently spelled 'off' as
'of' and 'there' as 'their'.

Letters from James Roberts and family to John and Mary Loxley,
Sheffield

Waterville, Conn., 30 Sept. 1849

DEAR CHILDREN,
   This is to inform you how & where we are. We are at Waterville,

11*

Waterbury. We have commenced making pocket knives for the Waterville Company. We are now living at Waterville in a street named Sheffield Street. There is myself, James & Matilda, Mary & little Tom. We have been at Williamsburg since the 4th of July doing verry little until we was compleatly tired and I set of into Connecticut to seek work and I got work at the before named. Now I will tell how we are. I ham as well as ever I was in my life. James has had the bowel complaint and is now better but has hapend a bad misfortune. We hammer our springs at one stroke under a stamp and he was hammering and got fore finger in the left hand crushed under the stamp, but I hope that will be soon better. Matilda is a little sick sometimes but no worse than usuel. Mary & Tom came on the 22 of this month. They was tired of Williamsburg and both verry well. I think Mary will get work at the works to wet knives & then we shal be all in work & in good circumstances.

We received your letters & was glad to hear you had plenty of work but was sorry to hear that you had no better prises for working wich is not the case here, for we have plenty of work and a good prise for it. I believe when we can take job for job we can get with ease 7 dollars each, and if Mary gets work I think she will get about 4 dollars. . . . Aaron Burkinshaw* is working here & wishes he had Tom Booth with him. The reason I mention is because Tom was apprentice to him. It would not be possible to discribe half the Sheffield people there are at these works. Ther is about 1000 people in the ville & I beleive there is a majority of Sheffield people.

Now I will give you a discription of the country. It is a country of hill & vale. It produces wood in abundance and also fruit in abundance, particularly aples, grapes, raspberrys, bilberrys, blackberrys, straw-berrys and nuts & all discriptions. I will just tel you what we did one day. We went out one day. We was from home about $1\frac{1}{2}$ hours and we got $1\frac{1}{2}$ pecks of grapes, 1 peck of nuts, and half peck of aples. The grapes we preserved. Their was three of us to get them. John Loxley stated that he would send me some rubarb seed. If he can I will be verry much obliged to him. I will be verry glad if he could send me some berry tree seed as their is no good berrys in the country.

The people that we work for are a company of people with a capital of 100,000 doallers in one thousand doller shares and is the largest spring knife manufactury in America and the best & convenientist shops I ever saw in my life. They have all their scales & springs made by machienry. The drilling is done by machienry except boring on, and we have power to do all the work we want to do by power and they find us

---

* Aaron Burnckenshaw, thirty-eight, cutler, English-born, was enumerated in the 1850 census at Waterbury.

every thing that we use to work with and soap and water to wash us with when we go to our dinner & when we give over.

Now I have a few old friends that I wish to mention. The first is Matthew Dodworth.* Tel him we have found out the land of the living but not in New York but the state of Connecticut. We do not need to go into the market to bye a hamper of apples. We can go a verry short distance from home & get what we please. I have been at Charles Boden's once and they were all well but as to circumstances I know not. I have been with Thomas Dodworth many times and I think they are verry well of. Him & me have been like old friends ought to be. He told me he had wrote to his brother Matthew & as I had a good deal of trouble with losing my wive & one thing or another I delaid writing until I was fixt in some situation. Now the friends are the committee of the St Georgs Ward. Tel them I should like to hear of them returning an overwhelming majority into town councel†. . . . [Greetings]

We have been living in part of the house with William Stones, but he has boght a house & a quarter of an acre of land & I believ him to flit on Thursday last so we have the whole of the house at preasant . . . [Greetings] The country is new to us & you may tell some of my Chartist friends that I have hardly got to know the politics of the country, but tel them when I get into them they shal have the whole of them. I have so much to say that I believe that I shal forget something at last. . . . [More greetings] So no more from your affectionate Father, Brother, sisters & nephew,

JAMES ROBERTS SENIOR, JAMES ROBERTS JUNIOR, MATILDA ROBERTS, MARY WILSON, THOMAS, for he will be called ROBERTS

Waterville, Conn., 14 Feb. 1850

DEAR CHILDREN,

We received your letter & was glad to hear you was all well. We are all in good health at preasant. You say trade is verry good. We are verry glad of that & hopes you are all doing well. We are still making knives & can have any quantity out that we think proper. We was cutting stag‡ 6 weeks up to the 1st of January at $1\frac{1}{2}$ dollers per day each. That is equal

---

* Matthew Dodworth was a pen and pocket-knife manufacturer at 30 Carver Street in Sheffield.

† In November 1842, two Chartists were elected to the Town Council in Sheffield. Six more were added in the election of November 1847. In the forthcoming election, to which Roberts refers, in November 1849, the Chartists filled eight of fourteen vacancies to hold twenty-two of the fifty-six places. Only small masters and well-to-do artisans among Sheffield's working men had the vote at this time.

‡ Stag was a material used for covering knife handles.

to 6 shillings & 3 pence English. We are now living in a house to ourselves wich we pay 40 dollers per year. We have one sellar, 2 low rooms & 2 chambers. Some say we have one acre of land but I think we have ¾ of an acre. We have about one thousand yards ploughed up for garden. We are all living together, James & Matilda, Mary & Tom & me. We should be as glad to mix with you but that cannot be at preasant. Mary is in our warehouse, but she does not like the country. If she did she might do well. Tell Elizabeth Thompson when you see her that now I ham in this country I oft think of down in the [valley?] under a tree, but she may call some Saturday night to go in the town with her. . . . [Acknowledges gifts]

Tell Mr Gilley I was glad to hear of the Town Councell from him for I know that the independent papers were not to be relied on. So it proved when we came to sample them together. That was the reason I wanted the truth. Give my best respects to my Chartist & Town. Councel friends. . . . [Weather] James & me went out to our dinner on Christmas day. We had turkey & every thing that was nice at William Green's, son of Colin Green of Soudergreen [Southeygreen?] So we have a day that they call Thanksgiving and if there is any person that has not a turkey that day they are thought nothing of. That day is on the 29 November so you see we was forced to have one. On Tuesday last was [Shrove] Tuesday & our James & 13 more went to play at cricket in the afternoon.

We have about one hundred seters in* at our place & 17 or 18 blade makers & I should think about 30 grinders. We have a man to kindle the fires & another to sweep out the shops once every day. It is not same here as in Sheffield, for if you go to the town as they call it their is no shambles† nor even a buchers shop to be seen. So if you do not get your meet of the buchers when he comes, you must go without.

The people of this country go quite oposite to what they do in England in mending roades. Instead of putting stone on the roades for the horses & carriges to run on, they throw the stone away & puts the dirt on the roads. So you see it makes verry bad for walking, for if it thaws you are up to the ankles in mud; then if it frizes it almost like walking upon spikes & it hurts my hangnails so that it makes it bad for me to walk. For you see I have not got in the Yankie fashon yet for the Yankees all wear boots one inch to long & half an [inch] to broad so they have no hangnails. But I have not had the good fortune to have had any Yankie boots for I not done with my changealley shoes yet so I must be content with my hangnails while my shoes is done. . . . [Presents] We

---

* Setters-in formed a distinct trade in Sheffield of men employed setting knife blades into hafts.

† A shamble was a bench or stall for marketing merchandise, especially meat.

have received 5 newspapers since the 12 of November & we return our thanks for them & want you to send us as many as you can if it is convenient for you to do so, for they are verry useful. For we have no newspapers no nearer than New York & we seldom see them, so what we get from you we keep reading them over & over again for want of more news. The winter now seems to be getting to a close, for the snow is disappearing. The buds is begining to be full & plump so we may expect that it will soon be time to begin of gardening & then you see I have plenty of work before mee for that that is broke up is verry stoney & I can break up as much as I like. Besides I forgot to tel you that we had a stable or cow house and we think of having a cow. So I must conclude by sending our best respects to you all.

JAMES AND MATILDA ROBERTS, MARY WILSON, THOMAS ROBERTS,
AND MYSELF, JAMES ROBERTS

Waterville, Conn., 13 April 1850

DEAR CHILDREN,

I write to you in advance that is two letters to your one. It is because we have more news than you have, at least we think so. The last time I wrote to you I told you that I thought that the winter was nearly over but the storms have returned many times since. Then the clouds have appeared. The sun has been overcast & every thing looked dull up to 30 of March when their was to our great joy a son broke forth, the son of James & Matilda Roberts. Since then their has been something else hapend, but before I tell you I shal let you know of the gloominess of Mary. She has been continually going to England. It was on the carpet at every verse end* untill I was quite tired & I told her that if she would wait untill the back end of August I would go to England with her & she almost agread but thought [it] to long to wait. But since then she has been rather more composed up to the 1st of April when to the great surprize of the whole ville she made a April fool of by marrying Mr Thomas Bradley† that was partner with Thomas Evans. Mary, or Mrs Bradley, received her Aunt Booths letter & was glad to hear they was all well & that trade was so good, but be sure to let her know that she does not want a place. So you see she does not need to come to Sheffield to seek a situation as she has found a Mr here.

* 'Upon the carpet', any subject that is uppermost for discussion or conversation.

† Thomas Bradley was enumerated in Waterbury in 1850, a cutler aged thirty. He went with other Sheffield Cutlers to New York state to establish the New York Knife Company, whose origins are described in James Roberts's next letter. By 1867, he was President of this company. He became President of the Board of Trustees of the village of Walden, Orange County, New York, in 1874 and the first vice-president of the Savings Bank of that village when it was incorporated in 1872. In 1875–6, he served as a state Assemblyman.

I forgot to let you know we are all living together & that is not all the increase in our family. We have six hens & one cock and we had a cow house & we thought as houseroom was so dear we would have a tennant. So we boght a cow, so you see we get on in farming wonderfully. Now I want to know if Wm Wright* and is family could like to come to America. If they think they could I should like them to send word & we will try to bring them out. I think they might do verry well here. If you think of coming write as soon as possible, because if you come we want you to bring two children with belonging to Marys husband. They are in the care Mr Joseph Wolstenholm, file manufacturer, 116 Broad Lane, near Red Hill†. . . .

Now I will just give you a little about the weding. Mr Bradley, me, a young man named Parson, with Mary took the cars, it being Easter as well [as] all fools day & went down to [New] York, but it so hapend that I was took with the bowel complaint at a place named Bridgeport & I was compeled to stop their untill the next train came up. That was 2 hours after, so I contented myself with walking about Bridgeport & eating oyster stew untill the train came up. They got into York at 20 minutes to two & I got into York at about four, but we was not to late for that job, so of we went to John Hadfields & John & me went to seek a parson & we soon found one that agreed to marry them at ½ past 7 oclock that night. So we went at the time named & made them 2 into one. We staid at York untill Thursday & then returned to Waterville, but I was not left behind going back. So here we are as comfortable as can be.

I could say plenty more but have no more room, so I must conclude by giving all our respects,

JAMES AND MATILDA ROBERTS, THOMAS AND MARY BRADLEY, THOMAS AND JAMES ROBERTS, AND THE LITTLE YANKEE

[Letter from James Roberts the Younger, 14 April 1850, about birth of son, omitted.]

Waterville, Conn., 6 Feb. 1852

DEAR CHILDREN,

We received your letter & was sorry to hear that William Wright has had so many misfortunes in their family, but we hope that by this time all will be well. He write to me also that trade is not so good as it has been & that the merchants &.manufacturers can either make trade good

---

* This was probably William Wright of Wright and Wragg, spring knife manufacturers, 23 Leicester Street, Sheffield.

† Joseph Wostenholme, thirty-three, file manufacturer employing twelve men, UK Census MSS, 1851.

or bad when they think proper. Well now I will let you know how we are fixed here. We have been setled of with every 6 months & and setling time was in January. We have to finish our work by the last of December, and on the first of January they told us we must begin to find our own files & tools of all kinds and if we refused to do it we might go about our business. So you see they have driven in the wedge & we do not know where it will end, but we are now going to form a company of our own & if it turns out well I hope it will be better for us all. Their is now sixteen of us that has paid 50 dollers each & has agread to make it up 2 hundred dollers by next July. So you see we are in right earnest. We expect a many more to come when they are able to pay the money, for we have left it open for any body to be proposed & they will become partners as soon as they have the money. We could have plenty of shareholders if we thought proper but we are determined to have nobody but working men, so you see we are determined to have no capitalists.

Myself is the only one that has entred the company in our family, but Marys husband intends joining as soon as he can make it convenient. I have been to our joiner and we asked him if he wood join & he said he was not able, but after all I think he will be proposed after July next. Since I wrote the other part of the letter we have two more joind us & they are all Sheffield men. . . [Messages] Now the last time I wrote to you I was living with Henry Deakin, but the wether was verry hot one washing day & it heated the blood of his wife so much that she wood have no borders, so I was forced to leave & half of the house that Mary & family was living in was to let, so I thought I would go & take it as nobody could turn me out any more & now Mary & family & myself are all living together, I bording with them. Just as I am writing this Bradley is pining two blade pearl on at home & Mary is making me a shirt & she thinks our Maryann has almost forgotten her but she wishes to be remembered to all her relations & friends. Although I have told you of the tyrany of the masters we are going on swimingly. You must know that we are not so bad of or we could not find money to begin with. But we are doubtfull if we do not look for ourselves that things will be a great deal worse. William Wright thought of coming out, but I think he had better wave the idea for a season as their has been so many come out of late. Beside they have been setting so many Yankee boys on that we was quite jamd up & if we said any thing they told us we might go about our buisiness.

. . . [Health] If you could send me a pair of spectecles, sixtys, from Cuts, I would send you the money by some means, steel frames not blued ones, such as I had before by Mrs Newton. I would be obliged to you for the Yankee make are all German silver & will not stay on my head. We are here now but I do not know where I shal be after next July. So I must conclude by wishing all the happiness the world can give you.

JAMES ROBERTS. . . .

Crawshaw Series 1853–66

When the 1851 census was taken, Titus Crawshaw was still living in his father's household at 1327 Taylor Hill, in Almondsbury Parish on the southeast border of Huddersfield.[1] His father, William Crawshaw, a man of forty-seven, was a handloomweaver of woollens. In spite of the rapid increase in power looms since the late thirties, it was still possible for handloom weavers to earn something at their trade, and William Crawshaw appears to have been one of these men who, entering the trade at the beginning of its long years of falling wages and irregular employment, persisted in it throughout the introduction of steam-powered looms. One can imagine that this family was poor in 1841, when William and Susannah Crawshaw had at least six children under the age of twelve. By 1851, all of their children were in employment, except for eight-year-old Emma, who was still a 'scholar'. Several of their children were working in a local woollen factory. The eldest daughter, Ellen, a young woman of twenty-two, was a steamloom weaver. Titus, aged nineteen, and Thomas, aged fifteen, were employed as cloth finishers, and Harriet, seventeen, as a piecer. The youngest son, Alfred, thirteen, was an errand boy and Elizabeth, eleven, was described as a 'nurse'.[2] William Crawshaw's reliance upon his children in the face of his own weak earning power is reflected indirectly in these letters by Titus Crawshaw's responses to his father's requests for money and the absence of any optimism about the condition of the family remaining in Britain. Most other industrial migrants' letters, at least at some point, referred to the 'good work and wages' being enjoyed by relatives in England – but not these.

Titus Crawshaw's own occupation of cloth finisher was no longer a highly skilled one. Whereas the croppers of the West Riding had been important in Luddism as they resisted the spread of gigging machines and shearing machines earlier in the century, that struggle had ended long-since. Nevertheless, Crawshaw regarded finishing as a better occupation than weaving, and he tried to gain entry into finishing rooms in the Philadelphia area. He succeeded in doing so most of the time until the depression of the late fifties, when he was (in his view) reduced to weaving at much lower wages than he had made earlier in the decade. By the end of the Civil War, he found he would rather spin than operate gigging machines in finishing rooms, work which he then found 'too damp'.

The manufacture of woollen cloth was still the largest single employer of labour in Huddersfield in 1851. During the forties, employment in the industry had expanded quite rapidly. In Huddersfield township the absolute increase in employment of adult men had been greater than that for boys or girls or women. During the fifties, employment patterns shifted radically. Overall employment in woollen manufacture ceased to expand in Huddersfield during that decade. The only group making gains in employment (and these were small) was adult women. The employment of young people under the age of twenty and of women rose from 486 in 1841 to 1,875 in 1861, while that of adult men rose from 1,347 in 1841 to 2,024 in 1851 and then fell to 1,917 in 1861. The employment outlook for a young man entering the woollen industry as an operative was, thus, not very promising in the 1850s; Titus Crawshaw and his brother Thomas were acting against the trend of shifting employment patterns in entering this industry as young men. At the same time, more jobs were being created in iron manufacture, engineering and machine-making and in railway work of various kinds, and the number of commercial clerks was growing. Titus Crawshaw's sister Harriet, was to marry William Meek, a booking office clerk in a railway station in Huddersfield.

There may have been genuine obstacles to Titus Crawshaw's obtaining work in engineering, both from the side of apprenticeship restrictions and his own indifferent health. In the event, Crawshaw and a number of other young men referred to in these letters preferred to try to stay in the woollen industry by emigrating. Population in Taylor Hill, an upland weaving fold, grew very little during the fifties, from 9,749 to 10,361, though nearby Huddersfield did not show this relative stagnation in population growth during that decade. Thus, Crawshaw's emigration seems to have been prompted primarily by economic motives. He did not have the ardent faith in an agrarian myth evinced by earlier industrial emigrants; he expressed no opposition to power-driven machinery. Although a reader of a co-operative magazine, who at one point justified his economic failure by pointing out that at least he was in the 'land of the free', he had neither the determination of the would-be farmers nor the fanaticism of a Chartist like Abel Stephenson. He seems to have had no social or political commitment to the United States on emigration.

Like Abel Stephenson, George Martin, Edward Phillips, and James Roberts the younger, Crawshaw emigrated from the parish of his own and his father's birth without any prior tramp in England. No other member of his family accompanied him when, in 1853, at the age of twenty-one, he sailed from Liverpool in a cholera-infested vessel. He did have friends from Taylor Hill in Philadelphia, however, and one of them helped him when he first arrived – another friendship subsequently shattered in recriminations about the amount of aid provided.

One dominant influence on Crawshaw's economic adjustment in America was his continued mobility. He came first to Philadelphia, where he worked in 1853 and 1854. Then he struck out for Rock County, Wisconsin, which was at that time, with over thirty persons per square mile, no longer frontier. In a few months, he was back again in Philadelphia, where he worked in 1855 and 1856. In response to an invitation from other immigrants from his home, in 1857 he went to Norristown, Pennsylvania, in Montgomery County, which is adjacent to Philadelphia County on its northwestern borders. Norristown was a town of nearly seventy thousand people. There Crawshaw spent some very difficult months in irregular work, frequently unable to collect his wages when he did work. 1859 found him back in the Philadelphia area, in Crescentville Way in the north-central part of the city. He remained there until 1861, when he volunteered for Civil War service. Discharged in 1862 for medical reasons, he returned to Philadelphia and then moved into Germantown in the northern part of the city, west of Crescentville Way, a district which in the 1850s had far more British than German immigrants, many of the English being stockingers and weavers. The next year he followed his friend John Wilson to Hespeler, Ontario, but in 1864 was back in Germantown. In 1865, he moved to Blockley, a town of about six thousand in 1850, which had been incorporated into the wards of the city of Philadelphia in 1854. In 1850, four times as many Irish as English immigrants lived in Blockley, and it was no doubt here that Crawshaw met his future wife. After their marriage, in 1866, the Crawshaws moved back to old Philadelphia.

These continued changes of location probably interfered with Crawshaw's prosperity and, at least in part, account for his pattern of irregular employment and his occupational downgrading. Not all of his moves were dictated by a search for better wages or more constant employment, although his depression move (from Norristown to Crescentville Way) probably was. On both occasions when Crawshaw made a stab at gaining independence, in Wisconsin in 1854 and Hespeler, Ontario, in 1863, he left a situation of full employment to do so. He was tempted to strike out for himself, in farming or in custom weaving, in boom rather than recession, probably because at these particular moments he had a little savings. The ventures cost him all those savings. By the end of the fifties, Crawshaw thought that he could have helped his parents more if he had remained in Huddersfield at sixteen shillings a week, even if employment had not been constant. He had no very clear aim for savings. As a single man he did not write about getting a house, an allotment, a cow or a pig. Throughout the fifties, the prospect of returning to England did not disappear from his calculations. His sampling of farming and his business venture were undertaken with little forethought and no determination. He used what savings he did acquire for remittances and for travelling.

Crawshaw's continued mobility was, no doubt, also an obstacle to his assimilation. In his early years in America, his friends were all immigrants, though not all of them from Taylor Hill. During this period, as he wrote, wherever he sought employment in the Philadelphia region he seemed to find someone he knew. During his months as a soldier, he was cut off from this immigrant community, and the most bitter letter he wrote, perhaps the most bitter in all these series, included here in spite of the fact that it is somewhat mutilated, reflects not only the indignities he felt himself to have suffered as a soldier and in the military hospital, but also the loneliness of an immigrant in a large city. Only when he himself married a woman from Northern Ireland who, like himself, was quite without family in America, did he seem able to break the link and support which letter-writing gave him. He also probably thereby discharged himself from the feeling of further responsibility to send remittances home.

The manuscripts of these letters are in the Library of the London School of Economics. I am grateful to John Halstead for reading and commenting upon this introduction.

Letters from Titus Crawshaw to his family at Taylorhill, near Huddersfield

Marshalls St., above Poplar St., Philadelphia, Penn., 18 Dec. 1853
DEAR FATHER, MOTHER, SISTERS, BROTHERS, RELATIVES,
    AND FRIENDS,

I therfore take up my pen to write a few lines and I hope they will find you in good health as it lieves me at preasent. I am working at Globe Mill in Philadelphia and I have one dollar a day at finishing and I think I shall stop this winter because it is better in the City in frosty weather but not in summer. It has been so very hot that many new landers as been struck dead walking up the street this summer. I am boarding at

Wm Hardy's. They came from Kirkheaton,* but he was brought up at [Glassel?] Hall. He know Richard Pollit.† Now you see I have not written soner because I wanted to work before I wrote. I went to learn to weave three days before I went to the finishing and I have ben working three weeks, but they pay monthly and we pay 10 dollars a month for board; and Allin Hey‡ is weaving at the same mill and boarding at the same place. He his in good health but he as no more beard and wiskers nor I expected you so [saw on?] me before I quit England. Well we are about both alike for that I like the apearance of the country. . . . [Weather]

I will tell you some little about my passage. . . . [Describes voyage] There were 200 passengers came on to our vessell. . . . Many of them slept on deck, all for fear of catching collary [Cholera]. We had between 80 and 100 deaths on board and they threw them over like dogs and they tied a bag of coals to thear feet, but it was not heavy enough. They went just with thear heads out. It was shocking to see them. . . . I thought when we got to the quarintine we should have better bed and board but I was mistaken. We had to throw all us men upon straw like a lot of hogs, the wommun the same in another room. . . . Advice to emagrants: never come here till you can come by steam in the second cabin. What I think at preasent I shall sail no more, only by steam. You cannot think. Sometimes you cant cook. Sometimes you put it on but a wave takes it of. Now you must send me word how you all are and what Thomas§ is doing. I guess all the others are at the same work. Send me word if the same hands his at John Rhodes yet and how they are for work. Send me word what books you have got and you may give over taking the *Reasoner*.¶ But pay into the club. It may be usefull. I remain your most afectonate Son and well-w[isher].

TITUS CRAWSHAW

Philadelphia, Penn., 6 May 1854

DEAR FATHER,

I was verry sorry that you had another round of liver complaint but I think that if you would keep yourself of geting cold it would be better and

---

* Kirkheaton is a township near Huddersfield, a handloom weaving area where population declined between 1841 and 1851.

† Richard Pollit, cotton warper, Almondsbury, was the father of Abraham Pollit, spinner, a friend of Titus Crawshaw.

‡ Allen Hey, born 1830 in Almondsbury, a cloth finisher, was the son of Stephen Hey, clothier.

§ Titus Crawshaw's younger brother, born 1836, a cloth finisher.

¶ *The Reasoner* was 'a secular and co-operative review', edited by George Jacob Holyoake in London, a monthly which appeared from 1846–72.

when you get cold if you would attend to Dr Coffins Works* it would do you good providing the liver complaint had not taken you from work; and when you are getting better you begin work to soon and then you cant stand it and you work against your strength, but you see that wont do either. Now Father be careful and keep your self as warm as possible and when you get wet take of your cloths and attend to yourself as well as ever you can.

Mother, I was glad to hear that you was as well as when I left home and I hope this will find you better still, for health his far before wealth; and I have been very hearty since I left home. I am working at the Globe Mill yet and finishing and I have one dollar a day and we have been very busy since I went there, and Webster Greenwood works here too. You want to know how I did for provisions. I got some of the Captain. I paid 15s for biscuits, flour and salt pork, and I lost them what I bought in Liverpool on the 4th of October, and I was filthey and add to throw some of my cloths away. . . . and when I landed I went to Wm Brooke's at Trenton, and Helen Brookes washed my cloths and made me comfortable. I was there 5 days before I went to Philadelphia and I have been there three times since. They behave very well to me. I had money till Allin Hey came and then he paid for all I wanted till I had earned some and I have settled with him now and bought some clothing. So I will send you some next time I write to pay my debts of there if there his not a stand for work. Father, I think you might as well give over paing in to the Club for me as I think it will do me no good here and if I come back in a while it will be as cheap to enter in again. I am boarding with a Scotch woman now. She his a widow. We have 12 boarders. The other man what I stoped with his moved of to Reading, a place about 60 miles of Philadelphia. That newspaper came but I was astonished who directed it. I cant make it out yet and you never mentioned one. . . . [Letter received]

I have seen Allen Haigh* and family and Francis Ellis, Joseph Ellis brother and he got work in Philadelphia. We work in Pensilvania and several other states only 10 hours a day that his 60 hours a week and trade his good at present and wages on the advance. But provisions his very high: 9 dollars for 200 lb. flour, and every thing in proportion. . . . [Weather] Allin Hey his weaving yet but he as not very good health. He

* *Coffin's Botanic Guide to Health and the Natural Pathology of Desease*, Leeds, 1845, by Albert Isaac Coffin, an American who had lived for six years in England. The guide advocated herbal remedies similar to those introduced in America by Samuel Thomson. (See above, p. 165.) The aim of the work was to give remedies which all could understand at a price low enough to place the work in the hands of 'the industrious classes'.

* Allen Haigh, born 1827 in Almondsbury Parish, woollen cloth dresser, who had also emigrated since the census of 1851 was taken.

keeps on with work but he complains of a pain in his back and he dont look so very well either. But he says he his best in summer. You have no occasion to trouble your self about those books because I dont want any of them now, and if I did you could not send them except by some one and there might be a great many people comming to America what would go thousands of miles of were I am. When you write send me particular word how you Mother Sisters & Brothers all are, and how my realatives and neabours all are and how trade his and provisions and how you all are for work and how Nicholas Cotton and family all are and weather they all work there at John Rhodes yet or not and John Rhodes and family his for health and if they get plenty of work yet, for I think this European War will stop the trade in England, and how Taylorhill lads all his and weather John Hodson* has heard of Wm Hodson yet or not and if he as, ask him if he will give you the directions because Webster Greenwood said he was with a fellow that goes to Jersey often about 2 months since and he would see him again in week or two, but he has not seen him. So I thought I would write and tell you he was there about 6 months since according to description. I therefore send my best respects to father, Mother, Sisters, and Brothers, all Inquiring Friends and Realitives,

TITUS CRAWSHAW

[undated]

DEAR FATHER,

I have pleasure in writing to you once more, and in seeing me in good health, and I hope this will find you all better nor any has done yet; I am working at the old place yet, and has the same amount of wages; but its awful hot. It his 124 degrees in the sun, where we have to [Tentor ?] pieces and it is 98 degrees in the shade, and has for sweating I knew nothing about that before. When we go up to bed its just like entring a stove room, and not a breath of air to be felt. I was verry sorry that Mother was so very sick, I should be very [glad] to hear that she was quite well. If I could do anything for her I should be very glad. You have my favourite work, the *Botanic Guide*, and if you refer to it, you will find something in the colds, that will relieve her a great deal I presume. . . . [Health] She has no occasion to say I have forgot either her or any one else because I dont mention their names seperately. I was also sorry to hear that we have got such relatives but its always the case the feeble

* John Hodson, born 1804 in Manchester, was a fancy weaver residing in Taylor Hill, Almondsbury Parish in 1851. He had thirteen children in his household, all born in Almondsbury, aged one to twenty-five; all those over the age of twelve were in employment. He was probably the father of William Hodson.

to attend to the dead. . . . [About Allen Hey] Tell James North* that if I stop another winter I will have some butterflys.† I have bought some bird skins. . . . [News of other immigrants. Address insufficient. Weather]

Keep this part of the letter to yourselves. There is a draft for £4. You will find it in there and you can get it at any of the public banks by going there. When you carry that paper they will give you another to go in three days after and then they will give you the money, but you must go to the same bank both times. When you go you must sign the same name there as there his on the draft. You see it is wrong. I sent the money down by John Wilson my bed mate. He was going with some for his wife and the clark spelt the name wrong. His wife lives at Farnley Bank.‡ She his Ben Walker's daughter. Allin Hey left the boarding house that we was stopping at and went were they wanted no more and so we have never boarded together since. But we live very near each other. John Wilson and me goes a good deal together. He his a Scotch man and a decent fellow for what I have seen by him and I have lived in the same house with him ever since I came to Philadelphia and I slept with him 14 weeks. Father, send me word what quanty a burned spunge & honey they mix for thaer necks, for mine is worse nor ever it was and if you was to see the Denby Dale doctor, if he would sell you a recete for it b[u]y one, if he dont charge too much, but dont trouble yourself so very much about it. . . . [Letter received] I remain your most affectionate Son,

TITUS CRAWSHAW

Philadelphia, Penn., 30 Nov. 1854

DEAR FATHER,

I am happy to inform you that I am in good health once more and able to follow my imployment and amusement as well as ever I was in my life, and I should be very happy to hear that you Mother, Sisters and Brothers were all as well as me. I was of work 18 days with the billious fever in October and the doctor gave me calomel till it salivated me and I was 5 days and no sleep and eating nothing, wich made me look very bad, and when I got round a little I whent up to Wm Brookes at Trenton and they was very kind to me. I was there four days but thanks I have

* James North, a shoemaker, born in Almondsbury Parish about 1828, was living in Close Hill in 1851.
† In their interest in natural history, these Yorkshire industrial workers resembled the Lancashire operatives of whom Mrs Gaskell wrote in *Mary Barton*. See also Rev. Samuel Green, *The Working Classes of Great Britain*, London, 1850, pp. 77–8n. On Yorkshire weavers, see Thompson, *Making of the Working Class*, pp. 291–4.
‡ Farnley was another township in Almondsbury Parish.

got quite well and work goes well too. I am working at the same place and we have plenty of work. Thats what hundreds is wanting in this city alone. It is likely to be a very hard winter. Now believe me provisions is dearer here nor they are in England. . . . [Prices]

Allin Hey is in on his way to England in the Wyoming. He set sail on the 28th of November. He has been sick too. . . . I cant advice any one to this country, for if they only see as much as I saw they will think they earn all they get here without working for three months anyway. I think the Lodge is very selfish when they begin to complain before I have been 12 months away, but I hope you will go on if you need it, but I should be happyer still to hear you had never wanted any help from them.

Please send me word whether Brother Thomas and Alfred is improving themselves in scholarship or no, and if they are not tell them they will want it whereever they be, and Sisters in housekeeping and sewing and other things. Thats good, for they dont no what will be wanted through life. I should think Emma is learning fast now. She is old enough now and tell them I wish them all well, and I could a liked very well to send them a small preasent each and Mother my daguerotype and you the bird skins, but he [Allin Hey] refused taking them so I got nothing else ready and if you, Father or Mother, thinks he has behaved like a gentleman, leting be a friend, I dont. And if he ever gets in as good friendship with me again he will have to mend his ways, for his ways and mine dont corrospond. I helped him down the warf night before but I lost no work with him. . . . [Greetings]

Father, if I was you I would not want to send anything by Allin and then he cant tell you he has got no room.

I have been thinking about going out West to Milwaukey in Wisconsin in March. I might as well go and see what kind of place that is before I come home, and then when I get home I cant wish myself there if I dont like, and if I like I shall stop a while. I like Philadephia better nor I did at first but I have been lucky in geting work and keeping it. . . . [Write] So no more at preasent from your affectonate Son and Brother,

TITUS CRAWSHAW

Please send a Huddersfield paper if any.

Town of Porter, Rock County, Wisconsin, 16 April 1855
DEAR FATHER, MOTHER, SISTERS, AND BROTHERS,

I once more write to you hoping to find you in good health. That is that I never have done since I left home. I am sorey for it but I cant help it. I am not so very well, but I am getting better, but I have been able to work all time since I got to Wisconsin, if I had add work. I have been six weeks without work and cant say when I shall get work. I got your letter January 20th and right glad I was to hear how you all was. I was glad to hear Allin Hey landed safe in England and if comes to America I hope he will prosper, though I never wish to come across him. . . . [A marriage] I got them pills which you sent by Allin Haigh. He fetched them right to the Globe Mill. I hope trade is beter nor when you wrote last because I cant send any money. I could have liked to. Now I think I shall have to come back to Philadelphia and work right steady for about three years and then get a steady wife and come west again. Anybody with three hundred dollars out here may live independent of anybody helping them. Been a farmer's man out here is as bad as been a slave. They wont hire anyone if they can help it for no less than six months and more than eight. Wages for good men 15 to 18 dollars a month and to pay it to you at fall. I have had the offer of 12 dollars a month. You must bear in mind they work all the daylight God sends and a little more sometimes, except Sunday. Then they only look after the cattle. If I can get a place by the month I shall stop and take it, but if I cant well then travel I must. And as for friends or neabours they are scarce. I live in the middle of a wood in a log house and pays 1 dollar and a half for board a week. It is just comming spring, so all is life, but I have been here a month with snow on the ground and every body apeared as if they were most as dead as the trees. I am afraid that I shall never like to work out here till I do get a place of my own. . . . [Direct to John Wilson, Philadelphia] So no more at preasent from your ever afectionate son,

TITUS CRAWSHAW

Philadelphia, Penn., 24 July 1855

DEAR FATHER, MOTHER, SISTERS, AND BROTHERS,

I was glad to receive your letter when I returned from the West, but I was sorry to see that you had trobled so very much about me since Allin got there and I hope this will ease your mind, for I am in good health and 1,400 miles nearer nor when I wrote last, and I have got work in Philadelphia at a place what gets a name like Dransfield at Moldgreen. I have 6 dollars a week when I work a week and I have the highest wages of any of the finishers at the place. I left work on the third of March and went west. All the money I earned west was 9 dollars and a half, and I left Wisconsin on the 14th of June and got to Philadelphia on the 23 of the same, commenced work at Joseph Garsides on the 2nd of July. I came on the railroad from Janesville to Chicago in Illinois. I left Chicago in the steam boat for Buffalo, went throug Lake Michigan, Huron and Erie, got to Buffalo in 5 days. I went to see the Falls of

Niagara about 18 miles from Buffalo. The falls is a great work of nature. I was on the Canadian side. Left Buffalo on the 21st at 5 oclock p.m. and got to Jersey City on the 22nd, 10 oclock a.m., left there at 12 the same noon, and got to Trenton at 4 p.m. on the same day, found Wm Brookes and wife all well and they appeared glad to see me safe back. I was glad to converse with someone what I was acquainted with. Left Trenton on the Saturday afternoon, got to Philadelphia at night. . . . I have got a friend or two yet, that is John Wilson and Brooke's. I have got aqainted with them both since I came to America.

My friend Mr Heyes and wife landed on the 4th of July and he came up to Wilson, but he never spoke about me till John told him I was in the house; but all he wanted with me was to know if his things was all safe. I never said anything to him that night but he came up for some of things in a night or two after and so I asked him how much money I owed him and he sayed you owe me nothing do you. I sayed not as I know off. I said what did you say in England about me. He sayed nothing. He says they tryed to pump something out of him but he would tell them nothing. I says didnt you tell someone that you sent me money to come to America and hadnt got it back yet. He said No. I asked how they got to now. He sayed I must have told his Father before I came because he asked him when e was there if I had give him that money back. He sayes he did not tell him. Father send me word how you got to know about that and whether he did tell any body or not and who it was if you can, and if there is any thing else that you know he sayed. Dont be afraid of telling me what you know because I have told him it is all over with me and he sayes its the same with him which pleased me much. Now he did not send me money exactly to come to America. He sent it to purchase some books for him which I did and he paid my board till I got some money, but I settled all with him the first three months. But Mother, you told me what he was before I came away and I would not have sent you any thing about him if he would have fetched a few thins for you and the rest, but there is more nor that to grieve me about him. Tell James North I will send him something yet. I have got a few butterflies about 6 inches accross the wings.

Thomas, I am very much obliged to you for your advice about the girls or women. I hope you will mind that your self, and I thought you must have heard something bad about me. If you have, send me word. Never fear for I am free for any body yet . . . [Messages] I will send the brothers something sometime if I can. But I am poor now. If I was anxious to come to England now I could not, but its no use coming back to starve. I see Allin had to come here again and if I come to England I shall want to stop. If I have to travel any more I would rather do it till

I am away. Give my respects to all inquiring friends, and tell the Taylorhill lads this is a whimsical country but I remain as ever to all and I hope it will last till death calls us all away. So no more at this time, from,

TITUS CRAWSHAW. . . .

Philadelphia, Penn., December [1855?]

DEAR FATHER, MOTHER, SISTERS AND BROTHERS,

I received your Sept. 22nd and right glad I was to hear you all was pretty well. I hope this will find you so still, as it lieves me at preasent. If I had ad good work all the time it would have been better. I have been playing* 7 weeks and I am likely to play 4 more before I get work. I expect to begin for my old master then. The time I was out West he failed, and he his going to commence next month. I should have wrote sooner but I thought I should get work and I did not like to write home when I was plaing. I could have got work on the railroad but that is about all, and there is very little moving at the factories in winter time, and when I wrote to Jack Cockroft I was working in the night and they stopped the night very soon after I wrote him. I expect trade to be a good bit better this spring in manufacturing wollen cloth nor it has been since I came to America, but I might be mistaken. I should not have wrote till I had got into work but I was geting very anxious to know how you was making out. You must not think because I am two years away from home that I have forgot any of you. The more I see in this country the more two-faced fellows I find and I know it was not so at home. That makes me think more about you. If anything goes wrong with me and the bosses here and you tell your neighbour he makes it worse in the place of simpythising, but if I live I shall learn if it dont cost me too much. I suppose James North got that note I sent in John Cockcroft letter. If John did not get the letter, send me word and tell James to send me word of one or two authurs on entimology. If he got the note he will know all bout it. . . . [Messages] from your affectionate Son,

TITUS CRAWSHAW

Excuse me for not writing more because I have to go out into the country 40 or 50 miles right away. It a letter I received and a little business.

Let Abraham Pollet see my letter this time and in answer to his own I

---

* Unemployed. Compare J.M.Ludlow, 'Account of the West Yorkshire Coal Strike and Lockout of 1858', National Association for the Promotion of the Social Sciences, *Trades Societies and Strikes*, London, 1860, p. 36: 'as the men say, they had rather play for nout than work for nout'.

have no idea of comming back till I can come on to [hill?] as good as when I went away.

Norristown, Penn., 9 March 1857

DEAR FATHER AND MOTHER,

I sincerely hope this will find you all well as it lieves me at preasant, but I here you are very sick. I come up to Noristown and Webster Greenwood told me you was very sick and I was to write home and that [is] the reason it is headed as above. I should have wrote sooner but I was waiting of John Rhoades's letter but its not come yet, and another thing I was wanting to send you a few shillings but I have had nothing but bad luck this two years, for I have played full half my time since I started for West. I should not have wrote yet if I had not heard of Mother been so very bad and the reson is I am ashamed to write because I know I could have helped you a little if I had never come to this country. But I am here and likely to stop for a short time. Yet Mother, dont trouble yourself about send anything to me of any value for I am as much pleased with the Parkin* as anything you could have sent, and dont trouble yourself about me for I have made some staunch friends since I came to this country and they are all teetotal. So you see I am all right on that score. . . . [News of other immigrants]

From your afectionate son,

TITUS CRAWSHAW

Norristown, Penn., 30 August 1857

DEAR FATHER, MOTHER, SISTERS AND BROTHERS,

I received your letter and the later part of June and right welcome it was but I was sorry to hear that you and Mother was, and had been, so very sick; but I hope when this reach you you will both be able to laugh and joke at your wandering sons mishaps. For I will give you a short history of my last twelve months cruise. Been healthy as I have been but strange to say I neither feed nor grow in any way, only about 4 years older since I left home July 56 [*sic*]. I left Norristown because I could not get into the finishing room and then I played three weeks and I got work about the middle of August in Philadelphia and worked there 6 months pretty steady, part of the time at 6 dollars per week and the remainder at 7 dollars; and then I was out of work 10 weeks and I was seeking work for about 50 miles north and south of Philadelphia and I was playing when Mrs Parker came home, but got work shortly after in Delaware State, about 50 miles south of Philadelphia. But I had not

---

* A kind of gingerbread made of oatmeal and treacle.

steady work and so I left when I had been five weeks. I did not like that place at all. It would do for desserters. Its so very secure. Delaware is a Slave State. Then I came to Philadelphia and played one week. Then Mr Samuel H.Needles sent John Wilson for me and I am working for him yet, but trade is not so very busy here at preasant. The fall sales is on and we shall know shortly whether trade will be brisk or not. Trade as been dull for 12 months now and its not likely to be pushed much before the spring.

Father, there is two pounds there and I would send more if I could spare it, but you know I must keep a little because I have had such a run of bad luck and there is no telling how long I might stop here. I have about doubled the amount I send you. That is pretty near two months board, and I board with John Wilson. Its a little cheaper and more like been at home nor living in a boarding house. There is no one lives with them but me. We have boarded together at three different.places and now I live with him. John Wilson is husband to that Sarah Wilson, Benj Walker's daughter, of Farnly Bank, what came here about 12 months ago. There is a note inside this letter for George Walker, son of the deceased Benjamin Walker, Farnlybank, and you will much oblige John and Sarah Wilson by taking it over; and if you are not fit to go, send it by Thomas; and, Father, if you go yourself with this note enquire who as got the small farm and let me know in my next letter. Thomas, I am very glad you write to me because I think it will improve you in your spelling and that is something you are very bad at. You ought to write a letter to me and show it Father and he should make every word with pencil what is spelled wrong and then you should find the words what is wrong in a book and commit the spelling of them to memory and set to work and write it all over again. It wont be wasting paper as you might emagine. That will both learn you to spell and write. You wish to know if I had my worst face on the Likeness was taken. How many faces do you think I have because I didnt know I had a great many to change on.

Webster Greenwood and wife both works at the same factory were I do and his Mother keeps house for him and looks after the boy . . . [News of other immigrants] Maryann and her husband were at our house to tea on Thursday last, and she said Stephen Hey, her Father, was stopping with Allin, and Sarah Wilson asked if Allin's wife was with him and she said yes, but she could do nothing, and Allin and her differed sometimes. But I asked about none of them only Stephen. . . . [Write] So no more from your affectionate Son,

TITUS CRAWSHAW

Norristown, Penn., 4 Dec. 1857

DEAR FATHER, MOTHER, SISTERS AND BROTHERS,

Your letter came duly to hand and I am very sorry that you and Mother as such very bad health, but I still think you might be benefited by a strict adherence to Coffins Botanic Guide under the respective heads of your complaints, and a great many of the most usefull herbs you may gather close to home. But I would advise you to buy you Cayenne Compostion Powder and Lobelia Inflata or Tincture of Lobelia from Clayton's Book Store in Huddersfield or any of Coffin's agents The reason I advise that is its greatly adulterated in most of the drug stores.

I am still in Norristown and in good health but there is a complete stagnation to trade all through the United States and you can scarcely imagine what a sore way all the manufacturing towns is in. A great many familys is receiveing charrity what was considered to be doing pretty well three months ago. At the mill where I work we have not drawn a cent these 15 weeks. We had worked six weeks and then we stoped six weeks and three days and then we commenced working at a reduction of 15 cents on the dollar with the promise that we was to be paid the old amount on Saturday week, but he did not come up to the promise and so we left of work again. We had only worked 9 days. We fully expect it every day. I have always had plenty of something to eat and if I get whats coming to me I can pay what I how [owe] and for other two months board besides, and if the mill commences I can save a little besides. So you see I have not run ashore yet. You wished to know if the last letter was paid. It was paid. I so [saw] the stamp, but I told you not to pay the letters what you sent away and I would do the same because I thought they would not be delivered as safe and I think so yet; but if there is any prepaing I think I ought to prepay. . . . [Reference to their letters] Thomas as no ocasion to quit writing because I told him to be carefull and spell his words better. I think he had better write oftener. He will do himself a great deal of good and I am sure e his not to old to learn. . . . [Greenwoods and Wilsons] John Wilson has the whole of Coffin's works and I peruse them a little. I am living with them yet and they are all pretty well as regards health except his Yankey.

Dec 7th The very latest   Monday

I am sorry to say we neither received our money on Saturday nor any better prospects. He only promises 3 weeks wages know. Before he promised 5 weeks as last Saturday week; but now we must wait another solitary week before we get these 3 weeks if he comes up then. A little will be accepable from him now I tell you.

But dont be allarmed for I believe the law is if he becomes bankrupt the work men gets their wages first, that is in Pensilvania, and there is as much stock in as will pay all hands without the machinery. . . .

Yours affectionate Son,

TITUS CRAWSHAW

Norristown, Penn., 5 May 1858

DEAR FATHER, MOTHER, SISTERS AND BROTHERS,

I received your letter last week and am very sorry to hear that Mother gets no better. Father, I expect Mother is troubled with coltiveness along with them pains and, if she is, make a decoction of Yarrow Velarian Ginger and Turkey Rhubarb of each an $\frac{1}{2}$ oz., boil gentle in one pint of water for 10 minute, to strain when cool and take two tablespoonful three times a day. And if that gives her any ease, make up some bitters for her four or five different kinds of herbs, say Yarrow, white Poplar bark, Horehound, Centuary and Clivers. Take morning and night. Them's good regulating bitters. I am also happy to hear that you are something better. I think the bitters would do you some good along with the bacon. I am also sorry to hear that you are nearly all playing, but I hope you will be doing better before you receive this. But I have very little better news for you nor I had last time. Some of the factories as commenced operation and some is idle; yet the factory I worked at as comenced with a new firm but they wont employ the old hands. Some as moved away and others is ready as soon as there is an opening. I have not got any work yet and, what is still worse, I did not get my wages for what was due me when Sam Needles signed over and the assignees as 12 months to pay in, from 2nd of December 1857, and then they say there will be only 50 cents the dollar. They owe me 32 dollars but then I shall owe it John Wilson for board very soon. I have got one blessing and that is the greatest good health. You did not get the paper but I will send another very soon and if you have not sent a paper when you receive this letter, dont do till you hear from me again because I shall have to move somewhere before long. . . . [Messages to brothers]

You say you think Wm Greenhalsh would not have send you word about the flies. Whether he had send you word or not I say he is a theaf because I told him that you would give him his flies when he had send you word, and he was to see that you did give him the very flies I gave to him, and I told Wm I was going to send a letter home to you, Father, and he was not to take a fly at all but wait till you gave them to him and he was not to have a fly at all out of James North's box, but he as taken the green Swallow tail, Emporer and a Drab Emporer out of your box and two Red under wings which he was not to have at all, and he as

TECHNOLOGICAL CHANGE IN FLAX HACKLING:
RONALDSON LETTERS

The manner of watering, breaking and hackling of hemp before mechanization from a print in *Universal Magazine* (p. 368).

Flax hackling after mechanization, showing also the change in the labour force, from *Pictorial Gallery of Arts* about 1860 (p. 368).

SCENES IN UPPER NEW YORK STATE

top: View of Rochester, New York, with falls of the Genesee River, from a coloured lithograph published about 1840. George Martin settled in Rochester in 1838 (pp. 275, 437–8).

above left: Charles Blondin, 1824–97, the celebrated tightrope walker, mentioned in Henry Petingale's letter of 12 August 1859 (p. 454).

above right: Spectators watching Blondin at Niagara Falls, photographed by William England in 1859 (p. 454).

taken 2 Camberwell Beauties, 2 Yellow and Black Swallow tails, and I believe 2 small Jamsons out of Jame's box. I think James would have mentioned them four particularly, [if] he had got them. The Yellow and Black Swollow tails is about 5 inches across the wings and the Small Jamsons is about the size of a humming bee. They are generly called the dumb humming bird here. They have part gauze wings and yellow and brown bodies, or rather olive and brown. I think it would be as well if you was to put him in prison for three or 6 months, and if you want any evedence there is both John Wilson and his wife heard me tell him he was not to take a fly at all but wait till you give them to him and they say they will take thear oath before a Justice of the Peace if need [be]. John Wilson is awful offended at him doing it because he wanted a Drab Emporer and I had just pairs. So John gave him one as I should not have to break into mine and you see he as taken one of your Drab ones when done. . . . [More about butterflies]

So no more at this time from your ever Affectionate Son,

TITUS CRAWSHAW

Cresent Ville Way, Penn., [1859?]

DEAR FATHER, MOTHER, SISTERS AND BROTHERS,

I hope this will find you all in good health as it leaves me at preasent. I was also delighted to find you in good health and happy to see there was plenty of work and I hope you have got more money for it nor when you wrote. I have got work but it is only poorly paid, but still I am doing some little better nor when I wrote last. Father, you speak encourageingly about me coming home, but I am the worst prepared for that ever I was since I came. I how about £6 for board and I have too much of a principle to leave the country before that is paid. I have paid £6 of the old board since August '58, and if I had been able to meet all demands I would have come back now when trade is midling good, but before I shall be able to come back trade might be bad and you know that would be another impedement. I think there is not the price of the passage betwixt this country and around Huddersfield when they are both in midling good trade. But still if ever I am able to come back I will do, that is if I have no better luck nor I have had this last four years; but if I never do come back home there is some consolation in knowing that you still have a place for me at your home, and I wish I was able to help you to keep it. I may be yet.

I got two newspapers, the Huddersfield *Chronicle* and Halifax *Guardian*, but I prefer a Huddersfield paper to any of them. The advertisements appears familiar but if the Huddersfield paper is contrary to your political opinions, dont purchase it, because every copy they sell strenthens thears. Please send me word how trade is around there and how you all are making out. Send me word how the Taylorhill lads is all making out. . . . [Messages] Give my respects to all the rest of the sisters and brothers and tell Mother I have lived as well all the time I was playing as working. So you see them was all feast days but not Honley feast.* So no more from your ever affectionate Son,

TITUS CRAWSHAW. . . .

Crescentville, Penn., 28 Sept. 1859

DEAR FATHER, MOTHER, SISTERS AND BROTHERS, . . . [Letters and newspapers received]

All the letters I have received as been paid letters, so I am compeled to pay mine or you would say as the American girls say 'You are a stingy young man'. Father, I see by your letters you are becoming a regular traveler. I further see Harriet has got a good home and you say it is nicely furnished, which makes me think she must have a steady man; and I heartely wish they may agree and enjoy thear nice home and never break it as long as they may live, neither to go to Austrailia or to come to America. If they do they might never get another fixed home. . . . I see according to Thomas's letter that he his dissatessfied because he cant get the wages he could like, but he dont say how much he as; but I can say safely if I had stoped in Huddersfield and worked four years out of the six I have been away at 16 shillings per week I should have been better off to day. Thomas, if you are discha[r]ged from John Rhoads, try and get something to do in the neabourhood. It might pay better nor been where you are. . . . [Enquires about sisters]

I will tell you how I have made out since I wrote last. I caught a cold last March and I commenced work to work it of but I strained my right side in the attempt and I played three days for the strain and then I commenced work and worked till about 9 weeks ago but I always had a pain in my side since March last, sometimes pretty severe. I had an in-flamation in my right kidney. I was of work two weeks. After that I went to work and worked very near two weeks, and I had a return owing I thought of my work being too heavy so I gave it up. I am ready for work when I can fall in with some, though I am no so very strong, but you know I shall never feel strong till I have worked a few days. So you see as regards money matters I am all on my beam ends again as it were; but John Wilson sticks to me for all my misfortunes. I must say with Paddy: 'Bad luck is better nor no luck at all at all'.

Crescentville, Jan. 18th 1860. I have been very long winded over this but

* Honley was a village near Huddersfield.

I will tell you the reason. I was out of work at the time I commenced this letter and so I started in quest of work that same day and I have been back in this village about 5 weeks so I thought I would conclude this. At the time I was playing for warp so you see I am only a weaver, but I like power looms better nor the ingrain carpet and I can make out as well. But you know weaving is only weaving. I have not seen any of the Greenwoods for over 12 months, but there is an old Talorhiller works at this mill and lives in the same village. His name is Wm Bedford, Benn Bedford's brother. So you see go where I will there is always somebody what knows something about the place as small as it is. . . . [Messages] So no more at this time from your affectionate Son,

TITUS CRAWSHAW

Crescentville, Penn., 11 August 1860

DEAR FATHER, MOTHER, SISTERS AND BROTHERS, . . . [Excuses for not writing]

I think they are all careless about writing since I became poor, but if I am poor they should bear in mind I am in the land of the free. I am not positive whether me or Thomas is in the fault but if I was sure would not he catch it (I guess he would). I think Thomas should have wrote first. I will tell you a little about myself. I am weaving yet, but the pay is very poor, but its better than nothing. I have averridged $4.60 per week this last 7 months and my board & washing is $2.75 per week. That leaves me for clothing and other expenses $1·85 per week. I am clear in the world once more and if no one would trust me I should stop, so I cant tell how long I shall stop clear without, but if sickness keeps away and no more panicks appears I will try what I can do. I have got no one but myself to keep thats one comfort. I have been in pretty good health since I wrote last. . . . [Asks about old workmates]

Father, you would very likely like to hear something about how different tradesmen are paid. I will give a list of as many as I can: for ten hours weavers from 3.50 to 6 dollors; spinners from 5.00 to 9.00 dollors; feed boys from 2.00 to 3.50; no peasers in woollen; finishers from 5.00 to 6.50; blacksmiths from 6.50 to 9.00; carpenters the same; shoemakers from 5.50 to 7.50; taylors about the same. . . . [Prices] [Greetings] I remain as ever your affectionate Son,

TITUS CRAWSHAW . . . [News of other emigrants]

Crescentville, Penn., 18 Sept. 1861

DEAR FATHER,

You will think me very neglegent in not writing home before this time, but I didnt want to write bad news every time. I really could waite no longer although things dont look so promiseing yet, but the North must win and the Union must be saved even if I have to help. Liberty must and shall win is the cry of all the North. And rather nor they should be short of soldiers theres thousands at home ready and willing to help, but not so hot as the soldiers what volunteerd at the President's first call. Nevertheless they might fight as well when they are tried. We have made some very good moves since the Battle at Bulls run, and General McClellan in a speech to the soldiers last week was we have made our last run. We have met our last retreat. Stand by me and I will stand by you. I think the fighting will be all over by Christmas and if it is over it will be in our favor. I expect you know as much about the fighting what as been as we know. So its no use me going into details.

Crescentville Mill is runing full time and nearly all the woolen mills in and around Philadelphia making army cloth, but I tell you theres been some hard times in this country since the war broke out and I tell you they are not all over yet. The cotton mills are all stopt and likely to be as long as the Southern ports is closed, but we think they suffer most. So we keep them shut. But as for me I kept somewhere straight yet and I think I can keep so long as Government work lasts. . . . [Greetings] So no more at preasent from your ever affectionate Son,

TITUS CRAWSHAW

Fort Worth, Va., 10 Nov. 1861

DEAR FATHER,

You must excuse me for not telling you that I had volunteered my services to the Federal Government. I did not want you to know anything about it, but in my opinion I have done just right. I hope the Secessionists will be wipt till they will behave themselves for at least 100 years. If the Unionists let the South secede now the West might want to seperate next Presedential Election, & they would be justified in so doing because if one goes out the Union is broke and there would have to be another form of a constitution wrote and after it was written who would obey it? Its hard to tell but I think the Government has got the better of them Rebels now in a fair way for been defeated. We have a very large fleet started from Fortress Monroe* better nor a week since and we should have heard from it before now, but we have had some very stormy weather most of the time since the fleet set sail and passing vessels as brought word that most of the fleet had arrived in Balls Bay, South Carolina,† and if that be true we shall hear of something been done very soon. I think yet we shall have all the fighting done this

---

* Fort Monroe, near the mouth of the James River in Virginia, north of Norfolk.
† Probably refers to Bull's Bay, just to the north of Charleston, SC.

winter. I sincerely hope so for the country is in a deploreble way; but I expect you will know all about this. Father, I hope you wont have to accuse me with cowardice and I am sorry for it if you thought I would send you a falsehood when you asked me whether I was a soldier or not. You said tell me the truth and nothing but the truth. I wrote before for you to think I was a citizen and would be a soldier if they wanted me. I never expected you to hear from me by any other source nor myself, but when you have heard I will tell you the truth and I am glad you take the same light of it you do. I was mustered (or swore in to the United States service) on the 25th May 1861 for the term of three years if not sooner discharged. The Federal forces as had to fall back from another place they attempted to take called Leesburgh with a great slaughter according to the number engaged, and we lost another man out of our Crescentville squad, but he was in a New York Regement. There was 7 out of 14 went into the 3rd Regement of N.J.V. and we are all here yet and in pretty good health. We have been laying from two to 5 miles off the enemy for the last 3 months, but I have never shot at one yet nor one at me and I have been within two hundred yards of the enemy's pickets many a time when I have been on picket duty. We have had 5 killed and 12 wounded when on picket out of our Regement and 4 killed with carelessness and two died a natural death and about 20 discharged for not been able to stand the fatigue. . . . [How to address letters] I see Alfred is in a fare way to have a large family, but I should have been better pleased if he had had a better situation.* . . . [Messages. About John Wilson.] I cant pay this letter so very well been in Virginia. I am only about ten miles of Washington. Still I could not get there for 20 dollors so long as the enemy is before us. Give my respects to all enquiring friends and tell them I shant always be a soldier. At least I dont expect to be. So no more at this time from your Affectionate Son,

TITUS CRAWSHAW

Fort Worth, Va., 15 Feb. 1862

DEAR FATHER,

I received your kind and welcome letter on the 6th inst., and if I can make it convenient I will try and let you know how I am getting along once a month as you wish it, but Father, I would like to know how you & all the rest of the family are in return. . . . I might not suffer in body & mind as much as you & Mother, but nevertheless I have time to think of both you & Mother, likewise all absent friends these long hours when I am on watch. Our Co. went out on picket on the 3rd of this month & come in on the 14th. So you see we was out on picket guard when I got

* Alfred Crawshaw was returned as an agricultural labourer in the census of 1861.

your letter. You would very likely like to know where we are stationd and who we are under. We are stationed along the Potomac in Virginia between the enemy & Washinton City, and our Commanding General is Lieu. Major General George B. McClellan. Commander of Division, Brigadier Gen. Franklin. Brig.Gen. of our Brigadeis Gen. Kearney, and Col Taylor is our Col and our Capt. is named Gibson. We have been quieter along our front nor any front in the whole Army, for the last 3 or 4 months. I think if things goes on as they have done these last 8 days the rebelion will be crushed. Our army and navy as been very successful. They have taken Roanoke Island in Pamlico Sound,* Fort Henry on the Tennesse River,† Fort Donolson on the boundary of Tennesse & Kentucky‡ with about 5,000 prisoners, camp tents, cannon, horses & wagons, and lots of worthless small arms.

You want to know why I volunteered in the American Army. When the south just bombarded Fort Sumtor there was a call for 75,000 men for the Federal or Union Army. We very soon raised that amount of men and when Col Smalls Regement was going to the protection of the Capitol they was attacked at Baltimore and drove back to Philadelphia. That showed our leaders that there was more Secessionists nor they ever thought off. The President called out 500,000 men for three years if not sooner discharged and I am one of those. I among many hundred never expected we should be wanted more nor about 5 months, but we have been disaointed. Anyway, I think the war will be all over and most of the volunteers discharged before next Christmas. I was in work, but I left because I thought the Capitol of Washington was in danger of falling into the hands of the rebels. I went and volunteerd in Col Small Regt for three months, but that blunder at Baltimore caused Col Small to be censered and then he could not go for three months. So I thought I would go anyhow. That is the reason I got in a Jersey Reget. I was not forced to go, but I thought it my duty to do so. You want to know what pay we get. We get 13 dollors a month. That is sufficient for spending money. . . . [Write]

T. CRAWSHAW

3rd Regiment N.J. Volunteer Infantry,
Colonel George W.Taylor, Commanding Camp,
near Fort Worth, Va., 28 March 1862

DEAR FATHER, . . . [Letters]

I am in pretty fare health and you must know I am in full employ. You know there is scarcely any kind of work we can go to that we

* Taken by federal forces on 8 February 1862.
† Fort Henry was captured on 6 February 1862.
‡ Fort Donolson was captured on 14 February 1862.

always like, and I think by the time my term of servitude is up I shall be tired of soldiering. But you must bear in mind that I am for a good cause or I shouldnt be carrying a rifle. I dont expect we shall be wanted more nor half our three years the way we are driving them before us. The Union troops is wining every battle they fight and you know that is good for us. The Southerners (or Rebels) as we call them as evacuated some of thear strongest places. On the 21st of July 1861 they wipt us at Bull Run and ever since that they have been fortifying around there for 7 miles and they have left there without a strugle. They have left Winchester, Columbus, Bowling green, Centreville, Bull Run, Mannassas, Nashville, all without fireing a shot; and a good many other places what they thought they could keep us from they found thear mistake. I think there has been some fighting as good as was at the Crimea. . . . [Newspapers] I think the fighting will be all over and peace declared by the middle of July. Anyway I hope so for the good of the working classes both of this country and the European countries. I know very well the poor cant help but be very poor as long as this war lasts. I am sorry you are doing so very little work and more so that you are not in a fit condition to work even if you had it to do. I am astonished to think Alfred thinks more about labouring nor serving a country in as glorious a thing as keeping the Union safe and sound and not letting any portion of the United States turn to anarchy. If the preasent Government was to let any State secede others might want to follow next week and this country would be as bad as the German states. I think that wont be. If it does its no place for me. . . . [Greetings] Your affectionate Son,

T. CRAWSHAW

DEAR FATHER, . . . [Letters]   Camp near York Town, 29 April 1862

Enclosed I expect you will find an order for two pounds. I sent ten dollars to John Wilson for him to get a draft in Philadelphia, in a legal manner, and I have great confidence in him doing anything for me of that kind what I ask of him. I will also tell him to send you a paper so as you can see for yourself how the war is progressing. I am in midling health at preasent considering how I am situated. We have not got one of the most splendedest grounds in America for a Camp ground tis true, but you know we cant pick our ground where we wish. We have got to pitch our camp in front of the enemy wherever they choose to make a stand, I hope they will choose to stop here long enough for our Army to kill a few thousand.* I dont see as we can make them come to terms in

* This letter and the succeeding one were written from points along the James River while Crawshaw was in the army which McClellan led into the first peninsular campaign against Petersburg and Richmond. It is curious that he seems to have no notion that this was a federal initiative.

any other way. Thear leaders are as stuborn as a jackass, and the soldiers, poor fools, thinks they are heroes to fight for them. Thear leaders knows well if they give it up they will be hung, and its not likely they will give themselves up to sure death. But they must have known a good while that they was wipt. We had a great battle at Pittsburgh Landing on the 6th and 7th of this month.* First day our forces was taken by surprise and we came pretty near suffering a defeat, but before night reinforcements arrived and the next day our forces drove the enemy right back to Corinth. I expect before very long we shall have three or four big fights, the sooner the better, for it begins to be very warm in the middle of the day. Down about New Orleans it will begin to be sickley in a short time. . . . [Greetings] Your Son,

TITUS CRAWSHAW

Harrisons Landing, 20 July 1862

DEAR FATHER,

I dare say you are ancious to hear from me after all the hardships and fighting on this Peninsula. Well I have past safely through. Not a scratch of any kind have I received. Since the march was over I have been a little sick, but nothing serious. I am on duty again. Our officers says its all lazyness to get of working in the trenches. There is a good many officers sick just now, so we call it cowardice. The officers when they get sick gets a furlough for 30 days and some as high as 60 days, but the poor privates, that is most of them as to get better on the Peninsula. We are laying here aperantly waiting on reinforcements, but they keep us busy picketing and digging as if they was affraid of us getting rickety, but there is not much danger of a soldier dying of that decease in the army in the time of war. We move about a good deal. I think thats the cause of so many men been sick.

Father, you gave me good advice when you told me that temperance and cleanliness was essential to good health. The temperance as regards spirituous liquors is concerned I never taste. I am as staunch a teetotaller as the day I left home. Cleanliness, thats another thing. As for washing all over every morning, its quite impossoble. We are for three days and cant take our belts of quite often, with the exception of going to the sink. Still I wash myself all over as often as ever I can and I either wash my shirt and drawers mostly every week or gets someone else to wash for me. . . . [Messages] from Your ever Affectionate Son,

TITUS CRAWSHAW. . . .

* Usually called the Battle of Shiloh after the country meeting house known as Shiloh Church at the riverboat settlement of Pittsburgh Landing on the Tennessee River.

North 4th St., Philadelphia, 9 Dec. 1862

DEAR FATHER, . . . [Letter received]

I am sorry that trade is so very bad. You wish this war was over. I wish so to but wishing does no good. I have tried other things besides wishing but that as done little good either yet. Well, Father, I dont know whether you will like it or not but I am no longer a soldier. Dont think I was afraid of the balls. It was not that. It was because the doctors thought if they send me down to the Army, it would be a loss to the Government. I am not sorry at them thinking I am unfit for duty. Believe me its not so pleasent playing soldier in winter time: winter or summer, I am tired soldiering. Little did you think when you wrote your last letter that I should be out of employment when I got it, but such is life, and I am not sorry to lose my last situation. I am mending very fast since I got to Philadelphia. You know I get something good to eat, and plenty of it, and that is the way to get strong if there is any getting strong in me. I have got all my pay. I shall not look for work this month. It wont do for me to exert myself for some time yet, but you know I have money enough to keep me for 2 or 3 months. So I think I had better get a little more strength before comencing to work. Whether I get work or not, I am not sorry at leaving the soldiers. . . . [Photographs] Alfred keeps working with his Father yet. I think he will have to work steady to keep bread for the youngsters. . . .

James North wished the war was over so as I could collect some flies. I have chance to collect flies now and the war is continuing, but the cuntry is in to much morning for shows of flies, birds, and eggs. I wish the war was over so as the working class of both this country and England could get plenty of work and plenty to eat. As bad as we are I think you in England are worse off. It makes me feel bad to read of the suffering in Lankishire, but you know I am glad to hear how they all are getting along also. I am glad they have got something to amuse themselves with. It is a very nice science. . . . [Greetings] Goodbye.

TITUS CRAWSHAW. . . .

Germantown, Philadelphia [undated]

DEAR FATHER, . . . [Letter received]

I am sorry you have had . . . to lose your Grandson Meek,* but . . . the best for the little fellow, he wo . . . many hardships what he would have had to encounter if he had stopt in this earth and another thing. It was God's wish He should die in his youth. Also it will make his Father & Mother cling closer to the land of his birth, nor if they still held him in

---

* Son of his sister Harriet and her husband, William Meek, clerk in the railway booking office in Huddersfield.

their embrace. England is a very poor country for poor people I know, but this country is not worth what it costs to get here. Its not the amount alone you lost, but you lose all friendship of your youth. One almost fancies himself in a wilderness walking the street of a large city, what he as lived in for many years. The streets and houses gets familiar, but the inhabitants look on you as though you was infirier to the native born. You must bear in mind I have been 13 months in Virginia, . . . Republic, and when I was taken . . . looked down on by the natives what . . . forst to do duty as long as I . . . ny beat. The Doctor as send me North . . . health, and I am getting along very . . . here four weeks and I expect to . . . ave hurt my back and as soon as . . . I shall have to join my Regt. My back . . . me to have come North. It gets . . . now, even in the hospital, I am looked . . . because I am an Englishman, so . . . not advice anybody to leave home and not know where they are going to. I have left the subject somewhat, but to return, I am sorry for both his Father & Mother. . . . [Where to write]

You must also bear in mind John Wilson as left Phila. and gone to Canada. His family as not gone from Philadelphia yet. I expect they will go before very long. . . . [About his regiment since he left it] Father I think wars are the greatest curse that ever came to a nation. Panicks are bad, but nothing like wars. You apear to think the North cant subjugate the South. I say they will do, if they have to kill all the whole population in the south what are able to bear arms, yes, if it costs as many from the North. It will never do to let the States suffer a seperation at this time after all the preperations and loss of life what the North as gone to, to supress this rebellion. There is plenty of drunkenness in this Army, as well as any other Army when they can get liquor to drink, but its not so very easy to procure, and when they do get it they never offer any to me, and if they do I refuse politely, and there is nothing more of it. There is also plenty of filth. I cant escape that as easy as liquor. . . . [Greetings] Tell Mother there is nothing seriously the matter with me if I am in a hospital. Also give my respects to Mr Meek and all what asks about me. Your well wishing Son,

TITUS CRAWSHAW

1303 North 4th St., Philadelphia, 3 Feb. 1863

DEAR FATHER, . . . [Letter received]

Tell Mother not to worry about me. There is no danger of me having to go again to the wars. I have got an honourable discharge, and another thing they cannot draft me till all the able men under 45 and over 18 as been in the Army. It is no use me thinking about comeing back. It would take 26 dollors and then I should get only 18 dollors in gold for my 30 dollors of paper. I would have sent you £2 but it would take so much to send it at preasent. It is all paper money that we get here. I use to give 10 dollors to send you £2 but I should have to give 18 dollors at preasent. I hurt my back when I was carrying wood. I had to cross a railroad; the rails was through a cutting; there was a gutter at each side [of] the track to keep the road dry and it was a very muddy time so the gutter was full of mud. I jumped across; the stick caught the bank and drove me back; and I fell on the railroad. The stick was just as much as I could carry and fell on the top of me, but I have got midling strong again. When I was sent away from the Regiment I had the fever caught in the swamp. The doctor called it mallario. My back and head was very painful. They tortured me with blisters. They made me as I could not make water for 36 hours. When they got me well again they discharged me. I have not commenced to work yet but I am looking for work. Very likely I shall be in work when you get this. Things look very bad for the future. I would not advice any one [to come] here if they can made bread and coffee with a place to sleep in in England, and if they cannot make that it makes very little difference where they are. Father, I cant send anything from the wars relating to my adventures but hardships, so its no use writing them. I had many a narrow escape, but I did escape, thank God. . . . [Greetings and messages] My love to all the family,

TITUS CRAWSHAW

[Hespeler], Canada, 31 July 1863

DEAR FATHER,

I got your letter of July 5th this week, also the letter you posted to Phila., May 11th, three weeks ago. I should have answered that one before I got this, but I was ashamed of myself for not been able to help you along. I know it is my duty and if I would send you the money in place of traviling it would be far better, but I will see if I can mend my ways. I have played half my time since I came to Canada and nót done well when I was at work. I have commenced to work again but I am a little bad. When I get that paid I would like to send some to you. I dont say I will do because I think it is wrong to promise anything when a person cant fulfill it. Father, I supose you cannot help thinking and talking about me, but I am not worthy of it. But I never thought you was careless and would not write to me, but it paind me to see what was the reason and me been so careless when I was able. I know sickness is a very bad thing, but when accompanied with poverty it makes it worse to bear. I am in good health. If I had only plenty of work, and I could have if I would go into the harvest field, but as healthy as I am I am afraid of the sun. Otherwise I am to lazy. I think I will try and shake of this laziness, I see it wont do. I must go at anything. Other people stands it and why not me?

You want to know if I was forced to come to Canada or go again to the wars. I came to Canada on my own free will and if my back is always good they cannot draft me till they have taken all the able-bodied young what as not been to the wars. I believe if I had stopt in Phila. it would try this climate. It agrees with me so far very well as far as health Philadelphia and John Wilson was in Canada here so I thought I would try this climate. It aggrees with me so far very well as far as health goes, but pecuniary I am bad enough. If I had been in Philadelphia when the Southern Army forced their way into Pennsylvania I should have gone again for six months. I am pleased now that I did not go. If that gives you a good deal of uneasyness I am glad to ease your mind for once. I also got that paper you posted to Phila. for me. Father, dont waste your money sending me papers. We get all the particulars sooner nor you can send it, except Huddersfield local news. . . . [Greetings] So no more at this time from your negligent Son,

TITUS CRAWSHAW

Germantown, Penn., 19 July 1864

DEAR FATHER,

I never was more ashamed to write since I left your house as I am this time. The last time I wrote to you I said I would try and send a trifleing present with the next letter. I cannot fullfill my intention. The last time I wrote to you I was in Canada and I had started a little buisiness, but I could not make it pay. I was at it 7 months and lost one hundred and fifty dollors besides my time and labour. When I give it up I had left just money enough to bring me to this city. Since I got here I have been unfit for work for about 3 months, not all together, but at different times. . . . [Apologies] When I was in Canada I borrowed 50 dollors from John Wilson. I spent that with the other. If I was compeled to pay some of it now I should have to give 3 dollors for 1 dollor Canada. If any one as got to send money to England at this time they will have to pay 15 dollors for £1 where it use to be only 5 dollors. Wages are good but I think both provisions and clothing is dearer in proportion since this rebelion broke out nor they was before it. I am in good work and I think I could make out good if I was only kept fully employed. I work in the night. The place runs night and day, and if there is any play we always get it. . . . [Health and more apologies] I partly wrote a letter for you some time back but, thinks I, what good is an empty letter? So I put it in the fire. Give my best wishes to Mother, Sisters, and Brothers and accept the same yourself from your Son,

TITUS CRAWSHAW

Germantown, Penn., 19 Sept. 1864

DEAR FATHER,

I received your sad but welcome letter on the 26th of last month. I am sorry for keeping you in misery so long with not writing when a few lines would set you at rest and ease your mind with regards to me as long as there is a war on this Continent, especially Mother, for I have no doubt but a few lines from me would have eased her considerable those six weeks day and night when she was forced to sit up not daring to lay down for fear of been suffocated. Father, I hope you will forgive me. It is too late to ask it from Mother for been so negligent. I know it is nothing else but negligent. I have promised to be better till I am ashamed of myself, and many times have I promised you a present and not fulfiled them till I know you cant credit my letters as a Father ought to do from his Son. You say you would rather have a letter without present nor be minus both. Well I can't plead for want of a clerk. I am my own. You learned me how to write and I am to neglectful to send you a specemen of it. I hope you will forgive me. I can't forgive myself. I ought to be able to help you having nothing but myself to keep, but you see I am no good either to your or anybody else. I am a blank on the face of the earth.

You want to know what I was doing in Canada. I was weaving Balmoral or those high coloured striped skirts. I had one loom with nedles and one 50 needle Jacquard. Some of the skirts had a small figure. I believe if I had tried in Philadelphia the figured skirts would have paid well. I could not make it pay in Canada because the stock was to clear, and I had to much runing about. I bought the yarn at one place and I had to take it 9 miles to dye. I could have made it pay I think if I had add plenty of money to lay in a big stock. I am working night work at Germantown, spining. We are not kept busy every night. I have averaged 7 nights in the fortnight since I commenced here and I have made as much money nearly as if I worked all the time at the gigs or power loom. We work 5 night for a full week. We dont work Saturday nights or Monday mornings. My health is midling good. I believe I am better at either spining or weaving nor giging.* The gigs are to damp. . . .
[Greetings]

TITUS CRAWSHAW. . . .

Blockley, 6 May 1865

DEAR FATHER,

It is with pleasure that I take a pen in hand today to write to you. You

---

* Gigs are rotary cylinders covered with wire teeth used in finishing woollen cloth by raising the nap or 'teazing' before shearing. Crawshaw says he is better at either spinning or weaving by machine than at finishing cloth.

must bear in mind this is my 34th birthday. I am getting to be an old bachelor. Well to speak the truth I have never seen any chance to keep a wife yet. I am waiting patiantly to see others do well, but I believe I shall have to wait till doomsday. . . . [About his misfortunes] I am working at Blockly at the place those men came to with Mallison. I have been working here 4 months and I am enjoying midling good health. Things are looking rather bad at preasent. A good many factories as shut down all together, others working short time. We are keeping on so far but it is uncertain. We have nearly finished this rebelion and made a good many of the Southerners surrender. All their leading Generals as give it up. In the midst of the rejoycing we was all turned to moarning. Our good Preasident Abraham Lincoln was assassinated. Father, I send you an Order for £2.0.0. I wish I was able to send more but I am not at preasant. I expect you will wonder what I do with my money, but to tell you the truth I cannot save any . . . I am sending you an envelop directed. I was thinking you might make a mistake. It is rather a quear name but the man as allways made me welcome at his house whenever I go, and I have been in his house more nor any other out of the place where I board this last 7 years. He is a North of Ireland man. . . . [Greetings]

TITUS CRAWSHAW

Philadelphia, 18 June 1866

DEAR FATHER,

You must excuse me for not answering your's dated March 23rd sooner. I put it of two or three weeks waiting on Eliza having her likeness taken. After that we had the appearance of stoping so I thought I would wait till I got another situation. I have been playing four weeks. So I made up my mind to write before I get work. A good many woolen mills are stopt and the others not doing much around Philadelphia. . . . [Father's rheumatism] You want to know a little about my wife. I will tell you as well as I can. You know we always think best about our own.

She was born in Ireland. She came to this country along with her parents when she was about 6 or 7 years old. Her parents are both dead. Her mother died since I got acquainted with Eliza. She as been dead about two years. Eliza does the best she can to help along. I think she can keep the house with as little money and give as good victuals as most of women could. She can make all her own clothes and some of mine, besides making dresses for other girls occasionaly. She is not very well acquainted around here. She as made two dresses this last week besides doing house work. We have not quarield yet nor I have not had any occasion, but you know we have only been wed eight months. You also wished a small likeness. So you will find one in this letter. You will see she is not a regular beauty, but she is as good looking as me. I agreed with her because I thought we should agree and live midling comfortable together. I was sorry to hear that sister Emma was doing badly. I hope this will find her with plenty of work and good health to do the work. You said Elizabeth had plenty of work, and all my sisters and brothers was in good health. I am glad to hear they are all in good health. I wish you could say the same for yourself. I also see by your letter that Alfred might get along very well if he had a mind. It is a bad thing following after raceers when their own family wants them at home. Give our best respects to Sisters, Brothers, Aunts, Uncles, James North, Gibson Thornton, and all inquiring friends, and accept the same yourself. I conclude with wishing you good health as it leaves us at preasent, from your Son and Daughter,

T. AND E. CRAWSHAW

Laing Series 1873-6

David Laing is one of two cases which have been found in the emigrant letters of a man who came out from Britain as a labourer, without industrial skills, and entered the industrial sector of employment in America.[1] Undoubtedly very large numbers of emigrants from England and Scotland, especially during the last half of the nineteenth century, followed this pattern which was typical of much of the Irish and continental immigration, but in the nature of things, their letters are less likely to have survived than those from farmers and skilled workmen.

Laing's origins are rather obscure.[2] He was born in a small village in Scotland which cannot be identified on a modern atlas. His mother was born in Dunbar, East Lothian, a village on the North Sea coast, east of Edinburgh and the Firth of Forth. Laing emigrated as a very young man. Born in 1830, he was already living in Pennsylvania by 1848. There he married a Pennsylvania-born woman with whom he had four sons and a daughter before they decided to move west.

Sometime between 1856 and 1858, the Laing family moved to Monticello, Indiana, where David Laing and his family appeared in the 1860 census. He gave his occupation as day labourer to the census enumerator. Between 1860 and 1870, Laing did not change his occupation which was still given as labourer in the census of 1870. While his personal property did not increase in value between those dates, the value of his real estate rose from $500 to $1,500. He thus followed the same pattern of other settled industrial workers of investing savings in a house and garden. His two eldest sons, Edwin and George, aged nineteen and twenty-one, were working as farm labourers by 1870, but the younger children, including William, aged seventeen, were attending school.

Indiana was not a state favoured by the foreign-born in America. It consistently trailed behind its neighbours, Illinois, Ohio and Michigan, in the percentage of its population which was foreign-born. In 1870 only about eight per cent of its inhabitants had been born abroad, and only one in two hundred was English-born. Indiana was both more rural and more agricultural than its neighbours to the east, west and north. In 1870 over four-fifths of its people still lived in towns of fewer than twenty-five hundred inhabitants or in the open countryside, and three-fifths of its labour force was still occupied in agriculture. There were no industrial opportunities in the town of Monticello in White County where the Laings settled, and only five Englishmen and one other Scotsman were to be found in its labour force in 1870. Thus, not only had Laing married an American, but he was also more isolated from other immigrants than any other of the letter-writers discussed to this point except Thomas Wozencraft and Edward Phillips. It is possible that this fact helps to explain the inadequacy of his social adjustment. When this series of letters begins, his marriage has broken up, and he feels that his children have been turned against him. These few letters were written as a means of coping with a profound loneliness.

Laing's decision to leave his wife in 1871 proved a salutary one for his occupational upgrading. He arrived in Logansport in Cass County, Indiana, in the wake of its most rapid growth. During the sixties this town not only increased its population by extending its boundaries, but also showed about a fifty per cent growth of population within its old boundaries to reach nearly nine thousand people in 1870. By 1880, it had passed 11,000. The seventies proved to be a decade in which Indiana attracted British immigrants. While the foreign-born population of the state rose by only two per cent between 1870 and 1880 the English-born population rose by nearly twelve per cent. Now, after a sojourn of twenty-three years in America, during which time he had become a citizen, David Laing secured employment in a railway maintenance shop, where the foreman and many of the workmen were immigrants from England and Scotland. During the depression he did not lose his job, though he accepted a reduction in his wages; and in 1876, he was promoted to the position of foreman, significantly, not in the machine shop where he had been working, but in shipping and receiving materials.

During the years when these letters were written, Laing's private life was crashing round his ears, accentuated by the death of his youngest child and only daughter. However, he had now arrived in a community of immigrants and was achieving some economic success through remaining in the same firm. One need not seek farther to explain the lapse in this correspondence after 1876.

The Laing letters were lent to me by Mrs Doreen Noble, who permitted me to make copies of them and who has kindly consented to their publication. Photostats are in the Collection of Regional History at Cornell University (812).

Letters from David Laing to his sister

Logansport, Indiana, 19 Feb. 1873

MY DARLING LITTLE SISTER,

I was made happy (last evening) on going to the Post Office by receving your letter dated Jan 26. I had given up in dispare ever hearing from any of you again, having writen many times but receved no answer. . . . I am happy to hear that my dear sisters are all happy & comfortable & may they allways be so is my sincere wish. I do not know theyr name except sister Isabella & I think it is Cheese. My daughter Isabella was married last Oct. to a young man named Hankee, a carpenter by traid. Let me know the girls' husbands names & theyr busness. . . . [Asks for news] I am so hungry to hear from you all I am starving. I have read your letter at least twenty times since I receved it. Now I supose you want to hear a little about my *unworthy* self. You are suprised to see my letter dated at Logansport. I am working here & have been for about two years. I am working in a large rail road shop at the machine busness. We have 86 locomotive engins to keep in repair & four hundred miles of road to keep up. Our formen are nearly all English & Scotch men & many of the men allso. I am runing a machine & have good easy situation. This town is twenty miles from Monticello. It has about ten thousand inhabitats. I have not been much at home the last two years. When Isabella gos to house keeping, she will live here and then I shall have a home & get out of a boarding house. If I were only able, I should be so happy to go over to see you; but my health has not been good since I was in the Army, I have had several spells of illness. I think a trip *home* would do me good but I must not think of it. It only makes me more unhappy but, Johan dear, I do want to see you all so much. I am bearly forty-three years of age & can feel that age is coming on. Well, I must submit, I have three sons young men: Hugh 24, George 22, William 20 past. Isabella will be nineteen in March, Charles was 14 1st Jan, Benjimin will be 13 1st Aprial. James & John died when babes. This is my family. Isabella, being the only girl, is pas pet & she is a good girl to her Father, God Bless her, & may she be a happy wife. Now here am I writing my thoughts to you in maters that perhaps you care nothing about. Oh how I wish I could see you & tell you my thoughts but I am afriad that will never be unless you come here & I would not ask you to come as you might not like the country & I would be to blame. I have not been to Monticello the last two months, but I hear the family are all well. They forwarded your letter to me here. . . . [Please write]

I am writing in a cold room (my bed room). It is geting late & I am sleepy & do not feel very well. So good night, dear. Your loveing Brother,

DAVID LAING

Pittsburgh, Cincinnati, St Louis Railway,
Logansport, Cass County, State of Indiana, 8 June 1873

MY DEAR SISTER, ... [Letters and photographs received]

You are one of my sisters that I have never seen. But if God is willing I will see you yet before I die. My Isabell is not liveing here. I am still in lodgeings, have *no home*. How I wish I could talk to you without writeing & I could tell you all about it. Well, I must not trouble you with my unhappiness. I am not lodgeing at the same place I was when I wrote my last. I am much better suted in a privat family with a widow lady and her son. They are very kind to me. He and I are both Freemasons, if you know what they are, & they treat me as one of the family; but he is about to marry & I supose that they will break up this home again as he will not wish to trouble his bride with a lodger. Well such is life, so I have allways been driven about in the world. I do not know how I will stand it to leave my mother. We both call her mother. You would laugh to hear us in the evening, as when we come home from work (we both work at the same shop) and changes our cloths, one will call Mother where is my clean shirt, the other where is somthing els. (The Old Lady) you two *Boys* are more trouble to me than all my money. We have lots of fun over it. Mrs Hendricks (that is our mothers name) sends her regards to you and says she will do the best she can for your brother. Isabella sends her love to you and all her Aunts. She says she would so love to see you. I fritened her verey much. I told her I was going to England to see you. She said now Pa you should have gon befor I got Married so I could have gon with you. Now I cant go & we might never see you again if you went. My oldest boy Edwin Hugh will be married next Thursday June 12 & so they go. There is more older than I was when I was married. ... [Sends pictures] from your loveing brother,

D. LAING

Logansport, Indiana, 8 Feb. 1874

MY DEAR SISTER. ... [Letters received; sending pictures]

Now my dear, you spoke of Isabela coming to this country. I would not advise them to come now. Times are harder here now than in England. Money matters are very unsettled and effect all the business of the country. There are thousands here that are out of employment this winter and those that have work are working at reduced wages. I have not been reduced yet, but all around me have and I am looking for it every day. The engin drivers on our road were reduced in Dec. and they struck the day after Xmas. We had a very severe time. The soldiers were called out to quiet them. Theyr places are all filld now and they are out of employment but the Company have lost a vast amount of money by the strike, aside from lossing the services of 1,300 good men. I am more comfortable noŵ. I am liveing with Isabela. Her husband is working in the car department in the same shops that I am. He is working at wood work. My son G. David is working in the machien shop with me. Mrs Hendricks sends her respects to you. Her son is married and she lives with him. If I could talk to you I could tell you a great many things I cannot write. My hope is that I will see you befor I die. Well, my Dear, I am not used to writing and my fingers cramp so I can hardly write. So I will close. Good bye & God Bless you. Your Brother,

D. LAING

P.S. If it would not be too much cost and trouble, I should be pleased to have paper but would sooner have letters oftener. D.L.

Logansport, Indiana, 12 July 1874

MY DEAR SISTER, . . . [Letter received]

You say you are so bussy but you have never told me what busness you are *engaged* in. I wish I could come and stay with you a few weeks as Christena is. I would have a good time if I *am* geting *old*. I am *Grand Father*. Isabella had a fine young son on the 18th of March, but her health has not been good ever since her bab was born. Her husband is not now working in our shop, & they have moved so far away that I could not stay with them and work here. . . . [Mrs Hendricks] I have receved a paper allmost every week for some time, which I must thank you for. Some of my shop mates are allmost as glad to get it to read as I am. There are a great many English working here. There is one man going home frome here in a few days. He has promised to call & see you for me. His name is Joseph Lee. I have only seen Edwins wife twice since they were maried. (I seldom go *home*) I beleve they are doing verey well, but times are verey hard here now. I am working for smaller wages now than I have for many years. There are thousands of men out of work. If I only had the means I should pay you a visite this sumer while times are so hard. And it might be end my life there if I could find busness, for I find that the minds of those I loved the dearest have been posined against me, and you are all the one I have left. My boys George & Charles are both working for our Company & boarding at the same house that I do. George is working in the shop, and Charley is runing on one of the trains. I had hard work to get them the places but suceded at last.

Well, my Dear Sister, I do not know what more to write. If I could talk to you I could say much more that I cannot write. If it would not be too much trouble please find out for me what a good black sute of cloths would cost there. I need a sute verey bad and they are out of my reach here. I find some of my freinds get things from there by express. Now, my Dear, I will bid you good bye for the present, hopeing that you will answer this sooner than you did the last, Your loveing Brother,

D. LAING

Logansport, Indiana, 16 May 1875

DEAR SISTER,

It is now about fourteen months since I receved any letter from you. I have writen two letters and receved no answer. I will try it once more & see if I can get any reply. . . . I am still working in the same shops & am in good health. . . . [Write soon], Your loveing Brother,

D. LAING

Logansport, Indiana, 11 July 1875

DEAR SISTER, . . . [Letter received]

You say you have left your situation. You have never told me what you were engaged in. *Oh I should be verey happy* to have you come over here, but my poor Mother was so disgusted with this country, that I am afraid to say come to you (Much as I wish to see you).*

Edwins wife had a daughter on Christmass morning. I have never seen it yet. Isabella is in very poor health. I am afraid she is going into a decline. She is going home to her Mother next week. She is not able to attend to her household affairs & her little boy. He is the dearest boy in Logansport (at least I think so) & he thinks his Grand pa is the only man there is. I shall miss him verey much. I go there every evening after work hours. He is my *pet* and he know it.

George and Charley are runing on the rail road for this Company. William and Benie are in Monticello. . . . [Greetings]

Now, my Dear Sister, I wish you would write to me oftener. I shall be very lonesome when Isabella & Albert gos away. I would send you a paper if I thought our papers here would interest you any. I get one from you sometimes & thank you for remembering me that much. Give my regards to your friend. You did not tell me her name. I should be happy to have you both over here if I thought you would be content.

* David Laing's mother was living in his household in Monticello at the time of the census of 1860.

I would certainly do the best I could for you. . . . [Write] I will close
with much love to you, your Brother,

D. LAING

Logansport, 13 July 1876

MY DEAR SISTER,

   I receved your kind and welcom letter some weeks ago, and was glad
to see you had not forgoten me alltogether. I had heard of the death of
our sister soon after the death of my own dear daughter who left me
allmost without hope in this world, for she was my best loved in this
world. She left one little boy, 18 months old when his mother died. He
is a sweet little darling, and loves his Grand pa so dearly. I only see him
about once a month, but he does not forget me, comes runing to me
with open arms. His name is James Albert Hankee. I am afraid I will not
see him now verey much unless I go where I am not wellcome. His
father married again about a month ago and I think his wife does not
wish to see me often. She has a fine farm and a good property in
Logansport in which they live. She was an *Old Maid* and supose it was
her last chance. If she only uses Berty well is all I ask of her.

   Isabelle never was well after her baby was born. She knew that she
was dieing and made all her arrangements, talked about it as calmly as if
she were going on a journey. Her only regret was leaveing her husband,
baby and me. I had all the advise I could get for her but it was no use.
Death was there and we could do her no good. The evening befor she
died, she called her brothers one by one to her bed side, bid them far-
well, giveing each advice for future life. Then my trial came, I being last.
She held to my hand untill the last breath left her. Johan Dear, it seems
to me as I write as if it were only yesterday I parted with her. I am pros-
pering in life but still I am so *lonely*. The boys are grown up all men.
They loved theyr sister, but cannot mourn her loss as I do, for all the
love of a warm nature was concentrated on her. Charley & George are
runing on the same railway that I am working for and are boarding at
the same house that I do, rooming in the same room when in Logansport.
They are on the road tonight so I am all alone. I have dreaded to answer
some of your questions, was siting here *alone*, thinking of you & my
Bell; took courage and thought I would spend a hour writeing to you. I
was promoted on the 1st of Aprial, am forman of a gang of twenty men
receveing and shipping all the stores & material; have 20 men and locomotive engine under my charge. Now you wish to know something
about my domestic affairs. It is something that I do not like to speak of,
but I supose *you* have a right to know something about it. In the first
place we have no thought or act in comon. She is ill natured and cross. I

suport her, give her all I earn after my board & clothing are paid for; but *I cannot* live with her nor excuse me from saying any more about this. If I could talk to yourself I would tell you more how she used my dear Mother when she was here. I can never forget that. I have seen her twice since Isabella died last September and then I was compeld to go there to attend to some busness. My property is there and she is liveing in it, but I have to pay taxes & keep it in order. . . . [Will send photos of sons] I live in hope that I will see you yet before I die.

The evening is verey warm and the musquetoes trouble me so. I can hardly write. There is an Englishman named George Ash in the same busness here that you are in. He is doing verey well. We have a man employed in the railway shop making cushions for the railway coachs & engines. He is busey all the time. . . . Your Brother,

D. LAING . . .

Ronaldson Series 1852–4

These letters were written by a Scottish emigrant to his wife. John Ronaldson was a flax hackler. Hackling was the last process in preparing flax for spinning and was carried out after flax had been steeped, dried and separated from the woody part of the stalk. A hackle was a steel-toothed comb on which the strip of flax was teased out to remove coarse fibres and divide up the filaments of flax. Hackling was regarded as a very skilled craft, requiring a high degree of experience and knowledge. Skilled hacklers had been brought to Scotland from Flanders by the Board of Trustees for Manufactures in the early 1730s. At first they travelled around the countryside working for farmers. In the early nineteenth century, hackling was still a handicraft though hacklers were coming to be concentrated in lint mills at water power sites. Others still worked on their own account or for manufacturers in workshops, sometimes called hackleries. During the second quarter of the nineteenth century, machines for hackling began to be introduced. One authority attributed the effort to develop machinery for this work to the fact that 'the hacklers were generally a rough lot of men, who were continually making unreasonable demands, and "striking", when these were not complied with'.[1] Once as important to the linen industry as the croppers had been to wool manufacture, their position was being undermined by new machinery. The displacement did not come suddenly. As late as 1864, a Dundee merchant in the linen trade noted that machine hackling was now practised extensively, suggesting that it was still not universal in Scotland.[2] John Ronaldson emigrated during a period of slow technological displacement of men in his trade.

Ronaldson probably emigrated from the Kirkcaldy district in Fife, though migration may well have been a feature of this family's life before he emigrated to America. His first letter to his wife, Eliza, was addressed to her in care of George Haywood, Kinghorn Mills, Fife.[3] Since the late eighteenth century, linen manufacture had been declining in western Scotland to concentrate mainly in the counties of Forfar, Fife and Perth, north of Edinburgh. Kirkcaldy, a few miles north along the North Sea coast from Kinghorn, was the centre of the trade in Fife. It had held an annual market for the sale of linen cloth since 1739, and in 1838 was making £200,000 worth of linens, much of which was exported to America, the West Indies and Australia. Steam power had been used in the spinning process here as early as 1807. During the 1830s, population had been expanding in both Kinghorn and Kirkcaldy; the census enumerator in 1841 attributed the increase in population in Kinghorn to the prosperous state of flax manufactures and the influx of visitors for seabathing. John Ronaldson had been a man in his twenties during this decade of vigorous growth in the Kirkcaldy district. In the county of Fife as a whole, employment in linen manufacture continued to expand during the 1840s, though employment for women was increasing very much more rapidly than for men. In 1841, fewer than four thousand women of all ages were listed in the various branches of linen manufacture as compared with nearly seven thousand men. By 1851, the number of women workers was approaching ten thousand whereas male employees had barely passed this figure. However, in the Kirkcaldy district itself the industry remained stationary, with fluctuations, for twenty years after 1840. The output in 1869 was the same as that in 1842. And the growth of Kinghorn was arrested in the forties.[4]

A note on a scrap of paper in the Ronaldson Letters indicates that John Ronaldson had had disagreements with his father. 'About my Father,' he wrote, 'any anger that I had has melted into pity.'[5] Ronaldson was also a man of strong political opinions, probably a Chartist sympathizer, though, because he did not believe such topics proper for discussion with a wife, we gain little insight into his views. There is, however, nothing to suggest that either his political opinions or his attitude towards his father were important in his decision to emigrate. Both technological change in his trade and a local stagnation in the industry in which he worked probably prompted him in 1852 at the age of twenty-nine, and very soon after his marriage, to try his hand in America.[6] His wife, whom he left in Scotland, also removed from the Kirkcaldy district, a few months after her husband emigrated, to work at the Mallery Mills in Balerno, a village in Currie Parish, a few miles southwest of Edinburgh.

John Ronaldson carried a sheet of paper with him on which were noted several addresses in towns in New York state.[7] Contacts in his trade, or related industries, determined his destinations in the United States. One or two of these contacts were also relatives. The intimacy of this community is indicated further in another fragment in the Ronaldson Letters: 'they have put on 3 extra hands. Jack Millar from the Links is one and Bob Mount from the Links is another. If A^r has been short of money I could have sent him any amount he required for his voyage, as I can command a few pounds at any time, thanks to my own Temperance.'

Ronaldson's first stopping-place, Schaghticoke in Rensselaer County, New York, just east of the Hudson River, north of Albany, was located in a flax-growing district. With an output of 269,000 pounds of flax, Rensselaer County produced nearly a third of the flax grown in the state in 1850. This town had a small flax-dressing industry. In 1850, one Scots and four Irish flax-dressers were enumerated in the town, which lost population during the ensuing decade. Since he was looking for work for his wife and other female relatives as well as for himself, Ronaldson moved on in January 1854, after he had been out of work for a fortnight in Schaghticoke. He wanted to find 'berths' for himself, his wife, and Jean and Nancy (possibly his sisters) in Andover, Massachusetts, north of Boston, near Lawrence. In this town of seven thousand people were concentrated in 1850 no fewer than sixteen English-born, sixteen Irish-born and thirty-two Scottish-born flax-dressers and hacklers. Failing to find work in this community, Ronaldson proceeded to East Braintree in the southern outskirts of Boston for a few months, and then returned to Scotland at the end of July. East Braintree returned only two Scotsmen in its labour force, no flax hacklers and eighty-nine Irish inhabitants in 1850; to Ronaldson it had the same disadvantages as Schaghticoke.

John Ronaldson's letters are very explicit as to the strength of the influence of community opinion in Scotland on a migrant's decisions. Samuel Mearbeck and Titus Crawshaw of the West Riding of Yorkshire also expressed sensitivity to what was said about them at home. Ronaldson was able to return to Scotland without loss of face because he did succeed in saving a modest sum from his earnings in New York and Massachusetts. He even felt prepared to indulge in spending on a few 'articles of fancy' before he returned home. Ronaldson used other criteria as well for judging whether to remain or to return. In considering the relative advantages and disadvantages of life in America he paid attention, not only to wages and employment, but to hours of work, to employment opportunities for others in his family, and also to the quality of life.

He remained in the United States about two years, never settling down nor purchasing property there. The last letter in the collection, dated 16 August 1854 at Liverpool, announced his return. Little is known about his later career in Scotland. When a daughter was born to him and Eliza in 1857 he gave his occupation as hammerman, Leith and Hull Company in North Leith. Family tradition holds that he became a whitesmith. He died in 1899.

The Ronaldson letters are owned by Miss Elizabeth MacDaid of Kilmarnock whose father as a boy knew the writer of these letters. I am grateful to Miss MacDaid for additional information and advice about John Ronaldson's life. Photostats are in the British Library of Economic and Political Science and in the University of Edinburgh. The letters have become illegible in places through lying folded over the years, but they contain so many interesting features that it has been thought worthwhile to present them in spite of their mutilation.

Letters from John Ronaldson to his wife, Eliza

Greenock, 21 May 1852

ELIZABETH,

I arrived safe in Glasgow, got things arranged the best way I could. We left the pier, then stuck in the river for a couple of days, landed here on the 20th. We are taking on part of our cargo here. My expenses left me with 17/6d. It will carry me into the country so far at any rate. There is 320 of us so you may consider the confusion in the ship. I can get no liberty to write for people jumping over my back, so you must excuse the shortness of this scrawl. . . . I am yours etc.,

JOHN RONALDSON. . . .

Schaghticoke, NY, 30 Oct. 1852

DEAR ELIZA,

After encountering the buffetings of the mighty Atlantic I am sat down to scrawl a few lines to you. . . . [Brief account of voyage. Landed 12 July] I left the ship on the 13th and the same day took my passage away into the interior. So I had little opportunity of seeing New York. After getting 160 miles up the country and knocking about a day or so in search of work, I got the promise of a little work at hackling. My success since then has been moderate in the extreme. Change of climate has been sore against me in health and money affairs. At the present time I am thinking of removing along with another man either to the far west or to the south, and there pick up what chance may throw our way for there is no going ahead here, being nothing but a colony of the Irish.* For me to say or lay down any settled plan for the future would be rash. I have a long and severe Arctic winter before me. In the meantime I am getting into the manners and customs of the country so that

* In 1850, there were 163 Irishmen in the labour force in Schaghticoke, New York, most of them farmers and labourers, as compared with only four immigrants from Scotland and seventeen English-born wage earners.

should be of some use to me and, if I keep anything strong, I have no fear of ultimate success either in one quarter or another. People thinks nothing of shifting a few thousand miles here, but I want as little shifting as possible myself, but in the meantime I must look about.

I think I shall be out of this in 3 weeks. If I am successful you will soon hear from me again. I remain yours,

JOHN RONALDSON. . . .

Schaghticoke, NY, 9 April 1853

. . . . I have a average share of health just now but nothing to brag about. Yours of the 27th Feb. reached me on the 7th. I am glad you are well. You complain bitterly of my long [illegible] I cannot blame you for so doing. I could give reasons for [illegible] as I have done, and [illegible] it serve to write you in the [illegible]. Viz. I have had a fever of the cold at one time, dysentry at another, loss of appetite, off work &c., and of all these I have had my [illegible], change of diet and climate is severe on some, but I hope it is [illegible] with me. This is a great country but many are sadly dissapointed. They come here and I consider myself one of the fortunate hacklers. I could tell you something about things but [illegible] to make a home in this western world for you and the rest. [illegible] reccolect that is not done in a short time under ordinary circumstances. [illegible] I am [illegible] the best in this country, but there is not a house to be got unless you have a family for the factory. The wages given to factory hands is not in proportion to the work performed. How would Jean like to work from sunrise to sunset in summer and from 7 a.m. daylight untill 8 p.m. in winter. But there are better places than this in America for women, and I must look about me. I shall state here as I have said to you on former occassions that I am doing my duty to the utmost of my ability, and I have no hesitation in saying to you that things shall end well if I keep well. [Trust?] me that understands a little of this country and allthough I tried to enter into detail you could not draw comparisons for this reason, things in this country dont resemble things at home. It dont signify in what department of life it is, and you shall see that when you come. So you must [cease?] longwind stories. You say that [? son] has kept you from dieing by cheering up your spirits. It wont [do to?] speak of dieing yet. Then you say your patience has been great. [It] dont look like it when you speak of departing this life in [whole line illegible] the Yankees and [illegible] Dont speak that way again. . . . [Describes fire in mill in which he worked]

I was 4 weeks idle but I got plenty [to do?] and boild all the same. This is the country for high feeding [every?] meal, of course you must pay for it. I pay about 2 pounds . . . [illegible words] I mend my own clothes . . . [illegible words] It would make you laugh but I can darn a stocking just [as well as] any woman I ever saw tried. Tell Wm Ogilvie that I often think of him as my passage. What a treat it would have been to him [illegible] rising and setting of the sun, and the different latitudes we passed thru and a great amount of scientific phenomena, nautical, geographical and astronomical theories practically exemplified. I took some notes of them in my own way. . . . [Messages]

Now Jean tell me what you think of Mallory. I dout you think more of Charlies Close yet. And run along the [illegible] even although [illegible] was ordering you home to bed. But you must be a good girl and do as I have told you before, and I would [words illegible] Eliza as you going to church on Sunday. This may appear a strange advice from me, I think will [illegible] you, although it was for nothing also than cleanliness and pleasure. I almost forgot Jenny Bell. If she is not started tell her to take a bushel of potatoes if she wants pleasure on board, also a net to boil them in. Give her my adress. A salt fish is a grand thing with potatoes. 99 passangers out of every 100 [illegible] taking the above. Jenny will thank me for the advice yet. Geo & Ednie circulated lies in [illegible] 20 people knows me here. If I had intended to pass myself off for what I am not I would likely go whare I was unknown and there is thousands of retreats. [Two lines illegible] I am &c.

JOHN RONALDSON

Schaghticoke, NY, 4 Dec. 1853

ELIZA,

Yours of Nov 13th reached me on the 30th. You want a few explanations of my seeming coldness. In the first place I could never see the consistency of people using terms in their letters they did not use in common conversation. It smells too much of flattery I think. Hence my letters to relations begins with Ar. Fr. Wm. Js. &c. I have no exemptions when I know the party. You seem offended. I must say tis a pity; with regard to my depending on Ar. it was not money I meant, it was family arrangements. I have always considered myself bound to help them that need my help. You next tell me of Mary recieving [£]2 from Ar and also that is more than I ever sent you, and that I might have mentioned it by this time. What would you be at? I could never see the use of sending money unless you needed it. Do you think it will be best for me to send you my surplus money? [illegible line] have got all my own way. Well I think my ways have been blameless since I came to this country. The only thing I have erred in is attempting to make money when I should have been in bed. I could say more of what I have done but I am rather vexed. What is the cause of you asking am I to be with you or not. And I am requested to give you an explicit Yes or No? Well. I here ask you to recolect if ever I gave you any assurance to that effect before, both by letter and word of mouth. You next say your meat is good, tis me that reduces your body by making your mind uneasy. That is replied to above. Me speaking about getting news from Scotland was given in good part I hope, but it seems it was not taken so. Blankets when needed can be bought in 5 minutes. You conclude by saying that you are to resume your complaints, abuse, and insinuations at another time. At any rate it means as much. Jean and Nancy is angry too at me for the form of my adress. Tell them their anger is vain, because I will never encourage caprice untill I am a pauper, and Jean thinks it is time you was beside me. She reasons well, but I know my own affairs best. The time is when I have places suiting. If places was right the money is right. We are nearly out of flax and it is not to be got and there is a great many tramps on the road. Ar has been out of work above a month. No news from Fn. yet. Jean did well in the links. You have all done well upon the whole, too much; but recolect it was my intention not to answer the first part of your letter at all, but people does not know how to do at times, so I have explained myself as cooly as I can do. Tis a good thing Peter has been mindfull of Annie. He has been a long time here but some men can save 4 times more money in this country than others, let them do their utmost, I know it. I have sat down to this several times this day but I cant write. It feels like [illegible] to me somehow. I have no news of any interest for you nor any one else. I hate too many promises. One is as good as a thousand, so you must all be of good cheer for the present. I think this will leave York on Wednesday. I tell any friend that I am comparatively well. Hoping this will find you in good health. I am &c.

JOHN RONALDSON

P.S. I might have lengthened my letter about sundry little things such as my brothers, sisters, and several things in this country; but I dont think it suits at present considering the letter I got. I cannot help thinking of it. Good night, tis late.

Oct. 26th. I have been waiting ever since I received yours expecting a letter from Ar but up to this none have come, but I understand that Hunter and Ar have left Andover and have gone to a twine factory called Braintree, 10 miles from Boston. I dont know his motive for moving. As it is it rather overturns my plans. Andover was a good opning for Jean and Nancy, and this is no place for them at all. I have a few months before me yet and if he is so placed that he can do nothing to help the family then I must do it. Only it is a pity I am not stronger than I am. When you get this either send it to Nancy or a copy of it, the meaning of it I mean, and tell her to be more plain in the next she send to me, what she means 'by keeping her distance from her', 'that they have got to much already' &c. I rather think it smells of ill feeling. If there is occasion for it, keeping at a distance is the best, but for my part I prefer good agreement among relations if possible. I hope this will find you all well. I remain your &c.

JOHN RONALDSON

East Braintree, Mass., 5 Feb. 1854

DEAR ELIZA,

I received yours on the 31st Jany. It found me well. If you pay attention you will understand the following. On the 20th of Dec. I was out of work. I wandered about the town untill the 8th of Jany. I got tired hanging around, so I packed up and took the train for Boston; we halted 1 night in Vermont. I arrived in Boston next day. I took the train for Andover, then went to the employer. He needed no one. I then took the train for Boston. From there I went with the train to this place and by good chance Ar had a berth for me. My ride and other necessary expenses cost near 9 dollars. It is nothing uncommon for a hackler to travel 6 or 7 miles here. It runs away with money, nothing without it . . . The people has good meat here, but they are generally as hard up as in Scotland. Thats them that keeps house. You mention Go. Ednee. I saw him yesterday here, but he had no chance of work. He was thinking of going to Mechanicsville. He has been sailing on the Lakes all summer and has had good pay. There are thousands in this country would be better at home, but then them at home wont believe it, so before they would submit to jeering at home they stop still. For my part my chance has been average, when you take sickness and other expenses into account; and I may tell you in secret that I have at present some 22 pounds sterling, and I always trying my best to see if I can get a place to settle in. I am trying hard to get a place in Andover. I would rather give you cheery news than gloomy ones. Still I must tell the truth.

You must understand that at present there is a duty of 20 pounds on every 100 pounds worth of linen goods that comes to this country.* The President is trying to take that duty off. If he succeeds, it will certainly destroy our trade. I am waiting the result. . . . [Sickness. Weather] This is a country for them that is very ill off at home or a young man of

* The tariff of 30 July 1846 placed linens of all kinds on Schedule E bearing a twenty per cent *ad valorem* duty. In 1857, the duty on linens was reduced to fifteen per cent, but the timing of Ronaldson's departure was not, as it turned out, the result of a lowering of the tariff.

certain trades that is determined to make every cent a prisoner, but if I had talents or influence I would advise them that is anything right to stop where they are. But I know people must see for themselves. There are other ways of convincing them. People may say you can leave, some gets conected here, others does leave in large numbers every ship. Some is always waiting for something to turn up and it seldom does turn up, but then you know their family generally reaps all the advantage and that is something to a good parent. Then there are others who can't bide the jeering of their relations and shopmates after they do return. Still I am one of the kind that says there are good chances and I think I may catch one and if not it don't matter much, for my prospects are far from good in Scotland. . . . [Messages] We pay about 12/– sterling per week for board. Things are very high at present. Nancy must try and battle away for a time, for I am just doing so myself. At the same time I don't like to hear she is so hard dealt with. You are still mentioning about money. You know I would send the money if you said the word. Mentioning the like of Ar. is nothing to me. You know he has more need to send home money, I should imagine, and with regard to me giving him money, you know I was obliged to him in the price of the boat and I don't think he owes me one cent, rather me him if anything. I never receive any papers I may say. I think the post-office keeps them I think. It is useless wasting money on them I should say. You speak of a man being hung. I am against people hanging each other. Education and oatmeal would answer better among the young than keeping it from them and then killing them. . . . [Postage] Ar. lives upstairs above me. . . . [Messages] I may tell you that I travelled some 400 miles coming here one day and another in the first class. They have no 2nd class at time. I have no particular news to give you, only that I am prepared to give you a statement of necessary articles when things suits. It is surely strange that I never receive any news from Kirkcaldy. . . . This is a small country mill, 12 miles south from Boston. I don't know much about it yet, only I can see the sea from the hills, being 4 miles from it. I see a ship at times. . . . [No more news] I am yours &c.

JOHN RONALDSON. . . .

East Braintree, Mass., 27 March 1854

DEAR ELIZA,

Yours of the 5th reached me this day. It found me in excelent health. I would say your letter was the best, the most common sense one you ever sent me. I hope you may agree with me in the following plan. I hope it may be for the best. You say Nancy is far from right, likewise Jean. Now if Nancy is no better we want her to leave Edinburgh instantly, and

I here enclose six pounds to you for the purpose of carrying the same into effect. My plan is this. You and Mary may appoint a day to meet in Edin. for to get this order cashed; then go to her employer, state the case. If they are against it she must leave all the same. Her wages must be no consideration. . . . [passage of four lines mutilated] and I am surprized to see you you can save so much money. Excuse me for thinking you are not doing yourself justice. Nothing pains me so much than to think that any of you are hurting your health because you must bear in mind that my all is at your command. So do not live mean. Nancy thinks she is like Christian. Well perhaps she may soon be, if she dont attend to the laws of health. Christian was a girl of a splended constitution, but bad fashion's pride and foolhardiness murdered her. In winter she wore thin soled shoes, light clothing, and drew in her waist with tight laceing all the time so that she hurt her stomach, confined her lungs and then blamed God. At any rate tis often said. My advice to you all is, and Nancy must adopt it, also Jean, and you. Let your clothes hang more loose (and I may state here that no person in this country wears stays) and wash the body every morning with cold water, all the body nearly. Then dry it well with a towel. It expands the lungs, and assists the digestion, and keeps away colds. A great many does it here. I do it myself and have felt well ever since. It takes firmness, and I am sure it will do you all good. Jean and Nancy must be sure and do it as they feel bad at present. I sent you a few lines in Marys letter. Things looks no better in this country for the hackler. Eliza, you mention about coming out and about wearying to see me. I believe you. Tis high time. This wont do long, I have money; still I am at a stand;. . . . [passage of four lines mutilated]. You mention Wm being in America. Sailors are strange chaps and Cecillia is dead. Nothing but changes. I pity poor Haycocks misfortune. Now Eliza, I hope you will agree with us and bring Nancy with you. Take no excuses, and mind, spend the money. You must all take more pleasure. Take a jaunt some opportunity. Here I will add another pound, 7 in all, and if you find a chance give our poor friends in the Links a bit [of a] present again. Dont be angry with me because I want to see you all happy. I hope this will find you all well and my little namesake John R. not forgetting his Mother. Write soon. I am yours &c.,

JOHN RONALDSON

East Braintree, Mass., [May ?] 1854

DEAR ELIZA,

Yours of the 16th reached me on the 5th of May. It found me well. I was happy to see you was all well in Mallery and that Nancy was **no** worse. Before I got yours I was induced to change my lodgings. There are about forty of us there in different nations. I then deposited the most of my money in the Savings Bank because chests and pockets are often rifled of money. The rules of the bank says money will be given out the first Mondays of July, Oct., Jany., and May, so you see how I am placed. There is no hurry for a few weeks . . . [Because of ice in the Atlantic] This will leave about the 17th and I think if you write the same day you receive it I will get an answer about the 17th of June and with all the news of importance, especially how our trade is likely to be affected by the war. You say that I will have a chance of work with my neighbours, true, but are there many chances? You may be satisfied. I am little satisfied as you are with putting off from time to time. Still I must reason on present appearances and again ask your opinions. I am making a pretty good wage and am saving a deal at present, and that is what few hacklers can say in America at present. To be honest I like home but I would be telling a lie if I said money was trash. I have not rued coming to this country. I have seen a deal and learned to govern myself in my estimation, a great acquisition to any mans happiness. Since we parted in Edinburgh intoxicating drink has only approached my lips twice and one of these occasions saved me from a stroke of the sun last summer, just three days before I saw Ar. I am sending you *Gleasons Pictorial* every week.* They leave every Wednesday with the steamer. Show Wm the papers. He used to like the *London Illustrated News* if I remember.

There is to be a number of hands here leaving for England, at the end of this month. They have work to go to there. The warm weather has set in, the parks are beginning to look green within these last few days, which is very refreshing after six months of ice. This is Sunday and to give you an idea of things, the factory girls are dancing and singing. Still they are very moral and religious. Sunday is not so gloomy here as in Scotland but more virtuous, at least to appearance. You see I am at a loss for something to fill this paper with. This is a country village and there is little to be seen. I might write about many things in this country but you have no interest in the public topics of this country. I mean the most of women don't bother themselves about some subjects, I think tis as well. We had a fast day on the 6th of April all over this state. A number of us hacklers took a jaunt into the city of Boston. We visited the shipping and all the public places of any note. I visited the museum and saw Uncle Tom's Cabin performed and then came home with the 2nd last train. I think I will soon be there again getting a few necessary articles of clothing and perhaps of fancy. I think I will buy a book or two. If you

* *Gleason's Pictorial Drawing-room Companion* was published in Boston, Mass.

could mention any trifling article that any of you might fancy I would get it.

I got Reynolds paper and it is very popular among the hacklers here.* All the papers that comes here from Britain has only one postage stamp on them and yours has 2. You see I don't pay this letter. I see 'tis best not to pay them until they arrive. Twas very obligeing of Mr Jervis in doing what was in his power. I must conclude and I must say the above has been a severe task. I am &c.

JOHN RONALDSON. . . .

* George W.M.Reynolds was one of the pioneers of mass journalism of a less elevated variety than that afforded by Charles Knight or the Chambers brothers in the 1830s. The pro-Chartist *Reynold's Miscellany of Romance, General Interest, Science and Art*, which included a weekly address to the 'industrious classes', was published in London between 1847 and 1849. *Reynold's Political Instructor* appeared in 1849 and became *Reynold's Weekly Newspaper* in 1850. This was the paper which Ronaldson read.

Lister Series 1883–4

Born in 1860, in Deptford, London, the son of a journeyman bricklayer, Ernest Lister was an unmarried man of twenty-three when he travelled to New York City on the *Persian Monarch* from London. He travelled intermediate class, with but one piece of luggage, and told the ship's captain that he intended to make a protracted stay in the United States. A sign-painter by occupation, Lister was returned in the ship's lists as a labourer. He landed in New York on 25 July 1883, just five days before this first letter to his brother-in-law and sister in London was written.[1]

Like most of these industrial workers, he arrived in New York without any fixed intention of remaining either in the City itself or in the United States. His journey was a kind of speculation, and his motives a mixture of economic ambition and a desire to see something of the world. Wage-rates and the cost of living were uppermost in his calculations. He succeeded in finding patrons, only the first of whom, the agent for the Monarch Line who came from his district in London, was clearly an Englishman. Within a very short time he was working for Americans, and by October 1883 was living in a boarding house kept by Americans in Jersey City where, as he said, he was treated as one of the family. But his economic success was limited. Although painters were making three dollars a day in New York City, he took employment at two dollars partly because he found the work entirely different from that to which he was accustomed. During his second winter in Jersey City, when he had no work to do for contractors, he lost the money his sister had sent him to enable him to return to London by undertaking work on his own account. He considered moving to other towns and even undertaking railway labour when he first arrived in order to keep himself in employment. When the labour market tightened with the depression which began in 1884, however, Lister returned to London.

Neither John Ronaldson nor Ernest Lister, who returned to Britain after about two years in the States, showed any interest in the agrarian myth which haunted the industrial emigrants of the first half of the century. The possibility of getting to a farm did not seem to enter into their calculations at all. They were both interested in making the best money they could at their trades. Lister seems to have been more modern and urban in his outlook than any of the other industrial migrants we have considered. He took an interest in his work, something hardly anyone else except George Martin expressed, and he also thought of earnings as available for spending on clothes and admired fine articles of consumption.

The Lister manuscripts are in the possession of his son, Ernest Lister of Ilford, Essex, who permitted me to copy these passages from them in 1949, and they are reproduced by his kind permission.

Letters from Ernest Lister to relatives in London

Monarch Hotel, 121 Pav-ave., Jersey City, NJ, 30 July 1883

MY DEAREST SISTER AND BROTHER,

What a lucky dog I am. I send word to say I have got work the first day I went to seek for it. I started at 1 o'clock. It was a surprise to me, for I did not expect to get any so soon. I am working as a handy man taking everything & I find there is a lot to learn in New York, for Americans go in for a superior kind & there are workmen from all nations & kalsoming* is used a great deal, but it is unknown to this child. My bos tell me to keep every thing to myself & he gives me some good advice & he work with us. His name is Charles Fleury, House Sign & Decorative Painter, 201 West 23 Street, corner, 7 avenue, N.Y.† He has started me with 2 dollars a day for 1 week & after 3 dollars, $12 & then $18 = £62.3.2, dont only count 4 shillings. He said he can't give more for it is late in the season, for he suits his prices to the changes of the year so as to have something to do.

There are no end of workmen out of work & every one seem to say I am lucky, but the Agent for Monarch line put me up to the moves. We chum together. He is a rich young fellow, but there some points I dont like but I shall stick to him. He came from our quarter & he has a great many people he knows & he think that if I don't have any thing for the winter he can put me on for working on the Erie Railway.

The people are very very wicked here. You must be sharpe with them ... 7 a.m. to 6 p.m., Saturday 5 p.m., to work. I can buy things pretty

---

* Calcimining, a trade name given to a kind of white or coloured wash for walls.

† Charles Fleury, painter, was listed in the 93rd volume of the *New York City Directory, 1879–80*, p. 491, as a painter at 224–7th Avenue, with a separate residence on West 17th Street.

cheep for the agent goes into the stores not shops here & you set on the counter & talk & then strike to bargan.

.... I cross in the ferry 3 cent each way any distance. From

ERNEST

It will cost about ½ wages for living &c. I shall write soon. I dont feel up to it. Summer heat & some days hotter.

Monarch Hotel, Jersey City, 20 August 1883

DEAR BROTHER AND SISTER AND BABY,

You wonder how I got on the ship. Well I got on fine. I did not feel very queer & when I saw plum pudding I was overjoyed, for it took my fancy on the first Sunday, plum pudding & fresh beef stew, porridge, potatoes, new bread, every meal pickles, rice &c. & marmalade for tea, tea or coffee which you like, cheese biscuits. . . . [Sea very rough] It was very foggy on the banks for 3 days. We had a draw for 3 pounds for the pilot boat. It was this. There are 24 boats belonging to the pilots and all are numbered. They put the number in a hat & names in another & then draw /Piece 1s/. Than comes the fun, looking for boat. All eyes are strained & a spek is seen. Than the ship makes for it & puts up a flag & the other boat the same if it is a pilot & the number is marked like the fishing boats. We picked them up 300 miles from shore. About 12 are on a boat & than they put 1 on & look out for another one. 20£ was his fee.

I am still busy & at $12 week which seem good, but I must be very careful. I pay $2 for my room now but if there was about 3 or 4 together it is best to [get] 3 or 4 room & then buy food & provide for all which would be about half if not less for one. House rent is the largest sum to pay. The hous wher I have been at work is let for 2,700 dollars [per] year, 20 rooms. The owner has taken a fancy to me & when I am out of work he will take me to some great firm & see what he can do for me. He has lots of houses. People say he is one of the richest of citizens, but you would not think so. I have been to his house & he would like to see a London paper. Do send me a weekly paper, for the papers here have no foreign news but plenty of murders &c. I will send some later on. This gentleman is coming to London in the summer. He would like you to show him about. He says he would pay for every thing & perhaps you could find him a bed with you. I don't know what good he might do me. He sold me a fine watch for 3$.50c & gave me a chain. He is going to try & get me evening work & I am very busy all the week for Monarch Hotel. I painting all there rooms below till 11 oclock at night, going to decorate them so I will have a dollar to bank. I put 7£ into the Greenwich Bank. The other money went quick for clothes. Boots to work is 2 calicow suits. I must get you to send a good thick suit for winter, for cloth here is very dear, about 4£ for anything. You might measure old trowsers & than they would know what kind in size round the waist & down the leg inside. I will send some dollar notes. You can change them easy. I cannot get a gold dollar yet for they are scarce. All are silver now. . . . [Describes pieces of money and elevated trains in New York City]

ERNEST

Monarch Hotel, Jersey City, 23 Sept. 1883

MY DEAREST BROTHER AND SISTER, . . . [Two newspapers received but no letter]

This morning I took a look at the 18 wonder of the world, Brookling Bridge, for they are now running very fine cars upon the endless cable principal to be open for people next week. I am working at a larger bier brewery & doing some fine work. Two of us are picking the ceiling out in colour & gold & black wallnut & finishing all the woodwork in hard oil like a polish, something fresh to me but I have got hold of it very quick. There is a great demand for painters for this fall of the year. Painters are look upon in a different light here than in London. To be a good one means a great thing for all kinds of ornamental work like gilding, graining, &c. It is one of the best trades here. Plumbers get 4$ a day but it is hard for them. Painters as a rule get 3$ and pretty easily. I keep at 2$ but I am looking up the different ways.

. . . . Just past by a funeral with about 200 people passing, a Society I think. The Sons of St George are after me for English only, a Society 20 [$] for death, $6 for sickness weekly & doctor for 4$ a year with a library & a place to obtain work & to look to one another generally. Would you join it? You know doctor charge 6$ or about that just a look. How are things with you. . . . But American hate English one way for making money & going away with it . . . I shall bank 5.00$, getting my rent free. I start another room Monday to decorate. . . .

Monarch Hotel, Jersey City, 7 Oct. 1883

MY DEAR SISTER AND BROTHER, . . . [Letter received]

You ask if I pass to & through the docks. Well, yes, I do but the dock are arranged in a different manner & you dont see ships gathered together like London docks. You know that N.Y. is an Island this shape. [draws a rough sketch] Well the ships are drawing up to quays like this. [sketch] Clean boats fit their ends in like this. [sketch] They draw a boat up in about 1 minute by hooking a chain upon the end & turning a wheel which draws all up close. Ships come & load & return direct. When the *Persian* comes in I allways go on board. I did the last time &

had a fine supper with Stuart, but I think that he is not comming next time. I had to buy some boots, got a nice pair for 4$. I think I will buy clothes here for they are in American style. I find I can get a suit for 14$ or 20$ to be pretty fair, I have gon in for 3 suits of underware. They are a sort of flannel trousers & 1 vest, a regular thing here for winter. I felt very warm in them & it is pretty cold first & last of the day. I give 1$ each for them. It is splendid healthy weather.

That gent has given me another week's work & a house. Two of us are to do next May the 1st. What do you think getting work in advance like that? You ask what about the mountains. Well I took the boat to Fort Lee & than is what they call the mountain, but to day I went right up town further end of N.Y. to Harlum for 5c. It is a cheep ride, 1 hour going by car, & came back on the elevated cars which run over the horse cars which is very fine to ride in the steam cars for quickness & horse cars below for stoping where you want to reach. Elevators run on a level with first or second floors just above the edge of pavement. No small houses to be had, all in flats. You all dine at public tables, but when I get through the winter I shall go into private boarding house. I stop at Hotel for I get work of them. I am geting my room for nothing & last night I took a celing & wood work to do up but have got to give price in about 6$ a week. I live & board on. If you were out here or I with you in London so you could do for me I could make money, but a single man as to pay for things, wher if I had a room I could cook & manage for about half in living. You can buy beef at 3 pence [per] lb. & when I have it at table it is $2\frac{1}{2}$ to pay, so there's the difference. Newspapers I read every morning & evening. Schools are established for every trade & free of charge, for women as well for dress making &c., but if I do little jobs in evening what time do I have? I leave work at $\frac{1}{2}$ 5. start at 7 a.m. Saturdays leave $\frac{1}{2}$ 4, or some place they let me go at 4 p.m. [pays?] us up till $\frac{1}{2}$ 5 money allway ready. Have been do some fancy work but cannot get any writing to do. Done a celing of gold & picked out in crimson & blue & wallnut [work] wood look fine. Gent gave a 1$ at finish & plenty of work to do for him. I wish that other gent had not sent for me for its like takes me from a good job to a short one. So I might not get sent back, but he will have I & another & no one else, so it is a good thing one way but not in another. . . .

Jersey City, 27 Oct. 1883

MY DEAR SISTER AND BROTHER,

By this time you will have received my last letter & surprised you are no doubt of me shifting my address. Your letters will come all right for [I] gave in a removal notice. Well I like my room well. The things are in fine style & lace covers worked upon the bed pillows & in fact it is like a gentlemens home. I am still working for my boss & he told me today that he had more work for me when I finish at brewery. I don't know ardly what arrangement I shall come. If I think it best to stop, I shall, for I am looking for No 1. . . . All the houses are kept fine & warm & the steamboats in fact are too warm sometimes. There are not many dull days & when it rains you would think that it was a water fall for you get soaked through in now time. . . . I get oatemeal & milk for breakfast 10c & for dinner beef stew & brown bread pudding & beet root preserved for 15c. When I get home hot meat & potatoe balls & all kinds of preserves served upon silver things. It is a fine family. You ought to see the Yankey soldiers. You could knock them out of time after seeing ours. They are somwhat like the French & in small bodies. You make the Yanks wild when I tell them they are no good. . . .

Jersey City

MY DEAR BROTHER AND SIS,

Glad to hear from you so soon again & somwhat surprised of you going without your holday for my sake of sending me money. Now I will take your advice & come home as soon as I am not doing any thing. I am still painting some nice carriages of traps. I shall finish 2 this week. 14 $ will I than take, for I go 2 $ on account & I am to paint another for 10 $. I can do one in 3 days or if I get two to 3 to work on I can do 3 a week which if I can only get would be from 20 $ to 30 a week. I am out of debt, for I keep all things clear & now I am at work on these buggies. My boss wants me but I shall work on this till I cant get more & than if he has no work shall get to another city & find some. . . . [incomprehensible sentence]

In this country it is all about the new coming President, banners hang accross the street with the competing pictures of them 200 feet squar they say they are. All the lettering is wrote on string netting, pictures in the centre. Now in N.Y. the street look funny with telegraph poles all along both side of the street with hundreds of wire strung & you find pols crooked in all styles but fine strong trees they have been . . . I have got the money safe & I will keep it by me till I find I will not get any thing to do then return home. I think I will go as fare up the Hudson River as possible by steamer. They take you 150 miles for 50c & than could stop at some place & see if there is work & thus see the places. . . .
[Fire at Pennsylvania Railroad Depot]

Jersey City, 21 Feb. 1884

MY DEAREST SISTER AND BROTHER,

You wish to know if I have seen any old fashoned English houses. No,
13*

I have not in the style we know of, for the American method is different to our system of building. Out of the towns they are all frame houses (i.e.) all wooden constructions. They first make the shape of the house in framework & then nail the wooden boards upon them with paper (oiled, brown) underneth so as to exclude all draught. They than nail the lathes up inside thicker than what English builders use & plaster thereon. The roof as a rule is flat on the slant, that is, just enough for the rain to run off & covered with tin, but when you see a regular slanting roof they cut pieces of wood in the shape of fancy slates and paint them red or slate colour & fix them just like slates & they look like them too. But there a great number of fancy houses with there turrets & old fashoned styles & certainly pretty designs. Allways as a rule in every country house you see a very nice verander or piazya out of 1st floor & a nice stepps up to them & they are a necessity in hot summer, for you find it too hot indoors. So they take a chair & set outside in the shade. There is a great deal of taste about these houses & especily about picking out the painting of them. For one thing is done to harmonize in colours & general look & ornament is introduced. All roofs are painted red where they are tin & flat. Generally cornices are built of galvanized iron, that is, the [coping] of the house, for they can buy them ready made & alas there's still numbers made of wood. These cornices as a rule are a deep moulding supported by 4 or 6 brackets or trusses & in between a pannel is formed. Some put an ornament in & some are left blank. These cornices are painted a brown to look like the stone that abounds here. They are about 6″ deep & length of houses. So this is the coping. Next thing is every window has wooden blinds open like shutters painted green or brown & you can move them open or shut in this way. There is a frame of wood to each half shutter (that is there are two to a window & close in the centre) and in from side to side thin laths reach accross like a venetian blind & then a thin stick is connected to the edge of every one & by pulling it down it opens the strips of wood so the light comes in & you can regulate them for the sun or similar to your venetian blinds. Now the doorways are nice. Double one are arranged vestibule is formed, [word illegible] or grained a black walnut, but I think white door predominate.

Everyone put fire ashes out side every morning to cart away. Now in New York no more frame houses are to be built. The houses are on an average much larger & tawler than London ones, bath room in all. Now every brick hous is painted a dull flat looking red brick colour & striped with white paint to form joints & they look very nice to look at, but the grand houses are very large & of brown stone & numbers of white marble with great deal of carving finished inside with hard wood, wallnut, ash, mahogany, &c., stained & pollished. Celing are frescoes with splendid designs. French Germans & Italian as a rule are the frescoers & designers. I have picked up a good deal by watching them. You will never seen a London celing with flower ornaments, butterflies painted in water colour. They set fine panel &c. all up the stairs. I wish you could see these celings at some of these houses & hotels. The north end or up town are the finest mansions &c.

Now there are another class. These are the flats where you can hire a floor or a few rooms. You pay according to the height, back or front for money matters. But I dont like them much. There is a janator or porter who collect rent & see every thing is kept clean & right who live below of course. The high class flats are fine, but not with the poorer one for there are hundreds of (brown light) beetles & they swarm the rooms, for the dont try to get rid of them. The sight is enough in the holes. Now in the general run of houses they are boarding establishments like this you pay $10–$12 – $7–$8 to sleep [and] have your meals in these place. I think the New York run of price is 10$ per week for to live. Male & femail both eat or dine at one long table & you have splendid dishes & everything served proper. This is what makes the Americans so familliar with one another. Now they did have regular table where I am living & we all dined together, but now they only let the rooms, a large room for 10$ and 2 other rooms for 12–10 dollars, two rooms at 5$ a month. One I have & do not board. Am one, but they treat me like one of the family for I go & set with them & doo what I like & I have what I like to eat for my one meal & I get two meal sometimes 3 meal, that is, the landlord & his wife & landladys brother & wife & a niece of theres & your [illegible words] chicken & pigeons, green peas, potatoes, jam [guinses] for desert & cake for tea. I enjoyed it. We are going to ketch some moor pidgeon at a shooting match outside of shooting ring can ketch them. The folks are just gone to a ball or a reception.

Now the roads are in a dirty condition. They keep the roads in a very bad style. It is mud slush & mud &c. All round here the country is a vast swamp, water last all the year round. There is no systemn of dranage for it is this. There are some large rivers & canals & they run over. I think the rocks arrise in all ways to huge cliffs. It is a bluestone and [they] blast. All of N. York was a vast stone island. North end there [are] large rocks of marble. It takes a good time to bore & blast the rocks for to build thereon.

. . . . Now I have earned 12$ this week, for a house owner had me to fix his painting up through Mr Bray who is not very well, for climate does not aggree with him. He looks very queer & Mr Dr Spellmire & I think that I will get a tin roof to paint for another man & there might be some inside work. Cannot tell yet. I think 12$ is pretty fair with me breakfast & dinner as good at 250c. If I could let myself out to people like that I could do I shall charge 3$ or 4½$ for the roof, but your money will be very handy, for I cannot tell how I will manage yet, for you know it is very hard to be in a strange land & no money, for I shall have to get clothes somehow &c. But the busy time will soon be here. I think in the spring all is rush. . . . [Notes a sign printing he has done]

Jersey City [1884?]

MY DEAR BROTHER AND SISTER, . . . [Describes Barnum Circus he has attended]

I am still at work for 3£ per week & riding money, for I get all about the outside of the city, but I have been 2 weeks whitewashing & tinting wall. Fancy paying 3£ for whitewashing. I dont work over much, nothing like I did for 12$ per week. I think if I dont ask for 18$ per week I can have work for long time. Could get work for 400c per day but not steady. I will write more later on. I will be quite clear of debts next week. I am 4 weeks in advance with board & lodging. . . .

[Autumn, 1884?]

The greatest of all is election for our next President. It is a great time they have praids every night. Men dress up in all kinds of costumes with bands of music, every thing to make a show. For the Republicans & Democrats & teetotlars have there men to run for office & the arguments in great paper print & libel one another & call the opposite parties thieves & liars without restraint &c.

Our house is to be illuminated for the final parad with Chinees lanterns. Republican we are.* About 30,000 people to join prade come from all quarters. I have been & see all the place to be seen arround us for a good many miles. I have worked in the Crange mountains† & a sight you would never see in England owing to the finess of climate to tints that to autumn paints the leaves. Rocks covered with moss is beyond description, red, yellow, pinks. Colours are grand amongst rock which the places are covered with the marshes & swamps & long tracts of country allmost treeless give these grandure as well, for tall grass arrise with bull rushes & wild flowers & wid rivers with railway track & factory where & these are pleasing. . . .

---

* Ernest Lister's son believed that his father had voted in the American election of 1884. If he did, he could not yet have been a qualified voter.

† This probably refers to Mount Crane in Warren County, New York, west of Lake George.

Jersey City, [Autumn, 1884?]

MY DEAREST SISTER AND BROTHER, . . . [No letter received]

Now I guess you are looking for my coming but I think I must put it off till spring, for I have spent some of the money which I could not help doing, & another reason is I think I will get through winter all right for I known about Jersey City. Now, I seem to be getting along pretty good. Well that is I don't owe a cent and have a few dollars in hand. I think I have managed for I have not worked for any boss for 3 months, for work is slack; but I have obtained it on my own account & some work I have done which I have got left on. That is no money. So it put me back & I used your money & well you know with the result. You will be very cross I know, but I thought I would make but lost. Well I have paid 45 dollars out since for rent & food in 3 months & during the last 3 weeks I have spent 100 dollars, for I painted a house up but took it too low, only made 20 dollar for myself which I now must lay out for rent &c. I have a front door to varnish for 3 dollars, two sleighs to commence on Tuesday for spring, if I stay, a house with 40 rooms to do up for my friend Dr Spellmeyer residence.

Cold weather is now coming on. About November snow will appear. (I have got a bare room at a stable with a fire all for no rent to work in). . . .

ERNEST

PART III

THE UPROOTED: IMMIGRANTS IN
PROFESSIONAL, COMMERCIAL AND
CLERICAL OCCUPATIONS

1

Background to Emigration

The letter-writers in this final group were not very different in social origins from those considered in the first two sections. They came from families of farmers, skilled workers, small tradesmen and manufacturers. They are distinguishable from the migrants in our other groups by the occupations they chose to enter in America, and also by the fact that they broke more ties in emigrating than did most of the farmers and industrial workers.

Except for Wozencraft, the immigrant farmers whom we have discussed migrated in a family network and maintained ties with their families after they came to America. Those who had been farmers or agricultural labourers in England or Scotland did not break the continuity of occupation when they emigrated. Farmers who came from urban and industrial backgrounds in Britain were sustained at least for a while by a cluster of values brought from Europe which I have called an agrarian myth. Almost without exception, these immigrants in agriculture maintained links with the religion of their youth and settled in communities where the immigrant population was large enough that they could find friends, and frequently wives, among other immigrants from Britain who understood their assumptions and attitudes.

In contrast, the industrial workers whose letters we have broke family ties more frequently, at least temporarily, when they emigrated, though a family network of distribution clearly had some importance for many of them, especially those emigrating before 1840. In a few cases, family disagreements played some part in the decisions to emigrate. Furthermore, the industrial workers, especially those who left from the 1840s onwards, may have been somewhat less likely to maintain religious connections after they emigrated. In spite of attitudes which approved of occupational mobility, the industrial workers did retain ties with the same occupations they had practised in Britain, and they tended to settle in communities in America where other immigrants were present in considerable numbers. In my view, it is significant that few emigrant letters have turned up from the many British industrial workers who settled in large immigrant communities like Lawrence, Fall River and New Bedford, Massachusetts, and Patterson, New Jersey. Such people had greater opportunities for maintaining contact with immigrant communities in America than did the very mobile men we have considered.

The individuals to be discussed in this section usually cut more ties in emigrating. They may be compared in some respects with agricultural migrants who settled in areas where they were isolated from other immigrants, and to David Laing, who not only moved to a part of America where there were very few British immigrants but who was also occupationally mobile, progressing from labourer to foreman. Obviously, all emigrants severed certain connections with their native place, and those who remained in America eventually became citizens of another country. In addition, with this particular group, migration brought a disruption of family, friendship and occupation. These emigrants tended to select their places of settlement in America without regard to the presence of family or friends from their communities at home. Most of them were mobile both geographically and socially. These men may well be described in the words of Pitirim Sorokin: 'He becomes less and less attached to anything and to anybody. He begins to remind us of one down driven by the wind in the air. He becomes "free" and, as a consequence, lonely as a socially unattached atom.'[1]

The white-collar workers whom we are to consider now were not part of what might be called a migratory elite. They brought no certificates of professional qualification with them to assist them in finding employment in America. In the early part of the century, as we have seen, some immigrants who could claim professional qualifications came to the United States in order to try to become landowners and farmers. There can be little doubt that at the very end of the century, when the number of recognized professions was beginning to expand in Britain, men were arriving in the United States who expected their paper qualifications to assist them in getting a start. In Seattle, Washington, for example, a town which grew from a tiny village after 1870, at least six of its eminent citizens listed in the local history of 1916 had come from England or Scotland in the eighties and nineties with qualifications as mining engineers, accountants or solicitors. In contrast, in two cities whose growth took place earlier in the century, Dubuque, Iowa, and Newburgh, New York, the English and Scots immigrants who appeared in county histories had been farmers, small tradesmen or skilled industrial workers before they emigrated.[2] The commercial, clerical and professional workers, whose letters are presented here, were not professionally qualified before they emigrated. Though some of them entered white-collar and even professional positions in America, they brought no specialized skills with them. Since the farmers and industrial workers, whose letters we have, were also able to read and write, this group cannot be especially distinguished by its literacy. Nor can we say that these men differed very much in their social origins from the other migrants we have been considering. They did not exhibit 'bourgeois' or middle-class attitudes in a unique way. As we have seen, most of the farmers and industrial workers were very interested in owning property and showed a marked tendency to save, attitudes usually associated with the bourgeoisie, which the men in this group did not exhibit in any significantly greater degree. We have found a common denominator in the occupations these men sought to enter in America – clerical work, the professions and independent business. They had greater social ambitions.

When it is possible to assess the reasons for emigration in this group of letter-writers, one is impressed, first of all, with the relative absence of any references to economic pressures. The most notable point of contrast between these migrants and most of those considered in the other sections is the predominance of personal, family and status reasons for emigration. The Petingale brothers all seem to have been trying to prove something to their father about their ability to make their own way in the world. Disappointment with a wife's dowry and other marital difficulties led Nathan Haley to emigrate. Juan Pattison, an engineer whose letters have not been included, also emigrated because his domestic life was shattered.[3] In the case of Andrew Mattison, a knowledge that he could never aspire to marry the girl he loved in England because her social status was higher than his own, led him to emigrate.[4] In Radcliffe Quine, an unhappy childhood, during which he felt that he had been woefully neglected, produced a powerful urge to emigrate.

Status considerations were sometimes intertwined with these family difficulties. William Petingale did not relish the life of a journeyman industrial worker, nor Thomas Petingale that of a draper's clerk, after educations which they felt fitted them for somewhat more elevated positions in life. Juan Pattison thought that if he could perform a remarkable engineering feat which brought him to the attention of the whole world, his wife and son might come back to him.[5] A vague, restless ambition also prompted James Vickredge, the son of a china dealer in Malvern, Worcestershire, to emigrate. Later in life he explained his emigration in these words:

on Jany 6th 1850 I sailed in the Good Ship London in the Steerage from

London Docks to come to the Land of Promise America Why did I come there were 6 of us in family Walter was in business at Chestnut William was with Father Fred was in Business at Camberwell Ted your Father was at Dulwich Lizzy was at School and I was clerk 2 years at Henly 2 years at Hamstead and no hope of being anything else. I was successful as a clerk and had good positions and good salary but it did not satisfy my ambitions. . . . Cousin Toucks and Miss Taylor who kept school at Battersea Gave up and Mrs Touks came to America to visit her married sister, a year after Miss Taylor joint her and I had made up my mind to go too but my Boss offered me more Sal. and I agreed to Stay and did for one year but I had the fever on and finally I started. . . .[6]

These migrants seem to have been more concerned with their long-run prospects in life, especially the eventual social status they might enjoy, than they were with short-term assessments of wages and cost-of-living differentials, such as governed much of the thinking of the industrial workers. Some of them cherished dreams of a really big breakthrough into either fame or fortune not characteristic of emigrants who chose to enter industry and agriculture.

The individuals in this group had been more mobile geographically within Britain before they went overseas than were most of the other letter-writers. When Nathan Haley deserted his family he went first to Liverpool for a time. William and Thomas Petingale both tried to find jobs away from their father's farm in Norfolk before they finally decided to emigrate. Other cases of clerks whose uprooting began in Britain have been encountered. J. Holmes, who was born in 1863 in Lyme Regis, Dorset, was apprenticed to a draper at Seaton, Devon. After that he went to London for nine years before he finally emigrated to New York at the age of twenty-six.[7]

Not only had many of these people already begun to uproot themselves from their native communities before they left the country, but they were also, like the industrial workers, mainly single men when they emigrated. Either they went out as young unmarried men, as did Quine, Mattison, the Petingales and James Vickridge, or else they left their families in Britain, as did Nathan Haley, Juan Pattison and others whose letters we have.[8]

Because of the highly individualistic motives for emigration, and the fact that many had already loosened their family and community associations before they left Britain, these individuals did not move within a social network of distribution either of family or of a trade. They did not go to join friends or relatives in America. The three Petingale brothers, who emigrated within about seven years of each other, migrated to different places in America and took their separate ways after they arrived. Although Radcliffe Quine emigrated in 1844 with relatives from the Isle of Man, his 'characteristic' emigration occurred within the United States when, in 1854, he left wife, child, and the rest of the family in the east and took off on his own for California, never again to rejoin his family. Sometimes brothers went to different parts of the world, as well as to different regions within the United States. One of the Petingale brothers emigrated to New South Wales, and one of Radcliffe Quine's brothers went to New Zealand.

2

Economic and Social Adjustment

Because they travelled without reference to an emigrant network, these people frequently settled in areas where there were very few other British immigrants. Andrew Mattison settled in Paducah, Kentucky, which had only nineteen English-born inhabitants in 1850. Robert Hesketh in Robeson, Pennsylvania, is another example. Others remained for many years outside any organic community of which they were members. This was the case with Juan Pattison and Henry Petingale, both of whom moved from one engineering project to another. Pattison quite consciously sought social isolation during the early years after his emigration: 'that I should have in just measure isolated myself as it were ... living in the wilds & selecting such an occupation as necessitates such seclusion – viz pioneering new railroads.'[9] Radcliffe Quine had only fleeting contacts with other immigrants during his years on Vancouver Island and in the gold mines of British Columbia. Nathan Haley, on the move within the trading economy based on the Ohio and Mississippi Rivers during the 1820s, was similarly cut off from a settled community. Even those who remained in large urban communities, such as the Reids in New York City and Brooklyn, seem to have been isolated from any continuing contact with other immigrants.

The want of family solidarity and the highly developed individualism of these migrants made them bear the entire burden of the migration experience and adjustment themselves, with little assistance from their compatriots. The immigrants in this group consequently sought help more frequently outside the immigrant community when they were in difficulties. William Petingale was tended in his illness in Rochester, New York, by a doctor obtained through the British Consul. A tavern-keeper in New York City helped Thomas Petingale try to trace his brother whom he believed to be dead. Radcliffe Quine had to call upon official agencies to prove his identity when he tried to claim an inheritance many years after he had cut himself off from his family. An American-born grocer interceded for Robert Hesketh with his family in

England. Juan Pattison called upon the British Consul in New York City to establish his credentials with his family in England.[10]

In spite of the fact that they did not depend upon other immigrants to assist them in getting a start in America, these immigrants had certain advantages in making an economic adjustment. Some of them were able to take jobs not ordinarily open to immigrants because they had had an education which made writing far easier for them than it was for many of the people in the other two groups. Most emigrant guidebooks continually warned prospective British emigrants that there was an oversupply of clerks in America and that clerical employment was rarely open to old countrymen. Yet we have a letter from an immigrant from Pontypool in Wales who had little difficulty in finding employment as a book-keeper in a wholesale drug firm in Cincinnati.[11] The Petingale brothers were able to get positions as assistant engineers and surveyors on southern railways during the late 1830s, without any previous experience of this kind of work, and to use this practical training to obtain positions as civil engineers in the north on railways and public works. When Thomas Petingale opted for a more settled married life, he secured a job as a clerk in the United States Treasury in Washington. The opportunities which British immigrants with a fair education might find, in helping fill the need for rudimentary skills in the undeveloped American economy during the first half of the nineteenth century, are illustrated in some of the remarks of James Knight, a country storekeeper in Nelsonville, Ohio. Commenting upon the want of material success gained by John Rochester, another literate Englishman, Knight observed that a man of Rochester's general education could easily set himself on the road to affluence by reading up a little surveying and commencing as a land surveyor.[12] Clearly an untrained but literate Englishman had more opportunities than similar immigrants from other countries.

In addition to their relatively high level of literacy, several immigrants in this group had another advantage in economic adaptation in their willingness to change both occupation and location. While migrants in agriculture preferred to take on by-occupations rather than continue moving and migrants in industry moved about rather than change occupation, this group of migrants demonstrated a flexibility in both respects. Their economic goals were less clearly formulated than those of the farmers and industrial workers, and their freedom from social ties at the time of migration also contributed to an initial mobility of occupation and location. In the relatively unspecialized local economies in the west in the early nineteenth century such flexibility was an asset in economic adjustment, perhaps even more useful than a specialized skill. As a lead miner, whisky distiller and trader along the Ohio River in the twenties, Nathan Haley followed his precept: 'A man in this Country must do everything if he mean to do good business.'[13]

With these particular migrants, mobility in the United States was not always simply a method of reaching a decision as to where finally to settle down. They did not regard a return to England as an alternative when meeting reverses. Though several of them did visit England from time to time, Nathan Haley was the only individual in this group who contemplated for a considerable time the possibility of returning per-manently to Yorkshire. Partly because their emigration resulted from a family quarrel or crisis, they emigrated for good and persisted in trying to make an economic adjustment in the New World. In contrast to the mobile industrial workers, they did not look upon America and Britain as alternative arenas in which to practise given skills. The acquisition of property finally stopped the geographical mobility of some of them – Mattison, Hesketh and Vickridge – but Mr Reid, Juan Pattison, Henry Petingale and Radcliffe Quine never achieved stability in their economic lives. Although flexibility about job and location and a fair determina-tion to remain in America could be economic advantages, they might prove self-defeating, even in an economic sense, if the immigrant's goals were too amorphous or too ambitious.

It is very difficult to generalize about the economic goals of these few migrants. Out of about fifteen migrants, whose letters we have, a wide variety of aims is represented. The simple goal of economic independ-ence to be gained from farming was rarely mentioned. There is a fairly wide gap between the more conservatively inclined men in this group, like Hesketh, who sought land and property as security in old age, or the Reids, who took a small grocery business in Brooklyn for the same reason, and Thomas Petingale, who finally settled down in a job without prospects but with maximum security, on the one hand, and the specu-latively-inclined men like Nathan Haley, Radcliffe Quine and James Vickridge on the other. Vickridge employed twelve clerks in the shop he bought in Norwich, Connecticut, when he went there from Newburgh, New York, but then for two years he claimed to have made nothing.[14] His career as a store-owner over a period of about twenty-four years in New York and Connecticut was punctuated by great ups and downs in his fortunes. Among the agriculturists, we found that often the more speculatively-inclined immigrants came from the more slowly growing, less industrialized parts of Britain. There is a suggestion of the same pattern among these immigrants in commercial occupations. John Hesketh, from Manchester, was a careful saver and prudent investor. A Yorkshire immigrant, who established a brewery business in

Pittsburgh, noted that he and his wife never lived up to the advances in their income, always ploughed back savings; and he criticized his American neighbours for their careless and wasteful housekeeping.[15] An almost incredible, and possibly very much exaggerated, instance of the savings instinct of a Lancashire immigrant in Connecticut was described by James Vickridge:

Mr Eccles came from Lancashire about 60 years ago he was earning 8/ per week there and came here to try and earn more he was a good Weaver and got work and saved his money and he rose by hard work and economy till he was Supt of Taftmill Hill I knew him there, he died in Norwich and left $445,000 about £90,000 to Charity, their Hospitals and children Houses & Baltic church, he had no children. a good Weaver here can make 22 dollars pr Week but he cannot do it but one week but 14 to 18 doll he can do every Week and if he saved his money he could Do as much Good as Mr Eccles did. . . .[16]

In his penurious old age, James Vickridge, from Surrey, admired such a feat of savings, so different from his own hazardous career in self-employment. One can also contrast the attitudes of John Hesketh, from Lancashire, with those of Radcliffe Quine, from the Isle of Man, who was at the other end of the spectrum, always willing to take a risk until he found himself in his declining years with nothing but gold mine claims which were rapidly deteriorating in value. Perhaps nothing more was involved in these contrasts than purely personal differences, the timid versus the confident individual, the pessimist versus the optimist. However, among the migrants in agriculture and other businesses, it is at least interesting that the most adventurous and speculatively-inclined individuals whom we have encountered rarely came from the more highly developed economic regions in Britain. Possibly the type of entrepreneurial migrant produced in industrially mature and urban Britain was the man who was less adventurous and more conservative in his economic outlook than the man who remained at home. The emigrant from a more slowly growing region at home might be more likely to have been a man who chafed at restraints to enterprise and insufficient opportunity and who had a tendency to take bigger risks in America. One cannot push this contrast very far, in view of the limited number of cases.

Another characteristic which these commercial and clerical workers shared with some of the farmers was their expectation that the flow of capital should be from Britain to America. Unlike the industrial workers, these people never considered sending remittances home. Some brought capital with them to set themselves up in business in America. Others borrowed on their prospects when they needed capital. James Vickridge bought his first store for $1,300 on loans raised from a cousin and on his expectations from his father's estate.[17] A former boy of Shrewsbury School who was living in North Carolina in the eighties tried to borrow money from his solicitor in Shropshire to enter a partnership in a store, since he thought that to mention such a use of capital raised on his prospects for inheritance would upset his mother, whereas in America to enter trade was not considered 'infra dig'.[18] The Petingale brothers had the idea that once they had proven to their father their ability to earn money, he should be willing to send them money. Not all of these efforts to obtain money from Britain succeeded. Juan Pattison and Radcliffe Quine, who more thoroughly than most had severed ties with their families at home, were conspicuously unsuccessful in their efforts.[19] These letters suggest that loans and remittances sent to immigrants in commerce and trade were as likely to be unwisely used as those sent to farmers. In this group, probably not altogether by chance, more individuals who had expectations that money from home would be available to rescue them were caught in economic dependence in old age. Radcliffe Quine's last letters from Seattle were begging letters, in which he made no effort to conceal his economic and physical dependence. Similarly, James Vickridge, who lived to be a very old man, had to write when he was in his eighties that he was poor and dependent on others for support. He could scarcely believe that his nephew, a Yorkshire wool merchant, had suffered such reverses in 1908 that he was unable to send his customary remittances.[20]

In spite of the initial economic advantages which they had in their acceptance of migration as a permanent step, their consequent flexibility about jobs and places of settlement, and in their ability to import capital or to seek aid from home in difficulties, this group of migrants was not outstanding for economic success. Their inadequate social adjustment is perhaps even more remarkable. The unhappiness concealed or expressed in so many of these letters cannot be attributed to a hostility on the part of Americans towards them. As isolated middle-class immigrants, most of them gained acceptance quite easily in the American communities in which they settled. John Hesketh felt his neighbours greeted him warmly as 'the Old Englishman'. He and Radcliffe Quine were both aided by Americans when illness and poverty made them dependent. Thomas and Henry Petingale married American women of 'good' families and obtained government appointments, Henry from a Know-Nothing government in New York state. Juan Pattison boasted that he had entrée into the best society during his sojourn in Syracuse 'but that does not always make a fellow happy'.[21] As an old man James Vickridge felt very sorry for himself because he had no relative within three thousand miles, except for some fourth cousins in Pennsylvania. In 1905, he noted that English immigrants were leaving the woollen mills in Hanover, Connecticut, where he had bought a house and allotment many years earlier. 'Mr Rodgers Family had left and are working in Norwich town, 7 of the help have gone to England and others have left for other Mills, so I have lost all my Friends in Hanover'.[22] Yet for all these complaints of total isolation, one finds that Vickridge received money from friends, visits and food from the pastor and members of the church he used to attend in Baltic, Connecticut, and even a cheque from the owner of the woollen mill at Hanover as his birthdays piled up.[23] These particular migrants were accepted by the American community because they usually placed themselves in situations in which they had more contact with Americans than did the farmers and industrial workers whose letters have been considered.

Nor were these individuals prejudiced in their adjustment by attitudes of contempt or superiority towards the Americans whom they met. William Petingale, the only one in this group to complain that Americans had 'an unnatural antipathy' to Englishmen, actually disapproved of what he took to be the attempts of Americans to create the same distinctions between rich and poor as existed in England.[24] Others expressed a strong feeling of identification with America very early in their stay in the country, sooner than farmers and industrial workers. See, for example, Andrew Mattison's statement soon after he had arrived in Kentucky, that the name of the United States 'makes my heart bound with such a feeling of joy that it is out of my power to express'.[25] Within three years of his arrival, Nathan Haley had decided that with all its disadvantages, this country 'is a great deal better country than England'.[26] John Hesketh was referring to 'our manufactures' and 'our rights', identifying with America before he had been ten years in the country. If his amanuensis was an American, who turned these phrases for Hesketh, nevertheless the closeness of his contact with native-Americans is demonstrated by the situation.[27] While Thomas and Henry Petingale tended to remain aloof from American politics, partly perhaps for professional reasons, Thomas approved of the American government and people before he had been in the States very long, and when later in life he took issue with the form of his sister's will he remarked that no American would have made such a will.[28] Thus these migrants, whose occupations and residence put them more constantly in touch with the American community, seem to have been less prone to the idealization of the place of their birth than other migrants, and quite willing to accept and defend American ways of doing things.

All these circumstances – the ease of obtaining employment without special qualifications, the friendliness of the American community towards British immigrants in such jobs, and the positive attitudes of the immigrants themselves expressed towards America – were favourable to assimilation in a new society. It is paradoxical that this small sample of immigrants produced more instances of family disruption and dependency than the other groups. Five marriages broke up irretrievably, three of them after the migrants came to America. Excessive drinking formed part of the background to these unsuccessful marriages, no doubt both as cause and effect. Juan Pattison confessed: 'I am like other men in all respects – but one that is I will be at the pint & that has sometimes militated against me – never socially, never morally but always pecuniarily . . .'[29] In all of the broken marriages, at least one of the immigrant parents became seriously estranged from his own children, and we have three additional cases, Thomas Petingale, James Vickridge and John Hesketh, of conflict or alienation between father and children. This estrangement from children was linked with another feature of this group of migrants. John Hesketh, John Norman, Radcliffe Quine and James Vickridge all spent lonely years as old men in some degree of real want.

It is quite possible that these social failures can be explained away without reference to the effects of migration. Since most of these people had already experienced a disruption of the family in some form before they emigrated, a pattern was merely repeated in America. Some of these people might be dismissed as chronic misfits, as deviants who mistakenly sought salvation in emigration. In the nineteenth century, overseas migration was a course open to such individuals, and they inevitably formed part of the migrant stream. Their very susceptibility to the indulgence of self-pity and their tendency to be disappointed in other members of their families suggest indirectly some of the strengths in adaptation of migrants who moved within networks of family or trade.

In some instances, the problems can be traced directly to the migrant's situation in America, however. Mrs Reid maintained that her husband had not been given to excessive drinking until they arrived in New York City, though we gain no insight into the specific difficulties. Stresses arising out of the close contact with American society are evident in other cases. In explaining his brother Henry's inability to settle down and live with his family, Thomas Petingale mentioned that Henry was 'too much of a John Bull' for his American relatives. Thomas Petingale himself lost his self-respect as he felt himself obliged to turn over the supervision of his children's investments to their mother's family in Cleveland. His own uneasiness among them is apparent in the letter he wrote after a visit to their home on Euclid Avenue. Juan Pattison also suffered from tension associated with his status among Americans. 'The higher a man climbs,' he wrote, 'the more difficult it becomes to sustain his place.'[30] The poverty-stricken ex-store-keeper, James Vickridge, who lamented that he had no family within three thousand miles of his home in Hanover, Connecticut, actually had an adopted son who was post-master in Norwich, less than ten miles away, and claimed that his two daughters had married into two of the best families in Norwich. Yet these children did not visit him. One explanation can be found in Vickridge's clear disapproval of the fact that his adopted son per-sistently lived up to his income and even sent a son to Yale to mix with young men who had larger incomes. Such spending was an anathema to the old man, not only because he himself was in dire need, but also because it transgressed the savings precepts which he valued.[31]

The origins of these family breakdowns can also be seen in attitudes about family responsibility formed by these people before they emi-grated. More ambitious to rise in status or wealth than the farmers and industrial workers, they abandoned many possible family impediments to their upward mobility, an effort which migration simplified. Most of our farmer-immigrants accepted an unlimited responsibility for any relatives who came to them in America. Industrial workers who had not yet acquired families of their own also felt some obligation to members of their families left in Britain, though sometimes this was expressed in nothing more concrete than apologies. Until the burden became too great because of the want of norms for such assistance, they were willing to aid both friends and other members of their families to get estab-lished in America. Most of these clerical and commercial workers showed a greater degree of individualism in that they recognized no fixed rules of accountability to other members of their families and none, so far as one can tell, to friends and acquaintances who might want to emigrate. Nathan Haley expected either his parents or his estranged wife's father to care for his children, whom he deserted, and he made no contribution himself towards their upkeep. Radcliffe Quine and Juan Pattison did not even know how their children were faring. John Hesketh is the only immigrant in this group who expressed a willingness to care for a sister or for motherless nieces, should they come to America, and who thanked his brother for looking after their mother. Most of these people kept in touch with parents or siblings in Britain, not to make a contribution to their well-being, but to avoid losing possible remit-tances or legacies. One should also note that because these people emi-grated largely for personal reasons they were not so likely to find themselves in a position where they might be called upon to aid other migrants from their families and communities. They were not part of a larger migration movement rooted in economic circumstances.

Their strong individualism is also to be seen in attitudes towards their own wives and children. Most of the farmers and industrial workers, whose letters give us insight into the circumstances of their marriages, chose a moment when they could afford a wife, or when they badly needed one, and then found as suitable a mate as they could. There is a practical, down-to-earth quality about their discussions of marriage. These white-collar workers were inclined to be far more effusive about the attributes of their wives. This kind of passage was rare in the other groups of letters:

My dear wife and children since I left England I have had many aching heart – you my dear, dear wife and my dear children, you may think because I am at a distance that I've forgotten you, but no, my love. As long as I live my dear wife and children cannot be forgotten. Although in a distant land I see you often in my dreams, my nights are short at the best of times but of late no sleep can I get for nights together thinking of you my dear wife. Volumes would contain what I've got to say to you, nor can tongue expres my feelings, but I must conclude for my heart is ready to burst with what I've already written. . . .[32]

The ambitious Juan Pattison considered marrying for a second time, but decided to let his prospective bride visit Paris, as she had intended to do, in order that he might judge her suitability from her letters: 'that would enable me to see how she wrote – I could not marry a woman who was not excellent in Education – and also writing shows the human mind I think better than conversation'.[33]

The same individualistic attitudes were expressed towards their children. The Lancashire merchant, James Stott, greeted his children separately in his letter:

I often had you in remembrance during my long and tedious passage, and many times in the night I have seen my children come prancing towards me. Frances generally outstripped her sister Hannah to meet me, (with eyes like two diamonds of the purest water), with all the freedom she ought to do. Hannah next, with blushing cheeks, appeared half pleased and half afraid. Next Maria, with the same careless indifference as usual. Then Eliza came skipping with her pretty little face, much in the same manner as her sister Frances. James generally, after slyly looking at me, laid himself upon a chair, and threw up his heels and looked again, etc. . . .[34]

The irony of all the effusion of attention and concentration of hopes in children, which can be seen in the letters in this group, is that, since the children gained no deeper a sense of family responsibility than their fathers had had as young men, the parents were disappointed in them. While his son William was growing up, John Hesketh's letters revealed his emotional reliance upon the boy. Yet this son went off to California and broke all contact with his ageing parents.

Because these migrants were so often isolated from other immigrants, isolated partly because of their ambition, they expected to derive more satisfaction, status and companionship from their children than did most of the farmers and industrial workers whom we have considered. The former labourer, David Laing, came closer to this kind of dependency on children than any other migrant previously considered. He too was upwardly mobile, married an American and suffered a broken marriage. Expecting too much of their families, this group of migrants did not develop the 'security in the family' which Donald Cole emphasized in his study of the adjustment of immigrants in the city of Lawrence, Massachusetts.[35] Nor did these people have the other supports which sustained migrants who moved at least partially within a community. Few had a religious faith of the fundamentalist or evangelical kind noted among so many farmers, which might support them. Their cultural interests seem to have been thinner than those of people like John Fisher or George Martin. Although they did read newspapers, in common with all the migrants whose letters we have, they did not have wider interests in music, botany or literature which we found among several of the skilled industrial workers. As far as can be ascertained, they did not join social, political, religious or benefit societies for English immigrants, although most of them settled in cities.

Nineteenth-century English society was so fluid that nearly every class in the population could turn up such individualists who did not conform to group norms or who visualized emigration as a means of upward social mobility. Such Englishmen were to be found all over the world and formed a part of the extremely complex stream of English emigrants. Their exposure to personal tragedy, in spite of their greater acceptability as immigrants, illustrates the importance of the transfer of institutions, the creation of new ones, the conscious reformulation of values, in short, the functions of the immigrant community itself, in making the migration experience bearable for the mass of immigrants. Because these few people did not migrate within a conventional network, or settle among other immigrants, the social and psychological adjustment for them was greater. The tendency to regard British immigrants as easily assimilated, because in many places they did not settle in conspicuous and distinct communities, overlooks the essential role these communities and their institutions played in the accommodation of the first generation immigrant and in the long-run assimilation of his children.

Letters from Immigrants in Professional, Commercial and Clerical Occupations

Haley Series 1820–5

Nathan Haley came from Great Horton, a village in the clothmaking district of Yorkshire near Bradford. His father, Jeremiah Haley, was a farmer.[1] Great Horton's population was growing much more rapidly than the population of England as a whole during the period when Haley emigrated, from 4,423 inhabitants in 1811 to 7,192 in 1821 and 10,782 in 1831. The rapid growth of his native community tends to confirm Haley's admission that he emigrated for personal reasons. An unsuccessful marriage, drinking, and small debts formed the background to his departure for Baltimore in 1820. Haley did not complain of social or economic disadvantages in England, and he quite complacently expected his parents to care for and educate his children when his father-in-law refused to do so. Though he made profuse protestations about his love for them, Haley made no effort to contribute to his children's welfare during the five years covered by these letters. He did not go to the United States penniless. He had property to mortgage to pay his debts, and appears to have arrived in America with more than six hundred dollars. His sister, Mary, was listed in Horton Road, in the 1841 census, as living on an independent income. The various bits of evidence suggest that the Haleys were people of comfortable means.

Fleeing from his responsibilities and problems, he intended, like the prodigal son, to remain in the States for seven years, though in spite of his limitless self-pity and resources for excuse-making, he probably did not intend to return penniless. In the United States he made his way to the lead-mining region of Missouri, which was at its peak of development. The output from the mines between the Big River and the Francis River, where lead ore was also smelted to be carted into St Genevieve and Herculaneum on the Mississippi River, was estimated at nearly five million pounds in 1819. About 1,130 men were thought to have been employed in the industry, as miners, teamsters, blacksmiths and wood-cutters.[2] Haley combined work as an ore miner and woodcutter with that of trader on his own account. He worked for lead in New Diggins near Potosi in Washington County, Missouri, and took it to Cincinnati, where he exchanged it for tobacco and flour, which he took back to Missouri. He also made two trading trips to New Orleans. From his account, only his recurrent bouts of ague prevented him from making a fortune in the river trade. His complete personal and familial uprooting gave him both geographical and occupational mobility. Unfortunately we know nothing about his later career.

The originals of the Haley letters are owned by John R.Rudd of Calverley, near Leeds, Yorkshire, who has kindly consented to their being published. Photostats are in the British Library of Economic and Political Science.

Letters from Nathan Haley to his father, Jeremiah Haley, of Great Horton, near Bradford, Yorkshire, and other relatives

Liverpool, 3 July 1820

DEAR PARENTS AND RELATIONS,

I am unaccustomed to letter writing and know not what to say, but the best way that I do know is to write truth. I have had a very bad home for many years and at a great expence. I have for years gone any were to weep, when some men would perhaps have done what Oldfield did. I have done nothing rong but getting into debt that I cannot pay and telling untruths the same as men in bad credit do. I have done very little but weep since I left home. But am getting better of that as well as other things. I have not been well for some time through troubles and drinking. Johnathn Anderton is my greatest creditor and all I owe [is] one shilling to [him] for wool. James Howett & John Scholfield* must be mesured of and see what they will want. They must be paid out of what is left on the morgage made from me to my father and Jonas Got, now lodged at Lamberts Office in Bradford and registered at Wakefield, for two hundred pound [illegible] and him, will have to pay to Halifax Bank, the rest for my family and friends who should be so unfortunate as want anything of me. I have very little time and much to say; but my heart is full, my eyes oreflows, my hand trembles, farewell.

No. I have not yet done. I see when I look over I have found to much fault in what is writen. But my children, my children, strikes me as much that it does unman me. I am weeping, My feelings are softer than some mens and after weeping for you and my family a long time I go on. Will you look at them? Now I see them in rags weeping for bread. What and an only daughter and him no wife. If he should have to keep them it

---

* John Schofield was keeper of the public house, the White Hart, Thornton Road, Bradford, in 1847.

is his duty, and then he is but the same as a married man with three children and he has good wages. If he will do that while I have it in my power to do it,   I will fly to some vast wilderness

> Some contiguity of shade
> Where rumer of oppresion and deceit
> Never shall reach me more.

I can ask the above faviour with boldness of him because Mary told me that I was to have three hundred pounds when I married, he having but her. I prest not the matter, considering it safe and this I never mentioned before. So are some men deceived. You perhaps begin to think me mad. I have thought so myself. Therefore we agree. This reminds me of Milton in his *Paradise Lost.*

> 'some [natural tears they dropped] but wiped them soon,
> The world was all before them, where [to choose]
> their place of rest, and Providence their guide,'*

again

> When this you see remember me
> And keep me in your mind
> Let all the world say what they will
> speak of me as you find.

Now, now, now. I am writing this in my bed room, but when I deliver this it will be to the Pilot after he has steered the Liverpool Packet out to sea, bound to Baltimore in North America, for which place I have paid my pasage. It is not possable for you to hear from me in less than three months from this date, but so soon as I land I will write to let you know. Weep not. It is true. Make yourselves happy, and that will be happyness to me. You know I am no fool. Therefore do be content, will you? Do, I beg you wouold. I have ere allmost persuaded myself you will then. Say with the hymn

> Fare thee well, sweet gift of heaven
> Tho to lose thee pains the mind
> Thou to us by God wast given
> And to him thou art resigned. . . . [Says farewell with

more verse and reference to prodigal son] Your unworthy son,

NATHAN HALEY

Baltimore, 20 Sept. 1820

DEAR PARENTS,
    From all I can learn this is a bad place to write from as nearly all the

---

* This quotation from Milton's *Paradise Lost,* lines 645–7, continues:
    'They, hand in hand, with wandering steps and slow,
    Through Eden took their solitary way.'

letters put in here for England are lost. I have sent before some perticulars, and will send you the same over again when I get to weeling in Ketucy on the Biks River* with different accounts to entertain you with if any thing can. . . . [Letters he has written] I have never been in liquor since I left England. Pardon all blunders in spelling and inditing as I am assisting the Captain with writing or any thing I can. If you have not received the other letters you will think this a strange letter to a father and mother, and if I have left you there never was a son loved his parents better than me. My fate is to be what it is, make yourselfes happy on my account and that will be happyness to me. Perticulars of Baltimore next letter. I had only 30 minutes to write in when I began and must finish with the good wishes of your son, Adieu,

NATHAN HALEY. . . . [Will write again soon]

Cincinnati, 16 Jan. 1821

DEAR PARENTS AND FRIENDS,

I often write to you to let you know I am well which is still the case. When you see me do not let me have to say the same as the 25 chapter of Matthew and 45 verse.† You shall not be a loser by what you do for my children. I hope you and them are well. I have traveled five states nearly every one as large as England. I should wish my traivels to be published. I have been amongst numbers of Indians. I have seen slavery in all its forms. I dare not say more. If I do you will not get to see it. I am your son,

NATHAN HALEY

P.S. I am going 700 miles from here immediately, WEST.

St. Louis, 12 April 1821

If I say, dear Parents, it gives no ease. My feelings are such I cannot. I must write but little at once if I wish to receive the same. The greatest part of what you read of this countrey is not‡ . . . . . Land speculators have got men to . . . never did see this countrey. I have . . . day three hundred barrels of flourr sold . . . doller per barrel in this place you . . . not judge this a good countrey . . . are cheap. How can any man get on . . . of flour if he has not one doller. . . . The weather is subject to sudden change . . . as you never knew this was other thin . . . much sickness and still people will . . . and say this Western countrey is . . . Paradise if such

---

* There was no Wheeling in Kentucky, nor a Biks River, so far as I can ascertain.

† 'Then he will answer them, "Truly, I say to you, as you did it not to one of the least of these, you did it not to me".'

‡ The deletions in this paragraph are all illegible words.

was paridise . . . might our first Parents fall. . . . There is nothing but gaming going. . . . People nearly all French here & at a Genea. . . .

I have frequently had to sleep in the woods without cloathing but what was on my back. This with you would be considdired very hard, particularly when the wolfs eyes are seen at a short distance, and the howls saying as much as that your fire does protect you from them. The Indians are still more to be feared than all the beasts of the forest. I have been amongst several tribes in this state. Yesterday I gave a poor man some money that came from Frederick Town, Maryland, named John Williams. He had been a prisoner seven years to the Manden tribe.* They gave seventeen wounds at different times and then cut out his tonge. He could write. All the Indians I have yet seen paint very much, and go nearly naked. Some of them have a blankett which they throw over the shoulders. They are not to be trusted . . . [Where to write. A mutilated passage] but I am your son

NATHAN H. I hope you are all well.

New Diggins, Washington Co., Missouri,† 1 March 1823
DEAR PARENTS, RELATIONS AND FRIENDS,

Have the goodness to see my children do not want for any thing in your power to do that you think is nesserery to with regard to education. Perhaps I shall be able to pay for the same when you see me which will be seven years from the time you did see me last. Some time ago I had a very bad fever and I did expect to die. If I had died I have a friend here that would have let you know my fate, but it now appears my work was not done as I am in good health and making money for somebody in a honest manner. I send lead from this place to Cincinnati and get anything I want from that place and likewise from Louisville in Kentucky at the cheapest price. The most respectable merchants are my agents, but no man owe me any money; neither do I owe any man. Perhaps I do not spell right but I mean I am not indebted to any body. I live well and will if I can which I have at present in my power and I am thankfull for the same. A man in this countrey must do every thing if he mean to do good business. Sometime I dig lead ore, some times I cut wood, some times I take a dram of wisky myself, some times I sell twenty barrels at once

---

* The Mandan Indians were known as a peaceful tribe in the late eighteenth century. Lewis and Clark spent a winter among the Mandans, one thousand six hundred miles from the mouth of the Missouri River in what is now North Dakota.

† Washington County is in East Central Missouri, near but not on the Mississippi River. Haley writes from a place he calls New Diggins near Potosi, the county seat of Washington County. Potosi was in the centre of a rich lead-mining district. Lead smelted at the mines in this region had to be transported in carts and wagons to towns like St Genevieve and Herculaneum on the Mississippi River.

of wisky or flower &c. Sometimes I think of you, and allways in the night I am with you; but when I awake behold it is a dream like John Bunyan. My expences since I came to this country has been a large sum, but I still make money. I keep one horse and two dogs and can hunt where and when I will which I sometimes do. What you want to know I would wish to write but I cannot tell what it is. From the day I left you I did keep a jurnal of every thing for you to read, but I had a small misfortune on board the steam boat *Mars* and that was lost in the Mississippi River. . . . [Hopes to live]

Them that have a home, let them keep it. But this is a great deal better countrey then England. Dear dear Parents if you think me worth writing to Direct for me at the New Diggins near Potose, Washington County, Missouri, America. Give my respects to J.A.Illenworth* and all friends and I remain with all the respect that a son can have for his parents your son

NATHAN HALEY

Herculaneum, Jefferson Co., Missouri,† 20 May 1823

DEAR FATHER,

Trouble not yourself about the lad. He is not dead – I am in good health and I hope you and all that is near and dear to me is the same – but this country is not so healthy as England. Fever and ague are very common and bilious fever are sometimes fatal, some parts of the country more healthy than others. The best and richest land is most sickly, poor high land more healthy than low bottom land. I have not seen many persons with red cheeks in this country. They are generly pale or yellow, particularly in this state which are French of a mixture of Indians and French – Slaves in this part are well off, better than your paupers, and their children is not sent to work in factorys as white children is with you sixteen hours per day – I supose you will think I wish to come and live on the old sod, but I do not. This country with all its disadvantages is a great deal better country than England – There is plenty of land to sell at one dollar and a quarter per acre and will be, for people who love the woods, a great many years to come, and sometimes a good farm can be purchased at the same rate or a little more with improvements on the land so that a family could live comfortable as soon as they did arrive at the place. But you must not think this is near any large old settled town but where game is plenty and money scarce. I wish not to give any encouragement to any person to come to

* Jonathan A.Illingworth was a surgeon in Bradford. A neighbour of Jeremiah Haley in Great Horton, John Illingworth, farmer, was possibly the father of the Bradford surgeon.

† Herculaneum was a town on the Mississippi River a few miles south of St Louis, to which lead was carted for shipment by river.

America. If I did before they did get settled they would wish me all the bad wishes that men could wish. If they have money every one they meet will take an advantage of them as new comers and give them all the assistance that is in their power in words but no further. . . . [Has received only one letter] If you would be so good as direct for me at Cincinnati, Ohio, I can get the letters there better than any other place. I shall be here in a little time and remain until next summer or perhaps longer.

NATHAN HALEY . . .

Cincinnati, 9 Dec. 1823

DEAR FATHER,

I yesterday received your letter dated June 30th and Mr Gotts dated June 18th, 1823 informing me that death had taken five of our family away – and that my dear mother was not well. I hope she soon did recover. These letters I got from the mines in Missouri and they make me very unhappy. The contents of Mr Gotts in perticular give me great trouble and he gives you and me a good scoulding. I will write to him in a short time. I sometime ago received your letter dated July 31 1823. It was the second I had received since I left you, and you may judge, better than I can express, my thankfullness to you for the same. The reason I did not write in return was at the same time I received one from Missouri stating there was two English letters for me that would be sent on which is the above two and likewise stating that Theo. B. Watthal of the mines died suddenly. He was a rich man and my best friend on this side of the Atlantic. He has no children and was from Nashville, Tennessee. Is not all this sufficient to affect me, yes, to tears? But to myself I must admit and by so doing I shall effect you. I was taken sick on bord a kech boat near the mouth of Ohio River in July coming up with lead. My disorder was feaver and ague which continued four months, and I am not yet as strong as I was before this; but I am in good health and geting stronger allmost every day – is not this more than some would let you know? Yes, so it is; but it is my duty to inform you of it and docters, medicines, wines and other expences amount to a large sum, but is paid. I am thankfull my hand is not hurt the least. Who tried to deceive you with this tale I dare not judge. Take care perhaps the same party may try some other plan. Do not some of them live near you? I am glad they did not succeed.

I have a quantity of pig lead to make into bars of one pound each and the same to dispose of to the best advantage, purchase wiskey, tobacco and different things of less value. The wiskey I shall rectify here before I go with it and shall go on board a steam boat to near the mines. This is plenty at once on my own account. But you must direct your letters here

14*

and I shall get them whether I am here or not. . . . Dear Mother, I think about you. I can say no more. I am crying, or weeping, as you call it – Look at my children. I wish they was here. There would be no bare meals for them, as Mr Gott says Mary and him has. . . . [Greetings] To Timothy Whitaker give my best respects and inform him I have not once played at cork and farthing since I left Horton. It will not answer amongst strangers . . . [More greetings] There is no fairs in this country, and this is Bradford fair today, and I am there but not see or hear but only in thought about shows and other things. . . . [Distances in USA.]

40 miles back in the country from the river at St Geneave* and 70 miles from St Louis is what is called the lower mine, containing about 70 miles from north to south, and 50 miles from east to west. In this track of land is some small lots of good land, but is in general very poor and thinly wooded with a great many small praries producing course grass in abundance which the cattle eat very [well?], but no one try to raise many cattle or hogs but [go?] on digging and purchace what they want. Some persons have claims to different parts of the land, but it nearly all belong to the United States cannot be sold, but people dig on this land and no one enterfers with them. A man with a common pick and wooden shovel is fitted for work and rules to abide by, which are: if he discover mineral a distance from any other diggins he gets 80 feet of ground all round his shaft; other persons gets 12 feet of ground around their shaft, each alowing 4 feet for the shaft.† If the discovery is good 10 or 20 acres are sometimes taken up on one day, in such lots as above stated of 28 feet. No man can hold more than one lot – Some will sink down perhaps 10 feet, some not so much, others more, according as the rock is hard or soft. The ore is sometimes on the surface or in the soil, in the clay, in the gravel, in the rock and sometimes in caves. If not successfull, they will take their pick and shovel and try some other place. . . . [Prices]

I remain your son,	N. HALEY . . .

Wheeling, Virginia, 10 Sept. 1825

DEAR FATHER, MOTHER, SISTERS AND BROTHERS . . . RELATIONS AND
FRIENDS,

If we are separated by distance of places we are not separated by

---

* St Genevieve was another town on the Mississippi River important in the lead trade. It was farther downstream than Herculaneum, about forty miles from St Louis. Its population in 1850 was only 718.

† In describing these rules, Henry Schoolcraft said that a person making such a discovery of minerals could claim twenty-five feet of ground in every direction around his shaft or fifty feet square. Otherwise details given by Haley do not conflict with Schoolcraft's account (Henry Schoolcraft, *A View of the Lead Mines of Missouri*, New York, 1819, p. 107).

difference of feeling. My thoughts are freequanly with you, both by day and night, awake and asleep. Do not forget to remember me to my children and let them know I have not forgotten them. When I wrote to you from New Orleans, which is more than two thousand miles by water from this place. I hear you say what a distance. I have been there twice and wrote to you and sent you a few newspapers boath times which, if you did receive, would be some little entertainment for you. The first trip to Orleans I did very good business which caused me to try last December again, expecting to do still better, in which I was very much disapointed. Agu[e]s [will?] appear to be my lot. This I know you will understand without me saying any more on the subject.

I bought at Cincinnati last fall flower, the best quality, at three dollars per barrel, cheese at from three dollars and a half to six dollars per hundred pounds, that is very little more than your two pence per pound. Great part the round of good beef with the bone taken out before it is weighed I give two dollars per hundred for and whould not have any but good at that price. You will say such things at such prices will pay great proffets. So they sometimes do, but last winter the market was overstocked to such a degree that, instead of me selling my cheese immediately, I bought Boston cheese at auction which is better than Ohio cheese and gave no more than one dollar per hundred.

You say this is plenty of this kind of information. Let us know something of the country. Well so I will, but neither you or any other person can get a good or right knowledge of this country unless you make a debtor and creditor account of all the information you can get and then see how the ballance stands. As I have been saying something of New Orleans I will say a little more about that place. It do make me tremble to relate the wikedness of the place. Sunday not respected, business is carried on the same as other days, publick and private, and Sunday is allways the best and largest market. There is gaming houses and Sunday is the best day for them. They pay a great sum to the United States for license. This is not all. Gaming is going on continneously in allmost every house. Robberys are common and murders frequent. If Hell is on earth, New Orleans is not far from it, if it consist in wikedness of almost every kind. New Orleans produces sugar, cotton, corn, rice, indigo, fig, orange &c. Two or 3 years ago there was a frost in Orleans, which killed a great many orange trees – Sugar do not answer well two hundred miles north of Orleans. Part of December 1824, January 1825, Febr., March and part of April, I was in this climate. Of course I did not see any winter weather and I was almost copper colour with the sun, when I found it wisdom to go north for the sake of keeping my health, before which I went to all the grave yards where it can be said truly that the dead find a water grave. The country is low and no hills or stone [except?] such as man convayed there. As [soon?] as you dig one spade full of soil the [earth?] will fill with water immeadiately. 42 graves was ready in one yard and all full of water, coffins in great numbers ready made and all prices. Some are buried, if so it can be called, in small brick vaults built on the surface of the ground to keep them from the water. [You] will understand from the above [what] a place of death that is Orleans. How can it be otherwise laying so low, and the River is confined in its bounds by banks of earth placed there by man. The water can be suffered to run through the streets at pleasure, the land being lower then the river. Near this place, Jacksons victory over the English. But I have not room to give you the information I wish. With regard to religion plenty is it for me to say they have one splended church under the pope and one monastery, I forgot what order. . . . [Greetings] with my best wishes for you Adieu,

NATHAN HALEY

P.S. It has been your Horton Tide or Fair. Hear what Burns says
A last request permit me then
When yearly you're assembled a'i
One round ask it with a tear
To him your friend thats far awa*

---

* From the poem by Robert Burns, 'The Farewell to the Brethren of St James's Lodge, Tarbolton', see *Poetical Works,* Bicentenary edition, 1958, p. 198. I am indebted to Professor Marion Stocking for assistance in identifying quotations.

Hesketh Series 1837–45

John Hesketh, who was born in Lancashire about 1786, had emigrated to the United States by 1832. The circumstances of his emigration differed from other migrants in this group of letters in that he did not leave because of a family dispute, and he took his wife to the United States. Hesketh seemed to take a serious interest in the welfare of the family in Manchester, offered to pay the passage to America of a sister, and to provide a home for some of his nieces. Since his father was dead at the time these letters were written, John Hesketh stood in a role of authority towards his brother Robert nearly twenty years his junior. He advised about family problems, practically forbade his brother from selling some of the family property in order to enter a speculation in 1842, and returned home to supervise the disposition of his mother's property after her death in 1845.[1]

It is difficult to believe that economic hardship, or even a want of opportunity, prompted his emigration from the county of Lancashire. He referred to the house he had bought near Pittsburgh at the age of fifty-four as smaller than the one in which he had spent his childhood. His brother Robert, to whom these letters were written, was working as a salesman in Cheetham, Manchester, in 1841, and was able to keep a servant in his household. Indeed, John Hesketh considered a clerk's position there at eighty or ninety pounds a year as better than could be obtained near Pittsburgh, since 'every one in America wishes to be clerks'. And there is other evidence in the letters that the rest of the family in Lancashire lived in comfortable circumstances.

One is inclined to think that John Hesketh, like so many other emigrants from industrial parts of Britain during the generation following the Napoleonic Wars, was attracted to America by the agrarian myth. He expressed ideas similar to those of industrial workers whose letters we have examined. In 1837, he professed never to want to have any more to do with trade. Considering land the safest investment for money and farming the safest business, he was at that time on the lookout for a plantation to buy. Like Abel Stephenson and Richard Hails, other emigrants from industrialized counties, he distrusted banks and paper money. Hesketh was ambiguous about the nature of the trade which he had abandoned for five years by 1837. It seems possible that he might have referred to an industrial craft, since in the same letter he noted that he was 'doing a good business and making money'. Even after he left Pittsburgh for a home and land on its outskirts, he noted that he was carrying on business as a confectioner. The 1850 census returned him as a grocer. Thus, it is possible that Hesketh had been an industrial worker and had by the 1830s obtained his independence, as a small tradesman and money lender. He differed from the other industrial workers who aspired to be farmers in that his enthusiasm for farming diminished perceptibly during the depression of the late thirties and early forties, and he was not prepared to buy unimproved property in order to get a farm quickly.

While Hesketh shared with industrial workers from Lancashire and Yorkshire attitudes which condemned speculation and applauded the security of land ownership, he seems to have been somewhat more concerned with social status than the men who went to the frontier. By 1839, he had left the rapidly growing town of Pittsburgh for a situation on its outskirts; and the next year he bought another piece of property about six miles due west of Pittsburgh on the Steubenville Turnpike in a township called Robeson. He exuded satisfaction on his successful removal to this wealthy and 'moral' neighbourhood. Continuing his business, he organized his life around improving this property, worth $2,000 in 1850, for his beloved son to inherit.

The town of Robeson had nearly two thousand people in 1850, but did not increase its population by more than about two hundred between that date and 1860, while nearby Pittsburgh expanded from 31,204 people in 1840 to 77,923 in 1860. When Hesketh arrived in Robeson in 1840, nearly everyone there was gaining a livelihood from agriculture.[2] Thus, John Hesketh continued his migration away from industrial growth after he came to the United States.

In this township Hesketh found few of his compatriots. Out of a total labour force of 576 in 1850, only seventeen were English, and eight of these were miners and four more labourers. There were 130 Irish in the township, and 78 other immigrants, chiefly from the German states. Robeson was not attracting British immigrants during the years of heavy immigration in the 1850s. Between 1850 and 1860, the English share in the labour force of the township fell from three per cent to one per cent, and even the number of Irish declined considerably. Hesketh was not isolated from the American community in a network of immigrant companions. His friend, Christopher Slade, a grocer, who still lived in Pittsburgh and who wrote the last letter in this collection, was almost certainly American-born.[3] Hesketh placed his hopes for companionship in his old age in his son, whose education he watched with meticulous attention, encouraging him to get a better education than his father had. His social ambitions came largely to focus upon this only son. The last letter in this series reports the tragic denouement of John Hesketh's life.

Only the first two of these letters were written by Hesketh himself. With the third letter, written from his first suburban home, a new handwriting appears with better spelling and punctuation. The fourth letter, written from his home in Robeson, bore still another handwriting and also a florid style in keeping with his rising social pretensions. By 1845, his son William was able to write his letters for him. It seems possible that Hesketh himself gave birth to a more stilted form of address when he had a better speller than himself writing his letters for him. Photostats of the Hesketh Letters are in the British Library of Economic and Political Science; they were made from originals in the possession of the late J.L.Baldwin of Birkdale, Southport, Lancashire.

Letters from John Hesketh to his brother, Robert Hesketh, in Manchester

Pittsburgh, 5 August 1837

MY BROTHER,

I receved your letter on the 24th July and was verry glad of it, not having heard from you so long. Am happy to hear you are all well. Gives me great pleasure to hear of your happyness. You say you have made some improvements for mother. It is my wish that she be made as comfortable as can be in her very old age. If she was here I could keep her and not feel the wors. Not a day goes over my head but I think at you all. I should like to see your children. Hope I shall somtime. My William is often talking about them. He is a smart boy. He will write to you next spring. He can write better then me. He is the best speller in the class. I intend him to be a farmer as it is the safest business. Mary is very well and looks as well as ever, onley older, but she is quite stout and spiritfull. We are sorry to [hear] of Brother Dobs death. She wishes his daughter was here. Sorry to hear Richard Withinton is dead. Give our love to them all.

I myself am very well in body, mind, spirits, quit stout. I weigh 182 lbs so you may think how I am, a man of my sise. Am verry corpulent. You may think I am slothfull, but I am not. Am as smart as ever I was. I am always moveing about. Yesterday I rode twenty miles round the countrey seeing the farmers busy in there feelds. They all made much of me. They sing out here comes oure old friend Englash man. I love this country well. I feel verry verry thankful I came to this country. We are doing a good buisness and making money. We have saved a good lump these four years past. Am looking out for a plantation to buy. It is the safeast way to put money out these times. Have been twise in Ohio this spring. I was at Edward Jones last Aprile. He went round with me one day but cant suite myself yet. . . . [Greetings from him] If I could write as well as you I would write to you evry month a long letter and give you plenty of news. Trade hear is bad, but I have had nothing to do with trade these five years and never will no more. If I could I would send you som of my newspapers as I take 3 per week. You will see I am against the banking principal in evry shape and form. As my old friend Jackson says, it makes the rich richer and the poor poorer. My friend Jackson is not hurt by these times. He never had a nephew and not given bale for any man these 14 years nor even speculated in any thing these 14 years. No, he is too much a man. The banks have all suspended specie payment and yet the have more gold and silver in the country than ever there was before, and yet we have nothing but paper agoing. It is no better that swindleing the people out of their rits . . . So no more at present from your loveing brother,

JOHN HESKETH

Pittsburgh, 3 May 1838

MY DEAR MOTHER, . . . [Letter received]

There is nothing in this inconstant world give me more pleasure than to hear from my affectionate mother and brothers. . . . [Glad mother lives] Yes, my dear brother, I congratulate you with respect to my aged mother birthday. Oh what pleasure would it have given me to celebrate the anniverscy with you, and I hope she may live to celebrate many more. My wife indeed is very sorry to hear of her brothers death and about the children he has left, but she is glad to hear there are in comfortable situations and she also very sory to hear of her sisters husband death but her heart seems cheered to think that [he] has left them comfortable off. . . . William is a fine boy and goes to school and learns fast and will make a fine boy and is indeed a great comfort and company to us both in our old days; and I hope what he learns, if he lives to be old, be of service to him. He is no doubt a promising youth possed of talents and those talents wich improved all hear after will be benificial to him, which I hope it may. Trade here is good but money scarce, and also many failures have taken place in Pittsburgh. I think shortly that things will ware a more favourable aspect than they do at present time. The currency question in America at this present time is bad. Nothing passes but what we call shinplasters. No silver at all. . . . [Greetings] No more at this present time. But remain your ever affectionate brother,

JOHN HESKETH

Pittsburgh, 7 May 1839*

DEAR BROTHER, . . . [Letter received]

I have purchased a house and lot near Pittsburgh which will convince you that I am not dissatisfied with the country or its institutions generally. Nothing you know can be perfect in this world; but we may approximate toward it.

On the subject of the Canada question I presume that you have heard ere this that all danger of a national conflict between the United States and Great Britain is completely obviated by the pacific measures mutually adopted by the two powers. The interest of the United States in plainly to be at peace with all the world. This all well informed men among us agree in, although on matters of international affairs they may widely differ in opinion; yet we are very tenacious of what we consider our rights. Let them be invaded from any quarter, or (which is the same thing) we consider them invaded 'party spirit' is lost, and Federalists, Democrats, Whigs, Masons, anti Masons, Radicals, abolitionists, colonisationists &c. (which are a few of the names by which we are distinguished) would be lost in a moment and known no more untill we were at peace with all the world. This is American Republicanism.

My wife and William who is a very promising boy join with me in giving our love and respect to all our friends. I will write you more fully in a short time. I remain your affectionate brother,

JOHN HESKETH

Stuebenville Turnpike Road, near Pittsburgh, 6 July 1840†

MY DEAR BROTHER,

Yours of may 11th is now before me and I hasten to answer it. Your letter of last August of which you speak was duly received, but a pressure of business prevented me from answering it. Agreeably to your request I answer at once.

I regret exceedingly to hear of mothers indisposition, but at her advanced period of life it may be expected. I hope it will be only temporary and that a kind Providence will smooth her descent to the ground and vouchsafe to her a triumphant death and glorious resurrection. To

---

* This letter is in a different handwriting from the first two and is better spelt and punctuated.

† This letter is written in still a third handwriting.

her we stand deeply indebted, and we will find it difficult, if not impossible, to discharge the claims of gratitude which she holds upon us. If she were within reach of me I would tender my best efforts to render her comfortable. Separation from those whom we love seems to be inseparable from this existence. You will present to her my grateful recollections and assurances that, though absent from her, I remember her to that being who can supply to her all the kind offices of a son and put her in possession of a hope full of immortality. . . .

I have removed a short distance from the place which I lived before. I bought a parcel of ground between five and six miles from Pittsburgh. I have remodelled the house & put the whole premises under a course of improvement. From my past experience I have found that it is far cheaper to buy than to erect buildings; however when we build we can place things according to our mind. My location is beautiful & [handsome ?], being on the side of the Pittsburgh and Steubenville Turnpike. I sell confectionery and intend to enlarge my establishment. My business has indeed faild some, but nothing like almost all kinds of business. For nine months or more money has been scarce & business dull. Crops of wheat have been some affected by the Hessian fly, but so far as I can learn the present crop, which is being cut, will be quite good. Within the last fourteen months wheat has fallen from one dollar & twenty cents per bushel to fifty cents, oats from $62\frac{1}{2}$ to $18\frac{3}{4}$, and other grains proportionably. The political parties, Democratic & Whig, predict a faverable change in the times according to their partialities. Every bank has gathered all the silver it can and also its own paper. In Pittsburgh it is almost impossible to obtain any of the paper which has been issued by the banks of that city. Politicks run very high among us.

William is a fine boy & promises to comfort us in our old days. He is becoming a good English scholar and would be very glad to see all of you. . . . [Greetings] Farewell. Your brother affectionately,

JOHN HESKETH

[Brief messages from William follow]

Pittsburgh, 20 May 1841*

MY DEAR BROTHER, . . . [No Letter since May 1840]

I rejoice greatly to hear of your family's welfare. Our William reciprocates the kind wishes of his cousins, but I fear that their mutual wish to see other will not be realised. William has studied arithmetic, English grammar & geography, reads correctly and writes a fair hand. He is a dutiful boy and promises to become a useful man. A twelvemonth past, the first of last April, I removed about a half mile fa[r]ther from

* Written in a fourth hand.

Pittsburgh on the same Steubenville Turnpike. For eighteen months the times have been oppressive on almost all classes of citizens. Failures have occurred among all grades of merchants and traders, from the most extensive to the most limited. Many manufactories have been closed for months and there exists but little prospect that they will shortly go into business vigerously; nor have the farming community escaped the general pressure. Grain and vegetables have fallen fifty per cent within two years, wheat from one dollar & twelve cents to fifty cents per bushel and all other grains in like manner. Many farmers purchased land when grain was at a high price, hoping to pay for it speedily, but have been sadly disappointed by the change. General confidence is at such a low ebb, in consequence of so many unexpected failures, that those in debt find it difficult, in many cases impossible, to borrow money.

You attribute your national difficulties to our not having bot so liberally from you as we used to do. You are no doubt right – but our scarcity of coin & general derangement of banks may be ragarded as the necessary and unavoidable result of our having bought *too much* from you. Of England & America it holds true as of many another mother & daughter, their interests are incompatible. While we encourage your manufactories we suffer means to languish on our hands – promote among our citizens idleness & luxury – prepare the way for national subjection & furnish the causes of future depression and difficulty to ourselfes. Of these results our statesmen are becoming convinced & are putting forth vigorous means to guard against them in future. No doubt Congress will shortly renew the protection once given to our manufactories by imposing a heavy duty on foreign fabriks. The necessity for this measure will be increased if'a war between the two nations occur, which I hope may not be the case.

But I have employed more paper & time in these speculations than I had assigned to employ. Crops look unfaverable – the spring has been unusually cool & backward. Many of your countrymen have lately come on & joined the Mormons – a deluded set of people – at Nauvoo, in Illinois State. They have been driven from Missouri State by the citizens from whom they had stolen horses, cows, hogs, &c. I feel ashamed that my countrymen should united with such knaves. . . .
[Greetings] Very affectionately your brother,

JOHN HESKETH

Pittsburgh, 28 April 1842

MY DEAR BROTHER, . . . [Letter received]

The mountains rise, the boisterous Atlantic rolls & many miles intervene between us, yet in the present exercise our hearts are brought into close union and our fraternal feelings are drawn forth. I regret exceedingly to hear of the catastrophe of Mr Hudson which you detail & which you justly attribute to his own imprudence. Your surprise at learning his condition must have been very great & not less was the embarrassment into which you were thrown. I rejoice that you were so soon extricated from your perplexing circumstances and I feel pleasure in expressing the hope that you will find your new house very agreeable and be allowed to enjoy it so long as you may wish, and that nothing will occur in your present relation to impress you with regret at the change. I cannot however suppress the fear that before long a difficulty similar to that from which you have escaped may over take you. Most sincerely do I hope & pray it may be otherwise. But you will do justice to my painful apprehensions when I tell you that I entertain not the least confidence in *the apparent* condition of business. Mere industry, frugality and ordinary caution have not furnished to business men in this nation any security against disaster, for they were constrained to practise on the credit system & you know that one whose means are in the hands of others can feel but little confidence in his ability. Such is the condition of most of our traders. From Maine to Georgia, from the Atlantic to the Pacific, we are in a state of suffering either endured or apprehended. Our paper currency is about being brought to a specie basis, which operation is leaving on our community a very large amount of paper money which is not available. As I have trusted but little, I shall lose but little, if any thing.

I have a pleasant situation on the Steubenville Turnpike, six miles from Pittsburgh, in a thickly settled, wealthy, moral neighbourhood and am engaged in beautifying my property which yields to me much comfort & will, I trust, be thankfully enjoyed by my good boy William, after I shall have gone hence. He is already improved in education & gives flattering promise of yielding us additional comfort as the necessities of our age may increase. . . . [Mother]

With regard to R. Heywood, relative to whom you ask my advice, I have to say that it is better, in my judgment, to let the matter rest until her decease, lest a law suit might disquiet her mind, & thus the property can be disposed of advantageously to some one who will prosecute our rights. We should be sorry to do anything that might, even in a remote degree, give her pain. We are in the enjoyment of good health, thanks be to God & send our love to all our friends. I should be glad to receive any one of Mary's nieces who might think proper to come here & live with us; please communicate this to them. Be assured of our love.

JOHN HESKETH. . . . [Note from William appended]

Pittsburgh, 7 May 1843

MY DEAR BROTHER,

I read your letter dated March 24th on the 30th April and hasten as you request to answer it. I am truly sorry to hear of the difficulties you have to encounter – and the flattness of business – but I can assure you, however bad it may be in Old England, it is in this country – in a worse condition – in fact we have no money, no circulating medium. Every thing is done by barter. Mechanics wages of every kind is paid in it and persons like myself who have lent out their little funds which was saved in good times, for the sake of the interest, can neither get principal nor interest. If we try to collect at law the debtor goes into bankruptcy and all is lost – Employment even for labourers is bad to be had, and then poorly paid. My advise to you, dear Brother, would be from my experience in the world and the difficulties I have had to contend with, would be for you to get the best situation you could in Manchester, even as low as £80 or £90, for such sums here would be considered high for a clerk. Every one in America wishes to be clerks so that the country is over run with them. I regret to hear of my mothers continued affliction, but these things are in the hands of an all-wise Providence and past our control. We can only sooth and comfort her.

Your proposal to sell the property and invest it in business in Manchester as times are now, would, I am sure of it, be a bad speculation. All the avenews of trade are in your place already filled up, and I feel convinced it would end in your loosing whatever you might invest, particularly as it is a business with which you are unacquainted – you have nothing to fall back upon, and therefore I am sure would not be for your own good. Whilst it is there the rents are always something certain and the advantage it will give your credit will be more than the small sum it would sell for in these times. I must therefore, in kindness and duty to you and the family, decline a sale of the property from these views of the matter. I do this not on account of thinking the money would be missaplied or badly spent by you, but from a conviction that the slight advantage it would be of to you in the meantime would nothing like compensate for the sacrafice. I have lived so long in the world and felt the difficulty of scraping together enough to build a very small house compared to our old one, that I would not willingly let it slip from my hands. I am satisfied when you maturely reflect upon the matter, you will see it in the same light.

I am very glad to hear of all your healths. You mention sisters living with you being a little draw back. Should my dear sister wish to come to this country, I will be able to advance enough to bring her here and make her a comfortable home afterwards. I do not mention this with a desire to seperate you but only if it is the wish of all of you. Far be it from one to say any thing to wound your feelings, but I have said nothing that is not thorough conviction. Myself, wife and William are all well and join in love to all your family. And so no more at present from your affectionate brother,

JOHN HESKETH

Pittsburgh, 20 Nov. 1845

MY DEAR BROTHER,

I received your letter on the 7th of June, dated May 14th, stating the particulars of the death of dear mother which gave me great satisfaction of all you have done. I believe kind Providence will reward you for it. . . . [Letter gone astray] In regard to my father will I shall not say much at present as I intend comeing over in the spring, as I am anxious to see Old England once more. I wish Mr Lawrence Fogg to receive all the rent of the property untill May next and to pay it to my sister Mary, and she can use it as she thinks proper. Further I wish you to write as soon as this comes to hand and let me know what the property will fetch in cash as near as you can. If you can find a purchaser do so, as I cannot stop more than a month. I will start about the first of Aprile. My wife and William are all well and wish to be kindly remembered to you all. I am, Brother, your sincerely

JOHN HESKETH. . . .

My William wrot this letter.

Letter from Christopher Slade, grocer, to Robert Hesketh of Manchester

Pittsburgh, 21 July 1856

RESPECTED SIR,

You will excuse the liberty a stranger takes in writing to you, but I cannot refrain, knowing that you are the next of kin to my much respected friend, Mr John Hesketh, although I am a messanger of ill news. You are aware that your brother has been blind in one eye for a long time. Early last fall a cataract formed in the other eye so that he lost his sight entirely. Early in spring while yet the cold lasted he had an opperation was performed. Now either it was in consequence that the opperation was performed too soon or the weather was too cold he has not found such relief as he expected. He remains dark; yet he lives in hopes, although it is very doubtful of his ever seeing again. To make the matter worse his wife was taken sick in May and she had a paralectic stroke on the 10th of June last when she gradually declined and died

Thursday, July 10th, at 8 oclock a.m. and on Friday, the 11th, we burried her. She was speachless from the first stroke, so that for one month he could not see her nor could she speak to him. We are pleased to believe that she fell asleap in Jesus and that this trying dispensation of Providence will ultimately ensure to your brother everlasting happiness. Your brother has not heard from his son in Calafornia for a long time. His wife is no more. He is blind and you might say alone, for he has no one with him but an old woman we procured for him. I should not have written to you had I not reason to believe your brother wished it. I know he always speaks of you with kindness. I shall be obliged by your writing to your brother soon either through me or directly to himself. With great respect believe me to be yours,

CHRISTOPHER SLADE

Petingale Series 1833–83

Through this remarkable collection of letters it is possible to follow the entire careers of three brothers who emigrated to the United States.[1] The father of these emigrants, George Petingale, farmed on a large scale in the county of Norfolk. Born in 1778 in West Bilney, educated in Yorkshire, George Petingale married Ann Crisp in his native town in 1804. According to family papers, George Petingale was the son of John Dalton, banker and landowner of Swaffham, Norfolk, who bought Petingale out of the army during the Napoleonic Wars, one year after he had enlisted, so that he could marry. The land which George Petingale farmed in West Bilney, a village a few miles southeast of King's Lynn, was owned by John Dalton.[2] On this farm all ten of his surviving children were born and spent their childhood.

In 1831, a few months before his wife died, George Petingale moved from the growing village of West Bilney to a spot in the northeastern part of East Anglia which was further removed from a sizeable village. There he rented from the Earl of Leicester the Manor Farm at Fulmodestone which he continued to farm, taking great pride in the size of his turnips and fulminating against the repeal of the Corn Laws, until his death in 1861. At Fulmodestone Petingale was an Overseer of the Poor and a Churchwarden. When the 1851 census was taken, he was returned as a farmer of eight hundred acres employing eighteen men. In his household were five unmarried daughters; Eliza, thirty-eight; Mary, thirty-six, who later became insane; Fannie, thirty-three, who died in 1861 leaving a will her brothers did not like; Elizabeth, thirty-one; and Anne, twenty-five, who later married a doctor. Only the youngest daughter, Jane, was married by this time, to the Rector of the Anglican church in the nearby village of Stibbard. In addition to all his daughters, George Petingale had three women servants living in his household. All four of his sons had emigrated before this, three of them to the United States and the eldest, John George, to New South Wales and from there to New Zealand where he died in 1870.

In an entirely rural but intensively developed agricultural area,

Fulmodestone was losing population in the 1830s and 1840s, and was, in this respect, the same kind of community which our other farmers' sons were leaving. About a hundred paupers had been sent out from Fulmodestone to America in 1836. Of course, William, Thomas and Henry Petingale were not among these paupers, though they emigrated about the same time. These young men emigrated for personal and social rather than straightforward economic reasons. In the first place, they clearly did not get on with their father. George Petingale appears to have been determined that his sons should make their own way in the world. They were to prove their worth, to demonstrate that they deserved what help he might give them. He regarded himself as an entirely self-made man, in spite of the assistance which John Dalton had given him as a young man. As his son Henry perceived, Petingale was probably suspicious of his own sons because he had felt a want of love and encouragement during his own childhood.

Unable or unwilling to take up farming, these young men felt that Norfolk did not offer them opportunities appropriate to their education. William, who was the first to emigrate, in 1835, at the age of twenty-three, had been working in a factory on the outskirts of Norwich. Forced by his father to rely upon his own resources to gain a livelihood, he was not inclined to continue to work as a common journeyman, since he felt his education had placed him beyond the rank of a common labourer. William had ambitions as a writer which were never realized. When he arrived in America in 1835, he was not much pleased with it, though he jumped immediately to a higher occupational status than he had enjoyed in Norfolk, where he had worked in a factory by day and gone to dances at night. Not much pleased with the genteel society in which he moved in Rochester, New York, William was the only one of the brothers to criticize America harshly, especially for the artificial and misplaced gentility of the people he met. He soon left Rochester for the south and continued on the move. Portraying a pitiful picture of their brother's hardship and pauper funeral in their letters home, his brothers reported him dead in 1840, on second-hand information. Yet William Petingale wrote home again in 1841 from Philadelphia when he was again planning to go south to work for a public works contractor. Continuously plagued by ill-health, he returned to Norfolk shortly thereafter. In the Petingale papers are some poems he wrote at West Bilney in 1844. When his health was restored, he again emigrated to the United States but died in 1847, after seeing some action in the Mexican War.

In spite of his brother's warnings that he could not like America, Thomas Petingale also emigrated by 1838, when he was twenty-two.

Thomas had gone to school in King's Lynn and also to a private school in Yorkshire. His friend and neighbour, James Emery, later recounted that Thomas was teased by old schoolmates when he was apprenticed to a silk mercer at Norwich, until he lost his place as a consequence. Thereupon his father gave him some money and sent him to America. His younger brother, Henry, having received the same education as Thomas, was not placed in an apprenticeship but sent to the States with two hundred pounds in 1836 at eighteen. Returning to England in 1838, Henry Petingale emigrated again in 1841, this time to stay.

Whether it was because of their reports of William's death or not, from 1841 onwards Thomas and Henry Petingale received a succession of gifts of money from their father. Between 1841 and 1858, they each received no less than £880. Thus, during the forties and fifties, neither man was entirely dependent upon his own earnings for his livelihood.

Throughout his first twenty-two years in America, Thomas Petingale did not settle down in one place. He started out in New Orleans in 1838. In the family scrapbook is a business card in which this erstwhile draper's apprentice announced his business as 'real estate plan drawing, auctioneers, notaries, surveyors, draughtsmen, 10 Bank Arcade Passage, New Orleans'. In 1840, he went north to work as an assistant engineer on the Boston and Western Railway and wrote home that this was a business 'I am pretty perfect in, having followed it in the South several years'. He was reported to be engaged in surveying plans for the city of Pittsburgh in 1841. In 1842, he was in Philadelphia. After a visit to England he spent 1843–5 in St Louis, where he met his first wife, the daughter of a doctor in Cape Girardeau, Missouri. By 1847, he was working for the Erie Railroad in New York as an assistant surveyor. The census of 1850 found him living in a boarding house in Friendship, Allegheny County, New York. In 1852–3, he was working, still as a railway engineer, in Avon Springs, New York; in 1854 he worked in Stafford, NY, where he met his second wife; in 1855, he returned to Avon Springs and paid a visit to England. His next stop was Milwaukee, Wisconsin. Sometime about 1860, when the remittances stopped coming from home, Thomas Petingale settled down as a clerk in the Department of the Treasury in Washington, where he remained until his death in 1888. Even in Washington, he did not show any inclination to invest in a permanent home but changed his residence at least four times. Thus, after his father's death, Thomas managed to change his nomadic way of life into a stable and respectable (Philistine) one, though he chafed at having to work very hard for meagre returns.

Henry Petingale's first few years in America were equally mobile, though most of his travels were within the state of New York. Like his brother, he managed to obtain appointments as an engineer without any previous training. In 1847, he was working for the Erie Railway in the same capacity as his brother. When that railway was completed in 1851, it almost seemed that Henry Petingale would settle down. He married Sarah Mecklem of Newburgh, NY, whose family Thomas referred to as Henry's 'American relatives'. Although Sarah Mecklem had been born in New York, both of her parents had been born in Ireland. George Mecklem, a shoemaker, had done very well, however, and reported $12,000 worth of real estate in 1850. After his marriage, Henry Petingale secured what seemed to be very good positions for a man with no training and only ten years' experience in engineering. He was given the task of constructing a new waterworks for the City of Newburgh in 1852, and in 1856 was appointed as assistant engineer for the New York State Board of Works. Although his home was established in Newburgh during these years, Henry Petingale's work kept him away from it through the week. About the same time that Thomas opted for security and stability, the remittances from his father ceased, Henry's career renewed its geographical mobility and became increasingly unstable. From 1860–3, he worked for a brewery in Newburgh, a job procured through his wife's relatives. In 1864, he left home to work as a railway engineer, as a civilian for the army in Virginia. Back in Newburgh in June 1864, he moved on to take employment with Swift and Company in Hartford, Connecticut, and Worcester and Salem, Massachusetts, for about four years. In 1869, he was again in railway work, employed on the Erie Railway shortcut. He was actually enumerated in Newburgh in the census of 1870. In spite of the remittances from his father in early years, his marriage into a comfortably-off family, and his series of professional appointments, he could report no real estate and a personal estate of only $300. His last years were spent in New Jersey, thoroughly estranged from his family, and probably in some poverty, though when he died in 1887 he was buried in Newburgh. It seems fair to assume that Henry Petingale's professional progress was hindered as the years went on, not only perhaps by his drinking, but more particularly by his want of a professional education.

Probably no more need be said by way of introduction to the careers of these two men which contrast so markedly with those of immigrants who arrived in America with specific goals, with a passion for saving and for acquiring property, and with a need to rely upon their own resources from the outset. Neither man had any contact with an immigrant community after he arrived in the United States. Having married American-born women, both were drawn into the vortex of their wives' lives and social relationships, in striking contrast to people like John

Birket, who absorbed their American-born wives into the small immigrant community of which they were a part.

The Petingale letters were given to the British Library of Economic and Political Science by the late Joseph L.Petingale, grandson of Henry Petingale. Mr Petingale also permitted me to examine scrapbooks and other documents in his possession, from which some of the details about this family have been drawn, and generously shared the fruits of his own research into his family's history. The letters are reproduced with the kind permission of his widow, Irene F.Petingale.

Letters from William Petingale to his father, George Petingale, Fulmodestone, near Fakenham, Norfolk, and sisters

[Bawburgh?] Mills,* 14 Jan. 1834

DEAR FATHER,

Amongst all the passions which compose my character I assure you obstinacy forms no part.

I am deeply sensible that my past conduct has been neither dutiful or affectionate; for the past, I entreat your pardon, with the assurance that, that of the future shall be more generally adapted to the rules of consistency.

I consider this apology due to you, and as it is the result of the conviction that I was much in error, and not the whinings of a person under the impulse of fear. Impressed *with that conviction* I sincerely trust you will forgive your affectionate son,

W. PETINGALE

[Bawburgh?] Mills, 8 Aug. 1834

DEAREST BESSY,

I am induced to commence our correspondence as I see no probability of your breaking silence. Indeed had there been a goddess of taciturnity I should say you were her sincerest votaries. I suppose you have had some information from Thomas. If so pray transfer it to me as I have heard nothing of him and am anxious to have some intelligence from John as it is so long a period since we recieved any.

But suppose I said I myself had an idea of going to America! Do not start, for it is very far from improbable. For if as it appears to be the case I am to depend upon my own resources I am not disposed to

* Bawburgh is a village on the western outskirts of the city of Norwich. This is the best reading I can get for this word which is not very legible in the letters. This letter was postmarked at Norwich.

[trib?] as a common journeyman in England when in other lands you may obtain a comparative competency if you do but exercise common industry, and I suppose I may be allowed to say I am not very deficient in genius or enterprise. I am not singular in these ideas for Jno Candler Jnr. has some intentions of the same kind and his father's opinion is not opposed to it. I am heartily tired of the prospects which present themselves here and am determined to try my fortunes elsewhere. My time expires next February and it is high time I should seriously consider what steps to pursue, and as the system of education &c. which I have recieved place me rather beyond the bounds of common labour I have thus resolved to see what a clear head and steady conduct can perform in the land of Independence. My [*pen?*] *may await there* but *the severest toil cannot raise me* from the *mud here*. How does harvest succeed in your district and how are the crops? I wish you would send me the *flute* as we have now a band forming in [Bawburgh] and as we want some *innocent recreation* as well as *work* Do not fail to send it.

Did you recover the silk handkerchief and shoes that we left at Mr Chamber's dance? If not I wish you would enquire for them as they must have been sent away by mistake. The Miss Candles are now home from London, and as they are going to relate what *sights* and *wonders* they saw, I must conclude for the present and wishing to hear that you are all well I am your affectionate brother,

WM. PETINGALE

Rochester, NY, 26 May 1835

MY DEAREST SISTER, [Elizabeth]

I suppose I shall not trespass upon your time in writing to you an account of a few things which I think would interest you.

First I will just sketch the city of Rochester. Fancy then a town built upon the banks of the Genese river, the houses overhanging the deep torrent which forms many waterfalls below over which 3 bridges and an aqueduct connect the two sides. The scenery is grand and such is not seen in England.

We have here a city containing about 15,000 persons,* about 10 churches, as many chapels and divers other places of worship, I really think Sir A.Agnew should come here.† He could not but be pleased by such a shew of religion.

I am sorry I cannot inform you of improved health for since I last wrote I have gradually got worse and have left my employment until I am better, but I trust I may be able to return to my situation shortly; or

---

* The population of Rochester increased from 9,207 in 1830 to 20,191 in 1840.

† Sir Andrew Agnew, 7th Baronet, Lochnaw Castle, Stranraer, Wigtownshire.

I shall go to the seaside as I am advised by a physician who will receive no pay for his attendance, an act of generosity not often seen here. Mr Buchanan, the British Consul, told me to apply to him in case of any emergency. This gentleman is an honour to his countrymen affording every possible assistance to emigrants from his native country. . . . [Steamboat accident on Lake Erie. Season and prices]

I forgot to say we had a Museum in Rochester in which are shewn some dozen stuffed English crows, jackdaws, and sparrows and some more such articles, and every visitor is entitled to have his ears inflated by the most detestable creaking of an hand organ. A gentleman who appeared not well pleased asked him (the player) very politely to desist, when the other with a stare of wonder enquired if there was no music in the museums of Europe, a question put with such exquisite simplicity as to oblige the gentleman to hold his risibility by turning away his face. Hogarth might have found an abundant treat in this *embryo museum*. Music is scarcely taught amongst the ladies, their chief aim being to obtain (and they are mostly successful) some good *plain sense*, refusing in most instances all superficial knowledge in acquiring that which is useful. But in thus praising the fair sex here I do not wish to raise invidious comparisons. The fact is generally acknowledged by English people.

To gardening very little attention is given, being at present confined to raising potatoes and other culinary articles; but as every thing is carried on with enthusiasm when once thought of, so will gardening and floriculture be extensively patronised very shortly since one or two individuals here now turned their attention to it. One establishment is opened and begins to be much resorted to. All flowers bear an immense price, 300 per cent dearer than in England.

Fires daily occur from the nature of the materials with which the houses are built, many being entirely of wood, but all with wooden roofs and the air being so dry causes them to be easily ignited. An act of legislature of public property rendered this prohibition quite necessary. The mills here are very powerful and execute their work in a very superior style. If Mr Emery would just read the following he will perhaps feel somewhat astonished. In Rochester we have 2 mills in which are 10 pairs of stones in each. Now one pair grinds 15 bushels of wheat per hour so that 10 pair will grind in 24 hours, 3,600 bushels or in the six days 21,600 bushels and if you consider that we have 25 mills containing in all more than 100 pairs of stones, some imperfect idea may be formed of the immense trade done in flour in Rochester. The great number of bushels of wheat which can be ground at each pair of stones is owing to its fine quality, being all white wheat and *extremely* tender. I suppose this will astonish some of our Norfolk millers. This immense trade is mostly very profitable as [it] requires but little capital to commence: I wonder whether trade is this brisk in Van Diemans Land. . . . [Write]

Lodging and boarding is very cheap & comfortable and even respectable living may be had for 2 dollars – 2½ dollars per week, but when provisions are cheap they may be readily provided at 1½ dollar. All sorts of things are very expensive although most articles of home manufacture [work] in consequence of the high wages given to mechanics. . . . [A mutilated passage asking for news]

To know of all your continued happiness is most sincere wish of your affectionate brother,

WM. PETINGALE

I wish to know how Thomas is and what he is doing. I am sure he is much better in England than he could be here. I do not think he could like America. The general impression is so different from the reality; in fact the Englishman has no feelings in common with the Americans. The latter has an unnatural antipathy to the former, for what I cannot surmise. The excitement produced by the dissolution of the English ministry was very great. They think it will lead to no good. It is rather strange that, though such staunch republicans, they suppose the tories are the most eligible persons to govern the British Empire. The truth many persons are desirous to create the same distinction between rich and poor in America as there exists in England, this always the consequence when persons obtain immense fortunes. It is laughable to observe how tenacious of terms the mechanics are. They will not call their superiors (masters) but substitute the word (bos) which is in fact the Dutch word for master. To use a common expression they often gulp over a gnat and swallow a camel. The Amerigos are again very susceptible of delicacy. For instance, they dislike Byron's work because he uses some terms not found in the Bible. They dislike Shakespeare because he uses such plain language, and in fact their sense of propriety is so strong that many times they do not express their ideas because to do so would be compelled to use words which have other meanings. This is indeed false delicacy in persons so deficient in the *true material*. In Rochester there is now no theatre as the authorities had it pulled down because of its demoralizing influence. On this I will not comment. It may be right; it may be wrong. Temperance societies in abundance which they much need, especially as the town so intersected by water which might perhaps finish the work of spirits by drowning.

Letters from Thomas Petingale to his sister at Fulmodestone, Norfolk

New Orleans, 8 May 1839

DEAR SISTER, . . . [Apologies for not writing]

I have just finished a letter to my Father, bearing same date & also sent by the same conveyance as this; he no doubt is surprised at my dilatory conduct, in not corresponding more frequently. He must think that I had forgotten him. This is far from being the case. If my Father knew how hard I am striving to get along, he would not blame me, considering too that I am hazarding my life in this sickly country, & exposed to all the vicissitudes of life. Young men commencing the world on their own responsibilities frequently, or I may say always, encounter unexpected hardships & troubles which they little anticipated.

I have not heard from William for a long while. When he last wrote he was in Cincinnati, & spoke of going to New York. He was quite well at that time. John I hope is doing well in New South Wales. It would give me much pleasure to hear from him.

My fathers farm ought to look pretty well now, I am glad to hear he likes it so much. The farms in general here are on a much smaller scale – 100 acres is sufficient to support a large family in a very decent manner. The land costs $1.25 per acre equal to about 5s sterling & the wood cut off the land is worth as much. Many dissatisfied people return to their native country because as they say it is impossible to get along here. Such persons are too lazy to work & cant earn a living anywhere. Others cannot conform to the manners & politics of the Americans & consequently return more discontented than ever. This country offers greater inducements to the hard-working man than any other in the world. I shall write more fully upon this subject when I have leasure. . . . [Greetings] Your affectionate Brother,

THOS. PETINGALE

P.S. No probability of a war between the U.S. and Gt. Britain, we think, & I hope the two countries will see the impropriety of settling the question that way. . . . [Will write again in a day or two]

Albany, 10 December 1840

MY DEAR SISTER, . . . [This letter reports erroneously that his brother William died in New York City in December 1839 and had received a pauper's burial. Thomas had received the news in New Orleans and travelled to New York City to see a Mr Collins, keeper of a public house, to get details. He stopped on the way in Pittsburgh because of illness and in Albany to work in an attorney's office long enough to get money to proceed to New York City.]

My cash being very limited, I returned to Albany where I resumed my avocation, but which I have since left to obtain more permanent employment for the winter, and I am happy to inform you that I have succeeded. I am engaged by a railroad company as assistant surveyor. This is a business I am pretty perfect in, having followed it in the South several years. Twelve miles of the road is under contract to be finished by next Septr. It will ultimately extend to Boston, Massts. a distance of 180 miles. It will take three years to complete it. I shall stay in this state (*New York*) until I hear from home, though much to my disadvantage. Wages are not half as high as in the South, and being so used to a hot climate, the North does not so well agree with me.

The more I see of America the more I like it, not only the country but the people and government also, and whilst God gives me health, I can always earn my living in it. But let me not lead others astray by saying this, for most foreigners are too much prejudiced to settle well in the United States, especially the English. I shall constantly write to you now. You would not fail to answer my letters if you knew how happy it would make me, to hear of your all being well. My Father I hope approves of my stay in America. It would give me much joy to hear from him. When you write send two letters. Then there will be some probability of my receiving one of them. I am sure Jane would willingly copy them for you to any number. I hope that my stay in A[merica] has sufficiently proved to my Father my ability and desire to earn my own living. It is my attention to request of him a remittance to enable me to start in some kind of business or to furnish a small house which would much add to my comfort and profit. He cannot think me ignorant of the value of money, after the trouble I have had in earning it myself for the last few years. If my father can spare a few pounds, he can well dispose of it now. His son's happiness is yet in his hands. I shall not press this subject but leave it to his consideration . . . [Again asks for letter] My brother John, I hope, is doing well in N.S. Wales. Henry, I hope, is at home; let him take my advice and remain there. You will remember me affectionately to all at home, hoping that my Father, Sisters and Brothers are well. Remain dear Sister, Your affectionate Brother,

THOS. PETINGALE. . . . [How to direct letters]

P.S. Send nothing of value by letter, for it might not reach me. The post office department is badly conducted.

Letter from William Petingale to his father, Fulmodestone, Norfolk

Philadelphia, 15 Nov. 1841

MY DEAR FATHER,

I am happy to say I am now recovered from my long sickness which obliged me to leave Rochester and come to this city for advice. I am now as strong as ever. I am afraid you have not received our letters as we are without any from home. Thomas is in Pittsburgh and is busily employed in taking plans of that city. You will see his advertisements in the papers I have sent you. He is well and is perfectly satisfied with his present employment. Pittsburgh in Penna. is about 360 miles from this place, but here we consider that a short distance. A railroad unites the two places. It is about 20 hours journey. I am preparing to go South, being engaged to a person who is a large contractor there on public works and I am perfectly satisfied with my prospects. My salary amounts to 380 pounds independent of all expences. My money is at 7 per cent per annum with the best security. I hope my sisters will write of everything that can interest us, such for instance, the harvest, stock, our friends, &c.

Sincerely hoping you enjoy good health, be assured of our intentions to exert ourselves to the utmost in advancing ourselves in the world and that nothing can give us so much happiness as to hear of your own, my sisters, and Henry's. Love to all at home as well as to friends.

Earnestly desirous to hear from you I am once more, Your affectionate Son,

WILLIAM

Letters from Henry Petingale to his sister, Elizabeth Petingale, Fulmodestone, Norfolk

Rochester, 22 August 1842

MY DEAR BETSY, . . . [Ill health from hot weather]

I have been obliged to be out much in the evenings to meet the steam boats from Canada on business. But I hope yet to render myself acclimated; I may then reasonably expect tolerable good health. You would think to see me now that I had not eaten much *roast beef* or *pudding* lately. But not to subject myself to the charge of egotism, I will try to blunt the pangs of my individual misseries, by commenting on those of others. Poring over the column of a daily paper the editor declares the commercial population of the United States *Bankrupt* (in toto) N.B. He could not have collected his quarterly dues to his satisfaction. But though he probably pened this in a fit of splenetic indulgence there is a great deal more of truth than poetry in the remark. Most of the businessmen of Rochester are indirectly bankrupt, (i.e. they owe large debts they cannot now, & never mean to pay). Creditors here have a poor chance of obtaining their rights. The very laws appear to justify swindling & shape their lenity in accordance with the hard times. Thank God I was pretty conversant with American principle, or they might have added me to their many unsuspecting victims. It would do you good to hear them writhe under the anticipated malediction of Boz. They feasted & flattered him when over here, but he saw through their double dealings, & refused to sacrifise his principles at the shrine of sour wine, weak adulation and *apple sauce*;* I would add a few words on a more agreeable subject, the ladies of Rochester, but must limit my correspondence to another opportunity, as the doctor (ill-omened bird) has paid me a visit, and vetoed a long letter, from what he pleases to term mental excitability. I beg to express my sincere regrets for the loss of poor Avey's & I hope my Father will be able to replace so valuable a servant. I am on the eve of leaving Rochester, so do not answer this. . . . [Greetings] Your ever affectionate Brother,

HARRY

Newburgh, NY, 14 July 1847

MY DEAR BESSIE,

I deeply regret the necessity of communicating what Thomas tells me he has informed you of, relative to brother Williams death in New Orleans, as from source we received the information no doubt can exist of such being the case. Poor fellow, he must have experienced but little consolation, during his sickness from the solicitude of strangers. I was not much surprised at the news of his death, as previous sickness at different times had impaired his health very much. As soon as I can possibly procure particulars relative to his decease, I will forward the same to you. . . . [Letters] Thomas and myself are both actively engaged by the New York and Erie R Rd Co.† Thomas's little girl grows finely and is a beautiful child, now nearly 8 months old. He thinks all *the world* of it. It afforded me the greatest happiness to hear of dear Janes union with a gentleman so likely to insure her happiness, and I feel confident that he *cannot but appreciate* the value of the prise he has

* See Charles Dickens, *American Notes*, London, 1842.

† Begun in 1835, the construction of the Erie Railroad had been suspended for want of funds. In 1845, the state legislature agreed to release the road from its three million dollars debt to the state and authorized three million dollars worth of first mortgage bonds. Construction was then resumed on this 537-mile-long line, which reached its destination, Dunkirk, in 1851.

obtained.* My dear Bessie, I have often thought that the clouds, which appear to have lowered over us all, would yet be dissipated by a more congenial aspect. That such should be the case is, I assure you my most sacred wish. I would write more to father, but have supposed that it would *disturb him.* You must not suppose that because I am so far removed from you that your happiness is a matter of indifference to me, for such I assure you is not the case, and I earnestly hope that all little causes of domestic discord no longer exist, to disturb your future harmony.... [Greetings] and believe me, my dear Bessie, your affectionate

'BRO HARRY'

Letter from Thomas Petingale to his sister

Newburgh, NY, 31 Dec. 1848

MY DEAR SISTER,

My last addressed to my father left us all in good health. Since then it has pleased the Almighty to take from us our dear boy. He died on the 22nd of this month after lingering about 4 weeks. The complaint was consumption. His age 1 year & 18 days. During his illness our neighbours & friends were most kind to us & the funeral was very respectably attended. It took place last Sunday afternoon, just a week ago. His death has had a tendency to injure Mrs P's health. She has not been well since and complains much of her cough. Our little girl is quite well & is beginning to talk and run about, to say nothing of climbing chairs, tables &c. Henry is still in Newburgh. He pays us a visit nearly every day. He tells me that he has written home several times & has received no answers.... [Birth of Jane's son] I still fill the same situation upon the rail road & have every prospect of doing well. Should you hear from Brother John please write me how he is &c. There is no doubt the news concerning William is correct. Poor fellow, I fear it is too true.... [Greetings] Your affectionate brother,

THOMAS PETINGALE....

Letters from Henry Petingale to his sister, Bessie

Newburgh, NY, 5 Feb. 1849

MY DEAR BESSIE, ... [Letters. Death of Thomas's son and his wife's illness]

The all engrossing topic now is California, and Gold! Gold! Gold!

* Jane Petingale married Nicholas Mortimer Manley, a clerk in holy orders, son of Charles Manley, merchant, on 22 April 1846.

the only word that echoes in the street, the road, the drawing room, the ball room, and even the church grasps the glittering word as it affords their ministry a text to descant upon. You would suppose that the Ghost of Midas has been wandering over the plains of California, and distributing his golden curse there for expiation, for we hear of persons without a No 2 shirt in their possession finding lumps of gold weighing 25 lbs. Had I not been engineering now, which keeps me actively engaged, my location might have been changed to the Pacific, and cant tell yet how far I may escape this *Yellow Feaver,* as I often feel a sensation at the end of my fingers, as if I would like to employ these 'pickers and stealers' in the golden sands & mountains of California. Cant say at present, but if I make up my mind to do so I will write you to that effect before I start. I expect to be very busy this spring as we have a rail road to finish up by next Sept. . . . [Greetings. Severity of winter]

N.B. I want you to measure the dimensions of the largest turnip before you answer this, (as I think there must be some that astonish the natives) and be so kind as to let me know how large they are. . . . [Greetings] Your ever affectionate brother,

HARRY PETINGALE. . . . [Greetings]

Newburgh, NY, 30 May 1849

MY DEAR BESSIE, . . . [Letter acknowledged]

I should not have delayed answering your letter so long, had I not been so busily engaged engineering, my time being occupied from 7 in the morning, till 8 oclock in the evening, as we are in a great hurry to finish up a railroad by the 1st of Septr next. Egotistically I shall introduce my own affairs first. I have abandoned the idie of going to California at least for the present, and luckerly too I think, as the accounts of the difficulties and privations suffered by the emigrants in most instances are nearly incredible, added to which the cholera has in many cases swept off *nearly whole* parties. The cholera prevails to a considerable extent in the South & South western states, following the valleys of the Mississippi & Ohio Rivers & radiating off in different directions. It is generally supposed that its ravages will be less in the more northern & eastern states, as they have the advantages of a better climate & purer water. . . . [Steamboat disaster on the Hudson River]

I see by your letter that Jane is going to London (I believe for the first time) and I suppose also the young Revd Chas George I am sure I [hope] Jane will be delighted with her trip, and yet like the *quiet domesticity* of Stibbard Rectory none the less. . . . [Answer by return mail] Please to inform Eliza that 'that cake took the *premium* about *these diggins'* & that I lent the recipe to a young lady who, wishing to monopolize it, refuses to give it to me again, neither kissing nor scolding have the least effect upon her obduracy. Thats what I call calico gratitude. So please ask Eliza as a favour to enclose it in your next letter. I would like to see the bullocks & sheep feasting on those large turnips. I hope the rogues will get fat. Thats all the harm I wish them. Send over a bushel of the largest to Mr Emery and tell him to grow likewise. I mean the turnips, not him personally. (Give my best respects to Mr & Mrs E.). Last summer when I arrived in America I weighed 15 lbs more than I did when I started previously away from there. I have lost it again with the rather severe exercise my duties of engineering entail upon me, and am as black as a coal need aspire to be. 13 hours a day in the hot sun *cooks a person a little.* I am sorry to inform you that Mrs Thos Petingale's health still continues bad, but I hope the summer will restore her. . . . [Asks for letter] Your ever affectionate brother,

HARRY PETINGALE. . . . [Greetings]

Newburgh, NY, 6 Aug. 1849
MY DEAR BESSIE, . . . [Letters and weather]

I see the English papers complain of the heat at 86 deg. Here we have had the thermometer ranging from 96 to 100 deg in the shade; and as my duties, civil engineering, expose me a great deal to the weather, I am able to speak feelingly. It is very trying to the constitution, though I have enjoyed good health most of the time. Thomas's wife has been and still continues in a bad state of health; and I never expect her to recover, though she may still continue to linger for some time. His little boy & girl are both well. I suppose you are aware of his being presented with a little boy, as I am under the impression that he wrote to some of you to that effect. I have been so busy since last October, that I have not had time to go anywhere, not even to New York city – but I hope we shall finish our railroad by next Novr and shall then either go on some other R Rd or engage in some business in Newburgh (like a musty old bachelor, you will say). I have given over all idea of going to California, and much of the excitement is allayed, which existed, and pervaded all classes, though the *root of all evil* still continues to arrive in considerable quantities. I suppose you have been at Bilney since I was there last summer. Remember me to all the next time you see them, and to my scattering friends I may have on your side of the Atlantic.

I see by the foreign accounts that you have had a fine season for the farming interests, as regards the weather, and I have no doubt that Father will beat the county with his turnips again this year. It would do some of the Yankee farmers good to go over and see his mode of farming. I take great interest in farming, but have little opportunity to gratify the taste here, as the farms are all small and conducted on the milk, egg & butter pedling system. It is rather surprising that you do not hear from John. I am fearful that you will not again. If you have done so, write me full particulars. . . . [Asks for news.]

HENRY PETINGALE

Letter, bordered in black, from Thomas Petingale to his sister Eliza

Newburgh, NY, 2 Sept. 1849

MY DEAR SISTER,

Last week I sent you a printed notice, recording the death of my dear wife. Too true it is that the idol of my heart has fled, but oh, my restless soul be easy. I will turn to God and seek the Kingdom prepared for those who love Him. There alone can I again see my kind, affectionate & ever dutiful Margaret.* This hope is the only consolation left poor me, my only support in this hour of affliction.

It is now nearly a year since I first noticed a change in the health of Margaret, sufficient however to warrant a belief that her lungs were affected; & the death of our little boy, who died of inflammation of those parts shortly after, confirmed the opinion that she was consumptive. In Decr last the disease was plainly developed, & her physician told me her situation. I had still hopes that she would be cured & thought that her complaint might be mistaken & that it might be a winter cough; but when spring arrived I noticed that she continued to waste in strength & in the middle of May she was too weak to sit up or to help herself. This continued until Friday 8th June on which day (an awful one to her & a sorrowful one to others who were aware of her difficulties) she gave birth to a living boy. She endeavoured to nurse him but could not. A day or two afterwards the baby was taken to a lady who had just lost her infant & she promised to keep him until he was strong enough to feed otherwise. Margaret after her confinement declined more rapidly. The cough was incessant & discharges of mucus very copious. The physicians told me she could not survive long & on the 10th Aug at 12 noon she died, & an Angel was then added to the Heavenly Host. Many weeks previous to her death she expressed great anxiety concerning Eliza & wished me to send her to her Mother in the West to take care of. The climate of Missouri I do not think would agree with her & I do not know how to carry out her wishes in this respect. If I can, it will be done though.

* Thomas Petingale's first wife, whose death is here announced, was the daughter of Dr James O'Hara of Cape Girardeau, Missouri.

My little boy (Charles) is nearly 3 months old. He is said to be my 'very image' (nurses can talk). He is much fatter than either of the others were at his age. As for Eliza there can be no prettier child. She is courted by all the juveniles, whose good fortune it is to be acquainted with her, for where Jose (nickname for Eliza) is, there is sure to be plenty of sweetmeats, candies, &c. She too is Petingale dark eyes, Bessy's coloured hair, & a good figure, but requires care until she gets rugged. These two little Pets are all there are left to me. . . .

THOMAS PETINGALE . . . . [Letters not received]

Letter from Henry Petingale to his father

Newburgh, NY, 26 March 1850

MY DEAR FATHER,

I received yours of Feb. 14th in answer to mine, and was not surprised to hear of the depression that pervades the agricultural interest in England, which could not fail to be the result of the suicidal policy the British Government has pursued for the last few years. Americans, even with their *professed liberality*, are too cunning to make such sweeping concessions, and smile at the policy that enables them to feed the pauper classes of Great Britain with the surplus produce of their vast and fertile praries. They are fond of reciprocity when it does not conflict with their own interests, and advocate free trade in such articles, that with a large and almost prohibitory duty England can compete with them in. In matters of statesmanship America has been misunderstood and underrated in England, for though but a sapling from the parent tree, still a vigorous one, and one likely to stand the shocks that sweep over the political hemisphere unharmed, even where the more sturdy and resisting obstinacy of Gt Britain might be the cause of her prostration. Excuse my obtruding my thought on a subject unsolicited on your part and about a country that gave me birth, and one that I shall always love, though compelled by force of circumstances to abandon perhaps for ever. I am afraid you put a wrong construction on my letter from the wording of your answer about assisting 'any of your sons with another shilling', for the last assistance in a pecuniary way was foreign to the import that I meant to convey, as you have been liberal and even too generous, I often think, and I assure you I shall always thank and respect you for it. What I asked I could with propriety have asked of a stranger. I was sorry to perceive in your letter a brevity, and absence of all feeling of interest, a sort of business like compliance with a disagreeable duty in writing to me. I hope such were not the feelings that actuated you. I know that you have a proud yet a feeling heart, though your early contact with an unfeeling world, unaided, unencouraged, by even parental solicitude, taught you a sad lesson of mistrust, and yet a cold proud feeling of self-reliance, the offspring of your position, which has paved your way to success through life. Father, you have always undervalued the influence of a few words of feeling or kind solicitude. I do not write this with a feeling of reproach but of regret.

I have watched the foreign reports of current prices of grain &c for some time, and have been surprised that quotations of American flour &c have been almost as low at Liverpool &c as they have at the Atlantic cities in America. This indicates a larger proportionate supply on hand in Gt Britain than at the ports in America. There is not a large quantity of wheat on hand in the interior or more westerly depots, as a large quantity was bought on speculation for foreign ac/t and hurried to the seaboard early last autumn before the close of navigation by the canals &c.

America with an increased population *of consumers* could not produce such a large surplus supply of wheat as is generally supposed. Neither her soil or climate are so well adapted for cereal grains as that of Europe; and my professional duties leading me over large tracts of country, I have had some good opportunities of observing and gathering many facts which the statistics of the country do not afford, espeacially in the more northern districts. The greatest enemy to the wheat are the frosts, which are so penetrating that they destroy the wheat by heaving the soil & exposing the roots to the action of the frosts. Our summers are also too short, the reaction from cold to heat so sudden that it produces premature ripeness, not giving time for the ear to develop itself properly. Wheat which now looks dried and sear, without any apparent life, will be cut in the first week in June. It is rarely that we see here wheat with the fine heavy ear that we do in England. Excuse these few remarks, little worth paper & ink, for the subject is one I like, and find opportunities to study sometimes on my surveying excursions through the country, though the farmers generally are an unenterprizing set of beings inheriting their grandfathers notions of farming &c.

I have been engaged in the location of the part of the New York & Erie R Rd about 400 miles west of Newburgh. We have put 170 miles under contract, and intend opening the road through to Lake Erie in about a year. Whole distance 480 miles. This is the most important R Rd in the United States affording uninterupted communication from New York City to Lake Erie. This makes the 4th year I have been with the co. and shall probably be engaged till the road is completed and perhaps longer. Excuse my taxing your patience so long and hoping that you may live long and happily in the enjoyment of good health, I remain, Your affectionate son,

H. PETINGALE

Letter from Thomas Petingale to his sister, Eliza

Friendship, Allegany Co., NY, 6 May 1850*

MY DEAR SISTER, . . . [Letters]

I intend enclosing in this a sketch of our road, at least the work upon which Henry and myself are engaged. . . . I believe in my last it was mentioned that this work was to be completed to Lake Erie in a year from now, after which I should pay you a visit. There is no doubt it will be finished by next May, but I shall not be able to visit England for probably a long time to come, for since I last wrote you I have had an offer made me of an excellent situation upon a rail road, which I have 'provisionally' accepted. There is no doubt of my being able to obtain at all times profitable employment & consequently have held out for higher salary. My terms are £200 per annum 1st year & £250 2nd & 3rd years, but I shall not give up my present situation until the road is finished. After that the road of 2,500 miles, the 'St Louis and Pacific' will be commenced & upon this I expect to be employed.†. . . [Says Friendship is at a summit separating rivers running north and south]

My 2 dear children are well & in the same places as when I wrote you last. I expect to see Eliza in a few weeks & Charles next week. . . . [Greetings] Your ever affectionate and ardently attached brother,

THOS PETINGALE

Letter from Henry Petingale to his sister, Eliza

Newburgh, NY, 27 July 1852

DEAR SISTER ELIZA, . . . [Apologies]

I am happy in being able to send you good news, namely that Sarah presented me with a fine boy on the 15th of this month; who (at least

---

* The 1850 census manuscripts reveal that, apart from the railway construction taking place nearby, Friendship was a farming community with few British immigrants. In the household where Thomas Petingale was living were an Irish-born axeman and his family, the New York-born chief engineer and his family, a nineteen year old engineer from England, and a twenty-one year old engineer from South Carolina.

† The Pacific Railway Company obtained a franchise from the State of Missouri as early as 1843. In 1852, about five miles of track, from St Louis to Cheltenham, had been completed. The engineer in charge in 1852-3 was James P.Kirkwood who had been formerly with the Erie Railroad and through whom Thomas Petingale may have received this offer.

in our eyes) embodies perfection itself.* And I am still happier in being able to say that both mother & child are doing extremely well.

You naturally want to know his name. I will introduce you then to Master George Henry Petingale; I must account to you for the young gentlemans names by stating that Sarah having the *controul fully*, of this part of the performance wished him to be named George, after his grandpapas and squeezed in Henry as a middle name, as she says, in compliment to me; so there are the cognomens he will make his debut in the world with. Sarah at this time is up, and in good spirits and ready with cheerful alacrity to face the unavoidable troubles and anxieties of her young charge, but I shall leave Sarah to give you a fuller detail of particulars when she writes, which she promises to do in a short time. . . . [Sister Mary's removal from home]

I hear from Thomas nearly every week. He is at present engaged on a railroad, in the western part of the state, and is located at Avon Springs, Livingston Co. Fortuitous circumstances have favoured him in this instance, for Avon Springs is one of the pleasantest of the many fashionable resorts of the 'upper ten thousand'. Our profession insures all the vicissitudes of scene and life, sometimes domiciled in large cities, and sometimes 'roughing it' in the wilds of the partially cleared wilderness. Thomas looked extremely well the last time I saw him (a few weeks since). . . . [He will write]

As regards myself I am 'happy as a Lord', with lots of work on hand. I have been all summer engaged in engineering for the Commissioners of the Newburgh Water Works, whose object is to obtain a large supply of water from a beautiful Lake of nearly 100 acres and 4 miles from Newburgh.† I like the work much as [it] affords me a considerable experience in hydraulics &c. . . . [Greetings]

And so, Sister Anne is going to take charge of the pots & kettles of a household for herself, for better or worse, Good sis Anne. I congratulate her sincerely, and hope she may experience as much happiness as I have been the recipient of by taking such a step, and I think her prospects are decidedly in favour of her securing a kind and gentlemanly husband in Mr Drew (and not only that she will have no doctors' bills to pay). Remember me to all old friends, Mr and Mrs Emery and Mr James Emery particularly, as though I never expect to visit England again, still I hope never to forget the kindness of old friends there. . . . [Greetings]   HENRY · PETINGALE

* Henry Petingale married Sarah Mecklem, daughter of George Mecklem of Newburgh, on 20 May 1851.

† In March 1852 an act appointing commissioners to construct water works to increase the supply of water for Newburgh by using the Little Pond passed the State legislature and the works were put under contract in 1853.

[There follows a note from Thomas Petingale from Niagara Falls announcing his marriage to Frances Amelia Stage, daughter of Isaac Stage of Stafford, NY.]

Avon, New York, 1 Jan. 1855

MY DEAR SISTER, . . . [Apologies. Hopes of visiting England. Deaths of his mother's brother and John Dalton at Bilney, where the Petingales lived until 1831.]

What terrible changes have taken place in Bilney lately. Those tombstones in the old churchyard record the ravages of time upon our relatives and friends. Our old native place was deserted & desolate; still would I feel the same regard for it as I have constantly done, but I will dismiss this subject with a sigh & with but a ray of hope that I shall yet see the dear old spot once more. . . . [Sister Mary]

I am glad to learn that my Father's health has improved. Of course when I write to you it is my desire that he should see or know the contents of my letters. It saves the trouble of writing the same matter over twice, & I think I know his aversion for repetitions & long-winded epistles. It also pleases me to hear that Ann & Jane & their babies are well. You can inform them that I have been presented with a fine little fellow. He was born on the 18th November last. Frances and the boy are both enjoying excellent health. Only four added to the world in the space of a month or two by the Petingales!!!

You appear desirous to know something concerning the person I have married. Well then, her name was Frances Amelia Stage; her age is 26 years. Her disposition very kind, her birth American (not Indian though), her religion Episcopalian. In every other respect she is not unlike the English lassies, at least I suppose so. Joking aside, she is really the person I wanted for my wife, and I can truly say that the estimate formed of her at first acquaintance has been fully realized since my marriage. Perhaps (& *had I been a little more verdant*) I might have added to the above, good-looking, good figure & a few more 'components', but *how that would sound* when speaking of one's better half. . . . [A marriage in England]

No doubt you would like to hear how I am 'getting along'. It is easily told for I have not changed my situation for several years, but my salary is higher, and my duties lighter than formerly. On the score of business I cannot complain, though there are many in our midst who feel the pressure of the times severely. . . . [Write] and can you not send me occasionally a Norfolk Newspaper? I shall be happy to exchange with you. . . . [Greetings] Very affectionately yours,

THOMAS P. . . . [Write]

Letter from Henry Petingale to his sister Eliza

Newburgh, 14 Sept. [1856?]

DEAR SISTER ELIZA, . . . [Letters]

Mrs Sarah Petingale presented me last Friday (Sept. 12) at 11 oclock a.m. with a fine little girl, & both mother and child are 'doing as well as could be expected under the circumstances.' Our little boy is well & growing up a stout little fellow.

We live at Newburgh yet, but I am home only once a fortnight, as the Board of Public Works of the State of New York has thought proper to appoint me First Assistant Engineer (not forgetting to attatch a good salary to the office) which necessarily leads me away from home a great deal. As this appointment was made by a 'Know Nothing' administration (Know Nothing party means those opposed to foreign born citizens) I suppose they intended it as a compliment. So you see, dear Sister Eliza, your poor good for nothing brother Harry meets some encouragement, even from the hands of strangers. . . .

I have been anxious to hear from Fulmodestone for some time, how Father, sister Mary & all the rest of you were, & also how the crops were, particularly the turnips, as though I have been following the profession of Civil Engineering for the last 10 years, still I love to watch the crops; & as the nature of my business calls me over a vast extent of country I have good opportunities of doing so. Still I have seen no farming like the English. Brother Thomas is out West, in Milwaukie, state of Wisconsin. I have not seen him for nearly a year, but I sometimes hear from him. I believe he is doing very well & the last time I saw him he was looking extremely well, being both fat and hearty. . . . [Messages from Sarah] Your ever affectionate brother,

HENRY PETINGALE. . . .

Fragment of a letter from [Henry?] Petingale to his sister

12 August 1859

DEAR SISTER, . . . [Letters. Asks for news]

We are never without the commercial & political news of England & the Continent. The American papers abound in copious extracts from the European journals. The sudden termination of the war has not, it appears, given general satisfaction. In this country it is viewed as a good stroke of policy on the part of the French Emperor & writers on this side are generally lavish in their laudations towards him, whilst they, in the same measure, condemn the course pursued by Austria. But the editors here, (at least the greater portion of them) are subject to such mutation of sentiment and sympathy that very likely in a few days the praise they have bestowed upon France will be transferred to Austria. The French are proverbial for instability, but it would be hard for them to beat the Yankee nation in that respect. They remained me of the Irishman's flea, very difficult to find his real whereabouts.

But let's have a change of subject. The good people of the state of New York have lately had the pleasure of witnessing some very daring feats performed by a Monsr Blondin, a Frenchman. Mr B. is by profession a tight rope walker & dancer. The spot selected by Blondin to exhibit his abilities was at Niagara Falls. A rope 2 inches in diameter was stretched across Niagara River just below the Falls.* At this point the Bluffs are nearly perpendicular & rise to a height of 250 feet above the surface of water in the river. The distance across is about $\frac{1}{4}$ of a mile. On two occasions prior to that of last Wednesday, Monsr B. has walked across (& danced upon the rope) from the Canada to the United States shore. Last Wednesday he actually carried a man weighing 140 pounds across on his back. One false step would have precipitated them both into the water below, a distance of 250 feet, the drawing below will give you perhaps a better idea of the chasm walked over. [diagram]

There were 30,000 persons present to see Blondin walk last Wednesday, & next week he proposes giving another exhibition. Even Blondin has a competitor. He, too, is a Frenchman by the name of De Lave. Last Tuesday I saw him walk a single rope stretched across the Genessee Falls at Rochester. In this instance the rope was 100 feet above the water below. He performed the feat bravely & to the satisfaction of about 20,000 spectators. . . .

[The harvest] [HENRY P.? in his handwriting]

Letters from Henry Petingale to his sister, Eliza

Newburgh, 6 Feb. 1862

DEAR SISTER ELIZA,

I beg to acknowledge the receipt of your letter with £300 enclosed, being the am/t of a legacy left me by my father. I have also enclosed a receipt for same as I supposed you would require a voucher, as adminis-

---

* The Frenchman Jean François Gravelet, alias Charles Blondin (1824–97), is said to have been the greatest tightrope walker of all time. On 30 July 1855 he made the earliest crossing of Niagara Falls on a rope three inches in diameter.

tratrix of fathers estate, to place on file.* I received your letter on the 10th of June 1861.

I can hardly realize that dear Fanny is dead, & I assure you that Sarah joins me in heartfelt sympathy for the loss you have sustained, as she was doubly endeared to you, from the years of companionship that had existed between you. But we must bow to the will of God. . . . [Letters]

Sarah has presented me with a fine little girl, born Oct. 10th, 1861. It is considered a fine handsome child. We intend to name it Fanny Eliza. Our little boy is named Joseph Lawson & his sister is named Florence. You will find their photographs enclosed. Thomas has arrived at Stafford. . . . [Thanks for presents] As my left arm pains me . . . , having broken it by a fall . . . excuse me writing more at present. . . .

HENRY PETINGALE

Warrenton Junction, Virginia, 10 March 1864

DEAR SISTER ELIZA,

Your letter of Feby 4th containing remittance of £22.15.8 for the childrens interest was safely recd at Newburgh on Feby 22 & I must thank you for your punctuality in sending it. . . . [Dr Drew's share]

I did not receive your letter till the 25th of March, as I am at present located in the State of Virginia, about 600 miles from Newburgh, & it had to be sent to me that distance. Being in the government employment, engineering on the military rail roads. I have had ample opportunities of witnessing the desolating effects of the present war in America. The proud old state of Virginia, three years ago owned by a rich aristocratical class of planters, now present no evidences of cultivation, houses torn down, or burnt, fences distroyed, & its woods cut down, by the contending forces, who have both occupied it. It has truly been the battle ground of the Eastern Armies of America. Our forces are in winter quarters, but occasionally have a skirmish & I frequently go to sleep with a lullaby of booming cannon & rattling musketry, not pleasant, but we get accustomed to it & dont regard it much. When will this cruel war end is a question in every ones mouth, is still unanswered & likely to be, as the North has to contend with a proud, uncompromising set of people, who have thrown their all in the scale; & they have fought well & desperately & no doubt will continue to do so to the bitter end, whenever that may be.

* George Petingale died on 4 January 1861. He left two hundred pounds to each of his married daughters, with the stipulation that their husbands could never touch the interest. He left three hundred pounds to Henry Petingale and the rest of his estate to his unmarried daughters. His estate, valued at about seventeen thousand pounds was in farm produce, bank deposits and consols.

I sometimes run over to Washington to see Thomas. Eliza Caroline resembles sister Bessie much, is lively, good looking & pleasant. Sammy is a well grown, healthy, English looking boy, but resembles the Stages more than the Petingales. Mrs Thomas's eyes are not good & I think will not ever be strong. . . . [Greetings] Your affectionate Brother,
HENRY PETINGALE. . . . [Write]

[There follows a letter from Sarah, Henry's wife, complaining of his dissipation, that he obtained a good position through her brother but does not support his family, and that before that he was using the children's interest money for himself. She has been obliged to take in sewing. The letter refers Eliza to ministers and a bank manager to support her pleas that the children's interest be paid direct to her.]

Letter from Thomas Petingale to his sister, Eliza, Thorpe Hamlet, Norwich

Washington, D.C., 7 July 1864
MY DEAR SISTER, . . . [Comments on her letter]
I should not have written to you again so soon after my last had not I felt there was very good reasons for doing so. The principal one is that touching Henry's matters, or more properly speaking, his family affairs. I am indeed surprised at hearing that Sarah wrote to you in such terms. Yes, I say *surprised,* for it was the first impulse after reading your note, or that portion of it which alluded to him. Henry is the only brother that I have in this country and it is not my province to speak against him; others can do that it appears. It certainly appears strange to me that after he & Sarah have been married some 13 years that some new development in his nature is discovered, and that you must be as suddenly apprised of the fact. Henry is yet a good deal of a John Bull, and perhaps his habits may not be exactly approved of by some of his American relations; but it surprises me (and it would pain me too if true) to hear that he is *so* dissipated &c.
I will write to him first opportunity – likely to day – and will find out all. There are generally two sides to family jars and misunderstandings. As for the sewing machine, the first folks in this country use them. Sarah is industrious & I do not doubt tries to do her best for her family. I can scarcely believe that Henry is wanting in those feelings which impels a parent to take care of his own. I shall admonish him to give every penny you send, which is intended for the children, to them. He will at least see the propriety of his doing so for the future. It is very

strange to me, if he does not every year contribute three times as much as he receives from you on account of the childrens interest to their support. Being out of business for a short time might produce a similar state of affairs as those stated by Sarah, but I will not believe that Henry is so dissipated as he is represented to be. It looks to me as if Sarah had a bad adviser when she troubled you with such unwelcome details.

Of course Henry's children (if Sarah's statement of their poverty be true) will want every penny of what is due them, and that as soon as you can conveniently send.

My own salary is a pretty good one; but prices are so high that but little, if any, reservation can be made. *These are war times with us.* . . . [High prices] Yours affectionately,

THOMAS PETINGALE. . . .

Letter from Henry Petingale to his sister, Eliza Petingale, Norwich

Hartford, Conn., 20 Sept. 1864

MY DEAR ELIZA,

Your letter dated August 6th with the childrens dividend of £22.17.6 enclosed is duly received & please find receipt for the remittance enclosed.

I have been busily engaged engineering for a large company in the states of Massachusetts & Connecticut & find it pleasanter than being in Virginia, as well as much healthier, and also being within one day's travel of my family in Newburgh.

With regard to the letter Sarah wrote you, I am ignorant of its contents as Sarah simply told me she had written you but did not inform me further; but I am satisfied that if Sarah wrote anything reflecting on me, it was at the instigation of her mother, who is an ignorant, prejudiced woman, and has been the cause of much unhappiness to me, as she has exerted a mothers influence over Sarah, to my prejudice, whenever I have been proffessionally absent. . . . [Greetings]

The war in America rages with unabated fury on both sides, but I hope the Presidential election which takes place in November may have some effect in restoring peace again. Every thing is heavily taxed now, and the necessaries of life are increased in price about three-fold, & there will undoubtedly be a great deal of suffering next winter amongst the poor. . . . [Asks about brother John. Asks for letters. Children.]

Your affectionate brother,

HENRY PETINGALE . . .

Letter from Thomas Petingale to his sister, Eliza

Treasury of the United States, Washington, 2 Oct. 1864

MY DEAR SISTER, ... [Letter received]

Your letter, containing one to Prime & Co. of New York, has *not* yet come to hand, but that firm has paid me the sum of 22.17.6 and I have given them in return my draft upon Overend Gurney & Co. and I herewith sent you a receipt for the same amount. Henry writes to me under date of the 18th Sept. as follows: 'I have recd the childrens dividend from Prime & Co. who wrote me that the letter of Credit had been sent to them *by mistake*, and that the mistake had been rectified by their correspondents.'

Now in connection with the complaint made by Sarah per letter to you, I consider it my duty to quote from Henry's letter of 18th *ulto.* to me, replying to one I wrote to him on this subject. He says: 'I will explain to you the cause of Sarah's writing such a letter. You will remember that when I went with you to Jay Cook & Co's last spring that he advanced $120 (dollars) on the letter of credit I had received. I forwarded Sarah $100 (dollars) by draft on New York. On the reception of the above amt. by Sarah, without regarding the advices that I sent her that I would remit the balance soon, wrote me a severe letter and stated that she had written to Eliza, but did not state the nature of the communication. I forwarded Sarah before I left Washington nearly $200 (dollars) and have her acknowledgements for the same.' He adds in another part of his letter: 'I have forwarded to Sarah the amount of childrens dividend.' Of course this means the last one, the $200 (dollars) having reference to the previous one. Now I believe all that Henry states, and consequently must believe that Sarah has, (to use the mildest terms) been too precipitate, too severe entirely. That she is an industrious person, no one who knows her can deny, but are not other qualities equally as essential to domestic happiness as this? I have always been very friendly disposed towards Sarah, and cannot even now feel otherwise. Still I cannot regard her the higher since she wrote so about Henry. He writes: '*I can only attribute Sarah's action to one of those impulses which seem to govern at times.*' She knows that I have always been her friend, and why did she not write to me if she had complaints to make about H., or did she expect that such an announcement as she made to you would turn you against your own brother? If so, and in due deference to you, I must believe that she was mistaken. This I do know for a certainty, that last spring, Henry tried his utmost endeavours to earn a living for himself and family, that he was engaged upon a military rail way, during which time he suffered *all the privations peculiar to camp*

*life, often in danger of being killed by the enemy, and always under appre-
hensions of some mishap or other.* Indeed I was glad when Henry told me
that the government had dispensed with the services of those who were
then employed on this semi-civil, semi-military occupation, for I do not
think it possible for him to have stood it much longer. But am I not pro-
lix on this subject? If left to me I should say, no, for it is my purpose to
assure you by facts *that Henry has not become so dissipated that he has
had no idea of providing for his family.* He is now profitably employed,
but has to work hard. I could add more but I fear you will think me
tedious. . . .

We are on the eve of another Presidential election, and all the *political
machinery* of the nation is in motion. It is Lincoln vs McClellan, but I
have touched now upon a subject which would take at least a ream of
paper to explain. Suffice it to say that it will be the most important election ever held in this country, and I trust it will be conducted without
bloodshed. . . . [Brother John – Greetings to sisters] Your affectionate
brother,

THOS PETINGALE. . . .

Letter from Henry Petingale to his sister, Eliza

Newburgh, Dec. 1874

DEAR SISTER ELIZA,

I would call your attention to my son Joseph Lawson Petingales
application for the advance of £100, to enable him to further his views.
I hope you will return a favourable answer to same, as Joseph is ambitious to get along in the world, and I am glad to say, a young man of
good habits. I have not seen brother Thomas since his return from
England, but hear from him frequently. We are well and hearty. . . .
[Greetings] Your affectionate brother,

HENRY PETINGALE

P.S. If you decide to advance the amt. Joseph asks for you can remit the
same as usual. H.P. You can address me the same as Joseph's address
Henry Petingale, care of Micklem Brothers, 287, Greenwich St., New
York City, U.S.A.

Letter from Thomas Petingale to his sister

Washington, 3 Oct. 1875

MY DEAR SISTER,

I think I told you in my last letter that it was my intention to write to you again soon, when I should direct you as to the time and manner of sending the principal belonging to my Sam. He will be of age on the 18 of next Novr. and if you sell out his share, or interest, in the Consols, say about the 1st of that month, he can receive the proceeds by the time he is entitled to them. Now as to the manner of remitting, I would suggest, as the safest way, your procuring, *as usual*, a 'Letter of Credit' to the 'Agency of the Bank of British North America in New York.' The letter of Credit should be in his own name, Samuel Kimball Petingale. It will be my province to return a receipt for the money to you as soon as possible, signed by my son & properly witnessed.

Frances & Sam are still in Cleveland, but I expect them here about the 15th of the present month.

I have had no word from Henry for months, & I am at a loss to account for his reticence. It is to be hoped that his Joseph will make a good use of the money he so easily came in possession of. But of course my greatest concern is for my Sam, for he is entirely without experience in business matters, and I have seen so many, who really understood the world's ways pretty well, fail to succeed, and even unable to make a living. Turn your eyes to London and you will there see thousands of young, middle aged & old men, groaning under such a weight of despair that their very lives are a curse to them, & very much of this misery is the product of unwariness, heedlessness, & want of self-denial.

Fanny's will was both unjust & injudicious, but she made it under the belief that it was the very opposite. It was made without consideration & certainly not in accordance with the duty she owed her living *sisters & brothers*, or I should have said of the latter, the *unfortunates*; and if I am allowed to say more, would add, that her will was far from being in accordance with what my father told me when he called me into his study. His words to me then were, your sisters will have something to leave should any of them die before you, alluding I presume to his sons generally.

The law of the State of New York is this, when a man's wife dies (if intestate) her property goes to the children, if there be any & not to the husband, unless willed to him. If a husband dies, one-third of his property goes to his wife & the remainder is divided among the children, i.e. provided he died without a will. He cannot in any event deprive his wife of her right to one-third of his property.

The duty a brother owes to his sisters is very well understood, and it is the same that sisters owe to their brothers. Now was the will alluded to above consistent with such understanding? Will such a will produce the fruits expected of it? No, I answer most assuredly, no. Already it has had the effect of causing trouble – 1st by putting children above their parents; 2nd by raising questions between man & wife; and 3rd by making the head of the family the one of the least importance in it. Results not yet developed. 4th, but I have said enough, time probably will tell more. With kindest love to all, remain, your affectionate brother,

THOMAS PETINGALE. . . .

P.S. This being Sunday and the day being so very fine, I will not forgo the opportunity to visit the Merrills. They live somewhat over a mile from me. They were all well when I saw them last & that was only a day or two ago.*

Letter from Henry Petingale to his sister, Eliza

Clifton, Passaic Co., NJ, 14 July 1876

MY DEAR SISTER ELIZA,

Please to receive my sincere thanks for the twelve pounds you have lent me. I received it very opportunely, & it was of great service to me. I will try to return it as soon as possible. I have enclosed a letter to you from Florence who wishes you would let her have a portion of her coming legacy, for purposes she has explained. If you think it best to let her have about £100 I think it would be advantageous to her. . . . [Weather] The 4th of July has passed, with an unusual degree of festivity, as it was the Centenial celebration in America. Business of every disscription is as dull as it has been for the last two or three years. We live in hope things may take a turn for the better soon. We are all enjoying good health here, & send our united love to you all. . . . [Direct letters to Clifton] Your very affectionate brother,

HENRY PETINGALE

Letters from Thomas Petingale to his sister, Eliza

Washington D.C., 19 August 1877

MY DEAR SISTER,

In due course your favour of the 1st came to hand. The sight of your letter proved both a welcome and a surprise, for the interval between your former & present note was entirely too great, and was the cause of considerable disquietude. I am confident that I wrote twice to you since

---

* Thomas Petingale's daughter Eliza, by his first marriage, married Henry Stephen Merrill of Boston, Assistant Chief of the Division, Revenue Cutter Service, Treasury Department.

you sent me Sam'l interest & am also very sure that I received no response to either of my letters. But I am happy at hearing from you again & to be assured of your & Bessie's good health, and it affords me pleasure in being able to report favourably of my family's condition. I hear from the Merrills' quite frequently. They are enjoying the seaside at present but intend returning to this about the 1st *proxo*, when Mr M's leave of absence expires. I am all alone now; Frances is in Cleveland at her sister's* & Sam is in Missouri in the government employ. He likes his position very much & is strong & hearty. I spent 3 weeks of my furlough at Mrs Kimball's very pleasantly. Here I met with Mr Sheridan, Mrs S. & their two beautiful children. Mr S. is the son of the M.P. returned from Dudley, England.† I like Harry quite well, notwithstanding his peculiarities, which for the most part, I guess, are inherited. He is a fine looking fellow, & is as highly accomplished as most of the young men of his particular sphere. The Kimball family consists as follows: Mrs Kimball, widow, & mother of Clara (Mrs Sheridan), Saml Kimball & Jessie Kimball. Saml K. is married but Jessie is not, being only about 15 years old. Miss J. will in all probability be the richest in the family, for her property is accumulating all the time & cannot be touched until she is of age. Her interest in her Father's estate cannot be short of $100,000 or £20,000. Her interest in her brother Fred's estate (who was drowned some years ago) is the third of £20,000 *besides accruing* interest. So Miss J., if she lives, will be worth on her arriving at age not less than £50,000. They all have means. Mr Sheridan, I understand, has considerable expectations in the future. Mrs K. is passionately fond of articles of *virtu* & when in London expended a large amount towards the acquisition of such gems as suited her fancy. She seems to take pleasure in outvieing her neighbours (though many of them are much richer than herself). Well in this she has succeeded pretty well. She has a bed stead (I slept upon it all the time I was at her house) which, she says, formerly belonged to Prince Napoleon. It is a huge *affair* & carved all over, it cost her a pretty penny. I was told, but not by Mrs K., that it was the bridal bed stead of Master Louis Napoleon & Eugenie, but I experienced nothing uncommon when lying upon it. I know that I got many a sound nap, notwithstanding the romance which hovered about this peculiar piece of furniture.

But I must not waste time in detailing matters. Suffice it then to say that Mrs K. has some very rich things which money has purchased &

---

* Thomas Petingale's wife was the sister of Sarah Stage, widow of Samuel Kimball, of Euclid Avenue, Cleveland.

† Mrs Kimball's eldest daughter married the son of Henry Brinsley Sheridan, barrister, JP and Liberal MP from Dudley from 1857 to 1877.

which any one else could have, who had the cash & the disposition to obtain them.

You ask me about Henry. I have not heard from him for over a year, and I do not know his address. His Joe, or some of the family, must be able to tell where he is. I am not in correspondence with any of them, and my opinion must change very much before I feel that my attentions are due in that direction. I have heard of Joe, but what is the use of talking about him. I am in no need of cosmetics at present.* I have no very good opinion of a boy who talks against his father, let his faults be what they may. Henry is stubborn & is not likely to yield unless convinced that he alone is in error. I know his disposition well, yet better perhaps, than I know my own. I do not know how he is situated in any respect; but if I knew him to be in actual want, he is welcome to share my loaf. I do not know whether he is living with his family or not. . . . [Comments on people mentioned in sister's letter]. . . .

I shall look for Frances' return about the middle of Oct. when our warm weather will be quite over. You no doubt would think 650 miles quite a distance to travel & only to make a visit, but we think nothing of it. Cleveland is situated on the southern shore of Lake Erie, and is about 650 miles from Washington. Its population is about 150,000. Euclid Avenue is one of the most beautiful streets in this country. For four miles at least, on both sides, are 'semi-palatial' structures, the residences of men of wealth. My sister-in-law's house is on this Avenue, the grounds about which are kept in perfect order, but they are not ours. Will Penry not the possessor. A few years hence it will be all the same. It may be for our good that we are poor. . . . [About sister] Your affectionate brother,

THOMAS PETINGALE

Washington, 29 Oct. 1877

DEAR SISTER,

I wrote to you only a few days ago, but since then I have seen Joseph and have obtained from him (what he believes to be) his father's address. It is Clifton, New Jersey. I presume you have directed letters to him there. Joe took me entirely by surprise. He called at the office to see me, but I could not for the life of me tell who he was, until he made himself known to me, for he had changed so during the space of 15 to 16 years, and I had not seen him for that length of time. He stayed here only a

* Joseph Lawson Petingale, eldest surviving child of Henry Petingale, set up in business as a chemist in New York City in the 1870s and travelled in France and England for a New York drug firm after his own enterprise failed. After ten years in the drug business, he settled permanently in England, where he became a journalist.

day, for business in New York called him thither without delay. There seems to be an entire alienation of feeling between H. & his family, if I may judge from Master J's remarks. As there is generally wrong on both sides, I will not venture to decide, even in my own mind, as to where the blame attaches. I shall write to Henry likely today, and if my letter is as available as I should like it to be, it will stir him up & cause him to feel that he has at least one friend in this country who is willing to aid him, provided that he himself will put his shoulder to wheel.

An event. I have *this very moment* received a newspaper from my son, in which I discover a notice of his marriage. It reads:

> At Kansas City, Mo. Thursday Evening Oct. 18 Mr S.K.Petingale
> to Miss Jennie Ashdown.

This is all the information I have received at present concerning Master Sam's matrimonial alliance, but expect more soon.

With kindest love to you all, in which Frances joins, remain your affectionate brother,

THOS. PETINGALE. . . .

P.S. If you are in correspondence Mrs Shipp pray remember me to her. I cannot forget Fanny, nor any of my friends, nor the land of my birth. Do write soon.

Washington, 7 March 1879

MY DEAR SISTERS, . . . [Henry and his family]

My Sam's wife is staying with us. Sam is at present in Cleveland at his Aunts. His poor health obliged him to give up his situation which was yielding him $1000 or £200 per annum. His Aunt (Mrs Kimball) invests his money for him. I would not have any thing to do with it, for had I met with losses I should ever regret it. His mother did not approve of his getting married. We knew nothing of even his intention to marry until it was consumated. The person he selected was entirely unknown to any of us. F. says it could not have happened, had he not had some money & in this I fully concur, & would add, that the leaving to inexperienced children money more frequently injures than benefits them, beside taking it from those to whom it naturally belongs. . . . [Health. Mrs Kimball]

I hardly know what more to say to you & my desk is full of work and that must be attended to. . . . [Please write] Your affectionate brother,

THOS. PETINGALE. . . . [Greetings]

Washington D.C., 9 March 1883

MY DEAR SISTER,

It is but a few days ago that I wrote to you, the note was necessarily short owing to my limited time. I have now not much to spare but will use that little in saying a few words to you. Joe P. was here last week & stayed with us a day or two. His intention (he says) is to start for England tomorrow (10th *inst*.) His particular purpose for going there is not known to me, but I presume he sees something in that distance that allures him thither. Then again he has given up his business in New York, it proving unprofitable, (very, I should say). I do not feel inclined to say more concerning J. Nor would it edify you to hear more of him at this time.

Henry remains silent, but I hear from J. that he does not call upon his family though in the same city with them. Nothing now can bring them together, for after so many years' alienation it would seem unnatural that anything short of mutual concessions could avail any thing towards a reconciliation. Indeed I am sorry that such a condition as theirs exists. . . . [Sister's health]

Now as regards myself & family I have only to say that we are only just so – that is, betwixt and between health & no health – a kind of fluctuating condition, & very much like the weather & very much influenced by it. Sam is far from being strong. He has not yet regained his strength since his last sickness. He is with me at present. Frances says she begins to feel old. Still she continues to grow fat. She only weighs about 210 lbs. Her sight is no better than it was. I am doing all I can for them, & am grateful to God that I am allowed the strength & *will* to successfully confront obstacles of no ordinary nature. . . . [Greetings]

THOS. PETINGALE. . . . [Daughter's family]

Washington D.C., 18 May 1883

MY DEAR SISTER,

Now the question is, what shall I say to you? Well then, I shall presume that you have received my last two notes and also that you found them lacking in interest as no doubt you will find this. I think I told you of my hearing from Joe Petingale. He promised to write me again but I cannot say that I am disappointed at his not doing so. Indeed I hope he may find something to do that will remunerate him better than his former business, when ended in a failure. By experience he may learn more wisdom &c. Joe is smart enough.

The Merrills are getting along comfortably. They have 4 children, 2 girls & 2 boys, & they are nice children if *grand-pa says it*. Mr M. is a native of Boston, Massachusetts, & is considered by his friends to be a very good man. Indeed I join happily in the opinion. They own their own house & every thing about them bespeaks comfort & happiness. Nor is the money squandered that sister Fanny left them; neither has

Sam fooled his portion away. Kind act of Fanny's but hardly a wise one. It was anomalous. No American aunt would do the like, but enough of that.

I am still in the Treasury. It is now nearly 21 years since I commenced there. My duties are onerous, but I keep going in spite of consequences to my health.

How are you all? Do write soon. All unite with me in kindest love to you all. Remain affectionately your brother,

THOS. PETINGALE. . . . [Greetings]

Quine Series 1861–1885

Radcliffe Quine was born on the Isle of Man in 1826. His father, Thomas Quine, was a schoolmaster in the town of Peel, on the western side of the island. Radcliffe was the third son in a family of six children, which included five boys. In 1841, when he was fourteen, his elder brother William was serving an apprenticeship as a shoemaker, and the eldest son in the family, John Quine, to whom many of these letters were written, was working as a carpenter.[1] Radcliffe Quine emigrated in 1844 at the age of eighteen.

Since this series of letters begins in 1861, we have few clues as to the precise circumstances of his emigration. At the time of his departure for America, he expected ultimately to inherit some property. The population of the island was increasing during the forties, at about the same rate as that of the whole of England. Economic difficulties were appearing for the lead and silver miners, who combined mining with crofting in the upland areas of the island, but the Quines were not among these people.[2] Nor did he emigrate alone, after a rift with his family. He went out with relatives in the manner typical of farming emigrants. Yet the Quine family was not characterized by the family solidarity noted among our immigrants who went into agriculture. Radcliffe felt that he had been neglected as a child and was defensive about his own treatment of his parents. The scattering of the family through emigration, and the struggle over its small property, completed the disruption of good relations between brothers and sister.

The letters show Quine to have been a highly materialistic individual, concerned almost exclusively with money matters and economic prospects. Family, religion, place of birth, politics meant little to him. This concentration upon economic aims he shared with other migrants who left Britain from the 1840s onwards. If these letters be any guide, the purely economic motives sharpened with time among all classes of migrants. They were also more pronounced among emigrants from slowly growing regions than among those from areas of abundant opportunity.

We know little about Quine's life during his first ten years in America.

In 1854, severing his connections with the relatives with whom he had emigrated, he left for California alone. It is possible that his wife, who was the sister of one of the men in the party with whom he emigrated, had died; when he left for California this man took over the care of Quine's son. From that point on, Radcliffe Quine lived a relatively Bohemian life interspersed with periods of stability.

For fifteen years he kept up a considerable geographical mobility. After four years in San Francisco, he joined the first gold rush to British Columbia in the spring and summer of 1858, when between twenty-five and thirty thousand men set off from San Francisco for the newly discovered gold in the Fraser River Valley. For ten years Quine lived on Vancouver Island, but almost certainly made trips to the Fraser River Valley as well as to the Cariboo mines, even farther north into the transportless interior, after the rush to them began in 1861. Then he went off to South America and returned, about 1868 or 1869, to Seattle, Washington, where we find him at the time of the 1870 census, living in a boarding house with immigrants from Maine, Pennsylvania, Hungary and New York. At that time there were only thirty-five Englishmen in Seattle. His last days were spent in a hospital in Seattle as a charity patient.

Like other industrial workers, Quine did keep returning to his basic trade of ship's carpenter, to which he may have had some introduction in Peel as a very young man. He worked as a ship's joiner in San Francisco and decided to seek employment in Seattle, on the Puget Sound, because of its infant shipbuilding industry. During his years on Vancouver Island he not only built and operated at least one lighter boat for himself but also worked for a steamship company. In between he tried gold mining, considered farming, and invested most of his earnings in gold-mining claims which never paid off. In 1870, he had only $100 worth of personal property.

Incorporated in 1869, Seattle was a very small town of eleven hundred inhabitants in 1870. During the seventies, its population more than trebled. Quine arrived just about the time that shipbuilding was begun in this town. One shipyard was moved from Port Ludlow to Seattle in 1869, and another was established in 1870. During the seventies, several small shipbuilding concerns began and failed in the town, and by 1882, there were still just three shipyards in the city. All of these were small enterprises building wooden vessels, including steamboats.[3] In spite of the fact that his skills were appropriate for this new industry, its early insecurity afforded Quine very intermittent employment, especially during the depression of the seventies. By the time revival was under way in the eighties, when Seattle's population rocketed to nearly forty-three thousand and the building of iron ships was begun, Radcliffe

Quine was unable to profit from the city's growth, having been stricken in 1881 with epilepsy which left him virtually an invalid.

The Quine letters are in the Manx Museum. They were presented to it by Betty Qualtrough of Douglas, Isle of Man, who has graciously consented to their publication. Photostats are in the British Library of Economic and Political Science.

Letters from Radcliffe Quine to his family in the Isle of Man

Victoria, Vancouver Island, 22 April 1861

DEARE BROTHER AND SISTER,

I take this opertunity of adressing you for the first time hoping that those few lines will find you and your famely in good health, as my health is very good, thank God. When I look back to the date of my leaving my native home, I feel the most poignant sensations of shame and regret. I will not aggravate the impropriety of my omission by amusing you with childish excuses of illness and buisiness, but confess that an unaccountable negligence and foolish habit of procrastination have made me so inattentive. I throw my self on your kindness, to excuse my fault.

I came on this side of Continant in the sumer of 1854, to Callifornia, and stayed in this state untill the sumer of 1858 when the gold excitement broke out in British Callidonia, now British Collumbia. At that time the country was a perfect wilderness onely a few forts for the protection of the fur traders [from] the saveges. There wass great excitement at that time as there wass about fifteen thousand able-bodied men in the Collony less than three months, but the greates part got disapointed and left for a freer and beter government. At that time this terietory wass held by a chartered company, styled the Hudson Bay Company, for the last age or two, to trade with the Indians for their furs and oils.

This same company wass very arbitrry. The impost very hevey taxes on the miners. The consequences was that miners returned to Callifornia as fast as the left, but the home government, hereing of there doings, tooke the charter from them 1859 and threw the country open for settlement.*

* Vancouver Island was ceded to the Hudson Bay Company in 1849. British Columbia was still unorganized territory with no government, towns or roads. The authority of the Hudson Bay Company on the mainland extended only to the fur trade, but since the same individual, James Douglas, was both governor of the Island and the chief factor of the Hudson Bay Company, when the Fraser River gold rush began in the spring of 1858, Douglas tried to preserve for the Hudson Bay Company all the trade arising out of the gold rush on the Fraser River. In August, 1858, the Colonial Office appointed Douglas Governor of British Columbia (as well as Vancouver Island) but forced him to sever his connection with the Hudson Bay Company.

Consequently the country is improving with imegration from the states of Washington and Oregon and Callifornia and the Canidas, but very few from Europe. The climate on the Island is very mild, both in sumer and winter, rather milder in both seasons than the Isle of Man. This Island of Vancouvers is about 250 miles long by 60 wide. It is very rich with coals and I have found gold in several of the rivers, but not to pay wages. The soil is very good in parts and plenty of all kinds of timber. This island and several small islands adjacent composes the Victoria Colene. British Columbia is the main continent that composes a second colleneny in this last named. The gold mines are which there is a greate number of men gon this season to the Carriboo digings, but I tell you it it a harde roade to travel.* You have got to carey your o[w]n blackets and food for three hundred miles, and take the soft side of the roade for your lodgings, and at daylight get up and shake the dust of your blackets and cook your o[w]n food for the day, and take the roade again. When you get in the mines you have got to pay 4s and 5 shillings per pound for every thing you eate, as it has to be carried with mules and horses, on there backs, with a pack sadle. They carey generaly 300 lb to the animel. The one man drives 25 to 50 animels, traviel 15 to 20 miles pr day.

Rates of wages: ship carpenters, 5 dollars or one pound pr day; house joiners, 16s 8d pr day; blacksmith, do; brick layers and masons, 5 dollars or one pound pr day; labouring men, 3 dollars pr day or 12s 6d pr day; men on farms, 25 to 30 dollars per month, £5 to £6 pr month; hired girls, 15 to 20 dollars pr month, £3 to £4 pr month. In this part of the world men and women do not hire out more then month at a time, as that is long enough to find out a good master or mistress. We have got no fairs on the continant for men and women to go and stand like I have seen slaves in the southern states of America for the highest bider as I have seen your fair sex stand on Atholl Street, Peel, on Saint Patricks Day, 17 of March. We have terietory enough here for half the population of Europe, and our land sistem is very good. Land can be obtained at 4s 2d pr acre, and land that is not surveyed can be preempted. It is onley 18 miles across the Gulph of Georgia to our sister colleny, British Collumbia, and in the colleney the laws are the same, as there is onely one govener, the both colleneys. I shall have to conclude, as I shall give you a more detailed account when I here from you. I have not herd from eney of my brothers since I came this side, excepting Frederick, that he was in the Sandwich Island, 1858, aboard of a whaler. I understand my sister is married in Ràmsey but I do not know the name. Please

* The major gold rush to the Cariboo got under way in 1861. The only means of access to this region was by steamboat on the Fraser River as far as Yale. After this point supplies had to be carried overland.

give my compliments to them all and all inquireing friends. So no more at preasent from your brother,

RADCLIFFE QUINE

Seattle, Washington territory, 3 Oct. 1876
DEARE BROTHER AND SISTER,

I take this opertunity of writing a few lines unto you, hoping the same will find you and famely in the best of health as I am well. I received your letter dated September the fourth. I went wright to work and got a lawyer and got up my power of atorney and got it signed before a notary public and then had to send it to the capital of the teritory to get it indorsed by the secritory of the teritory. It was made out on September 28 and sent to the govenor on the 30 and it gos from there to one thousand miles south to the British Consul in San Francisco, Callifornia, and from there direct to the Isle of Man. So you will get my power of atorney about the same time you will recive this letter, and I want you to act for me the same as you would for your self; and what expence you will be put to, deduct out of the principal, as I do not want but what honerabaley belongs to me. Send money by draft and ether of the following named banks in registred letter.

Bank of British North America, Victoria, British Columbia; Bank of British Columbia of Victoria, British Columbia, aghents, Liverpool Bank of Liverpool.

Brother John, I send by this mail too papers and strange you did not get the paper I sent you. Mr Quine, I am not maried. Your brother,

RADCLIFFE QUINE

Seattle, Washington, 22 March 1878
DEARE BROTHER JOHN AND SISTER, . . . [Usual salutation]

Brother John, it is thirty-four years since I bid you farewell, on Douglas Peire and have been on the travle westward since. I wass ten years on the Atlantic side, and left in fifty-four for Callifornia, and staid four years. In fifty eight gould was discouvred in British Collumbia, a thousand miles north, witch caust greate excitement in Callifornia. Every availble steemship wass put on the route and crouded with pasenger. I tooke gould fevour and must go with the ballance of fools, and left a good situaison, working for a large steem navigation company, wages 25 shilling of your money pr day. Well, I got to Victoria, Van couver Island, and in three months there where 25 thousand men landed, all for the gould digins, and not one women in croud, provision four shillings pr lb for everything you eate and [you cook?] your [own] or starve. Shortly after geting here bad news came from digins, and the

Indians or saviges declared war aginst the whites, but we sone put an end to it, but meney hundred lives lost. So I found it would be of no youse to go to gould diging and nothing to do here no meterials for building and men returning from the gould digins in disgust and leaving for Yankey land. I made up my mind to make the best of it. I like the country for its butifull clymate. The Hudson Bay Company had a large forte here, trading with the savages for the furrs of wild animals. The had many servants to trade with the Indians. I made up my mind that I should see some of the cuntry for farming. I hired one of the servants at a guiney pr day and horse and went out 10 miles and found a butifull farming country, govemant prise, one pound per acre. When I got back to land office to take up too hundred acres and pay for it, the officials wood question you about the land. If it wass good they would make it out entred in sume stranger name, and it would be a lie. At times those Hudson Bay people were so pregudise that the took us all for Yankys. So I got no land.

I wass bound to go in some speculation and I see that ships would not come in harbour upon account of not being surveyed. The would anchor of the heads and all fright had to be lightered into harbour at one pound per time. So I went to work and built me a sixty toon lighter. Shee paid well for 10 days, 100 pounds per day off. After that, bankruptcy. So I went carpenter on steemboat at 20 pounds pr month, runing betwen the too collenys, Vancouvers Island and its independsy and British Collumbya, too seprate collenys in them days, with British Govner in each, wich lasted five years. Then the collenys here united under one represeniteve government, Capital, Victoria, Vancouvers Island. It hass two harbours, one for shiping of five hundred tons, the lower harbour for the wholle British Navy. It is on the Straits of Defence, forty miles from the Paccific Ocean, the rendesvew of the Paccific squadron. Size of island, three hundred long by 60 in weth. There is an archaplage of islands reaching cross to main continent dividing the straits from the Gulf of Georgy. This island has got all the resourse and British Collumby to make an independent nation, gould and silver, copper, iron, [lumber?] coals in eney quanty, and the finest timber in the world. Vesials loding for Suth America, Austrila, China, Japan, Sandwich Islands, and most of the Paccific Islands and loading spars for Greate Britan and France. As a farming country it is good, and for stock raising it cant be beate. Beef cattle run the winter in the valleys and come out in spring fat, living all winter on the wild bunch grasses. For fish there is no part of world can come up to it, for salman, haleybut, hering, codfish and other kinds too numerouse to mention. In the salmon season on the grate rivers of British Columbia the take them out by the tons. I have seen the netts so full the could not hall them ashore. The would let them lay until the tide reced. For cureing those fish the have large canery establishments employing from one hundred to three hundred in each. They parsearve the fish in quart cans and [careses?] and ships them to England, Austrila, South America, and the United States. It take considerable to go in this opration. It is only a new opration for the past two years, but capilist is going into very heavy this season.

John, I lived in British Collumby ten years. Part of the time I dun very well and part misrable. Invested too much in gould mining and got broke and meney hundreds like myselfe but still there is every season three thousand men working in the three gould destricts. Every season the are taking out gould, sence 62 up to the preasent, eight million sterling.* There is a grate rush to the mines just now from Callifornia upon account of quarts [quartz] rich in gould. John, I have wrote several letters the past six years to my sister in Ramsey but no aswer. There must be some thing wrong. John, give my respects [to] sister and brothers. So no more at preasant.

RADCLIFFE QUINE

Seattle, [2 June 1878?]

MY DEAR BROTHER AND SISTER, . . . [Letter received]

I find by your letter that you dout me as your brother, but you rest asured it is the original Radcliffe Quine, born 1826, June the 28, imegrated with brother William and Phillip Garrett and Mr John Quine [and] wife 1844, and lived on the Atlantick side of this contnant untill 1854; received my sister at the residence of my Aunt Crane, Geneava, New York, on my way to Callifornia 1854; worked four years in Callifornia at ship joinering and left the country for British Columbia and worked ten years in the both collenys; left British possesions 1868 for the United States teritory and South America and located here on Puget Sound on account of the ship building, but very little dune in shipbuilding the past three yeares. The principal buissines is coals, lumber and spars for the Europin and South American and Austrilian, Sandwich Islands and Callifornia. The wheat crope of Callifornia and the state of Oregon and this teritory will be very hevy this yeare. All crops looks well. Buissines of all kinds dull, waiting for English & Rusians to fight.

Brother, I understand by your letter referring to my counduct in British Columbia of me geting shoot at a gambling table that I have been a disperado. Is all folley as I have held the hiest stations as a mechanic and for morality in the colleny after a residence of ten years

---

* The Cariboo Road was opened in 1864, but from 1865 onwards the output of gold in British Columbia diminished rapidly and only a minority of the miners remained as settlers.

16

and calculate to spend the remainder of my days. I see by your letter that I am counted as a ded man, not herd of me in 20 years or my [friends]. If you had eney corespondanc with Uncle Phillip Crane, you could have herd of me 1865. I have too letters in my posesion from my sister and severial from Phillip Garrett, my wifes brother. You say in your letter of my brother William rasing my son. My boy was brought up from the agĕ of four years by Mr Phillip Garrett in Canida and I know that he was brought up better then is father. Let me know if my Uncle Thomas McDogle is living.

Brother, I mane buissines. When I left home in 1844 I read my father will which left the land occupied by my uncle Robert Quine to your brother Radcliffe. Likewise you informed me the knight of my laving the country. I want information what belong to me as I am going to give the powr of aturney to a young man from Ramsey that is going home in three months. As for my brother Francis takin out papers of adminis-trator. There is no legality about it. Brother John, I do not want to put you to [unnecessary] truble, but you have had a good time in the youse of the money. I sent a letter to Francis the 25 of March, Douglass, but no answer. . . . [Write]

RADCLIFFE QUINE

Seattle, 12 August 1878

DEAR BROTHER AND SISTER, . . . [Letter received]

I am very much surprised at that Court Document of administration over a suposition. It is nothing but perjeury to get that document. He must have positive proof of my demise wich he had not a shade of, but I see that it wass by your free will and concent he took the document out in 1870 and have not herd of his brother for ten years. Consequently I am a dead man with out the least shadow of proof, and I am very much suprised that you, in particular, would be led by the ninth part of a man that never had a principle. He wass a regular drain on my pocket in the west, all the time borowing money and never pay. The consequence was I had to up on him. In 1860 I sent a letter to my Uncle Thomas, Mr Doyle, to be sent to my sister in Ramsey and I new she was maried and did not [know] the name, and in that letter I requested her to see you and get my legusay sent to me in Victoria. The answer was that you would not pay one farthing unless I should come home after it. I have got too let-ters in my posesion from my sister and I have letters from my uncle Phillip Crane up to 1865. His son in law was in Victoria and worked for me on a new steam boat in 1860 and in my company, 1865, but to the best of my knoledge he went to Corribo mines. I have not herd of [him] since. My brother was in San Francisco 1860 and calculated to come to

Victoria to se me but, like all tars, got drunk and kidnapt and sent on board of a cliper ship to China. That is the last I have herd of my unfortunate brother Frederick. In 1862 a young man the name of Armstrong, a taner & courier [tanner and currier] by trade, from the Island direct, brought me out letter from my half sister, Ann, but the [Magistrate?] requesting me to give my legasay to her; but I sent no answer. 1859 on Frasher River I met James Morison, son of John Morison, Peel, gould mining. In 1863 I met a son of Robert Gracy of Peel gould mining and severial others from the North Part of the Island. There is three Manx men on the sound and too Manx women. My friend, William Gouldsmith, calculated to get of for the Island this month, but he cannot for some cause unknown to me. It will make little difriance to me. Brother John, I do not see that the Power of Atturney from me would be of eney servis to you in colection that money, as I have nothing to do with Francis. You are the responsble and have giving bonds to the trustes to carrey the articles out in faithful maner . . . Brother, you come very hard on me regaurd writing to my parents, and you wish I certainely did promise and send you a piece of sugar maple, but that timber was so comon and inconvenian to ship that I was satisfied you would not receive it. I allwes wrote to my parents untill Francis came out, when he took the corespondance. I do not understand the cause of my unfurtunate brother Frederick being blackbauld from his inheritance, as he was to come home when the trustys were apointed to my Fathers will. I send you a British Collumbia paper by this mail and I should be hapy to receive a Manx paper. . . .

Your Brother

RADCLIFFE QUINE

[Letter of 3 July 1879 about inheritance omitted]

Seattle, 1 Dec. 1879

MY DEARE BROTHER JOHN QUINE, . . . [Salutations]

I think there is something very misterious in your actions that you could not find time to write to me but once in thirteen months on such an important case. I wrote to you last July but no return. As I consider you have had ample time to bring this suit to an end if you went legmatly to work. I consider this case the moost disgrasefull pergeured swindling case that evere was recourded in my native land. Now, Mr Quine, you will be carefull how you act in the case, as it is of as much concern to you as it is to me. You do not want to pay this money twise as my money lays on the estate. You are the responsible party. So I hope you will collect the same, as you will have but litle trubile if you go to work wright about it. You have my papers and that is your only salvation, to collect, because you had no cause to devide my money . . . You stated in your letter of July the 3rd, 1878, that Phillip Garret and Mrs Quine were on the Isle of Man about the time you and Francis took out the dead mans letter of administration, but I have proof to the contrary. . . . [Cites letters] Mr Quine, that money you promised to send to me fifteen months ago it apeairs to be glued to your fingers. On receipt of this letter, sir, please write. I am respectfully your brother,

RADCLIFFE QUINE

You will find a paper in this mail.

Seattle, 29 Sept. 1881

MY DEARE FRANCIS AND MARIA QUINE, . . . [Letter received]

I have recived a letter from John Quine after he got my power of attorney and the second letter he promised me what money he had and what he cud raise, to send it along. I never got a sent. John Quine tould me that your ware paid 189£ to you and 38£ to John Quine, that where in 1870. At foure per cent it would amount to a consdrable sum of money. You will send me a copi of fathers will if you please. I have got four letters from Frederick Quine, and he is well in [New Zealand?], Canturbury, Port Levey. My Brother, it would take me 400$ to pay my pasage toward and back and I canot se the youse in me coming home if I could get my money I shoud of heme. But John Quine has done verey wroung towards me and I expected sumthing will be wroung.

Carpenters and joiners his not worth [their Pain?] in this country, no work from South America to the Strait of Alaskia. You will probaly get a week work in a mounth. Carpnters wages is three dollars pr dy. Along shoremen get twoo and half dollars pr day. There is about twenty mills, all Rusian, in the lumber buisines. Ships from all parts come heare. There is foure coale mines on the sound. The greates [bronister?] is in Seatle. Lots of ships com heare, load coale and other ship lumbear. We have a populatin of 5,000, church six, schoul house six, & a great collage for all your men.* I remain your brother

RADCLIFFE QUINE

Seattle, 26 March 1882

DEAR BROTHER FRANCIS QUINE AND WIFE,

I tak this opertunity of writing a few lines unto you, hoping this same

---

* Asa Mercer's one-man college for young men was founded in Seattle in the early 1860s when the town had not much more than two hundred inhabitants. The first school building was completed in the summer of 1870, and by 1880, when Seattle had five public schools and three private schools, her citizens boasted that she was the 'City of Schools'. The first church, a Methodist Episcopal one, was built in 1855, and by 1880 Seattle also had Methodist, Presbyterian, Roman Catholic, Episcopal and Baptist churches.

will find you in good health as I have bene miserable. I take the pisilpeas
[epilepsy] in the knight on the third of March, 1881, and I could not say
a centang with my toung for over a month, but still I have comoncence.
My arms is shaking . . . and my two hands is left gust three fingers. The
others are turned on my hand. When I send you my last letter in the
faule I thought I was well. But I have been trubled with the rumatisiam
for five months. There is every thing coming on me. I have lost 6000 in
eight year in gould mining claims.

Francis Quine, I take this to be a loung [four?] months for you to
send my fathers copy of his will to me. You wil please [send] it to me as
sone as posible. I rote you a letter in the fowle or winter and likwise to
John Quine in regards to my money, but have got no answer. Please to
let me know what is the truble of me in not keting any money . . . I am
rispicfuly your brother

RADCLIFFE QUINE. . . .

Seattle, 1 July [1882?]

DEARE BROTHER FRANCIS AND MARIA QUINE,

I tak this opertunity to writing untoo you hoping you are well. My
health is miserable. I am nott maried, lives in a bording house at five
dollars pr week. I sent to you too ket information in regaurds too the
High Balliff in Duglas, but you wil not wright. I sent a letter four week
ago to High Balife in Duglas to let him know what I have surfade
[suffered] and I expect too heare from him in three weeks. John Quine
have not wrote to me for three years and sixe months. I just got answere
when he got my power of aturney. I have rote serverial times too him but
no answer. He tould me before the power of aturney was isued that he
woud send me money if I coud get the Bank to do it. The Bank of
Liverpool, England, and the Banke of British Columbia or Bank of
British North Ame[ric]a in British Columbia, Victoria. Give me the
check in British Columbia, Victoria, and I shal get my money . . . [Repe-
tition] I have got a letter from the Vice Consul of San Francisco to let
me know if I coud send letter to the High Bailife in Douglas and likewise
I have sent it.

I have recived your letter and paper on the 21 of June and I rote to
John Quine on the 25 of June. I see you have got railrods in the Island.
The Canada and Pacifick Railrode have got 6000 Chinese and too
thousand white men in British Collumbia.

Now you send a copy of fathers will if you plase. I shall realey send it
back if it his your demand. I send you a paper.

RADCLIFFE QUINE

Providence Hospital, Seattle, 23 March 1885*

DEAR BROTHER JOHN, WIFE AND FAMILY,

I take this opportunity of writing a few lines to you, and hope it will find you all in good health. I regret to say that I am in a most miserable state of health myself. It is now four years this month, since I was seized with an attack of epilepsy, and for a considerable time did not know whether I was asleep or awake, having also lost the power of speech for some two months. Even at this date I have but partially regained it.

I have been here in this hospital for two years. It belongs to the Roman Catholic Sisters of Charity, of whom there are twelve resident.

Derral Quine has arrived in this country. He is a son of William Quine.

Brother John Quine, you will be pleased to send my money, and I will ever pray, your affectionate brother

(signed) RADCLIFFE QUINE

* This letter was written in another handwriting.

Reid Series 1879–87

These letters describe a serious family crisis in New York City among immigrants from Ipswich in Suffolk. Very little is known about the background of this family. The husband of Mrs Reid's sister, to whom the letters were written, was a stonemason who moved from Ipswich to Harwich about 1861. If her own husband had been an industrial worker, the second of these letters alludes to a change of occupation when the family moved from 56th Street in New York City to Brooklyn to operate a grocery shop. In her letters, Mrs Reid refers to no mutual friends or relatives near them in New York or Brooklyn about whom she can send news to the family in England. The Reids appear to be an isolated family group cut off in a large city from other migrants. Their hopes of upward social mobility are suggested both by the family's move to Brooklyn and the choice of fashionable Harlem by two of the children for their homes after their marriages in the 1880s. After having a family of eight children herself, Mrs Reid is against large families and early marriages.

Photostats of the Reid letters are in the British Library of Economic and Political Science.

Letters from H. Reid to her sister, Sarah Hampstead in Harwich, Essex

423 W 56th Street, New York City, 1 July 1879

MY DEAREST SISTER,

I feel very deeply for you in your great affliction, the more so as I myself have been very near becoming a widow since I last wrote you. May God in His mercy comfort and support you and you know, my dear, that He will if you only trust in Him. Your poor husband is at rest after a great deal of suffering, so you must not murmur as it is for the best for him and you also, as all things work together for good for those who love Him to those who are called according to His purpose.

I am so sorry I did not write you before but I have had so much trouble. I did not want to write till I could send you better news. My husband was so sick with congestion of the brain. I had him taken to hospital. He his home now and able to attend to bussiness. I got sick waiting upon him but am quite well now. As to your leg, my dear, it is better at our time of life for it to discharge than to dry up . . . [Greetings] I am afraid we shall not be able to come this year, but we still hope to come some time or other, so now my dear Sister, I will say goodnight and still remain your loveing sister,

H. REID. . . . [More greetings]

157 South 4th St., Brooklyn, NY [undated]

MY DEAR SISTER,

I have to apologise for my seeming neglect, but I have been in such a muddle and confusion for the last 6 weeks I have had no time for any thing. I am glad to see by your last that you and yours were well. I am happy to say that this leaves us all pretty well. We have removed to Brooklyn where we have taken a store and opened it in the grocery line & hope it will do well, as our children are getting well up and we cannot expect them to remain with us always and we want something to depend upon after they leave us. Give my kind love to Joe and tell him as I owed you both a letter I thought I had better write to you as they both contained very near the same news. I hope he wont feel hurt. I send him a weekly paper every week which I hope he recieved all right. In the bother of moving I believe I missed one week. I recieved my Suffolk paper regularly and I am obliged to him for it. . . . [Greetings] Tell [Ted] I hope he will stick to his pledge of total abstinence as there is nothing like it, no safeguard without it. If the tempting cup is indulged in at all any one is liable to fall a victim at any time. There is no safty in so called temperance. Give my love to Walter and his wife and son. I am sorry he does not take care of himself, for a constitution once lost cannot be regained. I am glad that they are not bringing a large family into the world to impoverish them. . . . [Greetings] Give my kind love to Harry. Tell him he is right to wish to come to America. It is a great country, but to wait a bit as we are in a very unsettled state at pressent. [unfinished]

Brooklyn, 28 March 1882

MY DEAR SISTER, . . . [Letters]

It does not seem as if I should ever have any grandchildren, for my children are in no hurry to get married. I am glad Alice has not married so young. It spoils all their enjoyment and makes old women of them before their time. I hope she likes her place. Give all our loves to her. I am happy to say my health is better than it has been lately and our grocery is getting along slow but I hope sure. Hattie is still working at dress and cloakmaking and making her pound a week. Nellie is stayeing home with me to do chief of the housework. Jamie is still working at decorating. Ralph is a journeman and in busy times makes 3 dollars per day. At pressent he is only making $2\frac{1}{2}$. Charles is earning 5 dollars per week. He is at home just now with a crushed toe, but his wages goes on just the same. Lillie is at home and the two youngest are at school . . . [Greetings] As to Ike's religion, my dear, you are mistaken. The Catholic does not worship the Image but look upon it as the representitive of the Saviour. At the same time I cannot help being surprized at Ikes turning. So now, my dearest Sister, I must say goodbye, and may you be happy in this world and the next is the sincere wish of your loving sister,

HATTIE

5 July 1882

MY DEAR SISTER,

I am in great trouble. My life has been one long series of misfortune ever since I have been a wife. I hid them from you as well as I could, knowing that it would only make you miserable without benefitting me; but now a climax as come and I have left him for ever. I only hope he wont come to England and annoy you. If he does, have nothing to say to him. He has got drunk once or twice a year ever since we came to the country and he called me such horrible names and told the children such disgusting lies about me till I could stand it no longer and I had him arrested and put in prison so many times that he was afraid to strike me any more, but he would threaten to kill me and some of the children so I got the habit of having him locked up as soon as he got drunk.

On 19th of June he began to drink and he pleaded so hard with me to promise that I would not lock him up that I did so, telling him at the same time that if he were violent I would leave the house to prevent him using violence to me, for if he did that I knew the boys would fetch a policemen; and I wished to give him the chance he begged for. I have sent you the newspaper acct. of what happened as being quicker than I could write it; also to let you see the public oppinion as well as ours since this happend. I left the house, taking all the children and furniture except enough for his use. On [blotted] July he sold out all the stock and fixtures for a mere song and left his trunk containing some of his clothing, the rest hanging about the house, and the furniture I left for his use in the house and went off, we heard, to England, but on 3rd he went to Charlie's work and demanded our address which the boy refused to give him. I hope he will not find us, for the house we live in is hired in Jamie's name, so that he cannot come as he could have done if

16*

it were in my name; and I am afraid if he comes he will try some violent measures and if he does the boys wont stand it any longer but will combine together against him. . . . [unfinished]

Letter from Frank Reid to his cousin, Alice Hayward

7 Strykers Lane, New York City, 3 Apr. 1887

DEAR COUSIN,

This is the first time I have ever written to you but with help of God it won't be the last. We are all well and hope you are all the same. I don't know whether she has told you or not but Nellie has just had a baby girl, now nearly two months old. We are spread out pretty well, my father being a steward on a steamship going to Savannah, Ga; Hattie and her husband, living in Harlem where Charlie and his wife have lately moved. Ralph and his wife and Nellie & her husband are living very near me, and Lillie and I are boarding in separate places. Willie has turned out just as Charlie was at his age, being very wild. He lately ran away out West. We dont know just where as he hasnt written, but is at least 1000 miles from New York City. We all pray that he may come back a better boy. I have just turned 16 and have been employed by the firm of Tiffany & Co., jewelers, for the past year and a half, who also have a store in number 5 Argyle Place, London. If you have any of the old letters which mother and father sent you from this country or if anyone else in the family have any, please take the stamps off and send them to me as I am a stamp collector. If you have any old letters of England please [send] me some of them also, but queer as it may seem the stamp of this country, that is of course the old ones, are rarer here than foreign ones, as those of the high denomination were not used much in this country, but were all used [to] carry letters across the ocean, the postage of course being more than in the country. So I trust there are some very good ones on the old letters of mothers. With fond love from and please accept the same from your loving cousin,

FRANK W. REID

P.S. Please write to me at Tiffany as it is better than the boarding house.

Notes

Introduction

1 For estimates of net and gross emigration from England and Scotland, see Brinley Thomas, ed., *The Welsh Economy, Studies in Expansion*, Cardiff, 1962, p. 7, and N.H.Carrier and J.R.Jeffery, *External Migration, A Study of the Available Statistics, 1815–1950*, HMSO, 1953, p. 14. For estimates of emigration from other parts of Europe, see Gustav Sundbärg, *Aperçus Statistique Internationaux 11e Année*, Stockholm, 1908, p. 105.

2 United Nations, Department of Social Studies, Population Division, Population Studies, No. 17, *The Determinants and Consequences of Population Trends*, New York, 1953, p. 99. E.C.Snow in Imre Firenczi and Walter Willcox, eds., *International Migrations*, National Bureau of Economic Research, 1931, II, p. 252. Stanley Johnson, *A History of Emigration from the United Kingdom to North America*, 1913, reprinted, London, 1966, p. 39.

3 Charlotte Erickson, 'Who were the Emigrants from England and Scotland in the 1880s?' in David Glass, ed., *Population and Social Change*, to be published shortly.

4 C.E.Carrington's *The British Overseas*, London, 1950, a study of the growth of the British Empire in the nineteenth century, touches upon emigration mainly in considering public discussions of emigration projects in relation to the growth of the Empire. W.A.Carrothers' *Emigration from the British Isles*, London, 1929, focuses upon emigration to what are now the Dominions, as does Helen Cowen in *British Emigration to British North America, 1783–1837*, Toronto, 1928, revised and enlarged edition, 1964. Like Stanley Johnson, these writers told their story primarily from government source materials; projects and assisted immigrants received more attention than did the quiet movement of private individuals and families. Wilbur Shepperson's *British Emigration to North America*, Oxford, 1957, is precisely a study of 'Projects and Opinions in the Early Victorian Period', as its sub-title suggests. The discussions of English emigration in Arthur Redford, *Labour Migration in England, 1800–50*, Manchester, 1926, second edition, 1964, pp. 171–81, and in Marcus Hansen, *The Atlantic Migration*, Cambridge, 1940, pp. 283–4, 264–6, 211, 144, do not look beyond the mid-century. For recent studies which do provide new evidence on the origins of British emigrants, see Philip A.M.Taylor, *Expectations Westward*, Edinburgh, 1966, and Ross Duncan, 'Case Studies in Emigration: Cornwall, Gloucestershire and New South Wales, 1777–86', *Economic History Review*, Second Series, XVI, No. 2, December 1963, pp. 272–89. Apart from these two works most of the comment on the origins of British emigrants in the last half of the nineteenth century has been left to economists in their study of long waves in economic growth: Brinley Thomas, *Migration and Economic Growth*, Cambridge, 1954; A.K.Cairncross, *Home and Foreign*

Investment, 1870–1914, Cambridge, 1953; H.Leak and T.Friday, 'Migration From and To the United Kingdom', *Journal of the Royal Statistical Society*, Part II, 1933, XCVI, pp. 183–239.

5 Frank Thistlethwaite, 'Migration from Europe Overseas in the Nineteenth and Twentieth Centuries', *Rapports du XIème Congrès International des Sciences Historiques,* Stockholm, 1960, pp. 34–57.

6 Oscar Handlin, *The Uprooted*, Boston, 1951. Arnold Schrier, *Ireland and American Emigration, 1850–1900*, Minneapolis, 1958. Donald B.Cole, *Immigrant City*, Chapel Hill, 1963.

7 W.I.Thomas and F.Znaniecki, *The Polish Peasant in Europe and America*, Chicago, 1920, 2 vols. All citations are to the second edition, 1958.

8 Oscar Handlin, 'Immigration in American Life, A Reappraisal', in H.S. Commager, ed., *Immigration and American History*, Minneapolis, 1961.

9 Letter from John Bayes, 18 December 1900, York, England, in Devonshire Association Papers, Exeter Central Library. For letters written by internal migrants within the United States, see Mildred Throne, ed., 'Iowa Farm Letters', *Iowa Journal of History*, LVIII, No. 1, January 1960, pp. 51–86; James W.Patton, ed., 'Letters from North Carolina Emigrants in the Old Northwest, 1830–4', *Mississippi Valley Historical Review*, XLVII, No. 2, September 1960, pp. 263–77.

10 Cf. argument that their backwardness and provincialism gave Russian-Jewish immigrants in the United States 'a basis for withstanding the pressures of an alien world'. Aaron Antonovsky, ed., *The Early Jewish Labor Movement in the US*, Yivo Institute for Jewish Research, New York, 1961, p. 132.

11 Theodore C.Blegen, *Land of Their Choice, The Immigrants Write Home*, St Paul, 1955. Alan Conway, ed., *The Welsh in America*, St Paul, 1961. Walker D.Wyman, ed., *California Emigrant Letters, 1849–52*, New York, 1952. George M.Stephenson, ed., 'Typical "American Letters"', *Yearbook of the Swedish Historical Society of America*, 1921–2, pp. 52–93. Henry S. Lucas, *Dutch Immigrant Memoirs and Related Writings*, Assen, 1955, 2 vols.

12 John Hales, *Settlers*, London, 1950. Wilbur S.Shepperson, *Emigration and Disenchantment*, Norman, Oklahoma, 1965.

13 S.N.Eisenstadt, *The Absorption of Immigrants*, London, 1957, pp. 9, 159, 166.

14 William Savage, *Observations on Emigration to the United States of America*, London, 1819. William Cobbett, *The Emigrants' Guide in Ten Letters addressed to the Taxpayers of England ... including authentic letters ... from English Emigrants*, London, 1829.

15 Lloyd Reynolds, *The British Immigrant, His Social and Economic Adjustment in Canada*, Oxford, 1935, p. 211. Robert H.Billigmeier and Fred A.Picard, *The Old Land and the New, the Journals of Two Swiss Families in America in the 1820's*, Minneapolis, 1965, pp. 12, 36.

16 Jerzy Zubrzycki, *Polish Immigrants in Britain*, The Hague, 1956, p. 165. The term 'accommodation' is used in a sociological, not an economic sense, to indicate a half-way house between assimilation and conflict, the case where the migrant group is tolerated, but the immigrants confine their primary group relations to their own nationality.

17 In 1952 the late Margaret Kiddle of Melbourne University found approximately twenty-eight collections of emigrant letters from Australia in the nineteenth century for the Victoria Public Library. In her report, a copy of which is in the Records Office in Edinburgh, she noted that some of the best collections she had found were records of failures.

18 For studies of skilled British emigrants, see especially Frank Thistlethwaite, 'The Atlantic Migration of the Pottery Industry', *Economic History Review*, Second series, IX, December 1958; R.T.Berthoff, *British Immigrants in Industrial America*, Cambridge, 1953; and C.J.Erickson, *American Industry and the European Immigrant*, Cambridge, 1957, ch.1, *passim*.

19 Brinley Thomas, *Migration and Economic Growth*, tables on pp. 269, 271.

20 Thomas and Znaniecki, *The Polish Peasant*, I, p. 98.

21 Peter Laslett, *The World We have Lost*, London, 1965. G.E.Mingay and J.D. Chambers, *The Agricultural Revolution, 1750–1880*, London, 1966, pp. 21–33.

22 Thomas and Znaniecki, *The Polish Peasant*, I, pp. 173, 191, 199.

23 *Ibid.*, I, p. 132

I THE SAFETY VALVE

1 How Typical are the Letter-Writers?

1 For distribution of immigrants see Charlotte Erickson, 'British Immigrants in the old Northwest', in David Ellis, ed., *The Frontier in Economic Development*, Cornell, 1969, pp. 327–8.

2 Statement based on New York passenger lists, 1830, 1831, 1842, 1849, 1854. Microfilm 237, Reel 14, No. 99; 11, No. 254; 49, Nos. 438, 531; 48, No. 184; 61, No. 321; 71, No. 328; 72, No. 397; 78, No. 237; 79, No. 560; 81, No. 878; 83, Nos. 1264, 1302, 1304; 82, No. 1066; 88, No. 349; 137, No. 347; 144, No. 1032; 145, No. 1275, National Archives.

3 In 1870 one in four of the English and Welsh inhabitants of Wisconsin lived in the lead-mining counties of LaFayette, Grant or Iowa. The English and Welsh-born constituted twenty per cent of the population of Houghton, Keweenaw and Ontonagon counties in Michigan, where mining was important, as compared with only three per cent of the state's population.

4 The story of the Burlend family who emigrated from Barwick-in-Elmet near Leeds to Pike County, Illinois, in 1831, was told by Mrs Burlend to her son, a school-teacher, about 1846 and printed as an emigrant guide under the title 'A True Picture of Emigration of Fourteen Years in the Interior of North America' in London in 1848. This volume was reprinted, with an introduction by Milo M.Quaife, Chicago, 1936. For private letters of Morris Birkbeck and other members of his family, see Gladys Thomson, *A Pioneer Family, the Birkbecks of Illinois*, London, 1953. Birkbeck's own *Letters from Illinois*, Philadelphia, 1818, almost pure propaganda, had very little to say about his farming operations, as distinct from his plans. Other unpublished sources include five letters from Robert Bowles, Hamilton County, Ohio, to his brothers, John and Richard, 1823, Ohio State Historical Society, Columbus, Ohio; the Meatyard Letters, four letters from Robert and Betsy Meatyard, Alton, Illinois, to his mother in Twyford, near Shaftesbury, Dorset, 1836–8, originals in the Dorchester Borough Record Office (NK); three letters from Robert Shedden near Elgin, Kane County, Illinois, to friends in Scotland, 1842–5, copies given to British Library of Economic and Political Science (cited hereafter as LSE) by the British Records Association; Rose Letters from Ohio to Inverness, 1822 and 1830, originals owned by Donald Beaton, Weymouth; four letters from Ann and her son, Alfred Jones, Normandy, St Louis County, Missouri, to C.R.Wace, solicitor, Shropshire,

1864–80, LSE; letter from John Dixon, Earlham, Dallas Co., Iowa, to his parents, 1871, *Bulletin of the British Association for American Studies,* New Series, No. 12, 1966. Somewhat exceptional in that they came from members of a family which farmed near Huddersfield, Yorkshire, are seven letters from Arthur and Fred Pickford, Nora Springs, Iowa, early 1880s, to their family in Yorkshire, Wisconsin State History Society Library. Hugh John Nudham, 9 February 1834, Monroe Township, Adams County, Ohio, to W.Barnes in Stapleton, Kent, photostat in LSE.

5 Copies of the Mearbeck letters made by Robert Leader, editor of the Sheffield *Independent,* in 1901, were deposited in the Sheffield Central Reference Library. Copies of that typescript are at LSE.

6 Letters of Archibald and Peter McKellar, Mt Hero, Vt., 1850; Farmersburgh, Clayton Co., Iowa, 1852–6; Taylors Falls, Minn., 1851–3, McKellar Letters, Minnesota Historical Society Library. I am grateful to Michael Brook for calling my attention to this collection.

7 Milo M.Quaife, ed., *An English Settler in Pioneer Wisconsin, the Letters of Edwin Bottomley,* Collections of the State Historical Society of Wisconsin, XXV, Madison, 1918.

8 Letters relating to the Freeman family are in the Thomas Steel Papers, Wisconsin State Historical Society Library. Other sources of letters and memoirs of industrial workers include Mabel Kalmbach Spencer, 'Sketch of John Spencer', undated typescript *c.* 1909, Wisconsin State Historical Society Library. Some information and a few letters relating to the English potters' colony in Wisconsin are in Grant Foreman, 'Settlement of English Potters in Wisconsin', *The Wisconsin Magazine of History,* XXI, No. 4, June 1938, pp. 375–96. See also Grant Foreman, 'English Emigrants in Iowa', *Iowa Journal of History and Politics,* XLIV, October 1946, pp. 385–420, and 'English Settlers in Illinois', *Illinois Historical Society Journal,* XXIV, No. 3, September 1941, pp. 303–33.

9 In addition to the propagandist volume by Richard Flower, *Letters from Illinois,* London, 1822, we have the more valuable account by his son, George Flower, *History of the English Settlement in Edwards County, Illinois,* Chicago Historical Society Collections, I, Chicago, 1882.

10 Jay Monaghan, ed., 'From England to Illinois in 1821, the Journal of William Hall', *Journal of the Illinois State Historical Society,* XXXIX, No. 1, March 1946, pp. 21ff. and No. 2, June 1946, pp. 208ff.

11 Pritchard Letters, Case 18, Folio 76, Friends House Library, London.

12 John E. Inglehart, 'The Coming of the English to Indiana in 1817 and their Hoosier Neighbours', *Indiana Magazine of History,* XV, June 1918, which includes extracts from a few letters. William Faux, *Memorable Days in America,* London, 1823, p. 234.

13 C.B.Johnson, *Letters from the British Settlement in Pennsylvania,* London, 1819. *Commemorative Biographical Record of Northeastern Pennsylvania,* Chicago, 1900, p. 111.

14 *The Courtauld Family Papers,* privately printed in a limited edition by Bowes and Bowes of Cambridge in 1916 in eight volumes, contain dozens of letters from America. The only one of George Courtauld's sons who did not go to America, Samuel, laid the foundations of the textile firm of Courtaulds during these years when the rest of the family was trying to farm in Ohio. I am indebted to Professor D.C.Coleman for calling my attention to these rare volumes.

15 Many of his letters to the Courtauld family are in the *Courtauld Family Papers.*

Charles Manning Walker, *History of Athens Co., Ohio,* Cincinnati, 1869, pp. 544–6.

16 Letters of Thomas and Catherine Steel, Genessee, Wisc., 1843–70, Steel Papers, Wisconsin Historical Society Library.

17 A few letters have also survived from immigrants of this class who settled in the United States during the seventies and eighties, again often in communities like Le Mars, Iowa, which made a great effort to preserve their Englishness. Like the founders of Wanborough and Albion these emigrants placed a great premium on the presence of good society, of people of their own kind from England, in the agricultural areas to which they went. See the Jendwine and Cowan letters, LSE. These groups are discussed briefly in Berthoff, *British Immigrants,* pp. 114–17, and his footnotes cite some of the literature publicizing these later colonies. See also Eve Packer, 'Middle-Class British Immigration to the Trans-Mississippi West, 1870–1900', M.Phil. Thesis, London, 1967.

18 Thomas Steel, 26 April 1834, Atlantic Ocean, to his father, James Steel in London, Steel Papers, File 1.

19 George Poulton, 10 March 1834, Troy NY, to his father and Mary Poulton, 26 May 1834, Lockport, NY, to Mr Poulton, manuscripts at LSE.

20 Joseph Hirst, 29 August 1829, Equality, Gallatin Co., Illinois, to his son, Samuel Hirst, provision dealer, Leeds, photostats at LSE.

21 See also 'God Raised us up Good Friends', *Wisconsin Magazine of History,* Vol. 47, No. 3, Spring 1964, 224–37. Letters of Robert Pollock, Lake Mills and Cambridge, Wisconsin, 1848–58, to relatives in Ayrshire, Collection of Regional History (805), Cornell University.

22 *Counsel for Emigrants, with Original Letters from Canada and the United States,* Aberdeen, 1834. John Knight, *Important Extracts from Original and Recent letters written by Emigrants in the USA to their friends in England,* Manchester, 1818. G.Poulett Scrope, *Extracts of Letters from Poor Persons who Emigrated Last Year to Canada and the United States,* London, 1831. A second edition, published in 1832, added more letters. Benjamin Smith, *Twenty-four Letters from Labourers in America to their Friends in England,* London, 1829. More such volumes were published to encourage emigration to Upper Canada. They formed part of the propaganda for emigration from southern England in the early 1830s.

23 Simon and Collyer Letter, North Royalton, Ohio, 184[?], Collection of Regional History (684), Cornell. Letter from Henry Craig, 7 September 1850, Ohio City, to his family in Kent, original owned by P.W.Steed, near Margate, Kent; letter from Isaac Goodchild, 21 September 1851, South Kingston, RI, to Richard Goodchild, Beedon, near Newbury, Berks.; E. Gilley, 28 September 1845 Union, Rock Co. Wisconsin Territory, to his sister in Whitton Tower, Rothbury Northumberland, photostats at LSE.

2 Motives for Emigration

24 Hubert G.Schmidt, 'Some Post-revolutionary Views of American Agriculture in the English Midlands', *Agricultural History,* XXXII, July 1958, pp. 166–75.

25 James Flint, *Letters from America, 1818–20,* Reuben G.Thwaites, ed., *Early Western Travels, 1748–1846,* Vol. IX, Cleveland, 1904, p. 25.

26 Quaife, ed., *True Picture,* p. 7.

27 Robert Meatyard, 22 March 1836, Alton, Ill., to his mother at Twyford, near Shaftesbury, Dorset. See also letter from Hannah Young, 8 January 1832, nr.

York, Upper Canada, to relatives at Ellerby-nigh-Whitby, Yorks., photostat at LSE.

28 Robert Shedden, 12 December 1845, Elgin, Ill., copy in LSE Library.

29 George Courtauld, 26 December 1818, Marietta, Ohio, to his son, Samuel, in Essex, *Courtauld Family Papers*, II, p. 465.

30 S.B.Van Stone, 9 January 1901, Manasguan, Monmouth County, New Jersey, Devonshire Association Collection, Exeter Central Reference Library. See also career of John Hurry discussed in Fisher series, 7 October 1835, 5 September 1837.

31 Compare the following description of how a labourer adjusted in Scotland without emigration: '. . . my husband having no trade . . . when he was young he used to work in the country and then he was on the Clyde in the [word illegible] machines and now he is in the Kelvinside Forge . . .', Jane McDonald, 7 August 1869, Glasgow, to her nephew, Archibald McKellar, McKellar Letters.

32 On the difficulties which weavers faced in trying to change occupation, see E.P. Thompson, *The Making of the English Working Class*, London, 1963, p. 310.

33 'The Autobiography of Hannibal Lugg', pp. 1–5, typescript in Wisconsin Historical Society Library.

34 James McKellar, 26 March 1842, St Louis, to his brother, Peter; Catherine MacLeish, 11 November 1848, Charleston, SC, to her brother, Peter McKellar; Catherine MacLeish, 12 July 1859, Charleston, to her nephew, Archibald McKellar, McKellar Letters.

35 Edwin Bottomley, 25 November 1842, Racine, Wisc., to his parents, Quaife, ed., *An English Settler*, p. 39.

36 Thomson, *A Pioneer Family*, p. 30. Undated letter from Robert Bowles, Harrison, Hamilton County, Ohio, Bowles MSS. William Faux, *Memorable Days in America*, p. 240.

37 *Advice to Young Men,* London, edition 1926, pp. 222–3. Robert Bowles, 5 August 1823, Harrison, Hamilton Co., Ohio. Marcus Hansen, *Atlantic Migration*, p. 64.

38 J.Monaghan, ed., 'Journal of William Hall', *Journal of the Illinois State Historical Society*, March 1946, p. 24.

39 Thomas Steel, 12 March 1847, 1 July 1845, Genessee, Wisconsin, to his sister, Lilly Steel, Steel Papers, File 4, *Courtauld Family Papers*, II, p. 899. Quaife, ed., *An English Settler*, p. 184. Smith, ed., *Twenty-four Letters,* pp. 31–2. See below, John Fisher, 11 June 1832.

40 Letter from Rev. John Ingle to his son, Inglehart, 'Coming of the English to Indiana', p. 100. See also Richard Flower, *Letters from Illinois,* p. 22.

41 Edwin Bottomley, 4 September 1848, to his father and mother, Quaife, ed., *An English Settler*, p. 186. Samuel Mearbeck, 1 January 1817, Boston, to his mother. See also petition from Scottish weavers cited in Hansen, *Atlantic Migration,* p. 164.

42 Robert Bowles, 11 October 1823, 20 April 1823, Harrison, Hamilton County, Ohio, to his brothers.

43 Charles Rose, 15 October 1822, Scotch Settlement, nr. Lisbon, Ohio, to John Rose, Colloden, Inverness.

44 For further discussion and examples of this use of the word, see C.J.Erickson, 'Agrarian Myths of English Immigrants', in O.F.Ander, ed., *In the Trek of the Immigrants*, Rock Island, 1964, pp. 76–7.

45 Chester E.Eisinger, 'The Freehold Concept in eighteenth Century American Politics', *William and Mary Quarterly,* Third Series, IV, No. 1, January 1947, pp. 44, 49, 63.

46 James Steel, 1 May 1845, London, to his son, Thomas Steel, Steel Papers, File 4.

47 George Courtauld, 26 December 1818, Marietta, Ohio, to his son, Samuel, *Courtauld Family Papers*, II, p. 471. William Cobbett, *Cottage Economy*, London, 1822, p. 65. Letter from a labourer, 10 February 1833, Ellensburgh, Allegheny Mts., *Sequel to Counsel for Emigrants*, Aberdeen, 1834, p. 22. John Garside, 17 January 1818, Salem, Ohio, to his father-in-law, John Knight, *Important Extracts*, p. 30.

48 Neil J.Smelser, *Social Change in the Industrial Revolution, 1770–1840*, London, 1959, pp. 278–9. E. P. Thompson, *The Making of the English Working Class*, p. 262.

49 Fred Chaney and Frank Johnson, Autumn, 1849, Fond du Lac, Wisc., to their wives, 'God Raised Us Up Good Friends', p. 226. James Parks, 16 March 1828, Greenbush, NY, in Smith, ed., *Twenty-four Letters*, p. 29. George Fewins, 21 July 1850, Kansas and January 1851, Uniontown, Missouri, to the Overseers of Cheriton Bishop, Devon, Devonshire Record Office, Exeter.

50 George Courtauld, 23 May 1820, Edinburgh, to his son, George, *Courtauld Family Papers*, II, p. 719.

51 See, for example, the Morris brothers and Abel Stephenson below. Samuel Mearbeck, 1 January 1817, Boston, to his mother, Mearbeck Letters. Matthew Beaumont, 1817, Lynchburg, Va., to his mother, John Knight, *Important Extracts*, p. 22. John Freeman, 21 June 1832, Gooderich, Lake Huron, Upper Canada, to William Dore, in Saxmundham, Suffolk, *Extracts from Various Writers*, Norwich, 1834, p. 12.

52 J.Tewsley, a former Dorking farmer, 9 November 1832, Geneva, Ontario Co., New York; George Hill, late a labourer at Sullington, Sussex, 5 August 1832, Ancaster; John Watson, 13 August 1820, Seneca, Ontario Co., NY, *Letters from Dorking Emigrants,* ed. by Charles Barclay, London, 1833, pp. 31, 40. Contrast the reactions of Titus Crawshaw in Wisconsin in the 1850s, Titus Crawshaw, 16 April 1855.

53 George Conner, late keeper of a public house, near Middleton, Lancs., 4 February 1818, Laughry Township, Dearborn Co., Indiana, to his brothers and sisters, John Knight, *Important Extracts*, Second Series, p. 6.

54 *Courtauld Family Papers*, II, pp. 489, 917; III, pp. 1002, 1022. Quaife, ed., *An English Settler*, p. 185. Also Hugh John Nudham, 9 February 1834, Monroe, Adams Co., Ohio, to W.Barns.

55 *An Englishwoman in America,* London and Liverpool, 1848, pp. cxv, cxvii. For another example of a woman whose resistance to emigration was broken by the threat of an unsuitable marriage from one of her daughters, see Henry L.Norton, 'The Travels of the Marstons', *Journal of the Illinois State Historical Society* LVIII, No. 3, Autumn 1965, p. 283.

56 G.D.H.Cole, *Short History of the British Working Class, 1789–1925*, London, 1927, p. 115. R.K.P.Pankhurst, *William Thompson*, Watts and Co., 1954, pp. 208–9.

57 Richard Hails, 21 May 1849; Titus Crawshaw, 16 April 1855; John Hesketh, 5 August 1837.

58 Andrew Morris, 5 February 1844. Fred Chaney, 29 May 1853, Fond du Lac, Wisc., to his brother, 'God Raised us up Good Friends', p. 236.

59 Compare Merle Curti and Kendall Burr, 'The Immigrant and the American Image in Europe, 1860–1914', *Mississippi Valley Historical Review*, XXXVII, No. 2, September 1950, p. 223. For expressions of interest in education, see John Birket, 14 December 1842; John Fisher, 23 July 1833; Thomas Morris, 7 February 1832; W.T.Corlett, *People of Orrisdale and Others,* Cleveland, 1918, p. 20.

60 'Emigration and the Image of America in Europe', *Immigration and American History*, ed., Henry S.Commager, Minneapolis, 1961, pp. 36, 47.
61 Quaife, ed., *An English Settler*, p. 57.
62 Thomas Steel, 29 May 1846, Genessee, Wisc., to his father, Steel Papers, File 4.
63 Robert Bowles, 20 April 1823, Harrison, Hamilton Co., Ohio, Bowles MSS.
64 The most devoted nationalists among the Polish people did not emigrate, according to Thomas and Znaniecki, *The Polish Peasant*, II, p. 1485.
65 This is not to deny that some English emigrants left for political reasons. On the one hand there were the founders of colonies like Birkbeck and Courtauld who were dissatisfied with their want of political influence at home and who hoped to become the natural leaders of self-governing communities. Courtauld feared that if he did not found his own community, other leaders might already have established themselves in a region in which he settled. On the other hand there were political *émigrés* such as the Chartists who emigrated in the late thirties to escape imprisonment. See R.T.Berthoff, *British Immigrants*, p. 104; Sydney Pollard, *A History of Sheffield Labour*, Liverpool, 1959, p. 8, Frank Thistlethwaite, *The Anglo-American Connection in the Early Nineteenth Century*, Philadelphia, 1959, pp. 47–75; Thompson, *The Making of the English Working Class*, pp. 132, 180, 562.

3 *Networks of Distribution*

66 John Dixon, 17 June 1871, Earlham, Iowa, to his family, *Bulletin of the British Association for American Studies*, New Series, No. 12, 1966, pp. 9–10.
67 See, for example, excerpts in Charles Boewe, *Prairie Albion*, Southern Illinois University Press, Carbondale, 1962.
68 Henry Newman, 20 May 1833, Wanborough, Ill., to George Newman, Pritchard Letters; Richard Birkbeck was also very critical of his father's farming: Thompson, *A Pioneer Family*, p. 64.
69 See *Advice to Emigrants who Intend to Settle in the United States of America*, Wright and Bagnall, Bristol, second edition, 1832, 24pp. Other such guidebooks which invited prospective migrants to particular colonies were John B.Newhall, *Sketches of Iowa or the Emigrant's Guide*, New York, 1841; *A Glimpse of Iowa in 1846 or the Emigrant's Guide and State Directory*, Burlington, second edition, 1846; *Emigration to Virginia East*, Virginia Land Agency, London, 1869; S.B. Johnson, *Letters from the British Settlement in Pennsylvania*, London, 1819; *Description of the Wisconsin Territory*, published by the British Temperance Emigration Society and Saving Fund, Liverpool, 1843; George Courtauld, 'Address to those who may be Disposed to Remove to the USA on the Advantages of Equitable Associations of Capital and Labour', Sudbury, 1820, *Courtauld Family Papers*, II, pp. 646–70.
70 *Courtauld Family Papers*, V, pp. 1905, 2071–9. A letter from Knight appeared in the *Hampshire Telegraph and East Sussex Chronicle*, 6 February 1832, p. 1, col. 3.
71 *Courtauld Family Papers*, V, pp. 2039–56.
72 *Ibid.*, IV, p. 1766. Knight was an energetic developer, remembered as such in Athens County histories. His activities in promoting canal construction, bridge building, schools, meeting houses and other endeavours are discussed in his letters to the Courtauld family. Like John Birket whose letters are printed here, Knight came from a relatively backward county in England to undertake

vigorous entrepreneurial activities in the United States: Charles Manning Walker, *History of Athens Co., Ohio*, Cincinnati, 1869, pp. 544–6.

73 Inglehart, 'The Coming of the English to Indiana', p. 177.

74 John and Mary Thomson, 24 January 1850, Wingville, Grant Co., Wisc., to his brother, David Thomson, in Fife, Wisconsin Historical Society Library.

75 A survey of the biographies of over six hundred English and Scots immigrants in the states of Iowa, Illinois, Michigan, Ohio and Wisconsin produced only three references to emigration in response to publications about projected colonies. William Alston of Lancashire attributed his emigration to one of Flower's pamphlets. (*Portrait and Biographical Album of Jefferson and Van Buren Counties, Iowa*, Chicago, 1890, p. 295.) Robert North emigrated from Derbyshire with the British Temperance Emigration Society. (*History of Dane Co., Wisconsin*, Chicago, 1880, p. 1052.) Joseph Winterbotham, a stonemason from Manchester, emigrated under the auspices of the Potter's Emigration Society in 1851 (*Ibid.*, p. 1067).

76 James Stott, 23 June 1820, New York City, to his wife in Lancashire, copy of letter at LSE.

77 These and other rarer emigrant guides are reproduced on microfilm in 'British Immigrant Guides and Pamphlets, 1819–1970', Micro Methods Ltd., East Ardsley, Wakefield, Yorks., with an introductory comment by the author. See *Cassell's Emigrant's Handbook*, London 1852; *The Emigrant's Manual, British America and the United States*, William and Robert Chambers Instructive and Entertaining Library, Edinburgh, 1851; *Emigration: Who Should Go; Where to Go; How to Get there; and What to Take*, W.Strange, London, 1843; *Tegg's Handbook for Emigrants*, London, 1839.

78 Catherine Steel, 12 July 1846, Genessee, Wisc., to her sister-in-law, Lilly Steel; Lilly Steel, 14 May 1845, Holloway, London, to her brother, Thomas, Steel Papers, File 4. Thomas Steel, 10 May 1844, Genessee, Wisc., to his sister, Lilly Steel, File 3. Ann Whittaker, 23 January [1851?] While the letters suggest the popularity of the Chambers publications as late as the 1840s they do not substantiate Marcus Hansen's claim that *Information for the People* 'attained a phenomenal circulation, especially among farm servants and artisans who had hitherto read little'. (Hansen, *Atlantic Migration*, p. 150. See also Robert K.Webb, *The British Working Class Reader, 1790–1845*, London, 1955, pp. 74, 79–80 on Chambers' readers.)

79 Shepperson, *British Emigration*, p. 10.

80 Charles Streeter, 21 June 1823, Hanover, near Wilkesbarre, Penn., to his mother at Sanders Green, Headley, near Liphook, Hants., copies in the author's possession.

81 Undated fragment from a letter of Arthur Pickford, Nora Springs, Iowa, sometime in the early 1880s.

82 Thomas Steel, 16 June 1846, Mequonego Post Office, Wisc., to his sister, Lilly, extended such a specific invitation to one Edward Williams, Steel Letters, File 4.

83 Quaife, ed., *True Picture*, p. 8.

84 In addition to letters in this volume, see also Robert Meatyard who intended to settle in New York near an uncle (Robert Meatyard, 22 March 1836, Alton, Ill., to his mother). Also the Rose and Pickford letters exhibit an uncles' network. Copy of letter from James Filmer, 10 February 1848, Binghampton, NY, to his father, Newnham, near Sittingbourne, East Kent, in author's possession. For the importance of the larger family in the westward movement of Americans, see

John H.Kolb and Edmund de S.Brunner, *A Study of Rural Society*, Cambridge, 1952, pp. 140–1.

85 Hannibal Lugg emigrated to Quebec in 1842 with a brother of the girl he courted and in the autumn of that year was joined in Wisconsin by two brothers-in-law with whom he lived until he married and bought land himself.

86 Peter McKellar, Clayton Co., Iowa, to his son Archibald, a pencilled note on a letter from Mt Hero, Vermont, which he forwarded to his son. The note was marked 'received April 1852'.

87 James Steel, 1 May 1845, 28 June 1845, London, to his son; Thomas Steel, 2 July 1844, Genessee, Wisc., to his father, Steel Papers, Files 3 and 4.

88 Thomson letter, 24 January 1850. Undated letter from Fred Pickford, Nora Springs, Iowa, to his father and mother on grandmother's death. See comments on the funeral of Peter McKellar's father, Colin Houston, 17 April 1851, Kilbarchon, to Peter McKellar; Jane McKellar, 10 September 1848, Partick, to her father, Peter McKellar, McKellar Letters.

89 John Griffiths made an offer to pay a passage after the Civil War. Archibald McKellar asked his father's advice about contributing half the fare to a cousin, but his father pointed out that their farm needed his savings more. (Colin Houston, 11 October 1854, Anderston, to his cousin Archibald McKellar.)

4 Economic Adjustment in Agriculture

90 On the abundance of capital of English-speaking immigrants in Trempeleau County, Wisconsin, see Merle Curti *et. al.*, *The Making of an American Community*, Stanford, 1959, p. 81. For injunctions to sell all property and convert to cash, see Quaife, ed., *True Picture*, p. 8; George Flower, *History of the English*, p. 98; Inglehart, 'Coming of the English to Indiana', p. 97; Smith, ed., *Twenty-four Letters,* p. 12.

91 Samuel Mearbeck, 1 January 1817, Boston, to his mother.

92 William A.Whitney and R.I.Bonner, *History and Biographical Record of Lenawee County, Michigan*, Adrian, 1879, II, pp. 13–14. S.P.Hildreth, *Biographical and Historical Memoirs of the Early Pioneer Settlers of Ohio*, Cincinnati, 1852, pp. 491–528. Emily C.Blackman, *History of Susquehanna County, Pennsylvania*, Philadelphia, 1873, pp. 446–7.

93 Thomas Steel, 29 May 1846, Genessee, Wisc., to his father, Steel Papers, File 4.

94 For Scots immigrants who saved earnings as miners in Maryland and Pennsylvania before coming to Wisconsin to buy land in the 1850s, see Curti, *Making of an American Community*, p. 92.

95 This was Clarence Danhof's much quoted estimate. In his more recent valuable study of *Change in Agriculture in the Northern States, 1820–70*, Cambridge, 1969, p. 114, Danhof notes that his earlier estimate of one thousand dollars as the farm-making cost for fifty acres of woodland does not reflect the original investments actually made by most farm-makers of the time, since some of the costs were met by applying their own labour to the land and its resources. This view is consistent with our findings for these British immigrants.

96 Peter McKellar, *c.* 1850, Mount Hero, Vermont, to his sister, McKellar Papers.

97 Archibald McKellar started at fifteen dollars a month in 1851 but in August 1852 was able to send sixty dollars to his father (Archibald McKellar, 13 October 1851, Taylors Falls, Minn. Territory, to his father; 10 November 1851; 11 August 1852, McKellar Papers).

98 Peter McKellar, 25 June 1855, Farmersburgh, Clayton County, Iowa, to his son, Archibald; 10 February 1856, McKellar Papers.

99 Courtauld Family Papers, III, p. 1482.

100 Peter McKellar, 18 August 1853, Paint Creek, Iowa, to his son, Archibald, McKellar Letters.

101 Erickson, 'British Immigrants in the Old Northwest', pp. 334–6.

102 See the Smith letters, the Morris letters, the Birket letters and Hannibal Lugg's 'Autobiography'. 'Almost every mechanic is a farmer and he works at his business to suit his own convenience . . .' (James Knight to George Courtauld, 14 March 1853, *Courtauld Family Papers*, V, p. 2331.) See also James Knight to George Courtauld, May 1835, *ibid.*, V, p. 2376.

103 Robert Pollock, 7 April 1854, Cambridge, Wisc., to his brother.

104 See Erickson, 'British Immigrants in the Old Northwest', pp. 336–8. In the Simon and Collyer families, the men were working for provisions as day labourers on farms while their wives and daughters plaited straw and made bonnets to accumulate savings for the purchase of farms. These families began by buying livestock, keeping a cow, some pigs and a few hens before they bought land. (George Simon and W.Collyer, 20 September 184[?], North Royalton, Ohio, to family.) On sharecropping, see also, Robert and Mary Wilson, 8 November 1829, Grafton, Loraine Co., Ohio, to John Walker, Hull, in S.H.Collins, *The Emigrants Guide to and Description of the USA,* Hull, fourth edition, 1830, p. 166. Peter McKellar, 31 May 1856, Farmersburgh, Iowa, to his son. Catherine Steel, 15 September 1846, Genessee, Wisc., to Lilly Steel, Steel Papers, File 4. Danhof, *Change in Agriculture,* pp. 77–8, 88, 92–3.

105 Thomson, *A Pioneer Family,* p. 70. For other attempts to obtain legacies for farms, see Smith letters below; Alfred Jones, 30 July 1864, 17 January 1880, Missouri, Jones Letters, LSE. Nathan Pooley, 23 December 1862, Goshen, Elkhart, Indiana, to his cousin, Fisher Letters, Ipswich and East Suffolk Record Office, 2815/4.

106 Thomas Steel, 15 September 1846, Genessee, Wisc., to his father, Steel Letters, File 4.

107 Thomas Steel, 13 April 1844, Genessee, Wisc., to his father, Steel Papers, File 3; 13 February 1845, Genessee, Wisc., to his father; 13 March 1845, Genessee, Wisc., to his sister; 15 September 1846, Genessee, Wisc., to his father, File 4.

108 George Courtauld to Sophia Courtauld, 2 July 1823, Englishtown, *Courtauld Family Papers*, III, p. 1049.

109 See also letter from Reuben Carpenter, 16 February 1842, Jefferson County, Ohio, to his father in Gloucestershire, Carpenter Letters, LSE.

110 Quaife, ed., *An English Settler,* pp. 108, 111, 125, 151. The dissolving effects which the poverty of the frontier had upon civilized morals are noticeable when people like Bottomley and Thomas Steel openly followed their neighbours in helping themselves to timber or hay from neighbouring government lands. (*Ibid.,* pp. 38, 40, 68. Thomas Steel, 11 August 1844, Genessee, Wisc., to his father, Steel Papers, File 3.)

111 Mrs George Courtauld, 25 May 1822, Bocking, Essex, to her daughter, Sophie Courtauld, *Courtauld Family Papers*, II, p. 894.

112 Quaife, ed., *An English Settler,* pp. 173, 204. Smith, ed., *Twenty-four Letters,* p. 48. *Counsel for Emigrants,* p. 31. *Courtauld Family Papers,* IV, p. 1899; II, pp. 850, 894. Polish peasants did sometimes try to borrow money in Poland to buy

land in the USA (Thomas and Znaniecki, *Polish Peasant*, I, pp. 97, 136, 141, 151, 267, 318, 420).

113 Robert Bowles, 10 August 1823, Harrison, Hamilton Co., Ohio, to his brother, Bowles letters. Peter McKellar was unable to get a loan when he first arrived in Iowa in 1852, but wrote, 'I can get money here by paying interest' three years later. (Peter McKellar, 9 July 1852, Manona, Iowa; 12 August 1855, Farmersburgh, Iowa, to his son Archibald, McKellar Papers.) See Merle Curti, *Making of an American Community*, pp. 157–9.

114 For local loans by immigrants, in addition to examples in the Birket, Fisher, Wozencraft and Morris letters, see Hugh John Nudham, 9 February 1834, Monroe, Ohio, to W. Barnes; Quaife, ed., *An English Settler*, pp. 25, 44, 53; Grant Foreman, 'English Settlers in Iowa', p. 388; Quaife, ed., *True Picture*, pp. 115–16, 118–19, 148; Jay Monaghan, ed., 'Journal of William Hall', *Illinois State Historical Society Journal*, June 1946, p. 214; March 1946, pp. 52, 62; Thomas Steel, 13 August 1845, Genessee, Wisc., to his sister, Lilly, Steel Papers, File 4.

115 The Collyer family was much less precipitate about land purchase than immigrants like Gilley, Bottomley and Courtauld who arrived with capital. They declined to attempt to take on shares the first farm offered to them and also the offer of an improved farm of thirty-three acres for three hundred dollars because they preferred to continue with day labour and by-employments until they were in a position to buy a larger farm farther west (Collyer letter, 184[?], North Royalton, Ohio). See also, Danhof, *Change in Agriculture*, p. 81.

116 Marcus Hansen, *The Immigrant in American History*, Cambridge, 1942, pp. 65–9. Allan Bogue challenged this judgement in *From Prairie to Corn Belt*, Chicago, 1963, p. 21.

117 See Birket, Corlett, Fisher and Morris series below. Also other unpublished letters including that of Edward Gilley from Porter, Wisconsin Territory, 1845; Joseph Hirst, 1829, Equality, Illinois; Robert Pollock, 7 April 1854, Cambridge, Wisconsin. Quaife, ed., *An English Settler*, p. 31. See also C. J. Erickson, 'British Immigrants in the Old Northwest', pp. 341–2.

118 Quaife, *True Picture*, p. 52. About three acres had been cleared and broken on Peter McKellars's first Iowa farm. Thomas Steel bought only twenty acres of unimproved prairie land. After a few years' experience both of these men, who had no prior acquaintance with agriculture, began trying to find improved farms to buy. The Freemans pre-empted their first forty acres (Thomas Steel, 12 November 1844, Genessee, Wisc., to his father, Steel Papers, File 3).

119 John Birchall in the Morris Series; Bishop Series; Hugh John Nudham, emigrant from Kent to Adams County Ohio, Nudham Letter, 1834.

120 Samuel Mearbeck, 6 February 1820, Beverley, Randolph County, Va., to his sister in Sheffield, Mearbeck Letters.

121 See, for example, Robert Meatyard, who moved from New York state to Alton, Illinois, in 1835, for this reason (Robert Meatyard, 22 March 1836, Alton, Ill., to his mother in Dorset).

122 Peter McKellar, *c.* 1850, Mount Hero, Vermont, to his sister.

123 One guide book published in London noted that while proximity to markets was not to be overlooked in selecting land, a healthy situation was to be preferred to a few miles of distance (*Emigration*, British American Land Company, London, 1834, p. 56). Thomas Steel, like Edwin Bottomley, was very much influenced by the location of a road with respect to his land. Peter McKellar considered

mainly the land's resources, its soil, water supply and timber. Mearbeck was impressed by a romantic and healthy situation.

124 Compare George Flower, *History of the English*, p. 45. Curti, *Making of an American Community*, pp. 208–9.

125 Thomas Steel, 9 September 1843, Genessee, Wisc., to his father, Steel Papers, File 3.

126 Erickson, 'British Immigrants in the Old Northwest', pp. 344–5. E.Gilley Letter, 1845. Robert Shedden, 12 December 1845, Elgin, Ill., to John Young, Cloich, Scotland, copies in LSE. The American prejudice against prairies was not so pervasive as was once thought (Douglas R.McManis, *The Initial Evaluation and Utilization of the Illinois Prairies*, 1815–40, Chicago, 1964, pp. 43, 50, 56, 83–5, 92–3).

127 Alan Bogue, 'Farming in the Prairie Peninsula, 1830–90', *Journal of Economic History*, XXIII, No. 1, March 1963, pp. 13–15.

128 H.J.Nudham, 9 February 1834, Monroe, Ohio, to W.Barnes. Richard Birkbeck, 12 November 1820, Wanborough, Ill., to his uncle, Thomson, *A Pioneer Family*, p. 70. See also Hubert G.Schmidt, 'Some Post-revolutionary Views of American Agriculture', p. 174. John Davies, 11 August 1832, Mount Jackson, Penn., to his mother and brother, Conway, ed., *Welsh in America*, p. 68. Extracts of letters of a Scottish farmer, 10 August 1833, Albany, NY, *Counsel for Emigrants*, p. 38. *Extracts from Various Writers*, Norwich, 1834, pp. 8–9. Erickson, 'British Immigrants in the Old Northwest', pp. 346–7.

129 Joseph Pickering, *Inquiries of an Emigrant*, London, 1832, p. 5. See also William Faux, *Memorable Days*, p. 97; *Sequel to Counsel for Emigrants*, p. 69.

130 Thomas Steel, 20 October 1844, Genessee, Wisc., to his sister, Lilly; 12 November 1844, to his father, Steel Papers, File 4.

131 Edward Gilley, 28 September 1845, Porter, Rock Co., Wisc., to his sister. See also Griffiths Series, below.

132 Thomas Steel, 10 May 1844, Genessee, Wisc., to his sister. See also Robert Meatyard, 22 March 1836, Alton, Ill., to his mother in Dorset.

133 Thomas Steel, 13 March 1846, Genessee, Wisc., to his father, File 4. John Birket, 7 December 1834. George Flower, *History of the English*, pp. 165, 350. Richard Birkbeck, 29 December 1819, Wanborough, Ill., to his uncle, Richard Bush, Thomson, *A Pioneer Family*, p. 64.

134 Thomas Steel, 15 May 1846, Genessee, Wisc., to his father, File 4. John Birket, 6 May 1833. James Knight, 14 March 1835, Nelsonville, Ohio, to George Courtauld, *Courtauld Family Papers*, V, pp. 2334–5.

135 19–20 April 1823, Jay Monaghan, ed., 'Journal of William Hall', *Journal of the Illinois State Historical Society*, June 1946, p. 230.

136 Quaife, ed., *True Picture*, pp. 63, 83, 112, 116.

137 James Knight, 3 August 1828, Nelsonville, Ohio, to George Courtauld, *Courtauld Family Papers*, II, pp. 1848–9; 6 December 1833, V, pp. 2188–95. See David McDonald's comments on Birkbeck's 'unwillingness to adopt the American system of farming', based on conversations with immigrants living in Edwards County, 'Diaries of David McDonald, 1824–6', *Indiana Historical Society Publications*, 1942, pp. 279–80. Thomas Steel, 1 September 1843, Milwaukee, Wisc., to his sister Lilly, Steel Papers, File 3.

138 John Fisher, 5 October 1835.

139 John and Mary Thomson, 24 January 1850, Wingville, Grant Co., Wisc., to David Thomson.

140 William Oliver, *Eight Months in Illinois*, Newcastle-on-Tyne, 1843, pp. 97–8, 99. Robert Shedden, 12 December 1845, Elgin, Ill., copies at LSE.

141 Fred Pickford, 2 December 1882, Nora Springs, Floyd County, Iowa, to his father, mother and brother.

142 Lilly Steel, 16 October 1845, Holloway, to Catherine Steel; James Steel, 30 October 1845, 28 June 1845, 28 December 1834, Holloway, to Thomas Steel, Steel Papers, File 4.

143 Thomas Steel, 13 March 1846, 12 August 1846, Genessee, Wisc., to his father; Steel Papers, File 4.

144 Thomas Steel, 27 March 1846, Genessee Wisc., to Lilly Steel, File 4.

145 Thomas Steel, 31 July 1845, North Prairie, Wisconsin Territory, to his father, File 4.

146 Thomas Steel, 27 April 1846, Genessee, Wisc., to his father. Catherine Steel, 12 April 1847, Genessee, Wisc., to Lilly Steel. Thomas Steel, 12 May 1847, Genessee, Wisc., to his father, Steel Papers, File 4.

147 Catherine Steel, 3 May 1851, Genessee, Wisc., to her sister-in-law, Lilly Steel, File 6.

148 Peter McKellar, 10 February 1856, Farmersburgh, Iowa, to his son, Archibald.

149 Robert Pollock, 16 April 1858, Cambridge, Wisc., to his niece. See also Martin Martin, 24 September 1832, Guelph, Upper Canada, to Mr Sparks, Felpham, Sussex; John Freeman, 21 June 1832, Goderich, Lake Huron, Upper Canada, to William Dore, Leiston, near Saxmundham, Suffolk, *Extracts from Various Writers*, pp. 13, 17. Richard and Margaret Pugh, 15 November 1876, Prairieville, to Rev. E. Jones, Aberystwyth, Conway, ed., *Welsh in America*, p. 102. Robert Bowles, 10 August 1823, 5 August 1823, Harrison, Hamilton County, Ohio.

150 See also English immigrants in Athens County, Ohio, doing the same (John Rochester, 6 January 1825, Englishtown, Ohio, to George Courtauld; James Knight, 17 March 1834, Nelsonville, Ohio, to George Courtauld, *Courtauld Family Papers*, III, p. 1248; V, p. 2226).

151 Robert Bowles, 5 August 1823, 10 August 1823, Harrison, Hamilton Co., Ohio, Bowles MSS. Samuel Mearbeck, 9 November 1818, Washington, to sister: 'I shall then be where neither afluence nor poverty is known, where every man may procure by his own industry every thing that is nececary in this world to make him comfortable. . . .'

152 This was true in the case of the Courtauld family. See Mrs P. A. Taylor, 4 August 1822, Galliopolis, Ohio, to Sophia Courtauld, *Courtauld Family Papers*, II, p. 919.

153 Flower, *History of the English*, p. 287.

154 Quaife, ed., *An English Settler*, p. 144. See also, for other instances of complacency about diet, Robert Bowles, 20 April 1823, Harrison, Hamilton County, Ohio; Grant Foreman, 'English Settlers in Illinois', p. 307; Mrs George Courtauld to her daughters, 25 December 1821, Bocking, Essex, *Courtauld Family Papers*, II, p. 863; Sally Simon, 20 September 184[?], North Royalton, Ohio, to her parents; Arthur Pickford, 188[?], Nora Springs, Iowa; Ann Cheyney, 6 May 1851, Fond du Lac, Wisconsin, to her mother, 'God Raised Us Up Good Friends', p. 234.

155 Quaife, ed., *True Picture*, pp. 60, 151. Another emigrant from the East Riding of Yorkshire, who arrived in Iowa in 1871, was also far from impressed with the standard of diet – only three meals a day and very little beef. (John Dixon, 19

June 1871, Earlham, Iowa, *Bulletin of the British Association for American Studies*, 1966, p. 27.)

156 31 July 1816, Milford, to his mother, Mearbeck Letters.

157 4 June 1818, Baltimore, to his sister.

158 Whittaker Series. Thomson, *A Pioneer Family*, p. 80. Quaife, ed., *True Picture*, p. 72. Foreman, 'English Settlers in Illinois', p. 329. Deborah Pritchard, 2 March 1829, Wanborough, Illinois, Pritchard Letters.

159 Thomas Steel, 15 June 1844, Genessee, Wisc., to his sister, Steel Papers, File 3. Same methods described by Sarah Kenyon, 23 February 1861, Oneida, Mildred Throne, ed., 'Iowa Farm Letters', *Iowa Journal of History*, 1960, p. 80.

160 G.T.T., *Gone to Texas*, Thomas Hughes, ed., London, 1884, p. 124. See also Percy Ebbut, *Emigrant Life in Kansas*, London, 1886, p. 107.

161 Throne, ed., 'Iowa Farm Letters', pp. 59, 65, 67, 86.

162 Foreman, 'English Emigrants in Iowa', p. 418. Smith, ed., *Twenty-four Letters*, p. 27.

163 Mary Jane Watson, 27 October 1825, Albany, NY, to her grandmother, Smith, ed., *Twenty-four Letters*, p. 21.

164 Quaife, ed., *True Picture*, p. 113. Thomas Steel, January 1844, Genessee, Wisc., to his sister, Lilly, Steel Papers, File 4.

165 Matthew Farrar, 9 February 1818, Hogan's Creek, Lawrenceburgh, Dearborn Co., Indiana, John Knight, *Important Extracts*, p. 32.

166 Henry Newman, 20 May 1833, Wanborough, Ill., to his brother George Newman, Leominster, Pritchard Letters. William Faux, *Memorable Days*, p. 252. Joel W. Hiatt, ed., 'Diary of William Owen', 22 December 1824, *Indiana Historical Society Publications*, IV, No. 1, p. 80.

167 Catherine Steel remarked that calicoes were not so cheap as in London on 12 May 1847, Genessee, Wisconsin, to her sister-in-law, Lilly Steel, File 5. Foreman, 'English Settlers in Illinois', pp. 318, 321. Nudham asked for worsted stockings, 9 February 1834, Monroe, Ohio.

168 *Courtauld Family Papers*, IV, p. 1727.

169 'Autobiography of Hannibal Lugg', pp. 1–2, 7.

170 Blegen, ed., *Land of Their Choice*, p. 57.

171 Quaife, ed., *True Picture,* pp. 48, 51. George Flower, *History of the English,* cited in Charles Boewe, *Prairie Albion*, Carbondale, 1962, p. 83. A Scots tenant farmer in Ohio in 1830 thought building was improving but that 'they might have improved more by this time'. (H. Rose, 2 February 1830, Scotch Settlement, nr. Lisbon, Ohio.) Thomas Steel described the log cabin of the socialists with whom he emigrated in which twenty-one people lived in a log cabin no larger than his father's parlour with wind pouring in from all directions. (23 October 1843, Mequonego Township, Wisconsin Territory, to his father, James Steel, Steel Papers, File 3).

172 Thomas Steel, 15 June 1844, Genessee, Wisc., to his sister, Lilly, File 3. Fred Pickford, 188[?], Nora Springs, Iowa, to his parents.

173 Quaife, ed., *True Picture*, p. 150. For the importance of improved housing to the adjustment of migrants, see especially the Whittaker Letters. Faux, *Memorable Days,* p. 240. Quaife, ed., *An English Settler*, pp. 97, 175. Conway, ed., *Welsh in America*, p. 129. Letter from Deborah Pritchard, 19 December [1828?], Wanborough, Ill., Pritchard Letters.

174 Foreman, 'English Settlers in Illinois', pp. 314–22, citing letters from 'S', spring 1844, Albion; William Brunt, Six Mile Prairie, Perry County, Illinois; Thomas

J.Fitcher, potter from Henley, 16 April 1843, Navou; Mary Harney, Kaskaskia, *Potters Examiner*, I, pp. 14, 56, 182, 79. Robert and Mary Wilson, 8 November 1829, Grafton, Lorraine County, Ohio, to John Walker, Carr Lane, Hull, S.H. Collins, *The Emigrants Guide*, p. 163.

175 Thomas Steel, 28 March 1845 and 13 February 1843, Genessee, Wisc., to his father, James; Catherine Steel, 12 March 1847 and 11 April 1849, Genessee, Wisc., to Lilly Steel; Thomas Steel, 12 March 1847, Genessee, Wisc., to his sister, Lilly, Steel Papers, Files 4, 5 and 6.

176 Simons and Collyer Letter, 184[?], North Royalton, Ohio. H.B.Rose, 2 February 1830, Scotch Settlement, nr. Lisbon, Ohio.

177 Boewe, *Prairie Albion*, p. 83. Compare Faux's description of Princeton, Indiana, in *Memorable Days*, p. 225. Simons and Collyer, 20 September 184[?], North Royalton, Ohio, to relatives: '. . . there is not the same convenience in this country having to boil in a pot on the log fire and no wash houses &c &c . . .' Catherine Steel, 17 November 1847, Genessee, Wisc., to her sister-in-law, Lilly Steel, File 5.

178 Edwin Bottomley, 31 October 1845, Rochester, Wisc., to his father and mother, Quaife, ed., *An English Settler*, p. 103. James Knight, 1 February 1832, Nelsonville, Ohio, to George Courtauld, *Courtauld Family Papers*, IV, p. 1922.

179 Thomas and Hannah Boots, 2 December 1828, Constantia, to their son, Smith, ed., *Twenty-four Letters*, p. 47. Flower, *History of the English*, p. 119. Adam Hodgson, *Letters from North America*, London, 1824, II, p. 11. James Steel, 31 August 1845, London, to Thomas Steel, advised them to continue to petition for a post office until they got one. (Steel Papers, File 4.) On the want of a store, see Thomas Steel, 12 November 1844, Genessee, Wisc., to his father, James Steel, File 3.

180 James Knight, 1 February 1832, Nelsonville, Ohio, to George Courtauld, *Courtauld Family Papers*, IV, p. 1922.

181 Thomas Steel, 5 November 1844, Genessee, Wisc., to his sister Lilly; 2 July 1844, 4 October 1844 to his father, James Steel; 15 January 1845, Milwaukee, to his sister Lilly, Steel Papers, Files 3 and 4.

182 Peter McKellar to Archibald McKellar, letter pencilled on back of a letter from Harriet and Edmund Knight marked 'Received 2 April 1852'.

183 Edward Gilley, 28 September 1845, Porter, Rock Co., Wisc., to his sister.

184 Edwin Bottomley, 29 October 1846, Rochester, Wisc., to his father, Quaife, ed *An English Settler*, p. 143.

185 James Knight, 16 May 1825, Nelsonville, Ohio, *Courtauld Family Papers*, III, p. 1297.

186 James Knight, 30 November 1831, 1 February 1832, 9 November 1830, Nelsonville, Ohio, to George Courtauld, *Courtauld Family Papers*, III, p. 1482; IV, pp. 1905, 1919, 1799.

187 James Knight, 10 December 1835, Nelsonville, Ohio, to George Courtauld, *Courtauld Family Papers*, VI, p. 2467.

188 James Knight, 3 June 1836, Nelsonville, Ohio, to George Courtauld, *Courtauld Family Papers*, VI, p. 2525.

189 James Knight, 10 December 1835, 5 June 1836, Nelsonville, Ohio, to George Courtauld, *Courtauld Family Papers*, VI, pp. 2468, 2522–3.

190 See also Robert Meatyard, 29 January 1838, Alton, Ill., to his mother.

191 John G.Clark, *The Grain Trade in the Old Northwest*, London and Urbana, 1966, pp. 154–5.

192 Peter McKellar, 25 October 1853, Paint Creek, Iowa, to his son, Archibald. Thomas Steel also sold his first claim of forty acres for twenty acres nearer a road.

193 James Frederick Chaney, 1 March 1851, Fond du Lac, Wisc., to mother and Charles, 'God Raised us up Good friends', p. 233. Robert Bowles, 10 August 1823, Harrison, Hamilton Co., Ohio. Peter McKellar, 25 October 1853, Paint Creek, Iowa, to his son Archibald. For adverse attitudes to continued migration see also H.J.Nudham, 9 February 1834, Monroe Co., Ohio. John Birket, 25 December 1841. Katherine Bond, 7 June [1898?]; C.J.Erickson, 'British Immigrants in the Old Northwest', pp. 350–2. In a survey of the biographies of 420 English and Scots farmers in the Old Northwest and Iowa, only five were found who clearly had bought farm land in another state before they settled down as landowners in the county in whose history their biographies appeared.

194 See also Laramy family described in a letter from Esther A.Cole, 21 January 1901, Belle Plain, Scott Co., Minn., Devonshire Association Papers, Exeter Central Library. Clarence S.Paine, 'Diaries of a Nebraska Farmer, 1876–7', *Agricultural History*, Vol. 22, No. 1, January 1948, p. 103. Katherine Bond, 1888.

195 Morris Letters. 'Autobiography of Hannibal Lugg', pp. 7–8.

196 Robert Bowles, 20 April 1823, Harrison, Hamilton Co., Ohio, Bowles Letters. Samuel Mearbeck, 6 February 1820. Bogue, *From Prairie to Corn Belt*, pp. 266–7.

197 Quaife, ed. *An English Settler*, pp. 58, 63, 69.

198 Isaac Goodchild, 21 September 1851, So. Kingston, RI, to his brother in Newbury, Berks.

199 James Knight, 4 June 1825, Nelsonville, Ohio, *Courtauld Family Papers*, III, p. 1307. For other instances of store-keeping in connection with farming, see *Ibid.*, III, pp. 1362–3; Inglehart, 'Coming of the English to Indiana', p. 97; Thomson, *A Pioneer Family*, p. 79; John Knight, *Important Extracts*, Second Series, p. 27; G.T.T., *Gone to Texas*, p. 15.

200 Foreman, 'English Settlers in Iowa', p. 413n. For other similar cases, see Inglehart, 'Coming of the English to Indiana', p. 176. Harcourt Horn, *An English Colony in Iowa*, p. 31; 'Sketch of John Spencer', Wisconsin State Historical Society Library. 'Burton is about leaving Mr Hunt to work in Milwaukee as a smith or engineer. Alfred and Arthur Johnson are also gone in, one as a smith the other as a butcher ...' (Catherine Steel, 22 November 1849, Genessee, Wisc., to Lilly Steel, Steel Papers, File 6). Her brother Alfred left to go into cabinet-making in the same town (Catherine Steel, 19 March 1848, to Lilly Steel, File 5).

201 Edwin Bottomley, 3 May 1847, Rochester, Wisc., to his father, Quaife, ed., *An English Settler*, p. 163. When sickness and want of skill threatened their farming enterprise, Eliza Courtauld Ash and her husband 'determined ... to remove to some town ... and to commence his business' of cabinet-making. (Mrs Ash, 8 August 1822, to Sophia Courtauld; 9 July 1822, Cleves, Ohio, *Courtauld Family Papers*, III, pp. 931–3; II, p. 914.) Her father tried to get back into manufacturing in Pittsburgh. (George Courtauld, 14 May 1823, Englishtown, Ohio, *Ibid.*, III, pp. 1020–1.) See also George Flower, *History of the English*, p. 135. Archibald McKellar left his Iowa farm to return to the Minnesota lumber camps after his father's death. (N.V.MacNeil, 21 December 1864, National, Clayton Co., Iowa, to Archibald McKellar, McKellar Letters).

202 *Letters of John Langton from the backwoods of Upper Canada*, 21 October 1844, ed. by his son, Toronto, 1926, reprinted in John Hale, *Settlers*, pp. 97–8.

203 James Knight, August 1827, Nelsonville, Ohio, to George Courtauld, *Courtauld Family Papers*, IV, p. 1577. John Rochester, 1 June 1829, Logan, Ohio, to George Courtauld, *Ibid.*, IV, p. 1721.

204 Thomas Steel, 12 July 1846, Genessee, Wisc., to his father, James Steel, Steel Papers, File 4.

205 See the discussion of a number of such individuals in Wilbur S.Shepperson, *Emigration and Disenchantment*, Norman, 1965, pp. 31–61; Thomson, *A Pioneer Family*, p. 71; *Courtauld Family Papers*, II, p. 84; Flower, *History of the English*, p. 150.

5 Social Adjustment

206 H.Rose, 2 February 1850, near Lisbon, Ohio, to his brother in Scotland. Maurice Farrar, *Five Years in Minnesota*, London, 1880, p. 212. William Oliver, *Eight Months in Illinois*, p. 255.

207 B.Meatyard, 29 January 1838, Alton, Ill. to her mother-in-law in Dorset. Morris letter, 30 December 1838. George Simons, 20 September 184[?], North Royalton, Ohio.

208 William Cobbett, *The Emigrants Guide in Ten Letters Addressed to the Taxpayers of England*, London, 1829, pp. 33–6. Quaife, ed., *True Picture*, p. 7.

209 Robert Bowles, 10 August 1823, Harrison, Hamilton Co., Ohio, to his brother. Smith, ed., *Twenty-four Letters*, p. 26.

210 Quaife, ed., *An English Settler*, p. 41.

211 *Courtauld Family Papers*, II, p. 848.

212 Robert Bowles, 11 October 1823, Harrison, Hamilton Co., Ohio.

213 Charles Streater, 31 December 1838, Chevy Chase Farm, near Baltimore, to his sister, Headley, Hants, papers in private possession, copies made for author.

214 See for example, Catherine Bond, 1888.

215 'God Raised us up Good Friends', p. 233.

216 Thomas Steel, 23 October 1843, Mequonego Township, Wisc., to his father, File 3.

217 Thomas Steel, 13 April 1844, Genessee Township, Milwaukee Co., Wisc., to his father; 5 November 1844 to his sister, Lilly, File 3.

218 Thomas Steel, 29 May 1846, Genessee, Wisc., to his father; Catherine Steel, 2 May 1846, Genessee, Wisc., to Lilly Steel, File 4.

219 Catherine Steel, 2 May 1846, Genessee, Wisc., to her sister-in-law, Lilly Steel; Thomas Steel, 8 January 1846, Mequonego P.O., Wisc., to his father, File 4.

220 Catherine Steel, 20 January 1850, to Lilly Steel, File 6.

221 Quaife, ed., *True Picture*, p. 45. After ten years in Ohio, James Knight was more critical of Americans than he had been at the outset; '. . . they are always trying to take advantage if you treat them ever so well.' (James Knight, 22 March 1830, Nelsonville, Ohio, to George Courtauld, *Courtauld Family Papers*, IV, p. 1769).

222 Mrs George Courtauld, 26 December 1821, Bocking, Essex, to her daughter, Catherine Taylor, *Courtauld Family Papers*, II, p. 866. See also Mrs Ash, 12 June 1828, Cleves, Ohio, to George Courtauld, *Ibid.*, II, p. 910.

223 Quaife, ed., *True Picture*, p. 70.

224 *Courtauld Family Papers*, II, pp. 863–4, 865, 910; III, pp. 938–9, 919. See also Faux, *Memorable Days*, p. 258.

225 *Counsel for Emigrants*, p. ix. William Faux, *Memorable Days*, p. 330.

226 See statements by Edwin Bottomley in Quaife, ed., *An English Settler*, p. 70, and Robert Pollock, 17 April 1854, Cambridge, Wisc., to his brother.

227 The exceptions among letter-writers were Thomas Steel and Rev. Thomas Corlett. Steel decided, after some years of observing American politics, that the world's 'redemption' would have to come from Great Britain. (29 May 1846, to his father, File 4.) Rev. Thomas Corlett, who emigrated with his parents from the Isle of Man as a boy, expressed the view that the English government was the best in the world (Thomas Corlett, 29 June 1875, Cleveland, Ohio, to his cousin, Betsy Kneen, Corlett Letters).

228 Thomas Corlett, who emigrated as a child from the Isle of Man, mentioned attending meetings of the Monas Relief Society and the Monas Benefit Society in Cleveland, in a letter of 25 January 1871, nearly fifty years after he came to America.

229 The first St George's Benevolent Society was organized in Janesville in 1871 in Rock County, an offshoot of the St Louis society. The Odd Fellows were organized much earlier, however, in the mining communities. When the first lodge at Mineral Point, Iowa County, was established in 1835, there were, as yet, no American Odd Fellow organizations. *Commemorative Biographical Record of the Counties of Rock, Green, Grant, Iowa and La Fayette, Wisc.*, Chicago, 1901, p. 664. Cf. Berthoff, *British Immigrants*, pp. 180–1; Cole, *Immigrant City*, p. 153.

230 Berthoff, *British Immigrants*, p. 111; Shepperson, *British Emigration to North America*, pp. 54–64, 87, 93, 96–9.

231 Fred Pickford, early 1880s, undated letter, Nora Spring, Iowa, to his father and mother.

232 E.H. Bonsall, 19 July 1856, Philadelphia, to Elizabeth Newman, Pritchard Letters. Most of these families in agriculture seemed to fit Eisenstadt's description of the 'isolated stable family' in his study of Jewish immigration to Israel. (Eisenstadt, *The Absorption of Immigrants*, pp. 148–9.)

233 Hannah Young, 8 January 1832, near York, Upper Canada, to Ann, LSE.

234 Smith, ed., *Twenty-four Letters*, p. 20. Robert Bowles, 10 August 1823, 20 April 1823, Bowles Letters. Henry Newman, 20 May 1833, Wanborough, Ill., Pritchard Letters. Thomas Steel, 2 June 1844, Genessee, Wisc., to his father, Steel Papers, File 3. 'God Raised us up Good Friends', pp. 227, 232. Margaret Griffiths, 4 March 1850. James Knight, 5 November 1829, Nelsonville, Ohio, to George Courtauld, *Courtauld Family Papers*, IV, pp. 1749–50.

235 Thomas Steel, 22 November 1849, Genessee, Wisc., to his father, File 6.

236 Thomas Steel, 20 January 1850, Genessee, Wisc., to his father, File 6.

237 Joseph Hirst in Equality, Illinois and H.J. Nudham in Adams Co., Ohio, were also instances of isolated immigrants in agriculture.

238 Robert Bowles, 10 August 1823, Harrison, Hamilton County, Ohio. William Hall referred to a house-raising in Wanborough 'at which only one Americ' was present (Monaghan, ed., 'Journal of William Hall', p. 60).

239 Catherine Steel, 3 July 1851, Genessee, Wisc., to Lilly Steel, File 6.

240 Quaife, ed., *An English Settler*, p. 39.

241 Thomas Steel, 20 January 1850, Genessee, Wisc., to his father; Catherine Steel to Lilly Steel, 20 January, 1850, 12 February 1850, File 6.

242 Thomas Steel, 7 February 1853, Genessee, Wisc., to his father, 14 January 1852, File 7. For meetings among the socialists to read socialist literature, see Thomas Steel, 27 March 1846, Genessee, Wisc., to his father, File 4. Inglehart, 'Coming of the English to Indiana', p. 153. Monaghan, ed., 'Journal of William Hall', pp. 214, 217.

243 John Fisher missed his book club and enjoyed reading poetry; William Corlett was described by his son as 'fond of reading and his favourite books partook of a prosaic trend such as Watson's Biblical Dictionary and the History of all Nations'. (T.W.Corlett, *The People of Orrisdale*, p. 56.)

244 Miles Carpenter, *Immigrants and Their Children*, Washington, 1927, pp. 234–44. Berthoff, *British Immigrants*, pp. 134, 255. Samples of intermarriage in twelve townships in 1850 and 1860 suggest that the English married Americans more frequently than did either the Scots or the Irish.

245 Henry Newman, 20 May 1833, Wanborough, Ill., to George Newman, Pritchard Letters. See also Esther A.Cole, 21 January 1901, Belle Plaine, Scott Co., Minn., Devonshire Association Papers, Exeter Central Library. Kinvig, 'Manx Settlement', p. 9.

246 'God Raised us up Good Friends', p. 237. Andrew Morris, 5 February 1844.

247 'God Raised us up Good Friends', p. 234. Simons and Collyer, 184[?], North Royalton, Ohio. John Fisher, 30 November 1836.

248 Deborah Pritchard, 2 March 1829, Wanborough, Ill., Pritchard Letters. The establishment of an Episcopal Bishop's residence near Nashotah, as well as a theological school, helped make Waukesha County a favourite location for English immigrants. (William F.Whyte, 'The British in Wisconsin', Milo M.Quaife, ed., 'Wisconsin, Its History, Its People', Vol. II, typescript in the Wisconsin State Historical Society Library.) For later history of religion of British immigrants, and their churches, see Berthoff, *British Immigrants*, p. 154.

249 R. and B.Meatyard, 27 January 1838, Alton, Ill., to his mother. John Fisher, 29 May 1838.

250 The religious individualism of the British immigrants contrasts also with the attitudes of Polish immigrants. See Thomas and Znaniecki, *Polish Peasant*, I, pp. 286–7.

251 John Birket, 2 February 1843. 'God Raised us Up Good Friends', p. 235. Quaife, ed., *An English Settler*, pp. 37, 57, 111, 119, 125, 151, 230.

252 Horn, *English Colony in Iowa*, p. 83. *Portrait of Rock Co., Wisc.*, 1889, p. 982. See below Thomas Whittaker; Thomas Morris.

253 Thomas Steel, 2 July 1844, Genessee, Wisc., to Lilly Steel; 9 December 1843, File 3; Lilly Steel, 16 October 1845, Holloway, to Catherine Steel; Thomas Steel, 14 April 1846, Genessee, Wisc., to father; 15 October 1845, North Prairie, Wisc.; 28 March 1845, File 4. Compare George Courtauld's report: 'Unitarian Society [in Philadelphia] wh[h] I believe is still more unpopular in America than in England. Rat[l] Relig[n] is, I fear, scarcely known in Western America. Calvinism of the broadest & disgusting kind is the religion of the backwoods.' (George Courtauld, 19 October 1818, Athens, Ohio, to his son, Samuel, *Courtauld Family Papers*, II, p. 424.) Since one of Courtauld's daughters was a proselytizing Calvinist, who ceaselessly pressed her views on him, he was very sensitive to the *genre*. (George Courtauld, 4 December 1818, Marietta, Ohio, to his wife and daughters, *Courtauld Family Papers*, II, p. 452.)

254 Arthur Pickford, 1880s, Pickford Letters. See also W.T.Corlett's description of his father: 'while fundamentally a religious man, he did not allow church

dogmas to dominate him, nor to prevent his using certain expletives of profanity when occasion arose. He seldom attended church.' (*People of Orrisdale*, p. 56.)

255 Compare the Wesleyan Mrs Burlend's criticism of Methodist enthusiasts in Illinois and H.Rose's horror at the substitution of Isaac Watt's hymns for the Psalms of David among Ohio Presbyterians with this statement of Isaac Goodchild, who was a Primitive Methodist: 'I have not had the privelige of hearing anay but Church people and Babtist But I feel thankful that God is the same.' (21 September 1851, South Kingston, RI, to his brother, Richard Goodchild, near Newbury, Berks.) See also John Fisher, 30 November 1836.

256 James Knight, 22 March 1830, Nelsonville, Ohio, to Sophia Courtauld; 30 August 1828, to George Courtauld, *Courtauld Family Papers*, IV, pp. 1662, 1776.

257 Clarence S.Paine, 'Diaries of a Nebraska Farmer, 1876–7', *Agricultural History*, XXII, No. 1, January 1948, p. 3. Compare the perceptive remarks of Professor Gerschenkron on the newcomer to a migratory society in *Economic Backwardness in Historical Perspective*, Cambridge, 1962, p. 324.

258 Robert Shedden, 31 October 1842, Udina, to Andrew Fouldes. Corlett, *People of Orrisdale*, p. 53. For examples of hesitation, see H.Rose, 5 February 1830, near Lisbon, Ohio, to his brother; Thomas Steel, 16 June 1846, Mequonego, Wisc., to Lilly Steel; 29 May 1846, Genessee, Wisc., to his father, File 4. Of these letter-writers, John Fisher was the most enthusiastic about citizenship, 11 June 1832.

259 30 August 1828, Nelsonville, Ohio, to George Courtauld, *Courtauld Family Papers*, III, p. 1660.

260 John Birket, 25 December 1841. William Morris, 14 July 1841. Thomas Steel, 13 March 1846, Genessee, Wisc., to his father, File 4. Quaife, ed., *An English Settler*, p. 146.

261 James Knight, 1 February 1832, Nelsonville, Ohio, to George Courtauld, *Courtauld Family Papers*, V, p. 1925. Corlett, *The People of Orrisdale*, p. 19. John Fisher, March 1838. Thomas Corlett, 10 September 1862, Collamer, Ohio, to his uncle, Thomas Corlett, Corlett Letters. Nathan Pooley, 23 December 1862, Elkhart, Indiana, to his cousin, Fisher Letters.

262 Janet Clausson, 31 July 1866, New York, to Archibald McKellar, McKellar Letters.

263 Thomas Steel, 7 July 1834, Louisville, Kentucky, to his father, File 3.

264 John Griffiths, 23 April 1865. H.V.MacNeil, 21 December 1864, National, Clayton Co., Iowa, to Archibald McKellar, McKellar Letters.

265 M.T.Williams, 19 April 1861, New Orleans, to Sydney Williams, letter in private possession. See also Janet Clausson, 31 July 1866, New York, to Archibald McKellar: 'I am proud to be a rebel, we have the bravest men that ever fought.' In a letter of 26 December 1868, Charleston, S.C., Archibald McLeish described Old Carolina as 'the real Sebastopol of the South'.

266 John and Mary Thomson, 24 January 1850, Wingville, Wisc., to his brother in Fife.

267 Smith, ed., *Twenty-four Letters*, p. 12. Quaife, ed., *An English Settler*, p. 161. Corlett, *The People of Orrisdale*, p. 56. Thomson, *A Pioneer Family*, p. 82.

268 Hiatt, ed., 'Diary of William Owen', p. 130. Cf. Allan Bogue, 'Social Theory and the Pioneer', *Agricultural History*, XXXIV, January 1960, p. 33.

Birket Series

1 Information about the Birket family has been obtained from the following sources: UK Census MSS., 1841, 1851. *Kelly's Post Office Directory, County of Lancashire,* 1858, pp. 313, 434; 1864, p. 359. *Slater's Directory,* 1851, p. 439. *History of Tazewell County,* Chicago, 1879, pp. 680–1. Aaron Wilson Oakford, *Peoria Story,* compiled 1949–57, I, pp. 34–6. *Portrait and Biographical Album of Peoria,* Chicago, 1890, p. 277. William Pooley, *Settlement of Illinois, 1830–50,* Madison, 1908, pp. 404, 413. C.Ballard, *History of Peoria,* 1870, p. 125. US Census MSS, Population, 1850, 1870.

Corlett Series

1 W.T.Corlett, *The People of Orrisdale and Others,* Cleveland, 1918, p. 41. The additional material on the Corlett family in this introduction has been obtained from the following: *Ibid.,* pp. 6, 22, 37, 42–3, 50, 56. R.H.Kinvig, 'Manx Settlement in the USA', *Isle of Man History and Antiquarian Society,* V, No. 4, 1955, pp. 5, 10. UK Census MSS, 1851. Thomas Corlett, 29 June 1875, Cleveland, to cousin Betsey Kneen in Manchester; 25 January 1871, Cleveland, to cousin E. Kneen; 7 May 1852, Gambier, Knox County, Ohio; 7 December 1853, Granville, Licking County, Ohio, to uncle Thomas Corlett in Kirk Michael, Corlett Letters. *Thomas Kelly and Family's Journal in the Year 1827,* Times Press and Anthony, Gibbs and Phillips, 1965, pp. 16–17. (I am indebted to Negley Harte for pointing out this volume to me.) US Census MSS, Population, 1860. E.H.Chapman, *Cleveland; Village to Metropolis,* Western Reserve Historical Society, 1964, p. 152. Gertrude Cannell, 'A Short History of Mona's Relief Society'. Hundredth Anniversary of the Mona's Relief Society, Cleveland, 1951, p. 7.
2 John G.Clark, *The Grain Trade of the Old Northwest,* Urbana and London, 1966, p. 60.

Fisher Series

1 The reconstruction of Fisher's life which appears here is based on the following sources: UK Census MSS, 1851. *White's Norfolk Directory for 1836,* p. 810; 1864, p. 469. *Post Office Directory for 1858,* p. 174. US Census MSS, Population, 1840. William A.Whitney and R.I.Bonner, *History and Biographical Record of Lenawee Co., Mich.,* Adrian, Mich., 1879, II, pp. 173–4.
2 According to a local directory for 1836, the land in Brooke parish was owned by many proprietors. It is possible that the Fishers owned at least part of their farm.
3 Cf. Lillie Marian Springall, *Labouring Life in Norfolk Villages, 1834–1912,* London, 1936, p. 103.
4 Cf. Warren Rasmussen in National Bureau of Economic Research, *Trends in the American Economy in the Nineteenth Century,* Princeton, 1960, p. 270, quoting Ulysses P.Hedrick, *History of Agriculture in the State of New York,* 1933, p. 110. This estimate that the average settler could clear and sow ten acres and erect a cabin on timbered land in a single year seems to have been well above the average for British immigrant farmers.
5 See below pp.189–94 for letters from Robert Smith to the Fisher family.
6 Copious extracts from the correspondence of John Fisher were published in *Michigan History,* XLV, No. 3, September 1961, pp. 220–36, with an introduction by Louis Leonard Tucker.

Wozencraft Series

1 Details about Wozencraft have been garnered from the UK Census MSS, 1851, and the US Census MSS, Population, 1830, 1840, 1850.
2 Kington was later transferred from the county of Radnor in Wales to that of Hereford in England. Wozencraft thought it was in England as he addressed his letters to Kington, Herefordshire.
3 Because of strife between Athens and Watkinsville about which should be the county seat, the southern half of Clarke County, which included the Farmington district where Wozencraft lived, was organized into a new county called Oconee in 1875.
4 Rev. Thomas Corlett wrote in 1853: 'The state of religion in this country is at a low ebb. The public mind seems to be all taken up with business. No time for religion.' (Thomas Corlett, 7 December 1853, Granville, Licking County, Ohio. See also similar comments in a letter dated 26 January 1857, Baraboo, Wisconsin.) After noting the depressed state of business in 1859, he commented: 'The past year has been a year of great religious awaking all over this country, and we have been favored with God's presence and blessing in my parish. The number of my communicants has doubled the past year.' (Thomas Corlett, 21 March 1859, Cullamer, Cuyahoga County, Ohio, to his uncle, Thomas Corlett on the Isle of Man, Corlett Letters.)

Morris Series

1 Information about the Morris family and their friends has been obtained from the following sources: Edward Baines, *Directory of the County of Lancaster*, 1824, I, p. 605. *Slater's Lancashire Directory*, 1851, p. 145. UK Census MSS, 1851. John Morris, 23 April 1832, Coppul, Lancs., to Jonathon Morris; 13 February 1832, Heath Charnock, Lancs., to his son, Morris Letters. *History of Washington County, Ohio*, Cleveland, 1881, pp .676–7, 682. Martin R.Andrews, ed., *History of Marietta and Washington County, Ohio*, Chicago, 1902, pp. 293–4. US Census MSS, Population, 1850; Agriculture, 1850; Population, 1880. Passenger Lists, Philadelphia, 425/44, No. 118, microfilm, National Archives.
2 Thompson, *The Making of the English Working Class*, pp. 309–10.
3 Attributed in the census of 1851 to the failure of a calico printing firm.
4 Robert L.Jones, 'Special Crops in Ohio before 1850', *The Ohio State Archaeological and Historical Quarterly*, LIV, No. 2, April–June 1945, p. 138. F.P. Weisenburger, *The Passing of the Frontier, 1825–50*, in Carl Wittke, ed., *History of Ohio*, Columbus, 1941, III, p. 65.
5 Paul C.Henlein, *Cattle Kingdom in the Ohio Valley*, Lexington, 1959, p. 73.
6 Jones, 'Special Crops in Ohio', p. 140.
7 When Noble County was formed in 1851, Aurelius township was reduced in size. It may be that the Morris family were thus transferred to Noble County, but I have not had an opportunity to check this possibility.
8 John Morris was listed in the 1850 census as a farmer, though since he did not appear in the agriculture schedules, he did not have a farm of his own. He was the only one of the entire clan to be identified in a later census. In 1880, he was listed as a merchant in the village of Elba in Aurelius township.

Butterworth Letter

1 *Slater's Directory for Lancashire,* 1851, p. 464.
2 Cf. Morris and Crawshaw letters.

Whittaker Series

1 Information about the Whittakers was found in: UK Census MSS, 1841, 1851. *White's Leeds Directory for 1847,* p. 131. US Census MSS, Population, 1850; Agriculture, 1860.
2 D.W.Mitchell, *Ten Years in the United States,* London, 1862, p. 323. William Cobbett, *A Year's Residence,* p. 531.
3 Quaife, ed., *An English Settler in Pioneer Wisconsin,* p. 49.
4 See *Chambers Information for the People,* edited by W. and R.Chambers, London, 1835. *Chambers Information for the People,* second edition, Edinburgh, 1842, No. 18.

Smith Series

1 Further information about Robert Smith and his family has been obtained from the following: US Census MSS, Population, 1840, 1850, 1860, 1870; Agriculture, 1850, 1860. (Extracts from the Agricultural Census for Lenawee County, Michigan, were generously provided by the Michigan Historical Commission, Lansing, Michigan.) Bonner and Whitney, *History of Lenawee County, Michigan,* II, pp. 173–4.
2 A nephew wrote of Robert Smith: 'If there is a true Christian this side of the Blew Ocean it is him. It does our Soal good to set down By their hearth stone and hear them sing & Prey of the goodness of God.' (Nathan Poolley, 23 December 1862, Goshen, Elkhart Co., Indiana, to his cousin, Fisher Letters.)

Griffiths Series

1 For sources of these details about the Griffiths family, see UK Census MSS, 1851. *Post Office Directory for 1858 for Gloucestershire,* p. 147. US Census MSS, Agriculture, 1860, 1870, 1880; Population, 1880. Illinois State Census MSS, 1855.
2 Cf. UN, Department of Social Studies, Population Division, Population Studies, No. 17, *The Determinants and Consequences of Population Trends,* New York, 1953, p. 111.
3 For further details on the Mormon mission in Britain, see Philip Taylor, *Expectations Westward, The Mormons and the Emigration of their British Converts in the Nineteenth Century,* Edinburgh and London, 1965, p. 19.
4 Philip A. M. Taylor, 'Why did the Mormons Emigrate?' *Utah Historical Quarterly,* XXII, July 1954, p. 260.

Bishop Series

1 For Bishop family, see UK Census MSS, 1841, 1851, 1861. US Census MSS, Population, 1850, 1860, 1870, 1880. Stafford C.Cleveland, *History and Directory of Yates County,* Penn Yan, 1873, I, p. 369.

2 The likeliest candidate as the husband of Aunt Baldry, referred to in the letters, was Isaac Baldry, listed in the census of 1841, 1851 and 1861, at Dennington as an agricultural labourer. There were two other Baldrys at Dennington, both agricultural labourers.

3 The other daughter, Alice, said in the letters to have married a livery stable keeper, might be Alice Nicholas, wife of Charles Nicholas who had been born in England in 1846 and who gave his occupation in the US Census of 1870 as 'huckster stand'.

Grayston-Bond Series

1 In addition to the census volumes, information has been obtained from Victoria County History, *Lancashire*, III, pp. 284–5.

2 One of his farm labourers was a young relative, William Grayston, aged thirteen; and a niece of eleven worked as a house servant in Robert Grayston's home. Details about these families from: UK Census MSS, 1851, 1861. *Kelly's Post Office Directory for Lancashire*, 1864, p. 42. US Census MSS, Population, 1870, 1880. Conversation with Miss Jessie Thompson, 10 June 1949. Letter from Miss Thompson, 9 April 1970, to the author.

3 Sefton was located six miles north of Liverpool. Its population in 1851 was only 433. The Earl of Sefton was Lord of the manor and principal landed proprietor (*Kelly's Post Office Directory for Lancashire*, 1858).

II TRAMPING ARTISANS

1 How Typical are the Letter-Writers?

1 C.J.Erickson, 'British Immigrants in the Old Northwest', pp. 327–8.

2 E.P.Hutchinson, *Immigrants and their Children, 1850–1950*, New York and London, 1956, pp. 82–4.

3 The exceptions are Jonathan Oakes, an engine-fitter from Lancashire, who wrote one of the letters in the Morris collection, Lancashire Record Office, and Titus Crawshaw, wool finisher, whose letters are reproduced below. The editor of the recently published Hollingworth letters claims that members of this family 'were well equipped to help promote manufacturing in America. Almost instinctively they gravitated toward central New England, where the machine shop and factory were already part of everyday life'. When the members of this family left Huddersfield in the late 1820s, only the finishing processes had been partially mechanized in the woollen industry of that town. Since the prior occupations of the various members of that family have not been discovered by the editor, who refers to them as labourers, it seems likely that they brought pre-industrial handicraft skills rather than knowledge of machinery. The experience of the Morris family, above, and of Abel Stephenson, below, also cast doubt on how 'instinctive' the move to the factory in America may have been (Thomas W.Leavitt, ed., *The Hollingworth Letters: Technical Change in the Textile Industry, 1826–1837*, Cambridge, Mass. and London, 1969, p. xx).

4 See for example the letters of Edward Phillips, the younger, and David Laing below. Also the letter of John Wilson, Lowell, Mass., 1849, to relatives in Halifax, Yorks., LSE photostats.

5 Henry Edward Price Diary, *c.* 1904, manuscript in Islington Central Library, p. 136.

6 C.J.Erickson, 'Who were the English and Scottish Emigrants in the 1880s?'

2 Motives for Emigration

7 Price, 'Autobiography', p. 57. See also George Whittaker, hatter, 21 July 1817, Philadelphia, John Knight, *Important Extracts,* pp. 34–5. George Martin, 7 June 1837.

8 Abel Stephenson, 21 November 1838.

9 William Winterbottom, 28 February 1895, New York, to his cousin Charles, letter kindly lent by Miss Joan Nuttall. See also Leavitt, ed., *Hollingworth Letters,* p. 38.

10 William Winterbottom, *loc. cit.*

11 George Martin, 1 June 1837. Edward Phillips, 22 July 1820. Edward Phillips, the younger, 4 October 1838.

12 Jonas Booth, 20 March 1829, New Hartford, Oneida County, New York, to his brother and sister in Bradford, copy at LSE. Abel Stephenson, 18 April 1838. George Hails, 21 July 1839. Leavitt, ed., *Hollingworth Letters,* p. 93.

13 Colin Houston, 17 April 1851, Kilbarcham, Scotland, to Peter McKellar.

14 Colin Houston, 3 July 1864, Kilbarcham, to Archibald McKellar.

15 George Martin, 9 February 1851. Leavitt, ed., *Hollingworth Letters,* p. 61.

16 Jane Peebles, 2 November 1849, Partick, to her father, Peter McKellar. Port records suggest that the emigration of skilled workers was more stable and continuous than that of labourers, whose migration fluctuated much more widely in accordance with trade conditions in the USA. See also Leavitt, ed., *Hollingworth Letters,* p. 42.

17 Tom Martin, 27 July 1851, Rochester, NY, to his uncle in London, Martin Letters.

18 Joseph Hartley, 21 October 1860, Lockport, NY, to relatives, Michael Drake, ed., 'We are Yankees Now', *New York History,* XLV, No. 3, July 1964, p. 234.

19 Abel Stephenson, 26 November 1838; John Ronaldson, 5 February 1854; George Martin, 20 September 1834.

20 James and Harriet Parks, 16 March 1828, Greenbush, NY, Smith, ed., *Twenty-four Letters,* p. 31.

21 Jane McKellar, 13 May 1849, Partick, to her father, Peter McKellar.

22 Price, 'Autobiography', pp. 152–3.

23 Alfred Green, 28 July 1857, New Rochelle, NY, to his mother, letter in private possession, photostat in LSE. Leavitt, ed., *Hollingworth Letters,* pp. 3–4.

24 Daniel Stephenson, 16 May 1864, Fairfield, Iowa, to his uncle, Stephenson Letters, photostats at LSE. 'I hope you are saving as well as you expected ...' (Colin Houston, 17 April 1851, Kilbarcham, to Peter McKellar).

25 Joseph Hartley, 28 November 1859, Lockport, NY, to his aunt and cousin; 12 September 1858; 27 August 1861, Drake, ed., 'We Are Yankees Now', pp. 228, 231, 234.

26 A.K.Hamilton Jenkin, *The Cornish Miner,* London, 1927, second edition, 1948, pp. 327–8. *BPP* 1841, VII, 205.

27 George Martin, 14 May 1849.
28 Thomas and Znaniecki, *Polish Peasant*, I, pp. 466, 508, 198–203. Ernest Lister, Henry Price and George Martin did display some interest in techniques of work.
29 Ronaldson, 27 March 1854. Richard Hails, 31 July 1849.
30 Richard Hails, August 1849. Ronaldson, 5 February 1854. Martin, 25 May 1850. Titus Crawshaw, 30 November 1854. Richard Hails, 21 May 1849. Jonathan Dawson, August 1849, Shullsburg, Wisconsin, to his brother-in-law, Hails Letters. Edward Phillips, 4 October 1838. Stephen and Elizabeth Watson, 29 March 1824, Albany, NY, to their parents, Smith ed., *Twenty-four Letters*, p. 20.

3 Networks of Migration

31 Jonas Booth, 20 March 1829, New Hartford, Oneida County, NY, to his brother and sister-in-law. Family disagreements also formed part of the background to the emigration of John Wilson and George Martin. George Lowe, 18 June 1896, Newark, NJ, to his brother Walter in Birmingham, letter in private possession, lent to the author. Leavitt, ed., *Hollingworth Letters*, p. 8.
32 Jane McDonald, August 1855, to her brother Peter McKellar. Peter McKellar, 25 June 1855, Farmersburgh, Iowa, to his son, Archibald McKellar. John and James McKellar had emigrated to the United States without their wives, and Peter McKellar was a widower when he emigrated with one of his sons.
33 Frank Crewe, 18 May 1839, at anchor, Plymouth, to his brother in Marylebone, London. This letter was found by Hugh Brogan who made a copy for me.
34 Jonathan Dawson, August 1849, Shullsburg, Wisc., to his brother, Hails letters; Alfred Green, 28 July 1857, New Rochelle, NY, to his mother, LSE; Jonathan Oakes, 20 June 1841, New York City, to Jonathan Morris, Tyldesley, near Manchester, Morris Letters; David Whyte, 15 February 1855, Watertown, Wisconsin, to his brother, Wisconsin State Historical Society Library, MSS/AW.
35 This conclusion is based upon the passenger lists of ships' lists on microfilm in the National Archives in Washington. Erickson, 'Who were the English and Scottish Emigrants'. See also Louis Copeland, 'The Cornish in Southwest Wisconsin', *Wisconsin Historical Society Collections*, XIV, 1898, p. 308.
36 John Worrall Williamson, 5 June 1848, Allegheny City, Penn., to his sister and brother-in-law, Charlotte and Samuel Ashton, copy made for me by the late Professor T.S.Ashton from family papers.
37 Drake, ed., 'We are Yankees Now', p. 223.
38 Joseph and Rebecca Hartley, 18 June 1866, Lockport, NY, to sisters, *ibid.*, p. 239.
39 Henry Craig, 7 September 1850, Ohio City, to his family.
40 Letter from his mother, 20 August 1846, to Henry Edward Price, pasted in his scrapbook, 'Price, Autobiography', p. 66. See also Colin Houston, 11 October 1854 ?, Anderston, to his cousin, Archibald McKellar.
41 George Martin, 7 January 1849, 18 January 1852. Richard Hails, 21 May 1849, 31 July 1849. Edward Phillips, 22 July 1820.
42 Jane McKellar, 7 January 1849, Partick, to her father, Peter McKellar.
43 Price, 'Autobiography', p. 58. George Fewins, 21 July 1851, Kansas, to Guardians of the Poor, Cheriton Bishop, Devon, 132 A/PO 40–45, Devonshire Record Office, Exeter.
44 Photostat copies of Wilson Letters, 1848–9, Lowell, Mass. to Halifax, Yorks., are in LSE. Archibald McKellar carried testimonials from two of his employers in

Scotland when he emigrated in the late forties. See also James Burn, *The 'Beggar Boy', an Autobiography*, London, 1882, p. 262.

45 Joseph Hartley, 9 June 1858, Medina, NY, to his aunt and cousin, Drake, ed. 'We are Yankees Now', p. 226. Also John Worrall Williamson, 5 June 1848, Allegheny City, Penn; Price, 'Autobiography', p. 88.

46 John Wilson, 3 February 1849, Lowell, Mass., to his father-in-law, Wilson Letters. George Martin, 7 January 1849.

47 Joseph Hollingworth objected to turning wages over to the family. (Leavitt, ed., *Hollingworth Letters*, pp. 53–5, 88).

48 Jonas Booth, 20 March 1829, New Hartford, Oneida Co., NY, to his brother and sister-in-law. See also Abel Stephenson, 18 April 1840; James McKellar, 26 March 1842, St Louis, to Peter McKellar; Richard Hails, 31 July 1849.

49 J. and E.Thorpe, 6 July 1828, Hudson, NY, to Thomas Cooke, Cripscorner, Sedlescombe, Sussex, Smith, ed., *Twenty-four Letters*, pp. 42–3. For another example of a New York City chapel serving as a kind of employment agency, see Price, 'Autobiography', p. 123, letter from George Birmingham, 7 March 1848, Buffalo, to Henry Price. On Methodist church membership in England as an aid to internal migrants in Britain, see Thompson, *Making of the English Working-Class*, p. 379.

50 Edward Thompson, 16 December 1948, Romford, to the author. Compare C.J. Erickson, *American Industry and the European Immigrant*, Cambridge, 1957, pp. 88–105.

4 Economic Adjustment

51 James McKellar, 15 March 1841, Boston, to his brother; 26 March 1842, St Louis, to his brother, McKellar Letters. For discussions of tramping artisans, see E.J.Hobsbawm, *Labouring Men*, London, 1964, pp. 43–4; Thompson, *Making of the English Working Class*, p. 24.

52 Crawshaw, 30 November 1854; Stephenson, 1838; Ronaldson, 30 October 1852. The following sorts of entries in the census manuscripts were common: Richard Jordan, forty-five, iron manufacturer, born in England, had children who had been born in Pennsylvania and Virginia as well as Kentucky. (US Census MSS, Population, 1850, Covington, Kenton Co., Kent., Vol. 12, p. 210.) Samuel Crawshaw, fifty-five, manufacturer of woollens, born in England, had two children who had been born in Massachusetts. (US. Census MSS, Population, 1850, Newburgh, Orange Co., NY, Vol. 2, p. 591). Leavitt, ed., *Hollingworth Letters*, p. xxiv.

53 Thomas W.Barrett, Clearfield, Penn., Devonshire Assn Papers, Exeter Central Library. Peter Clark, a stone quarrier from Stirlingshire, emigrated in 1849 to Hadley, Massachusetts, and continued his travels to New York City, to California, Australia, Peru and back to New York City before he settled on a Wisconsin farm in 1854. (*History of Dane Co., Wisc.*, Chicago, 1880, p. 1084). For other examples, see Copeland, 'The Cornish in Southwest Wisconsin', p. 305n, James Ogden's biography in *History of Hancock County, Illinois*, Chicago, 1880, pp. 887–8; Thomas Phillips, *Commemorative Biographical Record of the Counties of Rock, Green, Grant, Iowa and Lafayette, Wisconsin*, Chicago, 1901, p. 408; James Tapper, *History of Clayton Co.*, Chicago, 1882, pp. 823–4.

54 John Watson, Etna Mines, Tennessee, in a letter to the Durham *Chronicle*, 28 March 1879, p. 3.

55 Jonathan and June Dawson, August 1849, Shullsburg, Lafayette County, Wisconsin, to George Hails, Hails Letters. The county histories of south-western Wisconsin are full of such cases.

56 Hails, 21 July 1849; Stephenson, 1838. James Burn, *Beggar Boy*, pp. 270–1.

57 Crawshaw, 1855; 31 July 1863. Compare the remark of a London carpenter who settled in Fond du Lac, Wisconsin, in the forties: 'Of course I do not care what I do if I dont get work at my oun trade I go to labouring work. . . .' Frank Johnson, 16 December 1849, Fond du Lac, to his wife, Betsy, 'God Raised us up Good Friends', p. 227.

58 Joseph Hartley, 15 April 1859, Medina, and 3 May 1860, Lockport, NY, Drake, ed., 'We are Yankees Now', pp. 230, 232.

59 Alfred Green, 28 July 1857, New Rochelle, NY, to his mother in Mile End, near London. Burn, *Beggar Boy*, pp. 267–8, on his second probation as a journeyman hatter.

60 Ernest Lister, 30 July 1883. George Martin, April 1848. A mason in Pennsylvania, working at a dollar a day in 1833, remarked 'had I been acquainted with the tools and manner of working I could have got much more'. (*Counsel for Emigrants*, p. 60).

61 Archibald McKellar, 13 October 1851, Stillwater, Minn., to his father.

62 This was also the case with John Worrall Williamson, who tried to get a job as an overlooker when he failed to obtain the apprenticeship as a mechanic which he hoped for.

63 The wages which are cited by skilled workers tended to lie near the averages of wages in their trades as reported by Stanley Lebergott, 'Wage Trends, 1800–1900', in *Trends in the American Economy in the Nineteenth Century*, Studies in Income and Wealth, Conference on Research in Income and Wealth, vol. 24, National Bureau of Economic Research, Princeton, 1960, p. 462. The only complaint of outright discrimination which I have encountered is the following: 'Without you have influence and have been long enough in the Country to become a Citizen (5 years) you are sadly handicapped. They will not find employment for foreigners as long as naturalized citizens and people born in the Country are walking around doing nothing'. This was written during the depression of the nineties. (George Lowe, 18 June 1896, Newark, New Jersey, to his brother in Birmingham, copy of letter, supplied to the author.) See also letter of Joseph Hollingworth, *c*. 1829, 'I believe the reason we had to move, was the effects produced by Masonic power and Yankeeism . . .' (Leavitt, ed., *Hollingworth Letters*, p. 74).

64 Price, 'Autobiography', pp. 80–2.

65 John Worrall Williamson, 5 June 1848, Allegheny City, Penn., to his sister.

66 Joseph Hartley, 29 December 1858, Medina, to his aunt and cousin, Drake, ed., 'We are Yankees Now', pp. 228–9. James McKellar, April 1841, Boston, to his brother, Peter McKellar, McKellar Letters.

67 Ronaldson, 9 April 1853; George Martin, 30 September 1834; Leavitt, ed., *Hollingworth Letters*, p. 22.

68 See, for example, Frank Wostenholm, 21 March 1870, to William Abbott and Ned Armitage; Sheffield *Independent*, 6 April 1870, p. 4. *Mining Journal Supplement*, 26 June 1880, p. 732. E.H.Cawley, ed., *American Diaries of Richard Cobden*, Princeton, 1952, p. 94. Sheffield *Independent*, 2 December 1871, p. 8: 'To work sixty hours a week for fifty shillings in a country where there is no beer fit to drink, no holidays, none of the delights sweet to a Sheffield workman. It is insanity for Sheffield workmen to come to this country. He may live the life of a

stranger in a strange country, cut off from all that makes work tolerable, his special taste and habit unsatisfied and at the end of the year he is probably worse off financially than if he had stayed at home. . . .'

69 Jonathan Oakes, 20 June 1841. NYC, to Jonathan Morris, Morris Letters. Titus Crawshaw, 6 May 1854. A foundry worker in Pennsylvania wrote during the depression of the seventies: 'We are only making eight hours a day but glad to get that to do' (Owen Prosser, 21 May 1876, Mt Washington, Penn., to his brother and sister, private letters copied for the author).

70 Joseph Hartley, 3 May 1860, 27 August 1861, Lockport, to his aunt and cousin, Drake, ed., 'We are Yankees Now', pp. 232, 234. Contrast fear of Yankee superintendent, Leavitt, ed., *Hollingworth Letters*, p. 49.

71 Price, 'Autobiography', pp. 88–91. Titus Crawshaw, 31 July 1863.

72 Joseph Hartley, 29 December 1858, Medina, *ibid.,* p. 229.

73 Joseph Hartley, 27 August 1861, Lockport, NY, to his cousin, *ibid.,* p. 235, Ernest Lister, 20 August 1883, 7 October 1883. Titus Crawshaw, 30 November 1854. Edward Phillips, 5 January 1820.

74 Edward Phillips, 10 December 1842. A rather interesting series from a Welsh iron worker, in his fifties, settled in Cuyahoga Falls, Ohio, exists because his former employer continued to send him money. (See Lloyd Letters, 1846–56, photostats in LSE Library. I am indebted to Robin Craig for copies of these letters.)

75 George Martin, 9 February 1851. William Winterbottom, 28 February 1895, New York, to his cousin Charles. Cf. Joseph Hartley about brother James' coming: 'he must make up his mind to settel down if he wishes to be anything in this world. He will be respected if he is steady & carfull if I had have been carfull the first 2 years I might have been better . . .' 18 June 1866, Lockport, to sisters after ten years in the US (Drake, ed., 'We are Yankees Now', p. 239).

76 Erickson, *American Industry and the European Immigrant,* pp. 49, 56, 215n. Berthoff, *British Immigrants in American Industry,* pp. 17, 52, 80–4. Roger Simon, 'The Birds of Passage in America, 1865–1914', MA Thesis, University of Wisconsin, 1966. *Rylands Iron Trade Circular,* 11 February 1865, p. 16.

77 See the Price autobiography and the cases described in W.S.Shepperson, *Emigration and Discontent,* pp. 62–84.

78 Drake, ed., 'We are Yankees Now', pp. 233, 235, 253, 261.

79 Owen Prosser, 21 May 1876, Mount Washington, Penn., to his brother and sister.

80 John Worrall Williamson, 5 June 1848, Allegheny City, Penn., to his sister in Ashton-under-Lyne. Hails, 21 May 1849, 31 July 1849. Titus Crawshaw, 18 June 1866, 30 August 1857. John Wilson, 21 April 1849. James Roberts, 30 September 1849. John Ronaldson, 9 April 1853. Drake, ed., 'We are Yankees Now', p. 262.

5 Social Adjustment

81 Jonas Booth, 20 March 1829, New Hartford, Oneida Co., New York, to his brother, Joseph Booth, Bradford. John Knight, *Important Extracts,* pp. 42–3. Smith, ed., *Twenty-four Letters,* p. 28.

82 David Whyte, 15 February 1855, Watertown, Wisc., to his brother in Scotland. James Roberts, 30 September 1849.

83 David Whyte objected to contact with 'Irish of the coarsest stamp' on the Lake Erie steamer. See also, Leavitt, ed., *Hollingworth Letters,* p. 21.

84 Cf. Ernest Lister's remark: 'imagin paying 3£ for whitewashing' in his letter of 1884.

85 See also Leavitt, ed., *Hollingworth Letters*, p. 15.
86 William Winterbottom, 28 February 1895, New York, to his cousin Charles.
87 George Martin, 16 April 1848.
88 Daniel Stephenson, 18 May 1864, Fairfield, Iowa, Stephenson Letters. Leavitt, ed., *Hollingworth Letters*, p. 99.
89 Alfred Green, 28 July 1857, New Rochelle, NY, to his mother.
90 This subject is discussed in R.T.Berthoff, *British Immigrants*, pp. 132–3 where he maintained that Americans did not regard British immigrants as foreigners.
91 Jane Martin, 16 May 1852, Rochester, NY, to her father, Martin Letters.
92 David Whyte, 15 February 1855.
93 *Loc. cit.* Cf. letter from Jonathan Dawson, August 1849, Shullsburg, Wisc., to his brother: 'We are blest with Gospel means here on the Sabbath. We have two schools, 3 sermons, 2 class meetings and 2 through the week and two prayer meetings through the week which are all great priviliges. . . .' See also Rebecca Hartley, December [1870], Lockport, NY, Drake, ed., 'We are Yankees Now', p. 248.
94 Price, 'Autobiography', pp. 20, 68, 70, 80. For a discussion of the provision of churches among British industrial workers in large cities, see Berthoff, *British Immigrants*, pp. 154–9. These letters challenge his view that 'most English immigrants were, if anything, either Anglicans or Methodists'.
95 David Whyte, 15 February 1855. Edward Phillips, 2 January 1820.
96 Joseph Hartley, 21 October 1860, Lockport, NY, Drake, ed., 'We are Yankees Now', pp. 233–4.
97 Such statements appeared in a letter of George Lowe, 18 June 1896, Newark, NJ, to his brother Walter Lowe in Birmingham, and in a letter of Owen Prosser, 21 May 1876, Mt Washington, Allegheny Co., Penn., to his brother and sister.
98 For objections to working near Negroes, see Titus Crawshaw, 30 August 1857, and David Whyte's letter of 15 February 1855, in which he noted that they had decided not to go to Canada because they had learned that the Government land was in the immediate neighbourhood of free blacks. A Yorkshire-born brewer in Pittsburgh, who had emigrated in 1805, was definitely against emancipation, as were possibly other English immigrants of a higher social class. (*Letters from a Yorkshire Emigrant, Joseph Wainwright of Pittsburgh, USA*, Department of Local History and Archives, Occasional Publications, No. 1, Sheffield City Libraries, pp. 15–16).
99 Joseph Hartley, 3 May 1860, Lockport; Rebecca Hartley, 7 May [1867–8]; January 1868; 12 December [1870]; 9 September [1870–1]; 30 June [1873–5], Drake, ed., 'We are Yankees Now', pp. 232, 244, 242, 248, 252, 256.
100 Stephenson, 18 April 1840. George Martin, May 1844. Titus Crawshaw, 24 July 1855.
101 Titus Crawshaw, 16 April 1855.
102 Price, 'Autobiography', letter facing p. 68.
103 Edward Phillips, 4 October 1838.
104 Such as those described in Berthoff, *British Immigrants*, pp. 165–84.
105 Joseph Hartley, 12 September 1858, Medina, NY, Drake, ed., 'We are Yankees Now', pp. 227–8. Leavitt, ed., *Hollingworth Letters*, p. 30.
106 Kirtley Nixon, 22 August 1870, Enon Valley, Lawrence Co., Penn., to his niece. Smith, ed., *Twenty-four Letters*, p. 25.
107 Price, 'Autobiography', p. 80. Ronaldson, June 1854.
108 Rebecca Hartley, 5 April 1872, Lockport, NY, Drake, ed., 'We are Yankees

Now', p. 254. Letter from Hanover, West Meridan, Conn., *Rylands Iron Trade Circular*, 1 February 1865, p. 16. Alfred Green, 28 July 1857, New Rochelle, NY. Charles Johnston, 10 January 1833, Perth Amboy, NJ, to Thomas Tyron, Northants. Record Office. See also Burn, *Beggar Boy*, pp. 293–6.

109 See Ronaldson, June 1854. Rebecca Hartley discussed clothing fashions after thirteen years in America, during the period when her husband finally had steady work for several years. (Drake, ed., 'We are Yankees Now', p. 247).

110 Daniel Stephenson, 18 May 1864, Fairfield, Iowa, to his uncle, Stephenson Letters.

Phillips Series

1 Information about the Phillips family was supplemented from a copy of a letter from Mary Phillips, 30 March 1820, Manchester, to her brother-in-law, Phillip Phillips; copy of letter from John Phillips, 19 April 1820, Manchester, to his uncle, Phillip Phillips, Phillips Letters. US Census of Manufactures, 1820, Microfilm, Roll M, Delaware, No. 17, Document 21, National Archives. US Census MSS, Population, 1820, 1850. UK Census MSS, 1841. Francis Leach, ed., *County Seats of Shropshire,* Shrewsbury, 1891, p. 198.

2 In a total population of 6,328 in 1840, there were returned only ten schools and 280 scholars, and 942 persons over twenty years of age were given as illiterate.

Martin Series

1 Material about George Martin and his family has been found in: *Kelly's Post Office Directory of Six Home Counties*, 1845, p. 793. *Post Office Directory of London and Nine Home Counties*, 1846, p. 239. UK Census MSS, 1841, 1851. Letter from Jonathan King, 31 January 1853, Rochester, NY, to Peter Martin; letter from T. Martin, 28 October 1852, London; Mrs G.F. Martin, 19 January 1853, Rochester, to her brother-in-law, Martin Letters. US Census MSS, Population, 1840, 1850.

2 William Martin, the father of George Martin, was listed as a carpenter in the directory for 1845 and as a builder and cabinet-maker in 1846. It is possible that Thomas Martin, listed in the 1841 census in Chevening as aged eighty and as possessing independent means, was William Martin's father. This Thomas Martin had also been born in Kent.

3 Jonathan King was a man of between forty and fifty at the time of the 1840 census. Since King had only one child of his own, George Martin probably had good reason to expect that he would one day be able to take over his employer's business.

4 George Martin's real estate was valued at one thousand dollars in the 1850 census.

Stephenson Series

1 For biographical details, see UK Census MSS, 1841, 1851. Petition of Richard Stephenson, 28 March 1858, Fairfield, Iowa; letter from Daniel Stephenson, 17 July 1854, Fairfield, Iowa, to his uncle, Stephenson Papers. *The History of Jefferson County Iowa*, Chicago, 1879, pp. 258–9, 361–3, 517, 548. *History of Jefferson County, Iowa,* Chicago, 1912, I, pp. 46–7; II, pp. 126–7. US Census MSS, Population, 1850, 1860, 1870.

2 Lockridge, the township in which Stephenson bought his land, lost out to Fairfield as the location of the county seat and became a purely agricultural township.

3 Daniel Stephenson used this Robert Stephenson as a witness as to Abel Stephenson's wishes about the disposition of his land when members of the family in Yorkshire tried to claim shares of it. He referred in his letter of 1854 to 'Mr Robert Stephenson and wife, an Englishman who lives about two miles off'. This Robert Stephenson had emigrated to Lockridge township in 1841. His son Robert was also a farmer in the township and afterwards became county recorder and postmaster. In spite of the coincidence of name, this was almost certainly another family, and probably one which had come from agriculture in England.

4 In 1860 Daniel Stephenson reported his real estate as worth $1500 and personal property worth $200. Ten years later the value of his real estate had risen to $4000 and his personal property to $1500. In contrast, Samuel Stephenson, who remained in farming, had only $1600 worth of real estate and $562 of personal property in 1870.

Hails Series

1 This was the conclusion drawn by his sister and her husband who lived in Shullsburg, Wisconsin, after Hails had sent them a clipping on his marriage from a Lowell newspaper (Jonathan Dawson, August 1849, Shullsburg, Wisc., to George Hails, Hails Letters).

2 The 1841 census listed only two female potters and potmakers, both of whom were under twenty years of age in Tynemouth parish. It also gave five male pottery printers and painters under twenty and one adult male printer and painter. None of the Hails family has been identified in the 1841 or 1851 census manuscripts at North Shields. The census suggests a rapid expansion of earthware manufacture in North Shields during the forties, and it is possible that the family lived nearby but not in North Shields.

Roberts Series

1 G.I.H.Lloyd, *The Cutlery Trades*, New York, 1913, pp. 54–5.

2 Sydney Pollard, *A History of Sheffield Labour*, Liverpool University Press, 1959, pp. 42–3, 48, 49, 73.

3 Information supplied in part by F.L.Preston, who has read this introduction and helpfully corrected it from his own researches in the family history. *Post Office Directory of Sheffield*, Kelley and Co., London, 1854, p. 114. *General Directory of the Town and Borough of Sheffield*, William White, Sheffield, 1843, p. 162. Other material about James Roberts and others mentioned in these letters has come from: US Census MSS, Population, 1850, 1860, 1870, 1880. E.M.Ruttenber and L.H.Clark, compilers, *History of Orange County, New York*, Philadelphia, 1881, pp. 386, 400, 403. Letters from Thomas J.Bradley, 1867–70, Walden, New York, to John and Mary Ann Roberts and to James Roberts, in Sheffield, Roberts Letters.

4 Pollard, *Sheffield Labour*, p. 8. Robert A.Leader, ed., *Reminiscences of Old Sheffield*, Sheffield, 1875, p. 279.

5 Reports of George Wallis and Joseph Whitworth, *British Parliamentary Papers*, 1854, XXXVI, 9, p. 40; 103, p. 9.

6 Pollard, *Sheffield Labour*, p. 73.
7 It is not known precisely when the firm lost its co-operative structure, but it was advertising as early as 1863 as the New York Knife Company, Thomas J.Bradley, President (*Hardware Reporter*, October 1863, p. 1).

Crawshaw Series

1 Information about the Crawshaws and other families mentioned in these letters has been obtained in UK Census MSS, 1851, 1861, and US Census MSS, Population, 1850. A search for Crawshaw in the US Census MSS for Philadelphia in 1860 and 1870 had to be abandoned.
2 In 1861, Titus Crawshaw's father, William, was again returned as a woollen cloth handloom weaver. By that time Titus's younger sisters, who were still living at home, were working in woollen factories, Elizabeth as a piecer and Emma as a burler.

Laing Series

1 See also James Grayston in the Bond-Grayston series.
2 According to the owner of these letters, David Laing's grandfather had been a shipbuilder in Dunfermline. The family had disintegrated when David's father and one or two of his sons were lost at sea (Mrs Doreen Noble, 21 March 1970, to the author). Other clues about Laing were obtained from the US Census MSS, Population, 1860, 1870.

Ronaldson Series

1 D.Bremner, *The Industries of Scotland*, Edinburgh, 1869, p. 257. See also Henry Hamilton, *The Industrial Revolution in Scotland*, Clarendon Press, 1932, pp. 95–7.
2 Alex.J.Warden, *Linen Trade Ancient and Modern*, London, 1864, pp. 683–4.
3 He married Elizabeth Allan in Kinghorn, Fife, 16 February 1852, a few months before he emigrated (Copy of marriage certificate provided by Elizabeth McDaid). Further information has been garnered from: Passenger Lists, NY, Microfilm 237/116, No. 930, National Archives. US Census MSS, Population, 1850. John Ronaldson, 18 June 1854, East Braintree, Mass., to his wife; 16 August 1854, Liverpool, Ronaldson Letters.
4 Bremner, *Industries of Scotland*, pp. 224, 232, 237. Warden, *Linen Trade*, pp. 566–7. *Slaters Royal National Commercial Directory and Topography of Scotland*, London, 1852, p. 449.
5 Undated fragment in Ronaldson Letters.
6 On the ship *Statira Morse* which arrived in New York from Glasgow on 13 July 1852 was John Ronaldson, thirty-nine, flax-dresser. Miss MacDaid thinks that this was an error. Ronaldson was only twenty-nine years old.
7 List in the Ronaldson Letters.

Lister Series

1 New York Passenger lists, 9 July–7 August 1883, Microfilm 237/468, No. 937, National Archives.

III THE UPROOTED

1 Background to Emigration

1 Pitirim A.Sorokin, *Social and Cultural Mobility*, Free Press of Glencoe, 1927, Collier-MacMillan Ltd, London, paperback edition, 1964, p. 523. These people faced problems similar to those associated with mobile business executives and professional men as described by Frank Musgrove in *The Migratory Elite*, London, 1963.

2 Based on biographies in the following volumes: *Portrait and Biographical Record of Dubuque, Jones and Clayton Counties, Iowa*, Chicago, 1894; *History of Dubuque Co., Iowa*, Chicago, 1880; *Portrait and Biographical Record of Orange County, NY*, Chicago, 1895; Edward M.Ruttenber, *History of the County of Orange, NY*, Newburgh, 1875; E.M.Ruttenber and L.H.Clark, compilers, *History of Orange Co. NY*, Philadelphia, 1881; Clarence B. Bagley, *History of Seattle, Washington*, Chicago, 1916, 3v.

3 Juan Pattison, 23 January 1872, 58 Broadway, NY, to his brother-in-law, John Whittle in Chorley, Lancs., Pattison Letters, Cornell Collection of Regional History, Photostats, 866.

4 Andrew Mattison, 14 February 1843, Hopkinsville, Kentucky, to Clara Thompson, London, University of Kentucky Library, MSS 85. I am grateful to Dr E.R.R.Greene for calling my attention to this letter.

5 'They will come to me bye & bye perhaps when I am a public man.' (Juan Pattison, 23 January 1872, Pattison Letters). See also letter of 4 November 1873.

6 James Vickridge, 6 July 1914, Hanover, Conn., to his nephew, Albert Vickridge. Letters in private possession, photostats at LSE. The letter is quoted by the kind permission of G.Woledge.

7 J.Holmes, 13 January 1901, NYC, Devonshire Association Papers. More remarkable was the case of another Devonshire emigrant to Australia who summarized his career in a letter. H.E.Bond, fourth son of a merchant in Kingsbridge, lived in Totnes for six years, Plymouth for three, Kingsbridge for three, London for four and Torquay for eight years before he emigrated to Brisbane where he engaged in business as a commercial traveller and later as a real-estate commercial agent (H.E.Bond, 21 February 1901, *loc. cit*).

8 See also letter from Edward Trayes, 30 September 1833, Cleveland, Ohio, to his wife; James Stott, 23 June 1820, NYC, to his wife in Lancashire, LSE. Trayes was a land speculator and tavern-keeper in America, and Stott went out as a merchant.

2 Economic and Social Adjustment

9 Juan Pattison, 3 March 1867, Syracuse, NY, to his sister, Anita Whittle, Chorley, Lancs., Pattison Letters.

10 Juan Pattison, 4 November 1873, 58 Broadway, NYC, to John Whittle, Chorley, Lancs. See also the unsigned letter from 'E', 14 October 1851, Jail Hospital, Chester, Penn., LSE. This migrant referred to the fact that 'I who have been educated in affluence and every comfort to be now a wretched outcast among strangers. . .' and used the prison doctor as an intermediary with a clergyman in Penrith, Cumberland, who knew his family.

11 W.O.Williams, 3 March 1850, Covington, Kentucky, to his friend Edwards, in Pontypool, photostat in LSE.

12 James Knight, 5 November 1829, Nelsonville, Ohio, to George Courtauld, *Courtauld Family Papers*, IV, p. 1751.

13 James Vickridge, Radcliffe Quine, the Petingale brothers, Edward Trayes, Juan Pattison also showed flexibility both as to location and as to occupation.

14 James Vickridge, 5 July 1914, Hanover, Conn., to his nephew.

15 Summary of letters of Joseph Wainwright, 13 December 1850, 27 April 1841, Pittsburgh, in *Letters from a Yorkshire Emigrant*, pp. 10–11.

16 James Vickridge, 5 July 1914, Hanover, Conn., to his nephew.

17 James Vickridge, 5 July 1914.

18 J.W.Jendwine, 5 January [1888?], Bowman's Bluff, North Carolina, to Mr Wace, solicitor, Shropshire, Jendwine Letters, LSE.

19 Juan Pattison, 4 November 1873, New York, to John Whittle, Chorley, Lancs.

20 James Vickridge, 17 November 1907 and 4 October 1908, Hanover, Conn., to his nephew, Albert Vickridge. See also a begging letter from John Norman, an elderly immigrant in Harlem who had once been an indoor farm servant in Suffolk. (John Norman, 30 January 1848, Harlem, NY, to his brother-in-law, John Philpot, Whalpole, Suffolk, Norman Letters, LSE). The brother-in-law of whom Norman begged a few sovereigns on which to live was an elderly farmer of forty-six acres.

21 Juan Pattison, 27 September 1868, Syracuse, NY, to his sister, Anita Whittle, Chorley, Lancs. Andrew Mattison and William Petingale referred to their being able to attend American social functions shortly after their arrival in the United States.

22 James Vickridge, 1 July 1905, 4 March 1903, Hanover, Conn., to his nephew Albert Vickridge.

23 James Vickridge, 5 August 1908; [1910?], Hanover, Conn. See also statement by a company secretary who went out to Central City, Colorado, in 1872: 'I feel just about as much at home here as among the people in England.' (James Thomson, 31 May 1872, Central City, Colorado, to Mrs Charles Bradlaugh, Henry S. Salt, *Life of James Thomson*, London, 1889, p. 79).

24 William Petingale, 26 May 1835.

25 Andrew Mattison, 14 February 1843, Hopkinsville, Kentucky, to Clara Thompson.

26 Nathan Haley, 20 May 1823.

27 John Hesketh, May 1835, 20 May 1841. See also Thomas Petingale, 10 December 1840 and Radcliffe Quine, 22 April 1861.

28 Thomas Petingale, 18 May 1883.

29 Juan Pattison, 23 January 1872, 58 Broadway, NYC, to his brother-in-law, John Whittle, Chorley, Lancs.

30 Juan Pattison, 4 January 1869, Syracuse, NY.

31 James Vickridge, 10 March 1910, 20 August 1903, Hanover, Conn., to his nephew.

32 Edward Trayes, 30 September 1833, Cleveland, Ohio. Thomas Petingale, 2 September 1849.

33 Juan Pattison, 23 January 1872, 58 Broadway, NYC, to his brother-in-law, John Whittle, Chorley, Lancs.

34 James Stott, 23 June 1820, to his wife.

35 Donald Cole, *Immigrant City, Lawrence, Massachusetts, 1845–1921*, Chapel Hill, 1963, pp. 99–112.

Haley Series

1. What little we know about Nathan Haley and others mentioned in these letters comes from: *White's Directory for Leeds,* 1830, p. 483; 1847, p. 291, UK Census MSS, 1841.
2 Katherine Coman, *Economic Beginnings of the Far West,* New York, 1912, II, pp. 51, 53.

Hesketh Series

1 John Hesketh returned from England at the age of sixty on the *Susquehanna,* which landed in Philadephia on 31 July 1846. (Passenger Lists, Philadelphia, Micro-film 360/61, National Archives). He paid twenty pounds for a cabin passage (John Hesketh, 9 June 1846, Liverpool, to his brother, Hesketh Letters). Further details about Hesketh were found in UK Census MSS, 1841. US Census MSS, Population, 1840, 1850.
2 Two hundred and eighty-nine returned in agriculture, fifty-five in handicrafts and two in commerce in the 1840 census of Robeson township.
3 Christopher Slade, a man somewhat younger than Hesketh, was returned in the West Ward of Pittsburgh in 1840. He was apparently a friend from Hesketh's early years in Pittsburgh, since Slade did not move to Robeson.

Petingale Series

1 Information about the Petingales in the letters has been supplemented from: UK Census MSS, 1851. *White's Norfolk Directory for 1836,* p. 647. *Post Office Directory for Norfolk,* 1858, p. 128. US Census MSS, Population, 1850, 1870. *Boyd's Directory of DC,* 1870, p. 307; 1874, p. 367; 1875, p. 409; 1880, p. 663; 1881, p. 594. The family scrapbook was lent to me by the late Joseph Petingale.
2 George Petingale may have been a common law son of John Dalton, or an adopted son; but when John Dalton's son, John, died at West Bilney in 1854 at the age of sixty-three, Henry Petingale noted the death in words which implied that he knew of no family relationship with him.

Quine Series

1 For details on Quine, see UK Census MSS, 1841, US Census MSS, Population, 1870.
2 Kinvig, 'Manx Settlement', p. 18.
3 Clarence B. Bagley, *History of Seattle, Washington,* Chicago, 1916, I, pp. 614–23.

Index

All numbers in bold refer to illustrations

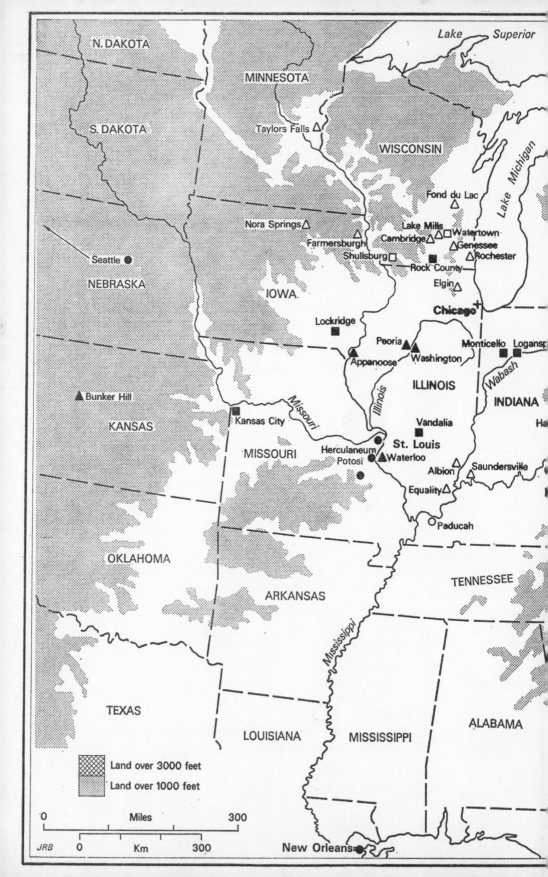

| N. DAKOTA | MINNESOTA | Lake Superior |

Taylors Falls △

WISCONSIN

Lake Michigan

Fond du Lac △

Nora Springs △

Lake Mills
Cambridge △ □ □ Watertown △
Farmersburgh △
Shullsburg □
Rock County ■ △ Genessee
△ Rochester

Elgin △

Chicago +

Seattle ●

NEBRASKA

IOWA

Lockridge ■

Peoria △
Appanoose △ Washington △

Monticello ■ Logansp ■

ILLINOIS

INDIANA

Wabash

Bunker Hill ▲

KANSAS

Kansas City ■

Missouri

Vandalia ■

Ha

MISSOURI

Herculaneum ●
Potosi ●
Waterloo ▲

St. Louis ■

Albion △ Saundersville △

Equality △

OKLAHOMA

Paducah ○

ARKANSAS

TENNESSEE

TEXAS

LOUISIANA

MISSISSIPPI

ALABAMA

Mississippi

▨ Land over 3000 feet
▧ Land over 1000 feet

0 Miles 300
0 Km 300

JRB

New Orleans ●